HOMER AND THE *ODYSSEY*

Homer and the *Odyssey*

SUZANNE SAÏD

OXFORD
UNIVERSITY PRESS

Great Clarendon Street, Oxford OX2 6DP

Oxford University Press is a department of the University of Oxford.
It furthers the University's objective of excellence in research, scholarship,
and education by publishing worldwide in

Oxford New York

Auckland Cape Town Dar es Salaam Hong Kong Karachi
Kuala Lumpur Madrid Melbourne Mexico City Nairobi
New Delhi Shanghai Taipei Toronto

With offices in

Argentina Austria Brazil Chile Czech Republic France Greece
Guatemala Hungary Italy Japan Poland Portugal Singapore
South Korea Switzerland Thailand Turkey Ukraine Vietnam

Published in the United States
by Oxford University Press Inc., New York

First published 2011

British Library Cataloguing in Publication Data
Data available

Library of Congress Cataloguing in Publication Data
Data available

Typeset by SPI Publisher Services, Pondicherry, India
Printed in Great Britain
on acid-free paper by
MPG Books Group, Bodmin and King's Lynn

ISBN 978–0–19–954284–0 (Hbk)
978–0–19–954285–7 (Pbk)

1 3 5 7 9 10 8 6 4 2

Contents

Note on Translations of Homer

The English translations of the *Odyssey* in this book are based on the translation by Walter Shewring, published by Oxford University Press. It has been necessary to modify Shewring's translation in several places to ensure that the English reflects the discussion of the Greek text. The translations by Martin Hammond (London, 2000) and Richmond Lattimore (New York, 1967) have also been consulted. Quotations from the *Iliad* are taken from the translation by Martin Hammond (Harmondsworth, 1987) with some slight modifications.

Ruth Webb

Introduction

Homer is the prime example of a 'first-class' author, the original sense of the term 'classic' (though this is too often forgotten). His was a towering presence in Greek culture. As tangible evidence of his importance, we need only mention the huge quantity of manuscripts (over 1,000 are known today) and papyri containing the Homeric poems, a far greater number than for any other author.[1] According to the grammarian and allegorist Heraclitus, author of the *Homeric Problems*, 'he accompanies man throughout all the stages of his life' (2). According to Lucian and Maximus of Tyre he was 'the best' and 'the greatest'. For Philostratus, 'he surpassed all the poets of his age in the domain in which each excelled: he practised the solemn style better than Orpheus, he surpassed Hesiod in charm . . . and Musaeus in verse oracles'.[2] He was the king of poets and the poet of kings, the only one whom Alexander the Great considered worthy of his attention.

Throughout Antiquity, Homer was constantly read and reinterpreted. He was considered to be the first historian and the ancestor of geographers, the origin of both tragic and comic drama, the father of philosophy, and the guardian of morality and religion. By isolating certain passages and reading them with particular aims in mind, ancient authors were able to claim Homer as an authority for everything. Readers in the modern era followed suit. Fénelon, the preceptor of the grandson of Louis XIV, wrote the famous *Adventures of Telemachus* between 1694 and 1696. This was extremely popular not only in France but throughout Europe and was quickly translated into several languages. In this *Bildungsroman* the young Telemachus together with his preceptor Mentor travels through various Greek

[1] On the Homeric papyri see Haslam 1997.
[2] Philostratus, *Heroicus*, 161K and 162K.

states which mirror contemporary France (his Idomeneus is modelled on Louis XIV himself) and learns the art of ruling from Mentor. In Victorian Britain, beginning with Gladstone, Homer was seen as an educator whose task was to promote the spirit of competition and to teach the young men who attended the exclusive public schools of the period to be 'good speakers of words and doers of deeds' (*Iliad*, 9.443). In sum, each period creates its own Homer.

Our own is no exception, as is evident from the sheer quantity of publications on Homer (of which the books and articles cited in this volume represent only a small part). One might well ask whether it was really necessary to add yet another title to a list that is already too long. But it can be difficult for specialists—let alone non-specialists—to find their way among such a plethora of titles. For this reason, particularly given recent developments in Homeric studies, it seemed important to provide a fresh overview that would both cover the critical approaches to Homer and do justice to the many and varied aspects of the work. The need for new works of synthesis is reflected in the publication of substantial collections of chapters and articles such as the second *Colloquium Rauricum* dedicated to 'Two hundred years of Homeric criticism' (*Zweihundert Jahre Homer-Forschung*), and the volume on Homer in the collection *Wege der Forschung*, both published in 1991; the *New Companion to Homer* published by Brill in 1997 to replace the first *Companion* edited by A. J. B. Wace and F. Stubbings in 1962, the collection of articles on the *Odyssey* alone, edited by S. Schein in 1996, entitled *Reading the Odyssey*, the *Oxford Readings in Homer's Iliad* edited by D. Cairns in 2001, the *Cambridge Companion to Homer* edited by R. Fowler, published in 2004, or the *Oxford Readings in Homer's, Odyssey* edited by L. Doherty in 2009.

The first part of the present volume also attempts, on a more modest scale, to review current approaches to Homer in three chapters (hence the abundant bibliographic references which are designed to allow the curious or the specialist to go directly to the sources for further information).

In order to understand the ways in which the *Iliad* and *Odyssey* are read today, it is essential to make a detour through the history of literary criticism and to trace the history of Homeric criticism; this is the subject of the first chapter. It was important to start with the ancient sources and the ancient biographies of Homer, partly to show that they are far from being historical documents that can be taken at face value but, most importantly, to arrive at a fuller appreciation of what they can tell us about the reception of Homer in Antiquity. It was also necessary to provide an overview of the evolution of the 'Homeric question' which dominated the study of Homer for over a century after the publication of the *Prolegomena ad Homerum* by Friedrich Wolf in the late eighteenth century, with the continued debates between the 'Analysts', who tried to distinguish different strata in the composition of the text, and the 'Unitarians', who tried to put back together what the analysts had deconstructed and defend the unity of the Homeric poems. It was also essential to show how the work of Milman Parry—which did not make a major impact until the 1960s although it had appeared thirty years earlier—reinvigorated the interpretation of Homer by showing how much the poetry owed to oral tradition and also how this work prompted new debates on the role that writing did or did not play in the composition of Homeric poetry and on the date at which the text we know today was written down.[3]

Chapter 2 focuses on the role of innovation and artistic creation in the Homeric poems. It proposes a more flexible definition of the formula and, in place of the image of a poet shackled by tradition and by a rigid system of formulae, it offers an image of a poet who is able to choose between different possibilities and to play on echoes and differences, who makes use of ellipse or amplification, combines traditional elements in an original way, and does not hesitate to employ unusual expressions to create new effects.

It was also important to address the question of the complex relationship between Homeric fiction and reality, a reality that is becoming better known thanks to archaeology. With Schliemann it was thought that Troy had been found. Since the work of Moses Finley it has been lost once more.[4] What is the current state of opinion concerning the Trojan War? Beneath the alterations and exaggerations of epic is there a kernel of historical fact? Chapter 3 approaches these questions, but its main focus is on the gulf that separates 'the world of Homer' from Mycenae and the Bronze Age, on the uncertainties surrounding its place in the intervening centuries, emphasizing everything that links it to the Greek renaissance of the eighth century. It is still the case that this world is by no means a pure reflection of reality. Rather, reality is the basis for

[3] Milman Parry's articles, published between 1928 and 1937, were collected in a volume by A. Parry published in 1971.

[4] See Finley's article 'Lost: The Trojan War' in Finley 1977b: 31–42.

'Homer's' depiction of a glorious past that exalts aristocratic values and validates the power of the elite who represent them. The Homeric poems are therefore not historical documents. And yet this reconstruction of the past made their author, long before Herodotus, the true 'father of history' in Greece.

The second part of the book is longer and is devoted to the *Odyssey*, which has always taken second place to the *Iliad* in Homeric studies.

Chapter 4 outlines the subject of the poem, analyses its composition, and demonstrates its unity. It also offers a detailed analysis of the treatment of space and time in this complex work, showing the subtle transitions and the importance of anticipations and flashbacks in broadening considerably the temporal horizon of the work. It then proposes a brief narratological study of this 'primitive narrative'[5] which examines the different types of secondary narratives that proliferate in the *Odyssey*, demonstrating the relationships between them and their narrators and audiences as well as underlining the points at which these narratives refer to each other or to the main narrative. Finally it seeks to use Homer in order to explain Homer, in accordance with the sound principles of Alexandrian criticism,[6] by presenting the image of poetry and poets contained within the *Odyssey* through the figures of two bards, Phemius on Ithaca and Demodocus on Phaeacia.

The next three chapters (5–7) aim to guide the reader through a work that can be divided into three blocks: the adventures of Telemachus (Books 1 to 4), the wanderings of Odysseus (Books 5 to 13), and finally the events on Ithaca culminating in the massacre of the suitors and the re-establishment of Odysseus at the head of his palace and of his city (Books 14–24). Rather than providing plain summaries of each book (which would duplicate the useful résumés to be found in the introductions to most translations of the *Odyssey*) these chapters provide a brief commentary which outlines the development of the plot and points out echoes and contrasts by comparing other passages from both the *Odyssey* and the *Iliad*. These comparisons make it possible to see how traditional or innovative each episode or expression is.

[5] Todorov 1977.

[6] Ὅμηρον ἐξ Ὁμήρου σαφηνίζειν. On this phrase, which is traditionally attributed to Aristarchus but which is found in the *Platonic Questions* of the Neoplatonic philosopher Porphyry, see Pfeiffer 1968: 225–7.

The final four chapters (7–11) offer a more thematic approach. We start with the world of men by contrasting Odysseus and his supporters—his son Telemachus, his faithful servants and devoted maidservants—to the group of suitors with their two leaders, their two 'good' members, caught up in the wickedness of their companions, and the unfaithful servants who have chosen to follow them (Chapter 8). In the light of developments in Women's Studies and Gender Studies it was important to devote a chapter to 'the distaff side'[7] with a series of portraits of female characters, Circe and Calypso, Nausicaa and Arete, and, last but by no means least, Penelope (Chapter 9). The world of the gods is the subject of Chapter 10 which makes a clear distinction between the scenes on Olympus and those in which the gods intervene in human affairs and which places great emphasis on the ways in which the gods are presented. Here, it is vital to distinguish what is said about the gods by human characters, what the gods themselves say, and what the main narrator says about their role in the action. Finally, I attempt to define the ethical system of the *Odyssey* and to identify the values that the poem depicts and attempts to inculcate in its audience. This is done first by trying to identify the rules that regulate relationships within the household, including both family members and servants. Then we move on to the community and to the gulf that separates the elite from the people within it, the relationships between these two groups, and the importance of social cohesion. Attention is also paid, given the importance of travel in this work, to the place of the stranger and the Homeric laws of hospitality.

The conclusion examines the relationship between the two Homeric poems. Should we consider the *Odyssey* as a mere epilogue to the *Iliad*? It is far from clear, given that there is so much that distinguishes these two works.

There is no doubt that this book will not tell the reader all that he or she wanted to know about Homer but never dared to ask. But it does aim to present the most important points. It is intended to be accessible to any reader with a basic grounding in the subject but also to be useful to students and specialists alike.

Because the repetition and variation in formulae is such an important part of Homer's art, it has sometimes proved necessary to quote the Greek text, but translations are provided throughout.

[7] Cohen 1995.

Given my firm belief that texts cannot be studied in isolation from their historical context, particularly when they are so far removed from us in time, I have tried as far as possible to make use of archaeological evidence and the most recent reconstructions of the Mycenaean world and the Geometric period to arrive at a better understanding of the world of Odysseus.

Because no text can be read entirely afresh and the *Odyssey*, in particular, has been on a long journey through the land of the philologists before arriving at our time, I have included a copious bibliography which has expanded even further since the original publication of this book in 1998.

If this book is able to inspire readers to reread the *Odyssey* in translation or, better still, in the original, my efforts and theirs will not have been wasted.

1

From 'Homer' to the Homeric Poems

1. THE POET AND HIS LEGEND

Throughout Antiquity the existence of the poet Homer was accepted as a historical fact. But nothing was known of the author, who only makes fleeting appearances in his own work in the form of the personal pronouns 'I', 'we', and 'me' and tells us nothing about himself.[1] As the Greek novelist Heliodorus said, 'he never mentioned his name, his country or his family'.[2] This silence may well be related to the deliberate omission of any references in the poems to a particular audience or performance context for the poems, as Mark Griffith and Walter Burkert have both suggested, an omission that allowed them to be recited at any time or place.[3] The first mention of Homer's name may be datable to the mid seventh century with the poet Callinus,[4] while the first securely datable reference, in the work of Xenophanes, belongs in the last third of the sixth century, and is followed by references in the work of Heraclitus and Simonides, coinciding with the emergence of a new interest in poetic creation and the personality of the author. It is this, it seems, that prompted the invention of an author for these epic poems that, up until then, had been transmitted anonymously.

[1] Homer refers to himself in the nominative singular (ἐγώ) at *Iliad*, 2.488 and in the nominative plural (ἡμεῖς) at *Iliad*, 2.486; in the dative singular at *Iliad*, 2.484, 489, 490 and 761; 11.218; 14.508; 16.112 and *Odyssey*, 1.1 and in the dative plural (ἡμῖν) at *Odyssey*, 1.10.

[2] Heliodorus, *Ethiopian Story*, 3.14. See also Pseudo-Plutarch, *On Homer I* (= *Life*, 3.1 West), Proclus (= *Life*, 5.2 West).

[3] See Griffith 1983: 42 and Burkert 1987: 210.

[4] Fr. 6 West (if the emendation of Sylberg for the *kalainos* of the MSS is right) and West 1999: 377.

There are however several ancient biographies of Homer, all of which were composed several centuries after the Homeric poems.[5] As early as the sixth century, Theagenes of Rhegium and Stesimbrotus of Thasus were interested in Homer's biography, if we are to believe the early Christian writer Tatian.[6] But the most detailed *Life of Homer*, which was attributed to Herodotus in Antiquity (an attribution that is false beyond any doubt), belongs to the end of the Hellenistic era at the very earliest and may well belong to the second century AD. Also from the second century are the works *On Homer* and *On the Life and Poetry of Homer* which were included among the works of Plutarch collected by Maximus Planudes in the thirteenth century, but which were no doubt written by a contemporary of Maximus of Tyre or of Numenius.[7] While it is clear that the story of the contest between Homer and Hesiod goes back to the fourth century BC at least and to the *Mouseion* of the sophist Alcidamas, the version we have belongs to the reign of Hadrian.[8] The other biographies of Homer, like those to be found in the *Chrestomathia* of a certain Proclus, in the *Souda*, or at the beginning of the manuscripts of Homer preserved in Rome and in the Escorial, are even later and can be dated to the Byzantine period.[9]

We can no doubt trace the origin of these biographies back to the rhapsodes who, in their recitations, 'sewed together' verses composed by others. More precisely, it can be linked to the 'Homeridae', a guild of rhapsodes based on Chios who claimed to be descended from Homer and specialized in reciting epic poetry, just like the Kreophyleioi on Samos, who recited the *Sack of Oechalia* and presented themselves as descendants of its mythical author, Kreophylos, or the guild of doctors on Cos who traced their origin back to Asclepius.[10] There is therefore no longer any question of reading the *Lives*, or the allusions to Homer's

[5] These biographies have been published in a useful collection in the fifth volume of the edition of the works of Homer by D. B. Monro and T. W. Allen (Oxford, 1902–12) and more recently, with an English translation, by M. L. West, *Homeric Hymns, Homeric Apocrypha, Lives of Homer* in the Loeb Classical Library (2003).

[6] Tatian, *To the Greeks*, 31.

[7] See Kindstrand 1990, Hillgruber 1994, Keaney and Lamberton 1996.

[8] See West 1967 and Richardson 1981.

[9] It is unclear whether this Proclus is the second-century grammarian or the fifth-century Neoplatonic philosopher. See Severyns 1963: IV: 67 (= *Life* 5 West); the *Souda*'s biography derives essentially from the Index of famous authors by Hesychius of Miletus (sixth century AD) (= *Life* 6 West); the *Vita Romana* is edited by West as *Life* 7; the two *Vitae Scorialenses* are *Lives* 8 and 9 in West's edition.

[10] See Pfeiffer 1968: 11, Burkert 1987: 206–7, and West 1999: 373–4.

biography in epigrams[11] and various other works, in order to try to separate out the wheat from the chaff and to extract a portrait of the 'real' Homer from the jumble of contradictory information they contain, as was attempted in the past by Raddatz, Wilamowitz, Jacoby, and more recently by Lambin.[12] We need to ask instead what the contradictions inherent in these various 'constructions' or 'inventions' of Homer can tell us about the reception of the Homeric poems, as the studies by Walter Burkert (1987), Martin West (1999), and Barbara Graziosi (2002) have done.

(a) Homer's names

Even the name 'Homer', which appears in all the *Lives* as well as in the oldest testimonia, raises questions. It has been noted that it is a real name, attested in ancient onomastics,[13] but as West (1999: 366) has rightly pointed out, 'No other person so named is known from before Hellenistic times'. It is clear that, for the authors of the *Lives*, the name itself was meaningful: it is always treated as a nickname, given to the poet for various reasons that reflect the different etymologies of the Greek word *homeros*. According to some, the poet was sent to the Greeks, or more precisely to the inhabitants of Chios or of Colophon, or to the king of Persia as a hostage (*homēros* in Greek);[14] alternatively, his father was sent as a hostage to Persia by the Cypriots.[15] According to other sources he went blind (*homēros* in the Aeolic dialect), an etymology that is used to support claims that Homer had Aeolian origins.[16] Or he agreed while he was still a child to 'accompany' (*homērein*) the Lydians when they left Smyrna (this interpretation is used to back up the links between Homer and Smyrna).[17] Or—proof

[11] See Skiadas 1965.

[12] See Raddatz 1913 Wilamowitz-Moellendorf 1916, Jacoby 1933, Lambin 1995. According to Latacz 1996: 24–30 such a reading is a 'false track'.

[13] See Bergk 1872: 1.447 and Latacz 1996.

[14] Lucian, *True Histories*, 2.20; Proclus (= *Life* 5.3 West), Hesychius (*Life* 6.3 West), and the anonymous *Life* of Homer (*Vita Romana*) (= *Life* 7.5 West) respectively.

[15] *Contest* (*Life* 1.3 West).

[16] *Contest* (*Life* 1.3 West); Pseudo-Herodotus (*Life* 2.13 West); Pseudo-Plutarch (*Life* 3.2 West) cites as his source Ephorus, himself a citizen of Cyme, an Aeolian city; Proclus (*Life* 5.3 West).

[17] Pseudo-Plutarch (*Life* 3.3 West) and Graziosi 2002: 79.

that ancient etymological speculation knew no bounds—his thigh (*ho mēros*) was covered in long hairs.[18]

Modern scholars, from Welcker to Durante, Nagy, and West, have tended to favour etymologies that reflect their own theories about the composition of the Homeric poems as a collective enterprise, as Barbara Graziosi (2002: 52) has pointed out. Welcker was the first to derive *Homēros* from *homou* and *arariskō* which he interpreted as meaning 'compiler' (*Zusammenfüger*).[19] He was followed by Nagy (1979: 297–300), who understood it to mean 'he who fits the song together'. Durante (1957), followed by West (1999: 375–6), linked *Homēros* to the term *homarion*, meaning 'the common assembly' of a people, supporting the argument that this was the type of situation in which the poems were recited. The name would thus refer to the performance context of the rhapsodes.

The *Contest* and the majority of the *Lives* give him a name that refers explicitly to his links with Smyrna and the river Meles (usually Melesigenes but also Melesagoras or Melesianax).[20] But the *Contest* also calls him *Aulētēs*, another significant name meaning 'flute player'.[21] Epigrams from the *Greek Anthology*[22] usually give him the name Maionides (son of Maion) and Lucian, who makes him into a Babylonian, invents the Armenian name Tigranes for him.[23]

(b) The genealogies

His genealogy is equally controversial. Usually his father (or adoptive father) is said to have been the river Meles, which flowed past Smyrna, or a man named Maion, who is also identified as his adoptive father.[24]

[18] Heliodorus, *Ethiopian Story*, 3.14.3.

[19] Welcker 1865–82: 1, 121.

[20] Melesigenes: *Contest* (*Life* 1.2 West), Pseudo-Herodotus (*Life* 2.3 West), Pseudo-Plutarch, *On Homer I* (*Life* 3.2 West), Proclus (*Life* 5.3 West), Hesychius (*Life* 6.3 West), *Vita Romana* (*Life* 7.5 West), *Vita Scorialensis I* (= *Life* 8.1 West); Melesagoras: *Vita Romana* (*Life* 7.5 West); Melesianax, *Vita Scorialensis I* (= *Life* 8.1 West).

[21] *Contest* (= *Life* 1.3 West) according to the manuscript reading but West, following Welcker, adopts the correction *Altēs*.

[22] See, for example, *Greek Anthology*, 5.30.2, 69.2; 7.2.2, 15.2, 138.3, 213.8, 674.2; 9. 28.2, 97.5, 192.2, 575.5.

[23] Lucian, *True Histories*, 2.20.

[24] Meles is given as the father in the *Contest* (*Life* 1.3 West) citing Euagion; Pseudo-Plutarch, *On Homer* II (*Life* 4.2 West); the anonymous *Life* of Homer (*Vita Romana* = *Life* 7.3 West), which states that this is the majority opinion; the *Vita Scorialensis I* (= *Life* 8.1 West) and *Vita Scorialensis II* (*Life* 9.1. West). Maion is

Other candidates for the role of father are Crethon and Alemon.[25] Some have meaningful names like Dmasagoras ('he who controls the assembly'), Daemon ('the clever one'), or significant professions, like 'the scribe Menemachus'.[26] Sometimes his father is said to have been unknown.[27] His mother's identity is equally fluid: she is sometimes anonymous but often she is named Cretheis, or Hyrneto, or Themiste.[28] She may also be given names that prefigure the poetic talent of her son: Eumetis ('The cunning one'), daughter of Euepes ('the man who composes beautiful verses').[29]

Homer was also considered in Antiquity to be the son of his own poems in that he is said to have been the son of 'Telemachus, son of Odysseus' (or the adoptive son of Phemius, the Ithacan bard).[30] His mother is likewise said to have been a daughter of Nestor named Polycaste, who appears once in the *Odyssey*.[31] Ancient authors also created genealogies linking him to Hesiod[32] or to the most prominent mythological poets: Thamyras, mentioned in Book 2 of the *Odyssey*, is said to have been his father while Orpheus, Musaeus, and Linus were counted amongst his ancestors.[33]

identified as the father in the *Contest* (*Life* 1.3 West) citing Hellanicus and Cleanthus; Pseudo-Plutarch, *On Homer I* (*Life* 3.2 West) citing Ephorus; Pseudo-Plutarch, *On Homer II* (*Life* 4.2 West); Proclus (*Life* 5.3 West); Hesychius (*Life* 6.1 West) citing the historian Charax; the anonymous *Life* of Homer (*Vita Romana*) (*Life* 7.3 West) citing Stesimbrotus and the *Vita Scorialensis I* (*Life* 8.1 West). See also *Greek Anthology*, 2.1.408; 7.5.3 and 16.292.1. Maion is given as the adoptive father in Pseudo-Plutarch, *On Homer* I (= *Life* 3.3 West).

25 *Vita Romana* (*Life* 7.3 West) citing Dinarchus and Democritus respectively.

26 *Contest* (*Life* 1.3, West).

27 Pseudo-Herodotus (= *Life* 2.2 West).

28 In the *Contest* (*Life* 1.3 West) she is said to be 'a woman from Ithaca' and in Pseudo-Plutarch, *On Homer I* (*Life* 3.2 West), citing Aristotle, 'a woman from Chios'. The name Cretheis in mentioned in *Contest* (*Life* 1.3 West), Pseudo-Herodotus (*Life* 2. 1 West), Pseudo-Plutarch I (*Life* 3.2 West) citing Ephorus, Pseudo-Plutarch II (*Life* 4.2 West), Hesychius (*Life* 6.1 West) citing Castricus of Nicaea, *Vita Romana* (*Life* 7.3 West) citing Stesimbrotus, *Vita Scorialensis* I (*Life* 8.1 West), *Vita Scorialensis II* (*Life* 9.1 West); Hyrneto in the *Contest* (*Life* 1.3 West), *Vita Romana* (*Life* 7.3 West) citing Stesimbrotus and Themiste in the *Contest* (*Life* 1.3 West).

29 Hesychius (*Life* 6.1 West) citing Charax.

30 Pseudo-Herodotus (*Life* 2.4 West), Pseudo-Plutarch I (*Life* 3.2 West), and the *Contest* (*Life* 1.3 West).

31 *Contest* (*Life* 1.3 West), cf. *Odyssey*, 3.464.

32 Pseudo-Plutarch I (*Life* 3.2 West) citing Ephorus.

33 *Contest* (*Life* 1.3 West), cf. *Iliad*, 2.595–601; Proclus (*Life* 5.4 West) citing Gorgias; Hesychius (*Life* 6.1 West).

Finally, the 'divine Homer' could also be considered the son of a god.[34] Sometimes anonymous,[35] this divinity may be identified as Apollo, who is said to have fathered the poet by a nymph or even by the principal Muse, Calliope.[36]

(c) Homer's country of origin

Both the *Lives* and the epigrams on Homer's biography often begin by admitting their ignorance and acknowledging that various cities laid claim to the poet:[37] 'Practically all cities and their inhabitants claim that he was born among them.'[38] For this reason, Homer is sometimes considered to be 'a man of many countries' (*polupatris*),[39] a 'citizen of the world' (*kosmopolitēs*),[40] or even a god who lived in the heavens.[41]

Attempts to arrange these various conjectures about Homer's origins into a chronological order, like those of F. Jacoby (1933: 24–37) and, more recently, B. Graziosi (2002: 51–89), show that Homer was originally considered to have been an Ionian poet: the author of the *Homeric Hymn to Apollo* (probably composed in 523 BC), in common with Simonides (fl. 514), Heraclitus (fl. 500), Damastes (fifth century BC), and Anaximenes of Lampsacus (*c.*380–320 BC), considered him to be a citizen of Chios. According to Stesimbrotus (fl. late fifth century BC) he came from Smyrna while Pindar (b. 518 BC) hesitates between Chios and Smyrna. Antimachus (*c.*380–320 BC) claims he was born in Colophon, where he is said to have composed the *Margites* according to the *Contest*,[42] Ephorus (*c.*405–330 BC) places his birth in Cyme,[43] while Aristotle places it on Ios.[44] These cities appear in almost all the lists of Homer's places of origin that are included in the *Lives*. They are even

[34] On the 'divine Homer' see Skiadas 1965: 65 and Graziosi 2002: 67 n. 48.

[35] *Vita Romana* (= *Life* 7.3 West).

[36] Hesychius (= *Life* 6.1 West) and *Contest* (*Life* 1.4 West).

[37] Pseudo-Plutarch 2 (*Life* 4.3 West), Proclus (= *Life* 1.4 West), *Vita Romana* (= *Life* 7.1 West), Pseudo-Lucian, *Encomium of Demosthenes*, 9, *Greek Anthology*, 9.97.4–6, 16.293.3, 294.1–3.

[38] *Contest* (= *Life* 1.2 West).

[39] Eustathius, *Ad Iliadem*, 1.6.7.

[40] Proclus (= *Life* 5.2 West).

[41] *Greek Anthology*, 16.295.8–9, 296.7.

[42] *Contest* (= *Life* 1.2 West).

[43] Pseudo-Plutarch 1 (= *Life* 3.2 West) and 2 (= *Life* 4.2 West), *Vita Romana* (= *Life* 7.2 West).

[44] Pseudo-Plutarch 1 (= *Life* 3.3 West) and 2 (= *Life* 4.2 West).

mentioned in the Pseudo-Herodotean *Life* which associates Homer firmly with Smyrna, while recognizing the existence of other traditions which it attempts to reconcile with each other. Thus the poet is said to have been born in Smyrna, but conceived in Cyme, and to have travelled to Colophon, Smyrna, and Cyme before dying on Ios. Modern commentators, starting with Wilamowitz, have proposed similar solutions.[45] As has often been noted, the various birthplaces reflect the nature of the Homeric dialect, which is predominantly Ionic with a high proportion of Aeolic features.[46]

This list continued to grow in Antiquity: the five potential birthplaces mentioned above grew to six and then seven, eight, even nine cities in the epigrams and in the *Lives*. The *Souda* records twenty cities, reflecting the expansion of Hellenism first to the eastern Mediterranean with Alexander's conquests (hence the legend of the Egyptian Homer[47]), then throughout the Roman empire (hence the legend of the 'Roman' or even 'Babylonian' Homer).[48] For the same reason, centres of Hellenic culture such as Salamis in Cyprus[49] which became a Hellenic outpost in the fourth century as a result of the efforts of its kings, Nicocles and Evagoras, and, of course, Athens were also claimed as the birthplace of Homer.[50] The choice of birthplace often reflects the place of origin of the writers and local pride, as Proclus was well aware: 'Each writer has indulged his inclinations with great freedom.'[51] Antimachus and Nicander from Colophon, Ephorus from Cyme, Lucian of Samosata, and the Egyptian priest in Heliodorus' *Ethiopian Story* all made Homer their compatriot.[52]

[45] Wilamowitz-Moellendorf 1916: 397 suggested that Homer was born in Smyrna, taught at Colophon, and then settled on Chios where he raised a family.

[46] See, for example, Graziosi 2002: 84.

[47] Pseudo-Lucian, *Encomium of Demosthenes*, 9; *Souda* (= Hesychius *Life* 6.2 West); *Vita Romana* (= *Life* 7.2 West); *Vita Scorialensis II* (*Life* 9.1 West); Clement of Alexandria, *Stromata*, 1.66; Eustathius, *Greek Anthology*, 7.7, 16.295.3; Heliodorus, *Ethiopian Story*, 3.13–14.

[48] Roman Homer: *Souda* (= Hesychius *Life* 6.2 West) citing Aristodemus of Nysa. See Heath 1998; Babylonian Homer: Lucian, *True Histories*, 2.20.

[49] Pseudo-Plutarch 2 (= *Life* 4.2 West), *Souda*, citing Callicles (= Hesychius *Life* 6.2 West); *Greek Anthology*, 16.296.3, 299.3.

[50] Pseudo-Plutarch 2 (= *Life* 4.2 West) and *Vita Scorialensis II* (*Life* 9.2 West) citing Aristarchus and Dionysius Thrax, *Souda* (= Hesychius *Life* 6.2 West); *Vita Scorialensis I* (*Life* 8.2 West), *Greek Anthology*, 11.442, 16.295.4, 297.2, 298.2.

[51] Proclus (*Life* 5.2 West).

[52] Pseudo-Plutarch 2 (= *Life* 4.2 West), *Vita Romana* (*Life* 7.2 West); see Pseudo-Plutarch 1 (= *Life* 3.2 West) and 2 (= *Life* 4.2 West), Lucian, *True Histories*, 2.20, Heliodorus, *Ethiopian Story*, 3.13–14.

In order to support their claims, ancient authors sometimes appealed to the names of the poet that linked him with the Meles, the river at Smyrna (see n. 24 above), or to the existence on Chios of the guild of the Homeridae,[53] while the inhabitants of Colophon showed visitors to their city 'the place where Homer had made his debut as a poet'.[54] The authors of the biographies of Homer also deduced his place of origin from the works themselves. Thus it is not surprising to find the Troad, Argos, Mycenae, Pylos, and, of course, Ithaca among his many fatherlands. The supposed presence of elements of the Attic dialect in his poems was also used as an argument in favour of an Athenian origin.[55] Some of the customs and rituals he describes were interpreted in the same way (Heath 1998: 28–32): lines of the *Iliad* (1.459–61) which omit any mention of burning the hip bone of the sacrificial animal were used to prove that Homer came from Aeolia (the region in which Smyrna was situated) 'because the Aeolians are the only Greeks who do not burn this'.[56] He is also said to have been Egyptian 'because his heroes kiss each other on the lips' in the Egyptian manner or because, like the Egyptians, Homer attributes a characteristic gaze and manner of walking to the gods.[57] Aristodemus of Nysa made him a Roman on the basis of 'certain games or customs which are particular to the Romans, like backgammon or the habit of social inferiors standing up when their superiors arrive'.[58] An analogous reasoning led Meleager of Gadara to make him a Syrian: like the Syrians, Homer's heroes do not eat fish.[59] Finally, Zenodotus of Mallos argued that he was a Chaldean on the basis of the knowledge of astrology to be found in the poems.[60]

(d) Homer's dates

Ancient readers were equally uncertain about the period at which Homer lived and worked. As Pseudo-Plutarch and Tatian, along with

[53] Contest (= Life 1.21 West); Eustathius, *Ad Iliadem*, 1.6.9–10.
[54] Contest (= Life 1.2 West).
[55] Pseudo-Plutarch, *De Homero*, II.12.
[56] Pseudo-Herodotus (= *Life* 2.37 West).
[57] *Vita Romana* (*Life* 7.2 West), Heliodorus, *Ethiopian Story*, 3.13.
[58] *Vita Romana* (*Life* 7.2 West).
[59] Athenaeus, *Sophists at Dinner*, 4.45 (Kaibel).
[60] Scholia to *Iliad*, 23.79.

the author of the *Praise of Demosthenes* attributed to Lucian, readily acknowledged, the answer was unclear (*asaphēs*), it was a source of perplexity (*diaporeitai*), and disagreement (*asumphōnia*) was rife.[61] Sometimes Homer is only dated in relation to other poets, particularly Hesiod, but even then the results vary widely as we can see from the opening of the *Contest between Homer and Hesiod*: 'Some say that he was older than Hesiod, others that he was younger, and related to him . . . Some, however, say that they flourished at the same time.'[62] Usually Homer was considered to have been older than Hesiod,[63] but Herodotus thought they were contemporaries.[64] This is also the solution favoured by the *Contest*, for the obvious reason that only then would a competition between the two have been possible.[65] Ephorus, on the contrary, held that Homer was younger than Hesiod.[66] The same conclusion is reached by the genealogies cited in the first Pseudo-Plutarchan *Life* and the *Contest*, according to which Homer was born one or even three generations after Hesiod.[67] If we are to believe Tatian, Homer was also said to have been the contemporary of Archilochus.[68]

The variations in the dates attributed to Homer can only be explained by the broader arguments that they are used to support, as Barbara Graziosi (2002: 109) has rightly pointed out. Those authors who make him a contemporary of Hesiod place the two poets on the same level whether to link them together, as in the case of Herodotus and Xenophanes who speak of them as the two poets who created the genealogy of the Greek gods, or to contrast them as the poet of peace and the poet of war, as does the author of the *Contest*. Similarly, one could see the association of Homer and Archilochus as the result of a desire to set up a parallel between the

[61] Pseudo-Lucian, *Encomium of Demosthenes*, 9; Pseudo-Plutarch, 2 (= *Life* 4.2 West); Tatian, *To the Greeks*, 31.4.

[62] *Contest* (= *Life* 1. 4–5 West). See Graziosi 2002: 101–10.

[63] According to Xenophanes and Philochorus, quoted by Aulus Gellius, *Attic Nights*, 3.11.2.

[64] Herodotus, 2.53; *Vita Romana* (= *Life* 7.4 West) citing Pyrandrus and Hypsicrates of Amisus.

[65] *Contest* (= *Life* 1.5 West).

[66] Ephorus, *FrGrHist*, 101 a (cited by Aulus Gellius, *Attic Nights*, 3.11.2).

[67] According to Pseudo-Plutarch 1 (= *Life*, 3.2 West), Homer was the son of Critheis, Hesiod's cousin, and of Maion, the brother of Hesiod's father. But according to the *Contest* (= *Life* 1.4 West) he was the grandson of Maion.

[68] Tatian, *To the Greeks*, 31.3.

poetry of praise and that of blame. By contrast, those authors who claim that Homer was the earlier of the two affirm his primacy and present him as the founder of Greek culture.[69]

The absolute chronology is equally revealing. Homer is placed both within a mythical chronology, in relation to the Trojan War or the return of the children of Heracles, and within a historical chronology, in relation to Ionian migration in the eleventh and tenth centuries, the first Olympiad, or a memorable event such as Xerxes' crossing of the Hellespont. The author of the *Encomium of Demosthenes* hesitates between the two when he places Homer either 'in the Heroic period' or 'in the Ionian period'.[70] Those, like Crates of Mallos, who have complete confidence in Homer and consider him to be a thoroughly reliable historian and geographer tend to place him close in time to the Trojan War.[71] According to Pseudo-Plutarch, 'Some say he lived at the time of Trojan War and saw it personally.'[72] Crates and his school were more cautious, however, and simply placed him close in time to the Trojan War and 'after the return of the children of Heracles', that is, less than eighty years after the end of the war[73] 'so that those who took part in the expedition could have been known to him',[74] while others dated his life to one hundred years after the war.[75]

Aristotle and Aristarchus, by contrast, brought Homer's dates forward to the period of the Ionian migration, sixty years after the return of the children of Heracles and 140 years after the Trojan War.[76] Others placed it 150 years after the war[77] or even later.[78] Herodotus held that Homer lived only 400 years before him, which would place him four centuries later than the Trojan War,[79] while Thucydides in the *Archaeology* (1.3.3) states that Homer lived 'long after the Trojan War'. Theopompus, for his part, placed Homer's birth 500 years after the

[69] See, for example, Tatian, *To the Greeks*, 31.1.

[70] Pseudo-Lucian, *Encomium of Demosthenes*, 9.

[71] Strabo, 3.4.4.

[72] Pseudo-Plutarch 1 (= *Life* 3.5 West).

[73] Proclus (= *Life* 5.7 West).

[74] *Vita Scorialensis* 2 (= *Life* 9.2 West). See also *Vita Romana* (= *Life* 7.6 West), Tatian, *To the Greeks*, 31.2, and Clement of Alexandria, *Stromata*, 1.21.117.6.

[75] Pseudo-Plutarch 1 (= *Life* 3.5 West).

[76] Pseudo-Plutarch 1 (= *Life* 3.3 West) and Pseudo-Plutarch 2 (= *Life* 4.3 West).

[77] Pseudo-Plutarch 1 (= *Life* 3.5 West).

[78] According to Pseudo-Herodotus (= *Life* 2.38 West), Homer's birth coincided with the foundation of Smyrna, 622 years before the crossing of the Hellespont by Xerxes.

[79] Herodotus, 2.53.2.

war.[80] Each author seems therefore to choose a date that reflects his opinion of Homer's veracity and his worth as an historical source: those who place him close in time to the Trojan War emphasize, by so doing, his value as a near contemporary witness while those who seek to distance him from the war thereby throw doubt on his version of events, as Barbara Graziosi (2002: 121) has noted.

(e) The Homeric corpus

For modern readers, Homer is the author of the *Iliad* and the *Odyssey*. But in Antiquity it was only after 520, the date of Hippias' decision to have 'the works of Homer and no other author' recited at the Great Panathenaea, that the Homeric corpus came to be officially restricted to these two poems.[81] Before that date, most of the poems in the Epic Cycle were attributed to him by 'the ancients' (*οἱ ἀρχαίοι*),[82] not only the Trojan Cycle (the *Cypria*, the *Aethiopis*, the *Little Iliad*, and the *Returns (Nostoi) of the Heroes*)[83] but also the Theban Cycle (the *Thebaid* and the *Epigoni*),[84] and other epic poems like the *Sack of Oechalia* or the *Phocais*.[85] Homer was also considered to be the author of all the Homeric Hymns[86] and of epic parodies like the *Margites* and the *Batrachomyomachia (Battle of the Frogs and Mice)*.[87] Homer's name was thus

[80] See Clement of Alexandria, *Stromata*, 1.21.117.8.

[81] Pseudo-Plato, *Hipparchus*, 228b and Lycurgus, *Against Leocrates*, 102.

[82] Proclus (= *Life* 5.9 West). See Pfeiffer 1968: 43, Burkert 1987: 216, Graziosi 2002: 184–200.

[83] According to Pindar, Homer gave the *Cypria* to his son-in-law Stasinus as his daughter's dowry (Aelian, *Varia Historia*, 9.15). See also Herodotus, 2.117. On the attribution of the *Aethiopis* see the entry for Arctinus in the *Oxford Classical Dictionary*. Pseudo-Herodotus (= *Life* 2.16 West) and Hesychius (= *Life* 6.6 West) attribute the *Little Iliad* to Homer. See also Hesychius, ibid., on the attribution of the *Nostoi*.

[84] *Contest* (= *Life* 1.15) Herodotus, 4.32. According to Pausanias, *Description of Greece*, 9.9.5, Callinus (fr. 6 West) had already attributed the *Thebaid* to Homer. On the *Epigoni* see also Herodotus, 4.32.

[85] Proclus (= *Life* 5.5 West) says that Homer wrote the *Sack of Oechalia* and gave it to Creophylus on Ios. See also Callimachus, *Epigram* 6 and Strabo, 14.1.18. According to Pseudo-Herodotus (= *Life* 2.15–16) Homer composed the *Phocais* at Phocaea, but the poem was appropriated later by Thestorides.

[86] Hesychius (= *Life* 6.6 West). Thucydides, 3.104.4, attributes the *Hymn to Apollo* to Homer. See also the *Vita Scorialensis 2* (= *Life* 9.3 West).

[87] On the Margites see *Contest* (= *Life* 1.5); Pseudo-Plutarch 1 (= *Life* 3.5 West); Pseudo-Plutarch 2 (= *Life* 4.4 West); Proclus (= *Life* 5.9 West), Hesychius (= *Life* 6.6). The attribution to Homer may go back as far as Archilochus (fr. 303 West). On

attached to the whole of archaic epic, making him the father of tragedy, but he was also considered to be the author of comic poems (*paignia*) which made him the ancestor of comedy, as Aristotle emphasized (*Poetics*, 1448b36–9).

(f) Homer's biography

The ancient depictions of Homer's personality and of some of the characters and events in his life were directly derived from his work.[88] This is a familiar strategy of ancient biographers, who tended to fashion an image of the man on the basis of his writings,[89] a method that is diametrically opposed to that of those nineteenth-century critics like the French philosopher Henri Taine who deduced the work from the man and tried to reconstruct the author's life as a way of explaining his writings.

According to the ancient sources, Homer's first teacher, or his adoptive father, was called Phemius, like the bard who sings for the suitors on Ithaca.[90] One of the members of his audience was a merchant named Mentes, just like the prince of the Taphians whose appearance is assumed by Athena in the first book of the *Odyssey*.[91] Upon his arrival in Ithaca, Mentes entrusted him to one of his best friends, who just happened to be named Mentor, like one of Odysseus' faithful companions.[92] Later, the cobbler who took him in, in the Cymaean colony of Neonteichos, has the same name as the man who made Ajax's shield of seven layers of ox-hide.[93] The link between the man and his poetry is mentioned explicitly by Pseudo-Herodotus who says: 'When he [Homer] turned his hand to poetry, he rendered his gratitude, firstly to Mentor the Ithacan in the *Odyssey*, for having tended him so assiduously when his eyes were ailing in Ithaca: he found a place for his name in the poem . . . He also repaid his teacher Phemius for his upbringing and education . . . He also recalls the

the *Batrachomyomachia* see Pseudo-Herodotus (= *Life* 2.24 West), Pseudo-Plutarch 1 (= *Life* 3.5 West), *Vita Scorialensis 2* (= *Life* 9.3 West).

88 See Latacz 1996: 28.

89 See Lefkowitz 1981: 98.

90 Pseudo-Herodotus (= *Life* 2.4 West), Pseudo-Plutarch 1 (= *Life* 3.2 West).

91 Pseudo-Herodotus (= *Life* 2.6 West).

92 Pseudo-Herodotus (= *Life* 2.7 West).

93 Pseudo-Herodotus (= *Life* 2.26 West).

shipowner [Mentes] with whom he sailed out all over . . . He rendered thanks also to Tychios, the cobbler who received him at Neonteichos' (*Life*, 2.26, West).

Furthermore, on his arrival at Chios, dogs are said to have given him a similar welcome to that received by Odysseus when he arrives at Eumaeus' house on Ithaca.[94] He is said to have planned to travel to mainland Greece, and to Athens in particular, as is shown by the praise of the Athenian heroes, Erechtheus and Menestheus, to be found in the *Iliad*.[95] But the most famous episode in Homer's life, the contest between him and Hesiod at the funeral games for Amphidamas—an anecdote that goes back at least to the fourth century and the *Mouseion* by Alcidamas, as we can see from two Michigan papyri,[96] or even as far back as the sixth century if we accept the date proposed by Richardson (1981)—has nothing to do with the Homeric poems. Rather, it is directly inspired by the passage in the *Works and Days* (lines 650–7) where Hesiod tells us that he returned victorious from a contest organized in Chalcis in Euboea.

Like Odysseus who 'saw many cities', the Homer of the Pseudo-Herodotean life is a great traveller who saw many cities and many countries.[97] He is also blind, like Demodocus.[98] Within the *Odyssey*, this blindness is compensated by a gift of knowledge which, like that of the seer Tiresias who is also blind, is not limited to the present. It thus serves as an illustration of the human condition in which good and ill are always intermingled. His blindness may also be explained by the division of roles between the Muse and the poet in the Homeric poems.[99] For it is the function of the Muses to see: if these goddesses know everything it is because they are everywhere and see everything.[100] The poets, for their part, must content themselves with the

[94] Pseudo-Herodotus (*Life* 2.21 West) and *Odyssey*, 14.29–35.

[95] Pseudo-Herodotus (*Life* 2.27–8 West).

[96] See West 1967: 433–8.

[97] *Odyssey*, 1.3 and Pseudo-Herodotus (*Life* 2.26 West).

[98] The blindness that characterizes Homer from the *Hymn to Apollo*, 172 onwards is mentioned by all his biographers with the exception of Proclus (= *Life* 5.6) and Lucian, *True Histories*, 2.20, two authors who consistently depart from the traditional biographies. On Demodocus' blindness see *Odyssey*, 8.62–5. The FV scholion to line 63 makes an explicit connection between Demodocus' blindness and that of Homer.

[99] For interpretations of Homer's blindness and their criticism, see Rabau 2001: 97–9 and Graziosi 2002: 132–46.

[100] *Iliad*, 2.485: *ὑμεῖς γὰρ θεαί ἐστε πάρεστέ τε ἴστέ τε πάντα.*

sense of hearing: they hear the Muses' tale[101] and thus have no need to see.

But there are two important elements of the biographies that can only be explained by the later reception of the text of Homer. The first is the way in which the image of the rhapsodes, who are normally credited with the invention of 'Homer', came to be projected upon the Homeric bard. The contrast between the ordinary everyday world in which the *Lives* of Homer are set and the aristocratic universe of the poets Phemius and Demodocus in the *Odyssey*, who sing their songs in the royal court, has often been noted (Jacoby 1933: 38). The Homer of the *Lives* is presented as a 'rhapsode' who travels from town to town to perform his songs in public or in private.[102] Another example is the tradition that presents him as a schoolmaster,[103] which can undoubtedly be explained by the importance of the Homeric poems in elementary education from a very early period (perhaps because these poems were the first to become available in the form of written texts (Burkert 1987: 216–17)) and by his role as the educator of Greece.

2. THE HOMERIC QUESTION

All the biographies of Homer present him as a poet who wrote his poems. But one or two sources suggest that he left others to make a unified whole out of scattered poems.

[101] *Iliad*, 2.486.

[102] *Contest* (= *Life* 1 West), 5: *Ὅμηρον περιέρχεσθαι κατὰ πόλιν ῥαψῳδοῦντα*; 15: *ὁ δὲ Ὅμηρος ἀποτυχὼν τῆς νίκης περιερχόμενος ἔλεγε τὰ ποιήματα* and 17: *ἐκεῖθεν* (i.e. from Athens) *δὲ παραγενόμενος εἰς Κόρινθον ἐρραψῴδει τὰ ποιήματα*. The *Contest* also portrays him performing his poems in Athens 'in the Council chamber' (17) and at the Festival at Delos (18) just as the Pseudo-Herodotean *Life* presents him as an itinerant poet who performs (*epideiknumi*) his poems at Neonteichos (10), Cyme (12), Phocaea (15), Chios (25–7), on Samos at the festival of the Apatouria and on Ios (34). See also Pseudo-Plutarch 1 (*Life* 3.4 West) where he sails to Thebes for the festival of the Kronia which was a musical contest. Proclus (*Life* 5.8 West) says that he 'travelled to many parts of the world'. See also Hesychius (= *Life* 6.6 West) and the *Vita Scorialensis 2* (= *Life* 9.5 West).

[103] Pseudo-Herodotus (= *Life* 2.5, 6, 24, 25 West).

(a) Taking Homer to pieces

In the Byzantine period the *Souda* claimed that Homer was not responsible for composing the *Iliad* as a whole but merely wrote 'rhapsodies' that he performed while travelling from town to town and which were later put together by several different people, including, most notably, Peisistratus, the tyrant of Athens.[104] Several centuries earlier, Cicero (*De Oratore*, 3.34) said that Peisistratus had been the first to arrange the Homeric poems in the order in which we now have them and that these poems had until then been 'in disorder' (*confusi*). In his *Against Apion* (1.2), Flavius Josephus explained the inconsistencies within the poems by the fact that they were only put together after the death of their author and even questioned whether 'Homer' had left any written poems at all. Aelian likewise accepted that the men of old had sung Homer's poems 'separately' at first[105] and that 'long afterwards Lycurgus of Sparta was the first to bring the whole Homeric poems to Greece . . . Later, Peisistratus published the *Iliad* and the *Odyssey* after putting them together.'

Since the eighteenth century at least, modern scholars have placed a great deal of weight on these traditions.[106] They began by taking the Homeric poems to pieces, without, however, questioning their authorship. The Abbé d'Aubignac, who composed a *Dissertation on the Iliad* published in 1715, and Charles Perrault, author of the famous *Comparison between the Ancients and the Moderns* (1692) as well as the famous fairy tales, both argued that the *Iliad* and the *Odyssey* were no more than a clumsy collection of poems originally composed as independent works by a single author. At about the same time, the great English philologist Richard Bentley[107] mounted a challenge to the myth of the poet named Homer who recorded his works in writing for posterity, proposing instead the image of a

[104] *Souda* (= Hesychius, *Life* 6.6 West): *ἔγραψε δὲ τὴν Ἰλιάδα οὐχ ἅμα οὐδὲ κατὰ τὸ συνεχές, καθάπερ σύγκειται, ἀλλ' αὐτὸς μὲν ἑκάστην ῥαψῳδίαν γράψας καὶ ἐπιδειξάμενος . . . ἀπέλιπεν. ὕστερον δὲ συνετέθη καὶ συνετάχθη ὑπὸ πολλῶν καὶ μάλιστα ὑπὸ Πεισιστράτου τοῦ τῶν Ἀθηναίων τυράννου.*

[105] Aelian, *Historical Miscellany (Varia Historia)*, 13.14: *Ὅτι τὰ Ὁμήρου ἔπη πρότερον διῃρημένα ᾖδον οἱ παλαιοί.*

[106] For the history of the Homeric question see Heubeck 1974, Turner 1997, and Fowler 2004a.

[107] *Discourse of Freethinking* (1713) by Eleuthereus Lipsiensis (quoted by Wolf, *Prolegomena*, chs. 39 and 27. See Grafton 1991: 225.

poverty-stricken poet who wrote 'a sequel of Songs and rhapsodies to be sung by himself for small earnings and good cheer at Festivals and other days of Merriment' (a portrait which, one might add, corresponds quite closely to the information conveyed by the ancient biographies); only after five centuries or so were these finally gathered together and made into a unified whole by Peisistratus.

(b) Wolf's thesis

But modern scholarship went further still along the path opened up by Bentley and the others. With his *Prolegomena to Homer* (1795), a groundbreaking contribution that opened a new chapter in the history of philology, the German scholar Friedrich Wolf laid the groundwork for the Homeric question when he 'gave up hope that the original form of the Homeric Poems could ever be laid out save in our minds, and even there only in rough outlines'.[108] A little earlier, an Englishman named Robert Wood,[109] whose 'brilliant audacity' inspired Wolf's admiration,[110] travelled all over the Ottoman Empire in order to 'read the *Iliad* and *Odyssey* in the countries, where Achilles fought, where Ulysses travelled, and where Homer sung'.[111] He not only demonstrated the accuracy of Homer's descriptions but was also one of the first to bring an ethnographic approach to the study of Homeric society with his comparison of the customs of the Homeric heroes with those of the Bedouins of Palmyra among whom he had camped.[112] Wood also noted the parallel between the Homeric poems and the poems of Ossian and suggested that both were examples of oral poetry that had been collected together and published at a later point. But the impact of Wolf's work was immeasurably greater. By applying the sophisticated methods that had been developed for biblical criticism to the study of Homeric texts, Wolf was able to identify the changes to which the original text had been subjected and thus to attempt a reconstruction of the history of the Homeric poems. This was all done in a limpid style that contributed greatly to the

[108] Wolf 1985: 47.

[109] An Essay *on the Original Genius of Homer*, 1769 (posthumous edition with additions and corrections London, 1775), ed. B. Fabian (Hildesheim and New York, 1976).

[110] Wolf 1985: 71.

[111] Wood, preface to the *Essay*, quoted in Myres 1958: 60.

[112] See Myres 1958: 60–3, Turner 1997: 124–5.

dissemination and success of his thesis. According to Wolf, the poems were oral compositions, originally transmitted by oral tradition and recited first by their authors, the *aoidoi* (or 'bards'), and then by rhapsodes (literally 'stitchers of song') who performed verse composed by others. They were first written down in Athens during the sixth century (under Peisistratus, to be precise) in connection with the creation of the Panathenaic festival at which the two Homeric poems were traditionally recited. Wolf argued further that they were not given their definitive form until the third century, as a result of the work of a series of scholars working at the library of Alexandria (the two most prominent of these being Zenodotus and Aristarchus) who were influenced more by aesthetic criteria than by scholarly analysis.

This mode of transmission, Wolf proposed, accounted for the repetitions and inconsistencies that are characteristic of Homeric poetry.[113] There are, for example, two descents to the Underworld, or *nekuiai*, in the *Odyssey*, one in Book 11 and one in Book 24. Furthermore, Books 16, 19, and 22 appear to contradict each other on a point that may seem unimportant to us today but which came to be vested with great significance by the Analysts.[114] In Book 16.281–98 Telemachus is ordered by Odysseus to remove all the weapons hanging on the walls of the great hall with the exception of 'a pair of swords, a pair of spears and a pair of ox-hide shields' which they themselves will use to fight the suitors. But, when the order is actually carried out in Book 19.3–33, it is clear that Telemachus and his father remove all the weapons. Moreover, when the battle commences in Book 22.101–12, Telemachus has to go and find shields, spears, and helmets 'in the room where the good arms were stored'. Such a lack of consistency was considered incompatible with single authorship, particularly when that author was as perfect as Homer. It was therefore seen as proof that alterations had been made by another hand.

In the light of the history of the Homeric text, F. A. Wolf was convinced that, given the history of the text of Homer, 'the sources cannot enable us to restore Homer's work to the genuine, pure form which first poured from his divine lips' (Wolf 1985: 45–6) 'The Homer that we hold in our hands now is not the one who flourished in the months of the Greeks of his own day, but one variously altered,

[113] See Grafton 1991: 227–33, Turner 1997: 125–31.

[114] Woodhouse 1969: 158: 'Perhaps the most formidable problem in the *Odyssey*.'

interpolated, corrected, and emended from the times of Solon down to those of the Alexandrians' (Wolf 1985: 209).

His successors, however, were less modest in their aims. In fact, critical studies of Homer throughout the nineteenth century and for a large part of the twentieth century were dominated by two approaches. Some scholars, following the path laid out by the work of G. Hermann, attempted to extract the original core of the Homeric poems from the morass of later additions or 'interpolations' which had disfigured it.[115] Others, inspired by the example of K. Lachmann and his *Betrachtungen über Homers Iliad* (1847), focused their efforts on identifying the different elements which had gone to make up the poems.[116] As Jean Bollack (1997: 32–3) has pointed out, Adolf Kirchoff's work *Die homerische Odyssee und ihre Entstehung* (*Homer's Odyssey and its Formation*), published in 1859, which tried to identify within the poem an original Return of Odysseus (or *Nostos*),[117] onto which the revenge of Odysseus and the Adventures of Telemachus were subsequently grafted, served as the foundation of the work of the later scholars who have been termed 'Analysts', such as Wilamowitz, Schwartz, and von der Mühll.[118] It also lies at the origin of those studies which tried to demonstrate the unity of its composition and consequently the existence of a single author (hence the name 'Unitarians' given to them).

(c) Analysts and Unitarians

Before giving some examples to illustrate this battle that was to rage for over a century, it is worth pausing for a moment to consider the very notion of interpolation and its implications, as Richard Tarrant (1987, 1989) and Sophie Rabau (1997a) have done. Claims that interpolations are always illogical and 'ruin the coherence of the text' or that they are inessential, repeating what has already been said, and unnecessary may well tell us more about the reader than about the work. Above all, they reveal the limitations of interpretative

[115] Hermann 1832. See Turner 1997: 134.

[116] Lachmann 1847. See Turner 1997: 131–3.

[117] This included, in addition to the last two stops on the travels (Calypso and the Phaeacians), the Ciconians, the Lotus-Eaters, the Cyclopes, and a short version of the *nekuia*.

[118] Wilamowitz-Moellendorf 1884, Schwartz 1924, von der Mühll 1940.

approaches that prove unable to explain the passages in question. For they allow the critic to excise from the text anything that proves resistant to commentary or, to be more precise, anything that the particular critic cannot explain by using his or her own critical approach. They thus attribute to the obtuseness of the interpolator what may in fact be a failing of the critic him- or herself. Finally, they authorize the construction of a 'perfect' text by rejecting as inauthentic anything that is felt to contravene the criteria of taste or morality, anything, in short that is judged to be 'unworthy of the author'[119] or, more precisely, anything that does not correspond to the reader's expectations of a 'great' author.

One consequence is that doublets are rejected. Where the same passage is repeated it is considered obvious that one occurrence is the result of an interpolation and this will be the one that is less 'natural' and less well suited to its context. One example will suffice. The same piece of advice, expressed in exactly the same terms and addressed both times to Telemachus, is found in Book 1, where it is spoken by Athena, and is repeated in Book 2, this time by Eurymachus. On the first occasion, Athena says, 'Tell the suitors they must disperse to their own estates; as for your mother, supposing her heart is set on marriage, let her go back to her father's house. They [the suitors] will prepare the wedding and the many gifts that should be given to a father in exchange for his daughter' (1.274–9). In Book 2, the suitor Eurymachus says: 'Let him bid his mother go back to her father's house. They [the suitors] will prepare the wedding and the many gifts that should be given to a father in exchange for his daughter' (2.195–7). In this case, critics note that these lines are appropriate to one of the suitors but hard to justify if spoken by Athena and lines 277–8 are thus removed from Book 1.

Other passages are condemned as inappropriate, like the story of the adulterous liaison between Ares and Aphrodite in Book 8 of the *Odyssey*.[120] Even in Antiquity lines 333–42 of this episode were condemned 'because they were not fitting'.[121] One scholion to line 778 of Aristophanes' *Peace* even gives the impression that certain

[119] Tarrant 1989: 152: 'passages where they [the techniques of elaboration, heightening, and capping] are ineptly or inappropriately used are therefore legitimately suspect.'

[120] See Hunzinger 1997 *passim*.

[121] *In Odysseam*, 8.333–42: *ἐν ἐνίοις ἀντιγράφοις οἱ δέκα στίχοι οὐ φέρονται διὰ τὸ ἀπρέπειαν ἐμφαίνειν. νεωτερικὸν γὰρ τὸ φρόνημα.*

ancient scholars had athetized the episode as a whole.[122] Modern scholars followed suit, but they mostly did so without reference to the question of morality (even if this in fact lies behind their refusal to attribute such a scandalous passage to an author who was at the same time an educator) and justified their condemnation by appeals to logic. They emphasized the 'different' and incongruous nature of a passage that 'creates a curious hiatus between the two dance scenes [of Book 8]' (Jaccottet 1982: 131 n. 6). They also noted the contradiction between this passage, in which Aphrodite is described as the wife of Hephaestus (8.268–9), and Book 18 of the *Iliad*, where the craftsman-god is married to Charis (*Iliad*, 18.382–3). In addition, they catalogued the rare forms of words and expressions which are all used as arguments against attributing these lines to 'Homer'.

Those who argue for the authenticity of the passage have adopted the opposite strategy and tried to demonstrate the coherence of the text as it is transmitted. They underline the fact that the subject of Demodocus' song is particularly well suited to an audience made up of lovers of 'dance' as well as 'the lyre' and 'the pleasures of the bed' (*Odyssey*, 8.248–9) and that it fits perfectly into the overall structure and organization of the text: 'it summarizes the themes and issues of the whole of Book 8'[123] and constitutes a *mise en abyme* in a comic register of a central theme of the *Odyssey*, that of the eternal triangle between husband, wife, and lover (represented in a tragic mode by the story of Agamemnon, Clytemnestra, and Aegisthus). The contrast with the Iliadic account of Hephaestus is justified by the difference in authorship, given that, as one ancient scholiast noted, Demodocus, and not Homer, is the author of the song.[124] The difference in tone is even treated as a virtue: the love affair between Ares and Aphrodite is interpreted as introducing into the *Odyssey* a certain note of realism that provides a welcome contrast to the ideal vision of the married couple embodied by Odysseus and Penelope (Olson 1989a) and helps introduce into the work a dialogism which is very modern (Peradotto 1993). Finally, Unitarians show that the language in this passage is not marked out by any significant irregularities.[125]

[122] Scholia in Pacem, 778.3: *ἀθετοῦντας τὴν ἐν Ὀδυσσείᾳ Ἄρεως καὶ Ἀφροδίτης μοιχείαν.*

[123] Pralon 1998, quoted by Hunzinger 1997: 134 n. 48.

[124] H Scholia to *Odyssey*, 8.267: *ὅλως δὲ Ὅμηρος οὐδὲ οἶδεν Ἥφαιστον Ἀφροδίτῃ συνοικεῖν, Χάριτι δὲ αὐτὸν συμβιοῦντα, Δημόδοκος δὲ τῇ ἰδίᾳ μυθοποιίᾳ.*

[125] See the references collected in Hunzinger 1997: 130 n. 26.

In sum, it is clear that all these arguments, or nearly all these arguments, can be made for or against a particular passage and serve only as a posteriori justifications of opposing readings of the text. It would take up too much space to provide a detailed recapitulation of the different results of this method of deconstructing the Homeric text and of the attempts at reconstructing it that it inevitably gave rise to. Here, it will suffice to give a short overview limited to the *Odyssey*.[126]

(d) The *Odyssey* between Analysts and Unitarians

The more moderate Analysts, such as Denys Page,[127] were content to identify a few minor interpolations and to follow essentially the Alexandrian scholars like Aristarchus and Aristophanes of Byzantium who considered the reunion of Odysseus and Penelope (23.296) to be the end of the *Odyssey*.[128] But their more daring colleagues did not stop at this. Wolfgang Schadewaldt (1991, originally published in 1959), for example, distinguished two authors: 'Homer' told the story of the return of Odysseus and was responsible for most of the *Odyssey* as we know it, whereas, he claimed, an interpolator with a very different turn of mind added Books 1 to 4 (the Adventures of Telemachus), part of Book 8 (the second day of Odysseus' stay at the Phaeacian court), and the whole of Book 24.

Others, like Peter von der Mühll, Friedrich Focke, and Reinhold Merkelbach, increased the number of authors to three by adding to the two poets a third one who combined their works into a single whole. But the resulting solutions differ widely. Von der Mühll (1940) proposed, in addition to the 'heroic poet' of the return of Odysseus and the more 'bourgeois' author of the Adventures of Telemachus, an Athenian 'arranger' or 'editor' ('Bearbeiter' in German) who combined these two poems into one at the beginning of the sixth century, thus creating the poem we have now. Focke (1943) suggested a different combination involving an Ionian poet of the second half of the eighth century who was the author of Odysseus' adventures, a

126 See the excellent summary by Heubeck 1974: 87–130.

127 Page 1955 excludes some parts of the Adventures of Telemachus, the second assembly of the gods, the second *nekuia*, and some episodes of the murder of the suitors.

128 See also Kirk 1962.

second author close to the *Iliad* who composed Books 5 to 23.343, and a third 'arranger' who put together the first two poems, adding in the process Books 1 to 4 (the Adventures of Telemachus) and Book 24. Merkelbach (1951), for his part, distinguished a poet who told of the revenge of Odysseus (from his arrival on Ithaca up to the recognition scene of Book 23) who might have been 'Homer', a later poet who added Odysseus' adventures, the account of his return to Ithaca, his stay at the house of Eumaeus, the return of Telemachus, and the recognition scene in Book 19, as well as the inevitable arranger.

Theiler (1950) increased to four the number of poets whose hand can be detected in the *Odyssey* in its current form: 'Homer', the heroic poet who was responsible for the account of the return and revenge of Odysseus; the bourgeois poet who composed the Adventures of Telemachus; a bucolic poet who composed Books 13 to 14, devoted to Odysseus' stay in the home of the 'godlike swineherd', and finally an arranger who put together these different sections with a greater or lesser degree of skill.

The 'Unitarians', by contrast, tried to show, often successfully, that the contradictions were only apparent and that the transitions between the various parts of the poem were too subtly handled to be the work of an interpolator who was, by definition, unintelligent. Here too a single example will suffice. The Analysts had frequently appealed to the structure of the account of Telemachus' visit to Sparta to support the argument that, originally, there were two separate works: the Adventures of Telemachus and an *Odyssey*. While it is undeniable that this episode is divided between Books 4 (1–624) and 15 (1–181), the Unitarians have been able to show that this is not a case of two fragments of a whole being arbitrarily divided by an interpolator, but of the use of two elements which echo each other in very precise ways to frame a central episode.

3. FROM ANALYSIS TO NEO-ANALYSIS

'Neo-analysis'[129] was invented by the Greek scholar J. T. Kakridis in a series of articles published in the 1930s but his influence was only felt

[129] On Neo-analysis see Heubeck 1974: 40–8, Kullmann 1984, 1992, and Willcock 1997.

much later, when his works were collected in a single volume published in Greek in 1944 and then translated into English in 1949 with the title *Homeric Researches*. Thereafter, his work had a major impact in Germany on scholars such as Heinrich Pestalozzi (1945), Alfred Heubeck (1991, 1st pub 1950), Wolfgang Schadewalt (1952), and Wolfgang Kullmann (1960). The Neo-analysts all wanted to find a middle position between the Analysts and the Unitarians. Like the Unitarians, they maintain the unity of the work but, like the Analysts, they recognize that there are inconsistencies within the Homeric text. But, instead of explaining these by the existence of multiple authors and distinguishing different layers in the composition of the text, they go back to the period before Homer, to Homer's own sources and to the tradition of which his work represents the culmination. They take their starting point from the perfectly reasonable hypothesis that the poems that make up the Epic Cycle and which are without any doubt later than 'Homer' (it has even been suggested that they depend very closely on the *Iliad* and the *Odyssey* and that they are continuations of these poems[130]) reflect an older oral tradition. They also claim, as Kullmann puts it, that 'the original use of motifs (i.e. the contexts in which they were originally used) can still be made out because the motifs are not thoroughly assimilated to their new context' (Kullmann 1984: 309).

The *Iliad* is thus related back to a tradition preserved in the *Aethiopis*, one of the poems in the Epic Cycle that we know of thanks to the résumé provided by Proclus in his *Chrestomathia*. In both epics, a friend of Achilles (Antilochus in the *Aethiopis*, Patroclus in the *Iliad*) is killed by a Trojan leader or one of the Trojans' allies (Memnon or Hector); Achilles then returns to battle in order to avenge his friend, although he knows that he will die shortly after his victim. The *Aethiopis* ended with the death of Achilles and it is possible to identify details that evoke this episode in the account of the death and funeral of Patroclus.[131] The presence of the Nereids and of Thetis seems to be borrowed from the account of the funeral of Achilles (*Iliad*, 18.35–66, cf. *Odyssey*, 24.47–59). In the *Iliad*, Thetis holds the head of her son in her arms, a gesture which is more normally associated with a person grieving over a dead body.[132]

[130] See Nagy 1990: 72.

[131] See Kakridis 1949: 65–95 and Willcock 1997: 176–8.

[132] *Iliad*, 18.71, compare *Iliad*, 24.724 where Andromache cradles Hector's head in her arms.

Moreover, the formula 'he lay there . . . huge and hugely fallen', used to describe Achilles' grief at the death of Patroclus,[133] is normally used to describe a dead warrior lying in the dust and is found in the *Odyssey* with reference to the death of Achilles.[134]

Neo-analysis does not simply seek to identify the sources of the *Iliad* but also shows how they have been transformed, thus contributing to a more balanced appreciation of Homer's originality. Thus the combat between Ajax and Odysseus during the funeral games for Patroclus can be seen as an echo on a smaller scale of their rivalry for the arms of Achilles (Willcock 1997: 188).

Also related to the Neo-analytical approach, even if they do not say so explicitly, are those studies that try to identify borrowings from folklore in the *Odyssey*.[135] Some of these studies simply attempt to find folktale motifs in the poem such as the departing hero who makes his wife promise not to remarry until their son is an adult, the figure of the sailor who, after a long absence, returns just in time to prevent his wife remarrying, not to mention enchanted ships and encounters with ogres and sorceresses.[136] Others have preferred to stress the various types of transformation undergone by these themes as they pass into the epic repertoire and contrast the 'folklore' version of the journey, in which a series of adventures each quite separate from the others can be multiplied *ad infinitum*, with the story of Odysseus, in which they are all interlinked and organized in such a way as to lead to a definite ending point.[137] In so doing, they attempt to distinguish between the old (the traditional elements used by the poet) and the new (the elements that are characteristic of his own particular talents) in each episode. Thus, in the *Odyssey*, the episode of the Sirens is no longer simply the story of monsters who, like the Sphinx, challenge travellers from their lair on top of a cliff and commit suicide when one guesses the answer to their riddle. Instead, the context is transformed and the heroic theme of glory is

[133] *Iliad*, 18.26–7: *αὐτὸς δ' ἐν κονίῃσι μέγας μεγαλωστὶ τανυσθεὶς | κεῖτο.*

[134] *Iliad*, 16.776 and *Odyssey*, 24.39: *κεῖτο μέγας μεγαλωστί, λελασμένος ἱπποσυνάων.*

[135] For a bibliography see Hansen 1997.

[136] Carpenter 1946, Germain 1954, Page 1973. See Hansen 1997: 446–57 who provides a list of the parallels between 'Homeric stories' and the analogous ones to be found in nineteenth- and twentieth-century oral traditions.

[137] Reinhardt 1996 and Hölscher 1988.

introduced as the Sirens try to hold Odysseus back by songs celebrating the sufferings of the Greeks at Troy.[138]

4. FROM THE HOMERIC QUESTION TO ORAL POETRY

Although they differed on almost everything else, the Analysts, Unitarians, and their successors, the proponents of Neo-analysis, were in agreement on one essential point. They all assumed that it was possible to treat the *Odyssey* and the *Iliad* like any other written text and to try to identify the individual or individuals who were their authors. This was to misunderstand entirely the very nature of the tradition from which the Homeric poems emerged, a tradition that was essentially oral, as Milman Parry brilliantly demonstrated in his thesis on *The Traditional Epithet in Homer* (1928) which revolutionized the study of Homeric poetry.[139]

In his study of the use of proper names and the epithets that are regularly attached to them in Homer, Parry noticed that for any given grammatical case, in a particular position in the line, and with a particular metrical value, the same formula is nearly always used. Thus, in the dative case, Odysseus is 'great-hearted' (Ὀδυσσῆϊ μεγαλήτορι) when his name occurs at the beginning of the line after a long and a short syllable, but at the end of the line he is 'godlike' (ἀντιθέῳ Ὀδυσῆϊ). Similarly, in the nominative, the name 'Diomedes' when it occurs at the end of the line can be preceded by a series of epithets which constitute a system given that they have different metrical values: short, long, short, short, long (βοὴν ἀγαθὸς Διομήδης, 'Diomedes, master of the war-cry'); two short syllables followed by a long (κρατερὸς Διομήδης, 'strong Diomedes'). There are very few instances of duplication (that is to say different formulae to express the same person in the same case with the same metrical value). Those that do exist such as Ὀδυσσῆος μεγαλήτορος ('great-hearted Odysseus', *Odyssey* 4.143) or Ὀδυσσῆος ταλασίφρονος ('enduring Odysseus', twelve occurrences) or, for Athena, Διὸς γλαυκώπιδι

[138] *Odyssey*, 12.184–91. See Pucci 1998: 1–11 'The Song of the Sirens'.

[139] Parry's thesis was published in French in 1928, the English translation was published in Parry 1971. See also Foley (1997).

κούρῃ ('the grey-eyed daughter of Zeus', *Odyssey*, 2.433) and *Διὸς κούρῃ μεγάλοιο* ('daughter of great Zeus', three occurrences) and, for Hera, *βοῶπις πότνια Ἥρη* ('ox-eyed queen Hera', fourteen occurrences) and *θεὰ λευκώλενος Ἥρη* ('the white-armed goddess Hera', nineteen occurrences) are exceptional. 'Of the forty different noun-epithet formulae only six are not unique in Homer.'[140]

The same applies to common nouns. Here, Parry limited himself in his thesis to samples.[141] He showed for example that, at the end of the line, the ship in the nominative singular can be called a 'swift ship' (*ὠκύαλος νηῦς*, two occurrences), a 'hollow ship' (*γλαφυρὴ νηῦς*, *Odyssey*, 4.356), a 'seafaring ship' (*ποντοπορός νηῦς*, four occurrences) or a 'well-made ship' (*νηῦς εὐεργής*, three occurrences). In the accusative it is a 'black ship' (*νῆα μέλαιναν*)—usually at the end of the line but it can also occur at the beginning, following an initial dactyl which may be *νῦν δ' ἄγε*, or *ἀλλ' ἄγε αἶψα δέ* (four occurrences). But we also find a 'swift ship' (*νῆα θοήν*, twenty-seven occurrences only two of which are at the beginning of a line), a 'well-made ship' (*εὐεργέα νῆα*, six occurrences, all at the end of the line), a 'very beautiful ship' (*περικαλλέα νῆα*, three occurrences, all at the end of the line), and, in one instance, a hollow ship (*νῆα γλαφυρήν*, *Odyssey*, 19.274). In short, 'the 23 epithets of ships in Homer present 70 different forms of which two only, *δολιχηρέτμοιο* (twice) and *κυανοπρῴροιο* (12 times), can be interchanged' (Parry 1971: 112).

Parry's conclusion was that Homer used formulae which, in the same metrical conditions, use the same words to express the same idea (in Parry's own words, the 'essential idea'). For a person setting out, Homer uses *βῆ δ' ἰέναι* 'he or she went on his/her way' (fifteen occurrences). The opening of a speech is often signalled by the phrase *ἔπεα πτερόεντα προσηύδα*, 'he or she uttered winged words' (107 occurrences), and its end by *ὥς φάτο*, 'thus he or she spoke' (138 occurrences), or *ὣς ἐφάμην*, 'thus I spoke' (thirty-eight occurrences). Milman Parry drew a broad conclusion from these results, claiming that Homeric poetry was entirely formulaic in nature: 'Generally speaking, whenever Homer has to express the same idea under the same metrical conditions, he has recourse to the same words or the same group of words' (Parry 1971: 22). For Parry, these formulae constituted 'a widely extended system only exceptionally presenting elements which are superfluous from the point of view of versification'

[140] See Parry 1971: 17. [141] Ibid. 109–17.

(Parry 1971: 17). This system was characterized by its extensiveness (the poet had formulae ready for every grammatical case, every position in the line, and every metrical pattern) and its economy (there is usually only one formula for a given essential idea with a given metrical value). It was not 'a common property of all hexametric poetry . . . A study of the heroic poems of Apollonius Rhodius and Virgil will provide us with sure evidence on this point' (Parry 1971: 24).

At almost the same time as Parry and entirely independently of his work, a German scholar, Walter Arend, drew attention to a similar phenomenon: the existence in Homeric poetry of what he named 'type-scenes'.[142] He noticed that certain actions or events (such as sacrifices, banquets, funerals, assemblies, oaths, journeys, deliberation, arming scenes, and baths) are narrated using the same expressions, always in the same order.

The best example is no doubt that of the sacrificial banquet. The description of this ritual act, performed according to a strict set of rules, always follows the same pattern. The description is divided into four sections each of which ends with a concluding line.

1. The first of these sections, which includes everything leading up to the slaughter of the victim, can be of greater or lesser length. It usually begins with the mention of the sacrifice or the hecatomb,[143] but can extend further back in time to include the moment at which the order was given,[144] with a description of the execution of the order and the arrival of the victim. It often includes the following elements:

a line evoking the bringing of the animal to the altar;[145]
a reference to the sprinkling of lustral water before the sacrifice;[146]
a mention of grains of barley being picked up;[147]
an allusion to the plucking of a few hairs from the victim's head which are then thrown into the fire;[148]
a prayer which follows one or other of these ritual gestures.[149]

[142] W. Arend, *Die Typische Szenen bei Homer*, published in Berlin in 1933.
[143] See, for example, *Iliad*, 1.447.
[144] See, for example, *Odyssey*, 3.421.
[145] See, for example, *Iliad*, 1.447, 2.410; *Odyssey*, 12.356, 14.414.
[146] *Iliad*, 1.449; *Odyssey*, 3.445.
[147] *Odyssey*, 3.446, 14.422; *Iliad*, 1.449.
[148] *Odyssey*, 3.446, 14.422.
[149] This follows the offering of the *oulokhutai* (*Iliad*, 1.450–6, 2.411–18; *Odyssey*, 3.445–6) or of the hair of the victim (*Odyssey*, 14.423–4) or, once, before them (*Odyssey*, 12.356).

The two most important moments in this sequence of actions are the offering of barley grains and the prayer, as is indicated by the closing formula: 'When they had prayed and had sprinkled the crushed barley grains' (αὐτὰρ ἐπεί ῥ' εὔξαντο καὶ οὐλοχύτας προβάλοντο).[150]

2. The second section describes the killing of the victim. It may be reduced to a single verb 'they slaughtered [the victim]' (ἔσφαξαν).[151] But equally, everything that occurs between the prayer and the slaughter of the victim may be described in detail, as in Nestor's great sacrifice (*Odyssey*, 3.448–55). After the moment at which the animal's throat is cut, the poet goes on to describe the following actions

the act of flaying (δείρειν)[152] the victim or, in the case of pigs, of singeing (εὕειν) the carcass;[153]
the preparation of the meat (ἀμφέπειν);[154]
the cutting up of the meat (διαχεύειν);[155]
the sacrifice proper, which consists of placing the parts to be burned on the altar;[156]
the burning of the sacrifice accompanied by libations;[157]
the cooking of the entrails;[158]

Here too the final formula, 'when the thighs were burnt up and they had tasted the innards' (αὐτὰρ ἐπεὶ κατὰ μῆρε κάη καὶ σπλάγχνα πάσαντο),[159] underlines the two most important moments in this sequence of events.

3. The third section is devoted to the culinary aspects of the sacrifice:

[150] *Iliad*, 1.458 and 2.421; *Odyssey*, 3.447.

[151] *Odyssey*, 12.359.

[152] *Iliad*, 1.459, 2.422, 7.316, 24. 621; *Odyssey*, 8.61, 12.359.

[153] *Iliad*, 9.467; *Odyssey*, 14.75 and 426.

[154] *Iliad*, 7.316, 11.776, 24.622; *Odyssey*, 8.61, 19.421.

[155] *Iliad*, 7.316; *Odyssey*, 3.456, 14.427.

[156] *Iliad*, 1.460–1, 2.423–5; *Odyssey*, 3.456–8, 12.360–1, 14.427–8.

[157] *Iliad*, 1.462–3, 11.772–5; *Odyssey*, 3.459–60.

[158] *Iliad*, 2.426 'They spitted the innards and held them over the flame of Hephaestus' (σπλάγχνα δ' ἄρ' ἀμπείραντες ὑπείρεχον Ἡφαίστοιο); *Odyssey*, 12.363 'They made a libation of water and roasted all the entrails' (ἀλλ' ὕδατι σπένδοντες ἐπώπτων ἔγκατα πάντα). The formula 'the young men stood by him with five-pronged forks in their hands' (νέοι δὲ παρ' αὐτὸν ἔχον πεμπώβολα χερσίν. *Iliad*, 1.463; *Odyssey*, 3.460) occurs at exactly the same point and may be substituted for the cooking of the entrails.

[159] *Iliad*, 1.464, 2.427; *Odyssey*, 3.9 and 461, 12.364.

the meat is cut up into small pieces which are then threaded onto skewers;[160]
it is roasted and the pieces are removed from the fire.[161]

This section closes with the end of the preparations for the meal and one of two formulae: 'when they had finished their work and prepared their meal' (αὐτὰρ ἐπεὶ παύσαντο πόνου τετύκοντό τε δαῖτα)[162] or 'when they had roasted the outer flesh and drawn it off from the spits' (οἱ δ' ἐπεί ὤπτησαν κρέ' ὑπέρτερα καὶ ἐρύσαντο).[163]

4. The fourth section is the shortest. Its core is constituted by the verb δαίνυσθαι ('to share a meal' which appears in the formulaic line 'They set to eating, and no man's desire went without an equal share in the feast' (δαίνυντ', οὐδέ τι θυμὸς ἐδεύετο δαιτὸς ἐίσης)).[164] It is not therefore the consumption of the meat that is the subject of the description but rather the way in which it is shared out, and this can be described in greater detail. This reference to the sharing out of the meat is sometimes replaced by another formula describing the gesture that immediately precedes the consumption of the food: 'They stretched out their hands to the food set ready before them' (οἱ δ' ἐπ' ὀνείαθ' ἑτοῖμα προκείμενα χεῖρας ἴαλλον).[165]

In the same way, in the *Odyssey*, we find nine examples of the codified sequence describing the reception of a guest.[166] On five occasions (in Books 3, 4, 5, 6, and 10) there is a reference to a bath then, once the guests are seated, the events are described in the following order:

1. ablutions: 'A maid brought water in a fine golden jug and poured it over their hands for washing, holding a silver basin below.' χέρνιβα δ' ἀμφίπολος προχόῳ ἐπέχευε φέρουσα | καλῇ χρυσείῃ, ὑπὲρ ἀργυρέοιο λέβητος, | νίψασθαι.[167]

[160] This action, which is described in detail in *Iliad*, 9.210–14, usually takes up a single line: *Iliad*, 1.465, 2.428, 7.317, 24.623; *Odyssey*, 3.462, 12.365, 14.75, and 430. In one case it only takes up half a line: *Odyssey*, 3.33.

[161] *Iliad*, 1.466, 2.429, 7.318, 24.684; *Odyssey*, 14.431, 19.423.

[162] *Iliad*, 1.467, 2.430, 7.319; *Odyssey*, 16.478, 24.384.

[163] *Odyssey*, 3.65, 470.

[164] *Iliad*, 1.468, 2.431, 7.320, 23.56; *Odyssey*, 16.479, 19.425.

[165] *Iliad*, 9. 91, 9.221, 24.627; *Odyssey*, 1.149, 4.67, 5.200, 8.71 and 484, 14.453, 15.14, 16.54, 17.98, 20.256.

[166] *Odyssey*, 1.113–43, 3.34–67, 4.22–68, 6.206–50, 7.139–84, 10.311–13, 14.29–111, 15.132–43, and 17.85–99.

[167] *Odyssey*, 1.136–8; 4.52–4, 7.172–4, 10.368–70, 15.135–7, 17.91–3.

2. Preparations for the meal: 'then she drew up a polished table for them.' *παρὰ δὲ ξεστὴν ἐτάνυσσε τράπεζαν.*[168]
3. Serving the bread: 'the trusted housekeeper came and put bread where they could reach it; she had many kinds of food as well and gave ungrudgingly from her store.' *σῖτον δ' αἰδοίη ταμίη παρέθηκε φέρουσα, | εἴδατα πόλλ' ἐπιθεῖσα, χαριζομένη παρεόντων.*[169]

By contrast there are no formulaic lines to describe the serving of the meat (or wine, where this is present), instead it is expressed in different ways:

'The carver lifted from his board the trenchers filled with all sorts of meat, put them before guest and host, put goblets of gold before them too, and again and again a page came up to pour the wine. *δαιτρὸς δὲ κρειῶν πίνακας παρέθηκεν ἀείρας | παντοίων, παρὰ δέ σφι τίθει χρύσεια κύπελλα, | κῆρυξ δ' αὐτοῖσιν θάμ' ἐπῴχετο οἰνοχοεύων* (*Odyssey*, 1.141–3)

He gave them portions of the innards and poured them wine in a golden cup. *δῶκε δ' ἄρα σπλάγχνων μοίρας, ἐν δ' οἶνον ἔχευε | χρυσείῳ δέπαϊ* (*Odyssey*, 3.40–1)

He took in his hands and set before them the fat chine of a roasted ox that had been reserved as his own portion. *καί σφιν νῶτα βοὸς παρὰ πίονα θῆκεν | ὄπτ' ἐν χερσὶν ἑλών, τά ῥά οἱ γέρα πάρθεσαν αὐτῷ* (*Odyssey*, 4.65–6)

4. The consumption of the meal and its conclusion: 'They stretched out their hands to the food set ready before them. Then, when they had put away their desire for eating and drinking. *οἱ δ' ἐπ' ὀνείαθ' ἑτοῖμα προκείμενα χεῖρας ἴαλλον. | αὐτὰρ ἐπεὶ πόσιος καὶ ἐδητύος ἐξ ἔρον ἕντο.*[170]

The libations, which serve to bring the gods into the human banquet, usually mark the close of the feast and themselves constitute a type-scene that can be divided into several phases:

1. An invitation to make a libation, which usually includes the name of the god to be honoured.[171] In three cases this invitation is explicitly said to be accepted by the guests.[172]

[168] *Odyssey*, 1.138, 4.54, 7.174, 10.370, 15.137, 17.93.
[169] *Odyssey*, 1.139–40, 4.55–6, 7.175–6, 10.371–2, 15.138–9, 17.94–5.
[170] *Odyssey*, 1. 149–50, 4.67–8, 15.142–3, 17.98–9. At 7.177 this formula is replaced by 'much-enduring godlike Odysseus began to eat and drink'.
[171] *Iliad*, 9.171–2; *Odyssey*, 3.43–8, 332–6, 7.163–5, 179–81, 13.39, 50–2.
[172] *Iliad*, 9.173; *Odyssey*, 3.337, 13.47.

2. Preparations for the libation, which can be alluded to briefly by allusions to the 'mixing' of the wine and the 'handing out' of the cups, or may be expanded to fill three lines as in Book 3 of the *Odyssey* (lines 338–40).
3. The libation itself, indicated by the verb λείβειν or σπένδειν, often accompanied by a verb meaning 'to pray' (λιτανεύειν).
4. A conclusion with the formulaic line 'when they had made their libations and drunk to their hearts' content'[173] αὐτὰρ ἐπεὶ σπεῖσάν τε πίον θ' ὅσον ἤθελε θυμός, or a variant.

It is usually after this that the guest is asked to reveal his identity. He is then offered a bed and sent on his way with a gift of hospitality.

Other scholars after Arend took up and developed the study of type-scenes. Battle scenes in particular have been the subject of studies by Armstrong (1958), Hainsworth (1966), Fenik (1968), Krischer (1971), and Latacz (1977). Mark Edwards (1986) has analysed the conventions of the Homeric funeral and others, including myself, have studied scenes of feasting and of hospitality.[174] The list drawn up by Edwards (1992) provides further proof, if this were needed, of the vital importance of type-scenes within the structure of Homeric epic.

Others have pointed out the existence of similar phenomena on a variety of different levels.[175] First of all, there are repeated motifs: during the suitors' last banquet, three of them, Antinous in Book 17 (lines 462–4), Eurymachus in Book 18 (lines 394–7), and Ctesippus in Book 20 (lines 299–300), all throw different objects at Odysseus (a footstool, a stool, and an ox-hoof). There are also duplicated characters: in the *Odyssey*, Eumaeus and Philoetius are both examples of the good male servant while Eurycleia and Eurynome embody the good female servant. These figures contrast with Melanthius and Melantho, two symmetrical figures, one male and one female, who represent the bad servant. Similarly, there are two leaders among the suitors, Eurymachus and Antinous, and two 'good' suitors, Amphinomus and Leodes, who suffer the same fate in the end as the others.

Moreover, the similes, which are one of the most characteristic elements of Homeric poetry, are themselves 'typical' to a certain

[173] *Odyssey*, 3.342, 395, 7.184, 228; 18.427, 21.273.
[174] Saïd 1979, Edwards 1975, Reece 1993.
[175] See Fenik 1974, Bader 1976.

extent, in the sense that they are constructed from identical elements and fulfil similar functions.[176] One example will suffice to illustrate this. In the Homeric poems, the most common simile is without doubt that of the lion (it appears fifty times in the *Iliad* and the *Odyssey*) which usually serves to emphasize the courage of a hero, given that the lion is the most courageous of animals in these poems. In nineteen cases, the comparison is reduced to the minimum: 'like a lion'. When it is more extended, it is developed in ways that represent variations on a single theme, that of the lion attacking flocks (in twenty-seven instances) or pursuing wild animals (in seven instances).

Such a system only makes sense as part of a poetic practice that is both *traditional* and *oral*. It is characteristic of oral poetry in that it allows the bard to compose his poem as he sings, thanks to the use of pre-existing formulae, hence the small number of enjambements (where the sense runs over from one line into the next) and the predominantly paratactic style of Homeric verse. It is traditional in that its complexity goes far beyond anything that could be created by a single individual. It can only be the result of a collective effort and the product of a tradition which the poet is bound to follow. This would explain both the inconsistencies in the story and the metrical irregularities of Homeric poetry since, as Parry pointed out, 'the bard, accustomed to expressing his thought through the medium of traditional expressions, will often have to choose between using two formulae which perfectly express his thought but whose junction entails a metrical fault, and renouncing formulae to make up expressions of his own. Given this fundamental contradiction between the rhythm and formulary technique, we can see what a temptation it was for the bard . . . to join together two formulae, even when he had to commit a metrical fault to do so' (Parry 1971: 196).

As a consequence, the arguments of both Analysts and Unitarians were dismissed and the 'Homeric question' became meaningless. It was no longer possible to distinguish, as the Analysts wished to do, between an original text, due to Homer, and later additions, since the repetitions are not the result of clumsy imitation but are part of the very essence of oral poetry. It is equally impossible to find evidence of the author's originality, as the Unitarians attempted to do. But, if Parry's work was to put an end to a debate that had dominated the

[176] On similes see Fränkel 1921, Buxton 2004 (who refers to Coffey 1957), Porter 1972–3, Moulton 1977, Edwards 1991: 24–41.

study of Homeric poetry for over a century, it opened up a completely new controversy. If 'Homer' was an oral poet, it was still necessary to explain when and how the text of the poems came to be fixed in written form. There was also the question of the vast differences between the Homeric poems and the South Slavic oral literature, used later by Parry and by Albert Lord as a parallel to support the idea of Homer as an oral poet,[177] and other similar poems. Researchers who wanted to understand how oral poetry functioned soon spread their net far further afield, turning to the past and to medieval poetry and, above all, broadening the geographical range of their enquiries to encompass Africa and the Middle East. They discovered, as was only to be expected, that oral traditions were more diverse than was previously thought and that it is difficult to generalize about the characteristics of oral epic.[178]

5. FROM ORALITY TO WRITING

Scholars were quick to point out the limitations inherent in the comparison between 'Homer' and the South Slavic *guslars*.[179] This parallel certainly served to show that it was possible to compose very long poems orally and that these poems could also be transmitted orally with minor variations. But these poems cannot be compared with the *Iliad* or the *Odyssey* in either length or quality. It was therefore necessary to propose the existence of a so-called 'creative' phase in the evolution of oral poetry, as did G. S. Kirk (1976: 28), for example, of which Homer just happened to be the only representative, in opposition to an earlier 'original' phase corresponding to the beginnings of the oral tradition (that is to say the Mycenaean period, in the case of Greece), and to a later 'reproductive' phase, illustrated by the South Slavic bards, which would have occurred in Greece in the mid seventh century (although Kirk is obliged to acknowledge that this must remain a conjecture since there is no trace left of it in

[177] Parry 1971: 439–64. See also Lord in Parry 1971: 465–78.

[178] Foley 1997: 159–61.

[179] Foley 1997: 161 nn. 38–40 refers to Kirk 1962: 86 and 95–8 and Dirlmeier 1971 who demonstrated the limitations of the analogy between Homeric and South Slavic poetry.

the record), and, finally, a 'degenerate' phase corresponding to the period of the rhapsodes.

If 'Homer', or rather the author (or authors) of the *Iliad* and the *Odyssey*, was an oral poet, the question of when and how the text of the two epics came to be fixed in written form remains to be answered. Oral poets' exceptional powers of memorization are well documented. But specialists in oral tradition nevertheless acknowledge that variations do occur from one performance to another. These are minor (around 4.4 per cent) in the case of two versions of the same poem recited by the same poet. But, on the basis of these figures, a poem that was transmitted over the course of six generations would show a total variation of at least 26 per cent in total. Moreover, more recent research into the workings of oral traditions showed that these traditions, precisely because they have to constantly adapt to changing conditions and to the eminently variable demands of the audience, are in a constant state of flux.[180] It is not surprising, therefore, that there is far from being a consensus concerning the date at which Homeric epic was fixed and 'crystallized'.

The problem is further complicated by the lack of agreement about the time and the place at which alphabetic writing first appeared in Greece and even about its original function. The first inscriptions, found at Lefkandi in Euboea and at Pithekoussai, in the Bay of Naples (on the famous Cup of Nestor which bears an inscription in hexameters) date to the second half of the eighth century. But it is not impossible to push the creation of the Greek alphabet back to a much earlier date, if one is prepared to allow that it was first used for record keeping in commercial contexts. As C. J. Ruijgh (1995: 38) has observed, 'The Greeks of the first millennium wrote their accounting records on wooden tablets . . . as well as on papyrus and animal skins (parchment). These are all perishable materials which have not survived in Greek soil.' An early date (around the eleventh century) would have the additional advantage of 'better explaining the very diverse processes of evolution that gave rise to the various local alphabets of the archaic period'. But the fact that the first known inscription is written in hexameters has also prompted the suggestion that the alphabet was in fact invented in order to record hexameter

[180] This is demonstrated by Jack Goody (Goody and Gandah 1972) in his analysis of the transmission of the Bagre, an epic poem from Ghana.

poetry and—which is entirely possible—the Homeric poems themselves.[181]

Recent scholarship has tended to place the borrowing of the Semitic alphabet and its adaptation to the needs of the Greek language in Euboea. Historically, the Euboeans were the first to establish contact with Phoenicia and it is possible that Phoenicians may have settled at Lefkandi. Here, Greek myth points in the same direction as the historical evidence since the most widespread legend concerning the invention of writing attributes it to Palamedes who was from Euboea.[182] But another possibility is Cyprus where there were already contacts between Phoenicians and Greeks (at Kition, for example), or Crete, or even Al Mina (at the mouth of the Orontes in Syria) which was the site of an important Greek trading post.

If we accept the thesis that Homer was an oral poet, there are several possible explanations of how the text came to be written down. One solution is that proposed by Kirk, who argued that the Homeric poems must have been recorded in writing long after they were composed as it is impossible to conceive of the use of writing being sufficiently developed by the eighth century BC to transcribe such long works. But this in turn raises the question of the transmission of the poems. A late date makes it necessary to suppose that archaic Greece was an exception to the general rule that significant variations occur when poems are transmitted orally. In this case the oral tradition would have to have been exceptionally faithful since, with just a few exceptions, the linguistic development of the Homeric text seems to have stopped very early and neither poem describes any objects or makes any allusion to social institutions that can be dated later than 700 BC. This is why scholars, including Milman Parry's own son Adam, were not convinced by his explanation.[183] Currently, the most ardent defender of a relatively late date for the 'crystallization' of the text of the Homeric poems remains Gregory Nagy who, after two centuries of controversy, has taken up the same position as Wolf.[184] He posits a 'relatively static phase' of oral transmission lasting at least two centuries, from the middle of the eighth century until the middle

[181] This was first suggested by Wade-Gery 1952: 11–14 and was developed and given greater currency by Powell (1991 and 1997).

[182] According to legend, his father Nauplius lured the Greek fleet onto the rocks at Cape Caphereus, at the southern tip of Euboea, in order to avenge his son's death.

[183] Parry (1989b): 126–31.

[184] See, for example, Nagy 1996: 65–106.

of the sixth century, and emphasizes the vital role played by Athens and the Peisistratids, attributing to the tyrants who are said to have instituted the recitation of the *Iliad* and the *Odyssey* at the Panathenaea the role of collecting together poems that had hitherto been scattered and fixing them in written form.

One solution to the problems raised by this thesis is to follow scholars like Albert Lord (1953) and Adam Parry (1989: 137–40) in situating 'Homer' at the threshold between orality and literacy and to imagine an illiterate Homer dictating his text to a scribe (a scenario modelled on the Yugoslav situation where Parry and Lord wrote down the poems of the *guslars* as they sang them). This solution is favoured by scholars such as Janko (1990), Powell (1991 and 1997), Ruijgh (1995), and Haslam (1997: 80–4). They suppose that the texts of the *Iliad* and the *Odyssey* were written down during the poet's lifetime, doubtless because important members of his audience, or his fellow poets, or his pupils wished to preserve the exact words of the two epics. Various factors such as the prominence of Euboea in the introduction of writing to Greece, the biographical traditions that situate the contest between Homer and Hesiod in the Euboean city of Chalcis, and the presence in Homeric Greek of certain dialectal features (like the presence of initial aspiration) that may well be Euboean in origin (Ruijgh 1995: 47–50) have been put forward as evidence that the wealthy admirer who had the Homeric poems recorded in written form may have come from Euboea.[185] As to the question of why it was felt necessary to write down the text of these two poems, it may be, as Ian Morris has suggested, that at a time of social change poems like these that exalted aristocratic values could serve an important ideological function (Morris 1986: 84–5).

But once one places Homer at a period when his poems could be written down, why not remove the scribe from the equation and suppose that the author himself was responsible for recording his poems in writing? Against this view, it has been argued on the basis of the South Slavic evidence that the transition to writing normally brings with it a marked fall in the quality of oral poetry.[186] But in fact, as T. B. L. Webster (1963: 157) rightly notes in his review of

[185] The role of Euboea in the recording of the Homeric poems has also been emphasized by West 1988: 165 ff. and Powell 1997: 21–2.

[186] This objection was made by S. Dow in a letter cited by Adam Parry 1989: 108 n.12.

Kirk's work, 'literacy killed the Yugoslav poets because it brought them into touch with a higher culture', which was hardly the case in eighth-century Greece. The theory that Homer was a poet steeped in the techniques of oral composition but who had also learned to write made it possible to account for the length and the unparalleled complexity of the Homeric poems, as well as their 'monumental composition' and their characteristic play of echoes and repetitions. It won over German scholars,[187] who had never truly accepted the orality of Homeric poetry, and also many critics in the English-speaking world, beginning with Milman Parry's own son.[188]

In short, we are now a long way from having any definite answers to these questions, a situation that is reflected in the title of the collected volume on *Homer: Beyond Oral Poetry*,[189] as well as the careful formulations of specialists in the oral tradition such as J. M. Foley (1990), who speaks of an 'oral-derived text', or specialists in epic, like R. Fowler (2004b: 222), who claims that 'the notion of a "transitional text", one partly oral and partly written, produced by an "oral-derived poet" . . . has much to recommend it'.

Even if we accept that the first written text of the *Iliad* and the *Odyssey* was made during the poet's lifetime, it is still necessary to acknowledge that it must have remained fairly fluid for a long period and that it may well have undergone major alterations (many critics still consider that Book 10 of the *Iliad* (the 'Doloneia') and Book 24 of the *Odyssey* are later additions). It is also clear, even if one does not accept the extreme arguments of Gregory Nagy, that the reorganization of the Panathenaic festival by Peisistratus and his sons represents an important stage in the history of the text of Homer, with the appearance of an official version of the poems, as a wide variety of ancient sources claim.[190] Finally, as Michael Haslam (1997: 56) has rightly stressed, the second and third centuries BC constitute a vitally important stage in the transmission of the poems with the work of the Alexandrian scholars Zenodotus, Aristophanes of Byzantium, and

[187] See for example Latacz 1996, Lohmann 1970, Friedrich 1975, Heubeck, West, and Hainsworth 1988.

[188] Parry 1989b (1st pub. 1966): 138. See also Garvie 1994: 15–17.

[189] Ed. Bremer, De Jong, and Kalff 1987.

[190] See in particular Pseudo-Plato, *Hipparchus*, 228b: 'Hipparchus compelled the rhapsodes to recite them in relays—one following the other' (ἐξ ὑπολήψεως ἐφεξῆς αὐτὰ διιέναι), Cicero, *De Oratore*, 3.317, Aelian, *Varia Historia*, 13.14, and Pausanias, 7.26.13.

above all Aristarchus, who produced the first 'critical' editions of Homer on the basis of the manuscripts collected together by the Ptolemies in the Library of Alexandria. Before this date, it is clear from other authors' quotations of the text and from the Homeric papyri that there were many differences in the tradition. These disappear almost completely from around 150 BC, which is the best indication that from this date onwards there was a vulgate which was considered authoritative.

6. THE LANGUAGE OF THE HOMERIC POEMS

This lengthy history has left its mark in the language of the poems whose complexity was remarked upon in Antiquity: the author of the *Essay on the Life and Poetry of Homer*, writing in the second century AD, was as aware of this as we are when he said, 'Homer mingled together elements of all the dialects of the Greeks.' But his explanation is very different: 'It is clear from this that he visited the whole of Greece and every one of its peoples.'[191] The analysis of Homeric language that he goes on to give, claiming that it is a mixture of Doric, Aeolic, Ionic, and, above all, Attic elements, would provoke the ire of modern philologists.[192] It is nowadays agreed that Homeric Greek is 'an artificial poetic dialect that includes, alongside Ionic elements contemporary with the poet, many older Aeolic elements and some Achaean elements dating from the Mycenaean period' (Ruijgh 1995: 1), not to mention a later stratum of Euboean and some Atticisms that were no doubt introduced in the sixth century when the official text of the Homeric epics was drawn up under the Peisistratids. The fact that the Ionic features that predominate in the Homeric dialect belong to an earlier form of Ionic than that used by the seventh-century lyric poet Archilochus has led some linguists like C. J. Ruigh (1995: 22) to propose an early date for the composition of Homeric epic and to situate it not in the second half of the eighth

[191] *Essay on the Life and Poetry of Homer*, 8. Translation by Lamberton and Keaney.

[192] Pierre Chantraine's monumental work, *Grammaire Homérique*, remains fundamental. There are also excellent surveys of Homeric grammar in Palmer 1962, Ruijgh 1995, and Horrocks 1997.

century, as is generally agreed today, but in the ninth century since 'a distance of a half-century is not sufficient to explain the radical differences between the Ionic of Homer and that of Archilochus'. The presence of older features can be explained above all by the demands of the metre. In most cases, the Aeolic forms have a different metrical structure from their Ionic equivalents and this explains why they were preserved by Ionian bards who borrowed the dactylic hexameter from their Aeolian neighbours in Asia Minor. We also find in Homer words and linguistic features which can be traced back to the old Achaean dialect since they are also found in Mycenaean Linear B tablets or in the dialects spoken in Arcadia (the only region of the Peloponnese that was left untouched by the Dorian invasion) and in Cyprus (an island that was colonized by the Achaeans around 1100 BC at the latest). The existence of strata earlier than Ionic in Homeric Greek is also confirmed by metrical anomalies like the existence of hiatus (where a word ending with a vowel is immediately followed by a word beginning with a vowel, something that is normally avoided) and the irregular lengthening of a final syllable. Both of these phenomena can be attributed to the disappearance in written Greek of a digamma that still often has an effect on the metre, or of an initial *h* that counted as a consonant in Mycenaean Greek, as in the formula *πότνια Ἥρη* (twenty-five occurrences). It is no doubt the study of the language of Homer that offers the most reliable grounds for the relative date of the epics within the corpus of archaic poetry, as the study by Richard Janko (1982) has shown.

After this rapid overview of a debate that is far from closed I would simply state, to conclude, that in this book I will take as my starting point the text of *Odyssey* as it has been transmitted and that my analysis will presuppose, to borrow the words of M. Charles (1995: 40), a belief in the unity and the identity of the text, without attempting to ask—still less to answer—questions about the origin of this unity, whether it is a man named 'Homer', a school, or an anonymous tradition.

2

The Art of Homer: Between Tradition and Innovation

The first champions of orality, Milman Parry and Albert Lord, tended to take the analogy between Homer and the South Slavic bards to the extreme and to present him as a prisoner of tradition, engaged in an almost mechanical process of putting together formulae that were shaped to fit the metre with no thought for their meaning. Parry for example wrote of the expression ἔπεα πτερόεντα ('winged words') that 'Homer uses πτερόεντα without thinking of its special meaning'.[1]

This image of the oral poet as a slave to tradition and to the system of formulae that it imposed is no longer accepted nowadays. In its place, the idea of choice—and thus of art—has been reintroduced into the study of Homeric poetry. The system of formulae is in fact less of a constraint than Parry's analyses suggested and there are exceptions to the principle of economy, as shown by the existence of doublets. Even where there is only one combination of noun and epithet to designate a hero in a particular grammatical case and in a particular place in the line, it is important to bear in mind that it was also possible to refer to the hero in question by name alone. The use of an epithet is not therefore a simple metrical lengthening device, devoid of any significance. It is increasingly acknowledged that, in the words of Jaqueline de Romilly (1985: 56), 'What was simply a matter of convenience for oral poets takes on a function in Homeric poetry and is used to create a particular effect.' Titles of works such as Mark Edwards's 'Some Features of Homeric Craftsmanship' (published in 1966), Anne Amory-Parry's 'Homer as an Artist' or Harald Patzer's *Dichterische Kunst und poetische Handwerk im homerischen Epos*

[1] Parry 1971: 414–18. See also Combellack 1959.

(both published in 1971), and Nicholas Richardson's 'The Individuality of Homer's Language' (published in 1987) as well as the two collections of articles published in 1978 (*Homer: Tradition and Invention* and *Homer Tradition und Neuerung*) reflected a new willingness to acknowledge the artistry of the Homeric poems. It is worth analysing this development in detail, even if the discussions can be extremely technical in places, as it led to the renewal of approaches to the Homeric poems and will form the basis of the interpretation of the *Odyssey* in this book.

1. THE FORMULA TRANSFORMED

It was Milman Parry himself who first began to broaden the notion of the formula when he recognized that, beyond the formula in the strict sense (that is a group of *identical words*, used in the *same case* and in the *same metrical condition*), there were also 'more general types of formulas' (Parry 1971: 313) which did not involve the use of identical words. This enabled him to treat expressions whose meaning was basically the same as variations on the same formula. Some examples are:

> 'Thus spoke [A], [B] was delighted' (ὣς φάτο, γήθησεν δὲ . . . 8 occurrences)
> 'Thus spoke [A], [B] was glad' (ὣς φάτο, χαῖρε δὲ . . . 1 occurrence)
> 'Thus spoke [A], [B] smiled' (ὣς φάτο, μείδησεν δὲ . . . 11 occurrences)

This applies equally to antonyms such as

> 'Thus spoke [A], [B] shuddered' (ὣς φάτο, ῥίγησεν δὲ . . . 4 occurrences)

Parry's follower, Albert Lord, followed him in this direction when he spoke of formulae as deriving from 'basic patterns' (1960: 35–45). It is now usual to find references to 'modifications of attested formulaic patterns' (Finkelberg 1989: 187) alongside discussions of 'formulae proper' in the context of comparisons between expressions like the following examples:

> 'Seeing them, lord Agamemnon was delighted'
> *Καὶ τοὺς μὲν (τὸν μὲν) γήθησεν ἰδὼν κρείων Ἀγαμέμνων* (*Iliad*, 4.283 and 311)

'Seeing them, the old man was delighted'
τοὺς δ' ὁ γέρων γήθησεν ἰδών (*Iliad*, 10.190)
'Seeing them, Odysseus was delighted'
τὴν δ' Ὀδυσεὺς γήθησεν ἰδών (*Odyssey*, 13.226 and 22.207).

There are in fact two possible ways of broadening the notion of the formula to allow more flexibility: one can retain the form (the syntax, the order of the words, and the metre) while sacrificing the content (the semantic content) or the reverse.[2] The first of these two solutions, with its 'abstract' definition of the formula, is the one that predominated initially. In an article published in 1966, Joseph Russo proposed in place of Parry's 'formula' a 'structural formula in which the same grammatical and metrical types are repeated'. He thus treats as two variations on a single formula such different expressions (different as far as the meaning is concerned) as 'Odysseus, son of Laertes' (Λαερτιάδεω Ὀδυσῆος, 12 occurrences) and 'Achilles, son of Peleus' (Πηληϊάδεω Ἀχιλῆος, 8 occurrences), because they are in the same case (the genitive) and have the same metrical value. He takes the process of abstraction still further when he considers expressions such as 'he (or she) imposed/gave/took away suffering/glory/triumph' as so many instances of the structural formula consisting of a noun (consisting of one long syllable followed by a short syllable) and a verb (consisting of a short syllable followed either by two long ones or, at the end of the line, by one long syllable).[3] Formulae in this definition are no longer fixed expressions but become instead 'abstract linguistic structures or matrices from which new epic formulas are generated' (Russo 1997: 246).

Some scholars have taken the opposite approach, privileging content and meaning over and above syntax and metre. Thus J. B. Hainsworth substituted what he calls 'phrase patterns' for Parry's formulae (Hainsworth 1993: 9). Here, it is the relationships between words that define the formula, while the case, the position, and the metrical form may change. In consequence, the formula loses all its fixity and allows for lengthening, going from 'red wine' (οἶνον ἐρυθρόν)[4] to 'red wine sweet as honey' (μελιηδέα οἶνον ἐρυθρόν)[5] and 'gleaming red wine' (αἴθοπα οἶνον ἐρυθρόν).[6] Formulae may be

[2] Russo 1997: 250.

[3] ἄλγε' ἔθηκε (*Iliad*, 1.2, 22.422), κῦδος ἔθηκε (*Iliad*, 23.400 and 406), κῦδος ἔδωκε(ν) (six occurrences), εὖχος ἔδωκε (*Iliad*, 11.288), εὖχος ἀπηύρα (*Iliad*, 15.462).

[4] *Odyssey*, 5.165, 12.327, 13.69, and 16.444.

[5] *Odyssey*, 9.208.

[6] *Odyssey*, 12.19.

combined: an expression like 'blessed immortal gods' (μάκαρες θεοὶ αἰὲν ἐόντες)[7] is seen as resulting from the combination of two formulae, 'immortal gods' (θεοὶ αἰὲν ἐόντες, 3 occurrences) and 'blessed gods' μάκαρες θεοί (6 occurrences). They also allow changes in the order of the words: ἀαπτους χεῖρας ('invincible hands', *Iliad*, 1.567) is a variation on χεῖρας ἀαπτους (10 occurrences). They may appear in different forms (thus we find two different forms of the dative plural: πᾶσι δόλοισιν and πάντεσσι δόλοισι, 'in varied stratagems')[8] and may change length by substituting one synonym for another αἷμα κελαινὸν (9 occurrences) αἷμα κελαινεφές (4 occurrences) both meaning 'dark blood'.

The most recent studies of the formula take the process of abstraction further still. Ahuvia Kahane, for example, made a statistical analysis of the factors dictating the use of the nominative 'Odysseus' in its two different metrical forms ('Οδυσσεύς with a long u and 'Οδυσεύς with a short u) in the *Odyssey* (Kahane 1997: 337–42). He was able to identify a norm: the verb precedes the subject or the nominative expression (the noun and its epithet or epithets). It is only in cases where this order is rendered impossible by the demands of the metre or by the presence of stronger patterns that it is inverted. More precisely, Kahane (1997: 340) established that in almost all the cases where 'Οδυσσεύς is found with a longer epithet and is immediately preceded by a verb of saying or thinking, it is placed at the end of the line.

The influence of the deep structures of Chomsky's generative grammar on the analysis of formulaic style is even clearer in the work of Michael Nagler, whose first article was entitled 'Towards a Generative View of the Oral Formula'.[9] Nagler posits the existence of 'traditional phrases'. These are preverbal structures ('preverbal Gestalt') that can be expressed in words in a series of different forms or 'allomorphs'.

Among the recent attempts to introduce greater flexibility into the notion of the formula, one final group of studies is worth mentioning. Their authors apply the results of linguistic analyses of the spoken language to poetry that was undeniably composed for recitation (even if some use was made of writing in the process). In contrast to the written language, which makes use of subordination, spoken language works by adding and juxtaposing independent elements. These

[7] *Iliad*, 24.99; *Odyssey*, 5.7; 8.306; 12.371 and 377.

[8] *Odyssey*, 9.19 and 13.292.

[9] Nagler 1967. See also Nagler 1974.

elements are, however, subject to a certain hierarchy so that it is possible to distinguish within the phrase a central core and peripheral elements. The same applies to Homeric language, which is simply a 'stylized' form of the spoken language.

One example is Edzard Visser's study (1988) of the lines describing killings and woundings. Visser noted that the names of the agent and his victim, which can appear in different metrical forms, constitute 'determinant' elements that dictate the choice of verbs used to signify 'kill' or 'wound' (there are twenty-seven different possibilities) as well as the nature of the conjunction that links them to what precedes (here there are nine possibilities). This study was developed further by Bakker and Fabricotti (1991) who analysed the expressions used to designate 'spear' in the dative case. They showed that for this element, which they call 'peripheral' (in contrast to the determinant 'nucleus' constituted by the name of the agent, that of his victim, and the main verb), the poet has a choice of three metrical forms meaning 'spear', δουρί made up of one long and one short syllable or ἔγχει, which can be scanned as two long syllables or a long followed by two shorts, without or without the addition of an epithet.[10] Thus the poet had at his disposal various combinations of words with different metrical values but identical meanings that could be used interchangeably within the battle narrative, enabling him to complete his lines with ease.

The result is a hierarchy of formulae that are more or less strictly defined and the recognition of different types of repetitions that are more or less literal. We can therefore continue to define Homeric style as essentially formulaic, since the notion of the formula has been broadened to the point where it can be defined as 'any expression that occurs at least twice in Homer or any unique expression that presents a modification of a recognizable formulaic pattern' (Finkelberg 1989: 181). It is even possible for an expression that only appears once in Homer like γεγήθει δὲ φρένα ('he was delighted in his heart', *Iliad*, 11.683) to be considered as a formula, or even the prototype of a series of formulae, given that it is attested elsewhere in epic poetry (in this case in the *Homeric Hymns*) (Finkelberg 1989: 185).

[10] The ἔγχος can be 'large' (ἔγχει μακρῷ), 'made of bronze' (ἔγχει χαλκείῳ), or sharp (ἔγχει ὀξυόεντι) while the δόρυ can be sharp (ὀξέι δουρί), shining (δουρὶ φαεινῷ), or made of bronze (χαλκήρει δουρί).

2. THE CHRONOLOGY OF THE FORMULAE

The scholars who came after Milman Parry focused on establishing a chronology for the formulaic style by distinguishing between older and more recent formulae. It had been known since the nineteenth century and the work of Adalbert Kuhn that Homer inherited a poetic tradition with Indo-European roots, since an expression like *κλέος ἄφθίτον* ('undying glory') has an exact equivalent in Sanskrit in the *Rig-Veda*.[11] The decipherment of the Linear B tablets made it possible to trace certain epic formulae back to the Mycenaean, or even the proto-Mycenaean, period due to the presence of metrical irregularities or morphological features which can only be explained as deriving from Mycenaean Greek.[12] At the same time, it has been possible to highlight the recent origin of certain formulae, thanks to comparisons with other parts of the Homeric poems themselves, and even to present these as Homer's own inventions.

3. FORMULAIC AND NON-FORMULAIC

In addition to proposing a more flexible conception of the formula and establishing a chronological order, scholars have also tried to nuance Parry's conclusions, rejecting, sometimes in categorical terms, the idea that 'Homer's diction is wholly formulaic and traditional' (Hoekstra 1965: 24). Lord's claim (1960: 142), based on an analysis of *Iliad*, 1.1–15, that 90 per cent of Homer's language was formulaic is no longer accepted today, nor is the idea that the choice of formula was guided only by concern for the metre and that it is therefore impossible to attempt any purely 'literary' judgement of the *Iliad* and the *Odyssey*.[13] In a groundbreaking article, Russo (1968) even replaced the picture of Homer enslaved by tradition by a 'Homer against his tradition'.

This tendency to acknowledge Homer's originality and to reintroduce the notion of choice, and therefore of art, into Homeric criticism

[11] See Finkelberg 1986 and the literature cited on p. 1 n. 1.
[12] See Ruijgh 1995: 75–91.
[13] See, for example, Combellack 1959.

can be seen even in the most technical studies. Thus Kahane, in both the title and the introduction of his book *The Interpretation of Order: A Study in the Poetics of Homeric Repetitions*, devoted to the subject of word-order, is careful to point out that his subject is the poetics of repetition and that he will try to show that 'some of these repetitions perform non-technical, literary functions', since his study is 'an attempt . . . to understand how particular formal aspects of Homer (i.e those to do with forms) relate to poetic themes such as disguise and recognition, to the heroic ideal, and to gods and mortals and the difference between them in the epics'. (Kahane 1994: 1–2).

From the late 1960s onwards, a certain number of scholars re-examined the question of the 'traditional epithet' in order to show that the formulaic system was less of a constraint than Parry's thesis suggested.[14] They started by underlining the fact that the flexibility of the Greek language allowed the poet a certain amount of room for manoeuvre, giving him the choice between, for example, forms of verbs with or without the 'ephelcystic' or 'movable' *nu* (the letter 'n' which can be added at the end of certain verb forms that would otherwise end in a vowel) (Hoekstra 1965: 71–112). They also pointed out that, as noted above, heroes could always be referred to by name alone, rather than by a fixed noun plus epithet formula. Statistical studies have shown that, in the case of proper nouns, there are more or less the same number of uses of the name alone as there are instances of the name plus epithet.[15] The proportion is higher still (almost two-thirds) in the case of common nouns, meaning that we cannot dismiss the epithets as simple metrical lengthening devices devoid of any further significance.

Moreover, it has been convincingly shown that epithets are not simply used to fill out the line and that their presence cannot be justified entirely by metrical concerns. Instead, they can also contribute to the meaning of the poem. Two examples will suffice here, one relating to a proper noun and the other to a common noun. First, Norman Austin (1975: 28–31) established that the formula πολύμητις Ὀδυσσεύς 'subtle-minded Odysseus', which appears sixty-six times at the end of the line within the *Odyssey*, is, with only two exceptions, always used with a verb meaning 'to say'.[16] Its use therefore contributes

[14] Whallon 1969, Austin 1975, Vivante 1982.

[15] See, in particular, Austin 1975: 11–80.

[16] The verb is usually προσέφη but on three occasions μετέφη is used. The two exceptions are *Odyssey*, 2.173 and 4.763.

to the meaning, given that it indicates a clever speech. Similarly, Tormod Eide has analysed the contexts in which the expression χειρὶ παχείῃ ('with a sturdy hand') is found (three times in the *Iliad* and five times in the *Odyssey*).[17] When applied to Penelope at *Odyssey*, 21.4, this expression which always indicates violent movement or fierce determination, is not merely a clumsy compromise, to be attributed to the demands of the metre. On the contrary, it serves to emphasize her determination at the moment when she takes hold of the key in order to enter the storeroom, take Odysseus' bow, and open the contest in which she herself is to be the prize.

Further evidence of the freedom with which Homer made use of formulae is provided by those cases where he does not hesitate to change an epithet when it is clearly unsuitable for the context. Thus in Book 16 of the *Iliad*, at the moment when Zeus 'disperses the clouds' (line 298), his normal epithet, 'cloud-gatherer' (νεφεληγερέτα), is replaced by 'lightning gatherer' (στεροπηγερέτα). As well as contributing to the meaning of the poem in themselves, formulae can also serve to link two passages. Thus, in the description of the combat between Ares and Diomedes in Book 5 of the *Iliad*, the repetition of the same expression 'with the bronze spear' (ἔγχει χαλκείῳ, lines 852 and 856) emphasizes the contrast between Athena's two interventions: the first time she deflects the spear, making it miss its target, while the second time she guides it home.

The repeated use of the same formula can also enrich the text and endow it with greater complexity and depth. The fact that a given formula appears regularly in a certain type of context means that each individual usage brings along with it a series of associations of ideas and provokes a certain set of expectations in the listeners, an effect that has recently been termed 'traditional referentiality' (Foley 1991: 15). In the *Odyssey*, for example, all the occurrences of the accusative noun ἄνδρα ('man') at the beginning of a line refer back in one way or another to the first word of the *Odyssey* and thus constitute a network of references or allusions to Odysseus (Kahane 1992).

At the same time as meaning was being restored to the formula, the idea of choice was reintroduced into Homeric poetics. Studies like those of Edwards (1970 and 1989), Patzer (1971), and Janko (1981) have demonstrated the sophistication of the poet, not to mention that

[17] Eide 1980. See also Eide 1986.

of the listeners who were able to appreciate these subtle variations, for example in the use of formulae introducing speeches or replies. One case study will suffice to show both that several different formulae may indeed express the same essential idea and that their use is guided by a deliberate choice.

To mark the start of the day, the poet has several possibilities among which he can choose:

1a. 'When early born Dawn appeared with her rosy fingers.' (22 occurrences)
ἦμος δ' ἠριγένεια φάνη ῥοδοδάκτυλος Ἠώς.

1b. 'As soon as rosy-fingered Dawn appears.'
αὐτὰρ ἐπεί κε φανῇ ῥοδοδάκτυλος Ἠώς (*Iliad*, 9.707).

1c. 'Rosy-fingered Dawn appeared.'
φάνη ῥοδοδάκτυλος Ἠώς (*Iliad*, 23.109, *Odyssey*, 23.241).

2a. 'Straightaway Dawn arrived on her golden throne.'
αὐτίκα δὲ χρυσόθρονος ἤλθέν Ἠώς (*Odyssey*, 10.541, 12.142, 15.56, 20.91).

2b. 'Dawn shone out on her golden throne.'
φαέ δὲ χρυσόθρονος Ἠώς (*Odyssey*, 14.502).

3a. 'Straightaway Dawn arrived on her beautiful throne.'
αὐτίκα δ' Ἠὼς ἦλθέν ἐΰθρονος (*Odyssey*, 6.48).

3b. 'Quickly Dawn arrived on her beautiful throne.'
αἶψα γὰρ Ἠὼς ἦλθεν ἐΰθρονος (*Odyssey*, 15.495).

4. 'Dawn in her saffron robe was spreading all over the earth.'
Ἠὼς μὲν κροκόπεπλος ἐκίδνατο πᾶσαν ἐπ' αἶαν (*Iliad*, 8.1 and 24.695).

5a. 'When lovely-haired Dawn ushered in the third day.'
ἀλλ' ὅτε δὴ τρίτον ἦμαρ ἐυπλόκαμος τέλεσ' Ἠώς. (*Odyssey*, 5.390, 9.76, and 10.144).

5b. 'When the tenth Dawn appeared with her rosy fingers.'
ἀλλ' ὅτε δὴ δεκάτη ἐφάνη ῥοδοδάκτυλος Ἠώς (*Iliad*, 6.175).

5c. 'When the tenth Dawn arrived bringing light to mortals.'
ἀλλ' ὅτε δὴ δεκάτη ἐφάνη φαεσίμβροτος ἠώς (*Iliad*, 24.785).

5d. 'When the twelfth Dawn after that came around.'
ἀλλ' ὅτε δή ῥ' ἐκ τοῖο δυωδεκάτη γένετ' ἠώς (*Iliad*, 1.493 and 24.31).

6a. 'Dawn rose from her bed beside the noble Tithonus to bring light to gods and men.'

Ἠὼς δ' ἐκ λεχέων παρ' ἀγαυοῦ Τιθωνοῖο
ὄρνυθ', ἵν' ἀθανάτοισι φόως φέροι ἠδὲ βροτοῖσι (*Iliad*, 11.1–2 and *Odyssey*, 5.1–2).

6b. 'Dawn in her saffron robe rose from the streams of Ocean to bring light to gods and men.'
Ἠὼς μὲν κροκόπεπλος ἀπ' Ὠκεανοῖο ῥοάων
ὄρνυθ', ἵν' ἀθανάτοισι φόως φέροι ἠδὲ βροτοῖσιν (*Iliad*, 19.1–2).

6c. 'The Sun rose up, leaving the lovely lake, into the bronze heaven, to bring light to gods and men on the grain-giving earth.'
Ἠέλιος δ' ἀνόρουσε, λιπὼν περικαλλέα λίμνην,
οὐρανὸν ἐς πολύχαλκον, ἵν' ἀθανάτοισι φαείνοι
καὶ θνητοῖσι βροτοῖσιν ἐπὶ ζείδωρον ἄρουραν (*Odyssey*, 3.1–3).

7. 'The goddess Dawn rose up to high Olympus to announce the coming of the day to Zeus and the other immortals.'
Ἠὼς μέν ῥα θεὰ προσεβήσετο μακρὸν Ὄλυμπον
Ζηνὶ φόως ἐρέουσα καὶ ἄλλοις ἀθανάτοισιν (*Iliad*, 2.48–9).

8a. 'When the morning star arrives to announce the coming of the day to the earth, after him Dawn in her saffron robe spreads over the sea.'
ἦμος δ' ἑωσφόρος εἶσι φόως ἐρέων ἐπὶ γαῖαν,
ὅν τε μέτα κροκόπεπλος ὑπεὶρ ἅλα κίδναται Ἠώς (*Iliad*, 23.226–7).

8b. 'When the brightest star rose, the one whose arrival announces the light of early born Dawn.'
εὖτ' ἀστὴρ ὑπερέσχε φαάντατος, ὅς τε μάλιστα
ἔρχεται ἀγγέλλων φάος Ἠοῦς ἠριγενείης (*Odyssey*, 13.93–4).

9a. 'And as they were weeping, Dawn would have appeared with her rosy fingers, if Athena, the gleaming-eyed goddess, had not had an idea. She held back the night for a long time at the edge of the world and kept Dawn with her golden throne over the Ocean and would not allow her to yoke the swift-footed horses that bring light to men, Lampus and Phaethon, the young horses that carry Dawn.'
καί νύ κ' ὀδυρομένοισι φάνη ῥοδοδάκτυλος Ἠώς,
εἰ μὴ ἄρ' ἄλλ' ἐνόησε θεὰ γλαυκῶπις Ἀθήνη.
νύκτα μὲν ἐν περάτῃ δολιχὴν σχέθεν, Ἠῶ δ' αὖτε
ῥύσατ' ἐπ' Ὠκεανῷ χρυσόθρονον, οὐδ' ἔα ἵππους
ζεύγνυσθ' ὠκύποδας, φάος ἀνθρώποισι φέροντας,

Λάμπον καὶ Φαέθονθ', οἵ τ' Ἠῶ πῶλοι ἄγουσι (*Odyssey*, 23.241–6).

9b. 'Straightaway she [Athena] made the early born one with her golden throne rise up from the Ocean to bring light to men.'
αὐτίκ' ἀπ' Ὠκεανοῦ χρυσόθρονον ἠριγένειαν
ὦρσεν, ἵν' ἀνθρώποισι φόως φέροι (*Odyssey*, 23.347–8).

Some of these formulae are, indeed, banal. 1a, which takes up a whole line, is by far the most frequent with twenty-two occurrences, and 1b is just a necessary variation to adapt it to contexts requiring the future tense. This formula can also appear in a shortened form which only takes up the end of the line (1c). The second (2a) involving a different epithet (χρυσόθρονος, 'golden-throned', also used of goddesses like Hera (three occurrences) and Artemis (two occurrences), instead of ῥοδοδάκτυλος, 'rosy-fingered') is found four times in the *Odyssey* and 2b is simply an abbreviated version that takes up the end of the hexameter line. The third, which takes up the first part of the line, substitutes ἐύθρονος ('with her beautiful throne'), which only applies to the Dawn (six occurrences), for χρυσόθρονος ('golden-throned') and is found twice in the *Odyssey* with a small variation (αὐτίκα δ', 'straightaway' versus αἶψα γὰρ, 'quickly'). The fourth, which uses the epithet κροκόπεπλος, 'saffron-robed' (which, like ῥοδοδάκτυλος, is only used of the Dawn (four times)) is found twice in the *Iliad*.

The fifth type of formula, which appears in four different forms, combines daybreak with an expression of the passing of time. The Dawn is said to be the third (three occurrences in the *Odyssey*), the tenth (two occurrences in the *Iliad*), or the twelfth (two occurrences in the *Iliad*) and she is associated with epithets like ῥοδοδάκτυλος, 'rosy-fingered', which is only used of her and always precedes her name at the end of the line (twenty-seven occurrences), or ἐυπλόκαμος, 'with lovely hair' which she shares with several mortal women and goddesses (twenty-four occurrences) and φαεσίμβροτος (once), 'who brings light to mortals', which is also applied to the Sun (on two occasions).

Another group of formulae (6) contains references to both gods and mortals and serves to link the two groups. The first (6a) is attested in the *Iliad* as well as the *Odyssey* and occurs once in each poem. The opening of *Iliad* 11 shows how it can be used to create a transition between men and gods: Book 10 closes with a scene involving mortal characters, as Odysseus and Diomedes offer libations to Athena, while Book 11 opens at daybreak with Zeus sending Eris, the goddess of strife, to the Achaean ships. Similarly, Book 4 of the *Odyssey* closes with the suitors waiting to ambush Telemachus on his return to Ithaca while Book 5, which opens with the Dawn, begins with an assembly of the gods. The second (6b) occurs at the beginning of *Iliad* 19 where it forms a transition between a scene set among the gods, as Thetis receives the arms made by Hephaestus for Achilles at the end of Book 18, and the beginning of the next book, where she arrives at the Achaean camp to give the divine presents to her son. In contrast, the combined reference to gods and men in the third (6c), which is also very different in form, rather than providing a transition between the human and divine spheres, serves to link two scenes in which gods and men are closely associated. Book 2 of the *Odyssey* ends with the libations offered to the gods by Telemachus and his companions, while Book 3 opens at daybreak with Nestor's sacrifice. The allusion to the 'lovely lake' can be explained by the fact that one of these scenes takes place on a boat, the other by the sea.

The seventh formula, which only mentions the gods, is highly unusual. It may be explained by the context, since the day whose arrival is announced in lines 48–9 of Book 2 of the *Iliad* follows on from the deceptive dream sent to Agamemnon by Zeus and marks the beginning of troubled times for the Achaeans. Formulae 8a and 8b are just as unusual. They replace the arrival of the Dawn with the appearance of the 'bearer of Dawn' (the morning star), a term which occurs nowhere else in the Homeric poems, or of the 'brightest star' (another Homeric *hapax*) which immediately precedes the dawning of the new day.

The unusual character of the description of the arrival of Dawn in Book 23 of the *Odyssey* (9a and 9b) may be justified by the nature of the event in question: a miracle brought about by Athena. The first line *καί νύ κ' ὀδυρομένοισι φάνη ῥοδοδάκτυλος Ἠώς* (*Odyssey*, 23.241) is formed from a combination of two formulaic half-lines: the first *καί νύ κ' ὀδυρομένοισι* is found three times in the Homeric poems,[18] but it is usually followed by a mention of the sunset *ἔδυ φάος ἠελίοιο* ('And as they were weeping the sun would have set'). Here it is followed instead by the hemistich describing the arrival of the Dawn *φάνη ῥοδοδάκτυλος Ἠώς*. The whole line leads into an account (which has no parallel elsewhere) of Athena holding back the horses of the Dawn to prevent them from bringing light to men (lines 242–6). Nature is

[18] *Iliad*, 23.154; *Odyssey*, 16.220 and 21.226.

only allowed to take its course once again a full hundred lines later when Athena allows Dawn to rise so that she can bring light to men (lines 347–8). It is precisely this type of interplay between tradition and innovation that makes certain passages stand out so remarkably.

Such variations are therefore extremely significant, as the following example shows. In the *Odyssey*, the verb 'to send upon' always occurs at the end of the line when it is in the future tense, whether it is in the first person (ἐφήσω), the second person (ἐφήσεις), or the third person (ἐφήσει). Its subject is usually Odysseus and its object is normally the 'horrible fate' (ἀεικέα πότμον) which he 'sends upon' the suitors (three occurrences) or his own hands (χεῖρας, four occurrences) and it is found in contexts where the hero's revenge, or the death of the suitors, is evoked. In line 576 of Book 19, however, Penelope also uses this verb to announce the 'challenge' that she is going to 'set upon' the suitors νῦν δὲ μνηστήρεσσιν ἄεθλον τοῦτον ἐφήσω. This ironic echo, with its unusual subject (Penelope) and its unusual positioning of the verb at the end of the line (a quality that is unfortunately lost in translation), reveals the true meaning of the trial of the bow which serves to mark the beginning of Odysseus' revenge and leads to the massacre of the suitors.

In fact, modern scholarship has focused more and more on precisely those aspects of the poems that were neglected by the pioneers of orality, that is, everything in Homer that is not formulaic. At the same time, these studies acknowledge the difficulties involved in providing a rigorous definition of this notion, given the transformations that the idea of the 'formula' has undergone in the last four decades. Thus Margalit Finkelberg (1989) has examined the terminology used to express joy which represents a clearly defined group of just three verbs: 'to be delighted' γηθέω, 'to rejoice' γάνυμαι, and to 'be glad' χαίρω. Despite using an extremely restrictive definition of the 'non-formulaic', Finkelberg found that 40 per cent of the phrases expressing the idea of joy are unique.[19] She also showed that the distribution of the two types of expression, formulaic and non-formulaic, is subject to certain rules. The formulaic expressions are found above all in the narrative sections, in the aorist tense, and in the third person (both singular and plural), while the unique expressions are most frequent in direct speech where they are in the present

[19] For Finkelberg 1989: 188 for an expression to be accepted as non-formulaic it is not enough for it to be unique, in addition it must also 'not [be] related to an attested formulaic pattern'.

tense, in the first and second persons, and, as one might expect, 'in unusual narrative situations' (Finkelberg 1989: 194).

As is clear, these conclusions do not undermine Parry's principle of economy, since a sizeable proportion of the non-formulaic expressions serve to fill in the gaps left by the traditional system of formulae. They are corroborated by studies on different aspects of the system, like the study by D. H. F. Gray (1947) on the epithets used to describe objects or that of William Sale (1989) on the epithets applied to the Trojans. The image of Homer, prisoner of tradition, has been abandoned and there is now a far greater awareness of the 'individuality of Homer's language', to cite the title of an excellent article by Nicholas Richardson (1987).

It is precisely in the similes, which constitute one of the most original aspects of Homeric poetry, as well as in the speeches, whose length and complexity make them one of the most striking and characteristic features of the poems, that we find the greatest number of *hapax legomena*. Their impact is made all the greater by the way in which they stand out from a background composed of formulae. Thus the presence of the *hapax* ἐρατεινός 'lovely' to describe the waters of the river Scamander precisely at the moment when they are full of the corpses of men slaughtered by Achilles (*Iliad*, 21.218) endows the river's complaint with an exceptional degree of pathos.

4. TYPE-SCENES: SIMILARITY AND VARIATION

We find the same progression towards more flexible definitions and more inclusive models when we leave the micro-level of the formulae to consider larger elements of the poems such as type-scenes. The definition of the 'type-scene' was, at first, relatively strict; 'the description of a simple, regularly-structured activity such as launching a ship, preparing and eating a meal, receiving a guest and the like' (Edwards 1975: 51). More recent studies have tended to introduce a certain flexibility into this notion: alongside these relatively fixed descriptions of ritual acts, it is now accepted that there are flexible 'sequences'[20] which leave more space for the author's own invention

[20] This term was first proposed by Emlyn-Jones 1984.

and allow for significant variations. It has even been suggested that the 'type-scene' is 'an inherited preverbal Gestalt for the spontaneous generation of a "family" of meaningful details' (Nagler 1974: 81–2). The use of terms like 'theme' and 'motif' also implies a far more flexible phenomenon.[21]

The interpretative models proposed have therefore become increasingly general in nature. The 'arming scenes', where the warrior puts on a cuirass and takes up his spear and his shield, are set alongside those in which archers take up their bows (*Iliad*, 15.479–82 and *Odyssey*, 22.122–5) and compared with episodes in which the gods prepare for battle (*Iliad*, 5.737–42; 8.384–91) and, more generally still, with scenes where a hero gets dressed (*Iliad*, 2.42–6) or a goddess puts on her finery (*Iliad*, 14.170–86). All these preparations fulfil the same function: they serve to focus the audience's attention onto the character who will be at the centre of the episode that is about to follow.

As in the case of formulae, too, it is acknowledged that the repetition of scenes or motifs is not just a consequence of the mechanics of the oral composition process with no discernible meaning. On the contrary this repetition can create effects and pave the way for important episodes. Thus, the appearance of the dog Argos, who dies after recognizing his master in the seventeenth book of the *Odyssey*, is prepared as early as Book 7 by the descriptions of the magnificent dogs that guard the palace of Alcinous (7.91–3), of the wolves acting like dogs at the entrance to Circe's house (10.214–19), as well as of Eumaeus' dogs, who come close to tearing the beggar Odysseus to pieces (13.29–31), recognize Telemachus (16.4–6), and flee in terror when Athena arrives (16.162–3).[22] Rather than treating type-scenes in isolation from the rest of the narrative, studies have shown how the presence or absence of significant details can also point forward to future events. Thus, in the arming scenes of the *Iliad*, the statement that weapons are 'shining' is an indication of victory (Russo 1968: 286) and in the *Odyssey*, the absence of libations to the gods before embarking on ship is a presage of a difficult journey (Greene 1995: 217).

The study of type-scenes has therefore undergone the same evolution as the study of formulae. In the case of the formulae, as we saw,

[21] See, for example, Segal 1971 (*The Theme of the Mutilation of the Corpse in the Iliad*) and Armstrong 1958 ('The Arming Motif in the *Iliad*').

[22] See Edwards 1987: 54.

interest shifted from the rule to the exception, from the formulaic to the non-formulaic. In just the same way, Homeric criticism has shown increasing awareness of the ways in which traditional schemas are modified by expansion or, on the contrary, by omission. It has been noted, for example, that the length of arming scenes varies according to the importance of the hero involved and of the *aristeia* which follows (Edwards 1987: 49). The arming of Patroclus takes up fifteen lines (*Iliad*, 16.130–44) and his exploits only take up part of Book 16; the arming of Achilles, by contrast, is told in twenty-seven lines (19.364–91) and his *aristeia* takes up the whole of Books 20 to 22.

The same applies to supplication scenes: Leodes' supplication of Odysseus is described in a few lines (*Odyssey*, 21.312–19) while Odysseus' own supplication of Nausicaa occupies a substantial passage (*Odyssey*, 6.149–85). Hospitality can also be described in one line, or even half a line, as when Telemachus and his companion arrive at Diocles' house in Pherae (*Odyssey*, 3.490 and 15.188b). But the account of the welcome given to Odysseus by the Phaeacians lasts for more than seven books. Conversely, infringements of the laws of hospitality may be expressed by the omission of all references to the usual giving of presents, or by the mention of incongruous gifts, as in the Cyclops' promise to Odysseus (who has given his name as 'Noman'): 'Noman then shall come last among those I eat; his friends I shall eat first; this will be my favour to you' (*Odyssey*, 9.369–70).

So instead of simply opposing 'tradition' and 'innovation', such approaches show how 'Homer' uses tradition as a basis for innovation, creating original scenes by combining elements borrowed from several different type-scenes. The arrival of Hermes on Calypso's island (*Odyssey*, 5.55–90), which starts off like a messenger scene, contains elements borrowed or adapted from the visit type-scene (Edwards 1975). Because it is possible to identify the various components of a type-scene with precision, we are able to pinpoint the differences which make a particular episode original. When he arms himself in Book 16 of the *Iliad*, Patroclus, like Paris in Book 3, Agamemnon in Book 11, or Achilles in Book 19, puts on first his greaves and then his cuirass and picks up a sword and a shield. But in contrast to Paris, who 'took up a strong spear' (*Iliad*, 3.338), he 'did not take the spear' (*Iliad*, 16.140) which Achilles alone is able to brandish and with which he later kills Hector (*Iliad*, 22.317–27). This simple detail suffices to reveal the vast difference between Achilles and his double.

The patterns inherited from oral poetry are therefore far from rigid, as we see from the example of deliberation scenes where the hero considers two or more options open to him.[23] Here the poet has several different possibilities to choose from. He can make use of a monologue introduced by the formula 'in distress he spoke to his own great heart'. He can also introduce the scene of pondering and decision with verbs like *ὁρμαίνω*[24] or *μερμηρίζω* (both meaning 'to deliberate' or 'to consider'). The second of these verbs can be used on its own (on six occasions) or in conjunction with several different types of expression. These include the neuter plural adjective *πόλλα* ('many things') as object of the verb, conveying the multiple options between which the hero hesitates,[25] adverbs, which serve (on four occasions) to emphasize the divided state of his mind (*δίχα* or *διάνδιχα*, 'in two'), or expressions which situate the deliberation in 'his mind' (*κατὰ φρένα*, *Iliad*, 2.3 or *φρεσί*, *Odyssey*, 22.433), 'his heart' (*κατὰ θυμὸν ἀμύμονα*, *Odyssey*, 10.50), or, most frequently (five times), both (*κατὰ φρένα καὶ κατὰ θυμόν*). The alternatives under consideration are then introduced with the words 'whether to . . . or whether to . . .' (*ἠέ . . . ἦ . . .*).

The ultimate decision may be the consequence of divine intervention (as happens four times in the *Iliad*) or may result from the character's personal choice, as is necessarily the case when the character is a god like Zeus (in *Iliad*, 2.5, 14.23, and 16.652) or Hera (*Iliad*, 14.161). This choice can be introduced by the words 'this seemed in his heart to be the best plan' (*ἥδε δέ οἱ κατὰ θυμὸν ἀρίστη φαίνετο βουλή*[26]) or 'as he thought it over it seemed more advantageous to him to . . .'(*ὧδε δέ οἱ φρονέοντι δοάσσατο κέρδιον εἶναι*).[27]

On occasion, however, the moment of the decision itself may be passed over in silence, either because some external action interrupts the character's deliberations, or because the poet passes on directly to the description of the resulting action.

Two episodes in which Odysseus reflects on a course of action can be analysed against the background of these type-scenes. In Book 17, Odysseus, who has been struck by the goatherd Melanthius, hesitates between

[23] Russo 1968: 289–94 who refers to Voigt 1933.

[24] *Iliad*, 14.20, 16.435; *Odyssey*, 23.86.

[25] *Iliad*, 16.647.

[26] *Iliad*, 2.5, 10.17, 14.161; *Odyssey*, 9.318, 424, and 11.230.

[27] *Iliad*, 13.458, 14.23, 16.652; *Odyssey*, 5.474, 6.145, 15.204, 18.93, 22.338, 24.239, and, with a variation (*μοι* in place of *οἱ*), 10.153.

two possible reactions: 'he wondered (μερμήριξεν . . . ἠέ . . . ἦ . . .) whether to leap upon him and beat the life out of him with his cudgel or whether to lift him by the middle and dash his head against the ground' (lines 235–7). But in the end he chooses neither of these solutions and instead 'he mastered himself and checked his impulse' (238). Odysseus' deliberation in Book 20, when he sees the maidservants going to meet the suitors, is longer: 'He wondered in his mind and in his heart whether he should leap out then and there and put every one of them to death or whether he should let them lie with the arrogant suitors this one last time. His heart within him growled with anger as a bitch with puppies, mounting guard over the strengthless creatures, spies a stranger, growls at him and prepares to fight him, so his heart growled within him in indignation at these wicked deeds' (lines 10–16).

But instead of concluding with a decision, the traditional pattern is no more than a prelude to a monologue that is close to a deliberative monologue, as Odysseus goes on to 'rebuke his heart' (κραδίην ἠνίπαπε μύθῳ, line 17). This is followed by a description of the thoughts which he turned over (ἑλίσσετο, lines 24 and 28) in his mind and a simile, whose unusual character is signalled by the use of the *hapax* αἰόλλειν ('to shift to and fro', 'turn over', line 27), comparing him to a man who 'turns (αἰόλλῃ) a spitted paunch of some beast, all filled with blood and fat over a blazing fire'.

In the case of the repeated recognition scenes that occur after Odysseus' arrival on Ithaca, it is even possible to speak of a systematic search for variation (Emlyn-Jones 1984, Edwards 1987: 54–5), as the ancient commentators themselves had noted.[28] But, as Emlyn-Jones (1984: 6–7) has remarked, this variety is created within a fixed structure: that of the recognition scene, which is made up of a series of eight sequences of events:

1. Odysseus in disguise.
2. A conversation in which Odysseus is pressed for his identity, in reply to which he tells a false story, in which he claims to have seen Odysseus in his travels and predicts his early return . . .
3. Odysseus tests the other's loyalty; the test is passed . . .
4. Odysseus reveals himself.
5. The other refuses to believe.
6. Odysseus gives a sign as a proof of identity.
7. Final recognition . . .
8. 'On to business'.

[28] Eustathius, *Ad Odysseam*, 2, p. 214 l. 2–12 cited by Richardson 1984: 229.

Usually, the recognition is brought about by Odysseus himself. But, as in Book 19, he may be recognized against his will. Sometimes it is the result of a mark on the body, as in the case of the famous scar that Odysseus received from a boar during a hunt,[29] or it may be brought about by a sign that is known only to Odysseus and the other person (like the secret of the bed that he shares with his wife or the number of trees that his father planted for him at his birth).[30] But it may even take place without any signs.[31]

In Books 21 and 24 it is Odysseus himself who, before revealing his identity, tries to find out the true thoughts of his servants (21.191–206) and 'makes thorough trial' (διαπειρηθῆναι 21.240) of his father. In Book 23, line 181, by contrast, it is Penelope who is said to be 'putting her husband to the test' (πόσιος πειρωμένη).

The contrast between two recognition scenes can even be underlined by the repetition of the same line in two different contexts. In Book 19, when Odysseus is recognized by Eurycleia, he obtains her silence with a threat: '*If the god delivers the suitors into my hands* (*εἴ χ' ὑπ' ἐμοί γε θεὸς δαμάσῃ μνηστῆρας ἀγαυούς*), I will not spare you, nurse of mine though you are, when I kill the other maidservants in these halls' (lines 488–90). In Book 21, by contrast, when speaking to his two loyal servants, he uses the same line but follows it with a promise to reward them: '*If the god delivers the suitors into my hands* (*εἴ χ' ὑπ' ἐμοί γε θεὸς δαμάσῃ μνηστῆρας ἀγαυούς*), I will find wives for you both and give you possessions and well-built houses near my own; and from henceforward in my eyes you two shall be comrades and brothers of Telemachus' (lines 213–16).

Finally, the study of the suitors' banquets in the *Odyssey* shows how the standardized motif of the feast, which is itself a poetic representation of a social practice, enables us to distinguish good from bad hosts by emphasizing the qualities of the former and denouncing, through a series of omissions and deviations from the norm, the crimes of the latter. In the *Odyssey*, good hosts invariably seat their guests in the place of honour, that is on the special seat next to that of the master of the house. Thus in Book 1, Telemachus seats Athena/Mentes next to himself and, when he arrives at Pylos and at Sparta, he is seated next

[29] *Odyssey*, 19.392–3, 21.217–20, 24.331–3.
[30] *Odyssey*, 23.205–6, 24.336–44.
[31] *Odyssey*, 16.186–214.

to Nestor and Menelaus respectively.[32] Similarly, Alcinous, in Book 7, invites Odysseus to sit next to him, in the place where his favourite son had been sitting (lines 169–70). Good hosts also give gifts, here the exceptional generosity of the Phaeacians is shown by the multiple episodes of gift-giving. In Book 8, Odysseus receives a first series of gifts from Alcinous and the Phaeacian princes who each give him 'a clean cloak and tunic, and a talent of precious gold' (lines 392–3) then, from Euryalus, a 'sword of bronze with its silver hilt and encircling sheath of freshly sawn ivory' (lines 403–5) and, from Arete, a chest, and a cloak and tunic (lines 424–5). Finally, Alcinous himself gives him a goblet made of gold (lines 430–2). The theme recurs in Book 13 where the Phaeacian nobles are all invited to give Odysseus further gifts of a cauldron and tripod each (lines 13–15). Good hosts are also pious and never neglect to honour the gods by pouring libations and making sacrifices. Nestor's outstanding piety is portrayed in the text through the repetition of the libation motif (3.40–64, 332–42, and 390–4) and by the length and detailed nature of the sacrifice scene (3.420–63).

By contrast, the impiety of the suitors and their transgressions of the code of hospitality are revealed through the series of omissions, changes, and distortions of the normal literary presentation of the banquet that characterize the four accounts of their feasts.[33] It is interesting to note that, despite their length, these four banquet scenes involving the suitors contain the greatest number of departures from the normal sequence of elements.

The first of the suitors' banquets, in Book 1, is by far the briefest of these episodes. It begins at line 106 with a tableau of the suitors amusing themselves against the background of the preparations for the feast and ends at line 150 with the usual formula, 'when they had eaten and drunk their fill'. It is worth considering in detail the account of the preparations: 'Heralds and servants busied themselves for them [the suitors]: some mixing wine and water in bowls, others washing tables with porous sponges and setting them in place, others dividing out large quantities of meat' (lines 109–12). This allusion to the division of the meat places us straightaway in the fourth part of the standard banquet scene,[34] and this is confirmed in line 147 by

[32] *Odyssey*, 1.130–2, 3.37–9, 4.51.

[33] *Odyssey*, 1.106–50, 2.299–397, 17.170–18.428, 20.249–21.433.

[34] See Chapter 1 above.

the detail of the bread being piled up in baskets, which also figures in the account of Eumaeus' feast precisely at the moment when he serves the meat,[35] not to mention the account in line 149 of the gesture that leads immediately to the consumption of the food: 'They stretched out their hands to the dishes set ready before them' (line 149). In the case of this first banquet, then, we only see the preparations and the sharing out of the food, which is nowhere said to be 'equal'.

The second of the suitors' feasts, in Book 2, starts further back in the sequence of actions that make up the sacrificial banquet. It opens in lines 299–300 with the scene of the suitors 'skinning goats and singeing fatted hogs', that is with the actions that normally mark the end of the second section and follow the slaughtering of the victims (see Chapter 1 above). (The combination of pigs and goats is worth noting in itself as the only other feasts to involve the mixture of different types of animal are the one held by Phoenix's relatives in the *Iliad* (9.466–8) and the banquet given by Alcinous in the *Odyssey*, 8.59–61.) In the lines that follow, there is only one allusion to the rest of the feast with the expression 'the suitors were preparing their meal in the house' (μνηστῆρες δὲ δόμον κάτα δαῖτα πένοντο, line 322), which is similar to the phrase normally used to mark the end of the third section of the banquet description.[36] Curiously, this banquet does not conclude with any of the formulae expressing the satisfaction of hunger or thirst but ends with Athena sending drowsiness upon the suitors at lines 395–8.

The third of the suitors' feasts takes up most of Books 17 and 18. It begins with the arrival of the animals that have been brought from their pastures (17.170–1). In the accounts of Nestor's and Eumaeus' feasts this moment is followed by a more or less lengthy description of the sacrifice itself.[37] Here in Book 17, by contrast, there is no reference to the preparations for the sacrifice and the second section, the slaughter of the animals, is reduced to two lines emphasizing the quantity and the quality of the victims: 'they slaughtered full-grown sheep, fat goats, fattened hogs and a cow from the herd' (lines 180–1).

The series of actions that make up the sacrifice proper, ending with the burning of the fat and bones, is missing, and the description

[35] *Odyssey*, 16.51.

[36] οἱ δ' ἐπεὶ οὖν παύσαντο πόνου τετύκοντό τε δαῖτα. See above, Chapter 1. n. 162. *Odyssey*, 2.322 is omitted by some editors and translators.

[37] *Odyssey*, 3.440–61 and 14.420–9.

moves on immediately to the preparation of the feast at line 182 with the phrase δαῖτ' ἐντυνόμενοι ('in preparation for their meal') which summarizes the whole of the third section of the sacrificial banquet in just half a line. Up until the libation made by Amphinomus, which marks the end of the banquet, the only evocations of the feasting itself are the three references to the sharing out of bread and meat which correspond to the fourth section of the standard banqueting scene, the distribution of the food.[38]

The last of the suitors' banquets, which is also the longest, treats the motifs of the preceding three banquets at greater length, but without correcting any of the omissions. It opens in Book 20 with accounts of the preparations made by the male and female servants, representing a slightly expanded version of the preparations for the first banquet.[39] The three lines describing the arrival of the beasts that follow (20.63, 174, and 186) echo the account of the same subject in the third banquet scene (17.71) and the description of the animals being slaughtered at 20.250–1 is an exact repetition of lines 180–1 of Book 17. However, in lines 252–5 the description is enriched by a series of further details: 'They roasted the innards and served them round, they poured wine into the bowls and mixed it. The swineherd gave each man his goblet, Philoetius brought round the bread in baskets, and Melanthius poured the wine.' When we read in the very next line, 'They stretched out their hands to the dishes set ready before them', we might well imagine that the scene is nearly at its end, given that this line is normally followed by the formulaic line marking the end of the banquet. But, in fact, this banquet continues after line 279 where we see how the guests, 'after they had roasted the outer flesh and drawn it from the spits, divided the portions and pursued the sumptuous feast', which takes us to the end of the third section (the preparation of the food) and the beginning of the fourth section (the distribution) of the standard sequence of events. There are even two further lines that serve to introduce the theme of the equal distribution of the food: 'Beside Odysseus, the servants placed a portion equal (μοῖραν . . . ἴσην) to the one they themselves had received' (20.281–2). But this is attributed directly to Telemachus: 'for Telemachus, dear son of godlike Odysseus, had commanded this' (20.282–3).

38 *Odyssey*, 17.358–9, 334–5 and 342–4.
39 *Odyssey*, 20.147–9 and 160–1.

In the case of the suitors, the accounts of the banquets are far removed from the ideal of the fairly divided feast (δαίς εἴση). The descriptions of feasts normally pass over the actual consumption of the meal, but 20.348 (which is without parallel in the *Odyssey*) shows the suitors in the process of eating 'flesh . . . fouled with blood'. This image, marked out as exceptional by the use of the Homeric *hapax* αἱμοφόρυκτα, reveals the true nature of the feast that is called, by an ironic antiphrasis, 'pleasant and plentiful' ἡδὺ τε καὶ μενοεικές (20.391). It also allows a smooth transition to be made between the banquet and the massacre, between the bloody meat and the thick jet of human blood (αἵματος ἀνδρομέοιο, 22.19) which spurts from Antinous' throat and leaves 'the bread and roasted meat befouled with blood' (σῖτός τε κρέα τ' ὀπτὰ φορύνετο, 22.21). The presence of the adjective 'human' (ἀνδρόμεος) which otherwise only appears in lines 297 and 347 of Book 9, describing the meal of Polyphemus as he feasts on human flesh, provides confirmation, if any were needed, of the close links between the suitors and the Cyclops.

Although the banquet is the context *par excellence* for hospitality, the suitors are never shown entertaining guests, in contrast to Telemachus who acts as the perfect host on several occasions. Another significant omission is that of the libations to the gods which are normally closely linked to the drinking of wine. During the first banquet, in Book 1, we see the heralds 'mixing wine and water in bowls' (line 110) and 'pouring water on the hands' (line 146) of the drinkers. But the libation which these actions seem to presage never occurs. Nor does the second banquet end with the guests performing a libation before returning to their homes, as is the case with Menelaus (3.395) or the Phaeacians (7.228–30), but rather with the suitors miraculously succumbing to the drowsiness sent upon them by Athena. The two later banquets, by contrast, do include libations as is indicated by the presence of the formula which normally brings the libation section to a close: 'Having made libations (σπεῖσαν) and drunk to their hearts' content' (18.27 and 21.273).

But if we examine these scenes more closely, we find that the first libation in lines 418–27 of Book 18 is attributed to the only righteous suitor in the group, Amphinomus. The libation in Book 21, by contrast, which is performed on the orders of Antinous, the chief suitor, involves the group as a whole. It contains all the elements of a classic libation sequence:

1. The invitation to make libations (lines 263–4);
2. The general approval of the suitors (line 269);
3. The ablutions and the practical preparations for the libation with the filling of the mixing bowl and the distribution of the drinking cups (lines 271–2);
4. The concluding formula (line 273).

The only missing elements are, in fact, the essential ones: the libation itself and the prayer that should accompany it. At no point is there any question of a god being the recipient of the ritual. It is therefore as if the only libation ascribed to the suitors as a group is nothing more than an empty gesture.

The same observations can be made concerning sacrifices: in the case of the suitors the sacrifice is only evoked by its absence: it is planned but never carried out or is simply omitted. Here again, the one exception is an exception in appearance alone and serves to confirm the rule. The only sacrifice carried out by the suitors has exactly the same status as the libation of Antinous and, like that example, is an empty gesture. What is more, the two are closely linked in the story given that, in Book 21, immediately after suggesting to the suitors that they make a libation, Antinous invites them to order Melanthius to bring the best goats in his herd so that they can 'offer thighbones from them to Apollo master of archery' (lines 265–8). But this normal sacrifice never takes place: the suitors are all massacred by Odysseus before they can carry it out.

A better understanding of the stereotypical scenes therefore leads to a more accurate appreciation of Homer's originality. Knowledge of the traditional pattern of the type-scene, arrived at through a process of comparison, thus enables us to measure precisely a series of departures from the norm and to arrive at a fuller appreciation of what is characteristic of each element of the sequence. In practice, what seemed at first to be a simple technical expedient becomes a demonstration of the poet's art.

5. SIMILES

In the same way, a fuller understanding of the tradition has made it possible to gauge more accurately the originality of the similes in

Homer. Through one of those circular journeys which are frequent in the history of criticism, modern scholars have come to many of the same conclusions as their ancient counterparts.[40] Like the scholiasts, they have shown how the similes introduce variety (ποικιλία) into the poem. This may well explain why they are three times more frequent in the *Iliad*, where they serve to break up the accounts of the battles, than they are in the *Odyssey* with its more varied subject matter. They also introduce sublimity (ὕψος) and serve as ornaments (κόσμος) to the style, endowing it with greater clarity (σαφήνεια) and vividness (ἐνάργεια), and underline the significance of certain passages (ἔμφασις).

Recent studies have underlined the freedom enjoyed by the poet, who had a whole range of equivalent similes at his disposal to convey the same basic idea. Thus, the rapidity with which the gods move can be expressed by comparisons with several different species of bird: a hawk (*Iliad*, 13.62, 15.237, 16.582, 18.616), petrel (αἰθυία *Odyssey*, 5.353), or seagull (ἅρπη, *Iliad*, 19.350) as well as by the image of the wind blowing (*Odyssey*, 6.20), of a lead weight plunging into water (*Iliad*, 24.80–2), or of a shooting star (*Iliad*, 4.75–7).

The analysis of groups of similes of the same type makes it possible to distinguish clearly the traditional and the original features. Of the seven lion similes to be found in the *Odyssey*, five are applied to Odysseus, one to the Cyclops, and one to Penelope. The most traditional of these, which is used on two occasions (*Odyssey* 4.333–40 and 17.124–30), is very close to the Iliadic tradition: it contrasts the courage of the hero, compared to a 'mighty lion' (κρατεροῖο λέοντος), with the cowardice of his enemies, who are compared to a deer (ἔλαφος), and serves to announce his forthcoming victory.

The comparison of Odysseus to a lion in Book 22, after the massacre of the suitors, is more original, however: the hero is 'spattered with clotted gore like a lion[41] that has devoured an ox; his chest and jaws are covered with blood on both sides, and he is terrifying to behold. Thus was Odysseus, with his feet and hands above spattered with blood' (lines 402–6). It expresses the hero's valour while at the

[40] On the treatment of the similes by the ancient commentators, see Clausing 1913, Richardson 1980: 278–91, and Snipes 1988. It is interesting to compare the remarks of the ancient scholiasts with those of Fränkel 1921: 103–5, Griffin 1980b: 11–12, and Rutherford 1992: 74–7.

[41] This line also occurs at *Odyssey*, 23.48 where it is also used of Odysseus.

same time drawing attention to the horror of the carnage that has just taken place.

In another example (*Odyssey*, 6.130–6) the novelty does not lie in the image itself but in the context in which it is used. Here, Odysseus is compared to a 'mountain lion who is confident in his strength' (λέων ὀρεσίτροφος ἀλκὶ πεποιθώς, line 130),[42] but here he is not a warrior falling upon his enemy, instead he has been washed up, naked, onshore and is approaching a group of girls and, far from being 'driven by his bold heart' (*Iliad*, 12.300) like Sarpedon, he is driven by his 'stomach'.[43] The contrast is far from being gratuitous but sums up perfectly the differences between the two poems and their heroes. In the *Iliad*, Achilles pays no heed to bodily necessities: he refuses to eat after the death of Patroclus and urges the Achaeans to fight on empty stomachs (*Iliad*, 19.48–153). Odysseus, by contrast, does not ignore the demands of his 'accursed belly' and gives in to them.[44]

In Book 9 of the *Odyssey* it is the Cyclops who is compared to a lion as he devours Odysseus' companions: 'Like a mountain lion, he devoured their flesh and entrails, bones and marrow, leaving nothing' (9.292–3). But there is nothing heroic about this lion and the simile, which reduces the Cyclops to the status of a beast, only serves to further emphasize his savagery and his monstrosity.

More remarkable still is the passage in which Penelope is compared to a lion: 'As a lion ringed by a band of hunters is filled with bewilderment and fear as they close their cunning circle round him, in such bewilderment lay the queen till welcome sleep came suddenly upon her' (*Odyssey*, 4.791–3). The implications are complex for, while the simile creates a subtle link between Odysseus—the lion *par excellence* of the *Odyssey*—and his wife, it also serves to emphasize the differences between them. In this simile, the lion is no longer the ferocious beast that knows no fear and spreads panic,[45] but is a vulnerable creature who is afraid (δείσας, line 792) and can only turn over thoughts in its mind.[46]

[42] ὥς τε λέων ὀρεσίτροφος occurs in three other places (*Iliad*, 12.299, 17.61, and *Odyssey* 9.292). At *Iliad*, 17.61 we also find the words ἀλκὶ πεποιθώς.

[43] *Iliad*, 12.300 (Sarpedon): κέλεται δέ ἑ θυμὸς ἀγήνωρ; *Odyssey*, 6.133: κέλεται δέ ἑ γαστήρ. See Pucci 1987: 222–4.

[44] *Odyssey*, 7.215–22, 15.344–5, 17.286–7, 473–4, and 18.364.

[45] *Iliad*, 12.45–6; 5.136, 476; 11.173; 17.67.

[46] Of the fifty occurrences of the lion simile in the Homeric poems only two involve a vulnerable lion that trembles with fear (τρεῖ *Iliad*, 11.554, 17.663).

By grouping similes together in this way we can also see the very moment at which a traditional phrase becomes an original image. For example, the comparison of a young man to a young plant, which is expressed in just two words (ἔρνει ἶσος) in the cases of Achilles and Telemachus,[47] is developed in the case of Nausicaa who is compared by Odysseus to a 'young palm tree' (φοίνικος νέον ἔρνος) that he once saw close to the altar of Apollo at Delos (*Odyssey*, 6.162–3). But, when combined with another of the typical images of the *Iliad*, that of the dying warrior who falls to the ground like a felled tree,[48] it takes on a pathetic note when the poet evokes the death of a young warrior during his first battle at *Iliad*, 17.53–60: 'As when a man nurtures a flourishing olive-shoot (ἔρνος) in a solitary place, where plenty of water wells up—a fine, healthy shoot it is, shaken by the breath of every wind that blows, and it blossoms thick with white flowers: but suddenly there comes a wind in a great storm, and uproots it from its trench and lays out its length on the earth, Such was the son of Panthous, Euphorbus of the ash spear, as Menelaus son of Atreus killed him, and set to stripping his armour.'

It is also possible to perceive variations in the content of the similes as well as in their tenor. In order to express Achilles' grief at the death of Patroclus, the *Iliad* compares him to a 'great bearded lion whose cubs have been stolen from the thick wood where he left them by a man out hunting deer: the lion comes back too late and is filled with anguish' (18.318–20). The *Odyssey* also contains comparisons of the tears shed by Odysseus and Telemachus with those shed by birds of prey, 'an eagle (?) or a vulture with hooked claws whose nestlings the hunters have snatched away unfledged' (16.216–18). But the simile is employed in an unusual manner: it no longer serves to convey the pain caused by the loss of a loved one but rather to underline the intensity of the emotions felt by father and son at their reunion and, perhaps, to imply that the pain of separation is not easily effaced.[49]

Finally, we can appreciate by contrast the originality of certain similes which do not belong to any group. Thus, in *Iliad* 21, the river Scamander, as he pursues Achilles 'with a great din' (line 257) and threatens to drown him, is compared to the water that flows through

[47] *Iliad*, 18.56, 437, and *Odyssey*, 14.175.
[48] *Iliad*, 5.560 (poplar); 13.178 (fir tree); 13.389–91 and 16.482–4 (oak or white poplar).
[49] See Buxton 2004: 148.

irrigation channels when the gardener removes the stones that were holding it back. This idyllic tableau, whose unusual nature is further underlined by the very high proportion of *hapax legomena*, is not simply an 'ornament' as one ancient commentator claimed.[50] By evoking the world of culture and man's efforts to channel the elements and use them for his own purposes, it focuses on the threat to mankind represented by the forces of nature when they are unleashed.[51] Similarly, the ironic assimilation of the victor to the vanquished in the comparison of the tears shed by Odysseus when he hears Demodocus singing of the sack of Troy with the tears of a captive woman about to be taken away as a slave as she weeps over the body of her husband (*Odyssey*, 8.521–31) is unparalleled.[52]

As understanding of the tenor of the similes grew so did awareness of their integration into the poem as a whole and of the role they could play. Similes can, in fact, help to articulate sections of the narrative. In Book 5 of the *Odyssey*, the two parts of the description of the storm, which is interrupted by the appearance of the marine goddess Ino, close with two parallel similes that of the north wind, 'sweeping thistle stalks over the plain' (5.328–30) and that of the wind 'tossing a heap of dry chaff this way and that' (5.368–70). Similes can also point forward to future events and serve to link episodes or characters. As the ancient scholiasts noted, the comparison of Patroclus to a 'lion who has been wounded in the chest' (*Iliad*, 16.752–3) at the moment when he leaps towards the body of Cebriones prefigures his own imminent death.[53] Similarly, at the end of the *Odyssey*, the image of the eagle flying high in the sky (24.538), which appears when Odysseus is about to achieve his revenge, refers back to the omens and dreams involving eagles that announced this revenge in Books 15, 19, and 20.[54] In the *Odyssey*, similes also serve to establish a link between Odysseus and Penelope. We have already seen one example: the comparison of Penelope to a lion. But there are also similes comparing her to a good king (19.108–14) or a shipwrecked man who arrives on dry land after a storm (23.233–9).[55]

[50] Scholia to *Iliad* 21.257–62: *Κόσμου ἕνεκα.*
[51] See the excellent comments in Richardson 1987: 172–3.
[52] See Buxton 2004: 148–9.
[53] BT scholia to *Iliad*, 16.752–3 cited by Richardson 1980: 280.
[54] *Odyssey*, 15.161, 19.538, 543, and 548, 20.243.
[55] See Foley 1978.

In the case of formulae, type-scenes, and similes, we can see how a better understanding of the techniques of oral poetry, the construction of categories series, and the systematic use of comparison have gradually made it possible to build up what has been termed a 'poetics'[56] or, alternatively, an 'aesthetics'[57] of orality. For the modern reader, appreciating Homer means recognizing in him the heir to a venerable poetic tradition that goes back to the Indo-European, as well as an innovative poet who can sometimes react against his tradition, a unique poet whose originality stands out even more clearly when we compare his poems to what we know of the other archaic epics.[58]

[56] This term was first used by Notopoulos 1964 and was taken up by Edwards 1997.

[57] See the title of Russo 1994: 'Homer's Style: Non-Formulaic Features of an Oral Aesthetics'.

[58] Russo 1968, Griffin 1977.

3

Homer and History

The Homeric epics are presented as historical accounts. They claim to relate a true story of past events by appealing to the Muse, and thus to tradition, as their source. In Antiquity, Homer was long considered to be an authority on historical matters and his poems were even used to back up territorial claims. According to Plutarch, Solon used two lines from the Catalogue of Ships that placed the Athenians close to the ships of Ajax, who was from the island of Salamis ('Ajax brought twelve ships from Salamis, and placed them where the Athenian lines were stationed,' *Iliad*, 2.557–8), when he wanted to defend Athenian claims on Salamis against the Megarians (Plutarch, *Solon*, 10.2). Modern readers, however, have been rather more sceptical and, for over a century, have questioned the historical value of the Homeric poems.

1. DID THE TROJAN WAR REALLY TAKE PLACE?

Although they argued over the date of the Trojan War, ancient readers never doubted that it was a real historical event.[1] Even a historian as 'rational' as Thucydides accepted it; in his overview of the ancient history of Greece, known as the *Archaeology*, his only criticism is that Homer exaggerated its importance: 'It is reasonable to think that that Trojan expedition was greater than all in previous history, but still short of the modern scale, if we can trust Homer's poems in this respect too (being a poet, he is likely to have exaggerated) τῇ Ὁμήρου

[1] Douris of Samos placed it in 1334, Herodotus around 1250, Ctesias and Eratosthenes in 1135. A distance of two centuries therefore separates the earliest and the latest dating.

αὖ ποιήσει εἴ τι χρὴ κἀνταῦθα πιστεύειν, ἣν εἰκὸς ἐπὶ τὸ μεῖζον μὲν ποιητὴν ὄντα κοσμῆσαι' (Thucydides, 1.10.3).[2]

For Diodorus, the Trojan War even served to mark the beginning of historical time, given that it was possible to give precise dates to all later events in relation to the war:

> As for the periods included in this work, we do not attempt to fix with any strictness the limits of these before the Trojan War, because no trustworthy chronological table covering them has come into our hands: but from the Trojan War we follow Apollodorus of Athens in setting the interval from then to the Return of the Heracleidae as eighty years.[3]

In the late nineteenth century the discoveries made by a German amateur archaeologist, Heinrich Schliemann, first at Hissarlik in north-western Turkey, and later at Mycenae in mainland Greece, seemed to provide material proof of Homer's veracity. But this turned out to be at the expense of both topography and chronology. The city identified by the archaeologists as Troy VIIa, which underwent a violent destruction at some point close to the traditional date of the fall of Troy (1184), was a small, poverty-stricken community that had nothing in common with the wealthy city described by Homer. What is more, there is no evidence that this destruction was the work of Achaean troops.

Is it even certain that Hissarlik was Homer's Troy? There are certainly enough discrepancies between the two places to prompt one historian to comment that 'there is something wrong either with Schliemann's Troy or with Homer's'.[4] The dates are no more certain than the places: the Trojan finds date to between 2,500 and 2200 BC and the treasure found in the Mycenaean tombs is certainly earlier than 1500 BC, placing it several centuries before the date of the Trojan War. We have even more cause for scepticism about the historicity of the events described in the *Iliad* and the *Odyssey* when we consider the extent to which epic can distort the events it relates. If the *Chanson de Roland* was able to transform the ambush of Charlemagne's troops by Christian Basques in the small mountain pass of Roncesvalles into a heroic battle against an immense horde of Saracens, if the *Niebelunglied* reversed the relationship between the

[2] The translation is adapted from that of Hammond (Oxford, 2009).
[3] 1.6.1. Translation by C. H. Oldfather (London and New York, 1933).
[4] Rhys Carpenter quoted in Finley's article 'Lost: The Trojan War' in Finley 1977b: 36.

Huns and the Burgundians, as Moses Finley (1964) pointed out, why should we give automatic credence to Homer?

There are however still archaeologists and historians who believe in Homer. At first, they based their arguments on Hittite documents.[5] The tablets found at Bogazköy contain mentions of people called *Ahhiyawa* who came to areas that the Hittite leaders considered to be under their control like *Millawanda* and *Wilasa* which at one time was ruled by a king named *Alaksandus*. It has been suggested that these *Ahhiyawa* can be identified with Homer's Achaeans given that the sphere of influence of the *Ahhiyawa*, as reflected in the Hittite texts, corresponds to that of the Mycenaeans as revealed by the archaeological record. *Millawanda*, in particular, has been identified as Miletus, where clear signs of a Mycenaean presence have been found. It has also been argued that *Wilusya* and *Tarwisa* are Ilion (or rather *Wilios, as the name originally began with the digamma) and Troy, respectively. *Alaksandus*, the ruler of *Wilusa*, would, of course, be Paris, also known as Alexander, of Troy.

But this sort of argument, even if it is defensible on linguistic grounds, flies in the face of both the chronology and the geography.[6] It is impossible to see in *Alaksandus*, the vassal of the Hittite king, the Alexander of the Trojan War who is an independent ruler, particularly when we learn that *Alaksandus* lived at the time of a king who fought Ramses II at the battle of Kadesh (1275 BC), that is, at least half a century before the generally agreed date for the Trojan War.

It is no longer even certain that the *Ahhiyawa* are Homer's Achaeans: the most recent attempts to reconstruct Hittite geography place them not at Mycenae but in western Anatolia or even in Thrace. The thesis that Hittite history confirmed the existence of the Trojan War has thus been seriously undermined and the specialists themselves remain divided between cautious believers and equally cautious sceptics.

Archaeologists also entered the fray. One of the leading experts on the Troad, J. M. Cook (1992; 1st pub. 1984), saw no reason not to accept the existence of Troy exactly where Schliemann and, after him, Dörpfeld and Blegen had excavated. He was also willing to admit that

[5] See Eaton 1984 and Güterbock 1986.

[6] Güterbock 1986: 34–5 and Watkins 1986: 48–50 argue that the name *Alaksandus*, which does not conform to the Anatolian onomastic tradition, must be a transcription of the Greek name Alexandros and that it is possible to identify *Wilusa* as Ilion.

this Troy was overcome by an attack by Achaean troops, even if he acknowledged, along with Thucydides, that the importance of the expedition was grossly exaggerated in the epic. The archaeologist Manfred Korfmann, who also carried out excavations at Troy, was amongst those who refused to see the Trojan War as a simple invention (Korfmann 1986a, and 1986b). The historian J. K. Davies concluded his discussion of oral tradition, in which he attempted to define criteria which would make it possible to decide whether a particular tradition was reliable or not, by admitting that 'in our *Iliad* we are dealing with a literary creation which reflects an orally transmitted tradition of an historical Trojan War' (Davies 1992: 225). And the results of J. B. Hainsworth's comparative study led him to claim that 'the great majority of traditions of heroic poetry are rooted in history' even if the historical content is distorted over time, the opposite conclusion to that of Moses Finley (Hainsworth 1984: 114). If the Trojan War had been lost, it was thus found again.

2. HOMER AND THE MYCENAEAN PAST

Schliemann's discovery of the Mycenaean world with its towering walls, its palaces, and rich burials, like Evans's excavations on Crete, inspired many to find ways of supporting the claim that the world described by Homer was that of the Bronze Age. There were, however, some sceptics like H. L. Lorimer who, as early as 1950, saw that the significance of the Mycenaean elements in Homeric epic had been greatly exaggerated (Lorimer 1950: 452). But it was the publication of the first edition of Moses Finley's *The World of Odysseus* in 1954 that dealt a fatal blow to the idea that Homer's world and the Mycenaean world were one and the same. Archaeological discoveries, as well as Ventris and Chadwick's deciphering of the clay tablets found in the ruins of the palaces at Cnossos, Pylos, and Mycenae in 1953, confirmed this view. The more that became known about the territory and the organization of Mycenaean society, the greater the gulf separating it from the world described by Homer appears to be.[7]

[7] The gulf between the Mycenaean world and Homer has since been underlined by Heubeck 1984, Crielaard 1995b, and Bennet 1997.

Despite claims to the contrary, the Catalogue of Ships in Book 2 of the *Iliad* contains almost no echoes of the actual geographical spread of Mycenaean culture. The names of the peoples who make up Nestor's contingent in the Catalogue (*Iliad*, 2.591–602) bear no relation to the names of the districts dependent on Pylos that are found in the Linear B tablets (Heubeck 1979: 231). The palace society of Bronze Age Greece with its palace-centred economy and its bureaucratic organization (which has much in common with that of other societies in the Ancient Near East), its 'ruler' (*wanax*) holding sway over vast areas and engaging in commercial contact with areas from southern Italy in the west to Egypt and Syria in the east, has nothing in common with the aristocratic society of the Homeric poems in which the 'king' was only the first among equals.[8] There is, moreover, a vast difference between the funerary practices of the Mycenaean world, where burial was the norm, and those of the Homeric world, where the dead are usually cremated.[9]

Indeed, it would be surprising if this were not the case, for reasons of both place and time. Place, because Homer is closely connected to Ionia while the great centres of Bronze Age civilization were located in mainland Greece and in Crete and the Achaeans migrated mostly to the mountainous regions of the Peloponnese (Arcadia) and to Cyprus, as is shown by the evolution of Greek dialects. But above all time: given that a span of at least twelve generations separated 'Homer' from the Mycenaean period, it is impossible to imagine that an oral tradition, which was by definition engaged in a constant process of revising its image of the past in order to make it conform to the ever-changing demands of its public, could have transmitted a faithful picture of such a distant period.

There are, however, still Mycenaean elements in the poem that need explanation. Their presence is undeniable, even if they are few and far between. It is true that excavations of Bronze Age sites have brought to light objects that correspond exactly to Nestor's cup with its depictions of doves (*Iliad*, 11.633–5), Ajax's shield, made of seven layers of ox-hide and covered with a layer of bronze (*Iliad*, 7.219–23), the helmet with boars' tusks worn by Odysseus (*Iliad*, 10.261–65), and the silver and ivory encrusted seat used by Penelope (*Odyssey*, 19.56), not to mention the bronze cuirasses and greaves worn by the

[8] See Heubeck 1979: 234 and Bennet 1997: 522–3.

[9] See Bennet 1997: 520.

Homeric warriors. The tablets found at Cnossos also reveal the existence of 'silver-studded swords', like the one given to Odysseus by Euryalus (*Odyssey*, 8.406–16). Finally, the chariots that played a major role in fighting during the Mycenaean period, as is shown in the inventories preserved on the Linear B tablets, are present in the epic, but they have become the ancient equivalent of the 'Marne taxis' that took soldiers to the front in the First World War, serving only to transport the heroes onto the battlefield.

Two types of explanation could be offered for such echoes of the past. They could be due to the presence of objects that dated back to the Mycenaean period in the treasuries of the great families or in temples, or to an unbroken poetic tradition dating back to the same period. The second of these explanations is more plausible. The continued existence in Homeric poetry of archaic linguistic features, some of which are paralleled in the language of the Mycenaean tablets, supports the idea that the poetic tradition of which Homer's poems represent the culmination had its roots in the Bronze Age. It has even been suggested that the scene represented on one of the walls of the building called 'Nestor's Palace' at Pylos may show a lyre player within a banqueting scene accompanied by a sacrifice. It is a short step from here to the argument that the Mycenaean rulers had resident poets at their courts whose status would have been similar to that of Phemius or Demodocus in the *Odyssey*, as has been suggested (Bennet 1997: 529).

3. HOMER AND THE 'DARK AGES'

If the world of Homer is not Mycenaean, should it be identified with a less distant past and read as a reflection of the social institutions of the period known as the 'Dark Ages' (because, until quite recently, very little was known about it or because it was held to be a backward culture), that is the tenth and ninth centuries? This was the view put forward by Moses Finley in *The World of Odysseus*. His thesis was based on two main arguments. First, he used comparative methods to establish that the society depicted in the Homeric poems was a coherent one in sociological terms and must therefore reflect historical reality. It was then easy for him to demonstrate that this society could not have been that of the Mycenaean period (for the reasons outlined above). He also excluded the possibility that it was the society in which the poems were composed, because he did not find in 'Homer' any of the characteristics of eighth-century Greece such as the arrival of the Dorians, the creation of the Olympic Games, the emergence of the city-state, the development of commerce with the Levant and colonization, the birth of alphabetic scripts, the existence of iron weapons and of cavalry. Only one possibility therefore remained: to place Homeric society in the historical black hole that was then the 'Dark Ages'.

But this thesis, which soon became a new orthodoxy, was itself called into question by archaeological discoveries that revolutionized our knowledge of the 'Dark Ages'. Excavations in Euboea and in Macedonia revealed that, as early as the mid ninth century, contacts were being made throughout the Aegean, trade was being re-established with the Near East, and that the regions that were at the centre of these developments, like Attica and the island of Euboea, were becoming more prosperous. At Lefkandi on Euboea traces of a large banqueting hall have been found, as well as rich burials that attest to a certain level of prosperity. The existence of trading links between the Greek world and the Orient was established by the finds at Lefkandi, as well as at Argos and Athens, of objects from Cyprus (a large bronze amphora) or even from the Near East (golden jewellery), and by the discovery of pottery from Euboea at Al Mina on the Syrian coast and at Amathus in Cyprus dating from the late tenth century. There are therefore fewer and fewer reasons to assume a complete break between the 'Dark Ages' (which are becoming less and less 'dark' as time goes on[10]) and what historians of Ancient Greece call the Geometric period (using a term borrowed from the classification of pottery).

4. HOMER AND THE GEOMETRIC PERIOD

The tendency has thus been to place Homeric society later and later in time and to situate it at the end of the 'Dark Ages', as in the work of Oswyn Murray (1980) who notes the presence in Homeric epic of relatively 'recent' elements like Phoenician merchants, or the function

[10] Morris 1997: 541 reduces the duration of the Dark Ages to a period of just fifty years: *c.*1075–1025 BC.

of tripods and bronze cauldrons as material signs of wealth, or the architecture of Homeric houses that is closer to Geometric period buildings than it is to the Mycenaean palaces. Murray was followed by Kurt Raaflaub who proposed the late ninth and eighth centuries (1997: 628). Ian Morris argued in an important article entitled 'The use and abuse of Homer' (1986) that it reflects Homer's own period.[11]

These shifts in date are not just the result of the progress made in archaeology. They also reflect a better understanding of the ways in which orality functions. Oral traditions do not aim to reconstruct the past 'as it actually was' ('wie es eigentlich gewesen ist', to quote the famous phrase of Leopold Ranke). Rather it recreates it on the basis of the present by adapting it to the demands of the listeners through a process of constant reimagining.[12] Once we admit this, it becomes difficult to accept that the society and institutions depicted in Homeric epic could possibly belong to a world that had existed two centuries earlier.

In fact, a more careful reading of the Homeric texts, combined with a more flexible conception of the Greek city and the institutions that characterized it, has made it possible to reveal a whole series of elements linking the world of Odysseus with the eighth century BC. In particular, the role of maritime trade in the *Odyssey* corresponds well to what is known about the increasing frequency of overseas contacts from the ninth century onwards. In the poem, merchants and pirates are familiar figures, as is shown by the classic question asked of strangers: 'Who are you? What land did you sail from, over the watery paths? Are you engaged in trade, or are you roving over the sea like pirates who sail at random, risking their lives and bringing ruin to other peoples?' (*Odyssey*, 3.71–4 = 9.252–6).

Trade with foreigners is a normal activity in the *Odyssey*: Athena, disguised as Mentes, has no problem convincing Telemachus that she is travelling with some companions to Temesa (which the ancient commentaries placed either in the west, at Bruttium, or on Cyprus, to the east) to trade iron for copper (*Odyssey*, 1.182–4). And Penelope is also ready to believe the beggar who tells her that Odysseus, after leaving the Phaeacians, continued to travel the world in order to

11 A revised version of this article is included in Cairns 2001: 57–91.

12 See Vansina 1965: 160 'Most tales merely express the ideals and ways of life of the present', and Ong 1982: 48 'oral traditions reflect a society's present cultural values rather than idle curiosity about the past'.

amass further wealth (*Odyssey*, 19.283–6). Nor is it as certain as it once seemed to be that the Homeric epics are devoid of all reference to writing. The mention of 'signs' 'inscribed' on the lots used to select the Achaean warrior who will fight the duel with Hector in Book 7 of the *Iliad* raises the question of their nature:[13] are they just symbols, designating each hero, or letters? It has also been suggested that the reference in Book 6 to 'baleful signs' inscribed on the tablet given to Bellerophon by Proetus might also be an allusion to a letter.[14] Opinions have been divided on this point: the linguist C. J. Ruijgh (1995: 39 n. 132) maintains that the 'baleful signs' of *Iliad* 6 are 'probably symbolic signs expressing the idea of death' whereas the historian J. P. Crielaard (1995b: 213), writing in the same volume, is willing to accept that the same phrase constitutes at the very least an explicit reference to writing.

The supposed absence of references to the city-state has also been questioned in studies that bring together all the elements of institutions and architecture that seem to point to the existence of the *polis*, at least in an embryonic form.[15] First, in the military sphere, there are the mass combats that form the background to the heroes' duels, as well as certain descriptions evoking something very close to the hoplite phalanx (a heavy infantry battalion which depends for its effectiveness on group cohesion and individual discipline).[16] It is interesting to read the account of the Myrmidons taking up their positions for battle at Achilles' orders in this light:

> And the ranks pressed closer together as they heard their king. As when a man builds a wall for a high house with the stones fitting closely, to keep out the force of the winds, so their helmets and bossed shields locked close. Shield then pressed against shield, helmet on helmet, man on man: the horse-hair crests in the bright ridges of their helmets touched when they moved their heads, so close to each other were they pressed. (*Iliad*, 16.211–17)

[13] *Iliad*, 7.175: *οἳ δὲ κλῆρον ἐσημήναντο ἕκαστος*; 187: *ἐπιγράψας*; 189: *γνῶ δὲ κλήρου σῆμα.*

[14] *Iliad*, 6.168–9: '[Proietus] sent [Bellerophon] away to Lycia, and sent with him signs of disastrous meaning, many lethal marks that he wrote in a folded tablet': *πέμπε δέ μιν Λυκίηνδέ, πόρεν δ' ὅ γε σήματα λυγρὰ | γράψας ἐν πίνακι πτυκτῷ θυμοφθόρα πολλά.*

[15] Since Finley, the most recent studies of Homeric society, such as Raaflaub 1997, make it contemporary with the birth of the *polis*.

[16] Since Latacz 1977: 68–74, the idea that Homeric warfare prefigures hoplite combat has become more widespread. See in particular Singor 1995 and Van Wees 1997.

And, in Book 13 of the *Iliad*, it is the Achaeans who close ranks to withstand the Trojan onslaught: 'spear was protected by spear, shield overlapped shield; buckler then pressed on buckler, helmet on helmet, man on man. The horse-hair crests in the bright ridges of their helmets touched when they moved their heads, so close to each other were they pressed' (*Iliad*, 13.130–5). Homeric epic can thus be seen to contain, in embryonic form at least, a characteristic institution of the city that reached its fully developed form in the middle of the seventh century.

Next, in the domain of politics, there is the dominance of the aristocrats who at times work together in harmony, as on Scheria, but who can also be torn apart by tensions and dissension, as on Ithaca. The *Odyssey* also shows knowledge of 'assemblies where decisions are made' (ἀγοραὶ βουληφόροι, *Odyssey*, 9.112) whose absence is seen as the sign of a lack of civilization, as is shown by the example of the Cyclopes in Book 9 of the *Odyssey*. These assemblies seem to have had, in theory at least, fairly wide-reaching powers: Antinous claims that the assembly on Ithaca could send the suitors into exile for conspiring to kill Telemachus (*Odyssey*, 16.376–92). They are dominated by the local aristocracy: on Ithaca it is Telemachus himself who orders the heralds to summon the assembly[17] and, in Book 16.361–2, the suitors prevent the ordinary people from attending. Assemblies like the one in Book 24 where the ordinary citizens arrive spontaneously,[18] in response to the emotions aroused by the massacre of the suitors, are the exception.

Certain elements in the Homeric narration also suggest the existence of a communal cult with ceremonies involving the citizens as a group. In *Iliad* 6, the Trojan women, led by Hecuba, go in a group to the temple of Athena, where Theano 'whom the Trojans had made priestess of Athena' (6.300) officiates, in order to make an offering to the goddess. At the opening of the third book of the *Odyssey*, Telemachus and Athena find the citizens of Pylos 'offering a sacrifice of black bulls to raven-haired Poseidon', and the way in which the participants are seated in 'nine companies . . . with five hundred men in each' (3.5–8) shows clearly that this sacrifice is conceived as a group activity.

[17] *Odyssey*, 2.6–8 (Telemachus summons the assembly), cf. 16.376–7 where the suitors fear that he may summon another assembly on his return.

[18] *Odyssey*, 24.420: αὐτοὶ δ' εἰς ἀγορὴν κίον ἀθρόοι.

It is also important to note that colonization, which presupposes the existence of a community acting collectively, is well known in the world of the *Odyssey*. This is shown first of all by the story of the Phaeacians as summed up by the poet in lines 4–10 of Book 6: in order to escape their aggressive neighbours, the Cyclopes, they left their original home to settle on Scheria and found a city. Their leader, Nausithous, did exactly what the founder of a colony would be expected to do: he surrounded the city with fortifications, built houses, erected temples, and divided the land between the settlers. In addition, the description of the island seen by Odysseus close to the land of the Cyclopes can only be understood in the context of colonization: 'The land is by no means to be despised; it might bring forth everything in season. Beside the shore of the whitening sea it has soft, moist meadows where vines might flourish and never cease. Its soil would make for easy ploughing; they might reap tall harvests there in season, for beneath the surface the loam is rich. Moreover there is a good harbour there; inside it you need no mooring tackle, no stones to be thrown down for anchors.' (*Odyssey*, 9.131–7) It is, in short, an ideal place to found a colony. Like Syracuse, for example, the Cyclopes' island has natural defences, a good harbour, and fertile land (essential for settlers who were first and foremost farmers in search of land).

The descriptions of the cities mentioned in the *Odyssey* correspond, moreover, to what is known about archaic Greek cities on the basis of the ruins of the old city of Smyrna and those of colonies like Megara Hyblaea in Sicily. Like these, Scheria is surrounded by walls, it has an open space where assemblies are held, as well as temples that are independent of the palace, like those that begin to appear in Greece at the beginning of the eighth century.[19] There are also some indications in the Homeric poems of familiarity with both Panhellenic games and Panhellenic sanctuaries. The *Iliad* contains a mention of a chariot race held at Elis (that is, Olympia) at 11.697–701 and the *Odyssey* refers to the existence of oracles at Delphi and Dodona, as well as at the Sanctuary of Apollo on Delos.[20]

All the features that characterize what has been termed 'the Greek Renaissance' can be found to various extents in the *Odyssey*. It is not

[19] *Odyssey*, 6.9 and 262–3, 7.44–5 (walls); *Odyssey*, 6.266–7, 7.44, 8.12 and 109 (assemblies); *Odyssey*, 6.10 (temples). Cf. Snodgrass 1980: 54 and Morris 1997: 546.

[20] *Odyssey*, 6. 162–3 (Delos); 8.79–81 (Delphi); 19.296–8 (Dodona).

surprising, then, that scholars like J. P. Crielaard, Ian Morris, and Kurt Raaflaub have been tempted to identify the world of Odysseus with the world in which Homer lived, or at the very least, to suppose that the two were close.[21]

5. HOMER AND THE RE-CREATION OF THE PAST

All the theses outlined above—that Homer was recording the Mycenaean age, the 'Dark Ages', or the Geometric period—were rejected by Anthony Snodgrass (1974) who undertook a radical re-examination of the historical value of the Homeric poems by attempting to demonstrate that, contrary to the arguments of Moses Finley, Homeric society was not a consistent system. He pointed out the existence of two different types of marriage in Homer: marriage involving a bride price in which the future husband gave gifts to the bride's family and a system similar to that in operation in classical Greece, where the bride's family paid a dowry to the husband which was supposed to be equivalent to the cost of her maintenance. In reality, however, these two systems are incompatible and never coexist within the same society, as anthropological studies have shown. Snodgrass made further use of anthropology and of the material gathered together in the *Atlas of World Cultures* (Murdock 1981) to show that practices drawn from two contrasting types of social organization, characterized by different modes of transmitting wealth from one generation to the next (the equal distribution of the inheritance between male and female offspring or the transmission through the male line only), coexist within the society depicted by Homer. This is therefore just a patchwork of different elements borrowed from different societies at different periods.[22]

Snodgrass's argument was, in general, well received by archaeologists and historians. It was welcome to all those who held, like Franz Hampl (1961), that 'The *Iliad* is not a history book'[23] and who recognized, as did Ian Morris in an important article, that 'it has

[21] See Crielaard 1995b: 273–4; Morris 1986, and Raaflaub 1997.

[22] As early as 1950, H. L. Lorimer had argued in *Homer and the Monuments* that the material culture of the Homeric poems was, like their language, an artificial amalgam.

[23] This is the translation of the title of his 1961 article 'Die *Ilias* ist kein Geschichtsbuch'.

not proved possible to identify a single region and period with a material culture exactly like that in the epics' (Morris 1997: 558). Several writers in the intervening period have spoken of an 'amalgam of anachronistic details'[24] or 'a poetic conflation of a number of diverse, contemporary societies' (Whitley 1991: 344). The world of the Homeric poems is artificial and composite, like their language which is itself the result of a long and complex evolution (Cartledge 1996: 687–8).

This image of a multi-layered text, composed of strata that vary in date, can also be explained as the result of oral transmission. It has been noted that certain elements of an oral tradition are more open to alteration than others (Sherratt 1995: 153–5). Descriptions of lost objects, which are preserved in fixed formulae, can be transmitted without change over a fairly long period of time. The similes, however, which draw on the audience's own cultural context, are closely linked to the present moment. The arming scenes, which are almost entirely formulaic and keep to a strict pattern, are more likely to preserve traces of older elements than the battle scenes whose structure is more flexible and thus more open to the inclusion of later features.

It is even possible to demonstrate these effects of chronological layering in the presentation of a single object, like the block of iron that is one of the prizes offered to the competitors in the funerary games held to honour Patroclus.[25] It is clearly considered to be a precious object, which takes us back to the period between the seventeenth and the twelfth centuries BC when iron was counted as a precious metal, used for jewellery and ornaments, sometimes in conjunction with gold. But, in his speech praising the qualities of the metal, Achilles says, 'the man who wins this iron will have the use of it for five succeeding years, even if his rich fields lie far out on their own—no shepherd or ploughman of his will go into town for lack of iron, but this will supply all their needs' (*Iliad*, 23.832–5). The emphasis placed in this speech on the use of iron in daily life corresponds to a much later period (beginning around the year 1000 BC) at which iron objects were commonplace (Sherratt 1995: 148–50).

[24] Coldstream 1977: 17: '[Homer's] epics, set in the heroic past are coloured by an amalgam of anachronistic details, accumulated over centuries of oral transmission.'

[25] *Iliad*, 23.261, 826, 839, 844.

Similarly, Hans van Wees (1994 and 1997) has shown that the *Iliad* combines two different methods of fighting: a series of duels between individual warriors fighting in the front line (πρόμαχοι) and a pitched battle, using missiles, fought by two bodies of massed troops. This could be explained as the juxtaposition of two types of warfare belonging to different periods: 'old-style' warfare in which the members of the elite face each other, while the troops just hurl their weapons from further back, and a 'modern' form of hoplite warfare.

Consequently, some scholars have adopted a 'diachronic' view of the epic and see the Homeric amalgam as reflecting the evolution of a long epic tradition within which older strata have been successively overlaid by more recent material.[26] Others have preferred a more 'synchronic' approach.[27] While accepting the existence of anachronisms, archaisms, and even of elements that go back to the Mycenaean period or to the 'Dark Ages', they defend the historicity of Homer and explain the juxtaposition of old and new by making the epic a reflection of a changing society and by placing Homer in an age of transition, marked by rapid transformation. The significance of the regional differences revealed by archaeological discoveries has also been underlined as has the Panhellenic nature of the epics, which are thus seen as a poetic synthesis of features borrowed from a range of contemporary societies.[28]

Whatever the case, it is clear that the world of Odysseus is not a direct reflection of any actual society but is an artificial construct. This picture of a heroic age transports the listener into another time (hence the almost total absence of any features that were felt to be modern, like iron weapons, writing, or the cult of the heroes[29]) and offers an idealized image of a glorious past which was more attractive and more noble than present-day reality. For the epic magnifies everything. Its protagonists are heroes whose physical strength and accomplishments far surpass anything in the modern world: by himself Hector can lift up with ease a rock that 'two men, the best in a township, could not easily lever on to a wagon from the ground, of the men that

[26] See Crielaard 1995b; Sherratt 1995.

[27] See Raaflaub 1991, and 1997, and Donlan 1997.

[28] Whitley 1991: 344.

[29] As Coldstream (1976: 16) remarked, there is only one unambiguous reference to a hero cult in the *Iliad*. This is the passage in the Catalogue of Ships where the poet tells the story of Erechtheus and notes that 'the young men of Athens propitiate him with sacrifice of bulls and rams in each year's circle' *Iliad*, 2.550–1.

live now at any rate' (*Iliad*, 12.447–9). They live in palaces whose splendour far surpasses anything that actually existed. Thus Menelaus' palace in Sparta stuns Telemachus by its beauty, 'a radiance like that of sun or moon filled the high halls of King Menelaus' (*Odyssey*, 4.45–6), and its wealth, 'these echoing halls are bright with the glittering of bronze and gold and amber and silver and ivory' (*Odyssey*, 4.72–3). They have splendid funerals whose rituals are an inextricable combination of contemporary realities and archaizing allusions, like the hero cults that grew up around the Mycenaean tombs at about the same period or the funeral processions and battle scenes represented on the huge geometric vases found in the Dipylon Cemetery at Athens with their parade horses and figure-eight shaped shields, both Mycenaean features.[30]

This reconstruction of an imagined past, made possible by the collapse of the Mycenaean palace societies and the consequent rupture between the Bronze Age and Homer's own period, has a precise ideological function: in a period of crisis, it serves to glorify aristocratic values, thus validating the authority of the elite who are held to embody them.[31] This defence of the status of the aristocracy is plain in episodes like that of Thersites in Book 2 of the *Iliad*. It is taken for granted that this man of the people, in contrast to the heroes, is a repulsive character: 'He was the ugliest man that went to Ilios. He was bandy-legged and lame in one foot: his humped shoulders were bent inwards over his chest: above, his head rose to a point, sprouting thin wisps of wool' (*Iliad*, 2.216–19). And when Odysseus puts him in his place and beats him for voicing criticisms of Agamemnon (which are identical in places to those expressed by Achilles in Book 1), his actions are applauded by the whole army: 'each man glanced at his neighbour and said: "Oh yes. Odysseus has done thousands of fine things before now, proposing good plans and leading in battle. But this now is far the best thing he has done among the Argives, putting a stop to this horror's rantings in assembly"' (*Iliad*, 2.271–5).

In the same way, the speech addressed by Sarpedon to Glaucus in Book 12 of the *Iliad* also lends itself to being read as a justification of aristocratic privilege as it explains how the advantages enjoyed by the

[30] On the simultaneous appearance of heroic cult and Homeric epic see Antonaccio 1995. On the geometric vases see Snodgrass 1997.

[31] The same argument has been made of other epics like the *Ramayana* which has been seen as 'a means of validating the monarchy'. See Thapar 1989.

'kings' are accrued as the reward for valour rather than being acquired by theft:

Glaucus, why is it that we two are held in the highest honour in Lycia, with pride of place, the best of the meat, the wine-cup always full, and all look on us like gods, and we have for our own use a great cut of the finest land by the banks of the Xanthus, rich in vineyard and wheat-bearing ploughland? That is why we should now be taking our stand at the front of the Lycian lines and facing the sear of battle, so that among the heavy-armoured Lycians people will say: 'These are no worthless men who rule over us in Lycia, these kings we have who eat our fat sheep and drink the choice of our honey-sweet wine. No, they have strength too and courage, since they fight at the front of the Lycian lines'. (*Iliad*, 12.310–21)

The relationship between epic and history is therefore infinitely more complex than Schliemann could have imagined. It is certainly possible to identify elements of historical *realia* in Homer and to find reflections of archaeological discoveries.[32] But we cannot deduce what Homer's world was like from his depiction of the world of Odysseus, nor can we use the Homeric poems as documentary evidence.

It is also vital to bear in mind the distance, or rather the radical discontinuity, that the epics constantly establish between the mythical past and the present inhabited by the poet and his audience. There are certainly many references to 'people to come' and to the good or bad reputation that will be associated with an individual, but these are always put in the mouths of the heroes themselves and never in that of the narrator.[33] When the poet does raise the question of the presence in his own world of traces of the heroic past, as he does once with regard to the wall built by the Achaeans, it is only in order to deny that such traces exist: the wall 'was built without the immortal gods' sanction, and therefore it did not stand long' (*Iliad*, 12.8–9). After the capture of Troy and the departure of the Achaeans it was totally destroyed by Apollo and Poseidon in a concerted action. They 'turned the power of the rivers against it, all the rivers that flow out to the sea from the mountains of Ida', while 'Zeus rained without ceasing, to wash the wall the sooner into the sea' (ibid. 17–26). From that point on, all trace of the wall was 'hidden' by the sand

[32] See, for example, Crielaard 1995b.

[33] *Iliad*, 2.119, 3.287 and 460 (Agamemnon); *Iliad*, 6.358 (Helen); *Iliad*, 22.305 (Hector); *Odyssey*, 3.204 (Telemachus); *Odyssey*, 8.580 (Alcinous); *Odyssey*, 11.76 (Elpenor); *Odyssey*, 21.255 (Eurymachus); *Odyssey*, 24.433 (Eupeithes, father of Antinous).

covering the shore, in order that its 'fame' (*kleos*) should not outshine that of the wall built earlier by Apollo and Poseidon for Laomedon (*Iliad*, 7.446–63).

6. HOMER AND THE INVENTION OF HISTORY

We should perhaps try to approach the problem from a different angle and to ask whether the question of the historicity of Homer, which has preoccupied archaeologists and historians since the nineteenth century, might not be connected to the very form of the narrative. If Homer was considered to be a reliable historical source might it not be because he was, before Herodotus, the true father of history?[34] This was suggested by Pseudo-Longinus in his treatise *On the Sublime*, 13.3, where he established a direct relationship between Homer and Herodotus, calling the latter the 'most Homeric' of authors. Likewise, the author of the essay *On the Life and Poetry of Homer*, 74–90, tries to demonstrate that Homer was the inventor of 'historical discourse' (ἱστορικὸς λόγος).

It is certainly the case that epic and history share the same subject matter. Herodotus describes his task as ensuring that the 'great and astonishing achievements of Greeks and Barbarians' are not forgotten (1.1) and Thucydides chose to record the Peloponnesian War because he saw it as an exceptional event that brought about 'more sufferings than have ever before occurred in the same span of time' (1.23.1).

Homeric epic, whose subject is a war, also seeks to preserve those elements of the past that are far from ordinary: it celebrates 'the glorious deeds of men' (κλέα ἀνδρῶν) and immortalizes the exceptional virtue of Penelope while stigmatizing the extraordinary crime of Clytemnestra.[35]

Like Herodotus, the bard guarantees the truth of his account, indirectly at least, by the existence of an eyewitness. In Homer's case it is the Muses, whose spokesperson the bard is, who see everything because they

[34] The question was raised by Georg Friedrich Creuzer as early as 1803 (pp. 114–17 of the third edition, published in 1845, quoted by Fornara 1983: 31). Since then it has also been discussed by Gomme 1954 and, more briefly, by Fornara 1983: 30–2. See the excellent article on Homer and the writing of history by Strasburger (1982).

[35] *Iliad*, 9.189; *Odyssey*, 8.73 and 24.196–201.

are able to be present everywhere (*Iliad*, 2.485). The accuracy of the bard's story can also be confirmed by one of his characters as when, in Book 8 of the *Odyssey*, Odysseus congratulates Demodocus for his account of the quarrel between Odysseus and Achilles: 'How accurately [literally 'in the right order'] you sing of the fortunes of the Achaeans—all they achieved and suffered and toiled over—as though you yourself were there or had talked with one who was'.

> λίην γὰρ κατὰ κόσμον Ἀχαιῶν οἶτον ἀείδεις,
> ὅσσ᾽ ἔρξαν τ᾽ ἔπαθόν τε καὶ ὅσσ᾽ ἐμόγησαν Ἀχαιοί,
> ὥς τέ που ἢ αὐτὸς παρεὼν ἢ ἄλλου ἀκούσας. (8.489–91)

We also find in the epics the distinction, familiar to readers of the Greek historians, between certain knowledge—what one has witnessed oneself—and second-hand knowledge, acquired through hearsay alone.[36] When Telemachus visits Nestor to find out what has happened to his father in Book 3 of the *Odyssey*, he makes a distinction between what Nestor has seen with his own eyes and what he has heard from another traveller.[37] Nestor's tale does in fact fall into two distinct parts: after recounting the events that he was involved in himself, from the sufferings of the Greeks before Troy to his return home (3.103–85) he then goes on to tell 'all that he has learned without stirring from his palace' (ὅσσα δ᾽ ἐνὶ μεγάροισι καθήμενος ἡμετέροισι πεύθομαι, 3.186–7). Narrators in the *Odyssey* may also cite their sources with precision. Thus, Menelaus quotes Proteus who told him he 'saw' Odysseus in tears in Calypso's home.[38] Similarly, Odysseus himself, disguised as a beggar, informs Penelope, who had earlier asked him via Eumaeus 'if he has gathered tidings of enduring Odysseus or has set eyes on him' (17.510–11), that he has 'heard of (ἄκουσα) Odysseus as returning, not far away, in the wealthy country of the Thesprotians' (19.270–1). Elsewhere, the speaker explains the chain of communications from which he derived his knowledge of events that he could not have witnessed directly: if Odysseus is able during his account of his travels to tell his listeners what took place between the gods after the cattle of the Sun were killed it is because he 'heard this from Calypso of the lovely hair, who herself had heard it,

[36] See Ford 1992: 105–9.

[37] *Odyssey*, 3.93–5: εἴ που ὄπωπας | ὀφθαλμοῖσι τεοῖσιν ἢ ἄλλου μῦθον ἄκουσας | πλαζομένου.

[38] *Odyssey*, 4.556: τὸν ἴδον.

so she said, from Hermes, messenger of the gods'.[39] Like a historical narrative, Homer's story is a carefully ordered account that situates events in time and in space, as was noted in Antiquity by the author of the essay *On the Life and Poetry of Homer*.[40] Homer usually identifies a clear starting point for his narrative. The Muse of the *Iliad* begins 'from the time of (ἐξ οὗ δὴ τὰ πρῶτα) the first quarrel which divided Atreus' son, the lord of men, and godlike Achilles' (*Iliad*, 1.6–7) and the bard Demodocus, in Book 8 of the *Odyssey*, sings the story of the wooden horse 'taking it up (ἔνθεν ἑλὼν) where the Argives had set their huts aflame, had boarded their ships and were under sail already, while the few left behind with great Odysseus were crouched inside the sheltering horse in the Trojans' own assembly-place' (*Odyssey*, 8.500–3). When he is about to recount the exploits of Agamemnon in Book 11 of the *Iliad*, the poet asks the Muses to tell him 'who was the first of the Trojans themselves or their famous allies to come out against Agamemnon?'

> ἔσπετε νῦν μοι Μοῦσαι Ὀλύμπια δώματ' ἔχουσαι
> ὅς τις δὴ πρῶτος Ἀγαμέμνονος ἀντίον ἦλθεν
> ἢ αὐτῶν Τρώων ἠὲ κλειτῶν ἐπικούρων. (*Iliad*, 11.218–20)

This is just one of several cases where the poet begins his battle narratives with the word πρῶτος, 'the first'.[41] By this means he establishes a clear chronology for the action of the poem as a whole: from the quarrel between Achilles and Agamemnon to Hector's funeral, with which the *Iliad* concludes, is a span of exactly nineteen days which are very clearly marked in the story.

Other features that came to characterize ancient historiography can also be traced back to Homer. One is the insertion of speeches into the narrative. Another is the interest Homer shows in identifying the causes of events, as we see particularly at the beginning of the *Iliad*, which is also paralleled in Herodotus and Thucydides. This aspect of Homeric epic was noted by the author of *On the Life and Poetry of Homer* who says: 'There are passages such as that at the beginning of the *Iliad* in which he describes the causes (αἰτίας . . .

[39] *Odyssey*, 12.389–90: ταῦτα δ' ἐγὼν ἤκουσα Καλυψοῦς ἠυκόμοιο | ἡ δ' ἔφη Ἑρμείαο διακτόρου αὐτὴ ἀκοῦσαι.

[40] *Essay on the Life and poetry of Homer*, 76–7: 'He also has descriptions of place (τόπου διήγησις) . . . and of time (χρόνου δέ).'

[41] See, for example, *Iliad*, 4.457, 5.38, and 6.5.

ἐμφαίνει) why something happens or has happened' (78). Before telling the story of the wrath of Achilles and the sufferings it brought about for the Greeks, the poet does indeed go back in time first to explain 'which of the gods set these two to their fighting' (*τίς τ' ἄρ σφωε θεῶν ἔριδι ξυνέηκε μάχεσθαι; Iliad*, 1.8) then to set out the reasons why Apollo was angered and sent the plague, 'because the son of Atreus had dishonoured his priest, Chryses' (1.11).

Finally and above all, it is the desire to tell stories of the past and to make a strict separation between it and his own time by eliminating almost everything that appeared modern to him, as we have seen, that makes Homer a historian. With the figure of Nestor he creates a complex image of this past, inviting us to imagine, beyond the time of the Trojan War, an even earlier period inhabited by 'better men still', 'mighty men who fought against mighty enemies' (*Iliad*, 1.260–72). Such tales of a bygone age are by no means gratuitous. On the contrary, they can serve as paradigms, like the story of Meleager in Book 9, told by Phoenix to Achilles in order to persuade him to put aside his anger and reconcile himself with Agamemnon. For this story has a moral, as Phoenix emphasizes in his introduction: 'This is what we have learned from the glorious deeds of the heroes of old (*οὕτω καὶ τῶν πρόσθεν ἐπευθόμεθα κλέα ἀνδρῶν*): when a raging anger came upon one of them, they were still ready to be appeased by gifts and words' (*Iliad*, 9.524–6).

It is precisely because it is only interested in the past in relationship to the present that Homeric epic is inevitably anachronistic. But this is also the reason why it can be, like Thucydides' *History* (1.23), 'a permanent possession'.

4

The *Odyssey*: Narrations, Narrators, and Poets

1. THE UNITY OF THE *ODYSSEY*

The *Iliad* told the story of the 'wrath of Achilles, son of Peleus, accursed wrath which brought countless sufferings to the Achaeans', beginning 'from the time of the first quarrel which divided Atreus' son, the lord of men, and godlike Achilles' (*Iliad*, 1.6–7), and its main action (Books 2 to 22) takes place over a period of four days. The *Odyssey*, by contrast, is presented as the portrait of man through the story of his wanderings, as the prologue makes clear:

> Tell me (ἔννεπε), Muse, of the man of many turns who wandered long and far after he sacked the sacred town of Troy. Many were those whose cities he viewed and whose minds he came to know, many the troubles that he suffered in his heart as he sailed the seas, labouring to save himself and to bring his comrades home. But his comrades he could not keep from ruin, strive as he might. (*Odyssey*, 1.1–6)

This prologue is as traditional as it is enigmatic. Traditional in that it contains, like other epics beginning with the *Iliad*, an invocation to the Muse who is invited to elaborate on a theme,[1] given in the accusative case. Enigmatic in that the hero in question is not named but is introduced by a periphrasis, 'the man of many turns', whose meaning is perfectly clear given that Odysseus is the only mortal in

[1] Homer, *Iliad*, 1.1: ἄειδε ('sing'); Hesiod, *Theogony*, 105: κλείετε ('celebrate in song'); Hesiod, *Works and Days*, 2: ἐννέπετε ('tell'); *Homeric Hymn to Aphrodite*, 1 and *Homeric Hymn to Pan*, 1: ἔννεπε ('tell').

archaic epic to be described as *polutropos* (the only other character to be given this epithet being the god Hermes).[2]

The prologue also contains an implicit contrast between the heroes of the *Odyssey* and of the *Iliad*: in Achilles we have a hero whose anger brings 'countless sufferings' upon the Achaeans (μυρί' Ἀχαιοῖς ἄλγε' ἔθηκε), in contrast to the hero of the *Odyssey* who 'suffered many troubles as he sailed the sea' (πολλὰ δ' ὅ γ' ἐν πόντῳ πάθεν ἄλγεα) trying to save others and bring his companions home (Pucci 1998: 14–19). A further difference from the *Iliad*, which has a very precise starting point, as we saw in the last chapter, is that the *Odyssey* appears to start from an arbitrary moment: the poet asks the Muse to tell him this story 'beginning where you will' (τῶν ἁμόθεν γε, line 10).

In fact, the *Odyssey* only relates the very end of Odysseus' journeys, a fact that earned it the admiration of Pseudo-Plutarch: *On the Life and Poetry of Homer*, 162: 'He started the *Odyssey* with the very last part of the wanderings of Odysseus, at the point at which it was possible to bring in Telemachus and to reveal the arrogance of the suitors. That which had gone before and all that had happened to Odysseus in his wanderings, he has Odysseus himself tell, and even these things seem more ingenuous and more credible narrated by the man who actually experienced them.'[3]

The poem commences 'when there came with revolving seasons the year that the gods had set for his journey home to Ithaca' (1.16–18) and takes up the hero's story when he is at the furthest point from home, detained by Calypso on the island of Ogygia at the edges of the world where 'there is not one town of mortals nearby to offer sacrifices and choice hecatombs to the gods' (5.101–2). His return voyage is announced in detail by Zeus at the beginning of Book 5: 'It will be on a raft firmly put together; on this, in spite of many troubles, he may come in twenty days' time to fertile Scheria; that is the land of the Phaeacians, a people whose lineage is divine; with all their hearts they will honour him like a god and will send him back by ship to his own dear land' (lines 33–7). The account of this return only takes up Books 5 to 13. It is preceded by the story of the adventures of Telemachus, which are set in motion by Athena and announced by her during the first assembly of the gods: 'As for myself, I will go to

[2] *Odyssey*, 1.1 and 10.330; *Homeric Hymn to Hermes*, 13.439. The Greek *polutropos* can mean both 'well travelled' and 'versatile', 'wily'.

[3] Translation by Lamberton and Keaney.

Ithaca to rouse his son and to put fresh eagerness in his heart to call together the flowing haired Achaeans and speak his mind to all those suitors who daily slaughter his thronging sheep and the swaying cattle with curving horns. Then I will send him to Sparta and sandy Pylos, to gather by hearsay what news he can of his father's homecoming and to win himself a good name in the world' (1.88–95).

This twofold start to the action is reflected in the two assemblies of the gods in Books 1 and 5, each followed by the departure of a divinity (Athena and Hermes respectively) who, with Zeus' consent, sets off to Ithaca or to Ogygia. The repetition puzzled several critics and prompted some of them to suspect the intervention of an editor (*Bearbeiter*). There are, however, two parallels in the *Iliad*. In Book 15, Zeus, using Hera as his intermediary, sends Iris to the Achaean camp to order Poseidon to withdraw from the battle and then sends Apollo to the Trojan camp to rouse Hector. Later, in Book 24, he sends Iris to summon Thetis so he can send her to Achilles (24.73–119) before dispatching Iris to Priam inside Troy to tell him to go and ransom his son's body (24.143–58).

But before following the travels of Telemachus, which take up Books 3 and 4 of the *Odyssey*, the narrative focuses in Books 1 and 2 on the situation on Ithaca. This way of organizing the narrative is also somewhat surprising. It is, however, essential, because it shows that there is nothing arbitrary about the timing of Odysseus' return. On the contrary, his return occurs at a decisive moment in the chain of events that has been unfolding since his departure. First, he returns just as Telemachus achieves adulthood, the moment at which Odysseus himself had authorized his wife to remarry, as Penelope reminds the suitors in Book 18: 'When you see this son of ours grown to bearded manhood, then leave your own palace and marry whom you will' (18.269–70). It is also the moment at which Penelope's stratagem to avoid remarriage is no longer effective: for three years she has managed to trick the suitors by promising to remarry as soon as she has finished weaving a shroud for Laertes, but 'when seasons passed and the fourth year came' (2.107) one of her maidservants found her undoing by night what she had woven during the day. At the point where the *Odyssey* begins she is therefore trapped, as she tells Odysseus in his beggar's disguise: 'Now I cannot escape a marriage; I can think of no other subterfuge. My parents press me to marry again, and my son chafes at this wasting of our wealth. He observes such things now; he is a man, he is of an age to take due care of a great house that Zeus makes glorious' (19.157–61).

For all these reasons, Odysseus is more than ever at the centre of all the characters' thoughts in the first two books of the *Odyssey*. When Telemachus makes his first appearance at the beginning of Book 1, he is seated among the suitors 'thinking of his noble father, wondering whether he might return from wherever he might be to scatter the suitors in the halls, to retrieve his honours and be lord of his own estate' (1.115–17). Penelope, likewise, speaks of her longing for her husband in the very first words she utters in the poem: 'so peerless a man is he I mourn for, he I remember always, a man whose fame has gone through the length and breadth of Hellas and of Argos' (1.343–4). Even the suitors are preoccupied by thoughts of Odysseus: when they see a stranger appear, they immediately ask Telemachus: 'Did he come to bring news of your father's return?' (1.408). And when Telemachus sets off on his voyages to Pylos and Sparta it is in order to ask the survivors of the Trojan War for news of his father.

At the end of Book 4, the story of Telemachus pauses temporarily (it will not be continued until Book 15) and the focus shifts to the story of Odysseus himself. This transition is handled with remarkable skill: a brief return to Ithaca at the end of Book 4 creates a link between the 'Adventures of Telemachus' and the *Odyssey* proper. The movement from one to the other is brought about in a few key lines which form the turning point, tying Menelaus' feast to the one taking place in Odysseus' palace on Ithaca:

> Such were their words to each other. And while they spoke, the diners came up to the godlike king's palace, driving sheep with them and bringing wine that cheers men's hearts: and at the same time their bread was sent up to the house by their mantled wives. So they prepared for the meal in the palace. Meanwhile in front of Odysseus' house the suitors were amusing themselves with games of discus and spear-throwing. (4.620–6)[4]

It is clear that the opening words of this passage (line 620), which follow on from a dialogue between Telemachus and Menelaus, can only refer to events at Sparta while line 625 with its reference to 'Odysseus' house' places the action unambiguously on Ithaca.

[4] The translation cited here is that of Hammond. Shewring follows those editors of the text who omit lines 621–4 (from 'the diners' to 'the palace') on the grounds that they are inappropriate to the context.

In Book 5, the action therefore starts afresh with a second assembly of the gods, which ends with Hermes being sent to Calypso's home on Ogygia to give her the order to allow Odysseus to return home. From Book 5 to Book 13, the story follows Odysseus closely, right up to the moment when the Phaeacians put him ashore on Ithaca (13.123). This end to his journeys is marked out by a sophisticated compositional effect involving a play of echoes between Books 5 and 13. For, with the departure of the ship that has transported the hero to Ithaca, the poet also brings his audience back to Phaeacia (13.125), that is, to the point where they had been brought at the end of Book 5. But, before the ship is in sight of the Phaeacian coast, the story changes setting again to Olympus and to the discussion between Zeus and Poseidon that forms a pendant to the divine assembly of Book 5. Moreover, as the hero is carried homewards on the Phaeacian ship we are told that 'the ship was carrying with her a man who was godlike in his counsels, who had suffered many troubles in his heart (*ὃς πρὶν μὲν μάλα πολλὰ πάθ' ἄλγεα ὃν κατὰ θυμὸν*), both in battle and on the sea' (13.89–90). The formula used here refers back to the presentation of Odysseus in the opening lines of the poem as the hero 'who suffered many troubles in his heart (*πολλὰ δ' ὅ γ' ἐν πόντῳ πάθεν ἄλγεα ὃν κατὰ θυμόν*) as he sailed the seas' (1.1). This play of echoes and allusions connecting the beginning of the poem with the moment at which Odysseus is about to reach his home serves as a type of ring composition that has the effect of framing the travel narratives within the poem as a whole.

Book 13, which focuses on Odysseus and takes place entirely on Ithaca, also marks the start of a complex interweaving of Odysseus' adventures with those of Telemachus. Its final two lines, describing Athena's departure for Sparta from where she will bring Telemachus home, are the beginning of a continual oscillation between Ithaca and Sparta: Book 14 returns to Ithaca and to Odysseus but Book 15 begins by shifting the action from Ithaca to Sparta by following Athena's movements (lines 1–3), before going on to describe (lines 4–181) Telemachus' last moments in Menelaus' house and then following his return journey back to Ithaca which takes him once more to Pherae and Pylos (lines 182–300). The story returns again to Odysseus in lines 301–494 before once again following the movements of Telemachus and his men (lines 495–557) up until the moment when the two narrative threads merge into one with the reunion of father and son in the hut belonging to the swineherd Eumaeus at the opening of Book 16.

From Book 16 onwards, the action takes place on Ithaca and can be identified with the new trials mentioned in the first lines of the epic (1.18–19) that Odysseus finds even in his own home, for he still has to wreak vengeance on the suitors. His revenge is not unexpected. It is announced by Zeus at the beginning of Book 5 (line 24) and later predicted by the seer Tiresias in Book 11 (lines 115–20). But Tiresias leaves open the question of exactly how the killing will be carried out by Odysseus, saying only that it will be 'by guile, or openly with the keen bronze' (l.120). The uncertainty remains until Book 13 where Athena and Odysseus together work out the plan which will allow Odysseus to go back to his palace incognito, disguised as a beggar, and to vanquish the suitors. This plan, revealed to Telemachus in Book 16, is put into action from Book 17 onwards and is fulfilled in Book 22 with the massacre of the suitors. Finally, the poem ends with Odysseus' reunions with his family, his wife Penelope in Book 23 and his father Laertes in Book 24, and with the final reconciliation with the suitors' families. This pattern is, in fact, the same as that of the *Iliad* where the death of Hector in Book 22 is followed by the scene of reconciliation between his killer, Achilles, and his father, Priam, in Book 24.

Despite its complexity, noted by Aristotle in his *Poetics*,[5] the structure of the poem is perfectly clear. Aristotle sums it up as follows:

> A man is away from home for many years and jealously watched by Poseidon and has lost his followers; moreover at home his affairs are such that his property is being wasted by suitors and plots laid against his son; he comes home in dire distress and after disclosing himself makes an attack and destroys his enemies without being killed himself. This is what is proper to the action; the rest of the poem is episodes.[6]

2. THE TREATMENT OF SPACE AND TIME

In order to understand the structure of the *Odyssey* it is necessary to go beyond the four main sections identified above and to examine in detail the twists and turns of the action and the changes in time and place.

[5] Aristotle, *Poetics*, 24, 1459b15 where the *Odyssey* is described as πεπλεγμένη ('twisted' like a rope).

[6] Aristotle, *Poetics*, 17, 1455b17–23 translated by M. E. Hubbard in *Classical Literary Criticism* (Oxford, 1989).

(a) The plan of the *Odyssey*

1.1–10 The prologue

1.11–21: The action begins as the gods decide that Odysseus, who is on Calypso's island, must return home.

The first day

1.22–101: On **Olympus**: the first assembly of the gods sets in motion two separate chains of events:

1. 84–7: 'Let us instruct the radiant Hermes, the Messenger, to go to the island of Ogygia and without delay to tell the nymph of braided tresses our firm decree that staunch Odysseus is to depart and journey home.'
2. 88–95: Meanwhile Athena will take care of Telemachus.
3. 96–101: Athena's preparations.

1.102: Athena travels from Olympus to **Ithaca**.
1.103–444: Athena finds Telemachus in the palace; the account of their meeting.

The next day

2.1–12: **From the palace to the assembly** with Telemachus.
2.13–259: **The assembly**. The suitors return to the palace.
2.260–97: Telemachus goes to the **beach**.
2.298–381: Telemachus returns to the **palace**: he prepares to leave.
2.382–92: Athena goes to the **harbour**.
2.393–419: Athena returns to the **palace** and accompanies Telemachus to the ship.
2.420–34: Telemachus sails from Ithaca to **Pylos** by night.

The next day

3.1–403: Telemachus at **Pylos**.

The next day

3.404–80: Telemachus at **Pylos**.

3.481–89: Telemachus leaves **Pylos** and travels to **Pherae**.
3.490: They spend the night at **Pherae**.

The next day

3.491–7: The journey **from Pherae to Sparta**.
4.1–305: Telemachus in **Sparta**.

The next day

4.306–619: Telemachus in **Sparta**.
4.620–4: Transition between **Sparta** and **Ithaca**.
4.625–847: On **Ithaca** with the suitors and Penelope.

The next day

5.1–42: The second assembly of the gods on **Olympus**.
5.43–54: Hermes prepares and leaves **Olympus** to go to **Ogygia**.
5.55–227: On **Ogygia** with Calypso and Hermes who departs at 148, and Calypso and Odysseus.

A period of four days

5.228–62: On **Ogygia**: Odysseus prepares to depart.

The fifth day

5.263–9: Odysseus leaves **Ogygia**.

After seventeen days at sea, on the eighteenth day

5.270–81: Odysseus arrives **near the coast of Scheria**.

Two days and two nights

5.282–389: The storm **off the coast of Scheria**.

The third day after the beginning of the storm

5.390–6.47: **On Scheria** first with Odysseus (5.390–493) then with Nausicaa (6.1–47), Athena's movements form the transition between the two.

The next day

6.48–7.347: **On Scheria.**

The next day

8.1–13.17: Odysseus in **Alcinous' palace** (Odysseus tells the story of his adventures).

The next day

13.18–69: The preparations for Odysseus' departure.

Indeterminate period of time

13.70–92: The voyage from Scheria to **Ithaca**.

The next day Odysseus lands on Ithaca

13.93–125: At **Phorkys**, the harbour on Ithaca.
13.125–58: On **Olympus** with Poseidon and Zeus.
13.159–60: Poseidon travels **from Olympus to Scheria**.
13.161–87: On **Scheria** with Poseidon and the Phaeacians.
13.187–439: On **Ithaca** with Odysseus, then Athena who transforms Odysseus into a beggar.
13.439–40: **From Ithaca to Sparta** with Athena.
14.1–533: On **Ithaca**: Odysseus in Eumaeus' hut.
15.1–3: Athena travels to **Sparta** (the continuation of 13.439–40).
15.4–42: Athena and Telemachus in **Sparta** (night scene).
15.43: Athena returns to **Olympus**.
15.44–55: In **Sparta** with Telemachus and Nestor's son (night scene).

The next day

15.56–181: At **Sparta**.
15.182–8: The voyage **from Sparta to Pherae** (see 3.486–90).

The next day the second day after Odysseus' arrival on Ithaca

15.189–92: The voyage **from Pherae to Pylos** (see 3.491–4).
15.193–281: At **Pylos.**
15.282–300: Telemachus sails home (15.287–91 echoes 2.422–6).
15.301–494: On **Ithaca** with Eumaeus and Odysseus as they eat their supper (they were last heard of asleep at the end of Book 14).

The next day the third day after Odysseus' arrival on Ithaca

15.495–549: **On Ithaca, on the shore** with Telemachus, Theoclymenus, and their companions.
15.550–7: Telemachus' companions and Theoclymenus sail to the town, Telemachus goes to the swineherd Eumaeus.
16.1–320: In **Eumaeus' house** with Telemachus, Odysseus, and Eumaeus. Eumaeus is sent to the palace (130–55). Odysseus, left alone with his son, is prompted by Athena to reveal his identity (155–219: *Recognition I*).
16.321–32: Telemachus' companions arrive **in town** and send a herald **to the palace.**
16.333–41: Eumaeus arrives **at the palace** at the same time as the herald and announces to Penelope that her son has returned.
16.342–408: With the suitors in the palace (342–57), then on the shore (357–360), then **at the agora** (361–406), finally **in the palace** (407–8).
16.409–51: **In the palace**: Penelope and the suitors.
16.452–81: **Eumaeus** returns home and rejoins Telemachus and Odysseus.

The next day the fourth day after Odysseus' arrival on Ithaca

17.1–25: **At Eumaeus' house.**
17.26–7: Telemachus goes **to the palace.**
17.28–60: Telemachus **in the palace** with Penelope.

17.61–83: Telemachus leaves the palace for the **town** where he meets his guest Theoclymenus.
17.84–165: Telemachus and Theoclymenus return **to the palace** where they find Penelope.
17.166–82: **In the palace** with the suitors.
17.182–253: Odysseus and Eumaeus set off **to the palace** and meet the goatherd Melanthius on the way (204–53).
17.254–60: Melanthius arrives **at the palace**.
17.260–327: Eumaeus and Odysseus arrive **at the palace**. Odysseus is recognized by his dog Argos (291–327: *Recognition II*).
17.328–491: **In the great hall of the palace** with Eumaeus, Odysseus, Telemachus and the suitors.
17.492–550: **In Penelope's room** first with Eurynome (492–506) then with Eumaeus, whom she summons (507–50).
17.551–89: **From Penelope's room to the great hall and back** with Eumaeus who serves as a messenger between Odysseus and Penelope.
17.590–606: In the great hall which Eumaeus leaves at line 605.
18.1–157: **In the great hall of the palace** with Irus, Odysseus, Telemachus, and the suitors.
18.158–205: **In Penelope's room**.
18.206–303: Penelope **in the great hall**.

304–426: In the great hall with Odysseus, Telemachus, the maid-servants, and the suitors.
427–428: The suitors leave the palace.
19.1–30: Odysseus, Telemachus, and Eurycleia in the great hall.

19.31–46: Odysseus and Telemachus take the weapons to the storeroom.
19.47–20.57: **In the great hall**.

19.47–52: Telemachus leaves the great hall while Odysseus stays there alone
19.53–4: Penelope arrives.
Odysseus is recognized by Eurycleia (19.386–507: *Recognition III*).
19.600–4: Penelope returns to her room.
20.1–30: Odysseus in the great hall.
20.30–53: Odysseus is joined by Athena.
20.54–7: Athena sends Odysseus to sleep and returns to Olympus.

20.57–90: **In Penelope's room**.

The next day the fifth since Odysseus' arrival on Ithaca

20.91–394: **In the great hall: the suitors' last banquet.**

- 20.91–123: Odysseus and the maidservants.
- 20.124–43: Telemachus arrives. Dialogue between Telemachus and Eurycleia.
- 20.144–6: Telemachus leaves the palace.
- 20.147–240: Preparations for the banquet.
  - 20.147–59: Eurycleia and the maidservants.
  - 20.160–1: Arrival of other servants.
  - 20.161–2: The women arrive.
  - 20.162–72: Arrival of Eumaeus.
  - 20.173–84: Arrival of Melanthios.
  - 20.185–240: Arrival of Philoetius the herdsman.
  - 20.241–7: The suitors prepare the death of Telemachus.
  - 20.248–56: The suitors feast in the palace.
  - 20.257–394: Telemachus, Odysseus, Theoclymenus who leaves at 371–2 and the suitors, while Penelope listens to them from her room at 387–9.

21.1–56: Penelope goes down to the storeroom to get Odysseus' bow.

21.57–22.456: **In the great hall**: the contest of the bow and the massacre of the suitors.

- 21.57–66: Penelope arrives in the great hall with the bow.
- 21.67–188: Preparations for the contest.
- 21.188–241: Eumaeus and Philoetius leave the great hall followed by Odysseus who reveals his identity (*Recognition IV*).
- 21.242–4: Odysseus, followed by Eumaeus and Philoetius, returns to the great hall.
- 21.245–55: The bow contest and the failure of the suitors.
- 21.256–73: Antinous proposes to postpone the contest, this proposal is agreed.
- 21.274–310: Odysseus asks to try the bow. He is rebuked by Antinous.
- 21.311–42: Penelope's intervention.
- 21.343–58: Penelope is sent back to her room by Telemachus.
- 21.359–79: Eumaeus gives the bow to Odysseus.
- 21.380–393: Eurycleia and Philoetius are sent to bar the doors.
- 21.393–434: Odysseus takes the bow and hits the mark.

22.1–33: Odysseus kills Antinous and is threatened by the suitors.
22.34–41: Odysseus reveals himself to the suitors (*Recognition* V).
22.42–67: Eurymachos proposes a reparation and is turned down by Odysseus.
22.68–118: The fight: the suitors are killed by Odysseus' arrows, while Telemachus goes to the storeroom to get weapons.
22.119–69: Odysseus and his allies fight with spears, while Melanthios goes to the storeroom to get weapons for the suitors.
22.170–99: Odysseus and his son hold off the suitors while Eumaeus and Philoetius seize Melanthios.
22.200–389: The end of the killing.
22.390–456: The great hall is cleaned by the disloyal maidservants.

22.457–79: **In the courtyard**: Punishment of the disloyal maidservants and Melanthius.
22.480–501: **In the great hall**.

22.480–94: Odysseus and Eurycleia purify the palace.
22.495–501: Eurycleia goes to find the loyal maidservants (*Recognition VI*).

23.1–84: **In Penelope's room** where Eurycleia has gone.
23.85–288: **In the great hall** (*Recognition VII: Penelope recognizes Odysseus*).
23.289–96: **In Penelope's room**: the couple are reunited.
23.297–9: **In the great hall** with Telemachus, Eumaeus, and the maidservants.
23.300–43: **In Penelope's room**: the night comes to an end (*Penelope and Odysseus tell their stories*).

The next day the sixth since Odysseus' arrival on Ithaca

23.344–8: The arrival of the dawn, which has been delayed by Athena.
23.348–65: **In Penelope's room**.
23.366–72: Odysseus, accompanied by Telemachus, the cowherd, and the goatherd, **leaves the palace**.
24.1–14: **From Ithaca to the Underworld** with the ghosts of the suitors.

24.15–204: **In the Underworld** with the suitors.
24.205–411: **In Laertes'** house with Odysseus and his companions.

205–20: Odysseus sends the others inside the house.
220–360: Odysseus goes to the orchard where he finds Laertes and reveals his identity (*Recognition VIII*).
361–411: In Laertes' house where Odysseus reveals his identity to Dolius and his sons (*Recognition IX*). Odysseus and the others share a meal.

24.412–19: The people of Ithaca hear of the suitors' deaths and their relatives go to retrieve their bodies.
24.420–63: The suitors' relatives go **to the assembly**.
24.463–71: More than half of the relatives set out to avenge their dead.
24.472–88: **On Olympus** with Zeus and Athena who descends to earth in line 488.
24.489–548: Return **to the countryside** and to the meal shared by Odysseus and the others: from the battle to the final reconciliation.

(b) The presentation of space

It is immediately clear from this breakdown that the spatial organization of the action of the *Odyssey* is extremely complex. But such a schematic presentation cannot do justice to the variety of the techniques used to create transitions. One way of moving from one place or character to another is simply to juxtapose the two, by presenting the actions as occurring simultaneously. Thus, at 4.842 we move from the bedchamber, where Penelope wakes up, reassured by the dream she has just had, to the suitors as they set out to prepare their ambush with a simple conjunction *δέ*, expressing the contrast between the two actions.[7] Similarly, the transition from Phaeacia to Ithaca at 13.185–7 is made simply by presenting the actions taking place simultaneously in each place: 'Thus then the chiefs and leaders of the Phaeacians (*οἵ μέν ῥ . . . δήμου Φαιήκων ἡγήτορες ἠδέ μέδοντες*) stood round the altars and made their prayers to Lord Poseidon. Meanwhile Odysseus woke from his sleep (*ὁ δ' ἔγρετο*) in the land of his fathers.'[8]

[7] See also, for example, *Odyssey*, 17.180–2: *οἱ δ'* (the suitors) . . . *τοὶ δέ* (Odysseus and the swineherd).

[8] See also, for example, *Odyssey*, 16.321–2, 17.166–7.

But there are more subtle ways of passing from one setting to another: at 17.261–2 the sound of Phemius' lyre is heard by Odysseus and Eumaeus from outside the palace, allowing a smooth transition to be made from one place to the other.[9]

Homer also makes use of the movement of a character between two places. In Book 1, Athena moves the action from heaven to earth by travelling from Olympus to Ithaca (lines 96–105); in Book 5.43–54 the journey of Hermes likewise forms a transition from Olympus to Calypso's island of Ogygia, while in Book 13.159–60 it is Poseidon who creates the change of place when he descends from Olympus to Scheria. In Book 16.328–32, the story moves from the harbour on Ithaca to Odysseus' palace along with the herald sent by Telemachus' companions to Penelope to reassure her that her son is safe. In Book 17 it is Eumaeus who serves as the intermediary between Odysseus and Penelope, providing the link between the great hall and the queen's chamber on several occasions.[10]

Another technique is to follow the respective movements of two characters who have just parted company. At the end of Book 13, Athena and Odysseus go their separate ways: the poem follows Athena first as she 'went off to sacred Lacedaemon to fetch Odysseus' son' (lines 439–40) before switching focus at the beginning of Book 14 to follow Odysseus as he follows Athena's instructions and 'leaves the harbour and takes to a rough woodland track, crossing the hilltops to where the good swineherd is' (lines 1–3).

The poet may also make use of a shared element to introduce one episode within another. The transition from Sparta to Ithaca in Book 4.620–6, mentioned above, is an excellent example of this. The transition between Books 5 and 6 also merits further attention: Book 5 ends with the tableau of Athena who has come to 'pour sleep upon Odysseus' eyes' while the next book opens with the goddess's further actions: 'So the much-enduring hero lay, overcome with toil and sleep. But Athena went to the land and the city of the Phaeacians' (6.1–4). The same action may even be carried over from one episode to another as the narrative shifts from one character falling asleep to another waking. This occurs in Book 20 where we move from

[9] A similar technique is used at 17.492–3 where Penelope in her room 'hears' (ἤκουσε) that the beggar has been struck in the great hall, and at 20.92 where Odysseus 'hears the voice (ὄπα σύνθετο) of his wife crying'.

[10] *Odyssey*, 17.507–41, 551–2, 574–5, 589–90.

Odysseus, sent to sleep by Athena before she returns to Olympus, to Penelope as she awakes: 'while sleep thus laid its hold on him, easing his limbs and easing his disquiet, his loyal wife on her soft couch returned to wakefulness and to tears' (lines 56–8).

(c) The presentation of time

The presentation of time is also extremely complex.[11] The action of the *Odyssey* takes up around forty-one days (Rengakos 2002: 176), if one leaves out the flashbacks and does not take account of the length of the sea voyage from Scheria to Ithaca which is not indicated by the poet. The chronology is entirely relative and is usually indicated in terms of the passing of days and nights (there are very few references to longer periods of time, such as seasons). In some cases, books begin with the start of the new day, as in Books 2, 3, 5, 8, and 17, but this is far from being the rule. Usually, the nights constitute a hiatus during which nothing happens (the night-time crossing of the Phaeacian ship that carries Odysseus back to his homeland (13.78–95) is an exception, appropriately enough given the magical nature of the journey).

The rhythm of the narrative is extremely variable: the seventeen days during which Odysseus sails uneventfully before being caught by the storm off the coast of Scheria are evoked in ten or so lines (5.270–81). By contrast, the penultimate day of the *Odyssey*, which ends with the massacre of the suitors, alone takes up more than three books (20.91–23.343), while the day during which Odysseus tells his story in Alcinous' palace fills over four books (8.1–13.17).

Overall, however, it is important to underline the remarkable extent to which the action is concentrated, in contrast to the poems of the Epic Cycle. As in the *Iliad*, the temporal frame of the work is considerably broadened by the use of a series of flashbacks and anticipations. The *Odyssey* contains a series of allusions to the story of Odysseus before his departure for Troy. These allusions, which are scattered throughout the poem, are introduced in an astonishing variety of ways. On occasion the principal narrator himself introduces them as a form of digression from the main narrative to which they are attached by the use of relative pronoun (19.393 and 21.13). Thus we move from Odysseus' scar, a

[11] See Delebecque 1958: 11–18; Hellwig 1964; Olson 1995; 91–119: ch. 5 'On Time and the Poet: The Chronology of the Odyssey'; Rengakos 1995, 1998, 2002.

passage made famous by the analysis in Auerbach's *Mimesis* (1968: ch. 1), to the circumstances in which he suffered the injury (19.393–466). In similar fashion, we move from the description of Odysseus' bow to its history, with the account of how it was given to him by Iphitus long before (21.13–41). More usually, however, the poet leaves these evocations of the past to his characters. Thus Athena, disguised as Mentes who claims to have often encountered Odysseus before he left to fight at Troy, tells a story of how Odysseus managed to find on Taphos the deadly poison that he had failed to find at Ephyra (1.255–64). Menelaus recounts Odysseus' victory in a wrestling bout on the island of Lesbos.[12] Penelope reminds Antinous of his father's debt to Odysseus, who once saved his life (16.424–30), and repeats in front of Eurymachus the instructions given to her by Odysseus when he set out for Troy (18.257–71). And finally, Odysseus, on meeting Nausicaa (6.162–7), recalls the palm tree he once saw on Delos and, later, tells how he made his bed out of an olive tree growing in the courtyard of his house (23.183–204).

The poet and his characters are also haunted by memories of the Trojan War. But, if we leave aside the general references to the sufferings of the Greeks in the plain before Troy made by Nestor and by Athena in the guise of Mentor (3.103–119; 22.226–30) and concentrate our attention on the precise events mentioned, some interesting choices emerge. The stories told in the *Odyssey* by the main narrator (4.187–8), by the bard Demodocus (8.73–82 and 499–520), or by participants in the war, whether survivors like Odysseus, Nestor, Helen, and Menelaus, or the deceased, like Agamemnon in the second *nekuia*,[13] mostly refer to episodes that are absent from the *Iliad* and tend to belong to the last phase of the war, with the possible exception of Odysseus' secret mission inside Troy, disguised as a beggar, which is not precisely located. Examples are the death of Antilochus, the quarrel between Odysseus and Achilles which signalled victory for the Achaeans, the death and funeral of Achilles, the quarrel over his arms and the suicide of Ajax, the episode of the Trojan Horse, and the exploits of Neoptolemus.[14]

[12] *Odyssey*. 4.342–4 =17.133–5 (in Telemachus' account to his mother of his visit to Menelaus).

[13] Odysseus: 5.308–11, 11.506–37, and 543–61; Nestor: 3.109–12; Helen: 4.242–64; Menelaus: 4.269–89; Agamemnon: 24.36–94.

[14] Antilochus: 3.111–12 and 4.187–8; the quarrel between Odysseus and Achilles: 8.73–82; Achilles: 3.109 and 24.36–94; the quarrel over the arms of Achilles and the

Two of these episodes deserve particular attention. The first is the episode recounted by Helen in Book 4. It is impossible to read of the manner in which Odysseus enters Troy 'having disfigured himself with ignominious stripes and thrown dismal rags over his shoulders' (lines 244–5) without thinking of the way in which he will later enter his own palace, disguised as a beggar, as was noted by the ancient commentators.[15] The second is the episode of the Trojan Horse told by Menelaus (4.269–89). Here, Odysseus was the only one of the Achaeans able to resist the lure of Helen's voice as she imitated the voices of their wives, in an attempt to make them betray their presence inside the horse. This ability prefigures the Odysseus of the adventures who does not succumb to the charm of the Sirens' song. When he puts his hand over Anticlus' mouth, to stop him from replying to Helen, he also foreshadows the Odysseus of Book 19 who will grip Eurycleia by the throat to prevent her from revealing his identity to Penelope (4.286–8 and 19.479–81).

To these reminders of the past we should also add the frequent allusions to the 'returns' of the Achaean leaders and the stories told by those leaders themselves who include, in addition to Odysseus himself, Nestor, Menelaus, and even Agamemnon in the Underworld. These stories will be examined in more detail below.

In the *Odyssey* the present is also linked to the future by means of a series of anticipations or flashforwards.[16] In what follows I will apply the distinctions used in narratology between 'internal' or 'intradiegetic prolepses' and 'external', or 'extradiegetic prolepses': the former serve to introduce events that fall within the temporal framework of the poem, while the latter allude to events that fall outside that frame. For the sake of completeness, we should also take into consideration the figure that the scholiasts call 'announcement by anticipation',

suicide of Ajax: 11.543–51; Odysseus at Troy: 4.242–64; the Trojan Horse: 4.269–88, 8.492–520, and 11.523–32; Neoptolemus: 11.506–37.

[15] See *Scholia vetera* Q to *Odyssey*, 4.245: *διὰ πολλὰ τῆς πράξεως ταύτης μνημονεύει ὁ ποιητὴς, οὐ μόνον ὅτι πρὸς τὴν ποίησιν συμφέρει τὰ μὴ δεδομένα τῆς Ἰλιάδος νῦν ἐμφανίζειν, ἀλλὰ καὶ πρὸς τὴν μνηστηροκτονίαν ταῦτα ᾠκονόμηται, ἵνα μηδὲ τοῖς μνηστῆρσι συνὼν ἐν τοιούτῳ σχήματι ἀπίθανον φαίνοιτο. τὸ πιθανὸν δὲ τοῦτο καὶ πρὸς τὴν Τηλεμάχου πίστιν. δεξάμενος γὰρ ταύτην τὴν διήγησιν, ἑτοιμοτέρως καὶ παρ' Εὐμαίῳ πιστεύει τοῦτον εἶναι τὸν πατέρα τὸν τοῦ πτωχοῦ πρόσωπον ὑποκρινόμενον.*

[16] See Schwinge 1991: 504–8 (who refers to Schadewaldt 1938: 103–18, 150ff. and Hellwig 1964: 54–8); de Jong 1987: 81–91; de Jong 1997: 319–20 (who refers to Duckworth 1966, Schadewaldt 1952 and Richardson 1990: 132–9; and Di Benedetto 1994: 24–32.

proanaphōnēsis. A single example taken from the *Iliad* will suffice here: in Book 5, when the poet comments on the wound suffered by Sarpedon, saying 'but his father [Zeus] kept destruction from him for the time', the word translated 'for the time' (ἔτι) may serve to indicate that Zeus' protection will not be there for ever and thus to announce indirectly the death of Sarpedon in Book 16.[17] The way in which themes are introduced and are then taken up and developed at greater length further on in the poem could be the subject of a far more detailed study. But here we will restrict ourselves to explicit allusions.

In contrast to the *Iliad*, which announces the death of Achilles and the fall of Troy on several occasions, the *Odyssey* contains very few allusions to events that fall outside the temporal framework of the poem. Apart from the generous reward promised by Odysseus to his loyal servants once he has achieved his revenge—'wives for you both and possessions and a well-built house near my own' (21.214–15)—there are only three allusions to the future destiny of the *Odyssey*'s characters to be found in the prophecies reported by secondary narrators. First of all, in Book 4, there is the prophecy given to Menelaus by Proteus according to which he will be sent to the Elysian Fields after his death (4.561–9). There is also the account of the fate that awaits the Phaeacians after they have conveyed Odysseus to Ithaca. When their ship is transformed into a rock by Poseidon as it comes into sight of the coast of Scheria, Alcinous recognizes that the miracle fulfils the prophecies made to his father in the past (13.172–83 and 8.564–9). These prophecies not only announced the destruction of the ship, they also predicted that the god would surround the Phaeacians' city with a mountain. In an attempt to appease the god's wrath, the Phaeacians make sacrifices to him but the narrative, which leaves them praying to Poseidon by the altar, says nothing about the effectiveness, or otherwise, of their prayers.

There is, above all, the strange prophecy given to Odysseus by Tiresias that Odysseus retells first in Book 11.119–37 as part of the story of his adventures narrated at the Phaeacian court and then repeats to Penelope when they are reunited in Book 23. His return to Ithaca will not mark the end of his trials: he will still have to undertake 'a vast labour, long and vexing' (23.248–53) that is, to travel to a land far away where the sea is unknown and make sacrifice to Poseidon before returning to enjoy his old age at home, surrounded by prosperity, before

[17] See *Scholia vetera* BT to *Iliad*, 5.662.

dying a gentle death that will come from the sea. This mysterious prophecy has provoked a good deal of discussion.[18] But one aspect that does not seem to have received the attention it deserves is the appropriateness of this end to the hero's character. If a hero like Achilles who constantly risks his life in combat (*Iliad* 9.322) must fall on the battlefield, a 'much-enduring hero'[19] like Odysseus can only undergo a final trial before ending his life peacefully, surrounded by his family.

If 'external' prolepses are rare in the *Odyssey*, internal prolepses are, by contrast, extremely common. It is not surprising to find that they are mostly concerned with the return and revenge of Odysseus (the two are usually closely linked) but they also concern, to a lesser extent, his son's adventures. As in the *Iliad* these anticipations may take the form of an ironic comment by the main narrator. Thus, at the end of Book 20: 'the suitors in merry mood had prepared a sumptuous meal to gratify their desires, so many animals had they slaughtered; but after this meal there was to come another, prepared by the goddess and the hero. That was to prove as sour a meal as could be, for they were the first to commit crimes' (lines 390–4).[20]

They are sometimes contained within a single word, as at the beginning of Book 21, where the narrator announces that the trial of the bow will be 'the beginning of the slaughter' (line 4). They are often attributed to the gods (Zeus, Poseidon, and above all Athena) who are, by definition, omniscient and reveal the hero's destiny to the audience in the conversations they hold with one another.[21] But the gods may also, when in disguise, reveal the future to the heroes, as Athena does on several occasions.[22] There are also the interventions of prophets like Proteus, the Old Man of the Sea, Circe, and Tiresias, who all know the future and reveal it to Menelaus or to Odysseus,[23] and, in addition, of those characters who know how to interpret signs or who have visions, like

[18] See, in particular, Peradotto 1990: 59–93.

[19] Odysseus' enduring nature is emphasized by the epithets used to describe him: πολύτλας ('much enduring'), ταλασίφρων ('stout-hearted'), τλήμων ('enduring').

[20] See also *Odyssey*, 17.364; 18.155–7 and 344–5; 21. 96–100; 21.418; 24.470–1.Similar comments can be found in the mouths of secondary narrators like Nestor (3.143–7) or Odysseus (10.25–7) when they are telling a story whose end they know. The same applies to the bard Demodocus who shares Homer's omniscience (8.506–10).

[21] *Odyssey*, 1.76–7 and 5.22–42 (Zeus); 5.290 (Poseidon); 1.81–95 (Athena).

[22] *Odyssey*, 1.200–5, 2.281–4, 15.36–42 (to Telemachus); 13.306–10, 394–415 (to Odysseus).

[23] *Odyssey*, 4. 561–9 (Proteus); 10.490–540; 12.37–141 (Circe); 11.100–37 (Tiresias).

Halitherses, Theoclymenus, and also Helen.[24] Odysseus' disguise and the knowledge of future events that he gains from Athena allow him too to predict his own return and the revenge he will wreak on the suitors, whether it is to reassure his loyal servants and his relations, like Eumaeus, Penelope, and Philoetius,[25] to warn a 'good' suitor like Amphinomus, or to threaten his enemies, like Eurymachus and Melantho.[26] He even reveals his plans and the way in which he will revenge himself on the suitors in great detail to Telemachus in Book 16.270–98. But it is important to note—as the Analysts, who drew predictable conclusions from it, certainly did not fail to do—that this plan does not coincide in every detail with the actual deeds.

To conclude this brief review of anticipations in the *Odyssey*, it is important to note that some of them are given twice, both before and after the event that they announce, as we have seen with regard to the Phaeacians. Others are only mentioned after the event. It is only when he hears Odysseus' real name that the Cyclops in Book 9 realizes too late that the old prophecies have been fulfilled:

> Ah, it comes home to me at last, that oracle uttered long ago.[27] We once had a prophet in our country, a truly great man called Telemus son of Eurymus, skilled in divining, living among the Cyclops' race as an aged seer. He told me all this as a thing that would later come to pass—that I was about to lose my sight at the hands of one Odysseus. (9.507–12)

In the same way, Circe recognizes in the man who resisted her charms 'Odysseus the man of many turns' whose arrival had already been predicted by Hermes (10.330–2) and, on Ithaca, the seer Halitherses proves the veracity of his prophecies by reminding his listeners at Book 2.172–6 (when the gods have decided that Odysseus will return but before his actual homecoming) that he had once announced to Odysseus that 'after many trials, after the loss of all his comrades, in the twentieth year, known by none, he would come back to Ithaca'. This use of the flashback, or analepsis in narratological terminology,

[24] *Odyssey*, 2.157–68, 24.454–62 (Halitherses); 15.531–4, 17.157–61, 20.351–7, and 367–70 (Theoclymenus); 15.172–8 (Helen).

[25] *Odyssey*, 14.151–2, 161–4, 331–3 (to Eumaeus); 19.269–72, 300–7, 585–7 (to Penelope); 20.233–4 (to Philoetius); 21.232–41(to Eumaeus and Philoetius).

[26] *Odyssey*, 18.145–50 (to Amphinomus); 18.384–6 (to Eurymachus); 19.81–4 (to Melantho).

[27] *Odyssey*, 9.507: *ὢ πόποι, ἦ μάλα δή με παλαίφατα θέσφαθ' ἱκάνει* (a line that is repeated exactly by Alcinous at 13.172).

is not just a simple reflection of a religious vision of the world and a belief in divine providence, it is also the sign of a structural complexity that makes the *Odyssey* the ancestor of the Greek novel.

4. NARRATIONS AND NARRATORS

There is no doubt that the predominance of direct speech is one of the most remarkable aspects of Homeric epic.[28] But in the *Odyssey* the poet does not just allow his characters to speak, he also entrusts them with the narration of much of the story. This multiplication of narrations and narrators struck the author of the treatise *On the Sublime* in Antiquity and has also been noted by modern narratologists.[29]

In addition to the main narrator, who is also the recipient of an original narration made by the Muse, the *Odyssey* contains many 'secondary' narrators or, to use a more technical term, 'intradiegetic narrators'. There are even complex layerings of stories within stories, involving two or three levels. Thus, Menelaus' narration in Book 4, which is itself a story within the story, contains within it a long narration made by Proteus. Odysseus' lengthy narration addressed to the Phaeacians contains a series of other stories of which Odysseus is either the narrator or the original audience. And Telemachus' narration in Book 17.142–6 quotes the story he heard from Menelaus who, in turn, reported the words spoken by Proteus.

Among the narrators of the *Odyssey*, it is important to distinguish first between the 'external' (or 'heterodiegetic') narrators, who tell of events in which they themselves played no part, and 'homodiegetic' narrators, who do play a role in their own stories. Sometimes the narrator is also the main character in his story, in which case we are dealing with 'autodiegetic' narrators. The first category is very small. In

[28] See the remark made by Aristotle in his *Poetics*, 24 (1460a5–8): 'Homer especially deserves praise as the only epic poet to realize what the epic poet should do in his own person, that is, say as little as possible, since it is not in virtue of speaking in his own person that he is a maker of *mimēsis*' (translated by Hubbard in *Classical Literary Criticism* (Oxford, 1989).

[29] Pseudo-Longinus, *On the Sublime*, 9.13: τὴς δὲ 'Οδυσσείας τὸ πλέον διηγηματικόν ('most of the Odyssey consists of narrative; translation by D. A. Russell in *Classical Literary Criticism*). The analysis that follows owes a great deal to Rabau 1995 and 2000.

addition to the main narrator and his source, the Muse, it includes the two bards, Phemius and Demodocus, whom we should perhaps not be too quick to consider as representations of the poet. For one thing, we are only told the subject matter of Phemius' song (the troubled return of the Achaean troops) but nothing is said about the presentation (1.326–7). Only the longest of Demodocus' three songs, the tale of the love affair between Ares and Aphrodite, reflects the style of the *Odyssey* in that it too combines narration and direct speech. Among the 'disinterested' narrators we should also count the seer Proteus, who is in exactly the same position as the Muse given that, like her, he is omniscient and can thus describe events that have taken place far away.

All the other narrators have participated, at least for a short time, in the story they tell. If they become storytellers it is usually in response to a request for information, introduced by one of two formulaic verses:

> 'But come, tell me this truly and in detail'
> ἀλλ' ἄγε μοι τόδε εἰπὲ καὶ ἀτρεκέως κατάλεξον[30]
> or 'and tell me this truly too, so that I may know'
> καί μοι τοῦτ' ἀγόρευσον ἐτήτυμον, ὄφρ' ἐῢ εἰδῶ [31]

There are also other shorter versions such as 'tell me in detail' (ἀλλ' εὖ μοι κατάλεξον, 3.97, 4.327) or 'come now, tell me in detail' (ἀλλ' ἄγε μοι κατάλεξον, 17.44). Nestor and Menelaus in turn tell the story of their returns from Troy in response to Telemachus' requests for information about his father's fate. In the second part of his narration, Odysseus satisfies the curiosity of Alcinous who asks him whether he met any of the heroes who died at Troy in the Underworld. In the same way, Anticleia responds to Odysseus' demand for information in Book 11 by recounting how she died and Eumaeus does likewise when he tells his story in Book 15. In Book 24, Amphimedon's account of the suitors' end is prompted by Agamemnon's question, 'what disaster has brought you all down to this land of darkness?' (24.106). Often, such narrations are the means by which the stranger can reply to questions such as 'Who are you? Where do you come

[30] This line occurs seven times: *Odyssey*, 1.169 (Telemachus to Athena/Mentes); 4.486 (Menelaus to Proteus); 8.572 (Alcinous to Odysseus); 11.170 (Odysseus to his mother); 11.370 (Alcinous to Odysseus); 15.383 (Odysseus to Eumaeus); 24.287 (Laertes to Odysseus).

[31] This line occurs three times: *Odyssey*, 1.174 (Telemachus' request, addressed to Athena/Mentes); 14.186 (Eumaeus to Odysseus); 24.297 (Laertes to Odysseus).

from? Where is your town and where are your parents?' (*τίς πόθεν εἰς ἀνδρῶν; πόθι τοι πόλις ἠδὲ τοκῆες*)[32] or 'Tell me the name that you were called there by your mother and father' (*εἴπ' ὄνομ', ὅττι σε κεῖθι κάλεον μήτηρ τε πατήρ τε*, 8.550), by declaring his identity. We see this in the cases of Athena/Mentes in Book 1 and of Odysseus in Book 8 (in response to Arete and Alcinous), Book 14 (on meeting Eumaeus), Book 19 (responding to Penelope), and in Book 24, when he meets Laertes.

An exception is the tale told by Helen in Book 4, 'which is solely motivated by the desire to tell a story' (Rabau 1995: 275) and is intended only to provoke a feeling of pleasure in the listeners as is clear from the formula used to introduce it: 'now I would ask you to remain here seated, taking pleasure in the feast and the talk (*καὶ μύθοις τέρπεσθε*)' (lines 238–9). Menelaus' tale, which follows on from that of Helen and tells of one of Odysseus' past exploits, is likewise offered without any explicit request for information having been made. It is tempting to place this pair of narrations alongside the tales exchanged by Penelope and Odysseus in Book 23, which are purely motivated by the pleasure of storytelling, as is once again clear from the introduction: 'They took pleasure in the stories that they told one another' (*τερπέσθην μύθοισι, πρὸς ἀλλήλους ἐνέποντε*, line 301).

Both speakers and listeners derive pleasure from the act of storytelling. Although the requests for stories are usually presented as requests for information, the comments made by the characters and by the poet frequently emphasize the feeling of enchantment that they create. Thus, following Menelaus' long story, Telemachus is so entranced by his words that he says: 'I would gladly sit for another year beside you and never fret for my home and kindred, so charmed I am as I drink in your words and tales (*αἰνῶς γὰρ μύθοισιν ἔπεσσί τε σοῖσιν ἀκούων τέρπομαι*)' (4.595–8). The Phaeacians are equally transfixed after hearing the first part of Odysseus' story: 'They all kept silence, held by the spell (*κηληθμῷ δ' ἔσχοντο*) in the shadows of the hall' (11.333–4). Eumaeus also succumbs to the charm of Odysseus' words, as is shown by the fulsome praise he gives when speaking to Penelope:

> Such are the tales the stranger tells, he would enchant your heart (*θέλγοιτό κέ τοι φίλον ἦτορ*). For three nights and three days I had him as guest in my own

[32] This line occurs seven times in the *Odyssey*: 1.170, 7.238, 10.325, 14.187, 15.264, 19.105, and 24.298.

cottage because he came first to me after escaping from a ship; but even so he did not finish the story of his sorrows. It was just as when one keeps gazing at a bard taught by the gods to sing pleasing songs (ἔπε' ἱμερόεντα) to mortals, and whenever he begins to sing, men gladly would listen to him for ever—so did this man enchant my ears as he sat beside me in the steading. (17.514–21)

This explains the prestige enjoyed by Odysseus the orator, despite his unattractive appearance, as he himself says:

A man may seem in outward aspect unworthy of much regard, yet heaven hangs beauty about his words, and those who hear him gaze at him in delight while he speaks unfalteringly and with winning modesty; he stands out among those assembled there, and as he goes his way through the city, men look at him as if at a god. (8.169–73)

But such expressions of admiration also reveal an acute awareness of the dangers of deceitful words and of seductive tales that are able to 'enchant' their audiences.[33]

The extraordinary power of words may help us to understand why the epic sometimes appears to invert the logical relationship between words and deeds. Alcinous, for example, seems to suggest to Odysseus that the remarkable talents of the Phaeacians exist solely to provide the subject for future tales:

But now you must listen to me in turn, so that later you may tell these things to some other chieftain as you sit and feast in your own halls with your own wife and your own children and recall what prowess is ours also, and what forms of excellence Zeus has bestowed on us ever since the days of our forefathers. (8.241–5)

After this analysis of the relationships between stories and their narrators and audiences, it is time to examine the ways in which they relate to the main narrative and to each other, given that it is only in exceptional cases that a story, like that told by Helen in Book 4, exists in isolation and does not intersect in some way with the main narrative. These connections are complex. The stories told by Odysseus to the Phaeacians only intersect with the main narrative at two points (his stay on Calypso's island and the episode of the Cyclops).[34] Others, by contrast, are a *mise en abyme* of the main narrative and

[33] See *Odyssey*, 1.56–7, 3.264, 14.387, 18.282–3.

[34] The Cyclops is mentioned by Zeus in Book 1.68–71 in order to explain why Poseidon is pursuing Odysseus. He is mentioned again in Book 2.15–20 when the poet introduces Aegyptius by saying that the Cyclops had killed one of his sons.

have also been called 'internal analepses or mirror-stories' (De Jong 1997: 309). These narratives provide summaries of events that have already been narrated by the poet. Thus, the story told by Odysseus to Arete of his stay on Calypso's island, the storm off the Phaeacian coast, and his meeting with Nausicaa (7.244–97) repeats the narrative content of Books 5 and 6, just as Telemachus' account of his travels, addressed to Penelope (17.108–49), constitutes a summary of Books 3, 4, and 15. One could also mention the account of the massacre of the suitors given by Eurycleia to Penelope (23.40–51) which sums up Book 22, as well as the long story told by the suitor Amphimedon to Agamemnon in the Underworld (24.120–90) which resumes the whole of Books 13–22.

Even though the formulaic language of the epic makes it possible to repeat whole sections of the main narrative with no change (other than a change from the third to the first person where necessary),[35] these summaries are far from neutral. They emphasize the details which are likely to interest the listener: when Telemachus tells his mother about his visit to Menelaus, for example, he only passes on the prediction he heard of the massacre of the suitors, the assurances he was given about the reliability of the information, and the fact that Odysseus is being held captive by Calypso.[36]

There are also discrepancies between the main narrative and the versions told by the characters. Sometimes the changes may be deliberate. In Book 6, for example, Odysseus enters the Phaeacian city alone at the request of Nausicaa who is concerned about the gossip that would be provoked if they were to arrive together (6.273–85). But when Alcinous criticizes his daughter for failing to accompany the stranger right up to the palace, Odysseus presents things differently in order to save Nausicaa from all reproach, claiming that she had indeed asked him to follow her but that he had refused out of 'respect and fear' (*δείσας αἰσχυνόμενός τε*) of displeasing her father (7.303–6). Such discrepancies may also result from the characters' particular point of view and their limited knowledge of events. According to Amphimedon, speaking in Book 24.149 after his death at the hands of Telemachus, Odysseus was brought back to Ithaca by 'some spiteful god' (*κακός ποθεν ἤγαγε δαίμων*) and Penelope, who

[35] *Odyssey*, 23.45 *εὗρον* (Eurycleia speaking in the first person), 22.401 *εὗρεν* (the poet speaking about Eurycleia).

[36] *Odyssey*, 17.124–41 = 4.333–50 and 17.142–64 = 4.556–60.

proposed the trial of the bow, must have been in league with her husband: the cunning Odysseus, he claims, 'told his wife to set out in the hall before us suitors his own bow and the axes of grey iron' (αὐτὰρ ὁ ἣν ἄλοχον πολυκερδείῃσιν ἄνωγε | τόξον μνηστήρεσσι θέμεν πολιόν τε σίδηρον, lines 167–8). The poet and his audience, by contrast, know that Athena was behind everything. It was she who welcomed Odysseus back to Ithaca and advised him to go to see Eumaeus at the end of Book 13. It was she too who, at the beginning of Book 21, 'put it into the queen's mind to place in the hall before the suitors the bow and the axes of grey iron' (τόξον μνηστήρεσσι θέμεν πολιόν τε σίδηρον, lines 1–3). Here, the contrast between the two interpretations of Penelope's decision is underlined by the repetition of the line describing it.

The secondary narratives can also display complex interconnections. One may be the *mise en abyme* of another. The story Odysseus addresses to Penelope of his adventures in Book 23 retells in indirect discourse the stories he told to Alcinous, summing them up in little more than thirty lines (23.310–43). They may also echo each other, as in the case of the three separate accounts of Penelope's stratagem. The first and last of these narrations are identical, which is hardly surprising given that in both cases the story is told by a suitor: Antinous denounces the queen's deceitful manoeuvres in front of the Ithacan assembly (2.93–110) while the ghost of Amphimedon tells the same story to Agamemnon in the Underworld (24.128–46). But the second narration, given by Penelope herself in Book 19, although it is exactly the same as the other two in most respects, has two significant differences, one at the beginning and one at the end, that serve to express her point of view: for Penelope, the idea was inspired by a god,[37] while the suitors attribute it to her alone,[38] and the woman who uncovered the deception is not described in neutral terms, as in the suitors' accounts, as a 'woman who knew the truth' (2.108 = 24.144), but as 'an impudent bitch' (19.154).

These tales may also fit together in interesting ways. Nestor's story, which recounts Menelaus' journey from Troy to Egypt via Sunium, Cape Maleia, and Crete (3.277–312), complements that of Menelaus himself who begins with the visit to Egypt (4.351–2). Similarly, the three stories dealing with the Trojan Horse each emphasize a different

[37] *Odyssey*, 19.138: φᾶρος μέν μοι πρῶτον ἐνέπνευσε φρεσὶ δαίμων.

[38] *Odyssey*, 2.93 = 24.128: ἡ δὲ δόλον τόνδ' ἄλλον ἐνὶ φρεσὶ μερμήριξε.

moment and a different character within the story.[39] The version by Demodocus, the Phaeacian bard (8.499–520), resembles the main narrative in that it is related by an omniscient narrator who knows what happened in both the Trojan and Achaean camps and who is mostly interested in the actions and the reactions of the different groups: Odysseus is only mentioned at the beginning (the Achaeans are clustered around him in the horse) and the end (he vanquishes Deiphobus with the help of Athena). The account given by Menelaus, by contrast, is centred around the figure of Odysseus: thanks to him, the Achaeans are able to resist Helen's charms as she imitates the voices of their wives and do not betray their presence (4.269–89). But Odysseus himself, when he evokes the episode briefly to Achilles, only includes those details that show Achilles' son in a positive light, such as his imperviousness to fear (11.523–32).

The complex interrelationships between these secondary narrations emerge even more clearly when we compare the different versions of the 'Oresteia' that occur throughout the *Odyssey* and serve to establish a parallel between the story of Odysseus and that of Agamemnon.[40] One returns to his kingdom to find a faithful wife and a grown-up son and manages, with the aid of the latter, to wreak vengeance on his enemies; the other returns to be killed by his enemy, with the complicity of his unfaithful wife, and is later avenged by his son. These allusions are all found in secondary narrations and we can see how the emphasis changes according to the listener's identity and the speaker's purpose.

The version of the story told by Zeus in Book 1.32–43 focuses on the figure of Aegisthus and serves to show that mortals are wrong to attribute the responsibility for their misfortunes to the gods. Aegisthus had been warned by Hermes of the fate that awaited him if he killed Agamemnon, he took no heed of the warning, and therefore deserved to die by Orestes' hand. Presented in these terms and within the context of the prologue, Aegisthus' destiny serves above all to represent the antithesis of the fate of Odysseus, the most pious of men (1.66–7), who does not deserve what has befallen him. It also prefigures the fate that awaits the suitors, who are as guilty as Aegisthus,[41] if we take the whole of the work into account (Hommel 1976).

[39] For a fuller analysis see Andersen 1977.

[40] See Hölscher 1988: 301–5; Olson 1990.

[41] The term 'crime' (ἀτασθαλίαι) is used both of Aegisthus at 1.34 and of the suitors at 21.146, 22.317 and 416, 23.67, 24.458.

Later on in Book 1, Athena/Mentes places the emphasis instead on the story of Orestes who acquired a glorious reputation among men by killing his father's murderer, thus inciting Telemachus to do likewise by avenging himself on the suitors later on (1.298–300). The same applies to Nestor in Book 3, who draws an explicit moral from the tale: 'How good it is that when a man dies, a son should be left after him just as that son took revenge upon the murderer, treacherous Aegisthus, who killed his father!' (lines 196–8). In both cases, Orestes serves as an example to Telemachus and the parallel between the two young men is underlined by the use of the same two-line formula in both passages: 'You too (*καί σύ*), whom I see so tall and handsome, must show your courage and win fame among future men' (1.301–2 = 3.199–200).[42] Telemachus' reply to Nestor shows that the lesson has not gone unheeded: 'Would that the gods would arm me also with such strength, to take my vengeance upon the suitors for their grievous crimes' (3.205–6). A little further on, Athena/Mentor alludes to the story of Agamemnon, but this time it is to contrast Odysseus' fate with that of Agamemnon and to declare that it is better to 'suffer many troubles and then to come home and see the day of return' like Odysseus, than to 'arrive and die in one's own home, like Agamemnon treacherously murdered by Aegisthus and his own wife' (3.232–5). This particular example adds another reference to Clytemnestra which needs to be understood in contrast to Penelope's fidelity.

The first detailed account of the fate of Agamemnon is to be found in Book 3, where it is given by Nestor as he tells how the Achaean leaders returned home (3.254–312). He begins by telling of the seduction of Clytemnestra by Aegisthus and passes relatively swiftly over the murder itself but places emphasis on the consequences of the absence of Menelaus, which allowed Aegisthus to reign over Mycenae for seven years, and on his return, which occurred just as Orestes was celebrating the funerals of Aegisthus and Clytemnestra with a banquet. In this case, the emphasis is justified by Nestor's comments to Telemachus which remind him of the dangers of a long absence: 'And you (*καί σύ*) my friend—do not travel long away from home, leaving behind you your possessions, leaving also those arrogant men in your own halls (3.313–15).

[42] Shewring's translation follows those editors who delete the second of these passages as an interpolation.

This first extended account is echoed and completed in Book 4.514–37 by the Old Man of the Sea who, as a seer, is able not only to tell what happened but also to identify the causes. He reveals that Agamemnon was able to escape unharmed from two storms, thanks to the protection of the gods (4.513 and 520). He describes Agamemnon's joy on his arrival at the 'edge of the fields'[43] and how he kissed the soil of his fatherland, using the same terms that will later be employed to describe Odysseus' joy at arriving first in Phaeacia and then in Ithaca.[44] But this initial parallel between the two heroes serves to underline the contrast that later emerges between Agamemnon, who walks blindly into the trap prepared by Aegisthus and is slaughtered 'at the feast, as one kills an ox at the manger' (4.535), and the foresight of Odysseus who arrives in disguise and slaughters the suitors during a feast.

In the *nekuia* of Book 11, Agamemnon himself tells Odysseus how he was murdered (11.405–34). His version is close to that of the Old Man of the Sea but he places more emphasis on the role of Clytemnestra, who killed Cassandra and then refused to close his eyes or mouth (11.426). He also develops the pathos of the murder at a banquet, not only repeating the image of the ox slaughtered at the manger (11.411 = 4.535) but completing it with the image of his companions 'mercilessly killed like white-tusked boars' (11.412–13) and creates a tableau that prefigures, through the detail of the blood-soaked ground, the massacre of the suitors.[45] This new emphasis can be explained by the context in which Agamemnon is telling his story: he is speaking to Odysseus who has also left a wife behind in his palace and the story is therefore designed as a warning: 'So you too (*καί σύ*) should never be too kind towards your wife and never tell her the whole of what you know but reveal part and leave part hidden' (11.441–3).

Odysseus heeds the warning. As soon as Athena tells him, on his return to Ithaca, that the suitors have been lording it in his palace for

[43] *Odyssey*, 4.517: *ἀγροῦ ἐπ' ἐσχατιήν*. (This is another point of contact with the story of Odysseus who arrives 'at the edge of the fields' at Eumaeus' cottage at *Odyssey*, 24.150.)

[44] *Odyssey*, 4.521–2 *χαίρων . . . κύνει ἁπτόμενος ἣν πατρίδα* (Agamemnon); 5.463: *κύσε δὲ ζείδωρον ἄρουραν* and 13.354: *χαίρων ᾗ γαίῃ, κύσε δὲ ζείδωρον ἄρουραν* (Odysseus).

[45] *δάπεδον δ' ἅπαν αἵματι θῦεν*: *Odyssey*, 11.420 (Agamemnon); 22.309 and 24.185 (the suitors).

three years and that Penelope has been encouraging them with empty promises, he cries out: 'I see I might well have perished in my own halls by the same evil doom as Agamemnon, had not you, goddess, told me the truth point by point' (13.383–5).

The final allusions to Agamemnon's fate are found in the second *nekuia* in Book 24, in the dialogue between Achilles and Agamemnon. Achilles' words to Agamemnon contain a reflection on the sad destiny of the man who was once a powerful ruler, turning Agamemnon's fate into an illustration of the uncertainties of the human condition (24.24–34). Agamemnon, for his part, is preoccupied by the contrast between his fate and the 'good fortune'[46] of Achilles and Odysseus. Achilles died a glorious death in battle and was honoured by a splendid funeral (24.36–94) while Odysseus has a virtuous wife whose fame will never die, in contrast to his own wife who will forever be an object of hatred for killing her husband (24.192–202).

This example shows how the emphasis of the story changes from version to version according to the context and to the addressee: at one moment the focus is placed on the role of Aegisthus and at another on Clytemnestra, and at yet another on their joint role. It is understandable that, when the vogue for Analysis was at its height, such differences were used to distinguish different authors with different versions of the myth and equally understandable that Neo-analysts should have seen them as signs of the poet's hesitation between several different versions of the story. But it is far more economical to explain such divergences as the result of the different intentions of the various narrators.

5. POETRY AND POETS

The best guide to understanding the very particular type of narration that is represented by epic poetry is without a doubt to be found in the *Odyssey* itself, with its portrayal of two bards: Phemius on Ithaca and Demodocus at the Phaeacian court.[47] Poetry in the *Odyssey* is an

[46] *Odyssey*, 24.36 (ὄλβιε Πηλέος υἱέ) and 192 (ὄλβιε Λαέρταο πάι).

[47] On the representation of poets and poetry in Homer see: Schadewaldt 1952: 54–86; Maehler 1963; Marg 1956, 1971; MacLeod 1983; Segal 1992b; Ford 1992b; Grandolini 1998.

aristocratic entertainment and an essential element of the banquet.[48] The lyre is referred to as the 'companion' and the 'ornament' of feasts.[49] Bards are a central feature of the good life as evoked by Odysseus in Book 9:

It is a happy thing to listen to such a bard as this, whose utterance is like a god's. Indeed I think life is at its best when a whole people is in festivity and banqueters in the hall sit next to each other listening to the bard, while the tables by them are laden with bread and meat and the cupbearer draws wine from the mixing bowl and pours it into cups. That, I think, is the happiest thing there is. (9.3–11)

When Menelaus celebrates the weddings of his son and daughter, a bard sings for the guests to the accompaniment of the lyre (4.17–18). On Ithaca, Phemius is present at the suitors' banquet in Book 1 and Demodocus enchants the guests at Alcinous' palace with his song in Book 8. Song even has a place at the banquets of the gods: the feast which forms the conclusion to the first book of the *Iliad* ends with Apollo taking up 'his beautiful lyre' and with 'the lovely singing of the Muses, voice answering voice' (*Iliad*, 1.603–4).

Although it is clear that the members of the social elite appreciate poetry, the status of professional poets is less clear. The bard who is entrusted with the task of watching over Clytemnestra's behaviour when Agamemnon goes to Troy seems to be a member of the household and a servant attached to the palace (3.267–8). The Phaeacian bard Demodocus, by contrast, appears to live outside the palace, as a herald has to be dispatched in order to bring him to Alcinous (8.47). In all cases, the bards seem to be totally dependent on the aristocrats who request their services: on Ithaca, Phemius is 'forced' to sing for the suitors[50] and, in Argos, Aegisthus apparently has no trouble ridding himself of Agamemnon's bard by abandoning him on a desert island (3.270–1). At the same time, they are counted among the experts whose knowledge is highly regarded and who are summoned from far away, as Eumaeus reminds Antinous, one of the leading

[48] See Segal 1992b: 5–7. Poetry is also associated with funeral ceremonies as we see from the presence of bards at Hector's funeral (*Iliad*, 24.720–2) and the chorus of the Muses at that of Achilles (*Odyssey*, 24.60–1).

[49] *Odyssey*, 8.99: *φόρμιγγός θ', ἣ δαιτὶ συνήορός ἐστι θαλείῃ*; 17. 270–1: *ἐν δέ τε φόρμιγξ ἠπύει, ἣν ἄρα δαιτὶ θεοὶ ποίησαν ἑταίρην*; 21.430: *μολπῇ καὶ φόρμιγγι· τὰ γάρ τ' ἀναθήματα δαιτός*.

[50] *Odyssey*, 1.154 and 22.353 where the term *ἀνάγκῃ* ('by force' or 'by necessity') is used.

suitors: 'No man of his own accord goes out to bring in a stranger from elsewhere, unless that stranger be among the masters of some craft (τῶν, οἳ δημιοεργοὶ ἔασι),[51] a prophet or one who cures diseases, a worker in wood, or again an inspired bard, delighting men with his song (θέσπιν ἀοιδόν, ὅ κεν τέρπῃσιν ἀείδων). The wide world over, men such as these are welcome guests' (17.382–6).

In what looks very like a case of self-interested pleading the *Odyssey* provides two examples of the great respect accorded to bards in Homeric society. In a society in which honour is expressed in material terms and the relative status of the participants in a banquet is made manifest by the *geras* or 'share of honour' they receive, Odysseus shows his esteem for Demodocus by sending him a choice piece of meat, adding by way of explanation: 'for among men all over the world, bards deserve honour and veneration, for the goddess of song has taught them lays and has shown her favour to all their brotherhood.'

> πᾶσι γὰρ ἀνθρώποισιν ἐπιχθονίοισιν ἀοιδοὶ
> τιμῆς ἔμμοροί εἰσι καὶ αἰδοῦς, οὕνεκ' ἄρα σφέας
> οἴμας Μοῦσ' ἐδίδαξε, φίλησε δὲ φῦλον ἀοιδῶν. (8.479–81)

And during the massacre of the suitors in Book 22 he spares Phemius, who has just reminded him of the importance of bards by saying: 'You yourself will repent it afterwards if you kill a man like me, a bard singing for gods and men alike' (lines 345–6).

The bard is at once a singer, as the Greek term *aoidos* (related to *aeidein*, 'to sing') shows, a musician who plays the lyre, and a composer who creates his poem as he performs it. In the *Odyssey*, his favourite subjects are the stories of the gods, even if they are scandalous, like the adulterous affair of Ares and Aphrodite, but most of all the 'glorious deeds of men' (8.73), beginning with the sad fate that the gods have spun for the Achaeans and Trojans 'so that they might be a subject of song for future generations' (ἵνα ᾖσι καὶ ἐσσομένοισιν ἀοιδή) (8.578–80). He also sings of related stories, like the quarrel between Odysseus and Achilles at the beginning of the war (8.75) and the story of the Trojan Horse which marks its end (8.492–93) (thanks to these two allusions, the *Odyssey* is able to encompass the whole of the war),[52] and the disasters that befell the Greeks on their return home (1.326–7).

[51] The Greek translates literally as 'one of the *demiourgoi*', that is, one of those who work for the people.

[52] See Rengakos 2002: 190.

The bard who is said to celebrate Penelope's virtue in a 'delightful song' (ἀοιδὴν . . . χαρίεσσαν) and lambastes Clytemnestra's crimes in a 'song full of loathing' (στυγερὴ . . . ἀοιδὴ) (24.194–202) seems also to be thought of as a sort of teacher, whose task it is to preserve and transmit elite ideology by distributing praise and blame.[53]

It is remarkable that none of the events celebrated by Phemius and Demodocus appears in the *Iliad*. But they still constitute indirect allusions to the poem. To cite just one example, it is clear that the quarrel that pits Odysseus and Achilles, 'the best of the Achaeans', against one another and the allusion to 'the calamity rolling towards both Trojans and Greeks because of the will of sovereign Zeus' (8.78–82) are modelled on the *Iliad* and on the quarrel between Agamemnon and Achilles that 'brought countless sufferings upon the Achaeans' (*Iliad*, 1.2).[54]

Contemporary events within the world of the poem may also be selected for poetic treatment by bards, providing that they are exceptional events, worthy of being kept alive in people's memories, such as Orestes' revenge (3.203–4), Penelope's virtue, or the crimes of Clytemnestra (24.195–201). It is therefore the nature of the act and its unquestionably memorable character that make it worthy of celebration in verse. In contrast to the modern poet, who chooses his or her themes freely, the Homeric bard is restricted to a range of subjects already selected by tradition or likely to be remembered because of their extraordinary character. This does not mean, however, that he is seen as being entirely deprived of any freedom of choice since he is able to select as he pleases from the traditional repertoire (he sings 'as his fancy takes him' or 'as his heart inspires him'[55]) or by divine inspiration (for the Muse may also 'move the bard to sing the deeds of heroes'[56]). He also must satisfy the tastes of a public who are avid for new songs (according to Telemachus (1.351–2), the most popular songs are the 'freshest' ones dealing with the most recent events) or specific requests from his listeners (as when Demodocus responds to Odysseus' request to change his theme and move on to a new subject (8.492)).

Whether his name is Phemius (a speaking name derived from *phēmē*, rumour), son of Terpias (another speaking name derived from the verb

[53] Watkins 1982: 112 notes that this is the function of the poet in Indo-European society.

[54] On the relationship between *Odyssey*, 8.77 and *Iliad*, 1.7, see Marg 1956: 22–4 and Pucci 1987: 303.

[55] *Odyssey*, 1.347: ὅππῃ οἱ νόος ὄρνυται and 8.45: ὅππῃ θυμὸς ἐποτρύνῃσιν ἀείδειν.

[56] *Odyssey*, 8.73: Μοῦσ' ἄρ' ἀοιδὸν ἀνῆκεν ἀειδέμεναι κλέα ἀνδρῶν.

terpein meaning 'to delight'), or Demodocus ('he whom the people (*dēmos*) welcomes (*dekomai*, the Ionian form of *dechomai*)'), the bard 'enchants' his audience,[57] through a power that is as magical as that of Hermes' wand (4.47, 24.3) or the Sirens' song (12.40, 44). When he sings, the room falls silent (1.325–6 and 339–40) and the guests enjoy a feeling of pleasure (*terpsis*) which is almost physical (the same word is used to evoke the 'pleasures' of food, drink, sleep, sex, conversation, playing, or hunting).[58] This account of the effects of song upon the listener is very close to what has actually been observed in societies with a living oral tradition such as Montenegro or Africa.[59]

This feeling of pleasure is only achieved when the listener enjoys a degree of detachment from the subject of the song (Segal 1992b: 9–10). Thus Odysseus can derive pure pleasure from the story of the affair between Ares and Aphrodite. In the same way, listeners who have had no direct experience of the Trojan War and its aftermath, like the suitors or the Phaeacians, can feel pleasure on listening to the tale of the 'sorrowful homecoming of the Achaeans' (νόστον... λυγρόν, 1.326–7) sung by Phemius or to the two dramatic incidents from the war celebrated by Demodocus in Book 8. Penelope, by contrast, suffers terribly on hearing Phemius' 'sorrowful song' (ἀοιδῆς ... λυγρῆς, 1.340–1) as it revives her feelings of loss and longing for the husband she cannot forget. And Odysseus, upon hearing Demodocus sing the story of his own adventures, is moved to tears (8.83–93 and 521–32). For Alcinous, who does not yet know Odysseus' identity, this response is an indication that the stranger has been personally involved in the events of the Trojan War, as we see from his questions: 'Did some kinsman of yours die before Ilium, some man of courage, your son-in-law or father-in-law... or was it a friend?' (8.577–86). This need for distance between the listener and the subject of the song is also illustrated in Eumaeus' words to Odysseus in Book 15: 'We two will find comfort in calling to mind one another's griefs and sorrows, for there comes a time when a man takes comfort from old sorrows, a man who has suffered much and has wandered far' (lines 399–401). We can compare the reaction of Penelope in Book 23: now that her suffering is over and she is reunited with Odysseus, she can

[57] *Odyssey*, 1.337: θελκτήρια; 17.521: ἔθελγε.

[58] On the pleasure derived from poetry see *Iliad*, 1.474, 9.186 and 189; *Odyssey*, 1.347, 8.91, 368, 429, and 542, 12.88; 17.385 and 606, 18.304.

[59] See Hainsworth 1984: 9.23 and Vansina 1985.

also 'take pleasure in listening' (ἡ δ' ἄρ' ἐτέρπετ' ἀκούουσ', line 308) to the account of the hero's trials (MacLeod 1983: 8).

If the bard is able to move to tears those listeners who have lived through the events he recounts in his songs it is because he tells them 'in the right order'[60] and 'skilfully'[61] and because his song is a faithful reflection of reality. The bard is comparable to the prophet in that he is a 'master of truth',[62] a 'divine' being with 'a voice like that of the gods' (1.371 and 9.4). His art is something that is 'taught'[63] or 'given' by the gods (Apollo and the Muses in particular) to those whom they hold dear.[64] And the Muses have the privileged position of being able to overcome the limitations of time as it is experienced by mortals. As eyewitnesses of everything that occurs, they have knowledge not only of 'what is' but also of 'what has been' (which may explain the tradition according to which the bard—whether Demodocus or Homer—is a blind man, since he has no need to see if the Muses are his eyes). Moreover, the poets who receive this information directly from the Muses can, in turn, speak as if they themselves had been present at the events they describe, as Odysseus says in his praise of Demodocus (8.491),[65] and give a 'detailed account'.[66] But there are limits to the poet's abilities: although he can name the leaders of the various Greek contingents in the Catalogue of Ships

[60] *Odyssey*, 8.489 (κατὰ κόσμον) and 496 (κατὰ μοῖραν).

[61] *Odyssey*, 11.368 (ἐπισταμένως).

[62] This is a quotation from the title of the book by Marcel Detienne, *Masters of Truth in Archaic Greece* (New York, 1996).

[63] *Odyssey*, 8.480: 'The Muse has taught them their songs' (οἴμας μοῦσ' ἐδίδαξε); 22.347–8: 'A god has implanted in my breast all manner of songs' (θεὸς δέ μοι ἐν φρεσὶν οἴμας παντοίας ἐνέφυσεν).

[64] *Iliad*, 13.730: 'God gives one man skill in battle, and to another he gives dancing, and to a third the playing of the lyre and song' (ἄλλῳ μὲν γὰρ ἔδωκε θεὸς πολεμήια ἔργα ἄλλῳ δ' ὀρχηστύν, ἑτέρῳ κίθαριν καὶ ἀοιδήν); *Odyssey*, 8.64: the Muse 'gave him [Demodocus] entrancing song' (δίδου δ' ἡδεῖαν ἀοιδήν) and 498: 'the god has given you ungrudgingly the gift of inspired song' (πρόφρων θεὸς ὤπασε θέσπιν ἀοιδήν). The Muse's love for bards is expressed at 8.62–3: 'the Muse loved the faithful bard above all others' (ἐρίηρον ἀοιδόν τὸν πέρι μοῦσ' ἐφίλησε) and 481: '[the Muse] has shown her love for all the company of bards' (φίλησε δὲ φῦλον ἀοιδῶν).

[65] The *Iliad*, 2.485–6 contains a similar opposition between the 'autopsy' of the Muses and the knowledge of the poets which relies on hearsay: 'You are gods and attend all things and know all things, but we hear only the report and have no knowledge', ὑμεῖς γὰρ θεαί ἐστε πάρεστέ τε ἴστέ τε πάντα | ἡμεῖς δὲ κλέος οἶον ἀκούομεν οὐδέ τι ἴδμεν.

[66] *Odyssey*, 8.496: καταλέξῃς. This verb is generally used in the *Odyssey* to introduce a list or catalogue (14.99, 19.497, 22.417) or a detailed narrative (1.169, 206, 224 for example).

in Book 2 of the *Iliad*, he cannot give the names of all the men who followed them: 'As for the mass of men, I could not tell of them or name them, not even if I had ten tongues and ten mouths, and in me a voice unbreakable and a heart of bronze' (*Iliad*, 2.488–90). This excuse can, of course, be explained by the very real limitations on what it is possible for the poet to express in words, limitations that require him, like any other narrator, to select elements for inclusion.[67]

The prologue of the Odyssey, like that of the *Iliad*, is therefore simply a dramatized presentation of this process of transmission of knowledge from the Muse to the poet, in which the bard asks the Muse to tell him about his hero, 'the man of many turns' (*ἄνδρα μοι ἔννεπε, μοῦσα, πολύτροπον*, 1.1), 'beginning where you will' (*τῶν ἁμόθεν γε, θεά, θύγατερ Διός, εἰπὲ καὶ ἡμῖν*, 1.10).

It is possible to express this representation of the personal relationship between the poet and Muse in more abstract terms and to suggest that the poet is presenting himself here as the conduit for a tradition that exists independently of him and that is far older than he is, a tradition that, moreover, confers authority upon his words. He claims to be doing nothing more than isolating within this tradition a single incident, 'the wrath of Achilles' in the *Iliad*, or a single figure, 'the man of many turns' in the *Odyssey*.

Such appeals to tradition can be found in oral poetry of every type. But it is usually identifiable with the authority of the 'poets of old'. Replacing them with the figure of the Muse, who is in direct contact with the poet, is, as Margalit Finkelberg (1990) has noted, a means of creating a marvellous alibi which serves to justify in advance any innovations the poet might choose to make. It is noticeable that the claims of submission to a tradition coexist with the bard's consciousness of his own originality: Phemius is able to attribute the entire responsibility for his song to the gods (that is, to tradition) while simultaneously claiming to be 'self-taught', doubtless meaning that he owes nothing to contemporary poets.[68] In the world of Homer, there is no contradiction, quite the contrary, between the craft and the inspiration, the god and the man.

[67] Ford 1992: 74–5 rightly compares these lines with the comments made by internal narrators in the *Odyssey*, like Nestor (3.113–14), Helen (4.240–1) and Odysseus (7.241–3) who preface their stories by noting the impossibility of providing an exhaustive account.

[68] *Odyssey*, 22.347–8: *αὐτοδίδακτος δ' εἰμί, θεὸς δέ μοι ἐν φρεσὶν οἴμας παντοίας ἐνέφυσεν.*

5

The Adventures of Telemachus

The adventures of Telemachus are the subject of the first section of the *Odyssey*, a section that is clearly demarcated from the adventures of Odysseus by the second assembly of the gods which opens Book 5 and marks a new beginning for the action.[1] Starting with the son is certainly a strange way to begin a work whose declared aim is to celebrate the father, Odysseus, 'the man of many turns'. But this choice becomes easier to understand if we consider the beginning of the *Odyssey* as a sort of indirect portrayal of Odysseus: his absence serves to arouse the listeners' curiosity about the rest of the story (Rengakos 2002: 181). We see exactly what he represents for the members of his household and for his fellow citizens when we hear of the catastrophic effects of his absence in Books 1 and 2. This bipartite construction has been compared to one of the works of the most Homeric of the tragic poets, Sophocles, whose *Trachiniae* also opens with the absence of the hero (in this case, Heracles) and its consequences (Latacz 1996: 143).

The Adventures of Telemachus are also an account of a young man's coming of age. This part of the *Odyssey* has often been seen as the first novel of moral and psychological development (*Bildungsroman*) in Western literature (by Fénelon, the author of the modern *Adventures of Telemachus*, for example). But this reading of the first part of the *Odyssey* is not entirely accurate. Telemachus does not go through a process of development, nor do we see him gradually becoming the worthy son of his father. Instead, the *Odyssey* uses a series of symbolic moments and acts to represent the transition

[1] See Klingner 1997, Reinhardt 1997b: 217–23, Austin 1969, Jones 1988, Heath 2001.

from childhood (νήπιος) to adulthood and the age of reason (πεπνύμενος).[2]

1. ITHACA

(a) Book 1: Odysseus' palace

Books 1 and 2, which constitute the first part of the adventures of Telemachus, give us a sketch of Odysseus' palace in his absence. Our first glimpse of Ithaca comes as Athena arrives at the palace disguised as Mentes, the leader of the Taphians. There she finds the suitors 'seated on the hides of oxen that they themselves had killed, amusing themselves with games of draughts' (1.106–8) while their meal is prepared. This tableau is highly significant, juxtaposing as it does the suitors' amusements with the ruin of Odysseus' household: the ox-hides are an indirect, but effective, way of evoking the suitors' consumption of Odysseus' possessions in a world where wealth is calculated in terms of livestock, and this theme is taken up and developed in many allusions throughout Book 1.[3]

One person's pleasure is another's cause for sorrow: as we saw in the previous chapter we first see Telemachus 'sitting despondently among the suitors, thinking of his noble father' (lines 114–15), dreaming of his return and an end of the suitors' depredations.[4] Penelope's first words too are a reminder of the sorrow she has been feeling ever since Odysseus left for Troy: 'so peerless a man is he I mourn for, he I remember always, a man whose fame has gone through the length and breadth of Hellas and of Argos' (1.343–4).

The dialogue between Athena/Mentes and Telemachus refers constantly to the absent hero and Telemachus never ceases to lament the father 'whose whitening bones are cast up, perhaps, upon some shore, mouldering in rain, or are wave-tossed in the salt sea itself' (1.161–2) and the state of his house whose resources the suitors are 'devouring' (1.248). Athena/Mentes, for her part, announces Odysseus' imminent return, evokes the long-standing relationship between him and his

[2] See Hölscher 1996: 137–9, Heath 2001: 129–31.

[3] *Odyssey*, 1.248, 250–1, 376–8.

[4] *Odyssey*, 1.115–17, 163–5.

own family, and recalls the heroic warrior in ways that prefigure the vengeance to come (lines 179–205).

The opposition between Odysseus and his family and the suitors goes further. The suitors think only of amusing themselves and of passing the time with music and dancing (1.151–2, 159) while the others are weighed down with nostalgia for the time when Odysseus was at home and the palace was 'rich and well-ordered' (1.232–3). Telemachus behaves as a good host should, inviting the stranger to eat and drink before asking him any questions and then offering him a bath and giving him presents before allowing him to leave (1.123–25 and 309–13), while the suitors' only contribution is to spoil the party with their uproarious behaviour (1.133–4).

In addition to providing a tableau of the two sides, Book 1 also sets the action in motion with Athena's advice to Telemachus to call an assembly: 'When tomorrow comes, call the Achaean chiefs together; make known to them what you have resolved and let the gods be witnesses to it. Tell the suitors to go back to their own estates' (1.272–4). She then suggests that he go to Pylos and Sparta to try to find out what has happened to his father (1.280–6). Athena disappears as soon as she has finished speaking, but her words have an immediate effect on Telemachus, filling him with 'strength and courage' (1.321). This change in Telemachus first becomes evident when he speaks to Penelope, assuming the role of master of the house and telling her in lines 356–9 to go back to her room to take care of her own affairs and get on with her weaving (the traditional female activity). He then announces to the suitors that he intends to call an assembly in lines 372–74. The 'amazement' felt by Penelope and the suitors alike emphasizes the unexpected nature of Telemachus' sudden transformation into a man.[5]

The conversation between Telemachus and the two leaders of the suitors, Antinous and Eurymachus, that follows prepares for the assembly of Book 2 and the transition from the private domain (Odysseus' house) to the public sphere (the leadership of Ithaca). Antinous expresses his desire to see a new royal family in charge in lines 386–7, while Telemachus declares his readiness to succeed his father in line 390 and Eurymachus leaves the decision to the gods in line 400. The arrival of night, coinciding with the end of the book, brings the argument to a close.

[5] *Odyssey*, 1.361: *ἡ μὲν θαμβήσασα* and 381–2: *οἵ δ' ἄρα πάντες . . . Τηλέμαχον θαύμαζον.*

(b) The assembly in Book 2

Book 1 showed what had become of Odysseus' house in its master's absence. The assembly, which takes up the whole of the first half of Book 2 (lines 1–256), reveals the ways in which public and private are intertwined and the political consequences of the king's absence and the resulting power vacuum.

It is Telemachus who orders 'the clear-voiced heralds to call the flowing-haired Achaeans to the assembly-place' (lines 7–8) at dawn, as usual (at 3.137–8 Nestor observes that it is 'abnormal' (οὐ κατὰ κόσμον) to call an assembly at sunset). The assembly is dissolved by Leocritus, one of the suitors, at 2.257. This process is quite normal. In both the *Iliad* and the *Odyssey*, the king usually has the power to call and to dismiss the assembly, through the intermediary of a herald or the divine equivalent, the goddess Themis who presides over the assembly. In the *Iliad*, all the assemblies of the gods are called by Zeus (*Iliad*, 8.2–3, 20.4) and it is Agamemnon who twice decides to call the Greeks together (*Iliad*, 2.50–2 and 9.9–11) just as, in the *Odyssey*, Odysseus summons his companions to an assembly.[6] But Agamemnon is not the only one: in *Iliad* 1 and 9 it is Achilles who calls and then dismisses the assembly,[7] and it is Hector, not Priam, who calls the Trojans together at *Iliad*, 8.489 and dismisses the assembly at 2.808. The men may also gather together spontaneously as in Books 7 and 18 of the *Iliad* and Books 16 and 24 of the *Odyssey*.[8]

The assembly usually discusses matters of concern to the community as a whole, news of 'an approaching army' or some other 'public affair' (δήμιον), as the first speaker in the Ithacan assembly of Book 2 points out (2.28–32). But here, the matter is a private one concerning the *oikos* of Telemachus alone and its destruction as a result of the suitors' demands. Telemachus' decision to put this question to a public assembly is, however, justified by the status of the victim and by the services performed by the family for the community as a whole: Telemachus is careful to point out that he is the son of the man who ruled over Ithaca 'as gently as a father' (2.47). It also signals Telemachus' inability to defend himself without help (2.58–62). His

[6] *Odyssey*, 9.171, 10.188, 12.319: καὶ τότ' ἐγὼν ἀγορὴν θέμενος μετὰ πᾶσιν ἔειπον ('Then, I summoned an assembly and spoke to them all').

[7] *Iliad*, 1.54 and 305 (with Agamemnon), 19.34–6 and 276.

[8] *Iliad*, 7.414–16, 18.243–5; *Odyssey*, 16.361, 24.420–1.

decision also implies that public opinion carries a certain weight, even if it is clear that the community is powerless to take any effective action against nobles like the suitors. In any case, this community never speaks and its reactions, which go from pity for Telemachus (οἶκτος δ' ἕλε λαὸν ἅπαντα, 2.81) to amazement at the omen sent by the gods (θάμβησαν δ' ὄρνιθας, 2.155), are merely evoked by the poet in as few words as possible.

The assembly consists of a series of nine speeches made by the following speakers: Aegyptius, Telemachus (I), Antinous, Telemachus (II), Halitherses, Eurymachus, Telemachus (III), Mentor, Leocritus. They are carefully arranged: Telemachus has three speeches, in contrast to the two given by the leading suitors, allowing him both to open the debate and to have the last word. The argument between Eurymachus and Telemachus is framed by the speeches of the two good counsellors, Halitherses and Mentor, both of whom are introduced by the formula reserved for speakers who represent the common good: 'With good intent [or 'with good sense'] he spoke and addressed the assembly' (ὅ σφιν ἐὺ φρονέων ἀγορήσατο καὶ μετέειπε, 2.160 and 228). The first to speak is Aegyptius, who appears nowhere else in the *Odyssey*, and the last is Leocritus, who is not seen again until his death at Telemachus' hands in Book 22.

Telemachus' first speech, in which he attempts to elicit a reaction from the people of Ithaca, is important for the way in which he appeals not only to their fear of the gods but also to their sense of honour as a group, asking them to 'feel shame (αἰδέσθητε) in the face of the men who live nearby' (2.65–6). This is in sharp contrast to the very personal sense of honour of the warriors in the *Iliad*, who only feel 'shame' in front of other warriors.[9] In his conclusion, Telemachus makes a gesture that echoes that of Achilles at the height of his anger in Book 1 of the *Iliad*: he throws his sceptre to the ground.[10] But although the gesture is the same, the meaning is entirely different: there is a world of difference between the divine wrath (μῆνις) of Achilles, which 'brought countless sufferings upon the Achaeans' (*Iliad*, 1.2), and the frustrated anger (χωόμενος *Odyssey*, 2.80) of a

[9] The contrast is clear from the comparison between Telemachus' words in *Odyssey*, 2.65 (ἄλλους τ' αἰδέσθητε περικτίονας ἀνθρώπους) and the sentiment expressed at *Iliad*, 5.530 and 15.562: 'in the raging battle feel shame in front of each other' [or more literally 'fear what the others might think or say'] ἀλλήλους τ' αἰδεῖσθε κατὰ κρατερὰς ὑσμίνας.

[10] *Odyssey*, 2.80 and *Iliad*, 1.245: ποτὶ δὲ σκῆπτρον βάλε γαίῃ.

young man who bursts into tears and only elicits pity from his audience.[11]

This speech by Telemachus is answered by Antinous (in lines 85 to 128). He transfers the blame for the situation to Penelope who, for three years, has been tricking the suitors. He urges Odysseus' son to tell his mother to remarry, explaining that the suitors will not leave the house until Penelope has chosen a husband. Telemachus refuses (2.130–7) because of the harm such a course of action would cause: if he sent his mother away he would have to return her dowry to her father and, more importantly, he is afraid both of his mother's curse if he ejects her from the house against her will and of being criticized by the people. For these reasons, Telemachus repeats his request to the suitors to leave the palace and concludes with an appeal for help this time addressed not to men, as in his first speech, but to the gods, repeating the conclusion of his speech to the suitors in Book 1 (2.139b–145 = 1.374b–380).

The gods' response comes in the form of an omen which is immediately interpreted, in lines 161–76, by the seer Halitherses who reminds the suitors that his predictions have proved to be true in the past (2.172–6). This divine warning is highly significant in a work whose prologue attributes the responsibility for evil doing to men and to their criminal madness: just as Aegisthus was warned by Zeus of the fate that awaited him and of Orestes' revenge if he killed Agamemnon after seducing his wife, the suitors are being warned of what is in store for them. At the same time, Halitherses tries to provoke a reaction from the people of Ithaca as a whole by urging them to put a stop to the suitors' excesses. But his speech has no effect, as is clear from Eurymachus' reply (2.178–207) with its threats and its request to Telemachus to return Penelope to her father so that he can arrange a marriage.

Telemachus' third speech (2.209–23) introduces a new theme as he asks for a ship to take him to Sparta and Pylos so that he can find out what has become of his father.[12] He announces his intention to arrange his mother's marriage on his return, if he finds out that Odysseus is dead. Mentor, who is the next to speak (2.229–41), takes up the themes of Telemachus' first speech, reminding his listeners of Odysseus' qualities, using the same terms,[13] and expressing his indignation at the

[11] *Odyssey*, 2.81: δάκρυ' ἀναπρήσας: οἶκτος δ' ἕλε λαὸν ἅπαντα.

[12] See Klingner 1997: 197–9.

[13] *Odyssey*, 2.234b = 2.47b.

Ithacans' passivity. The third suitor to speak, Leocritus, responds by repeating Eurymachus' threats to Halitherses, directed now against Mentor, and claiming that Odysseus himself, if he were to return, would be unable to overcome the suitors, due to their number. He ends by breaking up the assembly.

This lengthy episode, which has no equivalent in the *Iliad*, shows the role that can be played by the people in Homeric society and, above all, the limitations of that role. The fact that Telemachus can think of putting the matter to the assembly, and that a speaker can complain of the people's passivity, suggests in itself that it is not just a question of testing public opinion, as Moses Finley claimed (1977a: 80). Rather, it is important to note, as do Kurt Raaflaub (1997: 642–3) and Robin Osborne (2004: 212), that the people do have a political function, even if the assembly is dismissed without any decision being taken.

(c) Preparations for departure and the end of Book 2

The transition scene which follows on from the assembly immediately brings to mind the scene in the *Iliad* following the removal of Briseis from Achilles' tent: Telemachus, like Achilles, goes alone to the shore to pray to a divinity who responds to his prayer.[14] But, unlike Thetis in the *Iliad*, Athena only reveals herself in disguise. Here, she adopts the appearance of Mentor, the man who supported Telemachus at the assembly. The goddess promises Telemachus the ship and the crew he needs. But she also makes explicit the true purpose of the journey: to see whether Telemachus is a son worthy of his father who has inherited both his combative spirit (*menos*) and his resourcefulness (*mētis*) (2.271–80).

Telemachus' return to the palace to gather supplies is the occasion for a fresh confrontation with the suitors in a scene that emphasizes yet again how the house's resources are being depleted (he finds, in line 300, the suitors 'flaying goats and singeing fat hogs in the courtyard') and, at the same time, illustrates Telemachus' transformation. He is no longer the silent and sorrowful young man of Book 1 but an adult determined to complete his task who threatens the suitors and makes Eurycleia obey him. The end of Book 2, which focuses in its portrayal of the preparations for the journey on the activities of

[14] *Odyssey*, 2.260–6 and *Iliad*, 1.348–56.

Athena/Mentor, is a typical embarkation scene in which the presence of libations foretells a safe crossing (Greene 1995: 217).

2. TELEMACHUS' TRAVELS

The search for Odysseus is only the pretext for Telemachus' travels, which take up Books 3 and 4. They are above all a means for the son of 'a man whose fame has gone through the length and breadth of Hellas and of Argos'[15] to acquire 'a good name in the world' in his own right, as Athena makes clear in Book 1.[16] When he leaves Ithaca, Telemachus is just a young man who does not yet know how to behave in the wider world and is 'inexperienced in the shrewd use of words' (3.23). But thanks to the intelligence inherited from his father and with the help of the goddess who tells him what to say and puts courage in his heart (3.26–7, 76–7), he finds 'suitable words, such as you would not expect to hear from a young man' (3.124–5) and achieves recognition, not only as the living image of his father, as is clear from the reactions of Athena/Mentes, Helen, and Menelaus,[17] but also as a worthy son.

In the overall organization of the *Odyssey*, the short and uneventful journey that takes Telemachus from Ithaca to Pylos and then from Pylos to Sparta via Pherae functions above all as a contrast to Odysseus' adventures. It takes place entirely in a familiar world, at Athena's suggestion, under her protection, and, for the most part, in her company, while Odysseus' adventures, once he has rounded Cape Maleia, take place in mythical zones and the goddess only comes to her protégé's aid once he has left Phaeacia. Telemachus also encounters welcoming hosts, who have nothing in common with the Laestrygonians or the Cyclopes. The dialogue between Athena and Odysseus in Book 13 emphasizes their contrasting experiences. When Odysseus hears that his son has left for Sparta, he immediately thinks that the goddess plans to make his son undergo trials similar to his own: 'Did you want him as well to stray in misery over the barren sea?' (13.418–19). But Athena reassures him that his son's journey

[15] *Odyssey*, 1.344: *ἀνδρός, τοῦ κλέος εὐρὺ καθ' Ἑλλάδα καὶ μέσον Ἄργος.*
[16] *Odyssey*, 1.95: *ἵνα μιν κλέος ἐσθλὸν ἐν ἀνθρώποισιν ἔχῃσιν.*
[17] *Odyssey*, 1.207–9, 4.141–5, 148–50.

will be nothing like his: 'Don't be worried about him: I myself was his escort and wanted him to acquire a noble reputation from his journey. He is in no distress (*οὔ τιν' ἔχει πόνον*); he is seated at ease in Menelaus' palace and lacks for nothing' (13.421–4).

With the stories told by Nestor and Menelaus, which contain examples of all the possible types of homecoming (dying on the journey, like Ajax son of Oileus, being killed on arriving home, like Agamemnon, returning home uneventfully to live out one's life in peace like Nestor, or only after adventures that take the hero to exotic, but real, places, like Menelaus), Books 3 and 4 place Odysseus' return in a broader perspective and bring out the exceptional qualities of the *Odyssey*'s hero (Rutherford 1985: 140). These stories of homecoming were later the subject of a separate epic, the *Nostoi* or *Returns*, which is known only from its title and from the résumé provided by Proclus in the *Chrestomathia*.[18] Ajax, son of Oileus, had raped Cassandra while she was taking refuge at the statue of Athena, this sacrilegious act had brought the wrath of the gods down upon the Greeks, resulting in long and difficult homecomings.[19] But it is clear that poet of the *Odyssey* was already familiar with these legends, and does not hesitate to adapt them in order to underline their similarities to and their differences from the story of his hero. Despite his absence, Odysseus is therefore still present by implication in Books 3 and 4, just as he was in Books 1 and 2. But he is also made present through tales of his exploits told by the survivors of the Trojan War.

(a) Pylos

The visit to Pylos, which takes up almost the whole of Book 3, provides an illustration of hospitality and of a piety which earns the inhabitants the favour of the gods. When Telemachus and Mentor arrive, the people of Pylos are gathered together to perform a sacrifice. The ordered nature of this society is displayed in the way in which the participants are seated, which seems to reflect some institutional grouping: 'There were nine companies seated there, with five hundred men in each' (3.7–8).

[18] See Severyns 1963: 94–5.

[19] For Strausse-Clay 1997: 43–53. Athena's wrath is the key to the whole structure of the *Odyssey*.

The concern shown by all the men of Pylos for the new arrivals, who are immediately invited to share the feast and placed in the seats of honour next to Nestor and his son Thrasymedes (3.34–41), reveals their respect for the laws of hospitality and for etiquette as they invite the older of the two men, Mentor, to make the first libation before passing the cup to his younger companion. The length and completeness of the libation type-scene also serves to portray Nestor and his sons as exceptionally pious. Only later does Nestor ask the strangers about their identity, respecting the rule which he explicitly mentions: 'now that they have enjoyed the meal, we may rightly put questions to these guests and ask them who they are' (3.69–70).[20]

Telemachus replies by introducing himself and explaining the reason why he has come to Pylos, 'seeking news about [his] father' (3.83–4) and asking Nestor to give him a true and detailed account[21] of what he saw with his own eyes and what he was able to find out from others.[22] The tale that follows, in lines 103–200, does in fact make a clear distinction between what Nestor saw for himself (3.103–84) and what he found out later 'without stirring from my own house' (3.188–98).[23] His introduction, which tells of the Trojan War, begins by emphasizing how much the Greeks suffered and how many men they lost (3.102–20). Yet it also reveals Odysseus in a very favourable light as a hero unrivalled for his cunning and stratagems (3.120–2), but also for his sound advice, a quality which made him the associate of Nestor, the good counsellor *par excellence* (3.126–9).

The tale of Nestor's homecoming which follows conveys a moral and political lesson. Like Zeus' speech in Book 1.32–43, it provides a concrete example of the divine justice at work in the *Odyssey*, for men and men alone are responsible for their ills and the entire community has to pay for the crimes of the individual: 'Zeus devised sad homecomings for the Achaeans, since not all of them were wise or righteous' (3.132–3). Nestor's story also illustrates the dangers of dissension, an important point in the age of the birth of the city and the beginnings of colonization, both of which are collective

[20] This rule is respected by Telemachus (1.123–4), Menelaus (4.60–2), and Eumaeus (14.45–7).

[21] *Odyssey*, 3.97 (*εὖ μοι κατάλεξον*) and 101 (*καί μοι νημερτὲς ἐνίσπες*).

[22] *Odyssey*, 3.93–5: *εἴ που ὄπωπας | ὀφθαλμοῖσι τεοῖσιν ἢ ἄλλου μῦθον ἄκουσας | πλαζομένου.*

[23] *Odyssey*, 3.186–7: *ὅσσα δ' ἐνὶ μεγάροισι καθήμενος ἡμετέροισι | πεύθομαι, ἣ θέμις ἐστί, δαήσεαι, κοὐδέ σε κεύσω.*

enterprises. Once again, the Greeks' misfortunes stemmed from a quarrel, this time between the two sons of Atreus. Some stayed with Agamemnon, to try to appease the angry gods by offering a hecatomb, while others, including Nestor and Odysseus, set sail with Menelaus. At Tenedos a second quarrel further divided the Greek fleet: Odysseus left to find Agamemnon while Nestor and Diomedes, who continued their journey, were later joined by Menelaus. Only Nestor and Diomedes, who decided to travel by way of Euboea, arrived home after a journey that is the exact opposite of Odysseus'. It took place entirely within the real world and it is possible to follow their itinerary on a map: they sailed from Troy to Tenedos and then on to Lesbos. They then sailed past Euboea at Cape Gerestos before finally arriving at Argos and at Pylos respectively, after a three-day journey. What is more, they enjoyed ideal sailing conditions from beginning to end: 'the fair wind never slacked from the hour when the god sent it forth to blow' (3.182–3).

This first story is complemented by a brief review of the fates of the other heroes of the Trojan War who also arrived home without difficulty, like Neoptolemus, Philoctetes and Idomeneus (3.188–92), and by an account of the sad fate of Agamemnon, which Nestor relates at length at Telemachus' request (3.193–252). He also describes the beginnings of Menelaus' wanderings, which resemble those of Odysseus. Just like him, Menelaus was caught in a storm at Cape Maleia: 'but when he had launched his ships again on the wine-dark sea and came in his rapid course to the sheer headland of Maleia, thundering Zeus devised a distressing voyage for him, loosing upon him the violent breath of whistling winds and rearing huge waves as high as mountains' (3.286–90).

Like Odysseus, he lost many of his ships, but unlike Odysseus, who is finally left with a single ship after the Laestrygonian episode (10.131–2), which is then destroyed by lightning after the crew eat the cattle of the Sun (12.403–19), Menelaus managed to save five ships (3.299–300). He is also like Odysseus, who ends up on the 'far-off island' (5.55) of Calypso, in that he returned from far away 'from a land whence none would hope to return if a storm had driven him off his course into the ocean so vast that not even birds can return within a year, so vast and dangerous is it' (3.319–22) and brings back 'much wealth and much gold' (3.301), just as Odysseus returns with treasure from the land of the Phaeacians. Nestor's stories are not just designed to give Telemachus the information he wanted. They also convey a twofold lesson: Orestes' revenge on his father's murderer and the glory that results constitute an example for Telemachus to follow (3.195–200) while the story of Menelaus, who arrives home too late, shows the dangers of staying away too long (3.313–16).

After these lengthy stories, it is time to think about sleeping. But the evening does not end until a first libation has been made, at Athena's suggestion, to Poseidon and the other gods (3.330–42). This is followed by further libations and the promise of a sacrifice to Athena, whose presence has been recognized by Nestor (3.375–85). This double libation contributes further to the portrait of Nestor's piety and is emphasized by the repetition at lines 342 and 395 of the formulaic line 'having made libations and drunk to their hearts' content' (αὐτὰρ ἐπεὶ σπεῖσάν τ' ἔπιον θ', ὅσον ἤθελε θυμός), after which the guests normally return to their homes.[24] The next day is entirely devoted to a magnificent feast, and Telemachus is given a bath by Nestor's daughter (3.464–8), ensuring that the rituals of hospitality are fully observed.[25]

The disparity between the brief evocation of the meal itself in four lines (3.470–3) and the lengthy scene of sacrifice, taking up thirty-four lines (3.430–63) of detailed description unparalleled elsewhere in the *Odyssey*, further contributes to the portrait of Nestor's piety, which is one of the main themes of Book 3. This book ends with the preparations for Telemachus' departure (3.473–85) and his brief stay at Pherae where he stays the night (3.486–90) before leaving for Sparta at dawn and arriving there at nightfall (3.491–7).

(b) Sparta

Like Pylos, Sparta also offers an image of a harmonious universe, with banquets that are not an excuse for plundering other people's possessions, as they are on Ithaca. Telemachus and his companion find a king 'celebrating with many clansmen a wedding feast for his

[24] See *Odyssey*, 7.228–9 and 18.427–8.

[25] In accordance with this ritual, Telemachus and his companion are offered baths on their arrival at Menelaus' palace (4.48–50). It is also worth noting that Calypso bathes Odysseus before he leaves her island (5.264), Nausicaa offers him a bath (6.210–22), and that Circe bathes Odysseus (10.358–64) and then his companions (10.449–50). When Eurycleia washes Odysseus' feet at 19.357–92 she performs a version of this ritual.

daughter and his son' (4.3–4). It is also a world where the rules of hospitality are known. When a servant asks whether he should welcome the guests or send them elsewhere, Menelaus calls him 'foolish' (*nepios*, 4.31) and respects the rituals of hospitality to the letter. In lines 52–8 we find all the elements of the sequence describing the reception of a guest, as seen in Chapter 1 above: Telemachus and his companion are first offered a bath (4.48–50) and are then seated in the places of honour (4.51), next to the master of the house who shares with them the choice piece of meat that had been reserved for him (4.65–6).

But it is Menelaus' wealth, rather than his piety, that is emphasized. The splendour of his palace, which prefigures that of Alcinous,[26] amazes the new arrivals: 'They were filled with wonder at what they saw in the monarch's house; for a radiance like that of sun or moon filled the high halls of King Menelaus' (4.44–6). This impression of opulence is reinforced, in lines 71–3, by the list of the precious materials which were used in its construction—gold, bronze, amber, silver, and ivory—and by the reference to purple rugs which are only otherwise found in the palace of Alcinous and in Circe's home.[27] The list of the presents given to the Spartan king by the ruler of Egyptian Thebes 'where the houses are rich in precious things' (4.127), which includes two silver baths, two tripods, a golden distaff, and 'a silver basket with wheels to it and with rims finished off with gold' (4.128–32), completes this impression of opulence.

The reader might expect Menelaus to ask his guests to reveal their identity after the end of the feast. But the normal sequence of events is interrupted by Menelaus' speech in which he reminds his listeners of the heavy price he had to pay for his treasure and laments the warriors who died at Troy. This reminder of the past is the occasion for his first mention of Odysseus, who appears here too as a hero with exceptional qualities. But in contrast to Nestor, who emphasized Odysseus' intelligence, Menelaus draws attention to his powers of endurance: 'No other Achaean', he says, 'toiled as much as Odysseus or took so much on himself' (4.106–7).

This reference to his father causes Telemachus to weep and his tears do not go unnoticed by Menelaus. The same motif reappears in Book 8 where it is Odysseus who weeps on two separate occasions on

[26] *Odyssey*, 3.45–6a = 7.84–5a.

[27] *Odyssey*, 4.297–8, 7.336–7, and 10.352–3.

hearing Demodocus sing of his exploits and where it is Alcinous who notices. The comparison reveals Homer's art: the repetition sets up a parallel between father and son while the variations show how the same theme can be progressively developed. Thus, a motif that takes up three lines in Book 4 expands to take up twelve and then fourteen lines in Book 8.[28]

The arrival of Helen, who is immediately struck by Telemachus' resemblance to his father, leads to the revelation of his identity and prompts Menelaus to refer once again to Odysseus' trials and exploits (4.170), causing all present to weep. But Helen puts an end to this shared sorrow by two means that may appear to be very different at first sight but which in fact complement each other perfectly. First of all she pours a 'drug' (*φάρμακον*) into the wine which has the power to 'dispel all grief and anger and banish remembrance of every trouble' (4.220–1). Then she entertains her guests by recounting an episode from the Trojan War involving herself and Odysseus.(4.240–64).[29] This combination of remembrance and forgetting may seem surprising. But it is an exact parallel to the magical effect of the song of the Sirens who cause men to forget their homeland by telling them 'all the sorrows that the Greeks and Trojans bore in the plain before Troy by the will of the gods' (12.189–90).

Of all the legends surrounding Odysseus, Helen chooses a story that 'is suited to the circumstances' (*ἐοικότα*, 4.239),[30] since it illustrates his powers of endurance, already noted by Menelaus.[31] It also prefigures one of the most famous episodes of the *Odyssey*. For the Odysseus who enters Troy disguised as a slave is very similar to the Odysseus who disguises himself as a beggar when he enters his own palace. The encounter with Helen, who recognizes him, offers him a bath, and swears not to reveal his identity, corresponds to the scene in Book 19 where Eurycleia recognizes Odysseus while washing his feet and promises to keep the secret safe. The massacre of Trojans with which the story ends also prefigures the massacre of the suitors in Book 22. The story also serves Helen well. She emerges from it as a victim who stayed in Troy against her will and wanted nothing more

[28] *Odyssey*, 4.114–16, 8.83–94, and 521–34.

[29] See Rabau 1995.

[30] This is clearly the meaning of the Greek term at 3.125, but here as elsewhere it may also express the idea of 'likeness [to truth]' as when it serves to introduce a comparison or to describe a metamorphosis and expresses the idea of resemblance.

[31] *Odyssey*, 4.241: *Ὀδυσσῆος ταλασίφρονός*.

than to return to her homeland: 'I wept for the blindness that Aphrodite sent me when she made me go there, away from my own dear land, and let me forsake my daughter and bridal room and a husband who fell short in nothing, whether in mind or in outward form' (4.261–4). Her words are in harmony with the dominant theme of the *Odyssey*, homecoming, and with her current status as the worthy wife of Menelaus.

In lines 266–89, Menelaus responds to this story—whose appropriateness (though not its truth) he ironically praises[32]—by telling another story that is both symmetrical and contrasting. It is symmetrical in that it too illustrates Odysseus' 'endurance'[33] and self-control and also prefigures the Eurycleia episode of Book 19: here in Book 4 Odysseus stops Anticlus from responding to Helen and revealing the presence of the Greek warriors inside the wooden horse by 'pressing with his powerful hands on the man's mouth'. In the same way he grabs Eurycleia by the throat in Book 19 to stop her speaking out and revealing his identity to Penelope.[34] But it also contrasts with Helen's story in that it reveals a Helen who is in league with the Trojans and tries to trap the Greeks hidden in the horse by calling them by name, imitating the voices of their wives.

The evening comes to an end with these two stories. It is not until the next day that Telemachus repeats his request for information about his father in lines 322–31 and Menelaus replies in a long story that complements Nestor's tale, taking up the story exactly where Nestor had left it, with his arrival in Egypt.[35] In contrast to Nestor's homecoming, which was the very model of the peaceful journey granted by the gods to those who respect their decrees, Menelaus' tale of his return begins with a transgression (he is unable to set sail from Egypt 'because [he] had failed to offer the gods acceptable hecatombs' (4.352)) and involves a series of adventures that prefigure those of Odysseus. Like Odysseus, who has 'viewed many cities', 'come to know the minds of many men', and 'suffered many troubles', Menelaus has 'suffered much' and 'wandered far' and 'come to know

[32] *Odyssey*, 4.266: *ναὶ δὴ ταῦτά γε πάντα, γύναι, κατὰ μοῖραν ἔειπες*. The expression *κατὰ μοῖραν* is used in the *Odyssey* either to describe a speech that is appropriate to the circumstances (on ten occasions) or in praise of a story that relates the events accurately and in order (on three occasions).

[33] *Odyssey*, 4.270: *'Οδυσσῆος ταλασίφρονός*.

[34] *Odyssey*, 4.286–8 and 19.479–81.

[35] *Odyssey*, 3.299–302 and 4.351–2.

the thoughts and counsels of many heroes'.[36] It is true that his travels, unlike those of Odysseus, never take him into mythical realms but are confined to places that are real, 'Cyprus, Phoenicia, Egypt, the lands of the Ethiopians, Sidonians, Erembians and Lybians', even if they do display elements of the Golden Age, like Libya, where 'the ewes have lambs three times in the course of the year' (4.83–6). But they do involve very similar episodes. Like Odysseus, Menelaus is swept off course by a storm off Cape Maleia.[37] Both are saved by sea-goddesses who take pity on them: Eidothea enables Menelaus to continue on his journey after twenty days of dead calm just as Ino-Leucothea allows Odysseus to escape from the storm.[38] Both consult seers: Proteus tells Menelaus 'the path before him and the long stages of his journey and how [he] may return home over the fish-filled sea' (4.389–90), just as Tiresias will do for Odysseus, according to Circe.[39] Menelaus' despair when Proteus tells him he must return to Egypt to make a sacrifice prefigures the reaction of Odysseus and his companions when Circe tells them that their journey home must include a visit to the Underworld: all of them feel their 'hearts breaking'.[40] And finally, both Menelaus and Odysseus bring great wealth back from their journeys.

Proteus' prophecies do not just serve to tell Menelaus 'which god is pursuing [him] and how [he] may return home over the fish-filled sea' (4.423–4). They also complete the information already given by Nestor about the heroes' homecomings, as Menelaus asks the Old Man of the Sea about their fate: 'But tell me this too, in full and truly. Have all the Achaeans returned by ship unharmed, all that Nestor and I left behind when we sailed from Troy, or has one or another of them perished by some unkind fate on board his own ship, or in the arms of his kinsmen at the war's end?' (4.486–90).

The seer reveals in turn the fates of the lesser Ajax, Agamemnon, and Odysseus as well as Menelaus' own destiny after his death, for Proteus, like Calchas and the Muses, has a knowledge that transcends the boundaries of space and time: he can 'see' (*ἴδον*, 4.556) Odysseus weeping on Calypso's island. Like them, he can also identify which god is behind events (in contrast to normal mortals who can only

[36] *Odyssey*, 1.3–4 (Odysseus) and 4.81, 267–8 (Menelaus).

[37] *Odyssey*, 9.80–1 (Odysseus) and 4.514–15 (Menelaus).

[38] *Odyssey*, 4.363–424 (Eidothea) and 5.363–446 (Ino-Leucothea).

[39] *Odyssey*, 4.389–90 = 10.539–40.

[40] *Odyssey*, 4.481 (Menelaus), 10.496 (Odysseus), and 566 (his companions): *κατεκλάσθη φίλον ἦτορ*.

suspect divine intervention and attribute it, in a vague manner, to one god or several gods (θέος, θέοι), a divinity (δαίμων), or to Zeus).[41] He knows, for example, that it was Poseidon who caused Ajax's ship to sink, because he had incurred the wrath of Athena, and attributes Agamemnon's calm crossing to the favour of Hera.[42]

These two heroes' homecomings, as Proteus describes them, serve first of all as a contrast to that of Odysseus. The story of Ajax, son of Oileus, in lines 499–511 is dominated, like that of Odysseus, by Athena and Poseidon but the roles are reversed. Ajax is hated by Athena but is saved, at first, by Poseidon. Unlike Odysseus, his story ends in disaster: Ajax's insolence provokes Poseidon's anger and he drowns. Agamemnon, who is killed by his enemy working in collaboration with his unfaithful wife, is the opposite of Odysseus who finds a faithful wife on his return and succeeds in taking revenge on his enemies. But Proteus' revelation that Odysseus is a 'prisoner in the wide sea', weeping on Calypso's island, tells us nothing that we did not already know from the first assembly of the gods in Book 1.

The stories are followed by a dialogue which further emphasizes Menelaus' wealth, through the enumeration of the gifts he promises to Telemachus—'I will mark your departure handsomely; I will give you fine gifts, three horses, and a glittering chariot; and in addition to this I will give you a fine goblet' (4.589–91)—as well as Telemachus' observations about the contrast between the poverty of his island and the immense fertile plains of Menelaus' kingdom and, finally, through the description of the crater given to him by Menelaus: 'a finely wrought crater of solid silver rimmed with gold; Hephaestus made it' (4.615–17).

(c) From Sparta to Ithaca

As we saw in Chapter 4 above, the banquet that follows provides the opportunity for a subtle transition to be made between Sparta and Ithaca, as the suitors discover that Telemachus has gone and decide to ambush him on his return (4.624–74). The herald, Medon, allows a further transition to be made from the suitors to Penelope as he tells her about her son's departure and the suitors' plot (4.675–9). From

[41] Jörgensen 1904: 366–7, Strauss Clay 1997: 21–3.
[42] *Odyssey*, 4.500–2, 512–13.

then on the story moves back and forth between the suitors and Penelope and the book ends with a dream that reassures her about her son's fate but also prepares for the transition between Books 4 and 5, and from the adventures of Telemachus to those of Odysseus, with Penelope's question to Athena's emissary: 'If indeed you are yourself divine and have come at the bidding of a divinity, then tell me plainly about that other unhappy one. Is he still alive? Does he see the sunlight? Or is he already dead and in Hades' house' (4.831–4).

6

Odysseus' Travels

The second assembly of the gods marks the transition between the Adventures of Telemachus (Books 1–4) and Odysseus' homecoming (Books 5–13). As in the first assembly, Athena and Zeus speak and the gathering ends with the departure of a god who leaves Olympus to descend to earth. Once again, Athena pleads Odysseus' cause, this time using the same terms as were used by Mentor[1] (whose appearance she adopts at one point) in front of the Ithacan assembly. She also evokes the fresh danger that threatens his son, thus linking the adventures of Telemachus with the *Odyssey* proper. In his reply, Zeus sets out the course of Odysseus' homecoming and sends Hermes to Calypso to tell her of his decision.

This means that only the last two stages of Odysseus' return—the end of his stay on Calypso's island and the Phaeacian episode—are narrated by the poet. Most of the account of his travels is related by Odysseus himself as he replaces the main narrator and tells the tale of his own adventures in Books 9 to 12. His words are said to provoke the same effects as those of the bard, to whom he is compared by Alcinous in Book 11: 'You have told your tale as skilfully as a bard—the toils and trials of all the Achaeans and yourself' (11.368–9).[2] Like Telemachus and the suitors who listen 'in silence' (*σιωπῇ*) to the 'enchanting words' (*θελκτήρια*) of Phemius in Book 1, the Phaeacians are silent (*σιωπῇ*) and held by the spell (*κηληθμῷ δ' ἔσχοντο*) as Odysseus tells the tale of his adventures.[3]

[1] *Odyssey*, 5.8–12 = 2.230–4.

[2] We find the same comparison between Odysseus and a bard and the same emphasis on the 'charm' of his words in Book 17.518–21, where it is made by Eumaeus.

[3] *Odyssey*, 1.325, 339, and 337 (the bard); 11.333–44 (= 13.1–2): Odysseus.

But the hero does not share the omniscience of a narrator who is directly inspired by the Muse. In contrast to the poet, who is able to identify precisely which deity is intervening at any particular moment, Odysseus has no direct access to the world of the gods: he can only suspect divine intervention which he designates vaguely, using terms like *theos*, *theoi* ('a god' or 'the gods'), *daimon* ('deity'), or Zeus (Jörgensen 1904 and Chantraine 1954). The only exception, in 12.374–88, confirms this rule. Odysseus is only able to report the dialogue between the Sun and Zeus because he 'heard all this from Calypso of the lovely hair, who said she herself had heard it from Hermes' (12.389–90). There are further differences between this first-person narration and the 'objective' narration of the principal narrator, as has been shown by the detailed studies of Werner Suerbaum (1968) and Irene de Jong (2001: 223–7).

Since Antiquity, readers have been surprised by the way in which the narration is shared between the poet and his hero and have wondered about its significance. The author of the *Essay on the Life and Poetry of Homer* claims that Homer put the story of some of Odysseus' adventures into the mouth of their hero, for 'these things seem more ingenious and more credible narrated by the man who actually experienced them' (II.162). And, according to Theon of Alexandria, by making him tell his stories to the Phaeacians who were 'story lovers', he allowed him to tell them at length and with plenty of detail.[4] The fact that the author entrusts the narration of the most fantastic episodes to a character who is shown over and over again to be an accomplished liar has also prompted many readers of the *Odyssey* to ask whether Odysseus' tales, which do not emanate from the Muse, are indeed to be thought of as 'true'. The answer is probably 'yes', if one takes into account the fact that they correspond at several points—the story of the Cyclops, the stay on Circe's island, and, less directly, the allusion to Thrinacia and the cattle of the Sun in the prologue[5]—to the main story, as Glen Most (1989: 19) and Hugh Parry (1994) have pointed out, and that the main story is the only valid criterion of 'truthfulness' in the *Odyssey*.

[4] Theon, *Progymnasmata*, ed. M. Patillon (Paris, 1997), 4 (80.5–8).

[5] *Odyssey*, 1.68–75, 2.17–20, and 20.18–21 (the Cyclops); 8.448 (Circe); 1.7–9 (Thrinacria).

1. NARRATIVE AND TEMPORAL ORDER

The dual narrators create a subtle interplay between the order of the narrative and that of the events. The picture of Odysseus imprisoned on Calypso's island is established for the first time in Book 1, with the prologue (1.13–15) and Athena's speech (1.48–59). It recurs in Book 4 when Proteus tells how he saw Odysseus on an island 'weeping most bitterly, in the palace of the nymph Calypso who is keeping him there by force' (4.556–8). In Books 5 to 7.240, the poet narrates the end of Odysseus' stay with Calypso (5.43–269), his journey, including the storm that he endured for two days and two nights off the coast of Scheria (5.282–389), his arrival and meeting with Nausicaa (5.390–6.315), and his entrance first into the town and then into Alcinous' palace (7.1–239).

In Book 7.241–97, Odysseus gives a first account of his adventures, taking over from the poet. He begins by completing the poet's story: he describes Calypso's island (7.244–7), goes back in time to the storm lasting nine days which brought him to Ogygia (7.248–53), the welcome he received from Calypso, and the seven years he spent with her (7.253–60). Then he retells, in his own way, the story of the events that followed that has already been told by the poet: his departure 'when the eighth year came circling around' (7.261), the storm, and his arrival on Scheria. This first narration, which is addressed to Arete, is completed by a second narration (9.1–12.453) this time addressed to Alcinous, which goes much further back in time: it begins with the fall of Troy and ends exactly where the narration in Book 7 begins, as we can see from the almost exact repetition of 7.253–6 at 12.447–50. In the first of these passages Odysseus tells Arete: 'I was carried on for nine whole days; in the darkness of the tenth night the gods brought me to Ogygia where Calypso of the lovely hair, the dread goddess lives. She took me in and welcomed me kindly and looked after me.'

> *ἐννῆμαρ φερόμην: δεκάτῃ δέ με νυκτὶ μελαίνῃ*
> *νῆσον ἐς Ὠγυγίην πέλασαν θεοί, ἔνθα Καλυψὼ*
> *ναίει ἐυπλόκαμος, δεινὴ θεός, ἥ με λαβοῦσα*
> *ἐνδυκέως ἐφίλει τε καὶ ἔτρεφεν.*

And in Book 12 he tells his listeners: 'from there I was carried on for nine whole days; in the darkness of the tenth night the gods brought me to Ogygia where Calypso of the lovely hair, the dread goddess with the human voice, lives. She welcomed me and tended me.'

> *ἔνθεν δ' ἐννῆμαρ φερόμην, δεκάτῃ δέ με νυκτὶ*
> *νῆσον ἐς Ὠγυγίην πέλασαν θεοί, ἔνθα Καλυψὼ*
> *ναίει ἐυπλόκαμος, δεινὴ θεὸς αὐδήεσσα*
> *ἥ μ' ἐφίλει τ' ἐκόμει τε.*

Odysseus' next words also make this point: 'Why prolong the tale? Yesterday in this very place I recounted the rest to you and your noble queen, and it irks me to tell a second time a story already plainly told' (12.450–3).

It is also important to note that Odysseus' narration takes up the story where Nestor left it in Book 3. Nestor went further back in time, evoking the sack of Troy (3.130), the quarrel that broke out between the two sons of Atreus, the subsequent division of the fleet into two groups (3.132–57), and the way in which Odysseus at first set out with Nestor and Menelaus but then, after a second quarrel on Tenedos, turned back to join Agamemnon and his men at Troy (3.158–64). Odysseus' narration in Book 9 opens with this second departure from Troy. This interplay between the chronological order of events and the order in which they are narrated can be represented as follows:

Troy / storm / on Calypso's island / departure / storm / arrival at Phaeacia
5.1–6.331: narrated by Homer
7.241–297: narrated by Odysseus to Arete
9.1–12.453: narrated by Odysseus to Alcinous.

Further complexities emerge when we look more closely, particularly if we take account of brief allusions and references to earlier events. The first example to note is in the words of Athena/Mentes in Book 1: 'Surely Odysseus is somewhere still, not dead but alive—in some wave-washed island, it may be, with wide ocean all around him, held by brutish and unfeeling men whose prisoner he has become' (1.196–9). This information is half true (Odysseus is indeed trapped on an island, as is emphasized by the almost exact repetition of 1.197 at 4.198 where Proteus hints at Odysseus' fate) but it is also half false, given that Odysseus is the prisoner of goddess Calypso and not of 'brutish and unfeeling men'.

We may also note that several of the episodes of Odysseus' travels are foretold by Circe's prophecies in Book 10.488–540 and Book 12.37–141, and by Tiresias' prophecies in Book 11.100–37. In addition, Odysseus himself recounts the final stage of his journey in Book 16: 'I was brought here by the Phaeacians, famous seamen whose custom it is to take back to his own country any stranger who comes to theirs. They conveyed me asleep in their rapid vessel, set me ashore on Ithaca and gave me splendid gifts' (16.227–30).

Once he is reunited with Penelope in Book 23 he tells her the story of his adventures in a narration that condenses them all down to thirty lines (23.310–41) from the victory of the Cicones to his return to Ithaca on the Phaeacian ship. To conclude this formal analysis of Odysseus' travels, we must look in detail at the composition of the long narration that takes up Books 9 to 12, only being interrupted by a brief dialogue between Odysseus and his listeners.

9.39–61: The Cicones (with three indications of the passing of time: 'at dawn' (52), 'as long as it was morning and the sacred sun was climbing towards the zenith' (56), and 'when day sank down towards unyoking time' (58).

9.62–3: 'From there we sailed on with grief in our hearts; we were glad to be snatched from death, but had lost our dear companions.'

9.67–73: The first storm sent by Zeus.
9.74–5: 'Two days and two nights' spent on land (74).
9.76–9: 'When lovely-haired Dawn ushered in the third day.'
9.80–3a: The second storm off Cape Maleia which lasts 'nine days'.
9.83b–104: 'The tenth day', the land of the Lotus-Eaters.

9.105: 'From there we sailed on with grief in our hearts.'

9.106–564: The Cyclops: Odysseus arrives 'in the dark night' (143) and five days pass between his arrival and his departure, each of which is marked by the formula 'when early-born Dawn appeared with her rosy fingers' (152, 170, 307, 437, 560).

9. 565–6: 'From there we sailed on with grief in our hearts; we were glad to be snatched from death, but had lost our dear companions.'

10.1–27: The island of Aeolus where Odysseus is welcomed and stays 'for a whole month' (14).
10.28: 'For nine days we sailed day and night.'
10.29–55: 'On the tenth day' (29) Odysseus is close to arriving on Ithaca when he falls asleep. His companions open the bag of winds: the third storm which takes them back to Aeolus.
10.56–76: Second stay on Aeolus' island.

10.77: 'From there we sailed on with grief in our hearts.'

10.80: 'For six days we sailed day and night.'
10.81–132: 'The seventh day' (81): the land of the Laestrygonians.

10.133–34: 'From there we sailed on with grief in our hearts; we were glad to be snatched from death, but had lost our dear companions.'

10.135–568: The first stay on Circe's island, with several indications of the passing of time: 'two days and two nights' (142), then 'when lovely haired Dawn ushered in the third day' (144), 'when early born Dawn appeared with her rosy fingers' (187), 'every day, till the year's end' (467) and 'when the year was out and the seasons had circled round' (469), and finally, 'Straightaway Dawn arrived on her golden throne' (541).
10.569–11.13: The sea journey lasting 'the whole day' (11.11).
11.14–19: Arrival at the land of the Cimmerians.
11.20–332: The first part of the visit to the Underworld (or *nekuia*) with Tiresias' prophecies.

11.333–384: Odysseus' narration is interrupted by a dialogue with his hosts.

11.385–640: The second part of the visit to the Underworld.
12.1–10: The journey back to Circe's island.
12.11–143: The second stay on Circe's island lasting one day: 'when early born Dawn appeared with her rosy fingers' (8), with the burial of Elpenor (9–15), Circe's welcome and prophecies (16–141), 'straightaway Dawn arrived on her golden throne' (142).
12.144–165: The journey.
12.166–200: The encounter with the Sirens.
12.201–59: Scylla and Charybdis.
12.260–402: The stay on the island of the Sun with several indications of the passing time: 'When the third watch of the night had come and the stars had shifted towards their setting' (312), the fourth storm (312–15), 'when early born Dawn appeared with her rosy fingers' (316), 'for a whole month the south wind blew without ceasing' (325), while Odysseus is sleeping his companions kill the cattle of the Sun, they feast 'for six days' (397), and 'When Zeus, son of Cronus, brought the seventh day' (399), the storm comes to an end.
12.403–47: The journey from the island of the Sun to Calypso's island and the fifth storm: 'for nine days I drifted' (447).
12.448–53: Arrival at Calypso's island.

The first thing to note is the formulaic nature of the description of the journey which is organized around a series of storms and trials, where the decisive events often take place on the seventh or the tenth day or on the tenth night.[6] The repetition, on five different occasions, of the formulaic line 'from there we sailed on with grief in our hearts' is the most obvious sign of this but it is not the only one. Twice, a storm breaks out as Odysseus is within sight of the coastline of Ithaca[7] (in the same way, the storm in Book 5 begins at lines 279–80 just as 'the shadowy hills of the land of the Phaeacians' appeared). Twice the storms last for nine days.[8] Such repetitions are even discernible within episodes. In Book 5, the account of the storm that strikes Odysseus as he is within sight of the coast of Phaeacia can be divided into two parts, both with the same structure: first of all a monologue by Odysseus (297–312 and 356–64), then the arrival of a wave that destroys the raft or what is left of it (313–23 and 365–70), the hero clings on (324–32 and 370–5), and, finally, the intervention of a deity who brings aid (Ino, 333–55 and Athena, 382–7).

In addition to these formal repetitions there are also thematic similarities between episodes. The Lotus-Eaters, the Sirens, Circe's potion, and the gentle and deceptive words of Calypso all threaten to make Odysseus and his companions lose their desire to return home.[9] The Laestrygonians are, like the Cyclopes, man-eating giants who throw rocks at Odysseus' ships. On both the island of Aeolus and the island of the Sun, Odysseus' companions commit a fatal mistake while he is asleep: they open the bag of winds, thereby unleashing the storm, and sacrifice the cattle of the Sun, thus signing their own death warrants. The parallel between the Circe and Calypso episodes is clearer still and is even mentioned by Odysseus himself at the beginning of his narration: 'divine Calypso held me within her arching caverns and wanted me to be her husband, in the same way wily Circe kept me in her palace on Aeaea and wanted me to be her husband' (9.29–32).

Finally, Odysseus' arrival on Phaeacia, the last stage of his journey, prefigures his arrival on Ithaca in several respects: on both occasions,

[6] *Odyssey*, 10.81, 12.399 (seventh day); 9.83, 10.29 (tenth day), 12.447 (tenth night).

[7] *Odyssey*, 9.79–81, before the storm off Cape Maleia, and 10.28–30, before the bag of winds is opened.

[8] *Odyssey*, 9.82, before arriving at the land of the Lotus-Eaters; 7.253 and 12.447, before arriving at Calypso's island.

[9] *Odyssey*, 1.56–7 (Calypso); 9.94–5, 97, 103 (the Lotus-Eaters); 10.236 (Circe's potion); 12.41–4 (the Sirens).

he falls asleep near to an olive tree,[10] 'kisses the grain-giving earth'[11], and meets a guide who is either a princess (Nausicaa) or a prince (Athena disguised as a shepherd 'with the gentle air of a king's son').[12]

2. THE LOGIC OF THE JOURNEY

What distinguishes Odysseus' journey from ordinary seafarers' tales, in which the extraordinary adventures are more or less interchangeable, is above all the presence of order and progression (Reinhardt 1996: 72–3). It shows how Odysseus's companions are gradually lost: he leaves Troy with a fleet of twelve ships[13] but sees his fleet destroyed by the Laestrygonians[14] (a fact that makes this episode an important turning point in the story of his adventures). His last remaining ship is destroyed in the storm sent by Zeus to punish his companions' crime after the episode of the cattle of the Sun,[15] and he finally lands on Calypso's island alone, clinging to the keel of his last remaining ship. The story is organized around the list of his losses: the twelve times six men killed by the Cicones (9.60–1), the three companions who taste the fruit, sweet as honey, of the Lotus-Eaters, even if they are finally dragged back to the ships (9.91–8), the four companions eaten by the Cyclops (9.288–90, 344), the senseless death of Elpenor at Circe's house seems to be included entirely to ensure that this episode too counts among Odysseus' trials ('not even from there could I bring my companions away unscathed' (10.551), the six companions of Odysseus devoured by Scylla (12.245–46), before the final shipwreck in which all the remaining companions fall overboard (12.417).

Moreover, the different episodes are linked internally. Odysseus' triumph over the Cyclops is made possible by his visit to the land of the Cicones: the wine with which he makes Polyphemus drunk was a gift to him from 'Maron, Euanthes' son and priest of Apollo patron deity of Ismarus, because we protected him and his wife and child, out of respect because he lived in the god's leafy grove' (9.197–201). The Cyclops episode itself has a direct impact on Odysseus' further travels until he arrives at Phaeacia since it ends with Polyphemus' prayer calling down

[10] *Odyssey*, 5.476–87 and 13.122–4. [11] *Odyssey*, 5.463b = 13.354b.
[12] *Odyssey*, 13.223. [13] *Odyssey*, 9.159. See also *Iliad*, 2.631–7.
[14] *Odyssey*, 10.131–2. [15] *Odyssey*, 12.404–19.

Poseidon's wrath upon Odysseus (9.528–35). Poseidon's hatred not only explains the storms that afflict Odysseus but also the reception given by Aeolus when he returns to his island: if the master of the winds orders him to leave it is because he recognizes him as 'a man whom the blessed gods abhor' and whom divine law forbids him to help (10.73–5).

Although there is no obvious link between the Circe episode and the adventures that lead up to it, it dominates what follows. Circe's first prophecy, in 10.490–540, prompts Odysseus' visit to the Underworld in Book 11 and provides a great deal of detail: she describes the route he will follow as well as dictating the order in which he will meet the shades of the dead as she tells him not to allow any of them to approach the blood before Tiresias has spoken. The story of Elpenor, which brings Book 10 to its close, is above all a way of linking this first visit to Circe with the visit to the Underworld. Elpenor dies before they 'sail on to the house of Hades' (10.551–61) and his soul is the first to approach Odysseus at the beginning of Book 11 (line 51). In Book 12, when Odysseus returns from the Underworld, Circe resumes her role as prophetess (12.37–110): here she foretells the episode of the Sirens, the passage between Scylla and Charybdis (which she makes possible by advising him to sail closer to Scylla), and warns him of the dangers if he or any of his companions touches the cattle of the Sun. Odysseus' visit to the Underworld, which is in fact a long scene of necromancy, is integrated into his adventures as a whole by its place in the centre of the Circe episode and by Tiresias' predictions. The Theban seer explains the cause of Odysseus' past misfortunes—the wrath of Poseidon: 'he is angry because you blinded his son' (11.103)—and also warns him of the dangers that await him on the island of the Sun.

His arrival in the land of the Phaeacians may not be the end of his travels but it is the end of this part of his trials. It is the land where he will be delivered from his suffering, as both Poseidon and Leucothea say (5.288–9 and 345). It is there that Poseidon's power over him is broken.

3. THE GEOGRAPHY OF THE JOURNEY: MYTH OR REALITY?

The reality of the geographical setting for Odysseus' wanderings was a subject of debate in Antiquity. Modern tour companies who offer cruises following 'Odysseus' travels', like the old Baedeker guides that point out the rocks near Acireale that were thrown at Odysseus and his companions by Polyphemus and situate the bay where Odysseus met Calypso on the island of Corfu, are part of a very old tradition. The same applies to books like Victor Bérard's four-volume work on *Les Navigations d'Ulysse* (Paris, 1927–30), the photographs in F. Boissonas, *Dans le sillage d'Ulysse* (Paris, 1931), Ernle Bradford, *Ulysses Found* (1963), W. B. Stanford and J. V. Luce, *Quest for Ulysses* (1974), or Timothy Severin, *Ulysses Voyage: Sea Search for the Odyssey* (1987), and last, but not least Jean Cuisenier, *Le Périple d'Ulysse* (2003), not to mention the many internet sites offering maps of Odysseus' movements.

It is clear that Odysseus' journey begins and ends in real geographical space. He sets out from Troy, he lands in the country of the Cicones, who were mentioned in the catalogue of Trojans in Book 2 of the *Iliad* and who are situated in Thrace by the ancient scholiasts.[16] He then passes Cape Maleia and the island of Cythera. He finally arrives at Ithaca, which may well be the island which bears the name today.[17] But it is clear that Homer's geographical knowledge of Ithaca was somewhat vague: he situates it mistakenly at the north-western extremity of the group of islands made up of Doulichion, Same, and Zante and calls it 'low-lying' (9.25), when in fact it is mountainous, and the descriptions he gives of the island are far from precise. According to Telemachus, it is a land for goats, with no riding spaces or meadows, the exact opposite of a horse-breeding land like Sparta (4.605–8). For Athena, however, it is a model of equilibrium: 'It is rugged; it is no land for horses; it is not ample, yet not poor either; it has corn in plenty and wine as well; it is blessed with constant rain and copious dew; it is good for goats and cattle; it has varied woodlands and water-sources that never fail' (13.242–7).

Once he has passed Cape Maleia, Odysseus is indubitably carried westwards, while the final journey, from Ogygia to Ithaca via Phaeacia, is a movement from east to west. It is equally clear that Circe's island of Aeaea 'where early born Dawn has her dwelling place and her dancing-grounds and the Sun himself has his risings' (12.3–4) is located in the east. But what about the neighbouring countries, like the lands of the Laestrygonians or the Cimmerians? It is difficult to

[16] *Iliad*, 2.846, see also 17.73.

[17] See Bittlestone, Diggle, and Underhill 2005.

place them in a precise location. The Laestrygonians, whose city bears the meaningful name Telepylus ('gate of the far away people'), live 'where the pathways of day and night come close together' (10.86). The Cimmerians are located at the edge of the Ocean, in a place where the sun's rays never penetrate, on the other side of the world from the land of the Ethiopians which the sun never leaves.

These peoples clearly had no real historical or geographical existence, a fact that did not prevent ancient and modern readers from looking for their equivalents in the real world. Herodotus (4.176) situated the Lotus-Eaters on the coast of Libya. Thucydides refers to traditions according to which the Cyclopes and the Laestrygonians were the first inhabitants of Sicily (6.2.1) and the island of Aeolus was identified with the present-day Lipari islands (3.88.1). In the fifth century, the inhabitants of Corcyra (modern Corfu), who were famous for their navy, claimed to be the descendants of the Phaeacians (Thucydides, 1.25.4).

In Alexandria there was a fierce debate between the two leading grammarians, Crates, who considered the Homeric poems to be a mine of reliable information,[18] and Aristarchus, who, according to the scholia on the *Iliad*, maintained that everything the poet said was 'rather mythical, in accordance with poetic licence'.[19] He was followed by the geographer Eratosthenes, who also invited his readers not to look for historical facts in the 'old wives' tales' that are the Homeric poems because Homer, like all poets, only tries to charm his audience and not to instruct them.[20]

The geographer Strabo, for whom Homer was 'the founding father of geography',[21] adopted a middle position,[22] as the Byzantine scholar Eustathius was to do several centuries later in his commentary on the *Odyssey*.[23] Strabo excuses Homer for having combined myth with teaching and with historical information[24] and accepts that everything

[18] See Strabo, 3.4.4 C147.

[19] *Scholia vetera* D to *Iliad*, 5.385: *Αρίσταρχος ἀξιοῖ τὰ φραζόμενα ὑπὸ τοῦ ποιητοῦ μυθικώτερον ἐκδέχεσθαι, κατὰ τὴν ποιητικὴν ἐξουσίαν.*

[20] See Strabo, 1.2.17 C25, 1.2.3. C7, *γραώδη μυθολογίαν*, and 1.1.10 C7: *ποιητὴς πᾶς στοχάζεται ψυχαγωγίας, οὐ διδασκαλίας.*

[21] Strabo, 1.1.2 C2: *ἀρχηγέτην εἶναι τῆς γεωγραφικῆς ἐμπειρίας.*

[22] See Schenkeveld 1976, Dueck 2000: 31–40.

[23] Eustathius, *Ad Odysseam*, 1.1.6–7 ad proem: *νόμος τοῖς ποιηταῖς μὴ γυμνὴν τὴν ἱστορίαν ἐκτίθεσθαι, ἀλλὰ μύθοις καταπυκάζειν.*

[24] Strabo, 1.1.10 C6: *συγγνοίη δ' ἂν καὶ εἰ μυθώδη τινὰ προσπέπλεκται τοῖς λεγομένοις ἱστορικῶς καὶ διδασκαλικῶς.*

the poet says about the islands of Ogygia and of the Phaeacians, that is to say about lands at the end of the world 'in the middle of the Atlantic', is clearly invented.[25] But he uses the evidence of onomastics, geography, and the material traces left by Odysseus and the peoples he visited to locate most of his journey in the real world. He situates the Lotus-Eaters in Meninx (present-day Djerba) because 'what one sees there is close to the account of the Lotus-Eaters'.[26] Visitors are shown an altar of Odysseus and a tree called the Lotus tree on which delicious fruit grows in abundance.[27] Like Thucydides he places the Cyclopes and the Laestrygonians in Sicily, in the region of Etna and Leontini, and explains their hostile nature by the fact that 'the area around the straits [of Messina] was inaccessible in those days'.[28] Relying on Polybius whom he quotes repeatedly,[29] he also situates Scylla and Charybdis in the same region, because the method of fishing that Homer describes Scylla using resembles the way in which swordfish are caught in the region of Cape Scyllaeum[30] and because his account of Charybdis is reminiscent of a phenomenon known in the straits of Messina, where ships were reportedly sucked under by currents in the waters of the whirlpool, known as Charybdis.[31] He identifies Aeolus as the king of the Lipari islands, which are called 'Aeolian' by some.[32] He acknowledges that there is disagreement about the location of the Sirens, whom some people place on Cape Pelorias while others argue that their home was more than 200 stades away at the Sirenusae, the rock with three peaks separating the gulf of Cumae (present day Naples) from the gulf of Posidonia (now Salerno). But he emphasizes the fact that they are always associated with Sicily and southern Italy[33] and appeals, in support of this argument, to the existence at Naples of the tomb of Parthenope, one of the Sirens,[34] and to the name of the island of Leucosia, 'named after one of the Sirens who was cast ashore when the Sirens had flung themselves, as the myth has it, into the depths

[25] Strabo, 1.2.18 C26: *ταῦτα γὰρ πάντα φανερῶς ἐν τῷ Ἀτλαντικῷ πελάγει πλαττόμενα δηλοῦται.*

[26] Strabo, 1.2.17 C25.

[27] Strabo, 17.3.17 C834. See also 3.4.3 C157.

[28] Strabo, 1.2.9 C20.

[29] See Strabo, 1.2.9 C20, 15 C23.

[30] Strabo, 1.2.15–16 C24–5.

[31] Strabo 1.2.16 C25 and 6.2.3 C268.

[32] Strabo, 1.2.9 C20. See also 1.2.15 C24, 3.16 C57, 2.5.19 and 30, 6.1.5 C256, 2.11 C276.

[33] Strabo, 1.2.12–13 C22–3.

[34] Strabo, 1.2. 18 C26.

of the sea'.[35] Circe's island is identified with the Circaeum, 'a mountain that looks like an island because it is surrounded by the sea on one side and by marshes on the other', where roots grow in abundance and where there is an altar of Athena and a cup which, according to the inhabitants, belonged to Odysseus himself.[36] Finally, Thrinacia, the island of the Sun, is the same as Trinakria, a name for Sicily. The difference in spelling results from the change of τ ('t') to θ ('th') and the disappearance of the ρ ('r') for reasons of euphony.[37]

Modern scholars have continued these speculations. They have situated the Lotus-Eaters on Djerba, or in south Arabia and identified the lotus (rather prosaically) with dates, prickly pears, or jujubes (called *lotus* by naturalists in Antiquity).[38] They have moved the Cyclopes to Capri and the Laestrygonians to Sardinia, made Aeolus king of Stromboli, and made the Sirens sing at Capri. They decided that Scylla and Charybdis could be identified as the straits of Messina (or Gibraltar), that Circe lived on Monte Circeo, in western Italy, that the Phaeacians lived at Trapani, in Sicily,[39] and that the land of the Cimmerians and the entrance to the Underworld must be identifiable with the region of Pouzzoli and lake Avernus or, alternatively, with the British Isles. As for the mysterious island of Calypso, located at the end of the world, it has drifted from Crete to the British Isles via Italy, Malta, Gibraltar, and Madeira.

And why not? Or rather, why? Nothing will stop scholars from letting their imaginations run wild, contrary to the advice of Eratosthenes, the first ancient geographer: 'We will find the location of Odysseus' wanderings when we find the cobbler who sewed the bag of the winds.'[40] But the more sensible ones have long abandoned this quest and admitted that 'Odysseus' travels have nothing to do with geography, and there is more geographical truth in the "untrue" stories he tells to Eumaeus and Penelope than in all the stories told in Alcinous's palace.'[41]

[35] Strabo, 6.1.1 C252. [36] Strabo, 5.3.6 C232. [37] Strabo, 6.2.1 C265.

[38] For a fuller (but incomplete) list of the places proposed by modern scholars see Heubeck 1974: 118–20 and Rubens and Taplin 1989: 112–13.

[39] See Samuel Butler, *The Authoress of the Odyssey*. Heubeck 1974: 119 cites fourteen different locations for Phaeacia from Palestine to Heligoland.

[40] Strabo, 1.2.15 C24.

[41] See Vidal-Naquet 1906: 19.

4. THE STAGES OF THE JOURNEY

Odysseus' perilous return journey is framed by two episodes which are both firmly anchored in the real world: the battle with the Cicones and his arrival at the house of Eumaeus; but this world is the antithesis of the heroic world of the *Iliad*. Odysseus' expedition to the land of the Cicones, who are the Trojans' allies in the *Iliad* (2.846, 17.73), is anything but glorious. It can even be seen as the antithesis of the Trojan War, despite the fact that it is told using formulae that are found in the battle narratives of the *Iliad*. This battle is fought not for glory but for plunder and it is little more than a raid in which men are killed for their goods or their wives. It is followed by an equal distribution in which everyone receives the same share (9.41–2), in contrast to the practice of Agamemnon who, according to Achilles, always kept the best of the spoils of war for himself (*Iliad*, 1.163–7). Even the method of fighting is different. In contrast to the duels of the *Iliad* where the heroes are transported onto the battlefield by chariot, the battle against the Cicones seems to reflect contemporary realities such as the importance of cavalry and hoplite infantry: the Cicones fight 'on horseback' and 'on foot' (9.49–50), but also know how to 'stand firm' and fight 'with bronze-tipped spears' (9.54–5).

Odysseus' arrival on Ithaca and his departure for the hut of Eumaeus the swineherd which brings Book 13 to its close are also the antithesis of the heroic. At this point in the *Odyssey* (13.387–8), Odysseus' martial prowess and the sack of Troy are only evoked in order to underline the contrast with the *Iliad*. This Odysseus, who laments on the beach in Ithaca, unable to recognize his homeland and not knowing where to hide his treasure to keep it safe, is anything but heroic. Following Athena's advice, he then goes to the home of Eumaeus, 'where the swine feed . . . drinking from the deep dark water there and battening upon acorns—good wholesome fattening fare for swine' (13.407–10), details that also transport the listener into a very mundane world. The image of Odysseus the beggar with which Book 13 closes takes us further still from epic grandeur. With his bald head, his wrinkled skin, his dim eyes, and his rags (13.430–8), this Odysseus is closer to Thersites, the very model of the anti-hero, than to the noble warriors of the *Iliad*.

In contrast to this all too human world, the universe in which Odysseus' adventures take place is alternately superhuman and subhuman. To travel through it is to discover a succession of characters embodying the Other and the exotic. These are universal figures in whom several motifs from folklore have been identified, but also characteristically Greek figures who allow us, by contrast, to better understand the definition of normality and the representation of the human constructed by the archaic Greeks.

(a) Sirens and Lotus-Eaters

Situated at either end of Odysseus' wanderings, the Lotus-Eaters and the Sirens[42] are two parallel representations of inhumanity. In opposition to men who, in both Homer and Hesiod, are above all farmers who 'eat bread',[43] the Lotus-Eaters 'who eat flowers'[44] know nothing of working in the fields. And the Sirens' 'flowery meadows' (12.45, 159) have nothing in common with the meadows where the horses and rich herds of Pylos, or the Cyclops' island, graze. Covered with bones and human remains, they are closer to the 'fields of asphodel' where the souls of the dead wander (11.539, 573, and 24.13).

The Lotus-Eaters and the Sirens both make men forget and deprive them of what defines them as human beings, their awareness of belonging to a family and to a community. But they achieve this in contrasting ways. Men who eat the sweet fruit of the lotus 'forget their homecoming' (9.97 and 102) and think only of 'staying with the Lotus-Eaters', precisely because they have lost their sense of identity. The Sirens also prevent their victims from returning home but, to bewitch them, they have no need of plants, relying instead on their 'clear songs' and the 'pleasure' they cause (12.44 and 52). But, in accordance with the paradoxical nature of poetic language in archaic Greece, the song that causes oblivion is also a song of memory and knowledge: they deprive their listeners of their return home by promising that they will return as 'wiser' men.[45] In order to seduce Odysseus, the Sirens who, like the Muses, 'know everything that the Greeks and Trojans suffered in the plain before Troy by the will of the

[42] See Pucci 1998: 1–9, Segal 1996: 213–18, Doherty 1995a, 1995b.

[43] *Odyssey*, 9.89: *οἵ τινες ἀνέρες εἶεν ἐπὶ χθονὶ σῖτον ἔδοντες* and the adjectives *σιτοφάγος* (9.191) and *ἀλφηστής* (1.349, 6.8, and 13.261).

[44] *Odyssey*, 9.84: *οἵ τ' ἄνθινον εἶδαρ ἔδουσιν.*

[45] *Odyssey*, 12.188: *ἀλλ' ὅ γε τερψάμενος νεῖται καὶ πλείονα εἰδώς*. On the impossibility of return see 12.41–5 and Doherty 1995a: 83.

gods and everything that happens on the fruitful earth',[46] call to him with a line borrowed from the *Iliad*[47] and use the memory of his heroic past to compose a song which undermines the ethos of epic even as it imitates its outward form, evoking immortality in order to bring death.[48]

The originality of the *Odyssey* emerges more clearly still when we compare the Homeric treatment of these fabulous peoples with the folklore motifs which inspired them and which are infinitely more fantastical. The Lotus-Eaters seem to be the equivalents of the ghostly beings or evil spirits who offer a certain food to humans to stop them returning to the land of the living (this motif is attested in an extremely wide range of countries and at different periods, from Zulu and Maori legends to the Finnish epic the *Kalevala*) (Page 1973: 14–20). And the Homeric Sirens whose songs alone are mentioned (their physical appearance is never described) are infinitely less terrifying than their sisters depicted on Greek vases or on funerary monuments: the demons of the Underworld with the bodies of birds and women's heads (Page 1973: 86–90).

(b) Cyclopes and Laestrygonians

The episodes involving the Cyclopes[49] and the Laestrygonians, which frame the tale of Odysseus' visit to Aeolus, are both variations on a single theme that occurs in folk traditions from the Caucasus to the North African Berbers.[50] But, in the *Odyssey*, these stories of monstrous beings that serve to illustrate the triumph of intelligence and self-control over brute force[51] are merely a way of investigating the nature of barbarity and civilization.[52]

The Cyclopes are depicted in Book 9 as the antithesis of civilization, even of humanity itself. They know nothing of *themis*, the

[46] *Odyssey*, 12.189–91. For the Muses, see *Iliad*, 2.485.

[47] *Odyssey*, 12.184 = *Iliad*, 9.673; 10.544: δεῦρ' ἄγ' ἰών, πολύαιν' Ὀδυσεῦ, μέγα κῦδος Ἀχαιῶν.

[48] See Reinhardt 1996: 75 and Pucci 1998: 4.

[49] See Reinhardt 1996: 79–83, Page 1955: 1–20, Schein 1970, Calame 1977, Austin 1983, O'Sullivan 1987, Friedrich 1987b, Strauss Clay 1997: 112–25, Bakker 2002.

[50] See Page 1973: 28.

[51] Strauss Clay 1997: 122–4.

[52] See Calame 1977, Vidal-Naquet 1996, Strauss Clay 1997: 112–25, Pucci 1998: 113–30, Bakker 2002.

established rules upon which life in a community depends, and do not live in an organized society: 'They have no assemblies to debate in, they have no ancestral ordinances; they live in arching caves on the tops of high hills, and the head of each family heeds no other, but makes his own ordinances for wife and children' (9.112–15). These lines are of vital importance: in the list of features missing from the Cyclopes' world we can see the first definition of civilization as conceived by the Greeks. They show that, long before Aristotle, man was defined as a 'political animal' who is distinguished from animals solely because he lives in a society regulated by laws. The absence of laws goes together with the absence of religion: the Cyclopes care neither about Zeus who holds the aegis nor about the gods. They do not respect suppliants and have no conception of hospitality: instead of offering their guests a seat at a banquet, they devour them[53] and the only 'gift' (*ξεινήιον*) offered to Odysseus at 9.369–70 is the privilege of being eaten last, an utter perversion of the 'gift' (*ξεινήιον*) that is usually offered to a guest.[54] The fact that Odysseus holds an assembly (*ἀγορὴν θέμενος*) in line 171 and then a sacrifice (*ἐθύσαμεν*) in line 231 only serves to underline the barbarism of the island's inhabitants.

These beings, in addition to being without laws or religion, live in caves[55] and have no houses, which were associated with the birth of civilization for the Greeks.[56] Their primitive nature is also manifested in their lack of agriculture and ships (a detail which, one might add, only makes sense in a society in which navigation, and thus the commerce and colonization which it makes possible, are well developed, all of which points to the Geometric period). The text of the poem underlines this point at length: 'The Cyclops nation possess no red-prowed ships; they have no shipwrights in their country to build sound vessels to serve their needs, to visit foreign towns and townsfolk as men elsewhere do in their voyages' (9.125–9).

[53] Pucci 1998: 117.

[54] See *Odyssey*, 8.389: *ξεινήιον, ὡς ἐπιεικές*, 9.267–8: *ἱκόμεθ', εἴ τι πόροις ξεινήιον ἠὲ καὶ ἄλλως δοίης δωτίνην, ἥ τε ξείνων θέμις ἐστίν*.

[55] As Strauss Clay 1997: 115 has noted, caves in the *Odyssey* are never inhabited by humans but rather by monsters like Scylla or deities like Calypso, Proteus, Eileithyia, and the Nymphs.

[56] In the *Prometheus Bound* (lines 450–3) the birth of civilization is identified with the transition from 'deep sunless caverns' to 'brick houses warmed by the sun'.

If the Cyclopes do not cultivate their land or build ships it is quite simply because they have no need to, living as they do in a kind of Golden Age, in which the earth brings forth food spontaneously: 'The crops all grow for them with no sowing and no ploughing, wheat and barley and grapes that yield wine from ample clusters, swelled by the showers of Zeus' (9.108–11).

Polyphemus, the main character in this episode, is a sort of 'super-Cyclops':[57] 'A monstrous ogre, unlike any man who had ever tasted bread, he resembled rather some shaggy peak in a mountain-range, standing out clear, away from the rest' (9.190–2). Even more asocial than his neighbours, he has neither wife nor children: 'He used to pasture his flocks far afield, alone; it was not his way to visit the others of his tribe; he kept aloof with his mind set on unrighteousness' (9.187–9). But, like them, he combines contradictory qualities. On the one hand, he is a pastoral figure, a model shepherd (the poem describes at length the orderly nature of his stable and the manner in which he treats his animals 'according to the rules'[58]) who only drinks milk (9.248–9, 297) in contrast to humans, who are wine-drinkers. On the other hand he is a man-eater who, on three separate occasions (9.289, 311, 344), tears apart and swallows two of Odysseus' companions.

But this monster is defeated in the end, with the result that the whole episode can be read as a demonstration of the superiority of civilization over barbarism. The Cyclops is overcome by the effects of a wine that is not the 'natural' wine of his local vines, but the product of human skill. The two are entirely different entities, as Polyphemus himself acknowledges in lines 357–60: 'Earth is bounteous, and for my people too it brings forth grapes that thrive on the rain of Zeus and that make good wine, but this is distilled from nectar and ambrosia.' This solitary creature also falls victim to a group endeavour which shows, long before the myth of Plato's *Protagoras*, the importance of collective organization: Odysseus' companions work together to remove the bark from the olive stake which will be used to blind Polyphemus and to smooth it before they thrust it into his eye together. He is therefore defeated by a *technē* that combines cunning

[57] Eustathius notes this in his commentary I.331.28, describing Polyphemus as ἀθεμίστων ἀθεμιστότερος ('the most lawless of lawless beings').

[58] The animals are carefully divided into groups ordered (διακεκριμέναι) according to their age (9. 220–2) and the milking is carried out 'in the right order' (κατὰ μοῖραν, 9.245, 309, 342).

with technical know-how. Odysseus' deceptive speeches allow him to keep his ship safe and to stop the other Cyclopes coming to Polyphemus' aid. He also makes use of carpentry techniques to 'sharpen' the stake and 'harden it in the fire' and the account of how they plunged it into the Cyclops' eye compares their action first to the carpenter's art:

> I myself leaned heavily over from above and twirled the stake round, like a ship's carpenter boring through timber with a drill, while his mates below ply a strap between them to keep the drill spinning and running without a pause. In the same way we grasped the stake with its fiery tip and whirled it round in the giant's eye and the blood came gushing out around the red hot wound. (9.383–8).

He then compares himself to a blacksmith: 'It was as when a smith plunges an axe or adze into cold water, and it hisses loudly at the tempering, though this is what makes the strength of iron; so his eye hissed now with the olive-stake penetrating it' (9.391–4).

But Odysseus' victory is not just an illustration of the power of *mētis* ('cunning intelligence') in all its forms.[59] It also serves to demonstrate that respect for suppliants brings advantages sooner or later. The wine used to overpower the Cyclops was given to Odysseus by the priest of Apollo to thank him for sparing his life and those of his wife and children out of respect for the sacred grove of Apollo in which they lived. Finally, we should also note the moral that Odysseus draws from his opponent's defeat, a moral that is in complete accordance with the poem's emphasis on divine justice and, like the fate of Aegisthus, prefigures the fate that awaits the suitors:[60] 'Your sins were to find you out. You felt no shame to devour your guests in your own home; hence this requital from Zeus and the other gods' (9.477–9).

In essence, the Laestrygonians are simply another set of Cyclopes, as is suggested by the frequent verbal echoes between the two episodes.[61] Like them, they have nothing in common with bread-eating men and are explicitly compared to giants.[62] This cultural marginality carries over into their geographical situation: the Laestrygonians live at the end of the world, in a place where 'the pathways of day and

[59] See Strauss Clay 1997: 113.
[60] See Pucci 1998: 116.
[61] See Heubeck 1983: 228–9.
[62] *Odyssey*, 10.120: οὐκ ἄνδρεσσιν ἐοικότες, ἀλλὰ Γίγασιν.

night come close together' (10.86), with the result that there is eternal light there, in contrast to the land of the Cimmerians who live in permanent darkness.

Like the Cyclops, they know nothing of agriculture: when Odysseus climbs up onto a rock he sees no trace of cultivation in their fields (10.98). Like them, too, they are man-eaters and the parallel between the two groups is further emphasized by the similarities between the account of Polyphemus' meal and that of the Laestrygonian king. Polyphemus 'snatched up (*μάρψας*) two of them and battered them on the ground like puppies; their brains gushed out and soaked the ground. Then tearing them limb from limb he made his supper (*ὡπλίσσατο δόρπον*) of them' (9.289–91), while the Laestrygonian king 'snatched up (*μάρψας*) one of my men at once and made a meal (*ὡπλίσσατο δόρπον*) of him' (10.116).

Finally, the two episodes have similar endings: like the Cyclops, the Laestrygonians throw rocks at Odysseus and his men. But the results are different: Polyphemus only throws one rock at one of the ships in Odysseus' fleet and misses it (the other ships have remained hidden on the small island next to the land of the Cyclopes) (9.48–484, 537–41); the Laestrygonians, by contrast, pelt the fleet with rocks and manage to destroy it: only Odysseus manages to escape with his ship (10.121–4). The destruction of the fleet is, moreover, the only justification for this episode and makes it into an important turning point in the story of Odysseus' wanderings.

But we should not let the similarities blind us to the differences. Compared to the Cyclopes, the Laestrygonians are civilized savages. Whereas the Cyclopes have no political organization and know of no other community beyond the family group, the Laestrygonians live in an ordered society: they have a 'lofty fortress'[63] and a 'town'[64] to where paths lead down from the mountain; they have a 'king' who lives in a 'high palace',[65] not in a cave like the Cyclops; they even seem to be familiar with the assembly as an institution[66] and are capable of acting as a group: when their king summons them, they come running from all directions (10.118–20).

[63] *Odyssey*, 10.81: *αἰπὺ πτολίεθρον*.

[64] *Odyssey*, 10.104, 108: *ἄστυ*.

[65] *Odyssey*, 10.110–11.

[66] *Odyssey*, 10.114: *ἡ δ' αἶψ' ἐξ ἀγορῆς ἐκάλει κλυτὸν Ἀντιφατῆα*.

(c) Aeolus

Aeolus' world is also far removed from 'normal' Greek society, even if it does contain a 'city' and 'fine houses'[67] and prefigures in many ways the land of the Phaeacians. Like Scheria, it is cut off from the outside world: the bronze wall and the cliff that surround it (10.3–4) are the equivalent of the huge expanse of sea that separates the Phaeacians from the rest of humankind. Aeolus' practice of endogamy is even more extreme than that of Alcinous (who is married to his niece) since his six daughters are married to his six sons, in contrast to the usual practice of exchanging women between families as a form of currency that creates social bonds. He is also like Alcinous in that his life is a perpetual banquet and his hospitality is particularly generous: he looks after Odysseus for a month, during which Odysseus repays him with his stories, as he will do in the case of Alcinous: 'For a whole month Aeolus gave me hospitality and questioned me on all manner of things, Ilium and the Argive ships and how the Achaeans sailed for home. I told him each thing in order' (10.14–16). He is also like Alcinous in that he helps him to return home by giving him a bag containing storms and by making a favourable wind blow for him.

But, unlike the Phaeacian episode, this episode does not end with a trouble-free journey home, due to the actions of Odysseus' companions who open the bag of winds. Odysseus is carried back to Aeolus' island by the storm with the result that the episode is divided into two contrasting parts. When Odysseus returns to the palace and tells of his misadventure, the welcoming host is suddenly transformed into an implacable enemy who ejects the hero from his home because this 'friend of the immortal gods'[68] has recognized Odysseus as 'a man whom the blessed gods abhor', whom he is forbidden to help by divine law.[69]

(d) Scylla and Charybdis

Of all the threatening monsters encountered by Odysseus and his companions, Scylla and Charybdis,[70] who are first mentioned by Circe, are without any doubt the closest to the creatures of folktales

[67] *Odyssey*, 10.13: *καὶ μὲν τῶν ἱκόμεσθα πόλιν καὶ δώματα καλά.*

[68] *Odyssey*, 10.2: *φίλος ἀθανάτοισι θεοῖσιν.*

[69] *Odyssey*, 10.73–4: *οὐ γάρ μοι θέμις ἐστὶ κομιζέμεν οὐδ' ἀποπέμπειν | ἄνδρα τόν, ὅς κε θεοῖσιν ἀπέχθηται μακάρεσσιν.*

[70] See Reinhardt 1996: 102–4, Crane 1988: 149–51, and Danek 2002.

and fairy tales: Scylla is a true monster with six heads while Charybdis is a whirlpool which sucks in everything around it three times a day. But, as Circe makes clear when she warns Odysseus of this double danger and advises him to sail closer to Scylla than to Charybdis, one is more deadly than the other 'for it is better to lose six men' (if he sails close to Scylla) 'than to lose all your men' (if the whole ship is engulfed in Charybdis' whirlpool) (10.109–10).

But the primitive nature of the story is balanced by the sophisticated composition involving the splitting of the episode in two. Odysseus in fact makes this hazardous journey on two occasions, the first time with his companions, after escaping from the Sirens (12.201–59), the second time alone, after his companions have been struck by Zeus' thunderbolt (12.426–47). This repetition allows two different aspects of the hero to be highlighted. The first time, the emphasis is on Odysseus' valour, not without a degree of irony given that it makes him cast aside prudence for once. For the hero devotes all his attention to avoiding Charybdis but 'lets [him]self forget Circe's advice' that any armed resistance was futile.[71] He arms himself in preparation to do battle with Scylla and avoid losing any of his companions but, while his eyes are fixed on Charybdis, the monster seizes six of his best men (12.245–6). As Reinhardt (1996: 74–5) pointed out, 'the clash between the heroism of the *Iliad* and that of the fairy tale is nowhere else represented with such a fantastic sense of horror . . . Nowhere do we come across heroism that is so misplaced.' In the second episode, when Odysseus confronts Charybdis alone and clinging to the keel of his ship, he owes his survival to his endurance: he leaps onto the tall fig tree growing above Charybdis and clings on 'steadfastly' (νωλεμέως, 12.437) until the keel and the mast of his ship re-emerge from the deep. The presence of this same adverb in Book 4.288, in the episode of the Trojan Horse, in Book 9.435 in the Cyclops episode, and at the beginning of Book 20.24, when Odysseus resists the temptation to massacre the disloyal maidservants on the spot, is highly significant.

(e) Circe and Calypso

The episodes involving Circe[72] and Calypso[73] might, at first sight, seem to duplicate each other.[74] The two heroines do indeed have

[71] *Odyssey*, 12.116–20 and 226–7.
[72] See Reinhardt 1996: 90–9, Beck 1965, Segal 1968: 420–8, and Crane 1988: 31–45.
[73] See Crane 1988: 15–29.
[74] Crane 1988: 31 n. 1.

several points in common. Both are removed from humankind and associated with harmful powers: Circe is the 'sister of *baneful* Aietes' while Calypso is the 'daughter of *baneful* Atlas'.[75] Both live on wooded islands and invite the hero into their beds. This parallelism is also present in the way the two goddesses are introduced: when they first appear in the story both Calypso and Circe are singing with beautiful voices while they weave.[76] It is easy to see why critics, beginning with Wilamowitz, might have been tempted to assume that relationship between the two was one of model and copy, though without reaching any agreement.[77] But this is to forget that the two episodes are in fact very different both in content and function.

The island of Circe, 'the fearsome goddess with the human voice',[78] is described first of all as a world removed from civilization. Odysseus looks in vain for signs of 'human labour' (10.147) but finds instead 'dense oak trees and woods' (10.150). The forest is inhabited by strange creatures which look like wild beasts but behave like domesticated animals: 'There were lions and mountain wolves that she had herself bewitched by giving them magic drugs. The beasts did not set upon my men: they reared up, instead, and fawned on them with their long tails' (10.212–15). In fact they are men transformed into beasts by Circe's drugs and her wand. But the transformation is not complete as 'their minds were left unchanged' (10.240). Yet, in the end, Circe's dark magic only plays a minor role.[79] As Homer presents it, Circe's story is not only, or even mainly, a story of witchcraft, or to be more precise, a familiar story of a sorceress who transforms her lovers into animals. The marvellous only plays a small role in the episode as a whole. Both the transformation of Odysseus' companions into swine and their return to human form are evoked very briefly in just a few lines (10.238–40 and 388–96). As for the famous *moly*, the divine plant which is the antidote to Circe's magic, three lines are devoted to its paradoxical and divine nature (10.304–6) and Homer shows no interest at all in its workings.

[75] *Odyssey*, 10.137: *αὐτοκασιγνήτη ὀλοόφρονος Αἰήταο* (Circe) and 1.52: *Ἄτλαντος θυγάτηρ ὀλοόφρονος* (Calypso).

[76] *Odyssey*, 5.61 (Calypso): *ἀοιδιάουσ' ὀπὶ καλῇ* and 10.221 (Circe): *ἀειδούσης ὀπὶ καλῇ*. Their weaving is described at 5.62 and 10.222–3 respectively.

[77] For Wilamowitz Moellendort 1884: 122–3, Calypso was the model while Reinhardt 1996: 97–8 argued for the priority of the Circe episode.

[78] *Odyssey*, 10,136, 11.8, 12.150 and 449.

[79] See Heubeck 1983: 229–31.

In general, Circe's palace (*megaron*) has a great deal in common with the royal palaces of the *Odyssey*. It is built of polished stones (10.210–11), has 'shining doors' (10.312), a 'sumptuous bed' (10.347, 480), and 'silver studded chairs' (10.314, 366) with crimson covers (10.352–3). The way in which the goddess welcomes Odysseus' companions is also unexceptional: she invites them to sit down and serves them the same fortifying drink that Hecamede, Nestor's slave, serves to Patroclus in the *Iliad* (11.638–41). Like Penelope and Helen, she is surrounded by servants who prepare the meal and get baths ready for Odysseus and his companions. What is more, the story has a happy ending. As Gabriel Germain put it, 'the treacherous enchantress turns out to be a good fairy'.[80] Not only does she restore the companions to human form but she makes them 'younger, taller and more handsome than they were before' (10.395–6) and Ulysses stays with her of his own free will and spends his time feasting.

It is only when his companions urge him to remember his homeland (10.472) that he asks her to make good her promise to help him return (10.483–4). In fact the primary function of the episode is to facilitate Odysseus' return home. In Book 10, the goddess reveals that he must go to the Underworld, tells him how to get there (10.505–40), and gives him the black ewe and ram that he will need to sacrifice to Tiresias and to the dead (10.571–2). Then, at the beginning of Book 12, she foretells the new dangers he must face (12.37–141) and gives him the means to escape them.

Calypso, by contrast, forces Odysseus to stay with her (*ἀνάγκῃ ἴσχει*)[81] despite his tears and his sorrow.[82] Far from facilitating his return she delays it. True to her name (Calypso is derived from the verb *kaluptein*, 'to hide'), she 'hides' Odysseus for seven years, the time it takes for his return to coincide with his son's accession to adulthood. She keeps him on a remote island (5.55) far from the gods (she is separated from them by 'endless briny waters' (5.100–1)) and from men (she is also far from towns 'where human beings make sacrifice to the gods and offer choice hecatombs' (5.101–2)). And the mysterious name of Calypso's island, Ogygia, is also given by Hesiod (*Theogony*, 806) to the waters of the Styx, the river of the Underworld, and has sinister connotations.

[80] Germain 1954: 249 ('L'enchanteresse perfide finit en bonne fée').
[81] *Odyssey*, 4.557–8 and 5.14–15.
[82] *Odyssey*, 4.556, 5.13, 151–3.

Her island, however, is described in idyllic terms. At the beginning of Book 5 we enter, along with Hermes, into a world which is far removed from civilization. The 'house' (δώματα 1.51) or 'palace' (μέγαρα 4.557) of Calypso is in fact a 'great cavern' (μέγα σπέος 5.57) and the sight at which Hermes 'gazes in wonder' (5.75) is an entirely natural phenomenon. The description of the island (5.63–74) emphasizes the aspects which bring pleasure or delight to the visitor (τερφθείη 5.74)—its cavern surrounded by woods teeming with birds, its vine, its four springs, and its 'soft meadows'—and is the first of a long series of idyllic landscapes in Western literature and painting, from Theocritus to Virgil and from the Esquiline frescoes to Poussin. The traditional welcoming meal also has many marvellous features: Calypso welcomes Hermes by offering him the gods' normal food and drink, ambrosia and nectar (5.92–3). But this serves above all to bring out Odysseus' humanity by contrast. The meal shared by Odysseus, 'the man', and Calypso, 'the goddess' (θεὸς ἠδὲ καὶ ἀνήρ 5.194), has a symbolic importance: 'she put in front of him all manner of things such as mortal men eat and drink' (5.196–7) while she herself is served nectar and ambrosia by her handmaidens (5.199).

Her magic, like that of the Sirens, is entirely verbal and intended to make Odysseus forget his homeland and lose the desire to return. She tries to keep him with her by promising to preserve him from old age and death, a promise whose importance is clear from the fact that it is mentioned three times, in Book 5.135–6, Book 7.256–7, and Book 23.335–6. But she comes up against resistance from Odysseus,[83] who longs 'just to see the smoke rising up from his own land' (1.57–9) and prefers his mortal wife to a goddess's love (5.216–20). This choice of humanity over the divine is also a preference for culture over nature. The description of the natural beauties of the island stands in contrast to the long account of Odysseus' preparations for his departure, with a hero building his vessel alone and fulfilling the roles of woodcutter, carpenter, and sailmaker in turn.

(f) The land of the dead

The *nekuia*[84] that takes up the whole of Book 11 of the *Odyssey* and stands at the centre of the Circe episode is justified by Odysseus' need

[83] See Vernant 1996: 185–9.

[84] See Büchner 1937, Reinhardt 1996: 104–21, Segal 1962: 40–4, Bremer 1975, Crane 1988: 125, Matthiessen 1988, De Jong 2001: 271–95.

to consult Tiresias who will tell him 'the path before him and the long stages of his journey', 10.539–40). But the seer tells him far more than this. In addition to warning him what will happen if certain conditions are not respected during their stay on the island of the Sun, he explains to Odysseus, as Proteus had done for Menelaus,[85] the reason for his misfortunes, predicts the massacre of the suitors, and even goes beyond the temporal frame of the poem by announcing Odysseus' final trial, the journey to a land where people know nothing of the sea, followed by a prosperous old age on Ithaca and a gentle death.

But the *nekuia* is also a spiritual adventure and a moment when life and death are brought into contact. In a poem in which abstract ideals are always expressed in very concrete terms, the distance separating the living from the dead is shown in geographical terms: it is a land situated beyond the river Ocean which, for the ancient Greeks, delimited the inhabited world. As the soul of Anticleia says to Odysseus: 'My child, how have you come, still living, down to this murk and mist? These realms are perilous for a living man to see. They are separated by great rivers and fierce currents, Ocean in particular, which is impossible to cross on foot and needs a sturdy ship' (11.155–9).[86] The gulf separating the living from the dead is also clear from the description of the souls of the departed. In contrast to the living, who see the light of the sun and are defined by their vital energy and their bodily existence, the dead live in darkness, have no mental powers (*noos*) or strength (*menos*), and are no more than insubstantial shadows: 'The sinews no longer hold flesh and bones together; these are all prey to the great power of fire when once the life has left the white bones; the soul takes wing like a dream and hovers' (11.219–22). To emphasize this lack of material existence, the poet of the *Odyssey* compares the souls of the dead to shadows or to dreams, and Odysseus' vain attempts to embrace the shade of his mother, who eludes him (just as the soul of Patroclus eludes Achilles' attempts to embrace him in the famous scene in Book 23 of the *Iliad*), are a vivid representation of their lack of substance.

The spectacle of the dead also reveals the true value of human life, as we see in the dialogue between Achilles and Odysseus. The Achilles

[85] See Reinhardt 1996; 105–8, Matthiessen 1988: 21–2. The parallel is underlined by the use of the same line at 10.539 and 4. 389.

[86] Shewring follows those editors who delete the second half of this passage as an interpolation.

of the *Iliad* was a hero who valued his life less than his search for revenge and glory. He knowingly chose a short and glorious life over a long and uneventful one and was fully aware that he would pay for the death of Hector with his own life, given that his fate was to die immediately after his enemy. But in the *Odyssey* Achilles' perspective on life and death is the exact opposite. When Odysseus praises his godlike status and congratulates him for reigning over the dead after being honoured like a god during his lifetime, Achilles replies, 'I would rather be a servant on earth to a landless man who has little to live on than be lord of all the lifeless dead' (11.489–91).

If we bear in mind that the 'servant' (literally, *thete*, or 'mercenary') belonged to the lowest possible stratum of Homeric society, as he did not even have the advantage of belonging to a household as a slave did, and if we remember Achilles' indignant speech in the *Iliad*, reproaching Agamemnon for treating him as if he were a 'migrant without rights' (9.648), the full significance of these lines with their declaration of the priceless value of life could hardly be clearer.

This is not the only passage in Book 11 which brings together the hero of the *Odyssey* with the heroes of the *Iliad*. Odysseus' encounters with Agamemnon and Ajax also have an important symbolic function. Agamemnon's fate contrasts with that of Odysseus in every way. Clytemnestra, the unfaithful wife who kills her husband in league with her lover, is the complete antithesis of Penelope, and the murder of Agamemnon, slaughtered during a banquet 'like an ox at the manger' (11.411), while his companions are killed 'like white-tusked boars' (11.413), forms a counterpart to the massacre of the suitors which also takes place at a banquet. As for Ajax, his silent presence allows us to perceive the grandeur of the 'bulwark of the Achaeans', a warrior who was honoured as much as Achilles (in the *Iliad*, Ajax is explicitly said to be the best warrior after Achilles). It also reminds us of the famous quarrel over the arms of Achilles that broke out between Odysseus and Ajax and which was settled by 'the sons of the Trojans and Pallas Athena' (11.547) in the former's favour and completes the picture of the contrasting deaths of the heroes. In its implied rejection of life, Ajax's suicide stands in opposition to the deaths at the hands of others of Agamemnon and Achilles, even if the former was as ignominious as the latter was glorious. Alone among the souls of the dead, Ajax stands silent and aloof and does not rush forward to drink the blood that would give him the strength to speak.

These encounters with the dead are also the pretext for a journey through mythology as well as bringing in legendary material from outside the Trojan cycle, first with the catalogue of heroines (11.225–330) and then with the parallel catalogue of heroes (11.568–631). Like the Catalogue of Ships in *Iliad* 2, these two sections are composed of elements all introduced by similar formulae: 'first I saw . . . ' (11.235), 'then I saw . . . ' (11.260, 266, 306), 'and I saw . . . ' (11.271, 281, 298, 321, 326, 576, 582, 593), or 'then I recognized . . . ' (11.572, 601). This type of list is, by definition, infinitely expandable as Odysseus points out when he says: 'But I cannot name and tell every one of them, those princes' wives and daughters that I saw; the night heaven gives us would end too soon' (11.328–30).

In the catalogue of heroines, which has rightly been compared to the Hesiodic *Ehoeae*,[87] Odysseus restricts himself to a list of eight names followed by two groups of three, of which only the last is treated at any length. Each woman is defined by her family relationships, whether her lineage, her husband and (or) divine lover, and the children she bore, and each name can be accompanied by a brief biographical sketch. The order is far from random: Tyro (the first in the list) and Chloris (the sixth) are both related to Neleus, one as mother, the other as wife; Antiope (second in the list) and Epicaste (fifth) both play a part in the legends of Thebes, Antiope being the mother of its founders and Epicaste being the mother and wife of Oedipus; Alcmene (third) and Megara (fourth) are both linked to Heracles, one as his mother the other as his wife; Leda (seventh) and Iphimedeia (eighth) both had divine lovers, Poseidon and Zeus, and both bore twins.

The catalogue of heroes is organized in groups of three with three exemplary heroes framing a group of three criminals. In contrast to the treatment of the heroes of the Trojan War, which emphasized the gulf between life and death, the descriptions of Minos, Orion, and Heracles all show the deceased continuing the activities they practised during their lifetimes: Minos is a king who continues to dispense justice, Orion is still a great hunter, and Heracles continues to provoke fear with his bow. As for the three criminals, the poem only evokes the torments they now suffer and pays very little attention to their crimes. The only misdeed to be mentioned is that of Tityus who assaulted Leto, one of Zeus' lovers, which rather contradicts the moralizing message that some readers have attributed to this passage.

[87] See, for example, Crane 1988: 96–100 and Matthiessen 1988: 31–3.

(g) The island of the Sun

The element of the marvellous is also reduced to a minimum in the episode on the island of the Sun.[88] It is entirely confined to the end, at the point where the animals sacrificed by Odysseus' companions seem to return to life: their hides begin to move and the pieces of flesh on the spits begin to bellow. These 'wonders' (*teraa* 12.394) are far from gratuitous. They fulfil a clear didactic function, illustrating the anger of the gods against those who have offended them. This religious perspective dominates the episode which, like the story of Aegisthus with which it is closely linked in the prologue, plays a central role in the theology of the *Odyssey*.

Like Aegisthus, Odysseus' companions die because they have committed an offence that they were specifically warned against. By killing the cattle of the Sun the companions are guilty of harming the property of a god (this crime is far from being a purely mythological motif: in several parts of Greece, in Cape Tenarus in Laconia or Gortyn on Crete, there were herds consecrated to the Sun which it was forbidden to slaughter). They also break their oath, since Odysseus had made them swear solemnly that they would not touch the cattle (12.298–304). Finally, they commit multiple infractions of the proper ritual, as we see from the comparison with the 'good' sacrifice at Pylos in Book 3.430–63. Before killing the victim, Nestor makes a preliminary offering of grains of barley (these were normally scattered on the altar in front of the victims); Odysseus' companions substitute an offering of oak leaves 'because they had no barley-meal in the ship' (12.358). After the victim has been slaughtered, Nestor makes a libation and pours the flame-coloured wine over the meat but the companions use only water because 'they had no wine to make libation' (12.362).

(h) The Phaeacians: between two worlds

The last stop on Odysseus' journey is the one to which most space is devoted. Odysseus arrives on Scheria at the end of Book 5 and does

[88] On this episode as a whole see Schadewaldt 1960, Andersen 1973, Friedrich 1987a, Segal 1992a.

not leave the island until the beginning of Book 13.[89] This land which stands at the crossroads between two worlds functions as a transition between the mythical universe of Odysseus' adventures and the real world of Ithaca,[90] just as the Cicones formed the transition between Troy and the land of the Lotus-Eaters at the beginning of his voyage.

Scheria, with its fleet and its highly developed civilization, has been linked to Euboea,[91] where the epic dialect seems to have reached its final form[92] and where the *Odyssey* may have been composed.[93] Alcinous' palace has also been compared to those of the ancient Near East or Mycenae.[94] But Phaeacia is above all an idealized image. The Phaeacians are a people 'close to the gods' (5.35, 19.279) and are as mythical as the Cyclopes, who represent their antithesis in every respect. The Phaeacians are civilized beings who live in a city and are expert mariners and generous hosts, while the Cyclopes have no organized society, know nothing of seafaring, and hold the laws of hospitality in contempt.[95] As always in Homer, the distance that exists between the Phaeacians and the rest of humankind is expressed in concrete geographical terms. They live in 'shadowy mountains' (5.279, 7.268), 'far removed from bread-eating mankind' (6.8), 'apart, with the billowing sea all around, at the world's edge' (6.204). Like all Eldorados, their country is hard to reach: 'Here were no harbours for ships to rest in, no roadsteads either; only jutting headlands and reefs and crags' (5.404–5).

This place, situated outside normal geographical space, is a land of contrasts in which wildness exists side by side with the highest degree of civilization. This duality becomes apparent from the moment when Odysseus arrives. The island is covered in dense woodland and at first only affords him a natural shelter (5.478–80), more fitting for a beast than for a man (it is no accident that the same formulae are used at 19.440–2 to describe the lair of the boar that wounded the young Odysseus), and a simple bed of leaves. But it also has, growing alongside a wild olive tree, a grafted, cultivated tree, just like those

[89] On the Phaeacian episode see Mattes 1958, Reinhardt 1996: 121–32, Segal 1962, Rose 1969, Strauss Clay 1997: 125–132, Krischer 1985, Luther 2006b.

[90] Segal 1962: 27, Cook 1995: 240, Luther 2006b: 78.

[91] See Dougherty 2001: 143–57, West 1988: 166, and Ruijgh 2000: 217.

[92] West 1988: 166.

[93] Ruigh 2000: 217.

[94] Dougherty 2001: 104–11, Cook 2004.

[95] Segal 1962: 33–5, Vidal-Naquet 1996: 47–8, Dougherty 2001: 122–42.

that are grown on Ithaca,[96] as well as 'cultivated fields' (7.44–5) and a true city with 'long, high palisaded walls' (7.44–5) and an assembly-place 'set with huge blocks of stone bedded deep' (6.266–7). The parallel with Ithaca is further emphasized by Odysseus' reaction as he kisses 'the grain-giving earth' of Scheria on his arrival there, just as he will later kiss the ground on Ithaca (5.463 = 13.854).

The Phaeacians may be far away from other men, but they are the favourites of the gods and even share with the Ethiopians the privilege of entertaining them at their tables, as Alcinous remarks: 'in the past they have always appeared undisguised among us at our offering of noble hecatombs; they have feasted beside us, they have sat at the same table' (7.201–3). They inhabit a sort of Golden Age (Dougherty 2001: 86–91). Nothing illustrates this better than the description of Alcinous' garden as seen through the admiring eyes of Odysseus. It is a garden of marvels. In contrast to the carefully tended garden of Laertes (24.244–7), which only bears fruit in the right season, here 'the fruit never fails or flags all year round, winter or summer; here the west wind is always breathing—some fruits it brings to birth, some to ripeness. Pear upon pear matures to fullness, apple on apple, grape-cluster on grape-cluster, fig on fig' (7.117–21).

The splendour of Alcinous' palace far surpasses that of ordinary palaces. Even Menelaus' palace in Sparta, which also shines with a radiance like that of the sun and the moon (4.45 = 7.84), is no match. Alcinous' palace is the only one to have a 'bronze threshold' (ordinary palaces, like that of Odysseus on Ithaca, only have a 'stone threshold'), walls built entirely of bronze (which are perhaps a poetic elaboration on the bronze plaques that decorated Mycenaean palaces), and a frieze of blue enamel, not to mention the profusion of gold and silver.[97] And the only equivalents of the gold and silver dogs, the product of the divine craftsman Hephaestus' art, that watch over it, deathless and never ageing (7.91–4), are to be found in the world of the gods, with the golden statues used by Hephaestus as crutches in the *Iliad* (18.417–20). The furnishings are equally splendid, with golden torch-bearers and finely woven coverings (7.96–7) as well as

[96] *Odyssey*, 5.477 and 13.102, 122, 346, and 372 (see also 23.190, 195, 204) on the olive tree from which Odysseus made his bed and 24.246 on the olive trees in Laertes' garden).

[97] *Odyssey*, 7.84–97: on the relationship to Mycenaean palaces see Dougherty 2001: 104–11.

purple coverings on the seats as in the palaces of Menelaus and Odysseus.[98] And apart from Queen Arete only the Nymphs, who are deities, weave purple cloth.[99]

Conflict is naturally absent from this world where, in the words of Baudelaire, 'all is order and beauty, luxury, calm and pleasure'.[100] As Nausicaa explains, 'there is no man living—there never will be—who could come in enmity to the Phaeacian land' (6.201–3) and the Phaeacians' battles against the aggression of the Cyclopes who used to plunder their land are placed in the far distant past when they used to inhabit Hypereia (6.3–4). Athletic contests are the only form of conflict to be found on Scheria. For the Phaeacians 'there is nothing that brings a man greater glory than what he achieves by speed of foot and by strength of arm' (8.147–8). Among these contests, those that approximate most closely to fighting, like boxing and wrestling, are not their strong point, even if they are practised. The Phaeacians recognize this, as Alcinous makes clear when he says, 'We are neither boxers nor wrestlers of renown, but our feet are swift to run the race, and in seamanship there are none to equal us. Feasting we love and the music of strings and dancing; change of garments and warm baths, and the pleasures of the bed' (8.246–9)

The Phaeacians are presented in the *Odyssey* as seafarers first and foremost: 'they have regard only for masts and the oars of ships and the balanced ships themselves' (6.270–1) and their function in the poem is to transport Odysseus back to his homeland. Their strong link to ships (*naus* in Greek) is revealed by their names (their founder is called Nausithous and the king's daughter is Nausicaa) and by the formulaic epithets that are attached to them (in the *Odyssey*, only the Phaeacians, or ships, are described as 'having long oars' (δολιχήρετμοι),[101] they share with other maritime peoples, like the Taphians, the epithet 'oar-loving' (φιλήρετμοι)[102] and their outstanding navigational skills). The description of their city devotes a great deal of space to their two harbours and the only temple that is identified is dedicated to Poseidon. But the Phaeacians are no ordinary sailors. They 'give safe

[98] *Odyssey*, 7.337 (Alcinous), 4.298 (Menelaus), 10.353 (Circe), and 20.150–1 (Odysseus).

[99] *Odyssey*, 6.53, 306 (Arete), and 13.108 (the Nymphs).

[100] Baudelaire, 'L'Invitation au voyage': 'tout n'est qu'ordre et beauté, luxe, calme et volupté.'

[101] *Odyssey*, 8.191 and 369, 13.166.

[102] Taphians: 1.181, 419; Phaeacians: 5.386, 8.96, 386, 535, 11.349, 13.36.

passage to all men' (13.174) and their ships are magical: they need neither steersmen nor steering oars 'but understand by themselves men's thoughts and wills; they are well acquainted with towns and farmlands everywhere; swiftly they pass over depths of ocean, enveloped in mist and cloud' ((8.559–62). The speed and sureness which characterize their ships are conveyed by the two similes used to describe Odysseus' homeward journey (13.81–7). The first compares this voyage to that of a four-horse chariot, implying that the sea is as natural an element to the Phaeacians as the land is to other men. In the second, the ship's speed is compared to that of a hawk, 'the swiftest of birds', a comparison that assimilates it to the journeys made by the gods.

Phaeacia is not just a world in which everything is easier than in the ordinary human world. It is also a political utopia. As we saw above (Chapter 3, p. 485) the foundation of Phaeacia is a model of successful colonization. In contrast to Ithaca, with its conflict between the house of Odysseus and the other members of the aristocracy, the relations between Alcinous, 'on whom depends all Phaeacian power and prowess' (6.197), and the ten other 'kings' are entirely harmonious: the 'Phaeacian governors and counsellors' (7.136), who have the privilege of drinking the wine reserved for chieftains, are permanent guests of Alcinous. They approve all the measures taken by him to honour Odysseus (8.398, 13.16), even agreeing to make up for these gifts by raising a levy on their subjects, as Alcinous suggests at 13.14–15.

The Phaeacians are also pious and hospitable. Odysseus' time there is filled with libations and sacrifices. On the first day, the hero finds them in the middle of making libations to Hermes before retiring to bed (7.136–8). These libations are followed by a further one to Zeus, the protector of suppliants (7.163–6, 179–81). The second day is marked by the splendid sacrifice to Zeus that was announced in Book 7.190–1 and performed in Book 8.59–60 with exceptional magnificence. The third and final day begins with another sacrifice to Zeus (13.24–5) and Odysseus' departure is preceded by another libation to him (13.50–6). The last time we see the Phaeacians, they are preparing a sacrifice of twelve bulls to Poseidon (13.179–85). The only discordant note in this picture of harmony does not last long. Euryalus questions Odysseus' athletic prowess and accuses him insultingly of being a merchant who thinks only of profit (8.159–64). But he then obeys Alcinous and makes amends by giving Odysseus a bronze sword with a silver hilt (8.396–411).

Moreover, the Phaeacians are well aware that 'Zeus is patron of every stranger and every beggar' (6.207–8) and take due care of them: they immediately ask the suppliant to stand up and seat him at the place of honour, next to the king (7.162–71), give him a bath, a bed, and entertain him with the traditional banquet at which he is honoured by being given the chine of the boar, the choice cut, to eat as a sign of esteem (8.475) in addition to other precious gifts. The two-handled cup, silver mixing bowl, and richly embroidered robe given to Telemachus by Menelaus and Helen (15.101–30) are nothing in comparison to the robes, tunics, gold talents, cauldrons, and tripods—thirteen in number in each case—that Odysseus receives, not to mention Euryalus' sword and the golden cup contributed by Alcinous himself.[103]

There are, nevertheless, some discordant notes in this harmonious world.[104] These perfect hosts can also be 'overbearing' (6.274) and have the reputation of being hostile to strangers: 'they do not welcome or befriend someone who comes to them from elsewhere' (7.32–3). This fortunate people is also threatened by Poseidon, according to the prophecy given to their founder which told them that 'Poseidon was angry with [them] for giving safe passage home to all men; and one day when some nobly built ship of [theirs] was returning from such an errand over the misty sea, Poseidon would shatter it and block [their] town with a massy mountain' (8.565–70). But the *Odyssey* leaves the Phaeacians just at the point at which this prophecy is half fulfilled: the ship has been transformed into rock (13.160–4) but the mountain has not yet engulfed their city. It is precisely to escape this fate and to elicit Poseidon's pity that the Phaeacians perform a final sacrifice in his honour (13.184). We are told nothing about the god's response and the Phaeacians' fate is left in suspense (though the behaviour of the gods elsewhere in Homer gives little cause for optimism).

5. ODYSSEUS' TRUE AND FALSE JOURNEYS

In addition to the stories told by Odysseus to the Phaeacians, which supposedly give the 'true' account of his return journey, he also gives

103 *Odyssey*, 8.389–95, 396–411, 418–32, 13.13–15.
104 See Rose 1969.

many 'false' accounts,[105] presenting himself as a Cretan to Athena (13.256–86), Eumaeus (14.199–259), Antinous (17.415–44), and Penelope (19.172–299) and as a citizen of Alybas when he meets his father Laertes (24.265–79, 303–14). These stories are often closely modelled on Odysseus' actual travels and often use the same formulae.[106] They are however more realistic,[107] as is only to be expected given that a lie needs to be credible if it is to be convincing. They are not all heroic, as their hero's goal is profit rather than glory, and they are set entirely in real geographical space: the land of the Thesprotians, Dulichium, Crete, Cyprus, Phoenicia, Egypt, and Libya. They are also rich in genealogical and geographical information which helps to anchor these fictions in the real world.

Two of these tales are presented as the truth. In Book 14, Odysseus says to Eumaeus, 'I will tell you this exactly' (*τοιγὰρ ἐγώ τοι ταῦτα μάλ' ἀτρεκέως ἀγορεύσω*, 14.192). And, in Book 24, he says to Laertes, 'I will tell you everything exactly' (*τοιγὰρ ἐγώ τοι πάντα μάλ' ἀτρεκέως καταλέξω*, 24.303). Odysseus knows very well, like all good liars and like his patron goddess Athena, when she adopts the appearance of Mentes (1.179), that it is particularly important to claim to be speaking the truth when telling a lie. These introductory claims to truth are all the more convincing because they make use of a formula (or its equivalent) that usually serves to introduce a true story in Homeric epic.[108] But occasionally the poet warns his listeners, telling them that his hero 'did not tell the truth' (*οὐδ' ὅ γ' ἀληθέα εἶπε*, 13.254) or by adding a revealing comment at the end of the tale: 'As he spoke he made all these falsehoods seem like truth' (*ἴσκε ψεύδεα πολλὰ λέγων ἐτύμοισιν ὁμοῖα*, 19.203).

These stories share certain elements in common, like storms (13.276–7) and raids. They usually involve the Trojan War (13.263–6) and often refer to Crete, the Cretan king Idomeneus,[109]

[105] Trahman 1952, Blümlein 1971, Walcot 1977, Maronitis 1981, Emlyn-Jones 1986, Hölscher 1988: 210–34, Reece 1994, Grossardt 1998, De Jong 2001: 326–9, appendix E 596–7, Schmidt 2002.

[106] See Emlyn-Jones 1986: 4.

[107] Hölscher 1988: 211, Strauss Clay 2002: 78.

[108] *μάλ' ἀτρεκέως ἀγορεύσω* (seven occurrences in the Odyssey), *ἀληθέα πάντ' ἀγορεύσω* (*Odyssey*, 16.61), *μάλ' ἀτρεκέως καταλέξω* (two occurrences in the *Iliad* and one in the *Odyssey*, *ἀληθείην καταλέξω* (four occurrences in the *Odyssey*).

[109] *Odyssey*, 13.259, 14.237, 19.181.

Thesprotians,[110] Phoenicians,[111] and Egyptians.[112] But they are not interchangeable: each one is shaped to fulfil a particular function and to suit different audiences. It is worth examining them in more detail to show how the poet of the *Odyssey* masters the art of variation.

In Book 13, when he is speaking to Athena disguised as a young prince, Odysseus presents himself as a Cretan (perhaps, as an ancient commentator suggested, because the distance between Crete and Ithaca made it less likely that he would be caught out).[113] His invented story provides plausible explanations for his presence on Ithaca and for the treasure in his possession. He claims to have been forced to flee his homeland after killing the son of Idomeneus (leader of the Cretan contingent in the *Iliad*), a story that has several parallels in both the *Iliad* and the *Odyssey*.[114] He then begged a passing Phoenician ship to take him on board with the spoils he had won at Troy, but they were driven off course towards Ithaca where the Phoenicians put him ashore with his possessions.

The story is based on the true story of Odysseus who fought at Troy, killed enemies in a night ambush in Book 10 of the *Iliad*, suffered storms on his return journey, and was finally put ashore, asleep, on Ithaca with his treasure by the Phaeacians, who are the 'mythical' equivalents of the Phoenicians.[115] It also creates a portrait of its protagonist that is perfectly suited to the addressee: when speaking to the son of a king, Odysseus portrays himself as warrior chieftain (he refused to serve under Idomeneus and led his own troops to Troy) and a man worth helping (he killed the son of Idomeneus because he wanted to deprive him of his booty). But when he is speaking to Eumaeus in Book 14, Odysseus tells a tale of woe that is designed to elicit sympathy from a man like Eumaeus, himself a king's son who was enslaved after being kidnapped by Phoenician pirates. Odysseus claims to have been the son of a king by his slave and to have been brought up in luxury before losing everything on his father's death and then falling victim to a 'cunning-witted

[110] *Odyssey*, 14.335, 316, 335; 19.271, 287, 292.

[111] *Odyssey*, 13.272.

[112] *Odyssey*, 17.432.

[113] Scholia to the *Odyssey*, 14.199: ἐντεῦθεν δέ φησιν εἶναι φεύγων τὸν ἔλεγχον, ἐπεὶ πόρρω τῆς Ἑλλάδος.

[114] See the references provided by Heubeck and Hoekstra 1989 to 13.259.

[115] See *Odyssey*, 13.120–1 (the Phaeacians) and 13.282–4 (the Phoenicians).

Phoenician' (14.288).[116] But, in contrast to Eumaeus, the Cretan regains his status by marrying into a wealthy family.

From this point onwards, his adventures are close to those of the real Odysseus and of the Cretan of Book 13. Like them, he took part in the Trojan War and commanded troops alongside Idomeneus (14.235–9). But, like the real Odysseus, he did so against his will and under pressure from public opinion.[117] On his homeward journey a god dispersed the Achaean fleet, as in the real Odysseus' story and also that of the Cretan of Book 13, as we see from the reuse of the formula 'the god scattered the Achaeans' *θεὸς δ' ἐκέδασσεν Ἀχαιούς* at 3.131, 13.317, and 14.242. This Cretan nevertheless returns home without difficulty but then sets out after one month for Egypt (an obvious allusion to the story of Menelaus) where he is taken captive after a raid on the Egyptians goes badly wrong (an episode inspired by the story of the Cicones).[118] There are, however, two important differences. In the story of Odysseus, as told in Book 9, he is as responsible for the disaster as his companions, since it was his decision to attack Ismarus (9.40). But in the story he tells to Eumaeus in Book 14, he attributes all the blame to his companions (lines 259–65). Moreover, there is no comparison between the 'real' episode in which Odysseus only lost a few of his companions and the fictional battle which results in all his men being killed or sold into slavery. Only 'Odysseus', who made himself the king's suppliant, is spared. He then spends seven years in Egypt—exactly the same amount of time that Odysseus spends with Calypso—and amasses a fortune, as Menelaus did. He then sets sail with a Phoenician and, after spending a year with him, travels to Libya. Off the coast of Crete he is shipwrecked in a storm, described in exactly the same terms as the storm which kills Odysseus' companions after the killing of the cattle of the Sun,[119] and survives alone by lashing himself to the mast as Odysseus does in Book 12.[120] He then arrives at the land of the Thesprotians who are at first models of hospitality: his arrival there is exactly like Odysseus' arrival in Phaeacia, with the king's son greeting him, as Nausicaa greets Odysseus, taking him to the palace, and offering him

[116] On the parallels between Eumaeus' story and Odysseus' Cretan tale, see Grossardt 1998: 71–2.

[117] *Odyssey*, 14.238–9. There may also be a vague allusion to this episode at 24.115–19.

[118] See Emlyn-Jones 1986: 5–7.

[119] *Odyssey*, 14.301b–4 = 12.403b–406 and 14.305–9 = 12.415–19.

[120] *Odyssey*, 14.310–13, cf. 12.424–5.

a tunic and a cloak.[121] But, in contrast to the Phaeacians who keep their promise to take him home with his possessions, the Thesprotian mariners take his clothes as they near the coast of Ithaca, dress him in rags and tie him to the mast. He manages to free himself, with divine aid, and to swim to the coast, thus escaping his pursuers, a conclusion that explains his appearance.[122]

In Book 17, speaking to Antinous, Odysseus emphasizes his former prosperity and his generosity to beggars:

> I too had once a sumptuous house of my own; I was rich, and in those days I often made gifts to the wanderer, whatever he and his needs might be. I had servants without number then, and plenty of all those things that make life easy and make men count one as fortunate. But the son of Cronus, such was his will, shattered all this. (17.419–24)

The tale is designed to illustrate to Antinous the mutability of men's fortunes and to encourage him to follow his example and give to the needy.[123] The only part of the story told to Eumaeus that is retained is the raid on the Egyptians that turns out badly because of his companions,[124] but the ending is different: he claims to have arrived from Cyprus and not from the kingdom of the Thesprotians.

When speaking to Penelope, Odysseus claims illustrious ancestors: he presents himself as the grandson of Minos and the younger brother of Idomeneus, son of Deucalion.[125] The only story he tells about himself is his encounter with Odysseus in Crete after violent winds near Cape Maleia had blown the hero off course (παραπλάγξασα) as he made his way to Troy (an episode that is obviously inspired by Odysseus' experience on his return journey when 'as [he] was doubling Cape Maleia [he] was caught by wave and current and wind from the north and was driven off course (παρέπλαγξεν) and past Cythera').[126] This false story is corroborated

[121] *Odyssey*, 14.317–20, cf. 6.228 and 255–7.

[122] *Odyssey*, 14.342–3 ἀμφὶ δέ μοι ῥάκος ἄλλο κακὸν βάλον ἠδὲ χιτῶνα, | ῥωγαλέα, τὰ καὶ αὐτὸς ἐν ὀφθαλμοῖσιν ὅρηαι. See Grossardt 1998: 82–3.

[123] See Russo 1985: 182 and De Jong 2001: 428.

[124] On the relationship of this story to the episode of the Cicones and the story told to Eumaeus, see Emlyn-Jones 1986: 7–8.

[125] *Odyssey*, 19.180–2: this false genealogy is close to the reality described in the *Iliad* (12.117, 13.451–3, 17.608) where Idomeneus is descended from Minos and Deucalion. See Hölscher 1988: 210.

[126] *Odyssey*, 19.186–7, cf. 9.80–1. See also the storms that afflict Menelaus (3.287) and Agamemnon (4.514) off Cape Maleia.

by a whole series of true assertions about the geography and peoples of Crete (19.172–8), a detailed description of Odysseus' clothing with its golden brooch (19.224–34) and of his herald Eurybates (19.244–8), as Polybius and Strabo remarked in Antiquity and as Eustathius points out in his commentary.[127]

In the last and the briefest story, told to his father Laertes, Odysseus again emphasizes the prosperity of his household (24.304–5) and his unwillingness to set out on his journey (24.306–7). But now he no longer claims to be Cretan and transfers his story from east to west, presenting himself as an inhabitant of Alybas (24.304), a place which ancient readers placed in southern Italy, no doubt because of the mention of Sicily in line 307 (ἀπὸ Σικανίης). This is also the only one of the false stories not to have a Trojan connection. It resembles the stories he tells to Penelope, however, in its mention of Odysseus and the reference to the hospitality given to him by the narrator (24.309–13 and 19.185).

The relationships between these intertwined stories become still more complex when, as occurs in several of them, Odysseus himself is introduced as a character. When speaking to the hero's friends and family, the beggar is careful to mention that he met Odysseus at one point and that he shared bonds of hospitality or friendship with him. Thus he tells Eumaeus that, during an ambush, Odysseus managed to find him a cloak; he tells Penelope that Odysseus was his guest in Crete for a period of twelve days, and he claims, when speaking to Laertes, that four years earlier he had received Odysseus at Alybas and given him generous gifts. In conversation with both Eumaeus and Penelope, he reports rumours of Odysseus' imminent return that he claims to have heard from the Thesprotians (14.321–33 and 19.270–90).

The comparison between all these versions of Odysseus' return, which are all variations on the same theme, brings out clearly the virtuosity of the poet, Homer. In addition, it may help us to understand how he was able to create a new *Odyssey* by recombining traditional material in new ways.[128] But the fact that all these stories, true and false, are put into the mouth of the hero and not of the principal narrator serves to create a certain distance between the poet and his character and perhaps to throw doubt indirectly on the truthfulness of the *Apologoi*.[129]

[127] Strabo quoting Polybius, 1.2.9 C20; Eustathius, *Ad Odysseam*, 2.200.12–22.

[128] Trahman 1952: 43. The same argument is also made by Reece 1994, Roisman and Ahl 1996, and Danek 1998.

[129] Strauss Clay 2002: 79–83.

7

Odysseus on Ithaca

As the Phaeacians leave Odysseus sleeping on a beach on Ithaca we might imagine that he has finally come home, but this is far from the case. Odysseus only truly returns home at the very end of the *Odyssey*, when he re-establishes his authority first over his palace, where he is reunited with his faithful wife (Book 23), and then over his kingdom (Book 24), at the end of a chain of events that takes him from the harbour of Phorcys to the house of Eumaeus, where he meets his son and is recognized by him (Books 13–16), from there to the palace, which he enters disguised as a beggar to enable him to test its occupants (Books 17–21), before revealing his identity and wreaking vengeance on those who have been attacking his house (Book 22).

1. FROM THE CAVE OF THE NYMPHS TO THE PALACE

As has often been pointed out, Odysseus' arrival on Ithaca has much in common with his arrival in Phaeacia. In both places he falls asleep near an olive tree (13.122 and 5.476–7), does not recognize his surroundings, and asks himself the same question in the same words: 'Oh, whose land have I come to now? Are the people barbarous, arrogant, and lawless, or are they hospitable and godfearing?' (13.200–2 = 6.119–21). On both occasions he 'kisses the grain-giving earth' (13.354 and 5.463), meets a guide who is either a princess (Nausicaa) or a prince (Athena disguised as a young shepherd 'with the gentle air of a king's son', 13.223), and supplicates his interlocutors in almost identical terms, comparing them to gods (which is not without irony in the second case). Both times, the goddess brings about a similar miracle: on Ithaca she 'envelops the island in mist' to stop Odysseus recognizing it (13.189–91), while in Phaeacia she 'envelops Odysseus in a thick mist' so that he can go unseen by the inhabitants (7.14–17).

When he learns from the goddess that he has in fact arrived on Ithaca, Odysseus's first reaction is to demonstrate his cunning by inventing the first of his false life stories. Athena expresses her admiration as a fellow trickster before revealing her own identity. Like the divine assemblies of Books 1 and 5, the dialogue that follows has a programmatic function first and foremost: it sets the action of the following books in motion by sending Odysseus to the swineherd Eumaeus and preparing Telemachus' return to Ithaca. It also sheds light on the relationship between Athena and Odysseus and, in particular, the complicity that exists between two characters with such similar traits, as Athena makes clear: 'Both of us are subtle—you excel all mankind in stratagem and well-chosen words, I am renowned among all the gods for wiles and wisdom' (13.296–9).

This dialogue also serves to remind the audience of the help given to Odysseus by Athena both in Phaeacia and at Troy and shows their continuing cooperation in a way that combines the heroic and the mundane. The goddess begins by finding a safe place in the Cave of the Nymphs to hide the treasure Odysseus has brought from Phaeacia and arranges it carefully before sealing the entrance with a stone (13.366–71). She then tells the hero what is happening in his palace where the suitors 'have been lording it for three years now, wooing [his] noble wife and offering bridal gifts for her' (13.377–8). This information returns us to the depiction of Ithaca in the first two books and also enables Odysseus to avoid Agamemnon's terrible fate by forewarning him of the danger that awaits him. The idea of revenge is first evoked in heroic terms reminiscent of the *Iliad*, as Odysseus asks for Athena's help: 'stand by my side yourself to aid me, implanting in me such strength and daring as when we tore down from Troy the diadem of her glittering pinnacles' (13.387–8). But the means adopted are far from heroic as Odysseus is transformed into a hideous old beggar, a metamorphosis which is the starting point for an ironic exploration of the contrast between appearance and reality unparalleled by anything in the *Iliad*.

Book 14, with its pastoral setting and its humble characters, might seem to be out of place in an epic poem. It opens with a description not of a palace but of a model pig farm whose ordered nature has an important symbolic function. But this description, with its emphasis on the high number of sows compared to hogs, is also a reminder of the way in which the suitors have been depleting the herd, a theme that recurs throughout the book.[1] Odysseus' arrival is recounted in equally realistic terms. The beggar is nearly torn to pieces by 'savage looking dogs' (14.21) which are the exact opposite of the wild beasts who behaved like dogs outside Circe's house, fawning on visitors instead of attacking them. But Eumaeus' intervention restores order and marks the beginning of a passage that places great emphasis on his hospitality.

Here, it is possible to recognize several elements from the hospitality type-scene, but these are adapted to fit the unusual context. Eumaeus begins by inviting his visitor to sit down, but there is no question of offering a 'throne' as in the palaces of Odysseus, Menelaus, or Alcinous.[2] This seat is far more humble: a pile of brushwood with a wild goat's skin spread on top (14.49–50). Eumaeus then prepares the meal himself, in the absence of the usual servants, which makes it necessary for the formulae to be adapted from the plural to the singular form. The main dish is not of 'fatted hog', as these are reserved for the suitors, but of 'young hogs' (14.80–1), which are standard fare for servants. When he offers Odysseus a drink it is not from a drinking goblet (δέπας) but from his own humble cup (σκύφος).[3]

But Eumaeus, being a model host like Nestor, Menelaus, and Alcinous, also knows how to respect the rules of etiquette: he does not enquire into the visitor's identity until he has given him food and drink and takes care during the second meal he offers Odysseus not to forget the gods.[4] The only element missing from this rustic banquet is the bard's song, but this is replaced first by Odysseus' stories, which have the same effect on the swineherd as a bard (17.514–21), and then, in Book 15, by Eumaeus' tale of his own adventures which provoke a feeling of 'pleasure' through their evocation of past sufferings.[5]

[1] *Odyssey*, 14.26–8, 41–2, 81–2, 105–8.

[2] *Odyssey*, 1.130, 4.51, 7.169.

[3] This word is found only here in Homer, at 14.112, and seems to designate a roughly made cup of a type used by ordinary people.

[4] *Odyssey*, 14.45–7, 185–90, and 420–4.

[5] *Odyssey*, 15.391, 393, and 399: τέρπειν.

The dialogue between the swineherd and Odysseus is more than just an opportunity for the hero to display his skill in lying, through the longest and most complex of his false stories. It is the first of a series of tests which Odysseus makes the members of his household undergo:[6] he tests the swineherd to see whether he will extend his hospitality so far as to give him his own cloak to protect him from the cold, asking him indirectly before receiving 'the wide cloak that he [Eumaeus] kept in store as a spare garment to wear when some terrible storm arose' (14.520–2). The dialogue also reveals, through Eumaeus' lamentations, what the household servants feel about Odysseus. Finally, it provides a concrete demonstration of the impact of the suitors' pillaging of his property. It thus complements the picture given in Book 1 of the consequences of Odysseus' absence.

2. BETWEEN SPARTA AND ITHACA

As we saw above (Chapter 4) Book 15 is above all a transitional book that follows first Telemachus and then Odysseus, oscillating between events on Ithaca and at Sparta as it follows Athena's movements. It begins with Athena's advice to Telemachus, which corresponds to her conversation with Odysseus at the end of Book 13: as with Odysseus, she warns Telemachus of the dangers which await him on his return home and tells him what to do when he arrives (15.27–42). The account of the end of his stay with Menelaus (15.56–181) emphasizes the latter's wealth and generous hospitality with the long description of the gifts given to Telemachus (15.101–32) and a final feast followed by libations (15.133–47). It also prefigures the coming revenge through the appearance of an eagle holding a goose in its talons, a sign that is immediately interpreted by Helen in lines 160–78.

Telemachus' homeward journey follows exactly the same path as his outward journey and is without incident except for his meeting with the seer Theoclymenus in lines 223–86. The significance of this encounter is emphasized, as often in Homer, by its length which is here due to a lengthy genealogical digression about Theoclymenus' ancestors (15.225–55). After an embarkation scene following the

[6] *Odyssey*, 14.459: συβώτεω πειρητίζων.

traditional format, the narrative leaves Telemachus in the middle of his sea crossing in line 300 and returns to Odysseus in the very next line. Here, he tests Eumaeus' generosity for the second time (by offering to go to the suitors in the palace 'to see if the swineherd would still entertain him courteously and ask him to stay there at the farmstead, or if he would send him citywards', 15.305–6),[7] a test which Eumaeus passes with flying colours. He then asks him for news of his parents, which provides a new opportunity to dwell on the misfortunes that have befallen his house since Odysseus' departure. Finally, he asks him to tell his own story, which, like the story of Odysseus the Cretan, illustrates the mutability of human fortunes since Eumaeus is a king's son kidnapped and sold into slavery by Phoenicians.

The book ends in lines 495–557 with the arrival of Telemachus and his companions who go their separate ways: Telemachus disembarks and goes to Eumaeus' house while his companions, to whom he entrusts Theoclymenus, set sail again for the town. This arrival is also marked by a presage which corresponds to the one which occurred just before he left Sparta. Here too, a bird of prey (a hawk instead of an eagle) holding its victim in its talons (here a dove rather than a goose) flies to Telemachus' right and presages the victory of Odysseus and his allies, as the seer Theoclymenus reveals (15.525–34).

At the beginning of Book 16, Telemachus' arrival echoes that of Odysseus at the beginning of Book 14. It begins in lines 4–5 with an account of the dogs who fawn on him in silence instead of attacking him. The welcome Eumaeus gives to his master's son and the tears he sheds on seeing him prefigure the reunion between father and son and the tears which they will shed. This is emphasized by a simile which reverses the situation of Odysseus and Telemachus (given that it is not the father but the son who returns after ten years): 'As a father embraces lovingly an only and darling son, one for whom he has borne much sorrow, when after nine years he returns home from a far country, so now did the swineherd put his arms around the radiant prince, covering him with kisses as one who had escaped from death' (16.17–21).

[7] The repetition is emphasized by the repetition of the words *συβώτεω πειρητίζων* at 15.304.

The conversation that follows in lines 22–153 does not introduce any new elements. It recalls once again the crimes of the suitors and gives Telemachus the chance to prove (as he has already done with Athena/Mentes and Theoclymenus) that he knows how to treat visitors and suppliants: he promises gifts to the beggar and to take him wherever he wishes to go. At the end of this conversation, Eumaeus leaves to tell Penelope that her son has returned.

The arrival of Athena, who is visible to Odysseus alone and advises him to 'speak to his son and not hide anything' (16.168), leads to the first of a series of recognitions[8] and sets in motion a sequence of events that will lead to the suitors' deaths. This first recognition is brought about by Athena's wand as she reverses the transformation she had brought about at the end of Book 13 and restores Odysseus' true appearance.[9] Telemachus is incredulous at first and thinks that he is in the presence of a god,[10] but Odysseus manages to convince him (without needing to give him any proof of his identity). He simply repeats his claim to be Odysseus and alludes to the power of the gods who are able to make a man look like a beggar or a handsome young man. The intense emotion that takes hold of father and son is expressed by tears and cries as well as the paradoxical comparison to birds of prey who have lost their young.[11]

In lines 235–9 the two heroes set to work and draw up the plan which will allow them to kill their enemies. Their reunion thus represents the beginning of the war between Odysseus and his followers and the suitors. Readers of the *Iliad* will not be surprised to find a list of the participants on both sides which corresponds to the catalogue of Greek and Trojan forces in Book 2. On the side of the suitors there is a large force, totalling 118 individuals, while the other side consists of Odysseus and his son, with Athena and Zeus. Odysseus' plan is twofold. First he intends to make use of his disguise to test the justice and the generosity of the suitors, a test that will also demand great powers of endurance on the part of Odysseus himself and of his son. He then announces a battle plan that is only partly put into practice, a detail that exercised the Analysts as we saw above (Chapter 1, p. 23). Finally, he swears his son to silence so that he can test the loyalty of all the members of the household.

[8] See Chapter 2 above. [9] *Odyssey*, 16.172–6 and 13.429–38.
[10] *Odyssey*, 16.181–5 and 192–200. [11] See Chapter 2 above, p. 72.

By a simple statement of simultaneity ('thus they spoke... meanwhile the ship... ὣς οἱ μὲν... ἡ δ'... νηῦς... 16.321–2) the focus of the narrative switches from Odysseus and his son to the ship carrying Telemachus' companions. Then, with the account of the herald they send to Penelope and his encounter with Eumaeus (16.335–41), our attention moves to the palace, first to Penelope, who learns of her son's return in lines 335–9, and then to the suitors, who find out in their turn, with the arrival of Telemachus' ship, that their plan has failed (16.342–60). They then go to the agora to hold a 'closed' assembly, 'letting no one else, young or old, sit there with them' (16.361–3), a highly irregular practice. During this assembly, Antinous proposes a new attempt on Telemachus' life but the 'good' suitor, Amphinomus, insists that the gods should be consulted first as it is a 'serious matter' (δεινόν) (16.401–2). The others agree and they return to the palace. Penelope then appears and upbraids Antinous for plotting to murder Telemachus, the son of a man who once saved his father's life (417–33). The suitors' lack of gratitude is also evident in the falsely reassuring speech of their second in command, Eurymachus, who recalls how Odysseus had treated him like his own son in former times and had taken him on his knees (442–4). Penelope goes back up to her room where she falls asleep while Eumaeus, who left the palace in lines 340–1, rejoins Telemachus and Odysseus and tells them what is happening in the town and in the palace (452–3). The book ends with the three men retiring to bed after sharing a meal together.

Book 17 recounts the final stage of the journey that takes Odysseus from the Cave of the Nymphs to his palace. Telemachus arrives there first and is greeted by Eurycleia and the maidservants and then by his mother (17.28–56). He then goes to the agora to find Theoclymenus, whom he had entrusted to one of his companions at the end of Book 15, and takes him to the palace (17.61–83). Telemachus' hospitality is shown at this point, as in Book 1.136–50, in the account of the ritual actions using a series of formulae to describe the ablutions, the serving of the bread, and the sharing of food (17.91–9). The bath which preceded (17.87–90) is another important aspect of the rituals surrounding the reception of a guest. At this point, Telemachus gives a detailed account of his time with Nestor and Menelaus to Penelope, who is present at the meal; the repetition of certain lines from the narrative of his travels serves to demonstrate the reliability of his account.[12] Finally, Theoclymenus gives a more explicit interpretation of the portent seen at the end of Book 15.

The focus changes to the suitors in line 167. As in Book 1, we see them passing the time in front of the palace, this time with javelins and the discus rather than dice.[13] But the image of animals being brought from the countryside and then slaughtered in great numbers[14] serves as a vivid reminder of their excesses and symbolizes the way in which they are ruining Odysseus' household through their consumption. At line 182 there is another transition, which is particularly sudden in that it occurs in the middle of the line. We now return to Eumaeus' hut as he and Odysseus leave it as the evening falls, Odysseus carrying a stick to complete his disguise. Their journey into the town provides the opportunity for a series of contrasts to be drawn. To start with, there is the contrast between Odysseus' true status as the master and his appearance now that he is disguised as a 'miserable beggar'.[15] There is a further contrast between the idyllic setting with all the characteristics of the classic *locus amoenus* (trees, cool water, an altar dedicated to the Nymphs) and the scene of violence and sordid insults that follows as they meet Melanthius, the 'bad' goatherd. He hurls insults at the two men, accurately predicting that the beggar will have stools hurled at him by the suitors if he goes to the palace, and then hits him (17.215–34). This encounter serves as a prelude to the mistreatment that Odysseus will have to endure throughout Books 17 to 20, just as Eumaeus' prayer to the Nymphs that Odysseus may return and put an end to Melanthius' insolence foreshadows the fate that awaits the suitors.

The narrative then follows Melanthius as he joins the suitors in the palace and sits down to eat with them (17.254–60), before we return once more to Odysseus and his companion who have made their way to the palace in the meantime. There is a pause as Odysseus gives a description of his own palace (17.266–8), the building is described as

[12] Telemachus' visit to Nestor which takes up Book 3 is summarized in seven lines (17.109–15) and the visit to Menelaus which takes up most of Book 4 (lines 1–619) and the beginning of Book 15 (lines 1–181) takes up thirty-one lines (17.116–47). In lines 142–6 part of Menelaus' speech in Book 4.556–60 is repeated almost word for word.

[13] *Odyssey*, 17.167–8, cf. 1.106–7.

[14] *Odyssey*, 17.170–1, 180–2.

[15] The Greek text of 17.201–2 (*ὁ δ' ἐς πόλιν ἦγεν ἄνακτα πτωχῷ λευγαλέῳ ἐναλίγκιον ἠδὲ γέροντι*) underlines the incongruity of the transformation by juxtaposing the words *ἄνακτα* ('master') and *πτωχῷ* ('beggar').

large and well constructed but, in comparison with the splendid palaces of Menelaus in Book 4 and Alcinous in Book 7, the reader is struck by its ordinariness. The brief dialogue which follows (17. 269–89) once again emphasizes the mistreatment that awaits Odysseus and his endurance.

The episode which follows in lines 290–327, in which Odysseus' dog Argos dies immediately after recognizing his master, is justifiably one of the most famous passages of the *Odyssey*. This dog 'whom long ago Odysseus had brought up at home but had little pleasure in, because all too soon he had departed to sacred Ilium' (17.292–4) represents the long years he has spent far from his home. The account of his neglect by the servants, who leave him to sleep on the dung heap, covered in vermin, sums up the neglect suffered by the house in the absence of its master. But he is also a model of fidelity: as soon as he 'realizes' (ἐνόησεν) that Odysseus has returned, he wags his tail and drops his ears before dying.

3. ODYSSEUS IN HIS PALACE

With a simple conjunction (δέ) we move from the outside of the palace, where Odysseus waits, to the interior, where Telemachus welcomes Eumaeus and gives him his share of the food. Eumaeus' arrival is the prelude to Odysseus' entrance. This is a decisive moment whose significance is marked by a brief pause (Odysseus 'sits down' at the threshold) and by the contrast between the appearance of Odysseus who is 'in the shape of an old, wretched beggar' and the finely decorated palace (he rests his back against a 'cypress pillar which a master carpenter long ago had smoothed deftly and trued to the line' (17.340–1). At the suggestion of Telemachus and then of Athena, Odysseus begins to move from table to table, begging for food from the suitors (17.345–7, 360–3). But the goddess's words reveal the true motivation: the suitors' reactions will enable Odysseus to distinguish the good and the bad. In Odysseus' world, generosity is one of the essential qualities of a noble man. Here we see the beginnings of a division between two groups of suitors. Some take pity on the beggar and give him food (but one may question whether it is generosity to give without contributing from one's own resources and by distributing the property of others, as Antinous remarks in lines 450–52). At the other extreme stands Antinous, whose behaviour belies his appearance: he does not 'seem the meanest of the Achaeans, but the noblest—a kinglike man' (17.415–16) and yet he refuses even to 'take and give' as Telemachus urges him in line 400, preferring to keep another man's good for himself and to eat instead of giving.

On top of his refusal to give, Antinous makes an offensive gift. At the very moment when he refuses to take bread to give to the beggar, Antinous picks up a footstool and throws it at Odysseus. By using the stool 'on which he rested his feet in the hours of feasting' (17.410) as a missile, Antinous mixes categories that are utterly opposed: feasting and war, as the feast becomes the setting for fighting. But, the transition from one sphere to the other brings about a reversal of values. As Odysseus states in lines 470–2, 'there is no resentment and no distress in a man's mind when he receives a blow in a fight for his possessions, for cattle or for white sheep', and, at the same time, 'it is not right' (*οὐ μὲν κάλ'*, 17.483) to hit a beggar at a feast. The fact that Antinous is criticized by Odysseus and Penelope as well as by the other suitors, added to the structure of the narrative which twice (17.409–12 and 500–4) contrasts Antinous' action with the gifts given by the others, emphasizes the gravity of his crime. The threats he adds—the veiled threat of enslavement, with the allusion to a forced return to Egypt or Cyprus in line 448, or the open threat of death, with the allusion to the young men who could drag Odysseus out of the palace and flay him alive in lines 479–80—help to make this use of violence in the midst of the feast more scandalous still. The imprecations of Odysseus and then of Penelope, as well as the comments uttered by the suitors and by Eurycleia, serve as reminders that the gods are not indifferent and punish such insolent behaviour.[16]

From line 492 onwards, as Penelope learns what has happened, there is a continual movement backwards and forwards between the great hall and the queen's room, as the narrative follows Eumaeus' movements between these two locations before he leaves the palace to take care of his pigs. The end of Book 17 thus begins the preparation for the meeting between Penelope and Odysseus in Book 19, with the queen's request to Eumaeus to 'go and ask that stranger to come to me so he can speak to me face to face' (17.529) and Odysseus' reply: 'I would have you ask Penelope, eager though she may be, to wait in the hall till after sunset' (17.569–70).

[16] *Odyssey*, 17.475–6, 494, 496–7.

The structure of Book 18 is more complex. In one way it is the continuation of Book 17 with a new warning to the suitors and two more scenes in which Odysseus is insulted by a servant and undergoes further mistreatment at the hands of a suitor. But it also introduces two new themes with the confrontation between the real and the false beggars and Penelope's appearance before the suitors. The episode in which Irus, the official beggar of Ithaca, fights Odysseus is a parodic echo of the contest between Odysseus and Euryalus in Phaeacia. Here, the two men, one of whom is 'known all too well for his greedy belly' (*μετὰ δ᾽ ἔπρεπε γαστέρι μάργῃ*, 18.2) and the other simply concerned to 'fill [his] never-sated belly' (*βόσκειν σὴν γαστέρ᾽ ἄναλτον*, 18.364) according to Eurymachus, fight each other for a goat's paunch (*γαστήρ*) full of fat and blood (18.44–5). But there is nothing gratuitous about this episode. It is constructed so as to bring out the contrast between appearance and reality, one of the dominant themes of Books 17–22: on the one side is the braggart Irus who 'had no strength or vigour, though to look at him he was brawny enough' (18.3–4) and on the other the cautious Odysseus who looks like a ragged old beggar but when 'he tucks his rags around his loins, he reveals his fine sturdy thighs' (18.67–8). It also provides an opportunity for Telemachus to assert his authority by formally placing the beggar under his protection in lines 60–5.

This book also provides Odysseus with an opportunity to give Amphinomus, one of the two 'good' suitors who find themselves among the bad ones, a final warning. As with Antinous, Odysseus the beggar uses his own story as an example of the fragility of human happiness and the dangers of arrogant behaviour, in a tone that prefigures that of archaic lyric poetry: 'Earth mothers nothing more fragile than man . . . even I myself seemed once marked out as a prosperous man, but I committed many wicked acts, giving way to my power and strength, relying on my father and brothers. So let no man be lawless; let each quietly accept whatever gifts the gods may grant him' (18.130–42). But this warning will not be heeded, as the narrator makes clear: 'Yet even so he did not escape death; over him too Athena had cast her net, designing him to find death by violence from the hands and spear of Telemachus' (18.155–6).

The narrative then shifts with a *δ᾽ ἄρ᾽* ('and now' 18.158) from Amphinomus to Penelope. But the transition is made less abrupt by the presence of Athena in both episodes. It is the she who 'puts in the mind' (*ἐπὶ φρεσὶ θῆκε*, 18.158) of Penelope the idea of appearing before the suitors 'to open their hearts more widely and win more esteem from son and husband' (18.160–2). Athena's intervention is known only to the reader, since Penelope herself, 'forcing a laugh' (18.163), speaks to Eurynome of the desire that has entered her 'heart' (*θυμός*) to show herself to the suitors despite her hatred of them,[17] adding a further explanation for this strange decision which is equally surprising: she claims that she wishes to go down to the great hall to warn her son not to mix with the suitors. However, she refuses (paradoxically, given the context) to adorn herself and it is Athena's intervention that makes her more attractive. She also chooses this moment to say yet again how much she misses her husband (18.178–81 and 201–5), which seems equally out of place. When she enters the hall, she speaks first to Telemachus, reproaching him for allowing the suitors to mistreat the visitor, which has nothing to do with her original intention (18.215–25).

It is not difficult to understand the critical responses to this series of contradictions and the desire to restore a certain consistency to the text, either by cutting out the whole passage in which Penelope behaves 'almost like a courtesan' by requesting gifts from the suitors,[18] or by deleting one line or another, or by blaming the inconsistencies on the capricious and contradictory nature of female emotions. But the explanation is not to be found in Penelope's psychology or in the origins of the episode, but rather in her effect on the suitors and, above all, on Odysseus.[19] Penelope's appearance here, looking radiant, gives the suitors a new reason to continue their courtship, particularly as the queen tells them that the period of time she promised Odysseus to wait before remarrying is over, now that Telemachus has reached adulthood. Her criticism of their behaviour provokes them to give her magnificent gifts. But the whole spectacle is aimed at Odysseus, who sees his wife for the first time since his return: it is vital for him not only to hear her express in public her sorrow at the absence of her husband, but also to see her resplendent in her beauty and to witness the admiration of the suitors which is revealed in the precious gifts they give and can only 'win her more esteem from her husband' (18.161–2), as Athena planned. Odysseus

[17] *Odyssey*, 18.164–5: *Εὐρυνόμη, θυμός μοι ἐέλδεται, οὔ τι πάρος γε | μνηστήρεσσι φανῆναι, ἀπεχθομένοισί περ ἔμπης.*

[18] See, for example, Merkelbach 1951.

[19] See Hölscher 1996: 135–7.

even attributes his wife's behaviour to a duplicity that is equal to his own: 'patient Odysseus saw with glee how she lured them to make presents to her, stealing their souls with persuasive words, though her heart was set elsewhere' (18.281–3).

Once Penelope has returned to her rooms, Odysseus is once again subjected to insults, first from Melantho, the female equivalent of the goatherd Melanthius (18.321–36), and then from Eurymachus whose behaviour is reminiscent of that of Antinous (18.349–64). The latter's threat of enslavement is echoed in the offer of payment (*misthos*) that would transform Odysseus into a *thete* at the very lowest level of society. Also like Antinous, Eurymachus turns an item associated with the banquet into a weapon, seizing a footstool which he throws at Odysseus, but misses his mark, hitting the cupbearer instead (18.394–8). This earns him criticism from both Telemachus and Amphinomus. The narrative underlines yet again, through the words of the suitors, the inappropriateness of this violent outburst in the midst of the pleasures of the feast: 'We are quarrelling over beggars, and this fine feast can no longer give us pleasure' (18.403–4). At Amphinomus' suggestion, the evening draws to a close with libations and the suitors leave (18.412–28).

Book 19 which is—unusually for Homer—set during the night, represents for the most part a parenthesis in the story. However, it opens and closes with two episodes that move the action forward significantly. It begins with the first steps towards the realization of the plan announced by Odysseus in Book 16: with his son, and with the help of Athena, he takes down all the weapons that were hanging in the great hall (19.1–46). The book ends with Penelope's decision to propose that the suitors compete for her hand in marriage (19.570–99). But it is mainly devoted to the various tests that Odysseus, who is now alone after Telemachus' departure, uses to gauge the loyalty of Penelope and the maidservants.[20]

As in the previous book, Odysseus is insulted by Melantho and the repetition is underlined in the phrase that introduces her speech: 'For the second time, Melantho insulted Odysseus' (19.65). The hero's reply, with its emphasis on the mutability of human fortunes ('I too once lived among men in a sumptuous house' (19.75–76)), reiterates a theme that he had already used in his replies to Antinous and

[20] *Odyssey*, 19.45: ὄφρα κ᾽ ἔτι δμῳὰς καὶ μητέρα σὴν ἐρεθίζω.

Amphinomus. But here the lesson in morality is accompanied by threats which are echoed by Penelope.

Husband and wife are now in each other's presence and everything seems set for a recognition scene between the two. Penelope invites the beggar to sit down and immediately questions him about his origins, using the classic formula: 'Who are you? Where have you come from? Where are your city and your parents?' (19.105).[21] But Odysseus evades the question with a compliment and it is Penelope who tells her own story first, before repeating her request in line 162. Odysseus then spins another Cretan tale in lines 172–202, presenting himself this time as the brother of Idomeneus, king of Crete. But he restricts his story to the elements which are of interest to his audience and likely to win her goodwill, the hospitality he once offered to Odysseus on his way to Troy.

Instead of the expected recognition scene between husband and wife we have Penelope's recognition of the Odysseus of the story. After 'testing' the beggar's truthfulness by asking him to describe Odysseus' clothing and to name his companions (19.215–19), she 'recognizes the signs' he mentions,[22] the purple cloak with its golden brooch, as well as the name and description of the herald Eurybates, and assures him of her friendship and respect. But this reminder of the past only deepens her sorrow. Odysseus then tries to reassure her by saying that he has heard that Odysseus in on his way home, in the land of the Thesprotians, repeating, sometimes word for word, the tale he told Eumaeus but with new details taken from his true story, like the loss of both his companions and his ship after the episode on Thrinakia and the Phaeacians' generous gifts.[23] His story is met with incredulity on Penelope's part, but she repeats her offers of hospitality and begins by asking her maids to bring a footbath and prepare a bed for him. Odysseus refuses the bed, but accepts the footbath only if it is given by 'an old woman who is loyal and who has suffered as much as I have' (19.346–7).

It is now, when it is least expected, that the true recognition of Odysseus takes place, by his old nurse Eurycleia: 'She came closer and began to wash her master, and in a moment she recognized (*αὐτίκα δ' ἔγνω*) the scar. This was the mark made long ago by a boar's white tusk' (19.392–3). The long digression that follows recounts the origins of the scar. It is not merely the consequence of a style 'that knows only

[21] This formula occurs six times in the *Odyssey*.

[22] *Odyssey*, 19.250: *σήματ' ἀναγνούσῃ τά οἱ ἔμπεδα πέφραδ' Ὀδυσσεύς*.

[23] See above Chapter 6 (pp. 155, 183).

a foreground, only a uniformly illuminated, uniformly objective present' (Auerbach 1968: 7), but, like the genealogical digression inserted into the story of Theoclymenus,[24] it is a means of emphasizing the importance of the moment. This recognition, which is beyond Odysseus' control, also allows him to test the loyalty of his old servant, as he had intended at the outset, by insisting on her silence.

When Odysseus and Penelope resume their conversation in line 508, she tells him of the dilemma she is facing: 'My mind shifts hither and thither, wondering if I should stay with my son and keep everything unchanged—my estate, my waiting-women, my lofty-roomed house itself—respecting my husband's bed and the people's voice; or if I should now go with whatever Achaean lord seems noblest as he woos me and offers my kinsmen countless gifts' (19.524–9).

She then tells him of the dream she has had, which is unusual in many respects.[25] Of all the dreams in the *Odyssey* it is one of the few (along with the first dream of Odysseus the Cretan (14.495–6) and Penelope's last dream (20.87–90)) to be told only by the dreamer him- or herself. It is also the only dream in which the message from the gods is not communicated through the speech of a character, but is presented in the symbolic form of an image that must be interpreted.

> I have twenty geese belonging here, and I love (*ἰαίνομαι*) to watch them leaving their pond and eating their wheat; but a great eagle with crooked beak swooped down from the mountain-side and broke all their necks and killed them. So there they lay heaped up inside the house while the eagle soared skywards. Still in my dream I wept and moaned (*κλαῖον καὶ ἐκώκυον*), and Achaean ladies with lovely tresses came and stood round me as I lamented (*οἴκτρ᾽ ὀλοφυρομένην*) this eagle's slaughtering of my geese. (19.536–43)

The general meaning of this dream, which echoes the sign that appeared to Telemachus in Book 15 ('an eagle carrying in its talons a great white goose', 15.161–2), is perfectly clear. It is, moreover, made clear within the dream itself by the eagle, which begins to speak in lines 546–50: the eagle is none other than Odysseus and the geese must be the suitors, an interpretation that is immediately confirmed by Odysseus the beggar, who tries unsuccessfully to convince Penelope that the dream is not a deceptive illusion but is a true prediction of events to come. Penelope then makes a sudden

[24] See above p. 192. [25] See below Chapter 10 (pp. 336–8).

announcement, for which nothing has prepared us, that she is going to propose a contest for the suitors and will marry the winner:

I mean to make a trial of skill with the axes [Odysseus] used to set in line in the hall like the blocks for a ship's keel, twelve of them altogether; he used to stand well away from them and shoot an arrow through the whole line. And now I mean to send this ordeal upon (ἐφήσω) the suitors; whoever among them strings the bow with his hands most easily and shoots an arrow through all twelve axes, that man I will follow. (19.576–9)

This suggestion is greeted with enthusiasm by the beggar, who announces yet again Odysseus' imminent return. The couple separate as the evening draws to its close, Odysseus staying in the great hall while Penelope retires to her room to weep until Athena sends her to sleep.

The narrative then returns, at the start of Book 20, to the great hall where Odysseus is lying awake: he will not fall asleep for another fifty lines, when Athena 'pours sleep upon his eyes' (20.54). Before then, he sees the maidservants going to join the suitors, laughing and joking, in stark contrast to the image of Penelope crying as she falls asleep which closed Book 19. But this spectacle also prompts a deliberation scene whose unusual nature was noted above (Chapter 2, p. 63). It begins with Odysseus' famous address to his own heart: 'Have patience heart (τέτλαθι δή, κραδίη, literally, 'take it upon yourself'). Once you endured (ἔτλης) worse than this, on the day when the ruthless Cyclops devoured my hardy comrades; you held firm (ἐτόλμας) till cunning rescued you from the cave in which you thought to die' (20.18–21).

This monologue, in the form of a dialogue with the speaker's 'heart' (κραδίη), is closely comparable to the passage in the *Iliad* where Odysseus, again, hesitates between two options and speaks to his *thumos* before dismissing it 'but why does my heart debate this?'(ἀλλὰ τί ἤ μοι ταῦτα φίλος διελέξατο θυμός; *Iliad*, 11.407) and deciding for the only possible option. Here, however, we see a dramatic representation of the self-control that is, as we shall see in Chapter 8 (pp. 233–5), one of Odysseus' most important qualities. Here, it is defined as the ability to endure suffering without allowing the desire for short-term satisfaction (in this case the punishment of the disloyal servants) to triumph over the cautiousness which alone will bring success in the long term.[26]

[26] See Williams 1993: 55–8.

This all too human deliberation is followed by a divine epiphany which, like Hermes' appearance to Priam in *Iliad* 24, is very close to a waking dream. It opens with the formula, 'she stood above his head and said to him' (στῆ δ' ἄρ' ὑπὲρ κεφαλῆς καί μιν πρὸς μῦθον ἔειπε, 20.32), regularly used to introduce apparitions in dreams or visitations by the souls of the dead in both the *Iliad* and the *Odyssey*.[27] Athena's first words to Odysseus, 'why are you awake?' (τίπτ' αὖτ' ἐγρήσσεις, 20.33), also allude to this model, but they do so by inverting it. In Homeric poetry, the apparition begins by saying to the dreamer 'you are sleeping' (εὕδεις).[28] And the ensuing dialogue, like the dream sent by Athena herself to Penelope in Book 4, aims to allay the hero's concerns by assuring him of the power of the goddess who is protecting him.

As Odysseus falls asleep, reassured, Penelope awakes, weeps, and prays for death. She also recounts the dream in which she saw Odysseus lying beside her, attributing it to a malicious deity (20.87–90), just as she considered her dream in Book 19 to be a deceptive dream, from the ivory gates (19.564–5). Penelope's dream corresponds to Odysseus' waking vision of his wife standing 'by his head' and recognizing him (20.93–4). The hero then gets up and asks Zeus for a twofold sign, which is duly sent (20.97–121).

The narrative leaves Odysseus at this point and begins to describe the start of the day in the palace with the maidservants going about their business (20.122–3) as Telemachus wakes up in lines 124–7. This description, which also occurs elsewhere in the poem,[29] is expanded by the inclusion of a conversation between Telemachus and Eurycleia, which may be interpreted as a way of underlining the importance of the day that is about to begin and that will see Odysseus taking his revenge on the suitors. The preparations undertaken first by the maidservants and then by the menservants are also described in much greater detail than in the account of the first feast.[30] The account of the beasts arriving to be slaughtered for the suitors is also more elaborate here than in the description of the third feast where the quality of the sacrificial victims was only mentioned in

[27] *Iliad*, 2.20 (Agamemnon's dream), 23.68, and 24.612 (Patroclus' ghost); *Odyssey*, 4.803 (Penelope's dream), 6.21 (Nausicaa's dream).

[28] *Iliad*, 2.23 and 60.

[29] *Odyssey*, 20.125–6 = 2.2–3 (Telemachus) and 4.308–9 (Menelaus).

[30] *Odyssey*, 20.147–62 and 1.109–12.

the case of Melanthius' goats (17.212–14). In Book 20, by contrast, first we see the swineherd arrive bringing 'three fattened hogs, the best there were', then the goatherd brings in his turn 'the best goats in the herd', and finally, the herdsman Philoetius brings 'a heifer and fat goats'.[31] The arrival of the goatherd brings a fresh burst of insults which Odysseus endures as steadfastly as he did in Book 16. It also creates an opportunity for a contrast between the bad servant and the good herdsman, who is a parallel figure to Eumaeus and reacts in exactly the same way to Odysseus. At the same time, the references to the coming revenge become more frequent with the predictions of Odysseus (20.232–4), Philoetius' wish (236–7), and Eumaeus' prayer (238–9).

The transitional formula 'thus they spoke to each other. Meanwhile the suitors . . . ' (20.240–1) takes us from Odysseus and his companions to the suitors. They see a further sign of the vengeance to come (a bird flying off with its prey to their left) which forces them to abandon their plan to kill Telemachus (20.241–6). It is only then that the fourth, and last, of the suitors' feasts begins. It contains, in a more developed form, the motifs that were present in the accounts of the three earlier feasts[32] and, like them, betrays the suitors' transgression of the elementary rules of social interaction. One of them, Ctesippus, does begin by reminding the group of the rules of hospitality which require them to give an equal share to the stranger. He also states that it would be neither honourable nor just to mistreat him and even goes so far as to suggest that any gift given to a guest might prompt him to make further gifts in turn, setting in motion a wider process of exchange (20.292–8) (a reminder of the way in which Odysseus, during his time in Phaeacia, cuts off a large piece of the choice share of meat given to him by Alcinous which he gives to Demodocus, 8.474–83). But Ctesippus' gift (*ξείνιον*) is just as much of a travesty as that of the Cyclops, who promised Odysseus the 'gift' of being eaten last of all.[33] He throws a cow's foot at Odysseus, inviting him to share this 'prized gift' (*geras*) with other slaves like himself (20.296–300). The reproaches voiced by Telemachus, who intervenes here as he did

[31] *Odyssey*, 20.162–3 (Eumaeus), 173–5 (174–5 = 17.213–214) (Melanthius), 185–6 (Philoetius).

[32] See Chapter 2 above (pp. 65–8).

[33] *Odyssey*, 9.356 and 365. Along with 20.296 these are the only three instances of the word (*ξείνιον*) in the *Odyssey*.

in Book 18,[34] and the criticism voiced by one of the suitors, Agelaus, who echoes Amphinomus and repeats his words exactly,[35] emphasize the parallel with Eurymachus' behaviour in Book 18. A little further on, we also find an echo of the veiled threats uttered by Antinous in Book 17.458 and Eurymachus' insulting offer in Book (18.357–61) when the suitors suggest 'putting the two strangers [Odysseus and Theoclymenus] aboard a ship and sending them away to the Sicilians, where they might fetch a good price' (20.382–3). These words make explicit what had remained implicit until now and reveal the logical consequences of the suitors' treatment of strangers. The refusal to show respect to a stranger and to attribute some value (τίμη) to him reduces him to the status of non-persona and makes him into a commodity to be put up for sale.

This demonstration of the suitors' culpability is followed by an illustration of their blindness. The 'gentle words' (μῦθον . . . ἤπιον, 20.326–7) spoken by Agelaus to persuade Telemachus and his mother to accept a new marriage, since it is clear that Odysseus will now not return (20.333), and the good grace with which Telemachus accepts this proposal in lines 339–44, are deeply ironic in the circumstances. The suitors' lack of any moral sense even turns into madness with Athena's intervention:

> Pallas Athena roused among the suitors a kind of laughter they could not quench, because she had driven their wits astray (παρέπλαγξεν δὲ νόημα). The lips they laughed with seemed as it were not their own, and the flesh they were eating was foul with blood (αἱμοφόρυκτα δὲ δὴ κρέα ἤσθιον). Their eyes overflowed with tears, and all their thoughts (θυμός) were of desolation. (20.345–9)

This striking tableau shows a mental deviation (this is the literal meaning of the Greek term παρέπλαγξεν) and a complete lack of self-control: the suitors are unable to suppress their 'unquenchable' laughter and their mouths, which are laughing, are no longer governed by their 'hearts' which only wish to weep. Its significance becomes clear when we compare this to the portrait of Odysseus, the man who has been constantly deviated from his route home (the verb πλάζω and its compound form παραπλάζω meaning 'to push off course' in the active voice and 'deviate' in the middle voice are systematically applied in the *Odyssey* to Odysseus' wanderings, both

[34] *Odyssey*, 20.303–08 and 18.405–9.

[35] *Odyssey*, 20.322–5 = 18.414–17.

true and false) but who has always maintained his self-control. It also shows the suitors' feasts in their true light through its shift from the metaphorical level to the literal: the suitors who 'devour the wealth' (κτήματα δαρδάπτουσιν)[36] of Odysseus are not, as the Trojans are in the *Iliad*, simply compared to 'flesh-eating jackals in the mountains' devouring a stag (ὠμοφάγοι μιν θῶες ἐν οὔρεσι δαρδάπτουσιν),[37] but are said to behave literally like them by eating meat that is 'befouled with blood' (and therefore raw).[38]

It also prefigures the final massacre where it is human blood that mingles with the food, as is emphasized by the use of the verb 'to befoul' at the death of Antinous to describe the horrifying mixture of bread and roasted meats with the 'human blood' spurting from the wound in his throat.[39] The horror of this scene is enhanced by the vision of the prophet Theoclymenus, which follows immediately.[40]

After the seer's departure, Chapter 20 ends with fresh insults from the suitors to which Telemachus offers no response, and with the comments of the poet who contrasts 'the sumptuous meal to gratify their desires' (δεῖπνον . . . ἡδύ τε καὶ μενοεικές) prepared by the suitors with the 'bitter' (ἀχαρίστερον) meal which is about to be served up to them by the hero and the goddess and which is nothing other than the final revenge (20.390–4).

4. ODYSSEUS' REVENGE

Book 21 is dominated by the contest of the bow which will reveal Odysseus' unquestioned superiority over the suitors. But it opens with Penelope and her decision to 'place in the hall before the suitors the bow and the axes of grey iron' (21.3), a decision that is presented here as the result of divine inspiration. The decision has an immediate effect: Penelope goes to the storeroom, taking 'with her sturdy hand' (21.6) the key which opens it (see Chapter 2 above, p. 53). This detail has surprised critics who would prefer to think of Penelope as having a fine or delicate hand. But rather than explaining this as a 'mechanical

[36] *Odyssey*, 14.92 and 16.315. [37] *Iliad*, 11.473–80.
[38] The verb δαρδάπτω is only used in these three lines.
[39] *Odyssey*, 22.21: σῖτός τε κρέα τ' ὀπτὰ φορύνετο.
[40] See Chapter 10 below (p. 344).

use of the formula',[41] or as a sign of appreciation of the plump beauty of the heroine [42] it is important to remember, as Norman Austin points out (1975: 73–4), that this expression emphasizes here as elsewhere the activity of the agent and the energy he or she expends.

The significance of this moment is further marked in lines 13–38 by the story of the bow, a digression that slows the rhythm of the narrative.[43] In contrast to the arms of Achilles which were made by Hephaestus (*Iliad*, 18.468–613) the bow belonging to the character who is a 'man' *par excellence* is a very human object whose story is part of human history. It illustrates the continuity of the family: Iphitus had received it in the past from his father Eurytus. It also provides both good and bad examples of the characteristically human institution of guest-friendship. Odysseus had received this bow from Iphitus, to whom he gave in exchange a sharp sword and a spear to mark the beginning of their friendship. But this same Iphitus, while a guest in Heracles' house, will be killed by his host 'who did not heed the vengeance of the gods or the rites of hospitality' (21.7–9). This past history is entirely fitting for a bow that is to be the instrument of revenge for infractions of the laws of hospitality in the *Odyssey*.

It is Antinous who organizes the contest and he does so in strict order. The first contestant is the 'good' suitor Leodes, who will also be the last to be killed in the massacre in Book 22.[44] His failure is met with insults from Antinous and it prompts the suitors to try to make the task easier by warming the bow. But they all fail. Only Antinous and Eurymachus remain, 'the chief among the suitors and by far the strongest of them all' (21.187). Eurymachus tries and fails and his reaction to his failure reveals the true purpose of the test: 'I am less grieved about the marriage ... what shames us all is to find our strength no match for the strength of King Odysseus: we are not able to bend his bow, and this will be a disgrace to us that generations to come will hear of' (21.250–5). The test reveals unequivocally the superiority of Odysseus, who was able to make an arrow pass through the twelve axes 'standing well away from them' (19.575). From this perspective, the bow plays the same role in the *Odyssey* as Achilles' spear does in the *Iliad* where it is described as 'the huge, heavy,

[41] See Russo, Galiano and Heubeck 1992 ad loc.
[42] Wyatt 1978 followed by De Jong 2001: 506.
[43] See Schein 2002: 95–8.
[44] *Odyssey*, 21.144–66 and 22.310–29.

massive spear which no other Achaean could wield' (*Iliad*, 16.140–2). The contest also draws attention to the qualities of Telemachus who places the axes with admirable skill and would no doubt have managed to string the bow, after three failed attempts, if Odysseus had not stopped him (21.120–9).

Book 21 also prepares directly for Odysseus' revenge with the intervening episode in which he is recognized by his two loyal servants, Eumaeus and Philoetius, who promise their support (21.188–241). As Odysseus returns to the hall with the two men (21.242–4), the contest resumes with Eurymachus' attempt, which also ends in failure (21.245–56). Antinous' proposal to postpone the end of the contest until the next day is met with approval by the suitors (21.256–69) and the appearance of the formulaic verse 'having made libations and drunk to their hearts' content' (21.273), which is usually followed by the departure of the participants,[45] appears to signal the end of the feast.[46] But instead, Odysseus intervenes and asks to try the bow (21.274–84). His request is indignantly rebuffed by the suitors and their spokesman, Antinous, who makes use of one of the few mythological exempla in the *Odyssey* to back up his refusal. Believing that the beggar is drunk, he warns him against the effects of wine by telling the story of the Centaur Eurytion who 'committed crimes' (κάκ' ἔρεξε, 21.298) in the palace of the Lapith king Peirithous, while drunk on wine: 'The heroes were seized with indignation; they leapt up, they dragged the centaur across the courtyard and out of doors, where they lopped off his ears and nose' (21.299–301).

This punishment was not sufficient to deter Eurytion who sparked the conflict between the Lapiths and Centaurs to avenge his treatment and was killed as a result. Comparison with the *Iliad* reveals the sophistication of the *Odyssey*. When, in the *Iliad*, Phoenix uses the example of Meleager in his speech to Achilles in Book 9, or when Achilles uses the story of Niobe when talking to Priam in Book 24, the story contains a warning or a lesson that is completely suited to the listener: like Meleager, Achilles is in danger of losing prizes if he delays his return to battle for too long, and Priam, like Niobe, must agree to eat even after losing a child. The story of Eurytion, by contrast, prefigures ironically the fate of its teller by announcing the fate of the suitors and their allies. In Book 22, the goatherd

[45] See *Odyssey*, 3.342, 395, 7.184, 228, 18.247.

[46] De Jong 2001: 516 speaks of a 'mild form of misdirection'.

Melanthius will suffer a worse fate than Eurytion: he will not only have his nose and ears cut off, his genitals will also be thrown to the dogs.[47] Moreover, Antinous' father will lose his life for having tried to take revenge, like Eurytion, in Book 24.[48]

At this point in Book 21 we might expect Odysseus to respond, but it is Penelope who intervenes to defend the beggar and to criticize Antinous in lines 311–19. Eurymachus then tries to justify the suitors' attitude in Antinous' place (21.320–9). After Penelope's response (21.330–42) Telemachus ends the discussion, asserting his role as master of the house and ordering his mother to leave the hall (21.343–58). The swineherd then brings the bow to Odysseus, hands it to him and orders Eurycleia to lock the doors to the hall while Philoetius goes to fasten the doors of the courtyard shut, in accordance with the plan that Odysseus had shared with his two allies when he revealed his identity.[49] We follow Philoetius as he returns to the hall and watches Odysseus handling the bow, making the string 'sing out' after having strung it like a bard stringing his lyre (21.393–411), a comparison which had been made earlier by Alcinous in Book 11.368–9. This echo serves to underline the contrast between the feasts of the Phaeacians, where pleasure reigns (*χαριέστερον*) as the guests listen to the melodious song of the bard[50] (or his substitute, Odysseus), and the 'bitter' (*ἀχαρίστερον*, 20.392) banquet that Odysseus and Athena are about to serve up to the suitors, accompanied by the sound of the bow.[51] It is now that the hero manages to accomplish the trial of the bow with ease, 'without rising from his stool' (21.420), before giving Telemachus the sign to arm himself.

The vengeance begins in Book 22 with the killing of Antinous which forms the prelude to the general massacre and sets the tone. The death of Antinous as he is about to 'raise a fine two-handled golden goblet' (22.9–10) is more horrifying than the deaths of Euphorbus and Hector in the *Iliad*, even though they are killed in exactly

[47] The parallel is underlined by the partial repetition of lines 300–1 of Antinous' speech, describing Eurytion's punishment (*ἀπ' οὔατα νηλέι χαλκῷ ῥῖνάς τ' ἀμήσαντες*) in the account of Melanthius' punishment at 22.475–6 (*τοῦ δ' ἀπὸ μὲν ῥῖνάς τε καὶ οὔατα νηλέι χαλκῷ τάμνον, μήδεά τ' ἐξέρυσαν, κυσὶν ὠμὰ δάσασθαι*).

[48] *Odyssey*, 24.469–71 and 523–5.

[49] The plan is revealed at 21.234–41 and put into practice at 21.359–91.

[50] *Odyssey*, 9.5–7: *οὐ γὰρ ἐγώ γέ τί φημι τέλος χαριέστερον εἶναι | ἢ ὅτ' ἐυφροσύνη μὲν ἔχῃ κάτα δῆμον ἅπαντα, | δαιτυμόνες δ' ἀνὰ δώματ' ἀκουάζωνται ἀοιδοῦ.*

[51] *Odyssey*, 21.411: *ἡ δ' ὑπὸ καλὸν ἄεισε, χελιδόνι εἰκέλη αὐδήν.*

the same manner, by a spear whose point 'went right through his soft neck',[52] because of its setting: a banquet rather than a battlefield. It is followed by Odysseus' revelation of his identity and his statement of the offences committed against him by the suitors. The suitors make a final attempt to appease his anger, by offering the type of exchange in which they have, up until now, refused to engage. Through the words of Eurymachus they then attempt to attribute the entire responsibility for what has happened to Antinous, acknowledge their crimes, and offer compensation to Odysseus: 'We shall go to the people and gather goods enough to make satisfaction for everything eaten and drunk in these halls. Every one of us will bring his tribute of twenty oxen. We will give you bronze and gold until your heart relents, before that is done we cannot find fault with your indignation (*πρὶν δ' οὔ τι νεμεσσητὸν κεχολῶσθαι*)' (22.55–9). Eurymachus' final words are a formula, also used by Phoenix when he addresses Achilles in Book 9 of the *Iliad*, asking him to reconcile with the Achaeans now that Agamemnon has offered a suitable reward. But Odysseus, just like Achilles in the *Iliad*, refuses the offer of compensation saying: 'Eurymachus, not if you all gave me all your patrimony, whatever you have and whatever more you might come to have, not even then would I hold back my hands from slaughter till every suitor had paid for the whole of his transgression' (22.61–4).

It is now that the massacre begins and, like the suitors' feasts, it is the antithesis of a banquet. The suitors at their feasts were assimilated to wild beasts in their consumption of Odysseus' wealth by the use of the verb *βιβρώσκειν* ('to devour').[53] Odysseus' revenge seems to be similar in nature, as is implied by the signs that predict it as well as the images used to describe it. It is prefigured by the appearance of an 'eagle carrying in its talons a great white goose' (15.161) and then by the dream of 'the great eagle with crooked beak' which 'swooped down from the mountain-side and broke all the necks of the geese' as they ate their grain (19.538–9). It is also represented symbolically on four occasions (an exceptionally high number for a work in which similes are relatively rare) in similar terms. The first example occurs

[52] *Iliad*, 17.49 (Euphorbus), 22.327 (Hector), and *Odyssey*, 22.16 (Antinous): *ἀντικρὺ δ' ἁπαλοῖο δι' αὐχένος ἤλυθ' ἀκωκή.*

[53] This verb is used twice in the *Iliad*, once of a serpent (22.94) and once of Hera who wants to 'eat raw' Priam, his children, and all the Trojans (4.35). It is also used twice in the *Odyssey*, once of a lion who has just eaten an ox (22.403) and once of the suitors who devour Odysseus' wealth (2.203).

in Book 4 and is attributed to Menelaus (and thus corresponds to the eagle's feast of Book 15 which is a sign interpreted by Helen). When he learns of the suitors' excesses and their pursuit of Penelope's hand, Menelaus expresses his indignation at the idea that these worthless men could hope to occupy the bed of such a valiant hero and predicts a miserable end for them:

> As when a fallow deer leaves the twin fawns just born to her in slumber in some great lion's den, while she herself goes roving and browsing over the mountain spurs and the grassy hollows, but then the lion returns to his lair and strikes the two sucklings with hideous death, so will Odysseus strike these suitors with hideous death. (4.335–40)

The same image is repeated word for word by Telemachus in lines 126–31 of Book 17, when he presents his brief account of his voyages to Penelope. It recurs at the end of the massacre of the suitors with the image of Odysseus covered in blood like a lion who has just 'devoured' (*βιβρώσκειν*) an ox (22.401–6).

The massacre in Book 22 is, as Pietro Pucci has noted (1987: 183), the most Iliadic passage of the *Odyssey*. Like the *aristeiai* of the *Iliad*, it gives the hero and his son an opportunity to demonstrate their valour. It is also carefully divided into three parts: after a first episode in which Odysseus kills the suitors with his bow, we move on to a more typical hoplite battle, in which Odysseus and his allies fight using shields, helmets, and spears. The battle takes a further turn with the intervention of Melanthius, who goes to get arms from the storeroom, which allows the suitors to arm themselves and adds a new level of interest to the combat.

We find several of the characteristic elements of 'battle type-scenes' with the god who intervenes to turn the spears thrown at Odysseus away from their target and make them 'futile' (22.256 and 273) while the missiles sent by Odysseus and his allies always hit their mark (22.265–8), or the variations on the theme of the light wound (like the grazes incurred by Telemachus on his wrist or by Eumaeus on his shoulder) followed by the death of the enemy who inflicted it (22.277–86). We also find some similes that are familiar from the *aristeiai* of the *Iliad*. The first, that of cattle panicked by a gadfly (22.299–301), portrays the power of the goddess as she brandishes her aegis (in the *Iliad*, 15.323–6, the panic of the Achaeans when Apollo brandishes his aegis is similarly conveyed by the comparison with a herd of cattle or a flock of sheep harassed by two wild animals). The image of the bird of prey soaring up or swooping down to catch its victim also occurs several times in the *Iliad*.[54] The final simile, comparing the suitors to fish that have been hauled out of the water by fishermen and are dying on the beach (22.383–9), takes up and develops one of the most striking similes in Patroclus' *aristeia*, where he is compared to 'a man sitting on a rocky point [who] hauls a monster fish out of the sea with his line and bright bronze hook' (*Iliad*, 16.406–7) as he pulls an enemy warrior out of his chariot. But the change from the singular to the plural underlines the collective nature of the victory in the *Odyssey*, in contrast to the individual achievement that is so important in the *Iliad*.

We also find a series of three supplication scenes with contrasting results which are reminiscent of the *Iliad*, particularly the passages in Books 20 and 21 in which Trojans beg Achilles to spare their lives. The first of these scenes in *Odyssey* 22 is parallel to that involving Tros and, even more, to the scene with Lycaon.[55] But the different arguments used reflect the contrasting moral universes to which the two poems belong. In his attempt to elicit pity from Achilles, Tros emphasizes the fact that they are the same age in order to elicit some fellow feeling from his adversary. As for Lycaon, he simply reminds Achilles that his relationship to Hector was indirect and that his status as suppliant should bring him some respect. Liodes by contrast appeals to strictly moral values, emphasizing his innocence. But he is unsuccessful. Phemius, by contrast, is saved by his role as bard and by the fact that he only sang for the suitors against his will (οὔ τι ἑκών, 22.351) and under constraint (ἀνάγκῃ, 22.353), and above all by the intervention of Telemachus who points out his innocence (ἀναίτιον, 22.356). The same applies to Odysseus' herald, Medon (22.361–74).

At the end of Book 22, the contrasts between the *Iliad* and the *Odyssey* are clearer still. The victors are restrained in their responses: Odysseus stops Eurycleia from crying out in triumph because 'it is not right (οὐχ ὁσίη) to exult over the killing of men' (22.412). At the same time, the characters display a cruelty that goes far beyond anything in the *Iliad* when it comes to punishing the suitors' lowly accomplices: the maidservants are hanged and Melanthius' genitals thrown to the dogs (while in the *Iliad*, Hector's body is not touched by dogs). However, the book does not end with these horrific images but with

54 *Odyssey*, 22.302–9 and *Iliad*, 13.531, 17.460, and 21.251–3.
55 *Iliad*, 20.463–72 (Tros) and 21.74–96 (Lycaon).

a scene of ritual purification and the moving reunion between Odysseus and his loyal maidservants which serves as a prelude to his reunion with Penelope: 'they fell on Odysseus and embraced him, kissing his head and shoulders, seizing his hands. And a tender longing came upon him to sob and weep because he knew them all once more in his heart' (22.498–501).

Book 23 is dominated by the long-awaited recognition scene between husband and wife and a reunion that was considered by ancient scholars like Aristarchus and Aristophanes of Byzantium to be the true 'end' of the *Odyssey*. The narrative follows Eurycleia from the great hall, where Odysseus remains, to the upper floor where Penelope has been asleep since the end of Book 21. The nurse then tells her mistress that Odysseus has returned and the suitors are dead, but the news is greeted with incredulity by Penelope. For a reader familiar with Homeric poetry, this response is predictable from the moment when Eurycleia's speech is introduced using the line 'She stood over Penelope's head' (23.4) for this is the formula that regularly announces the nocturnal appearance of dream figures,[56] divine epiphanies,[57] or the ghosts of the dead in both the *Iliad* and the *Odyssey*. Penelope's doubts are also justified given the incredible nature of the events reported by Eurycleia: how could Odysseus, acting alone, have overcome the whole group of suitors in his palace (23.35–8)? Being a conscientious messenger, Eurycleia makes a clear distinction in her reply between the massacre itself, of which she has merely heard tell, as she was shut up with the other women 'at the back of their strong-built quarters' (23.41), and what she saw for herself from the moment when Telemachus called her into the great hall. The accuracy of her account is shown by its closeness to the poet's narrative.[58] However, the 'wise' Penelope still refuses to be convinced. In a world where gods can always take on the appearance of mortals, she suspects this to be a case of divine intervention: 'It must be some god who has slain these haughty-minded suitors, in anger at their outrageous pride and their evil deeds' (23.63–4). As often in Homer, this scene has been prefigured by another one involving a minor character. In Book 14 of

[56] *Odyssey*, 4.803, 6.21. See also *Iliad*, 2.59 (Agamemnon recounts his dream): *στῆ δ' ἄρ ὑπὲρ κεφαλῆς, καί με πρὸς μῦθον ἔειπεν.*

[57] *Iliad*, 24.682; *Odyssey*, 20.32.

[58] *Odyssey*, 23.45 = 22.401 (with the change from the first to the third person) and 23.48 = 22.402.

the *Odyssey*, the beggar who predicted Odysseus' return and backed up his claim with an oath met with a similar response from Eumaeus, as is emphasized by the use of the same formula 'your heart has always been unbelieving' (14.150 = 23.72).

Penelope then goes down to the great hall to meet her husband. This second meeting, which leads to the recognition scene, corresponds to the first and to the episode in Book 19 which led paradoxically to Odysseus being recognized not by his wife but by his nurse. But the roles are reversed. The first time it was Odysseus who, on the advice of Athena, was 'testing'[59] Penelope and had managed to control himself in the face of her tears: 'beneath his eyelids his eyes kept as firm as horn or iron; he still dissembled and showed no tears' (19.211–12). In Book 23 it is Penelope who 'tests'[60] Odysseus and is reproached by Telemachus and then by Odysseus for her 'endurance' in keeping aloof from her husband, her 'heartlessness', and her 'heart of stone' (23.100, 103, and 167).

The couple's conversation only begins once Telemachus has left them alone and after Odysseus has given further evidence of the superiority of his cunning intelligence (and the poet of the *Odyssey* has shown yet again his mastery of irony, since Book 23 represents a new wedding for Odysseus and Penelope). To hide the death of the suitors, he orders the members of his household to pretend to be holding a feast 'so that anyone listening from outside—a passer-by or one of our neighbours here—may think that it is a wedding feast' (23.135–6).

Before the recognition can take place, Odysseus needs to resume his original appearance, after taking a bath. Such a transformation, combined with Odysseus' statement 'I am your father', had been enough to convince Telemachus of his identity in Book 16. But it is not enough for Penelope. She needs the 'solid sign' (23.206) of the marital bed built by Odysseus from the trunk of the olive tree in the centre of his house, a sign known only to Odysseus, his wife, and the maidservant who guarded the door of their room. Thus, as Jean Starobinski very aptly said, 'the proof of Odysseus' being as a person, the *confirmation* of his true essence are to be found on the outside in

[59] *Odyssey*, 13.336: πειρήσεαι.

[60] *Odyssey*, 23.114: πειράζειν; 181: πειρωμένη.

the room and the bed he built'.[61] This bed symbolizes the union of nature and culture represented by marriage: it is still part of nature, since the tree from which it was carved still has its roots in the earth, but it is also a product of culture, as it has been crafted by a man from an olive tree which is, for the Greeks, the cultivated tree *par excellence*. It also demonstrates the central importance of marriage for the family, constituting as it does the secret centre point around which Odysseus' house is organized. Impossible to move, it is the embodiment of the union between Odysseus and Penelope. It is only now that Penelope is willing to recognize Odysseus as her husband and that Odysseus' return is truly accomplished. The paradoxical comparison of Penelope's joy to that of a shipwrecked man who touches dry land is further confirmation, if any were needed, that Odysseus' tribulations (and his wife's trials) have finally come to an end. However Odysseus and Penelope's second wedding night does not begin until Odysseus has told his wife of the fresh trials that still await him after the end of the *Odyssey*.

It is not difficult to understand why many ancient scholars, like Aristophanes of Byzantium and Aristarchus,[62] as well as modern critics like Wilamowitz, von der Mühll, and Page,[63] were tempted to place the true conclusion of the *Odyssey* at lines 295–6 of Book 23: 'And they passed on with much content to where as of old their bed awaited them' (οἱ μὲν ἔπειτα ἀσπάσιοι λέκτροιο παλαιοῦ θεσμὸν ἵκοντο). (This does not necessarily imply, for the ancient scholars at least, that the original text of the *Odyssey* stopped at line 296 but simply that this moment represented the true denouement of the plot and all that followed was just subsidiary episodes.[64]) However, it is hard to see how a poem could reach its conclusion in the middle of a phrase since this would leave a 'μέν' ('on the one hand') with no corresponding 'δέ' ('on the other'). Others, like Schadewalt (1991: 360–2), are a little more generous and are prepared to accept that 23.297–343, where the 'delights of storytelling', with Odysseus' account of his adventures in thirty lines, take over from the 'delights of love' before he falls asleep, are an integral part of the original *Odyssey*. But even this conclusion, which shows Odysseus re-established in his

[61] Starobinski 1989: 284.
[62] MV scholia to *Odyssey*, 23.296.
[63] Wilamowitz Moellendort 927: 70 ff.; von der Mühl 1940: 761–2; Page 1955: 114–15.
[64] Erbse 1972: 166–7 followed by Rengakos 2002: 181 n. 34.

own palace, would be incomplete as it does not show him meeting his father, whom he enquired about in Book 11 and Book 14, and does not resolve the tensions within the city and the problems between Odysseus and his fellow citizens provoked by the massacre of the suitors.

The last words addressed to Penelope by Odysseus after he wakes (23.350–65) serve a threefold purpose: they announce the restoration of Odysseus' house which will now recover its wealth and its flocks, they exclude Penelope, who must remain inside the palace, from the action that will follow, and they prepare for Odysseus' meeting with his father. Book 23 ends with Odysseus and his allies leaving the palace to go to the countryside where the aged Laertes lives.

Book 24 cannot therefore be described as superfluous. It falls into three distinct parts: the second *nekuia* (24.1–100), the reunion between Odysseus and Laertes (24.203–411), and the confrontation with the families of the suitors which ends with a general reconciliation, thanks to Athena (24.412–548). The transition from the world of men to the Underworld is facilitated by the parallel between the action of Athena, who, at the end of Book 23, 'leads' Odysseus and his companions 'out of the town' (ἐξῆγε πόληος, 23.372), and that of Hermes who 'leads' (ἄγε, 24.5) the souls of the suitors to the 'field of asphodel where the souls, the phantoms of the dead, have their habitation' (24.13–14).

We will pass over the arguments against the authenticity of the second *nekuia* put forward by Aristarchus and taken up by modern critics,[65] and focus instead on defining the role played by this episode in the text of the *Odyssey* as it has been transmitted and on what distinguishes it from the first *nekuia*. The visit to the Underworld in Book 11 brought a living man, Odysseus, into the presence of the dead, including Achilles and Agamemnon, and played a significant role in the plot, since the seer Tiresias told Odysseus 'the path before [him] and the long stages of [his] journey and how [he] might return home over the fish-filled sea' (10.539–40). The second *nekuia*, by contrast, has no impact on the ending of the *Odyssey* and this time only the dead speak: Achilles, who is accompanied by Patroclus, Antilochus, Ajax, Agamemnon,[66] Agamemnon, who is surrounded by those who died alongside him in Aegisthus' palace,[67] and Amphimedon,

[65] See the *schol in Od.* 24. 1 v and the discussion in Wender 1978: 19–38.
[66] *Odyssey*, 24.15b–18 = 11.467b–470.
[67] *Odyssey*, 24.20–2 = 11.387–9.

who is the representative of the suitors who died in Odysseus' palace. This *nekuia* is cut off from life and from the ongoing action of the poem and is entirely taken up by philosophical reflections on human life.

The dialogue between Achilles and Agamemnon (24.23–97) contrasts the fate of the two heroes whose quarrel was the subject of the *Iliad.* Achilles laments the fact that, instead of the solemn funeral honours that Agamemnon would have received had he died in the war, 'commander of so many brave-hearted men in the land of Troy' (24.26–7), he suffered the most pitiful end. The 'fortunate son of Peleus' (24.36), by contrast, enjoyed a glorious death and a magnificent funeral.

The dialogue between Amphimedon and Agamemnon which follows (24: 105–202) is not just an opportunity to provide a summary of all that has taken place on Ithaca from the beginning of the courtship of Penelope up to the massacre (a summary that reminds us of the one Odysseus gives of his adventures to Penelope in Book 23 and is not without a few distortions due to the limited point of view of the character, in contrast to the omniscient stance of the main narrator).[68] It also enables a further contrast to be made between the fate of Agamemnon (and, indirectly, that of Achilles) and the fate of the 'fortunate son of Laertes' (24.192) whose wife remained virtuous.[69]

In lines 203–6 we move from the dead to the living with the simplest of transitions: 'Such were the words that they spoke to each other in Hades' halls, in the secret places of the earth. But they (οἱ δ') descended from the city and soon came to Laertes' fine land . . . '

It is now time for the scene that will bring to a close the series of recognitions in the *Odyssey.* It is the result of Odysseus' desire to 'make trial of'[70] his father, exactly as he had earlier been tested by his wife. The similarity between the two scenes is underlined by the deliberations which precede them. Just as Penelope wondered in Book 23 'whether to stand apart and question her husband or whether to go up close to him and to clasp and kiss his face and hands' (23.85–7), Odysseus wonders 'whether to kiss his father, to embrace him and tell him all the tale of his coming home to his own land again, or to question him and make thorough trial of him

[68] See Chapter 4 above (pp. 120–1).

[69] See Wender 1978: 40–4.

[70] *Odyssey*, 24.216: πειρήσομαι.

(πειρήσαιτο). As he pondered it seemed the better thing to make trial (πειρηθῆναι) first with bantering words' (24.235–40).

One may well wonder what the motivation is for this final test at the moment when Odysseus has triumphed over the suitors and when there is no longer any need for caution and disguise. It is, once again, easy to understand why critics have asked this question and why many have been shocked by the cruelty which Odysseus seems to show towards his father in this scene. From here to condemning the whole episode as an interpolation, as Page did,[71] is an easy step to make, even if, as is so often the case, the aesthetic and moral arguments remain hidden behind more 'objective' linguistic criteria. But this is to overlook the fact that this episode has been prepared from the very beginning of the poem with the references to Laertes' despair since his son's departure made by Telemachus (1.188–93), Anticleia (11.187–96), and Eumaeus (15.353–7 and 16.137–45) and that Odysseus' reunion with his father is as essential to the conclusion of the *Odyssey* as his reunion with his wife and son.

The way in which this reunion takes place is also perfectly fitting to the character of Odysseus who here invents the last of his false stories (see Chapter 6, p. 188). As with Penelope, the recognition occurs thanks to a 'clearly perceptible sign' (σῆμα . . . ἀριφραδές, 24.329). First there is the tangible mark constituted by the scar (24.331–5) but there is a further sign that relies on the private knowledge shared by father and son: the trees which Laertes gave him in the past (24.336–44). Like the bed in Book 23, this sign has a highly symbolic function in a work in which children are often compared to young saplings (see Chapter 2, p. 72). The episode concludes with the transformation of Laertes who, after a bath, regains his former beauty and vigour (in an obvious parallel to the passage in Book 16 where Athena restored Odysseus' original appearance when he revealed himself to his son) and with a banquet attended by the loyal servants (24.361–411).

In the third and final section of Book 24, the domestic sphere gives way to the political sphere. The narrative leaves Odysseus and his household at their feast to follow the rumour of the suitors' deaths that is spreading throughout the town (24.412–14). A popular assembly then takes place, echoing that of Book 2. But in contrast to that

[71] Page 1955: 104–11. See the refutation by Wender 1978: 45–51.

earlier assembly, this one is not called in the usual manner by a member of the elite but is a spontaneous gathering of the people of Ithaca who arrive of their own accord (αὐτοί, 24.420). Eupeithes, the father of Antinous, one of the suitors' leaders, speaks first to call for revenge (24.422–37). The herald Medon, who was spared by Odysseus in Book 22, then intervenes to testify to the support given to Odysseus by the gods and to warn the people of Ithaca against making any rash decisions (24.439–49). The seer Halitherses, who had spoken at the first assembly, predicting the disaster that would befall the suitors, plays a similar role here, telling the people of Ithaca not to bring any further suffering on themselves (24.451–62). But he only manages to convince a little over half of his audience and the others decide to take up arms and to follow Eupeithes (24.462–71). The private dispute is thus in danger of leading to civil war.

As in Book 24 of the *Iliad*, the solution is provided by the gods. Athena intervenes to ask Zeus what he is planning. His reply, 'do as you please' (ἔρξον ὅπως ἐθέλεις, 24.481), seems to give free rein to Athena. But it is qualified by a piece of advice which has the character of an order: the conflict must be brought to an end, the citizens must forget and restore their former friendly relations, which are the guarantee of peace and prosperity (24.481–6). This is not the only place in the Homeric poems where the king of the gods gives free rein to another deity, using the same formula or its equivalent, as he does with Hera and Athena in the *Iliad* and Poseidon in the *Odyssey*.[72] But a closer comparison reveals the unusual nature of this particular passage. For in all the other cases, Zeus' response leads to the destruction of a city or of a man. By allowing Pandarus to break the truce in *Iliad* 4, he sets the seal on the destruction of Troy, in Book 22 he decides not to save Hector. Similarly, in Book 13 of the *Odyssey*, he allows Poseidon to punish the Phaeacians. Here, by contrast, Zeus' intervention puts an end to the conflict and saves a city.

In lines 487–8, Athena takes the action back down to earth from Olympus. The narrative finds Odysseus and his family at their feast. On seeing the suitors' relatives approaching, they arm themselves, seemingly in preparation for a fresh *aristeia* which will also be a collective one. Athena, disguised as Mentor, reassures them that the

[72] *Iliad*, 4.37 (to Hera): ἔρξον ὅπως ἐθέλεις, *Iliad*, 22.187 (to Athena): ἔρξον ὅπῃ δή τοι νόος ἔπλετο; *Odyssey*, 13.145 (to Poseidon): ἔρξον ὅπως ἐθέλεις καί τοι φίλον ἔπλετο θυμῷ.

gods are with them in this final battle, which is a clear manifestation of the unity of Odysseus' household with three generations ready to fight together against the suitors' families. The aged Laertes kills Eupeithes, the leader of the revolt (24.489–525), but a general massacre is finally averted due to the direct intervention of Athena and the two sides take an oath confirming their reconciliation and re-establishing order in the city (24.526–48).

8

The Human World

Homer's ancient readers were well aware of the importance of the depiction of character in the *Odyssey*. In his *Poetics*, Aristotle noted the complexity of this poem which was 'full of character'[1] and the author of the treatise *On the Sublime* compared it to a 'comedy of manners'.[2] The *Odyssey* does indeed present a whole series of characters, good and bad, nobles and slaves, often arranged in contrasting or symmetrical pairs. They are shown in action and are defined by the epithets attributed to them. It is important to note that the use of formulaic diction in their speeches does not preclude the expression of individuality, as several studies have shown.[3] Moreover, the inclusion of multiple secondary narrations allows the *Odyssey* to represent equally multiple points of view. We see Odysseus not only through the narrative related by the principal narrator but also as he is portrayed by the bard Demodocus and as he presents himself in the tales he tells, both true and false. He also plays a role in the recollections of his former companions, Nestor and Menelaus, as well as of Helen, and his memory and reputation are constantly in the minds of the members of his household.

[1] Aristotle, *Poetics*, 1459b 15–16: ἡ δὲ Ὀδύσσεια πεπλεγμένον . . . καὶ ἠθική. (Translation by M. E. Hubbard, Oxford 1989.)

[2] Pseudo-Longinus, *On the Sublime*, 9.15: οἱονεὶ κωμῳδία τίς ἐστιν ἠθολογουμένη.

[3] See. Parry 1989a, 1989c, Griffin 1986. Martin 1989: 160–205, Martin 1993: 222–8.

1. ODYSSEUS, HIS FRIENDS, AND FAMILY

(a) Odysseus

The hero of the Odyssey is represented by a name which is programmatic: in Greek, Odys(s)eus (Ὀδυσ(σ)εύς) means 'child of hatred'.[4] This name was given to him by his maternal grandfather Autolycus, because he himself 'hated (ὀδυσσάμενος) many people, men and women over the bounteous earth' (19, 407–8),[5] and it foretells the hero's destiny. In the prologue of the poem, Athena asks Zeus why he 'hates' (ὠδύσαο) Odysseus so much (1.62); later Ino asks him why Poseidon 'hates (ὠδύσατ') [him] so violently' (5.339–40), and Odysseus acknowledges on two occasions that the 'hatred' of the gods, first Poseidon, then Zeus and Helios, is the cause of the storms that beset him (5.423 ὀδώδυσται, 19.275 ὀδύσαντο).

Odysseus is also defined as a member of a dynasty, a family, and a city. In the *Odyssey* he is referred to thirty times as the 'son of Laertes' and his primary goal is to be reunited with his wife (1.13), even though Calypso, Circe, and even Nausicaa want him to be their 'husband'.[6] He is also the 'man from Ithaca' (2.246, 22.45) who wishes only to return home (5.220): there is no sweeter sight for him than his native land (9.27–8) and he 'would be content just to see the smoke rising up from his own land' (1.57–9). He was the 'king' of Ithaca (2.47: βασίλευε, 2.234, and 5.12: ἄνασσε) and is still considered their 'lord' (ἄναξ) by all the members of his household as well as by the companions who followed him to Troy, like the unfortunate Elpenor (11.71).[7]

Odysseus is portrayed in the *Odyssey* as a complex personality, a complexity that we can no doubt ascribe to the interaction of several different traditions.[8] He is related both to the trickster figure familiar from folklore and to the epic hero of the *Iliad*, who makes use of both

[4] See Dimock 1963, Austin 1972: 1–3, Strauss Clay 1997: 62–4.

[5] It is possible that the participle could have a passive meaning ('hated', see Chantraine 2009, s.v. ὀδύσσασθαι) and would therefore refer to the hatred felt for Autolycus by others.

[6] See *Odyssey*, 1.15 and 23.334 (Calypso), 9.32 (Circe), and 6. 244–5 (Nausicaa).

[7] See *Odyssey*, 2.47 (βασίλευε). See De Jong 1993: 290–7 on the importance of the title 'lord' (ἄναξ) with respect to Odysseus.

[8] On this point see Stanford 1954: 8–80 and the remarks of Strauss Clay 2002: 73–6 on the studies and Roisman and Ahl 1996 and Danek 1998.

his courage and his intelligence in the service of the community (he is 'a speaker of words and a doer of deeds' (μύθων τε ῥητῆρ' . . . πρηκτῆρά τε ἔργων, *Iliad*, 9.443)), because he has, as Telemachus remarks, 'the hands of a warrior and the mind of a wise counsellor' (χεῖράς τ' αἰχμητὴν . . . καὶ ἐπίφρονα βουλήν, *Odyssey*, 16.242). But this warrior, whose prowess is often referred to, also embodies other qualities which are further from the spirit of the war epic, like the capacity to endure situations that are far from heroic and a multifaceted intelligence which encompasses prudence, cunning, and technical know-how, not to mention curiosity and a desire for knowledge for its own sake.

The Odysseus of the *Iliad* was, like Achilles, a 'destroyer of cities' (πτολίπορθος),[9] a warrior capable of standing firm against the enemy on the battlefield, as well as being, when necessary, a cunning fighter who organized a night ambush in the *Dolonia*. Even if the *Odyssey* carefully omits any reference to Odysseus' contributions to the *Iliad*, it is still haunted by memories of the Trojan War. From the very start, it gives credit to Odysseus for destroying the holy city of Ilium,[10] reserves the epithet 'destroyer of cities' for him alone,[11] and presents him, along with Nestor, as the 'great glory of the Achaians' (μέγα κῦδος Ἀχαιῶν).[12] The glorious funeral that would have been his if he had died at Troy is also contrasted in the *Odyssey* to the ignominious fate of drowning at sea or dying unnoticed.[13] Odysseus himself does not fail to remind his interlocutors that he had the honour of being 'among the troops of Agamemnon, that son of Atreus whose fame is paramount under heaven because of the mighty town he sacked and the multitudes of men he slew' (9.263–66). In particular he describes his fight to protect Achilles' body from the Trojans (5.308–11) and reminds Athena of the time when, with her aid, he 'tore down from Troy the diadem of her glittering pinnacles' (13.388).

The bard Demodocus also celebrates Odysseus' valour when he sings of the quarrel between him and Achilles, a quarrel that echoes

[9] The epithet is applied to Achilles four times in the *Iliad* and twice to Odysseus (2.278 and 10.363).

[10] *Odyssey*, 1.2: ἐπεὶ Τροίης ἱερὸν πτολίεθρον ἔπερσεν.

[11] This epithet is applied to Odysseus eight times.

[12] This formula, which is used twice of Odysseus in the *Iliad*, is applied to him at *Odyssey*, 12.184. In the two poems the only other figure to whom it is applied is Nestor (four times in the *Iliad* and twice in the *Odyssey*).

[13] *Odyssey*, 1.237–40 and 5.306–12.

the one that broke out between Achilles and Agamemnon in the *Iliad*, but does so by inverting it (like the quarrel of the *Iliad*, its protagonists are both heroes who claim to be the 'best of the Achaeans'[14] but instead of 'bringing countless sufferings upon the Achaeans' it fulfils a prophecy and announces the imminent fall of Troy).[15] Helen, for her part, chooses to emphasize the cunning of a hero who did not hesitate to disguise himself as a beggar and to disfigure himself in order to penetrate inside Troy and massacre many of his enemies (4.240–58), an episode which clearly prefigures his transformation in Book 13 and the massacre of the suitors which follows. The story of the Trojan Horse is also alluded to in Menelaus' narration in Book 4, in Demodocus' song in Book 8, and in Odysseus' own account in Book 11.[16] This fragmented presentation of Odysseus allows all the different aspects of his character to be set out one after the other. His courage emerges when Demodocus tells how he confronted Deiphobus 'like Ares' and triumphed over him with Athena's aid (8.517–20). Elsewhere we see his cunning intelligence (Odysseus 'brought this trap', the horse, into Troy, 8.494) as well as his prudence and his powers of endurance (he prevented the Achaeans from falling victim to the seductive illusions of Helen's voice and held them back, when they were about to betray their presence by responding to her call or by breaking out of the horse, 4.271–89).

In the *Odyssey*, therefore, Odysseus continues to embody traditional heroic values. Even in Books 5 to 13, we cannot altogether forget the hero's hunger for glory. His account of his travels begins with an episode which demonstrates that the epithet 'destroyer of cities' is not gratuitous: he sacks the city of the Cicones and massacres the inhabitants (9.39–42). Clearly it is in Book 22, during the massacre of the suitors, that Odysseus shows his full prowess as an archer (when he begins to attack the suitors with his bow) and then as a hoplite, once he has shot all his arrows (22.119–25). The intervention by the goatherd Melanthius, which enables the suitors to arm themselves (22.142–6), is simply a means of further displaying the courage of a hero who is capable of 'containing' the suitors, with only Telemachus by his side (22.172). And Athena, who wishes to challenge Odysseus, only prolongs the fight in order to give him a better chance

[14] See *Odyssey*, 8.78 and *Iliad*, 1.91 (Agamemnon), *Iliad*, 1.244 (Achilles).

[15] *Iliad*, 1.2 and *Odyssey*, 8.79–82.

[16] *Odyssey*, 4.269–89, 8.499–520, 11.523–32. See also Chapter 4 above (p. 112).

to show that he has 'kept unflawed the strength and courage' that he had during the war (22.226–38). This demonstration is completed at the end of Book 24 when Odysseus and the members of his household—eleven men in all—confront the crowd of relatives of the suitors; a massacre is only averted by Athena's intervention: 'Odysseus and his son fell upon the first rank of fighters, thrusting with swords and two edged spears. And now they would have destroyed them all and taken away their hopes of home, had not the daughter of Zeus cried out and held back the whole throng' (24.526–30).

In the Homeric world, the athletic contests that pit members of the elite against each other are also an opportunity for the heroes to display their prowess, as we see in Book 23 of the *Iliad* with the description of the funeral games for Patroclus, where Odysseus achieves a draw in his wrestling match with Ajax thanks to his use of a cunning stratagem (*Iliad*, 23.700–39). In the *Odyssey*, we not only hear about Odysseus' past victory in wrestling over Philomedes on Lesbos, to the great joy of the Achaeans (4.341–4), but we also see two examples, one in Book 8 and one in Book 21.[17] When Odysseus is challenged by the Phaeacian Euryalus, who accuses him of not being athletic, he reacts as a hero should: he abandons his original decision to stay out of the contest and decides to participate, easily wins the contest in discus-throwing, and then challenges all the Phaeacians to compete against him in 'boxing, wrestling or running' (8.206) in order to 'display [his] prowess' (8.237). The contest of the bow in Book 21 takes up and develops the themes introduced in Book 8 and is the occasion for Odysseus to make a decisive demonstration of his superiority in a test which he alone is able to complete.

On several occasions, however, it is possible to see a conflict between the traditional heroic values and a caution that could even be taken for cowardice. In these conflicts, the desire for glory sometimes wins. Odysseus cannot resist the temptation to proclaim his victory over Polyphemus and to reveal his name, enabling the Cyclops to curse him by name and to call the wrath of Poseidon down upon him (9.492–536). As soon as he finds out that his companions have disappeared in Circe's palace, he slings his great bronze silver-studded sword over his shoulders, puts his bow on top, and sets off for the palace despite Euryalus' prayers (10.261–73). But the most significant episode is

[17] The concentration of instances of the ἄεθλος ('contest') in Book 8 (where it occurs ten times) and in Books 19–22 (eleven examples) is significant.

surely that involving Scylla. When Circe first describes the monster with her 'six long necks with a grisly head on each of them, and in each head a triple row of crowded and close-set teeth, fraught with black death' (12.90–2), Odysseus is not afraid and declares his intention to fight her (12.112–14). Circe tries to dissuade him by explaining why such resistance would be futile (12.116–20) but in vain. For once, the man famous for his foresight throws caution to the wind: 'I let myself forget that irksome command of Circe's; she had told me not to arm at all, but I put my glorious armour on, took a long spear in either hand and strode up to the half-deck forward' (12.226–30).

Odysseus therefore remains a courageous hero in the *Odyssey*. But he is also, above all, the embodiment of cleverness. No man can surpass him, or even equal him for his cunning intelligence (*mētis* in Greek) that ensures 'success in a particular sphere of activity'.[18] Both mortals, like Nestor and Telemachus, and gods, like Athena, recognize this quality in him.[19] While mortals usually have fewer ingenious plans than gods, Odysseus is the only one to equal Zeus in this respect.[20] He is also the only one to be described by a series of epithets that underline the depth and the multifaceted nature of his intelligence as well as his skill in devising stratagems.[21] In the very first line of the *Odyssey* he is called 'the man of many turns' (πολύτροπος),[22] 'ingenious' (πολύμητις, used sixty-six times), and 'intelligent' (πολύφρων, four times), qualities which he shares with Hephaestus, the divine craftsman;[23] he is also described as a man of many, varied wiles (ποικιλομήτης, six times) and is endlessly resourceful (πολυμήχανος, used seventeen times).

Odysseus is characterized first and foremost by his caution. He is able to foresee danger. After his raid on the Cicones, he fears the arrival of reinforcements and orders his companions to flee as quickly as possible (9.43–4). On their arrival at the Cyclops' island he takes Maron's wine with him: 'because from the first I had forebodings that the stranger who might face us now would wear brute strength like a garment round him, a savage whose heart had little knowledge of just

[18] Detienne and Vernant 1978: 11.

[19] *Odyssey*, 3.120–2, 13.296–9, 23.124–6.

[20] *Odyssey*, 13.89: ἄνδρα φέρουσα θεοῖς ἐναλίγκια μήδε' ἔχοντα.

[21] See Stanford 1950: 108–10, Strauss Clay 1997: 29–32, Pucci 1987: 58–60.

[22] *Odyssey*, 1.1, 10.330. See Pucci 1987: 24–5.

[23] Hephaestus is πολύμητις at *Iliad*, 21.355 and πολύφρων at Iliad, 21.367 and *Odyssey*, 8.297 and 327.

laws or of ordinances' (9.213–15). And, instead of drawing his sword and killing the Cyclops while he is sleeping, he decides to wait, realizing that he would be unable to move the rock blocking the entrance to the cave.[24] In the land of the Laestrygonians, he moors his boat prudently outside the harbour, instead of sailing inside, which enables him to escape and to avoid the huge rocks thrown by the giants (10.95–6). Although he is well aware of the dangers posed by Scylla, he does not tell his companions, fearing that 'the crew in fear might have left their oars and huddled down inside the hold' (12.223–5). He is also capable of making long-term strategic decisions: despite his desire to return home as soon as possible, he says he is ready to stay in Phaeacia for a whole year, if it means acquiring enough valuable gifts to earn him the respect and friendship of the people of Ithaca.[25]

He is also skilled in foreseeing all eventualities and weighing up the risks carefully. When he arrives on Scheria, he hesitates between spending the night by the river, where he is in danger of dying of cold, and taking refuge in the bushes, where he will be vulnerable to attack by wild animals (5.465–73). He suspects that apparently innocent enquiries may be a trap and responds accordingly: when the Cyclops asks him where he has moored his ship, he replies with a lie and claims that his ship has been lost in a storm (9.283–5). He is not swayed by promises and does not trust others before he has tested them or been given guarantees. Even when he longs to return home, he does not seize upon Calypso's offer to help him return, but immediately suspects a trick: 'Goddess, your purpose cannot be as you say: you cannot intend to speed me home. You tell me to make myself a raft to cross the great gulf of ocean—a gulf so baffling and so perilous that not even rapid ships will traverse it, steady though they be and favoured by a fair wind from Zeus' (5.173–6).

When he is caught up in the storm and Leucothea tells him to abandon his raft and wrap himself in her veil, which will protect him, he hesitates, asking, 'Can this divinity in her turn be laying a snare for me in her command to forsake the raft?' (5.356–7). And when Circe invites him into her bed he is afraid that she may be about to use this

[24] *Odyssey*, 9.302–5. On the contrast with Achilles in Book 1 of the *Iliad*, see Rengakos 2002: 185–6.

[25] *Odyssey*, 11.355–61. This trait is found in the 'false' Odysseus of Book 19 (283–6). See Redfield 1983: 228 and Di Benedetto 1998: 717–19.

as a chance to rob him of his virility (10.337–41) and demands guarantees from her. Before trusting the promises of Calypso and Circe, he makes them swear a solemn oath that they are not plotting against him (5.178–9 = 10.343–4), just as, inside Troy, he did not reveal the Achaeans' plans to Helen until he had sworn her to silence with an oath (4.253–5).

He shows a similar caution when he arrives on Ithaca. Instead of hurrying to his palace to be reunited with his wife and child as any other man would have done, as Athena notes (13.333–4), he chooses to wait and to 'put to the test' not only his wife and father but also all the other members of his household.[26] On two separate occasions he tests Eumaeus to see how far his generosity and hospitality will go (14.459–61 and 15.304–6). He orders Telemachus to keep his return secret so that he can test the loyalty of his other servants, male and female (16.30–7). When he fights the beggar Irus, he weighs up the dangers of an overwhelming victory which would risk revealing his true identity: 'Odysseus wondered whether to give him such a blow that the life would leave him there as he fell, or to give him a more merciful one and only stretch him upon the floor. As he asked himself this, the more merciful thing seemed the better, as the suitors would not suspect him' (18.90–4).

As well as being cautious, Odysseus is also cunning. Praise of his *mētis* is often accompanied by references to his pre-eminence in laying traps, practising deception, and telling false stories, as Nestor and Athena both say (3.120–2, 13.291–8). He even introduces himself proudly to Alcinous as 'Odysseus, son of Laertes, known among all mankind for my cunning' (9.19–20). He is skilled in deceptive speeches and expert in concealing his identity. Even before he is transformed into a beggar by Athena's magic wand at the end of Book 13, he has already tricked the Trojans by taking on the appearance of a slave (4.244–8). In Book 9 he gives a false name to Polyphemus and is able, thanks to this ruse, to escape the other Cyclopes who see no reason to rush to help the victim of 'Noman' (9.410–12). On his arrival on Ithaca, he is careful not to reveal his identity to the young shepherd who tells him he has arrived in his homeland and invents a false biography for himself (13.254–86).

[26] *Odyssey*, 13.336, 24.216, 238, and 240. See Rutherford 1986: 158.

Odysseus' skills are also of a practical nature, which is not surprising given that the same Greek word, *technē*, can designate both deceptive stratagems and technical knowledge. The hero is not only a sailor able to guide his ship 'in expert fashion' (5.270, τεχνηέντως). He can also do the work of a woodcutter, carpenter, and sailmaker when he needs to construct the ship that will take him away from Calypso's island in Book 5. The Polyphemus episode provides Odysseus with another chance to put his technical skill into practice, first of all in the preparation of the stake used to blind the monster (this is stripped and smoothed before its point is hardened in the fire, 9.319–28) and then when he does the deed, as we see from the similes comparing him first to a carpenter and then to a blacksmith (9.384–94).

Finally, it is important to note a more unusual aspect of Odysseus' intelligence that is too often overlooked. This is his curiosity and his thirst for knowledge for its own sake, qualities that make him the first tourist in Western literature. Even if Odysseus does not choose to travel and is more interested in returning than in leaving home, he remains the hero who 'viewed many cities and came to know the minds of many men' (1.3), and sometimes allows himself to be guided by his desire to know, as when he wishes to listen to the Sirens' song, or enter into conversation with the dead. In Book 11, only the dialogue with Tiresias is motivated by the need to obtain information that will help him complete his journey. When he allows 'the wives and daughters of great men' to drink the dark blood (11.227), he is motivated purely by the pleasure of hearing about their origins and their stories. Similarly, he abandons his attempts to make Ajax break his silence because his 'heart was eager to see the souls of the other dead' (11.566–7). And, after his encounter with Heracles, he waits a little longer 'hoping some other one might come from among the heroes who perished long ago' (11.628).

Odysseus stands out also for the suffering he endures,[27] as is shown by epithets such as πολυπενθής ('full of sorrow'), πολύστονος ('much sighing'),[28] δύστηνος (unhappy),[29] or ὀιζυρός (wretched) [30] as well as

[27] See Di Benedetto 2003: 101–2.

[28] *Odyssey*, 14.386 and 19.118 respectively.

[29] The seventeen occurrences in the *Odyssey* refer to Odysseus.

[30] Of the ten occurrences in the *Odyssey*, five refer to Odysseus.

nouns like ὀϊζύς (sorrow),[31] κήδεα (suffering),[32] ἄλγεα (hardship),[33] and the verbs ὀϊζύω ('to suffer grief')[34] and μογέω ('to suffer hardship').[35] In this sense, the hero who epitomizes what it is to be human also shows that suffering is the defining experience of the human condition.[36] But he is also characterized by the exceptional powers of endurance which enable him to survive trials (ἄεθλοι) which are comparable to the labours of Heracles.[37] This quality is shown by the use of epithets such as πολύτλας ('much-enduring'),[38] ταλασίφρων ('of enduring spirit'),[39] τλήμων ('enduring'), or πολυτλήμων ('much-enduring').[40] But this endurance is not solely a matter of being able to stand firm in the face of enemy assaults and having the courage to face death, as it is in the *Iliad*. Alongside this 'active heroism' Odysseus also embodies, to quote the title of an article by Erwin Cook, 'passive heroism'.[41]

Throughout the period when he is held by Calypso on her island, he can only put up a passive resistance to the goddess,[42] spending his time weeping and lamenting, even wishing for his own death.[43] Before this he 'suffered many troubles in his heart on the sea' (πολλὰ δ' ὅ γ' ἐν πόντῳ πάθεν ἄλγεα ὃν κατὰ θυμόν, 1.4) as well as in battle.[44] The story of his return home naturally emphasizes his ability to withstand the punishing demands of a long sea journey. In Book 12, for example, when Odysseus' companions beg him to make a stop on the island of the Sun they contrast his indefatigable spirit

[31] Of the fourteen occurrences in the *Odyssey*, seven refer to Odysseus.

[32] Of the ten occurrences in the *Odyssey*, seven refer to Odysseus.

[33] Of the fifty-one occurrences in the *Odyssey*, twenty-six refer to Odysseus.

[34] This verb is used twice in the *Odyssey*, both times of Odysseus.

[35] This verb is used twenty-seven times in the *Odyssey*; twenty times it refers to Odysseus.

[36] At *Iliad*, 13.569 and *Odyssey*, 4.197, mortals are described as 'suffering' (ὀϊζυροῖσι βροτοῖσιν); at *Iliad*, 22.31, 76, 24.525 and *Odyssey*, 11.19, 12.341, and 15.408 they are 'wretched' (δειλοῖσι βροτοῖσιν).

[37] *Odyssey*, 4.170, 241, 23.248, 261, 350 (Odysseus); 11.622, 624 (Heracles).

[38] Used five times in the *Iliad* and thirty-eight times in the *Odyssey* (in the case of Odysseus always in the formula πολύτλας δῖος Ὀδυσσεύς).

[39] Used once in the *Iliad* for Odysseus (11.466) and eleven times in the *Odyssey* (in the formula Ὀδυσσῆος ταλασίφρονος).

[40] In the *Iliad*, Odysseus or his heart are described as τλήμων three times and he is called πολυτλήμων at *Odyssey*, 18.319.

[41] Cook 1999-2000. See also Pucci 1987: 44–9.

[42] *Odyssey*, 1.49: πήματα πάσχει; 5.13: ἄλγεα πάσχων.

[43] *Odyssey*, 1.55, 5.82–4, 151–3, 156–8, and 5.11.

[44] *Odyssey*, 13.90–1.

with their own exhausted state (12.279–82). This spirit is also in evidence during the storms that assail him. As he says to Calypso, 'If this or that divinity should shatter my craft on the wine-dark ocean, I will bear it and keep a bold heart within me. Often enough before this time have war and wave oppressed and plagued me; let new tribulations join the old' (5.221–4). It is interesting to note that expressions such as 'I will stay here and endure my troubles' (*τόφρ' αὐτοῦ μενέω καὶ τλήσομαι ἄλγεα πάσχων*) and 'I endured and stayed' (*ἀλλ' ἔτλην καὶ ἔμεινα*) both occur in descriptions of storms, in Book 5 (before Odysseus' arrival on Scheria) and Book 10 (after the companions open the bag of winds).[45] Odysseus' endurance is also revealed in his ability to stand firm in situations that are far from heroic, as when he clings to the underbelly of the ram to leave the Cyclops' cave: 'there I clung in the rich soft wool, desperately holding on with enduring spirit (*τετληότι θυμῷ*)' (9.434–5).

He also displays a moral steadfastness that enables him to resist temptation: despite Calypso's repeated offers of escape from old age and death, she never manages to sway him (7.255–8). This quality is closely allied to his self-control which is the necessary condition for his salvation and that of his companions, according to Tiresias: 'You and your men may perhaps reach home, though with much misery, if only you have the strength of will to curb your own and your comrades' appetites (*σὸν θυμὸν ἐρυκακέειν καὶ ἑταίρων*)' (11.104–5).

Particularly after his return to Ithaca, Odysseus shows his ability to control his emotions on several occasions. He does allow himself to weep when he is reunited with his son, although up until that point 'he had held back his tears' (*πάρος δ' ἔχε νωλεμὲς αἰεί*, 16.191). But he shows no reaction when he sees Penelope's tears in Book 19: 'His heart went out to his weeping wife, but beneath his eyelids his eyes kept as firm as horn or iron (*ὀφθαλμοὶ δ' ὡς εἰ κέρα ἕστασαν ἠὲ σίδηρος ἀτρέμας ἐν βλεφάροισι*); he still dissembled and showed no tears' (19.209–12).

Although he is able to control himself, he does not always manage to control others, as we see in the story of the cattle of the Sun. But if we look beyond the story of his travels, there are examples. On Ithaca, in the past, he was able to restrain the people's anger (*ἀλλ' Ὀδυσεὺς κατέρυκε καὶ ἔσχεθεν ἱεμένους περ*, 16.430) when they wanted to

[45] *Odyssey*, 5.362 and 10.53.

lynch the father of Antinous. Later, inside the Trojan Horse, he was able to prevent Diomedes and Menelaus from answering Helen's calls and to stop Anticlus' mouth with his hands, as he does later with Eurycleia to stop her revealing his identity.[46]

But, from Book 13 onwards, once Odysseus is on Ithaca, his endurance takes on a new form. As a beggar, Odysseus now has to endure in silence the insults and humiliations thrown at him by the suitors, as Athena forewarns him (13.306–10) and as Amphinomus will acknowledge in the Underworld: 'for a while he endured (ἐτόλμα) being beaten and insulted in his own house with a patient heart (τετληότι θυμῷ)' (24.162–3). Telemachus is urged by his father to show a similar patience:

If they insult me in the house, your heart must be resolute within you, no matter what outrage comes my way (σὸν δὲ φίλον κῆρ τετλάτω ἐν στήθεσσι κακῶς πάσχοντος ἐμεῖο); even if they drag me by the feet along the hall and out through the doors, even if they hurl missiles at me—look on, be patient (σὺ δ' εἰσορόων ἀνέχεσθαι). (16.274–7)

Odysseus' endurance is put to the test for the first time in Book 17, when, on his way to the palace, he meets the goatherd Melanthius near to a fountain, who insults him grievously, calls him a beggar and a knave, and threatens him with physical injury if he goes to the palace before ending by kicking him (17.215–34). Odysseus' reaction to this first insult is typical: 'He stood firm, but wondered (μερμήριξεν) whether to leap upon the fellow and dash the life out of him with his cudgel or whether to lift him by the middle and batter his head against the ground. Nevertheless he mastered himself and checked his impulse (ἀλλ' ἐπετόλμησε, φρεσὶ δ' ἔσχετο)' (17.235–8). The self-control that Odysseus shows here is underlined by the comparison between this episode and the famous description of Achilles' anger in Book 1 of the *Iliad*:

Anger came over the son of Peleus. His heart in his shaggy breast was torn between two alternatives (διάνδιχα μερμήριξεν), whether to draw his sharp sword from beside his thigh . . . or to quell his anger and restrain his heart (ἦε χόλον παύσειεν ἐρητύσειέ τε θυμόν). While he was pondering this in his mind and his heart, and was pulling his great sword from the scabbard, Athena came down from heaven. (1.188–95)

[46] *Odyssey*, 4.284 and 19.479–81.

It takes the physical intervention of a goddess, descending from Olympus, to calm the fury of Achilles. Odysseus, by contrast, is able to restrain his anger by himself.

This aspect of his character is underlined again when Odysseus prepares to enter his palace. When Eumaeus warns him against the mistreatment he may suffer, the hero replies: 'I am no stranger to blows and peltings. I have a hardy temper (τολμήεις μοι θυμός); I have suffered much (κακὰ πολλὰ πέπονθα) from waves and wars, and now let this trial join the rest' (17.283–5). When he is hit by Antinous, 'Odysseus did not reel at the blow, he stood there still, firm as a rock (ὁ δ' ἐστάθη ἠύτε πέτρη ἔμπεδον). He only shook his head silently as he brooded evil in his heart' (17.463–5). In the same way, he urges his heart to endure the behaviour of the maidservants as they go to meet the suitors at the beginning of Book 20: 'Have patience, heart (τέτλαθι δή, κραδίη). Once you endured worse than this (καὶ κύντερον ἄλλο ποτ' ἔτλης), on the day when the ruthless Cyclops devoured my hardy companions: you held firm' (20.18–20). Later on, when attacked by Ctesippus, he simply dodges the missile hurled at him, with a bitter smile (20.300–2). These responses, which could not be further from those of Achilles, show the distance that separates the hero of the *Odyssey* from the hero of the *Iliad*.

A further difference between these two heroes lies in their relationship to the narrative itself. It is true that at the beginning of Book 9 of the *Iliad* we see Achilles, far from the battlefield, 'delighting his heart' by playing the lyre and singing, like a bard, 'tales of men's glory' (*Iliad*, 9.186–9). But the *Odyssey* does not just show Odysseus as an incomparable orator, as he was in the *Iliad*, capable of enchanting his listeners 'with the words which flocked down like snowflakes in winter' (*Iliad*, 3.222). Rather, he also becomes a teller of tales, a trait that is no doubt expressed in the formulaic epithet πολύαινος. Odysseus is alone in both the *Odyssey* and the *Iliad*[47] in being given this epithet which draws attention to his ability to tell αἶνοι, or stories with a hidden meaning which bring some benefit to their tellers, an ability that he shares in the *Iliad* with Nestor and his son Antilochus (*Iliad*, 23.652 and 795). It is particularly evident in the story that the Cretan Odysseus tells to Eumaeus in Book 14 of the *Odyssey* (469–506). This lengthy account of the ambush he mounted along with Menelaus and

[47] *Iliad*, 9.673 = 10.544, 11.430; *Odyssey*, 12.184. According to Chantraine 2009, *s. v.*, an αἶνος is a story with a meaning. See Pucci 1998: 2 n. 2 and 131–2.

'Odysseus' in the bitter cold and of Odysseus' stratagem to get him a cloak is not told without an ulterior motive, as the conclusion shows: 'I wish I had that fresh vigour now, that same strength of body undiminished. Then one of the swineherds on the farm would give me his cloak out of kindness and out of respect for a better man' (14.503–5).[48] Eumaeus' response shows that he fully understands the hidden purpose of these words: 'Old guest, this tale (αἶνος) you have told is excellent; not a word of it was misjudged (παρὰ μοῖραν) or went to waste (νηκερδές, literally 'brought no profit'), so you shall not go short for covering or for anything else a suppliant ought to be given when he comes one's way' (14.508–11).

For this reason, there is probably no need to draw the sharp distinction suggested by Tzvetan Todorov (1977: 62) between the two Odysseuses of the *Odyssey*, of whom 'one has the adventures' while 'the other tells them'. In contrast to the bards, Odysseus never tells stories for pleasure alone. As we saw in the analysis of his Cretan and Sicilian stories (Chapter 6 above, pp. 183–8), he constructs each time an image of himself that is perfectly shaped to suit his listener(s) and to create a particular impression. This even applies to the stories he tells to the Phaeacians. It is possible, as has been suggested by Glen Most (1989), that all these tales of bad hosts who want to destroy the stranger (like Polyphemus) or refuse to let him leave (like Calypso) serve above all as negative exempla, demonstrating how not to treat a guest. Be that as it may, through the tales of his adventures, Odysseus manages to acquire a new prestige in the eyes of the Phaeacians, as we see from the comments of Arete in Book 11: 'Phaeacians, what do you say of this man now—his air and presence and poise of mind?' (11.336–7).

Odysseus' intentions may be very different from those of a bard, but the effect he works on his listeners is the same. After listening to his stories, the Phaeacians are 'held by the spell' (κηληθμῷ δ' ἔσχοντο).[49] And Alcinous, like Eumaeus further on in the poem (17.518–21), does not hesitate to compare him to a bard: 'With you the spoken words are eloquent and the mind they come from is a wise one. You have told your tale as skilfully as a bard—the toils and trials of all the Achaeans and yourself' (11.367–9). The final comparison of

[48] Shewring's translation follows those editors who omit the second part of this passage.

[49] *Odyssey*, 11.333–4 = 13.1–2. See Chapter 4, pp. 128–30.

Odysseus to a bard occurs, paradoxically, just before the massacre of the suitors, as Odysseus strings his bow:

Like a master of lyre and song (ἀοιδῆς) who with utmost ease winds a new string round a peg, fitting the pliant sheepgut at either end, so did Odysseus string the great bow tranquilly. Then he put his right hand to the string to try it, and it sang out (καλὸν ἄεισε) beneath his fingers as clear as a swallow's note. (21.406–11)

This is an indirect, but very effective, way of revealing the unity between actor and narrator.

(b) The companions

Odysseus' companions exist above all as a group and are defined both in relation and in contrast to their leader, which is unsurprising in an aristocratic society like that of the Homeric world. There is, however, a fundamental difference between the *Odyssey* and the *Iliad* which it is important to point out. In the *Iliad*, the troops are above all a mass of fighters who are entirely at the disposal of their leaders but the *Odyssey* emphasizes the leader's responsibility for his men. Odysseus' companions are therefore a means by which an 'Odysseus-loving' (*philodusseus*) poet[50] can portray the qualities of a hero who 'suffered many troubles as he sailed the sea . . . trying to bring his companions home' and made use, in vain, of all his physical and mental resources to protect them from danger, as we see in the prologue (1.4–5) and as Odysseus himself reminds his companions (12.211–12). The episode on Circe's island, when Odysseus does not hesitate to go into the unknown to save his companions and where he refuses to touch the bread and wine until he has seen them safe and sound, is without doubt the best example of his concern for his men. And the simile that is used to describe the joy of his companions when they see him return from Circe's home emphasizes both their dependence on him and their affection for him:

Just as on a farm when the cows have had their fill of grass and the herd of them comes back to the yard, the calves all push their way out of their pens and run with much lowing to meet their mothers and frisk around them so, when they saw me with their own eyes, my weeping comrades crowded

[50] Eustathius, *Ad Odysseam*, 2.220,30.

round me and in their hearts it was as if they had reached their own land again and the very town of rocky Ithaca where they were born and bred. (10.410–17)

The companions are saved when they obey Odysseus' orders and row with all their might between Scylla and Charybdis (12.206–22). When they perish, it is as a result of decisions they have taken by themselves or because of their failure to obey the hero. In the land of the Cicones, when Odysseus asks them to raise the anchor immediately after their victory, 'they in their folly would not listen' (9.44), leading to considerable losses. Then, when they are within sight of the coast of Ithaca, they decide while Odysseus is sleeping to open the bag of winds, thus letting loose a storm (10.34–49). The episode of the cattle of the Sun, when Odysseus reports the prophecies of Tiresias and Circe and plays the role of the wise counsellor, is the last and clearest illustration of this theme. At first the companions 'obey' Odysseus and refrain from touching the cattle (12.324). But then, once again while Odysseus is asleep, they disobey and bring about their own destruction 'by their own wild recklessness' (σφετέρῃσιν ἀτασθαλίῃσιν, 1.7).

The companions' actions therefore usually serve to bring out the sagacity of their leader by contrast but on occasion the roles are reversed. They manage to stop him by their gentle words when he is tempted to commit a crime and to kill Eurylochus when he refuses to follow him to Circe's house (10.438–45). And it is they who tell him, after a year spent on Circe's island, that it is time to think of returning home (10.469–75). Despite the psychological inconsistency involved, they are even used to emphasize Odysseus' rare moments of rashness. In the Polyphemus episode, they beg Odysseus to leave the cave immediately, taking some lambs and some cheese, but this time it is Odysseus who refuses to listen (9.224–9). A second time, they try to stop him from provoking the Cyclops with his insults, again with no success (9.492–500).

Some individuals do emerge from the group, like Perimedes, Polites, Elpenor, and above all Eurylochus. Perimedes is little more than a name, twice linked to Eurylochus.[51] Polites emerges more clearly as a character: he is presented as a 'leader of men'[52] and the 'best and

[51] *Odyssey*, 11.23 and 12.195.

[52] *Odyssey*, 10.224: ὄρχαμος ἀνδρῶν. This expression is not reserved for members of the elite in the *Odyssey*, like Menelaus (six occurrences), Peisistratus, son of Nestor

dearest of the companions' (10.225), but he only acts once, in the Circe episode, when he suggests to the companions sent out on the reconnaissance mission with Eurylochus that they call out to the woman whose voice they hear (10.226–8). Elpenor, the youngest and most foolish of the companions who is neither particularly brave nor particularly intelligent, only appears in order to die a pointless death (10.552–60), perhaps because each stage of the journey, including the stay on Circe's island, needs to involve the death of at least one of the companions. Then there is Eurylochus. Twice he carries out Odysseus' orders during the sacrifice that precedes the *nekuia* and in the episode of the Sirens (11.23–4 and 12.195–6). At the beginning of the Circe episode, where he leads a group made up of half the companions and goes with them to explore the island, he seems at first to be Odysseus' double: he is the only one to suspect a trap (10.232) and to escape Circe's spell, while his companions are caught 'because of their foolishness' (10.231). But he becomes the antithesis of Odysseus because of his cowardice: he does everything to avoid returning to Circe's palace (10.266–9 and 429–37). Finally, he plays a vital role in the episode of the cattle of the Sun, where he is the leader of the opposition to Odysseus, first by obliging him to land and then by suggesting to his starving companions that they sacrifice the sacred cattle, thus leading directly to their deaths (12.278–94 and 339–52).

(c) Telemachus

In the *Odyssey*, Telemachus is first and foremost the son of Odysseus, that is to say his double, which is not surprising in an archaic world in which divine favour is shown above all by the fact that 'the womenfolk bear children that resemble their fathers'.[53] His physical resemblance to his father is so striking that those who knew Odysseus recognize him immediately as his son, even when seeing him for the first time. In Book 1, Athena, disguised as Mentes, asks, 'are you the son of Odysseus himself? Your likeness to him sets me wondering—the head might be his, and the fine eyes; I speak as one who had much to

(three occurrences), or Odysseus (once), but is also applied to servants like Eumaeus (on six occasions) and Philoetius (twice).

53 Hesiod, *Works and Days*, 235. Translation by M.L. West (Oxford, 1988) slightly modified.

do with him before he embarked for Troy' (1.207–9). And Helen has the same reaction in Book 4: 'Shall I hide or tell what I am sure of? Yes, my heart urges me to speak. Never, I think, have I seen such likeness in man or woman—amazement seizes me as I look. This boy looks far too much like Odysseus to be any other than his son' (4.140–4). To which Menelaus replies, 'your thought has become my thought as well. Odysseus had just such feet and hands; his head and hair were like this boy's; his eyes had the same glance' (4.148–50). But the resemblance is not only physical, it is also a question of character. This is suggested first of all by the epithet πεπνυμένος ('shrewd'), usually applied to the son of Odysseus,[54] as well as the adjective πολύμυθος 'with many words, eloquent' used to describe a good orator, which is used once, of Telemachus, in the *Odyssey* (2.200). It is significant however that, in contrast to Odysseus, Telemachus is never described using epithets that express cunning (*mētis*) or practical skill (*mēchanē*).

This is also the impression given by the poem as a whole. As we saw in Chapter 5, the Adventures of Telemachus do not, as has often been claimed,[55] show the various stages of his passage from childhood to adulthood. Rather, they show that Odysseus' son has now become an adult, exactly as Athena says. For the goddess does not claim to be educating the young man; she simply 'rouses' him and 'puts energy in his heart'[56] so that he calls an assembly, just as the gods in the *Iliad* 'rouse' warriors and 'put energy into their hearts' to enter the fray and to fight.[57] When she advises him to travel to Pylos and Sparta it is not in order to broaden the young man's mind but so that 'he can win himself a good name in the world' (1.95). When she speaks to him directly, disguised first as Mentes in Book 1 and then as Mentor in Book 2, it is only to remind him that the time for childish things is

[54] This occurs forty-six times in the two formulae used to introduce Telemachus' words. This epithet is not exclusive to Telemachus but is also used of his father (*Odyssey*, 8.388; 19.350), his grandfather (24.375), Nestor (3.20), Menelaus (3.328, 4.190), the good suitor Amphinomus (18.125, 19.350) (not to mention the ironic use of this participle by Telemachus who uses it to describe the two leaders of the suitors at 18.65). On the connotations of this epithet see Heath 2001: 135, 'πεπνυμένος is the mark of a man who has reached mature judgement and can speak and act accordingly'.

[55] See for example Millar and Carmichael 1954 and Austin 1969.

[56] *Odyssey*, 1.89: ὄφρα οἱ υἱὸν | μᾶλλον ἐποτρύνω καί οἱ μένος ἐν φρεσὶ θείω.

[57] Compare for exemple *Iliad*, 5.461, 'Ares spurred on the ranks of the Trojans' (Τρῳὰς δὲ στίχας οὖλος Ἄρης ὄτρυνε), and 21.145, '[Xanthos] put courage in the heart (of Asteropaios)' (μένος δέ οἱ ἐν φρεσὶ θῆκε) to fight against Achilles.

over (1.296–7), that he must now prove his worth so that people will speak well of him later (1.301–2), and that he is capable of accomplishing his project because he has the 'fearless spirit' μένος ἠΰ (2.271) and 'resourcefulness' (μῆτις, 2.279) of his father.

The *Odyssey* contains frequent reminders of the contrast between the Telemachus of former times, a 'foolish' child (νήπιος),[58] and the Telemachus of the present who 'knows how to tell good from bad'[59] and now sits among the adult men in the assembly (11.449). It is true that, at the beginning of Book 2, Telemachus still presents himself as a defenceless child when he asks the people of Ithaca for their help: 'there is no man left with the mettle of Odysseus to ward off ruin from the house. I myself am not able to ward it off; I fear I shall always be a weakling, with no skill to resist at all' (2.58–61). He continues to doubt his abilities when he arrives at Nestor's palace and is concerned that he is 'unpractised in subtle speech' (3.23). Penelope too, at the end of Book 4, thinks of Telemachus as 'a child with no knowledge of men's adventures or men's debates' (4.818). But when her son returns from his journey she realizes that he is no longer 'an unreflecting child' (19.530). He has now 'grown and reached manhood' and is henceforward 'of an age to take due care of a great house'.[60]

In fact, Telemachus asserts his authority over his mother and over the suitors several times during the *Odyssey*. In Book 1, when Penelope asks the bard Phemius to stop singing of the disasters that befell the Achaeans on their return from Troy, he tells her to 'school her heart and mind to listen' (1.353) before ordering her to go back up to her room: 'Go up to your room again and look to your own province, distaff and loom, and tell your women to ply their task: speech (μῦθος) shall be men's concern, and my concern most of all; authority (κράτος) in this house is mine' (1.356–9). In Book 21, when Penelope, whose idea it was to hold the trial of the bow tries to intervene in its organization and orders Eurymachus, one of the two leaders of the suitors, to give the bow to the beggar so that he can participate in the contest (21.336), she is again put in her place by her son. Telemachus reminds her that he alone has the authority to give the bow or to refuse to give it (21.344–5) and then repeats his command to her from Book 1.356–9 with just one change: he substitutes the word 'bow'

58 This adjective is applied to him seven times.
59 *Odyssey*, 18.228–9, 20.309–10.
60 *Odyssey*, 18.217 = 19.532, 19.160–1.

(τόξον) for 'speech' (μῦθος), saying now that 'the bow shall be men's concern' (21.352). What is more striking still is that these formulae are almost identical to the passage in which Hector tells Andromache to return to her room at the end of Book 6 of the *Iliad*. The passage is identical, except that here it is 'war' that is 'men's concern', and instead of referring to his authority in the house in the second half of the final line, Hector adds a reference to the 'men born in Troy', with whom he shares his concern for fighting.[61] Within the *Odyssey*, Telemachus' words also echo those of the Phaeacian king when he promises to take Odysseus home on the following day: 'your safe passage (πομπή) shall be men's concern, and my concern most of all; authority (κράτος) in this kingdom (ἐνὶ δήμῳ) is mine' (11.352–3).

This unexpected assertion of authority by a very young man stuns Penelope and its impact is expressed both times with exactly the same words: 'At this she withdrew to her room in wonder (θαμβήσασα), laying to heart her son's wise words (μῦθον πεπνυμένον)' (1.360–1 = 21.354–5). We should also note the order that Telemachus gives to his mother in Book 17: 'Bathe your face and put on fresh garments; pray, and promise to all the gods the sacrifice of unblemished hecatombs, in hope that Zeus will bring about requital' (17.48–51). The order is followed immediately, as we see from the repetition of the same formulae with a simple change of grammatical person: 'She bathed her face and put on fresh garments; she prayed and promised to all the gods the sacrifice of unblemished hecatombs, in hope that Zeus would bring about requital' (17.58–60).

Telemachus also asserts his authority over the suitors when he announces his intention to call an assembly to 'give them a forthright message (ἀπηλεγέως)' to leave his palace (1.373–4). His speech elicits amazement from the suitors, similar to that felt by Penelope: 'They bit their lips and wondered (θαύμαζον) at him, so fearless (θαρσαλέως) had been his words' (1.381–2).

For Antinous, there can be no other explanation for this sudden boldness than a divine intervention: 'Telemachus, it must be the gods themselves who teach you to speak so fearlessly and disdainfully (ὑψαγόρην τ' ἔμεναι καὶ θαρσαλέως ἀγορεύειν)' (1.384–5). Telemachus' transformation is also clearly revealed in Book 2 by his refusal to join

[61] *Iliad*, 6.490–3. See Rutherford 1991–3: 51–2.

the suitors at the banquet, as he had done in the past, and by the threats which accompany his refusal:

Now I am full grown, and with listening to this man's and that man's talk I have learned at last how things are, and all that I feel has gathered strength. So now I will strive as best I may to set the spirits of doom upon you, whether I go as far as Pylos or stay here in my own country. (2.314–17)

With his departure for Pylos, Telemachus begins to carry out this threat, which explains the suitors' decision, in Book 4, to kill him before it is too late, as Antinous states explicitly: 'Now he will go from bad to worse. I only pray that Zeus may cut short his recklessness before he can reach man's estate' (4.667–8).

On his return, Telemachus reaffirms his status as master of Odysseus' house. He reacts forcefully when Eurymachus throws the footstool at Odysseus in Book 18 and dismisses the suitors using the same formula as Alcinous, whose authority was uncontested, had used on Phaeacia: 'Go home to your beds' (18.408 = 7.188). Similarly, in Book 20, he invites the beggar to sit down beside him and proclaims his rights loud and clear: 'I myself will give you protection from the taunts and violence of the suitors, because the wealth of this house is not any and every man's; Odysseus won it, and I am his heir' (20.263–5). In both cases, the suitors react in the same way as they did in Book 1, the similarity being emphasized by the reuse of the same two formulaic lines.[62]

From Book 17 onwards, Telemachus also shows through his actions that he is truly the son of the father who revealed his identity to him in Book 16.[63] He does so through his self-control: Odysseus does not flinch when he is struck by Antinous but 'only shook his head silently as he brooded evil in his heart' (17.465); seeing this, Telemachus 'left his distress for the sufferer to swell within his breast without letting a tear fall from his eyes; he only shook his head silently as he brooded evil in his heart' (17.489–91). In Book 21, during the contest of the bow, he is almost his father's equal. He is able to set out the axes perfectly in preparation and 'amazement came upon all beholders as they saw the sureness of his movements, because he

[62] *Odyssey*, 18.410–11 = 20.268–9 = 1.381–2.

[63] Heath 2001: 144 draws attention to line 16.308 'His noble son answered him thus' (τὸν δ' ἀπαμειβόμενος προσεφώνεε φαίδιμος υἱός) describing it as 'a line unique in the Homeric corpus . . . that emphatically marks Telemachus' role as son'.

himself had never watched this thing being done' (21.122–3). He also almost manages to string Odysseus' bow: 'a fourth time he strained at it, and this time he would indeed have strung it, but Odysseus gave him a warning nod and stopped him short' (21.128–9). In Book 22, fighting at his father's side, he kills several suitors and is ready to stand against the people of Ithaca in Book 24 when Athena puts an end to the conflict. He thus shows, as Odysseus says, that courage is a characteristic quality of their family (24.508–9). But he remains subordinate to a father whose place he has only taken temporarily.[64]

(d) Laertes

Laertes only appears as a character in Book 24. But he is referred to on several occasions before this since, more than any other character, he embodies the disastrous consequences of Odysseus' absence. As Odysseus is told by his mother in Book 11:

> Your father stays on his own farm and never comes down to the city now. He has no bed to lie on, no blankets or shining rugs; in wintertime, he sleeps in the house just where his servants do, in the ashes by the fire, and the clothes on his back are wretched ones. When summer and mellow autumn come, his sleeping-places are on the ground, anywhere on the vineyard slope with its thick-strewn leaves. There he lies dismally, with grief in his heart ever more intense as he longs for your homecoming, and old age is hard for him besides. (11.187–96)[65]

When Odysseus finally sees him in Book 24, the detailed description of his clothing, beginning with his 'goatskin cap' (*αἰγείγ κυνέη*, 24.231) which contrasts with the 'well-made' 'bronze helmet' (*χαλκγργς κυνέη*) worn by noble warriors,[66] is a vivid illustration of his fall from grace. But, just as with Odysseus, when he is transformed into a beggar by Athena, Laertes' noble origins shine through his outward appearance, and he still has 'the look of a king'.[67] Once the recognition has taken place and he has had a bath and been dressed in clothing that is worthy of him, he looks 'godlike' (24.371). Thanks to Athena, who 'breathes strength into him' (24.520), his wish to become once more

64 See Thalmann 1998: 206–22.

65 See also *Odyssey*, 1.189–93, 15.353–5, 16.138–41, 24.226–31.

66 *Odyssey*, 10.206, 14.276 *ευτΰκτος*, 18.378, *πάγχαλκος*.

67 *Odyssey*, 24.253 (Laertes), cf. 20.194 (Odysseus).

the warrior he was before (24.376–82) is fulfilled and he kills the father of Antinous (24.521–5).

(e) The servants

The world of the humble subordinates, who depend entirely on their master and serve his interests, is much more prominent in the *Odyssey* than in the *Iliad*. But its representation is entirely shaped by the same aristocratic values. The division between 'the kings nourished by Zeus' and the 'common people' is very clear and 'there is no mistaking the child of a man whom the son of Cronos marked out for happiness at both birth and marriage'.[68] As William Thalmann puts it, 'the people of lower status . . . are imagined in accordance with the poem's ideological biases'.[69] But in the *Odyssey* the contrast between the 'good' servants who remain loyal to Odysseus and the 'bad' ones who have gone over to the suitors is just as important, as is made clear through a series of antithetical pairs, which give rise to a complex interplay of echoes and variations.[70]

First of all, there are the two good servants, Eumaeus[71] and Philoetius, 'the two servants of Odysseus, the cowherd and the swineherd' (21.189) who retain their affection for Odysseus and his family and carefully tend his livestock. Once Philoetius is introduced in Book 20, they are often linked together by conjunctions such as ἠδέ, καί (both meaning 'and'), and ἠέ ('or')[72] or by a dual verb,[73] and act in very similar ways. In Book 20, they arrive at the palace together: first we see Eumaeus ('then the swineherd appeared, driving three fat hogs, the best he had', 20.162–3) and then Philoetius ('After these two came a third, Philoetius, bringing the suitors a calfless heifer and fatted goats', 20.185–6). Once inside the great hall, they both serve at the feast: 'The swineherd gave each man his goblet, Philoetius brought round the bread in baskets' (20.253–4). In Book 21 they both weep on seeing Odysseus' bow and are both insulted by Antinous as a result (21.80–95). They leave together with Odysseus who,

[68] *Odyssey*, 4.207–8, cf. 4.63–4.
[69] Thalmann 1998: 13.
[70] See Fenik 1974: 172–5.
[71] On Eumaeus, see De Jong 2001: 341, Collombier 2002, and Schmidt 2006.
[72] *Odyssey*, 21.193; 22.103–4, 359, 435, 454; 23.297, 367, 24.359, 363.
[73] *Odyssey*, 21.86, 188, 222, 223; 21.188; 22.114, 173, 181, 187, 202.

satisfied that they are loyal, reveals his identity to them and gives them identical roles in the battle to follow: Eumaeus is given the task of ordering the maidservants to bar the doors to the hall while Philoetius is told to bolt the entrance to the courtyard (21.233–41). In Book 22, during the massacre of the suitors, they put their armour on together and both stand by Odysseus' side (22.114–15), they are both ordered to overpower and bind the goatherd Melanthius, which they do together (22.173–93), they kill some of the suitors together (22.284–5), and then scrape the floor of the hall clean after the massacre (22.454–6). In Book 23 they, along with Telemachus, create the false festivities that are designed to cover up the massacre, before going to bed (23.297–9), and set off with Odysseus and Telemachus to Laertes' farm at the end of the book. In Book 24, they prepare the meal for Odysseus and his family (24.359–64) and arm themselves to fight alongside them in the last battle that is interrupted by Athena (24.496–7).

Despite all this, the role of Eumaeus, who 'cared for his master's possessions more than any other servant of Odysseus' (14.3–4), is a great deal more important than that of Philoetius. He is introduced in Book 14, while Philoetius only appears in Book 20. The swineherd is given an extensive biography (15.363–70, 402–84) and has noble origins (as the son of a king who only became a slave after being kidnapped by Phoenician pirates and sold to Laertes), in contrast to Philoetius, whose story is summed up in two lines, telling us that 'when [he] was still a lad [Odysseus] made [him] the keeper of his cattle in the land of the Cephallenians' (20.209–10). The fidelity of the swineherd, who 'is as loyal to [Odysseus] as ever; he loves Telemachus and he loves Penelope' (13.405–6), and the care he has taken to protect his master's possessions, are emphasized on several occasions and his generous hospitality is illustrated in detail in Books 14 and 15. In the case of Philoetius, these themes are merely expressed in a few lines in his speech in Book 20.199–225. It is not surprising therefore that, during the contest of the bow, it is Eumaeus and not Philoetius who hands the bow to Odysseus.[74] This imbalance only changes once in Philoetius' favour, when the poet makes him speak as he kills Ctesippus (22.287–91).

[74] *Odyssey*, 21.359, 366–7, 378–9.

A pair of loyal maidservants corresponds to this pair of loyal servants.[75] But, in contrast to Eumaeus and Philoetius, these women do not act together, except in Book 23.289–91, where they both prepare the bed for Odysseus and Penelope before one of them guides them to their room. Moreover, the imbalance between the major figure of Eurycleia, who appears in Book 1, right at the beginning of the poem, and Eurynome, who is only mentioned from Book 17 onwards, is much greater. 'Eurycleia, daughter of Ops, son of Pisenor' has an aristocratic name,[76] a genealogy, and a story: 'Laertes had bought her long ago as a girl, giving twenty oxen's worth of goods for her; in the household he paid her no less regard than he did his wife, but he never lay with her in love, fearing his wife's anger' (1.430–3). Eurynome, by contrast, is only defined by her function as 'housekeeper' or 'chambermaid'.[77] And while Eurycleia serves the men of the household above all, Telemachus and then Odysseus,[78] the second is particularly closely associated with Penelope.

The relatively important role played by Eurycleia in the Adventures of Telemachus,[79] can be explained both by her close relationship to the young man ('Among all the maids she was always the fondest of Telemachus; in his childhood she had been his nurse', 1.434–5) and by her function as a housekeeper ('day and night she was near [the storeroom], using her shrewd wits to watch over everything', 2.345–7). She secretly prepares the provisions for Telemachus' voyage (2.348–80) and swears to him that she will not tell Penelope 'until some dozen days have passed or she herself misses [him] or hears from another of [his] going' (2.374–5). She keeps this promise scrupulously, only telling Penelope the truth two books later, at 4.742–7, when Penelope has already heard about Telemachus' departure from the herald, Medon. Her special relationship to Telemachus is also evident in Book 17.31–3, where she is the first to see him on his return, and at the beginning of Book 19 (lines 15–30), where she follows his orders to lock the

[75] See Scott 1918, Fenik 1974: 189–91, Pedrick 1994, and Thalmann 1998: 74–83.

[76] *Odyssey*, 1.429, 2.347, 20.148. See Thalmann 1998: 75.

[77] *Odyssey*, 17.495, 18.169, 19.96, 23.154 (*ταμίγ*) and 293 (*θαλαμγπόλος*).

[78] See Thalmann 1998: 78.

[79] See Thalmann 1998: 74–81.

maidservants into their quarters while he removes the weapons from the great hall.

From Book 19 onwards, the emphasis is on her relationship with Odysseus.[80] It is she who washes his feet, recognizes him from his scar, and promises to remain silent, as she promised Telemachus in Book 2, adding that she will provide him with the names of the disloyal maidservants. She is present, in the background, during Books 20 and 21 and makes her own contribution to his revenge, closing the doors of the great hall to prevent the sound of the massacre from spreading throughout the palace. She returns to the foreground in Book 22, at the end of the massacre, first to show up Odysseus' own self-restraint when he stops her from rejoicing at the sight of the dead bodies (22.407–16). In this episode she also keeps her promise to identify the guilty maidservants, brings the sulphur and fire needed to purify the palace, and announces to the loyal maidservants that their master has returned.[81] Finally, is it Eurycleia who tells Penelope at the beginning of Book 23 (lines 1–84) that her husband has returned and taken his revenge and receives the order from Odysseus and then from his wife to prepare the bed, which will lead to the recognition between the two.[82]

If we leave aside the brief curse that she pronounces against Antinous (17.495–7), Eurynome simply carries out Penelope's orders in Books 17 to 19. In Book 20 (line 4), she shows her concern for the queen's guest when she covers him with a blanket. She also gives him a bath after the massacre of the suitors, but this bath, which is far from having the dramatic significance of the one given to him by Eurycleia, is recounted in just three lines (23.153–5). Throughout the poem, Eurynome is little more than a pale shadow of Eurycleia.

Finally, we should not forget Dolius, his wife (the old woman who looks after Laertes),[83] and their children. Given to Penelope as a wedding present by her father (4.735–6), Dolius 'epitomizes the contrast between good and bad slaves through his two sets of children',[84] on the one hand Melanthius and his sister Melantho who have taken the side of the suitors,[85] on the other his six sons who

[80] *Odyssey*, 19.357–8, 386–93, 467–505.
[81] *Odyssey*, 22.417–25 and 480–96.
[82] *Odyssey*, 23.171–2, 177–80.
[83] *Odyssey*, 1.191–3, 24.211–12, 389–90.
[84] Thalmann 1998: 67.
[85] *Odyssey*, 17.212, 18.321–2,22.159.

work with him on Laertes' farm and are ready to fight alongside Odysseus and his family.[86]

2. THE SUITORS AND THEIR SUPPORTERS

Like Odysseus, the suitors are members of the elite (*aristoi*)[87] but they also serve as the villains of the story in the *Odyssey*.[88] The whole lexicon of terms for crimes and excesses is applied to them. We hear of their 'wrongdoing' (ὑπερβασίη, ἀταλασθία) and their violence (ὕβρις); they are labelled 'criminals' (ἀλείτης and ἀτάσθαλος) and described as 'overbearing' (ὑπερφίαλος, ὑπερηνορέων) and shameless (ἀναιδής). They are criticized for their disgraceful acts (αἴσχεα) which break all the rules of decent behaviour (ἀεικέα). They certainly pay no heed to the concern for the appropriateness whose important place in Homeric ethics has been pointed out by A. A. Long (1970: 135–9). They also have little concern for justice (δίκη or θέμις) and fear neither the criticisms of men (νέμεσις) nor the wrath (μῆνις) of the gods.

Their motivation has been understood in various ways, as the thirst for power (Thornton 1970: 63–7) or sexual desire (Halverson 1986: 124–6). It is no doubt best to acknowledge that, in the words of Thalmann (1998: 182), 'It is the notion of honor, together with the competitive ethos it engenders, that connects Penelope herself, Odysseus' wealth, and his status as objects of desire . . . the text emphasizes now one now another of the suitors' motives and it leaves the relation among these goals largely to be inferred.'

Their actions, however, are clear. The suitors act aggressively towards Odysseus' household and thus Odysseus himself. Their aim is to take his place in his wife's bed. They force their presence upon his son, 'against his will',[89] and even try to kill him at one point. They sleep with the women of the household. Finally they pillage his possessions in a manner that is depicted in very concrete terms as outrageous and scandalous throughout the poem. They threaten to 'devour' Telemachus' wealth (2.203) using the verb βιβρώσκειν, a rare word which elsewhere in Homeric epic is applied to the feasts of wild

[86] *Odyssey*, 24.222–5, 387–411, and 497–501. [87] *Odyssey*, 1.245–7 2.50–1.
[88] Whitman 1958: 306–7. [89] *Odyssey*, 2.311, 3.213, 15.19, 16.94.

beasts (*Iliad*, 22.94, *Odyssey*, 22.403) or used to express Hera's hatred for the Trojans whom she would like to devour raw (*Iliad*, 4.34–6). They tear to pieces (δαρδάπτειν) his goods (*Odyssey*, 14.92, 16.315) another rare word, used once elsewhere in Homer to describe scavengers tearing a stricken stag to pieces (*Iliad*, 11.479). This image has a literal force as the suitors are always eating and the impact of their excessive consumption is expressed throughout in terms of the bread they eat, the wine they pour from jars and drink, and, above all, the herds of beasts that are brought to the palace to be slaughtered by them. This last theme, which is the most important given that livestock equates to riches in Homeric society and is the accepted measure of worth, is explored from Book 17 onwards with an artful use of variation that has rightly been compared to the 'art of the fugue'.[90] In so doing, they cause the breakdown of the system of exchange which normally underlies the banquet. Instead of eating at each other's houses in turn, as Telemachus suggests they do,[91] or organizing 'contribution feasts' (ἔρανος, 1. 234) where the cost is shared by all, they find it 'a better thing, a more desirable thing, to waste one man's substance and go scot-free'.[92]

From the moment when the beggar first enters the palace, the suitors are also guilty of repeated breaches of the laws of hospitality. In an aristocratic world, in which generosity is an important virtue and where one wins honour through giving just as much as through receiving valuable gifts,[93] the suitors are so avaricious that they even refuse to be generous with other people's possessions[94] and subject Telemachus' guests to insults and blows. It is easy to see why Odysseus, and then Penelope, say after their deaths that 'They had no regard (τίεσκον) for any man, good or bad, who might come their way' (22.414–15 = 23.65–6).

The suitors are most often referred to as a group. They usually appear in the plural and the 'catalogue of suitors' given in Book 16.247–51, in contrast to the Catalogue of Ships in *Iliad* 2, does not include a single name. They act in concert and often speak as one, as is shown by the formula 'This is what one of those arrogant youths would say' (ὧδε δέ τις εἴπεσκε νέων ὑπερηνορεόντων)[95] and its variant

[90] See Bader 1976 and Chapter 3 above (pp. 65–9).
[91] *Odyssey*, 1.374–5 = 2.139–40.
[92] *Odyssey*, 1.376–7 = 2.141–2.
[93] See Finley 1977a: 121.
[94] *Odyssey*, 17.400–4.
[95] *Odyssey*, 2.324; 4.769, 17.482; 20.375.

'Then another of the arrogant young men would say' (ἄλλος δ' αὖ εἴπεσκε νέων ὑπερηνορεόντων).[96]

Some individuals, however, do emerge from the group. Some of these, like Euryades and Elatus, are only mentioned in Book 22 (line 267) as they are killed by Odysseus and his followers. Others, like Demoptolemus and Polybus, are more visible as they are mentioned by name twice, once in the list of the 'most valiant suitors' (22.242–3) and then at the moment of their deaths (22.266 and 284). Their sole function is thus to bring out the strength and courage of their opponents since, in the Homeric world, an anonymous victory is not a true triumph: it is vital that the victim know the name of his vanquisher, as we see in the episode of the Cyclops, but also that the vanquisher be able to name his victim. In comparison to the 'minor combatants' in the *Iliad*, studied by Gisela Strasburger (1952), these suitors are 'very minor combatants': they are not even accorded a brief biography or a description of the fatal wound. They are reduced to names, sometimes with the addition of an epithet, like 'warlike Polybus' (22.243). Others appear in two different places, but their textual existence, so to speak, is confined to three or four lines. Eurynomus appears first as one of the four sons of Aegyptius, the first man to speak at the assembly, and he only reappears in the list of suitors in Book 22.[97] Both Eurydamas and Peisander, son of Polyctor, are singled out for the splendid gifts they offer to Penelope in Book 18 before being killed in Book 22.[98]

Others have a more substantial existence. Before being killed by Telemachus, Leocrites son of Evenor speaks at the assembly in Book 2.[99] In his speech, which is the final one, he insults Mentor and boasts that he would be able to vanquish Odysseus himself, if he were to return secretly to his palace. Amphimedon, who recounts the massacre to the inhabitants of the Underworld in Book 24, is given a brief one-line genealogy: he is the 'son of Melaneus, illustrious Amphimedon' and even has an embryonic biography: he once played host to Agamemnon on Ithaca (24.103–4). But he achieves little in battle: he 'wounded Telemachus on the wrist, though the bronze did

[96] *Odyssey*, 2.331, 21.401.

[97] *Odyssey*, 2.22 and 22.242.

[98] *Odyssey*, 18.297–8 and 22.283 (Eurydamas); 18.299–300 and 22.243, 268 (Peisander).

[99] *Odyssey*, 2. 242–57, 22. 294–5.

not pierce below the skin' before being killed by him,[100] a pattern that is familiar from the battle narratives of the *Iliad*. Finally there is Ctesippus, who is introduced at some length in Book 20: 'There was among them a lawless-hearted (ἀθεμίστια εἰδώς) man who was called Ctesippus and lived in Same; confident in his vast possessions (κτεάτεσσι πεποιθὼς), he was wooing the wife of the absent king' (20.287–90).

This portrait clearly alludes to Polyphemus, who is the epitome of 'lawlessness' in the *Odyssey*.[101] But it is also tempting to see a parallel between this suitor, 'confident in his vast possessions', and the man that Odysseus pretends to be in Book 18 when he tries to warn Amphinomus against 'lawlessness' by offering his own story as an example: he claims to have committed crimes 'relying on my father and brothers' (πατρί τ' ἐμῷ πίσυνος καὶ ἐμοῖσι κασιγνήτοισι, 18.139–40). This introduction is perfectly suited to a man who will offer Odysseus an insulting 'gift of hospitality', suggesting that he share it with the other servants: instead of the usual gift of a choice piece of meat, which he can then share with whomever he wishes to honour in his turn (as Odysseus does with Demodocus), he throws a cow's foot at him which, luckily for him, misses its mark for otherwise Telemachus would have killed him then and there.[102] In the end he gains little from the delay. In Book 22 he merely grazes Eumaeus' shoulder with his spear before being killed by the cowherd, in a fine example of poetic justice.[103]

By comparison with these minor characters, Antinous and Eurymachus 'the foremost of the suitors who excelled in manly prowess' (4.629 = 21.187) stand out. They sometimes form a pair,[104] and speak one after the other: in Book 1, they reply to Telemachus in turn.[105] During the assembly in Book 2, Telemachus replies to each of them, one after the other (2.129–45, 208–23). On occasion they seem interchangeable: in Book 16 and in Book 21, Penelope speaks to Antinous but it is Eurymachus who replies.[106] In Book 18, Penelope's speech is framed by that of Eurymachus and that of Antinous and they present

[100] *Odyssey*, 22.277–8 and 284.
[101] *Odyssey*, 9.189 (ἀθεμίστια ᾔδη) and 428 (ἀθεμίστια εἰδώς).
[102] *Odyssey*, 20.291–300 and 303–7.
[103] *Odyssey*, 22.279–80, 285–6.
[104] *Odyssey*, 4.628; 18. 65; 21.186, 277.
[105] *Odyssey*, 1.383–7: Antinous; 399–411: Eurymachus.
[106] *Odyssey*, 16.417–47 and 21.311–29.

their gifts one after the other.[107] In Books 17 and 18 they both insult the beggar and throw objects at him: a stool and a footstool.[108] In Books 21 and 22, they are the last two to attempt the trial of the bow and the first two to be killed.[109] Their wounds and their deaths are described in detail, in the style of the *aristeiai* of the *Iliad*, which they surpass in horror.

They are also equally forgetful of the good deeds that have been performed for them in the past. In Book 16, Penelope denounces the ingratitude of Antinous whose father's life was saved by Odysseus (16. 424–30). And Eurymachus, who recalls shortly afterwards that Odysseus once took him on his knees and treated him like his own son, is equally ungrateful (16.442–4).

But here too there are limits to the parallel. It is Antinous who instigates the worst crimes. It is his idea in Book 4.669–72 to ambush and kill Telemachus on his return journey and he thinks about killing him again in Book 16.383–4, where he suggests to the suitors that they try to kill him in the countryside or on the road. He is also the first to strike the beggar in Book 17. His authority over the other suitors is visible in other details. In Book 18, he organizes the fight between Irus and Odysseus and gives the prize to the winner;[110] he also suggests to the suitors that they give presents to Penelope (18.286–7). In Book 21, he is the one who dictates the order in which the suitors attempt the trial of the bow and then decides to put off the end of the trial until the next day.[111] Eurymachus is only truly in charge during the brief interval between the death of Antinous and his own death, when he tries, in vain, to make a truce with Odysseus (22.44–78).

As they are portrayed in the *Odyssey*, these two suitors are therefore something of a paradox which is no doubt what makes them interesting as characters. They are members of the elite. Eurymachus, 'far-famed son of wise Polybus', is regarded 'with reverence like a god' by the people of Ithaca and is 'by far the best (*aristos*)' (15.519–21). Antinous is similarly considered to be 'the best (*aristos*) of his age-group for words and counsel' (16.418–20). He looks like 'the best of the Achaeans', making him like Achilles, and is a 'kinglike man' (17.415–16). But their behaviour is in stark contrast to their glowing

[107] *Odyssey*, 18.244–89 and 292–6.

[108] *Odyssey*, 17.462–3 and 18.394.

[109] *Odyssey*, 21.186–7, 22.8–21 (the death of Antinous), and 79–88 (the death of Eurymachus).

[110] *Odyssey*, 18.34–50, 78–87, 118–19.

[111] *Odyssey*, 21.140–3 and 256–69.

reputations. Eurymachus deceives Penelope by posing as Telemachus' protector, as the narrator says, 'So he spoke in disarming phrase, but he himself was plotting destruction for Telemachus' (16.448). Antinous plots the death of the son of the man who once saved his father's life and has no respect for suppliants (16.420–32). He speaks in a manner that is unworthy of his status.[112] He is the 'harshest' of the suitors,[113] in a world in which kings are supposed to be 'gentle',[114] and is compared by Penelope to 'some black spirit of destruction' (17.500).

The villainy of Antinous and the suitors in general is thrown into sharp relief by the presence among them of two 'good' men, Amphinomus and Leiodes, who, like Antinous and Eurymachus, form an asymmetrical pair. The priest, Leiodes, who was 'the only one among them to hate unrighteousness, and was indignant with all the suitors' (21.146–7), is the less important of the two and is characterized as much by his ineffectiveness as by his sense of justice. He appears only in Book 21, at the moment of the trial of the bow, which he is the first to attempt and to fail (21.144–66). And this first cameo appearance seems designed solely to prepare for his prayer to Odysseus in Book 22.310–19 and to validate in advance a speech that reflects the story: 'I tell you; I spoke no evil and did no evil to the serving-women in your halls; far from it, I strove to check the others when they were guilty of such things' (313–15).

Amphinomus plays a much more prominent role, not unlike that of Amphiaraos in Aeschylus' *Seven against Thebes*. Like him, he is a just man caught up among the impious, even if he finally suffers the same fate as them. Like Leiodes, he is introduced in a way that contrasts him with the other suitors: 'He was the son of Nisus and grandson of Aretes; he was moreover chief of the suitors from Dulichium, that island of pasture and wheat, and he above all the rest of them could please Penelope with his words, for he had sound sense' (16.395–8).

His genealogy also hints at his excellence as he boasts a king named Aretes ('the excellent one') among his ancestors and his father is Nisus, whose qualities and good reputation are mentioned by Odysseus later

[112] *Odyssey*, 17.381: Eumaeus says to Antinous, 'high-born you may be, Antinous, but your words do you no honour' (οὐ μὲν καλὰ καὶ ἐσθλὸς ἐὼν ἀγορεύεις).

[113] *Odyssey*, 17.388 and 395: χαλεπός.

[114] *Odyssey*, 2.47, 230, 234; 5.12: ἤπιος.

on in the poem (18.126–7). His reactions are consistently opposed to those of the other suitors. In Book 16, when the suitors hear of Telemachus' return, he greets the news with 'gentle laughter' (line 354) which contrasts with the other suitors' shocked and downcast appearance (line 342). He is the only one to reject the idea of killing a man from a royal family without Zeus' consent and to oppose Antinous' plan to ambush Telemachus (16.400–5). It is also Amphinomus who draws the conclusions from the unfavourable omen sent by Zeus and forces the other suitors to abandon their project (20.244–7). In Book 18 he is the only one to welcome Odysseus disguised as the beggar: he gives him bread and greets him by giving him a cup of wine (18.119–23), earning Odysseus' compliments for his 'good sense' and 'courtesy' and a helpful warning that is, however, given in vain.[115] He then protects Odysseus from Eurymachus' blows, approves of Telemachus' action in sending the suitors home and criticizing their behaviour, and suggests a libation be made to the gods.[116]

But the figure of Amphinomus is also the best example (though by no means the only one) of the epic's indifference to psychological coherence. The Amphinomus who takes over from Antinous and Eurymachus as the suitors' leader and charges at Odysseus before being killed by Telemachus in Book 22.89–94 is simply a warrior whose defeat allows Telemachus to demonstrate his superior prowess. The same could be said of Agelaus. When he is mentioned for the first time, in Book 20, he is the double of Amphinomus in Book 18: the four lines of verse in which he approves of Telemachus' decisive action are exactly the same lines that had been attributed to Amphinomus on the earlier occasion.[117] But in Book 22 he is above all a fighter who shows courage and initiative, first in trying to raise the alarm, then in leading the resistance.[118] At this point, the restraint he showed earlier has entirely disappeared and he threatens Athena/Mentor with reprisals against his entire family (22.212–23).

Alongside the suitors we need to mention the two disloyal servants, Melanthius and Melantho.[119] They are introduced into the narrative in identical ways: in Book 17, Melanthius encounters Odysseus and

[115] *Odyssey*, 18.125–56.
[116] *Odyssey*, 18.394–6, 412–27. See Chapter 2 above, p. 67.
[117] *Odyssey*, 20.322–5 = 18.414–17.
[118] *Odyssey*, 22.131–4 and 247–55).
[119] See Fenik 1974: 174–8.

kicks him before returning to the palace and sitting down beside Eurymachus 'whom he liked more than any other' (line 257).[120] In Book 18, it is the turn of his sister Melantho, 'mistress and bedfellow to Eurymachus' (18.325), to throw abuse at Odysseus.[121] In Book 19.65, Melantho 'renews her insults to Odysseus' and in Book 20 it is the turn of Melanthius, in a scene which echoes the first since it takes place as the goatherd is once again 'bringing the finest beasts from his herds to make the suitors' morning meal, along with two herdsmen'.[122] But this second scene is less violent as there are no blows.

These parallels in fact serve to bring out the differences in Odysseus' reactions to the siblings. He suffers Melanthius' insults and blows in silence (17.235–8 and 20.183–4), but he threatens Melantho (more violently the first time) (18.337–9 and 19.70–88). Moreover, after Book 20, Melantho fades back into the group of disloyal maidservants destined to be hanged at the end of Book 22 (430–73), while Melanthius, who actively helped the suitors in Book 22 by going twice to the storeroom to fetch arms for them (135–46,182–5), before he is overpowered by Eumaeus and Philoetius (22.186–93), is horribly mutilated. What was, for the heroes of the *Iliad*, a threat that was never realized becomes a reality for this member of the lower orders:[123] 'They cut off his nose and ears with the ruthless bronze, tore out his parts to be eaten raw by dogs and in savage fury lopped off his hands and feet' (22.475–7).

Finally, there is the 'real' public beggar, Irus, who is a counterpart to the 'false' beggar Odysseus in Book 18 in an episode where the language of blame replaces that of praise.[124] Odysseus, who is distinguished in this episode for his *mētis* and his clever speech,[125] is a beggar in appearance alone: his rags hide 'his fine sturdy thighs . . . his broad shoulders . . . and his chest and stout arms' (18.67–9). Irus' appearance is deceptive in a different way: he looked tall but had neither strength nor vigour.[126] Their fight, which provokes laughter, is a mere parody of heroic combats or athletic contests, like the boxing match between Epeius and Euryalus in the funeral games for Patroclus (*Iliad*, 23.685–99): the beggar is driven to fight by his

[120] *Odyssey*, 17.212–57. [121] *Odyssey*, 18.321–36.
[122] *Odyssey*, 20.174–5 = 17.213–14. [123] Thalmann 1998: 95.
[124] See Nagy 1979: 225–6, Pucci 1987: 161–4, De Jong 2001: 437–42.
[125] *Odyssey*, 18.51: τοῖς δὲ δολοφρονέων μετέφη πολύμητις Ὀδυσσεύς.
[126] *Odyssey*, 18.3–4: οὐδέ οἱ ἦν ἴς | οὐδὲ βίη, εἶδος δὲ μάλα μέγας ἦν ὁράασθαι.

poverty and by his 'stomach'[127] and the prize is nothing more than a goat's paunch stuffed with blood and a promise of food in the future (18.44–9). But it also announces the coming victory of Odysseus over the insatiable suitors. This final example therefore reveals yet again the play of echoes and variations that is central to the depiction of the characters of the *Odyssey*.

127 *Odyssey*, 18.53–4: ἀλλά με γαστὴρ | ὀτρύνει κακοεργός.

9

Women in the *Odyssey*

The importance of the female figures in the *Odyssey*, beginning with Penelope, was noted by ancient readers of the epic. An epigram in the *Greek Anthology* (9.192) contrasts the *Iliad*, with its two male heroes Achilles and Hector, with the *Odyssey* which tells of the 'travails of Odysseus and the tears shed by virtuous Penelope over her empty bed'. In 1713, Richard Bentley, in his *Remarks upon a Discourse of Free Thinking*, contrasted the *Iliad*, written for a male audience, with the *Odyssey*, which he claimed was composed with a female audience in mind. Over a century later, Samuel Butler (1897) even suggested that the poem had a female author, given the prominence of women in the poem, a hypothesis that was taken up rather more recently by Raymond Ruyer (1977). Despite all this, it was still possible in the 1970s to complain, as did Charles Rowan Beye, that the female side of the *Odyssey* had received little critical attention: 'the feminine component or facet of the *Odyssey* has never been stressed, talked to, or accounted for. The generations of male critics apparently did not know how to accommodate women into the epic tradition.'[1] This gap has been well and truly filled in the intervening years by numerous articles[2] and by books such as *The Distaff Side: Representing the Female in* Homer's Odyssey (1995) or *Siren Songs: Gender, Audience and Narrators in the Odyssey* (1995) as well as five books on Penelope published

[1] Beye 1974: 93. Beye cites (99 n. 1) Wehrli 1959, Harder 1960, and Allione 1963. See also Büchner 1940 and Segal 1968.

[2] Bergren 1981, Beye 1974, Doherty 1995a, Dupont-Roc and Le Boulluec 1976, Emlyn-Jones 1984, Felson-Rubin 1996, Felson and Slatkin 2004, Foley 1978, 1995, Helleman 1995, Holmberg 1995, McDonald 1997, Murnaghan 1986, 1994, 1995, Naerebout 1987, Slatkin 1986, Thomas 1988, van Northwick 1979, Whittaker 1999, Winkler 1990, Wohl 1993, Zeitlin 1996.

between 1975 and 2003.[3] Some of these readings, like those of Jack Winkler[4] and Helene Foley,[5] even present Penelope as the true heroine of the *Odyssey*. In this chapter I will outline the female figures of the *Odyssey* and the role played by women in the action of the poem, starting with the women who appear during Odysseus' voyages (Circe, Calypso, Nausicaa, and Arete), followed by Helen and Clytemnestra, before focusing on Penelope, a complex character who will serve as a basis for an investigation of how the feminine is represented in the poem.

1. CALYPSO AND CIRCE

Calypso and Circe, who both wish to make Odysseus their husband,[6] have much in common, as we saw in Chapter 6 (pp. 171–2). But these two characters have too often been interpreted in ways that assimilate them a little too closely to ordinary women,[7] and may tell us more about the psychology of male readers than about Homer's poem. William Stanford preferred by far the 'warm affectionateness' of Calypso, who 'does all she can to keep' Odysseus, to Circe whom he characterized as 'a dispassionate enchantress intent on having her own way' and who seems to show 'nonchalance in parting with Odysseus'.[8] Charles Segal, by contrast, prefers Circe, who 'seems to understand her man better than Calypso. Rather than keep him, a pining, unwilling lover in her bed . . . she sends him off at the first sign of uneasiness',[9] while Calypso tries selfishly to condemn Odysseus to an immortality that he does not want. In place of these very personal

[3] Mactoux 1975, Katz 1991, Papadopoulou-Belmehdi 1994, Felson-Rubin 1994, Clayton 2003.

[4] Winkler 1990: 133; 'the real center of the *Odyssey's* plot . . . is the way in which Penelope, constrained as she is by the competing and irreconcilable demands of social propriety, exerts some degree of real control over events and makes possible the homecoming of her husband.'

[5] Foley 1995: 32: 'The central moral decision on which the action of the *Odyssey* turns is Penelope's. She must decide whether to stay in Odysseus' house, continue to guard it, and wait for her husband to return or to marry one of the suitors.'

[6] λιλαιομένη πόσιν εἶναι, *Odyssey*, 1.15; 9.30; 23.334 (Calypso); 9.32: (Circe).

[7] This type of reading is rightly criticized by Segal 1968: 421.

[8] Stanford 1954: 47–8.

[9] Segal 1968: 422–4.

readings, we might prefer an interpretation that takes fuller account of their double nature as women and goddesses.

Calypso and Circe are characterized, as are ordinary women, by their physical beauty (like them, they have 'beautiful hair'[10]) but their clothing surpasses anything worn by mortal women in its splendour: they alone have cloaks of shining white and golden girdles.[11] Their occupations are also close to those of mortal women: when they first appear in the Odyssey they are both engaged in weaving.[12] They give baths to men,[13] provide them with clothes,[14] food,[15] or the animals they need for their sacrifices,[16] and serve their meals.[17] In short, they take care of them.[18]

But they are also dread goddesses[19] who exert a power over men that is entirely foreign to their human sisters, a dimension that emerges more clearly when we compare them to the temptress Siduri in the Akkadian epic *Gilgamesh*.[20] Both have the power to prevent Odysseus from leaving,[21] but only Calypso forces him to stay against his will.[22] In the end, both are transformed from obstacles to his return into helpers as they make favourable winds blow.[23] Calypso also helps Odysseus by giving him the tools he needs to build his raft as well as provisions for his journey, while Circe gives him advice on how to make the voyage safely.[24]

Both goddesses are also characterized by their cunning.[25] But this quality takes different forms and has varying results. Calypso makes use of 'soft and coaxing words' to charm Odysseus into forgetting his

[10] *Odyssey*, 1.86; 5.30, 58; 7.246, 255; 12.449 (Calypso); 10.136, 11.8, 12.150 (Circe).
[11] *Odyssey*, 5.230–2: Calypso; 10.543–5: Circe.
[12] *Odyssey*, 5.62 (Calypso) and 10.222–3: Circe.
[13] *Odyssey*, 5.264: Calypso and 10.449–50: Circe.
[14] *Odyssey*, 5.264, 7.259–60: Calypso, and 10.365: Circe.
[15] *Odyssey*, 5.265–67, 7.264–5: Calypso.
[16] *Odyssey*, 10.571–2: Circe.
[17] *Odyssey*, 5.196–7: Calypso, 10.370–2: Circe.
[18] *Odyssey*, 8.453: Calypso; 12.448–50: Circe.
[19] *Odyssey*, 7.246, 255, 12.449 (Calypso); 10.136, 11.8, 12.150 (Circe).
[20] See Nagler 1996.
[21] *Odyssey*, 1.14 and 55, 9.29, 23.334 (Calypso); 9.31 (Circe).
[22] *Odyssey*, 4.557, 5.14, 154, 17.143: ἀνάγκῃ; 5.155: οὐκ ἐθέλων.
[23] *Odyssey*, 5.268 (Calypso) and 12.148–50 (Circe).
[24] *Odyssey*, 5.233–7 and 265–7 (Calypso); 12.36–141 (Circe).
[25] Calypso: *Odyssey*, 7.245 (δολόεσσα Καλυψώ); Circe: 9.31–2 (Κίρκη... δολόεσσα), 10.339: (δολοφρονέουσα), 23.321: (Κίρκης κατέλεξε δόλον πολυμηχανίην τε).

homeland,[26] but without success. The sorceress Circe, with her 'deadly arts' (10.289), uses *pharmaka*[27] to 'enchant' men,[28] making them forget their homeland and turning them into beasts. She can also reverse her spell thanks to another *pharmakon* and even make them 'younger than they had been before, and taller and handsomer to the eye' (10.395–6). But her magic is powerless when confronted by the good *pharmakon* given to Odysseus by Hermes.[29]

This explains Odysseus' reaction to the promises made to him by Calypso and Circe. When Calypso announces that she will let him go after all, tells him to build a raft, and promises to help him leave, he does not believe her:

> Goddess, your purpose cannot be as you say (ἄλλο τι δὴ σύ, θεά, τόδε μήδεαι): you cannot intend to speed me home. You tell me to make myself a raft to cross the great gulf of ocean . . . I will not set foot on such a raft unless I am sure of your good will—unless, goddess, you take on yourself to swear a solemn oath not to plot against me any new mischief to my ruin (μή τί τοι αὐτῷ πῆμα κακὸν βουλευσέμεν ἄλλο). (5.173–9)

Similarly, when Circe invites him into her bed after her *pharmaka* have failed, he is equally suspicious and asks her in very similar terms to swear that she is not plotting to harm him:

> Circe, how can you ask me to show you gentleness? In this very house you have turned my comrades into swine, and now that you have me also here you ask me in your treacherousness (δολοφρονέουσα) to enter your room and lie with you, only that when I lie naked there you may rob me of courage and of manhood (ὄφρα με γυμνωθέντα κακὸν καὶ ἀνήνορα θήῃς). Never, goddess, could I bring myself to lie with you unless you take on yourself to swear a solemn oath not to plot against me any new mischief to my ruin. (10.337–44)

Goddesses here are treated in the same way as mortal women and Odysseus' suspicion prefigures the advice that Agamemnon, speaking from his own bitter experience, gives him in Book 11: 'You too must never favour your wife too far; when you have perfected some scheme, do not tell her the whole of it, but reveal part, and part leave hidden' (11.441–3).

[26] *Odyssey*, 1.56–7: αἰεὶ δὲ μαλακοῖσι καὶ αἱμυλίοισι λόγοισι | θέλγει, ὅπως Ἰθάκης ἐπιλήσεται.

[27] *Odyssey*, 10.213, 236, 276, 290, 317, 326, 327, 394.

[28] *Odyssey*, 10.213, 291, 318.

[29] *Odyssey*, 10.287, 292, 302.

The Calypso episode also shows that female figures retain a certain mystery and that it is difficult for men to perceive their motives unless they choose to reveal them themselves. We see this when Calypso claims that she is letting Odysseus go of her own free will and hides Hermes' role in his liberation (5.161). Not surprisingly, Odysseus is puzzled by her motives: 'She told me and urged me to return, perhaps because Zeus had sent her warning, perhaps because her own mind had changed' (7.262–3).

This episode also reveals the inferiority of goddesses to their masculine counterparts, who have multiple sexual liaisons with mortal women (as we are reminded in the catalogue of heroines in the *nekuia*[30]) while denying their female counterparts the right to do likewise with mortal men. This is no doubt in order to defend their privileges but may also serve to preserve the hierarchy between the sexes which might be threatened if the female partner had a higher status than her male companion:[31]

> You are merciless, you gods, resentful beyond all other beings; you are jealous if without disguise a goddess makes a man her bedfellow, her beloved husband. So it was when Dawn of the rosy fingers chose out Orion; you gods who live in such ease yourselves were jealous of her until chaste Artemis in her cloth-of-gold visited him with her gentle shafts and slew him in Ortygia. So it was when Demeter of the braided tresses followed her heart and lay in love with Iasion in the triple-furrowed field; Zeus was aware of it soon enough and hurled the bright thunderbolt that killed him. And now so it is with me; you resent this mortal man beside me. (5.118–29)

2. NAUSICAA AND ARETE

The women of Phaeacia live in a type of Golden Age, at the intersection between the human and the divine. Nausicaa and her mother Arete, like all the Phaeacians, may be 'close to the gods' (ἀγχίθεοι, 5.35) but they are still mortal, although they are distinguished by a godlike beauty. Nausicaa is so beautiful that she stands out among her servants who themselves have 'beautiful hair' and 'white arms'[32] and whose beauty comes from the Graces (6.18). She is even compared

[30] *Odyssey*, 11.235–70, 305–20.
[31] See Wohl 1993:26, Kearns 2004: 66.
[32] εὐπλόκαμοι, 6.135, 222, 238; λευκώλενοι, 6.239.

to a goddess more than once, both for her stature and for her appearance. She is compared to Artemis twice (6.102–9 and 150–2) and this leads her to be courted, like Penelope, by the young men of the elite (6.34–5 and 284). Her behaviour is a model of modesty and propriety: she is concerned about her reputation, which, for a young girl, depends on the care she takes of her family's clothing and the measures she takes to avoid censure by appearing in public with a man or by entering into a relationship with him without her parents' consent.[33] She greets the suppliant exactly as she should, with offers of a bath, clothing, and food.[34] And, as Odysseus remarks at 7.292–4, 'at no point did she fail in thoughtfulness (*ἡ δ' οὔ τι νοήματος ἤμβροτεν ἐσθλοῦ*). One would hardly hope to find such discretion in one so young, so often do youth and thoughtlessness go together (*αἰεὶ γάρ τε νεώτεροι ἀφραδέουσιν*).'

But her decisive act, which alters the course of events, is the result of divine intervention. She decides to go to the river to wash clothes, where she meets Odysseus, only because Athena gives her the idea in a dream, by reminding her that it is nearly time for her to be married (6.25–40). And when she alone has the courage to stand firm and not to run away when she sees Odysseus emerge, it is once again because Athena has given her boldness and has taken away fear from her limbs (6.139–40). Once she has fulfilled her function, she disappears and only makes one further, brief appearance before disappearing entirely from the narrative.[35] It is in this final appearance that she takes the initiative for the only time (when she bids Odysseus farewell and asks him to remember her at 8.457–62). But this act has no effect on the action of the epic.

Arete is mentioned first by her daughter, in Book 6, when she advises Odysseus to go to her mother and clasp her knees (6.303–15). She depicts her, just like Circe or Calypso, engaged in the typically feminine activity of weaving: 'she will be sitting in the firelight by the hearth, spinning the wool whose ocean-purple astonishes the beholder' (6.305–6). This advice is repeated at the beginning of Book 7, this time by Athena who insists on the importance of winning the queen's support.[36] She then recounts her genealogy (Arete is

[33] *Odyssey*, 6.26–30, 273–88. [34] *Odyssey*, 6.191–3, 209–10, 214–16, 227–8.
[35] Fenik 1978: 127. [36] *Odyssey*, 7.75–7 = 6.313–15.

Alcinous' niece as well as being his wife) and emphasizes her power and wisdom:

[Alcinous] has honoured [her] (*ἔτισ'*) as no other wife in the world is honoured (*τίεται*), of all wives who rule a household under their husband's eye. Such has always been, and such still is, the honour paid to Arete (*τετίμηταί*) by Alcinous and by her children and by the people here (*ἔκ τε φίλων παίδων ἔκ τ' αὐτοῦ Ἀλκινόοιο καὶ λαῶν*), who gaze at her as at a divinity (*θεὸν ὥς*[37] *εἰσορόωντες*) and greet her with loyal words whenever she walks about the town, because she is full of unprompted wisdom *οὐ μὲν γάρ τι νόου γε καὶ αὐτὴ δεύεται ἐσθλοῦ*). If she takes kindly to anyone—to a man no less than to a woman—she will be a peacemaker to his feuds (*καὶ ἀνδράσι νείκεα λύει*). (7.67–74)

This praise of the queen's wisdom, which is echoed in Book 11 by the Phaeacian Echenous, anticipates the terms in which Antinous and Agamemnon will later praise Penelope.[38] But here there is also a political dimension, unparalleled elsewhere with the exception of the reverse simile assimilating Penelope to a good king (19.107–14), since Arete is honoured by the people. In contrast to Hera, who claims the ability to calm a conjugal dispute in the *Iliad* (14.197–221 and 301–6), Arete is able even to calm quarrels between men. She is also the only woman in either the *Iliad* or the *Odyssey* to be given honours equal to a god.[39]

But, as has been pointed out, 'given this elaborate build up, it is Arete's powerlessness, rather than her power, that is most striking in her appearances in Books VII and XI',[40] and this has rightly been called a 'genuine discrepancy'.[41] For, while Odysseus approaches Arete as a suppliant in Book 7.146–52, it is the wise Echenous who, in lines 159–66, responds, urging Alcinous, and not Arete, to welcome the suppliant. In lines 167–96 it is Alcinous who raises him to his feet, seats him in the place of honour, gives the order for a libation to Zeus, the protector of suppliants, calls an assembly for the

[37] At *Odyssey*, 5.36 the Phaeacians will honour Odysseus like a god.

[38] *Odyssey*, 11.344–5: *οὐ μὰν ἧμιν ἀπὸ σκοποῦ οὐδ' ἀπὸ δόξης | μυθεῖται βασίλεια περίφρων*. Here it is also important to note the use of the adjective *περίφρων* which is usually associated with Penelope (44 occurrences). For Antinous' speech see *Odyssey*, 2.116–22; for that of Agamemnon see *Odyssey*, 11.445–6 and 24.194–8.

[39] This formula, which appears five times in the *Iliad* and twice in the *Odyssey*, is used exclusively of men elsewhere.

[40] Wohl 1993: 29 citing Pedrick 1988: 86–7.

[41] Fenik 1974: 106.

following day, and promises to return him to his homeland safe and sound. The feast ends with Odysseus' reply and with the Phaeacians' general approval of the king's proposals. It is only when Odysseus is alone with the royal couple that Arete speaks, in lines 237–9, to ask him about his origins and how he got his clothes, which she recognizes as the product of her own and her servants' craft, in which the women of Phaeacia are said elsewhere to excel (7.109–11).

Critics have found her long silence surprising, to the point that scholars like Reinhold Merkelbach (1951: 127) and Wolfgang Schadewaldt (1959: 14–17) concluded that lines 148–232 are an interpolation, introduced by the poet who shaped the *Odyssey* into the form it has today. Another solution is to suggest, as did Uvo Hölscher (1960: 263–5), that Arete's silence at this point is a means of building up tension and of giving more weight to her words, or alternatively to see it, along with Fenik (1974: 104), as an example of the 'interruption sequence . . . a standard Homeric, and especially Odyssean scene type'. But what seems to be the most important thing here is that the decisive action by Arete, which the remarks of Nausicaa and Athena lead us to expect is absent from Book 7. Moreover her question is not answered by Odysseus until much later (7.296). Then, Odysseus' reply is followed by a fresh dialogue between Alcinous and the hero and Arete does not appear again until the very end of Book 7 (lines 335–8), where she plays a typically feminine role, ordering her servants to prepare a bed for Odysseus. Similarly, when she appears in Book 8.423–45, Alcinous entrusts her with the task of placing a clean cloak and tunic in one of their best chests and bringing it to Odysseus before preparing his bath. She obeys immediately, as is to be expected since women are normally in charge of baths and of clothing in the *Odyssey*.

Her intervention during the interlude of Book 11, which interrupts Odysseus' account of the *nekuia*, is entirely unexpected:

> Phaeacians, what do you say of this man now—his air and presence and poise of mind? He is my own guest especially, but each of you is of princely rank. So be in no haste to send him from us, and do not be sparing with your gifts; his need, as you see, is great, and—heaven be thanked—the possessions housed in your halls are plentiful. (11.336–41)

But, as Fenik (1974: 105) argues, we should probably accord less importance to these lines than has sometimes been the case. It is true that she addresses her words to the 'Phaeacians' (336), presents Odysseus as 'her guest' (ξεῖνος δ' αὖτ' ἐμός ἐστιν, 338), and suggests that they give more gifts (339–41). But if she refers to Odysseus in this way it is because he approached her first as suppliant,[42] and her reference to gifts simply repeats the proposal made by Alcinous in Book 8.387–97. Her words are followed by more words of praise from Echenous, as in Book 7, who encourages the other Achaeans to do as she says (ἀλλὰ πίθεσθε) but also reminds them that it is Alcinous' role to speak and to act.[43] For this reason, I cannot agree with the argument of Victoria Wohl (1993: 30–1) that this is proof of 'Arete's unspoken authority' and of an equal division of labour between a queen who is responsible for speech (*muthos*) and a king responsible for action (*ergon*). This interlude serves, rather, to reaffirm the power of the king alone, even if Alcinous replies by saying τοῦτο μὲν οὕτω δὴ ἔσται ἔπος ('The thing she speaks of shall be done'), significantly using the neutral term *epos* in place of Echenous' μυθεῖται with its connotations of authoritative speech.[44] Arete's final appearance in Book 13.56–69 seems to confirm this interpretation. Here she plays an entirely non-speaking role: Odysseus gives her the golden cup that was used for the libations, she then sends three serving women to accompany him, 'one had the clean cloak and tunic, one was given the strong chest to carry, one was laden with bread and red wine' (13.66–9).

3. HELEN AND CLYTEMNESTRA

Even more than in the *Iliad*,[45] Helen remains an enigmatic figure in the *Odyssey*. Upon the figure of Helen of Troy, who is evoked at several points in the poem and is portrayed in the symmetrical stories of Helen and Menelaus in Book 4, is overlaid Helen of Sparta, now reinstalled in her home. Moreover, the text depicts her from multiple points of view: she is not only what she herself says and does, but also what men and women (such as Penelope) say about her.

[42] As the scholiast cited by Fenik 1974: 106 n. 126 noted.

[43] *Odyssey*, 11.346: Ἀλκινόου δ' ἐκ τοῦδ' ἔχεται ἔργον τε ἔπος τε.

[44] See Martin 1989: chapter 1.

[45] On Helen in the *Iliad* see Groten 1968.

The 'Argive' Helen[46] is still characterized in the *Odyssey* by her beauty with epithets such as *kallipareos* 'with beautiful cheeks',[47] and *kallikomos* 'with beautiful hair'.[48] Like Calypso, Nausicaa, and Penelope she is compared to Artemis.[49] Her outstanding beauty is further enhanced by the splendid objects around her: a silver basket (4.125), the perfume of the room which she leaves (4.121), and the magnificence of Menelaus' palace, which rivals that of Alcinous (see above Chapter 3, p. 89). She is also clearly associated with the typically feminine task of weaving, as were Calypso, Circe, and Arete. In the *Iliad*, when she appeared in the story for the first time in Book 3, Iris found her 'in her room, working at a great web of purple cloth for a double cloak, and in it she was weaving many scenes of the conflict between the horse-taming Trojans and the bronze-clad Achaeans, which they were enduring for her sake at the hands of Ares' (*Iliad*, 3.125–8). In the same way, at her first appearance in the *Odyssey* in Book 4 she is surrounded by attributes that clearly identify her as a weaver: a basket 'full of yarn that had been prepared for spinning' and a spindle 'with the violet wool already on it' (4.133–5).

Troy and the war of which she was both the cause and the prize, the war dead, and the suffering she brought upon others are as present in the *Odyssey* as they are in the *Iliad*.[50] But the question of Helen's responsibility remains open. In the *Iliad*, the Achaeans insult her and some members of Priam's family blame her,[51] but the Trojan elders consider that it is 'no shame that the Trojans and well-greaved Achaeans should suffer agonies for long years over a woman like this' (3.156–7). Priam himself removes all blame from her (3.164–5) and Hector always defends her (24.771–5). She herself blames the trickery of Aphrodite at *Iliad*, 3.399–405, but still acknowledges that her own actions have attracted shame and criticism (3.242), which is an indirect acceptance of responsibility. In *Iliad* 6, she twice refers to herself as a 'bitch' (344 and 356) but also as a victim of the gods who 'sent these evils upon her'.[52]

[46] *Odyssey* five occurrences; *Iliad*, eight occurrences.

[47] *Odyssey*, 15.123.

[48] *Odyssey*, 15.58. Iliad, *eukomos*: eight occurrences.

[49] *Odyssey*, 4.122 (Helen), 6.151 (Calypso), 6.102, 151–2 (Nausicaa), 17.37, 19.54 (Penelope). See also *Iliad*, 3.158 where the Trojan elders compare her to a goddess.

[50] *Odyssey*, 11.382–4, 438, 14.69, 17.118–19, 22.227–9, 23.223–4; *Iliad*, 2.161–2 = 2.177–8; 2.356 = 2.590, 3.126–8, 356 = 590, 19.326.

[51] *Iliad*, 3.242, 24.768–70.

[52] *Iliad*, 6.349: αὐτὰρ ἐπεὶ τάδε γ' ὧδε θεοὶ κακὰ τεκμήραντο.

In the *Odyssey*, Helen refers to herself once as a 'bitch',[53] Odysseus blames her 'will' twice,[54] and Eumaeus holds her responsible for the deaths that occurred in the war (14.68–9). But Penelope, in a passage of Book 23 which has prompted a great deal of discussion,[55] provides an excuse for her:

Never would [Helen] have lain with a foreign lover if she had but known that the warrior sons of the Achaeans were to carry her back again to her own land. But the god impelled her to do the shameless deed (τὴν δ' ἦ τοι ῥέξαι θεὸς ὤρορεν ἔργον ἀεικές); not till then did her mind conceive the fatal folly (τὴν δ' ἄτην οὐ πρόσθεν ἑῷ ἐγκάτθετο θυμῷ λυγρήν) that was the beginning of distress not only for her but for us also. (23.218–24)

As this passage shows, the recognition of *atē* always follows upon the experience of failure and represents the human being as the passive victim of a phenomenon that is attributed to some outside agency.[56]

But the most important sources on Helen in the *Odyssey* are Book 4 and the beginning of Book 15, in which she plays a major role, and the stories told by Helen and Menelaus. These relate the exploits of Odysseus, illustrating his cunning and his shrewdness (in Helen's story) as well as his ability to control himself and to stop others from acting rashly (in Menelaus' story), but speak of Helen at least as much as they speak of Odysseus.[57] As has been pointed out, these two stories are 'symmetrical in form' and 'woven in identical terms', but 'the roles and the meaning are reversed', since they give two contrasting images of Helen.[58] This contradiction was long explained as the result of the varying traditions about Helen.[59] The tendency now is to accept that the complex play of echoes and parallels between the two

[53] *Odyssey*, 4.145: κυνώπιδος.

[54] *Odyssey*, 11.384: κακῆς ἰότητι γυναικός, 437: γυναικείας διὰ βουλὰς.

[55] As noted by M. Katz (1991: 183), this passage was athetized in Antiquity (*schol. in* Od. 23. 218.1.2 v ἀθετοῦνται οἱ ζ ὡς σκάζοντες κατὰ τὸν νοῦν). Modern scholars from Kirchoff 1879: 531–2, Wilamowitz-Moellendorf 1884: 84 n. 8, to Schadewaldt 1970: 73, Stanford 1964–5 ad 23.218–24 follow suit. Zeitlin 1996: 49 notes that 'it must be admitted that Penelope's speech remains disturbing . . . the way it is framed seems at best a kind of non sequitur'.

[56] On *atē* in Homer see Saïd 1978: 75–88.

[57] See Dupont-Roc and Le Boulluec 1976, Olson 1989b, Katz 1991: 78–80, Wohl 1993: 32–5, Rabau 1995, De Jong 2001: 101–3.

[58] Dupont-Roc and Le Boulluec 1976: 31. On the symmetry between the two tales see also Olson 1989: 387–9, De Jong 2001: 101.

[59] Kakridis 1971: 49.

shows that this is the result of a deliberate choice.[60] But there is still no consensus about the meaning. Should pride of place be given to the 'true' story of Menelaus which serves as a corrective to the 'false' story of Helen?[61] Or should we try to reconcile the irreconcilable, as the ancient scholiasts attempted to do,[62] and see Menelaus' narrative as a 'defence of Helen' by putting all the weight on his mention of divine causality? Or, finally, should we speak of the complementary nature of the two stories, or of their fundamental duality and irremediable ambiguity?. In this case, their juxtaposition, far from providing an answer, would simply pose a series of questions,[63] thus prefiguring two potential outcomes for the second part of the *Odyssey* and the role given by Odysseus to Penelope in his revenge[64] (that is to say, he can either reveal his identity and involve her directly in his vengeance, as Helen's story encourages him to do, or he can continue to conceal his identity until the massacre of the suitors is accomplished, as Menelaus' story seems to advise).

Helen begins by claiming that she will speak 'fittingly' (ἐοικότα γὰρ καταλέξω, 4.239) thus introducing her speech as one that will be both 'like truth', 'plausible' and 'suited to the situation' (these meanings are both encompassed by the Greek term ἐοικότα and it is probably unnecessary to try to decide between them here).[65] Her story, naturally, presents her in the best light. She shows great perspicacity as she is able, unlike Penelope, to recognize Odysseus under his disguise as a beggar (4.250).[66] She acts as a perfect hostess, giving him a bath, anointing him with oil, and giving him clothes (4.252–3), just as Nausicaa and Arete did and as Penelope will do later. She also becomes his accomplice when she swears solemnly not to reveal his identity until he has returned to his ships and his camp (4.253–5). Above all, the joy she feels at his success (4.259–60) after he had killed many Trojans with his sword and taken precious information back to

[60] See the analyses in Dupont Roc and Le Boulluec 1976: 31–3, Bergren 1981: 207–10, Olson 1989: 389–90, De Jong 2001: 101.

[61] Olson 1989: 392–3, De Jong 2001: 101.

[62] *Schol. in Odusseam* 4.275.1 H: μὴ βουλόμενος δὲ τὴν Ἑλένην ἐλέγχειν τοῦτο παρενέβαλλεν.

[63] Dupont-Roc and Le Boulluec 1976: 34, Bergren 1981: 208–9, Goldhill 1988: 23–4, Goldhill 1991: 64, Wohl 1993: 34–5.

[64] Olson 1989: 391, De Jong 2001: 102.

[65] Rabau 1995: 279.

[66] Bergren 1981: 208.

his camp as his prize[67] shows that her feelings have changed: 'I wept, too late, for the blindness that Aphrodite sent me (ἄτην δὲ μετέστενον, ἣν Ἀφροδίτη δῶχ') when she made me go there, away from my own dear land, and let me forsake my daughter and bridal room and a husband who fell short in nothing, whether in mind or in outward form' (4.261–4). Her words here recall the Helen of *Iliad* 3 who wishes she had died before following Paris 'leaving behind the house of my marriage, and my family and my darling child and the sweet company of friends' (3.173–5)[68] and reproaches Aphrodite for the deceit and trickery she has used against her.[69]

Although he begins his own speech with praise for the 'appropriate' way in which his wife has just spoken,[70] 'Menelaus represents a Helen who is dangerous and untrustworthy towards the Achaeans.'[71] During the episode of the Trojan Horse, Helen, accompanied by Deiphobus (whom she married after the death of Paris, as the scholiasts point out), came close to the horse in which the best of the Achaean warriors were hiding and called each of them by name three times, 'imitating the voices of their wives' (πάντων Ἀργείων φωνὴν ἴσκουσ' ἀλόχοισιν, 4.279). Only the intervention of Odysseus saved the Achaeans (4.280–8). But if the facts of the story are easy enough to understand, Helen's motivation in approaching the horse and then withdrawing remains unclear. According to Menelaus, she must have approached 'at the prompting of some divinity who wished to give glory to the Trojans' and when she left it was because of the action of another deity, Athena.[72]

The Helen of Sparta who welcomes Telemachus in Book 4 is no less complex than Helen of Troy. From the start she has equal status to

[67] See Heubeck and West 1981 on line 4.258.

[68] See also *Iliad*, 24.764.

[69] *Iliad*, 3.399: ἠπεροπεύειν and 405: δολοφρονέουσα.

[70] *Odyssey*, 4.266: "ναὶ δὴ ταῦτά γε πάντα, γύναι, κατὰ μοῖραν ἔειπες. On the meaning of the formula κατὰ μοῖραν ἔειπες | ἔειπεν which occurs nine times in the Odyssey and seven times in the *Iliad* see Garvie 1994: 211: 'To speak in accordance with μοῖρα is to speak in accordance with the appointed order, that is in a way which is expected by society, "properly", "appropriately".' Dupont-Roc and Le Boulluec 1976: 30 explain its use here as meaning 'a speech that fits her current status' ('discours conforme à ce qu'elle est maintenant').

[71] Dupont-Roc and Le Boulluec 1976: 30: 'Ménélas met en scène une Hélène dangereuse et perfide à l'égard des Achéens.'

[72] *Odyssey*, 4. 289. Dupont-Roc and Le Boulluec 1976: 35 n. 37 compare Athena's intervention here with that during the sack of Troy that allowed Odysseus and Menelaus to defeat Deiphobus, as related by Demodocus (*Odyssey*, 8.520).

her husband. In Egypt, gifts of hospitality were not only given to Menelaus by the king, his wife offers 'lovely gifts' to Helen separately (χωρὶς) (4.130–2). When she first sees Telemachus, she shows the same perspicacity as she had in Troy and immediately recognizes him as Odysseus' son (4.140–6), a recognition that is made possible by a gap in the normal sequence of actions that make up the reception type-scene.[73] Normally, the guest's identity is only revealed after the end of the feast, as Nestor makes clear in Book 3.69–70 when he says, 'Now that they have enjoyed the meal, we may rightly (νῦν δὴ κάλλιον) put questions to these guests.'[74] Helen then weeps, along with the others, at the idea of Odysseus alone, 'deprived of his homecoming' (ἀνόστιμον) by a jealous deity (4.181–6). Menelaus then intervenes to urge his guests to stop weeping and think about eating, and puts off their discussions until the following day (4.212–15). The banquet scene then continues with the ritual ablutions followed by the formula used to express the consumption of food.[75] At this point, Helen's action interrupts the normal sequence of events (we might be expecting a bard's song or the announcement that the guests are retiring to bed): 'A new thought came to Zeus-born Helen' (4.219). She pours a potion (*pharmakon*) into their drinks that has the power to put an end to mourning and anger and 'banished remembrance of every trouble' (νηπενθές τ' ἄχολόν τε, κακῶν ἐπίληθον) (4.220–1), an effect that is more ambiguous than it might at first appear since it is both 'cunning' and beneficial,[76] like everything that comes from Egypt where 'the bounteous earth yields a wealth of drugs, both healthful and baneful' (4.229–30).

Helen's gesture here prefigures the episodes of the Lotus-Eaters (whose food also has the power to make those who eat it 'forget their homecoming'), of Circe (whose *pharmakon* also makes Odysseus' companions 'forget their homeland'), and the Sirens ('If a man in ignorance draws too close and catches their music, he will never

[73] See Saïd 1979: 28–30.

[74] See also *Odyssey*, 1.69–70: Telemachus to Athena/Mentes, 7.238: Arete to Odysseus, 14.187: Eumaeus to Odysseus. Significantly, this order is not respected by the Cyclops (*Odyssey*, 9.252).

[75] *Odyssey*, 4.216–18. On this point see the excellent commentary in Rabau 1995: 276–7 which notes the correspondence between line 216 and the ablution sequence mentioned in line 52 as well as the repetition in line 218 of the formula used in line 67.

[76] *Odyssey*, 4.227–8. This is the only time the adjective μητιόεντα is used in Homer, and it is unclear whether it has positive or negative connotations.

return to find wife and little children near him and to see their joy at his homecoming; the high clear tones of the Sirens will bewitch him').[77] The negative effect of Helen's potion is complemented by the *muthoi* whose avowed aim is to give pleasure to the listeners, as we see from line 239: μύθοις τέρπεσθε. In Antiquity, this complementary relationship between Helen's *pharmakon* and her *muthoi* was underlined by Plutarch in his *Table Talk*.[78] But does it prove effective? We may well wonder, seeing that Helen's story is not followed, as are the tales of Odysseus or the bards Phemius and Demodocus, by the enchanted silence of her listeners.[79] It is true that in line 266 Helen is praised for having spoken appropriately (κατὰ μοῖραν), but this compliment, which echoes the one paid by Odysseus to Demodocus (8.496), is immediately followed by Menelaus' new story (Sophie Rabau (1995: 283) has aptly described this as an example of 'narrative rivalry'). What is more, the only audience reaction that is noted in this episode, immediately after Menelaus' story, is that of Telemachus and shows that Helen has failed in her aim. Far from forgetting his misery, the son of Odysseus is suffering even more than before (4.292). He will only experience the combined effects of pleasure and forgetting much later, at the very end of Menelaus' story: 'I would gladly sit for another year beside you and never fret for my home and kindred so charmed I am (αἰνῶς . . . τέρπομαι) as I drink in your words and tales' (4.595–8).[80] After this narrative interlude, the end of the episode shows Helen, like Arete, fulfilling her role of mistress of the house by preparing a bed for her guests before going to bed to sleep beside her husband.[81]

When Helen reappears in Book 15 she is first and foremost the mistress of the house who is ordered by her husband to prepare a meal for their guests (15.93–4). Then we see her standing next to the chests holding 'the rich robes woven by herself' (15.104–5), a fresh reminder of her skills as a weaver. She then takes 'the amplest and the most richly broidered' (15.106–7) to give to Telemachus.[82] Here

[77] *Odyssey*, 9.94–5, 10.235–6, 12.41–5.

[78] Plutarch, *Table Talk* (*Moralia*, 614b–c); see Dupont-Roc and Le Boulluec 1976: 35 n. 42.

[79] *Odyssey*, 1.325–6, 339–40: Phemius, 8.367–9: Demodocus, 11.333, 13.1–2, 17.518–21: Odysseus.

[80] See Rabau 1995: 285.

[81] *Odyssey*, 4.296–301 (Helen) and 7.335–8 (Arete). See also 7.346–7.

[82] *Odyssey*, 15.123–9.

again the comparison with Arete is significant. The Phaeacian queen was simply obeying her husband's orders (8.424–5) when she gave Odysseus a coffer with a 'clean cloak and tunic' (8.438–40) while here the gift is the initiative of Helen alone. She intervenes one last time to give her interpretation of the omen sent to Telemachus: an eagle gripping a goose in its talons that flies up on Telemachus' right. In so doing she takes the place of her husband whom Peisistratus had asked for an interpretation (15.166–8). While Menelaus is still pondering, she speaks out saying: 'Listen as I expound this thing as the immortals put it in my heart and as I am sure will come to pass' (*κλῦτέ μευ· αὐτὰρ ἐγὼ μαντεύσομαι, ὡς ἐνὶ θυμῷ ἀθάνατοι βάλλουσι καὶ ὡς τελέεσθαι ὀίω*, 15.172–3). As should be noted, Helen is the only woman in the *Odyssey* to be given the gift of prophecy, but even here, this ability does not belong to her permanently, it is the result of divine intervention.

Should we therefore see Helen, as has been suggested, as 'the irreducible and incomprehensible force of female sexuality and creativity', or as subverting 'the male–female polarity'?[83] Or should we see in Homer's portrait of her an illustration of the nature of human action in general and of its ambiguities?[84] I would prefer to suggest another explanation. Helen is, as the poet of the *Odyssey* reminds us on several occasions, the daughter of Zeus[85] and she seems to derive certain privileges from this genealogy (if Menelaus is able to escape Hades and live in bliss in the Elysian Fields it is because of his marriage to her and his status as 'son-in-law of Zeus').[86] It explains in addition the relative degree of autonomy she enjoys compared to other women. Her sphere of influence is nevertheless very restricted and her motivation remains as opaque as that of the other female characters.

Clytemnestra is closely associated with her sister in Book 11. Like Helen, she is called a 'bitch' (*κυνῶπις*) by Agamemnon in line 424 and both are the instruments used by the gods to destroy the two sons of Atreus, according to Odysseus in lines 436–9: 'Alas, too surely has Zeus the Thunderer nourished unbounded hatred from long ago for the seed of Atreus, with woman's wiles for his instrument (*γυναικείας*

[83] Wohl 1993: 35 and Doherty 1995b: 59.

[84] Dupont-Roc and Le Boulluec 1976: 34.

[85] *Odyssey*, 4.184, 219, 23.218.

[86] *Odyssey*, 4.561–9.

διὰ βουλάς). How many of us have been killed for Helen's sake, and now there is this betrayal by Clytemnestra plotted (δόλον ἤρτυε) against you while you were far away.'

But, unlike Helen, Clytemnestra is only portrayed indirectly in the *Odyssey*, through the words of gods (Zeus in Book 1, Athena in Book 3, and the Old Man of the Sea in Book 4) and of men (Nestor in Book 3, Menelaus, who takes up the story told by the Old Man of the Sea in Book 4, Agamemnon and Odysseus in Book 11, and Agamemnon in Book 24). In the first assembly of the gods, she is merely an accessory to Aegisthus' crime, a status that is underlined by the fact that she appears as the grammatical object in the statement of Aegisthus' misdeeds: 'he took in marriage the wedded wife of the son of Atreus and killed her husband when he returned' (1.35–6). In Book 3, by contrast, Athena presents her as an equal partner along with Aegisthus in the treachery that led to Agamemnon's death (3.234–5). Nestor, however, emphasizes her passivity: she was the victim of Aegisthus who 'charmed her with his words' (3.264). Before then she had been a virtuous wife who 'would not consent to the shameful deed as her mind was sound' (3.265–6). But this virtue seems to have depended entirely on the presence of the bard left by Agamemnon to watch over her. As soon as he was removed from the palace, Clytemnestra followed Aegisthus' every wish:

> There was a bard in the palace whom the king as he took ship for Troy had earnestly bidden to guard his wife. But when the gods' purpose ordained that she [or 'he'[87]] should yield (ἀλλ' ὅτε δή μιν μοῖρα θεῶν ἐπέδησε δαμῆναι), Aegisthus carried the bard away to a desert island and left him there to become the spoil of birds of prey; the queen he took to his own home, and he and she were of one mind (τὴν δ' ἐθέλων ἐθέλουσαν ἀνήγαγεν ὅνδε δόμονδε). (3.267–72)

Nestor wavers in his version of events: he holds 'treacherous Aegisthus' (Αἴγισθον δολόμητιν) alone responsible for the planning of the murder (ἐμήσατο . . . λυγρά) and for its execution (κτείνας Ἀτρεΐδην) in lines 303–4, while reminding the audience indirectly

[87] Shewring, Hammond, Lattimore, and the P scholia all take the pronoun to refer to Clytemnestra. The E scholia, however, hesitate between Clytemnestra, Aegisthus, and Agamemnon. The immediate context would seem to suggest that it is the bard who is 'caught'.

that Clytemnestra was killed by Orestes at the same time as Aegisthus, and describing her a little further on, in line 310, as 'hateful'.

Clytemnestra is not mentioned at all in the story told to Menelaus by the Old Man of the Sea and then reported by Menelaus to Telemachus at 4.512–37. Once again it is 'treacherous Aegisthus' (*Αἴγισθος δολόμητις*, 4.525) who 'conceived the foul trap' (*αὐτίκα δ' Αἴγισθος δολίην ἐφράσσατο τέχνην*, 4.529), 'pondering the terrible deeds' (*ἀεικέα μερμηρίζων*, 4.533) that led to the death of the king.

In Book 11, Agamemnon begins by holding Aegisthus responsible for his terrible end: 'Aegisthus plotted death and destruction for me' (*τεύξας θάνατόν τε μόρον τε*, 11.409) but adds in the very next line that 'he killed me, he and my accursed wife'. He even claims that Clytemnestra and Clytemnestra alone killed Cassandra (*Κασσάνδρης, τὴν κτεῖνε Κλυταιμνήστρη δολόμητις*) in line 422. He then claims that she left after the murder and 'would not stretch out her hand to close my eyes and mouth' in lines 424–6. He finishes by describing her as guilty using an expression which recalls the words used of Aegisthus in 3.303, 4.533, and 11.409: 'Thus did my wife devise this abomination, contriving murder against her own wedded husband' (*οἷον δὴ καὶ κείνη ἐμήσατο ἔργον ἀεικές, κουριδίῳ τε τεύξασα πόσει φόνον*, 11.429–30). Finally, in Book 24, Agamemnon tells of his death for the last time, repeating the interpretation made by Odysseus in Book 11 and considering both Clytemnestra and Aegisthus as simple instruments of divine will (a perfect example of dual causality, which in no way exonerates the perpetrators since, in Homer's world, it is deeds that count: 'At my return Zeus plotted a horrible end for me at the hands of Aegisthus and my accursed wife' *ἐν νόστῳ γάρ μοι Ζεὺς μήσατο λυγρὸν ὄλεθρον Αἰγίσθου ὑπὸ χερσὶ καὶ οὐλομένης ἀλόχοιο* (24.96–7).

What are we to make of these contrasting interpretations that even occur within the same speech? It is clear that Clytemnestra is, as has often been pointed out, a negative example and 'the obvious inverse parallel to Penelope' (Wohl 1993: 35). But we can also see in her depiction in the *Odyssey* the image of a woman whose behaviour is controlled by outside influences (she is virtuous as long as she is watched over by the wise bard, and becomes evil when she is bewitched by Aegisthus' sweet words), and a demonstration of the profound uncertainty surrounding the motivations of female characters.

4. PENELOPE

Penelope is the most complete and the most complex embodiment of the feminine in the *Odyssey*. As Emlyn-Jones (1984: 14) aptly puts it, she is 'the most elaborately and searchingly portrayed of Homer's female characters'. She is defined first and foremost as a 'relative' identified through her relationships to the male characters. She is the 'worthy wife of Odysseus, son of Laertes' (on five occasions), the 'daughter of Icarius' (on fifteen occasions), and 'the mother of Telemachus' (17.554). Penelope also has qualities of her own. One is her beauty, which is always evoked through the use of abstract terms such as εἶδος ('form'),[88] μέγεθος ('tall stature'),[89] δέμας ('stature'),[90] and ἀγλαΐη ('beauty')[91] or by comparison with deities (even if, like all humans, she remains their inferior, as Odysseus acknowledges to Calypso (5.215–17)): thus she is 'like Artemis or Golden Aphrodite' (Ἀρτέμιδι ἰκέλη ἠὲ χρυσέῃ Ἀφροδίτῃ, 17.37). Her beauty is also suggested indirectly by the effect she has on the suitors: their knees fail them, an expression that is only used in the *Iliad* and *Odyssey* to express extreme emotional states, whether absolute despair or intense joy.[92]

Her qualities make her a wife worthy of Odysseus. Just as he is superior to other men, she is superior to other women, since Athena has given her every kind of gift: 'Skill in exquisite workmanship, a keen mind (φρένας ἐσθλὰς), subtlety (κέρδεα)—these she has, beyond anything we have heard of even in the ladies of older times—the Achaean ladies of braided tresses like Tyro and Alcmene and garlanded Mycene; not one of these had the mastery in devising things that Penelope has (ὁμοῖα νοήματα Πηνελοπείῃ)' (2.117–22).[93] The *Odyssey* places a great deal of emphasis on Penelope's intelligence and wisdom, as we see from epithets like περίφρων (wise, sage, prudent) (fifty occurrences), ἐχέφρων (sensible, discreet) (seven occurrences), and πινυτή (of sound understanding) (four occurrences). These epithets are also applied to Eurycleia (described as περίφρων four times), Arètè (περίφρων, once), Odysseus (ἐχέφρων, once), and the daughters of

[88] *Odyssey*, 18.249, 251; 19.124.
[89] *Odyssey*, 18.249.
[90] *Odyssey*, 18.251, 19.124.
[91] *Odyssey*, 18. 180.
[92] See *Iliad*, 21.114; *Odyssey*, 4.703, 5.297, 22.68, 147, 23.205, 24.345.
[93] See also 18.248–9.

Pandaros (πινυταί, once). Penelope's intelligence is also evoked through the use of terms and expressions such as νόον,[94] φρένας ἔνδον ἐΐσας,[95] φρένας ἐσθλὰς,[96] ἀγαθαὶ φρένες,[97] ἐπίφρονα μῆτιν,[98] εὖ φρεσὶ μήδεα οἶδε,[99] and κεδνὰ ἰδυῖαν.[100]

Some of these expressions are also used to describe Odysseus.[101] But their connotations, where the context allows us to judge, are quite different. The masculine wisdom embodied by Odysseus consists in sacrificing to the gods (1.65–7) and giving good advice to other men (3.128–9 and 16.241–2). For a woman like Penelope, wisdom is identified with conjugal fidelity. This is clear from the two speeches in praise of Penelope made by Agamemnon in Book 11 and in Book 24: if she is praised for her wisdom it is because she has preserved her husband's memory[102] (this may well explain why Agamemnon chose a bard, a guardian of memory, to watch over his wife). Just as Odysseus never forgets Ithaca, Penelope never ceases to think of Odysseus.[103] Even if she were to take another husband, she would maintain, even in her dreams, the memory of her house and her first husband, in contrast to most women who, once remarried, 'have no thought of their living children or the dead husbands they loved before' (15.22–3).[104]

Female wisdom also consists in honouring a guest in the correct manner and making sure he is comfortable by giving him food and wine, preparing a bed, and ensuring that he takes a bath and is given clean clothes before the meal, as we see from Penelope's reply to the beggar: 'How can you ever know, my guest, if I surpass other women in thoughtfulness and regard for others (εἴ τι γυναικῶν ἀλλάων περίειμι νόον καὶ ἐπίφρονα μῆτιν) if you sit down for a meal in this hall dirty and dressed in rags?' (19.325–8). More recently, however, scholarship has tended to focus on the last item in the list of Athena's

94 *Odyssey*, 2.124, 19.326. 95 *Odyssey*, 18.249.

96 *Odyssey*, 2.117. This is also one of the characteristics of Phaeacian women, see 7.111.

97 *Odyssey*, 24.194. 98 *Odyssey*, 19.326. 99 *Odyssey*, 11.445.

100 *Odyssey*, 20. 57, 23.182, 232.

101 νόον: *Odyssey*, 1.66; νόῳ καὶ ἐπίφρονι βουλῇ: 3.128; φρένας ἔνδον ἐΐσας: 11.337; ἐπίφρονα βουλήν: 16.242.

102 Penelope is praised for her wisdom at 11.445–6 and 24.194. At 24.195 Agamemnon describes her as ὡς εὖ μέμνητ' Ὀδυσῆος. On the importance of memory for Penelope, see Mudle, 2009.

103 *Odyssey*, 1.343–4: τοίην γὰρ κεφαλὴν ποθέω μεμνημένη αἰεὶ ἀνδρός.

104 *Odyssey*, 19.579–81, 21.77–9.

gifts to Penelope, the 'cunning stratagems' (κέρδεα) that make her the embodiment of *mētis*, along with Odysseus.[105] But if the vocabulary used to describe Odysseus throughout the poem makes him into a living example of this quality, the same cannot be said of Penelope. Her name, unlike that of Odysseus, is never associated with epithets containing the terms *dolos*, *mētis*, *kerdos*, or *mēchanē*. It is true that, at 19.326 cited above, she refers to her own 'good sense' ἐπίφρονα μῆτιν, but it is clear from the context, as we have just seen, that it is a question of 'wisdom' rather than 'cunning'. In contrast to Odysseus, whose mind is a store of wiles and stratagems of all kinds, Penelope seems only ever to have had one stratagem at her disposal. And this belongs to the past by the time the *Odyssey* begins. Once her stratagem has been foiled, she has no more options left, as she says at 19.157–8: 'Now I cannot escape a marriage; I can think of no other subterfuge (*mētis*).' It is certainly the case that in Book 4, when she learns of Telemachus' departure, the only plan she can think of is to send a servant to Laertes to tell him the news and 'see if he can weave some plan (*mētis*) in his mind' εἰ δή πού τινα κεῖνος ἐνὶ φρεσὶ μῆτιν ὑφήνας (4.739). The vocabulary of cunning intelligence is only associated with Penelope in the three tales of her single stratagem told by Antinous in Book 2, Penelope in Book 19, and Amphimedon in Book 24. Thus Antinous creates a picture of Penelope who is 'expert in cunning stratagems' (περὶ κέρδεα οἶδεν, 2.88),[106] able to 'devise a trick in her mind' (2.93)—a line that is repeated verbatim by Amphimedon at 24.128—and to say one thing while thinking another: 'She cheats her suitors' hearts. She gives hope to all, she promises every man in turn, she sends out messages here and there, yet her purpose is far removed' (2.91–2). When Penelope herself speaks of 'spinning a web of stratagems' for the suitors,[107] she is still referring to this one trick, recalling how she once duped them by asking them to wait until she had competed 'the long delicate robe',[108] 'which shone like the sun or

[105] In the *Odyssey*, with the exception of 2.118, κέρδεα are associated with Odysseus (13.255, 13.297, 19.285, πολυκερδείῃ 23.77, 24.167), Athena (13.297, 299), and Telemachus (18.216, 20.257).

[106] See also 2.117–18: ἐπίστασθαι . . . κέρδεα.

[107] *Odyssey*, 19.137: ἐγὼ δὲ δόλους τολυπεύω. On the use of the verb see Clayton 2003: 33 'τολυπεύω, a familiar metaphor from the world of war, has been reinscribed with an element of the real, or literal, from the domestic world of spinning and weaving.'

[108] *Odyssey*, 19.140, 24.130.

the moon',[109] which was to be Laertes' shroud, while secretly undoing by night what she had woven during the day until she was betrayed by one of the serving women. She then completed the robe 'unwillingly and under constraint'.[110] But the origin of this stratagem remains unclear. Antinous refers to it at one moment as a trick that she thought up in her mind,[111] and at another as 'an idea that the gods placed in her heart'.[112] Penelope herself, at 19.137, acknowledges her plan but in the very next line attributes the idea to a god who inspired the idea of the shroud.[113]

The shroud is not the only allusion to Penelope's weaving. In Book 1, as in Book 21, when Telemachus orders her to leave the great hall and return to her room he says: 'Go up to your room again and look to your own province, distaff and loom, and tell your women to ply their task' (1.356–8 and 21.350–2). At the end of Book 4 we see her surrounded by her serving women, busy with their 'work', that is, with their weaving (4.682–3). In Book 15, Telemachus justifies the advice he gives to Theoclymenus to avoid his palace by adding: 'My mother would never see you. She seldom shows herself publicly to the suitors; she keeps her distance, weaving her web in her upper room' (15.515–17). In Book 17, she is sitting in the great hall, 'spinning fine wool' (line 97). In Book 19, when she wants to test the truthfulness of the beggar who claims to have entertained Odysseus in his house, she first asks him 'if in your Cretan palace you did indeed entertain my husband and his comrades, tell me what sort of clothes he wore' (19.216–18). In his reply, Odysseus tells her that 'King Odysseus wore a thick double mantle; it was crimson, and had a clasp of gold with two sheaths' (19.225–7) which he goes on to describe in detail (228–35). When, in line 250, she sees 'what powerful proof he offered' (*σήματ' ἀναγνούσῃ, τά οἱ ἔμπεδα πέφραδ' Ὀδυσσεύς*) she explains that 'those garments were those I took from my store myself and folded and gave to him, with the glittering clasp upon the tunic to make his presence the handsomer' (19.255–7). This recognition is

[109] *Odyssey*, 24.148.

[110] *Odyssey*, 19.156 and 2.110, 24.146: *ὣς τὸ μὲν ἐξετέλεσσε καὶ οὐκ ἐθέλουσ', ὑπ' ἀνάγκης.*

[111] *Odyssey*, 2.92: *νόος δέ οἱ ἄλλα μενοινᾷ*, 2.93: *ἡ δὲ δόλον τόνδ' ἄλλον ἐνὶ φρεσὶ μερμήριξε* and 122 *τοῦτό γ' ἐναίσιμον οὐκ ἐνόησε.* Amphimedon, 24.128: *ἀλλὰ δόλον τόνδ' ἄλλον ἐνὶ φρεσὶ μερμήριξε.*

[112] *Odyssey*, 2.124–5: *νόον, ὅν τινά οἱ νῦν ἐν στήθεσσι τιθεῖσι θεοί.*

[113] *Odyssey*, 19.138: *φᾶρος μέν μοι πρῶτον ἐνέπνευσε φρεσὶ δαίμων.*

prefigured in Book 7 by the scene in which Arete asks Odysseus, 'Who gave you the clothes you are wearing now?' (7.238), as she had recognized 'the cloak and tunic that she herself had made with her waiting women' (7.234–5).

A close examination of Penelope's various appearances in the *Odyssey* will allow us to arrive at a clearer definition of this complex character and to evaluate the limits of her power within the house that she is supposed to be 'keeping intact'.[114] But first, there is one passage that has been overlooked in the past that should perhaps be mentioned.[115] This is 2.226–7, in which Mentor is introduced as a former friend of Odysseus, 'When Odysseus sailed, he had left all his household in Mentor's care, bidding him respect the wishes of old Laertes and keep them intact' (*καί οἱ ἰὼν ἐν νηυσὶν ἐπέτρεπεν οἶκον ἅπαντα/, πείθεσθαί τε γέροντι καὶ ἔμπεδα πάντα φυλάσσειν*). This description of Mentor seems to represent a serious limit to Penelope's authority, since it applies to Mentor the same expression that is used elsewhere to define her role.

At the beginning of the *Odyssey*, Penelope's ruse has been foiled; her suitors are occupying Odysseus' house, are eating up his wealth, and announce in Book 2 through their leader Antinous that they will not leave until Telemachus sends his mother away and orders her to take a husband, which he cannot do for several reasons: he would have to pay her dowry back to her father, he would incur the wrath of his own father[116] (if he were ever to return) and divine wrath if Penelope were to curse him, thus bringing the Erinyes down upon him, not to mention the criticism that such a course of action would earn him from other men (2.130–7). Penelope is also caught in a trap without any obvious solution: 'Although the thought of marriage is hateful to her, she dare not refuse outright and make an end of it' (1.249–50 = 16.126–7). In sharp contrast to Clytemnestra who was persuaded by Aegisthus to follow him 'of her own free will' (*ἐθέλουσαν*, 3.272) to his house, she does not leave Odysseus' palace and her movements are confined to going up and down between her room and the great hall.

[114] *Odyssey*, 11.178 and 19.525: *ἔμπεδα πάντα φυλάσσει | φυλάσσω*.

[115] Katz 1991: 40–1 simply mentions these lines and Foley 1995: 109 refers to them in a note.

[116] *Odyssey*, 2.134: *ἐκ γὰρ τοῦ πατρὸς κακὰ πείσομαι*, I agree with the scholia that the father is the father of Telemachus but Heubeck, West, and Hainsworth 1988 ad loc. thinks that it is Penelope's father.

Her first appearance, at 1.328–64, is prompted by Phemius' song of the disastrous returns of the Achaeans. Here, the image that predominates is that of the inconsolable woman in mourning for her husband, who never ceases her laments for the hero whose glory spread throughout Greece and the Argolid.[117] Here she orders Phemius to cease his melancholy song, using an imperative: *ταύτης δ' ἀποπαύε' ἀοιδῆς/λυγρῆς* (1.340–1). But this order is countermanded by Telemachus who tells his mother to 'school herself to listen',[118] using another imperative, and then sends her up to her quarters to attend to her work and leave *muthos* to the men, whose business it is, thus asserting his authority (*kratos*) (1.356–9). As has often been noted and as was mentioned above Chapter 8, pp. 241–2), these lines which repeat with a change of a single word (*muthos* is substituted for *polemos*) Hector's words to Andromache at *Iliad*, 6.490–2, reaffirm the distinction between masculine and feminine spheres, as well as male superiority.[119] Penelope is astonished and obeys without a word, going up to her room. The scene thus ends with a statement of female powerlessness.

At the end of Book 4, Penelope hears of Telemachus' departure at the same time as the suitors' plot against his life. Her response is to fall into a state of intense despair:

Her knees and her heart alike failed her; speechlessness came upon her; her eyes filled with tears and the clear flow of her voice ceased. (4.703–5)

> *τῆς δ' αὐτοῦ λύτο γούνατα καὶ φίλον ἦτορ·*
> *δὴν δέ μιν ἀφασίη ἐπέων λάβε, τὼ δέ οἱ ὄσσε*
> *δακρυόφιν πλῆσθεν, θαλερὴ δέ οἱ ἔσχετο φωνή.*

These expressions are striking for their violent imagery and their unusual nature. In one of the two passages of the *Iliad* in which it appears, the phrase 'his knees and his heart alike failed him' (*αὐτοῦ λύτο γούνατα καὶ φίλον ἦτορ*) expresses Lycaon's despair on realizing that he is about to die (21.425). In the *Odyssey*, where it is used seven times,[120] this expression serves to describe Odysseus' despair on two

[117] *Odyssey*, 1.336: *δακρύσασα*, 342: *πένθος ἄλαστον*, 343–4: *τοίην γὰρ κεφαλὴν ποθέω μεμνημένη αἰεὶ / νδρός, τοῦ κλέος εὐρὺ καθ' Ἑλλάδα καὶ μέσον Ἄργος.*

[118] *Odyssey*, 1.353: *σοὶ δ' ἐπιτολμάτω κραδίη καὶ θυμὸς ἀκούειν.*

[119] See for examples the comments of Heubeck, West, and Hainsworth 1988: 234 on lines 356–9, Katz 1991: 36, Clayton 2003: 36–7.

[120] *Odyssey*, 5.297, 406, 22.68, 147, 23.205, 24.345.

occasions (when he is beset by the storm sent by Poseidon and when he finds Melanthius taking weapons to the suitors) and once to describe the reaction of the suitors when Odysseus reveals his identity. It also expresses the violent emotion that overcomes the suitors when they see Penelope. The two other occurrences describe the reactions of Penelope and Laertes when they recognize Odysseus (23.205 and 24.345). The only other instance of the phrase 'the clear flow of her voice ceased' (*θαλερὴ δέ οἱ ἔσχετο φωνή*) belongs to a similar context, when Eurycleia recognizes Odysseus. This passage of Book 4 is also the only place in Homeric poetry where the term *ἀφασίη* ('speechlessness') is used. A little further on, we find the same type of striking expression in the second account of her despair. Expressions like *τὴν δ' ἄχος ἀμφεχύθη θυμοφθόρον* ('heart-withering anguish invaded her', 4.716) and *ἁδινὸν γοόωσα* ('lamenting without cease', 4.721) do not occur anywhere else in Homer. Penelope's words at 4.722–3 'Friends, hear me speak. To me, above all other women born and bred in my generation, Olympian Zeus has allotted sorrow' (*κλῦτε, φίλαι· περὶ γάρ μοι Ὀλύμπιος ἄλγε' ἔδωκεν ἐκ πασέων, ὅσσαι μοι ὁμοῦ τράφον ἠδ' ἐγένοντο*) inevitably make readers of the *Iliad* think of Thetis' words to Hephaestus in Book 18, when she realizes that Achilles' death is imminent: 'Hephaestus, is there any one of the goddesses on Olympus who has endured such misery in her heart as all the sorrows that Zeus, son of Cronos has given me beyond all others.'

> *Ἥφαιστ', ἦ ἄρα δή τις, ὅσαι θεαί εἰσ' ἐν Ὀλύμπῳ,*
> *τοσσάδ' ἐνὶ φρεσὶν ᾗσιν ἀνέσχετο κήδεα λυγρὰ*
> *ὅσσ' ἐμοὶ ἐκ πασέων Κρονίδης Ζεὺς ἄλγε' ἔδωκεν;* (*Iliad*, 18.429–31)

But Penelope's despair has no practical effect. As we saw above, Penelope can think of no other solution than to send Dolius to tell everything to Laertes to see if he can 'frame some plan' (4.739). She is dissuaded by Eurycleia in line 754 who tells her not to 'distress the old man further' and follows her advice, going up to her room to pray to Athena, after washing her face and putting on clean clothing (4.750–3 and 759–66).

After an interlude describing how the suitors put their plan into action, the narrative returns to Penelope in line 787 to describe her suffering, which this time is manifested in her refusal to eat (4.788). We are then told of her thoughts: 'she was asking herself (*ὁρμαίνουσ'*) if her blameless son would escape death or would fall prey to the arrogant suitors' (4.789–90). This type of deliberation is very different from the deliberation scenes that lead to a decision or an action, as in the *Iliad*, when Nestor weighs up two different courses of action and chooses one of them or Zeus decides to do as Hera wishes.[121] Penelope, like Telemachus at *Odyssey*, 15.300 who wonders 'whether he would escape destruction or meet it' (ὁρμαίνων, ἤ κεν θάνατον φύγοι ἦ κεν ἁλοίη), remains passive and has no effect on the action. We should also take note of the comparison of Penelope with a lion at 4.791–3 since, as we saw in Chapter 2 above (p. 71), this 'cowardly' lion which simply turns over thoughts in its mind is without parallel in the Homeric poems: 'As a lion ringed by a band of hunters is filled with bewilderment and fear as they close their cunning circle round him, in such bewilderment lay the queen till welcome sleep came suddenly upon her.'

> ὅσσα δὲ μερμήριξε λέων ἀνδρῶν ἐν ὁμίλῳ
> δείσας, ὁππότε μιν δόλιον περὶ κύκλον ἄγωσι,
> τόσσα μιν ὁρμαίνουσαν ἐπήλυθε νήδυμος ὕπνος.

In the *Iliad* the lion is the animal that epitomizes courage and always inspires fear in others.[122] He never feels fear himself, even when his bravery leads to him being surrounded and killed.[123] It is true that, in the *Iliad*, Ajax in Book 11 and Menelaus in Book 17 are both compared to lions when they are forced to retreat, much against their will. In both cases, the lion is said to be 'frightened back for all its eagerness' (τρεῖ ἐσσύμενός περ, 11.554 and 17.663), by the arrows and burning sticks, but he only retreats after an unsuccessful attempt to attack the men's flocks to devour their flesh. The lion to which Penelope is compared is the only one to be depicted as passive, able only to turn over thoughts in its mind which, like those of the queen, do not lead to action.[124]

Penelope's despair only ends when Athena sends sleep to her, in the first example of a recurring motif. As Charles Segal says (1994:

[121] *Iliad*, 14.20–4 and 16.435–58.

[122] *Iliad*, 11.172–4: οἳ δ' ἔτι κὰμ μέσσον πεδίον φοβέοντο βόες ὥς,/ ἅς τε λέων ἐφόβησε μολὼν ἐν νυκτὸς ἀμολγῷ | πάσας and 17.65–7: ἀμφὶ δὲ τόν [for λέων]γε κύνες τ' ἄνδρές τε νομῆες | πολλὰ μάλ' ἰύζουσιν ἀπόπροθεν οὐδ' ἐθέλουσιν | ἀντίον ἐλθέμεναι· μάλα γὰρ χλωρὸν δέος αἱρεῖ.

[123] *Iliad*, 12.45–6: τοῦ δ' [sc. κάπριος ἠὲ λέων] οὔ ποτε κυδάλιμον κῆρ | ταρβεῖ οὐδὲ φοβεῖται, ἀγηνορίη δέ μιν ἔκτα.

[124] I cannot therefore agree with Felson-Rubin 1994: 21: 'She is a ferocious potential victim besieged, but strong and resourceful.'

70): 'Penelope is more frequently associated with sleep than anyone else in the Odyssey. Her sleep often follows grief and weeping.' Here, sleep brings with it a reassuring dream sent by Athena which changes Penelope's mood and 'her heart was comforted' (4.840).

Penelope does not reappear until Book 16.130–1, when Telemachus returns and sends Eumaeus to tell her that he is safe and to give her the order to send the housekeeper to pass the news on to Laertes without anyone knowing (16.151–3). He is joined along the way by the herald sent from the boat with the same announcement (16.328–9). After they arrive, at 16.335, the herald delivers his message to Penelope, in line 337, and is followed in lines 339–41 by Eumaeus who tells her everything Telemachus asked him to say, before leaving. But we hear nothing of Penelope's reaction to this news. The narrative moves directly on to the suitors in lines 342–408. It is only after this that we return to Penelope and her thoughts. She has decided to show herself to the suitors, a decision motivated by what the herald Medon has told her about the suitors' plot to kill her son (16.409–12). Her entrance into the great hall is described in the same terms as in Book 1 (16.414–16 = 1.332–4). She then speaks to Antinous, criticizing him for plotting Telemachus' murder, reproaching him for his lack of gratitude, and ordering him (*κέλομαι*) to put an end to his plotting and to stop the others too (16.421–33). But Antinous does not reply to her speech and it is Eurymachus who tries to reassure her in lines 435–47. However, the text leaves us in no doubt of his true intentions in line 448: 'So he spoke in disarming phrase, but he himself was plotting destruction for Telemachus' (*ὣς φάτο θαρσύνων, τῷ δ' ἤρτυεν αὐτὸς ὄλεθρον*). Penelope's intervention therefore has no practical effect. She then returns to her room to weep for Odysseus again, until Athena sends sweet sleep to her (16.449–51).

To sum up, from Book 1 to Book 16 Penelope has no effect on the action. As has been pointed out: 'until [this] point . . . Penelope's conduct within the narrative is entirely one dimensional. She longs for her husband's return and remains resolutely steadfast and faithful.'[125] The narrative emphasizes her powerlessness and the despair she feels first at the absence of her husband and then at her son's departure and the dangers he faces.

[125] Katz 1991: 119.

In Books 17 to 21, by contrast, Penelope is at the origin of a series of actions that have a considerable impact on the way events unfold, like her order to Eumaeus to bring the beggar to her in Book 17, her appearance before the suitors in Book 18, and above all her decision to instigate a contest for her hand in marriage. These rather problematic passages (terms like 'inconsistencies', 'discrepancies', 'illogicalities', and 'incongruity' recur frequently in the critical discussions of them) have been central to the analysis of Penelope's character since Wilamowitz. It is worth summarizing briefly, as Katz (1991: 77–154), Murnaghan (1994), and Doherty (1995b: 31–63) have already done, the history of the interpretations of Penelope before proposing my own interpretation.

German critics from Kirchoff to Merkelbach, including Wilamowitz and Schwartz, turned to Analytical criticism to find ready answers to the problems posed by Penelope, as did their British followers like Kirk and Page.[126] They explained away the inconsistencies in the text (like the fact that Penelope proposes the contest of the bow just as the signs of Odysseus' imminent return are becoming more frequent) as the result of the complex tradition and of the combination of different versions. In one of these, echoed by Amphimedon in Book 24, husband and wife have already recognized each other and are in league against the suitors. According to this scenario, Penelope's idea of the contest is simply a trick, like that of the shroud, to escape a marriage she detests as well as being a means for Odysseus to achieve his revenge. In the other version, the recognition did not take place until after the massacre. These two were then combined (the Analysts argued) by an editor (*Bearbeiter*) with his usual clumsiness. In this view, we need to search for the origins of the text and identify the elements that belonged to the original *Odyssey* if we are to understand Books 17 to 23.

The Unitarians adopted the opposite approach, defending the text as it was transmitted by trying to find psychological consistency in Penelope's character. This type of approach has been robustly defended by readers like Hanna Roisman,[127] but has been rightly criticized (although not always for the same reasons) by Sheila

[126] The most detailed account of the Analysts' position is that of Katz 1991: 85 and 93–102.

[127] Roisman 1987: 60 n. 4 claims that the psychological approach is 'especially justifiable in the analysis of Penelope's behavior'.

Murnaghan and Nancy Felson. Murnaghan (1994: 80) draws attention to the anachronistic nature of this type of reading which treats 'her [Penelope] simply as a character without a setting, indeed not as a literary character at all but as a real person to whom the modern reader is free to attribute whatever qualities he or she believes real people possess'. Felson (1994: 126), by contrast, makes use of the distinction drawn by Roland Barthes between a figure ('an impersonal network of symbols combined under a proper name') and a person ('a moral freedom endowed with motives') in order to criticize psychological readings which confuse the two, 'taking a character's figuration in a text as though it existed in a stable and unchanging, if fictive, ontology' (even if she does abandon these principles on the very same page, saying that 'Despite her fictionality, Homer invites psychologizing about Penelope, especially concerning her decision to hold the contest of the bow').

The interpretation of 'Penelope' has thus become a sort of Rorschach test, onto which each reader projects his or her own vision of femininity. We can choose between the traditional image of 'the model wife' (as celebrated in the song 'Penelope' by Georges Brassens) and by William Stanford (1954: 39) who lauds her sacrifice: 'Her final submission to Odysseus is not a defeat. It is a paradoxical triumph of self giving' or a feminist Penelope *avant l'heure*, 'a character aware of the plots she creates and like Odysseus, cunning in securing her own best interests in terms of survival, duty, and pleasure'.[128]

The simplest solution, and the most radical, was proposed in 1950 by P. W. Harsh: Penelope in fact recognizes Odysseus in Book 19, but says nothing, which explains her decision to instigate the contest of the bow and justifies both Homer and Penelope at one stroke. Homer's apparent clumsiness is revealed as an astonishingly subtle narrative strategy while Penelope acquires the typically feminine gift of intuition. If Homer gives no reasons for the change in Penelope, and does not in fact even mention it, it is because an explicit explanation would be 'tedious and awkward'.[129] Penelope does not reveal that she has recognized Odysseus because of the presence of the maidservants (who could betray her). Her dialogue with the beggar, which leads to her decision to suggest the contest of the bow, is a coded

[128] Felson-Rubin 1996: 168. [129] Harsh 1950: 10.

conversation, as one might expect from two characters renowned for their duplicity. The dream (which is made up by Penelope) is a way of asking Odysseus indirectly whether he is prepared to kill the suitors. By confirming the interpretation of the dream suggested by Penelope, he conveys his assent. However, even those scholars, like Jack Winkler, who have been influenced by this thesis admit that it is untenable.[130] It is contradicted by numerous passages of the poem, like 23.94–5, where Penelope has difficulty recognizing Odysseus because of his rags.

Harsh's interpretation was adapted by Anne Amory (1963). She also suggests that Penelope's recognition of Odysseus actually begins in Book 19 but argues that it is done 'intuitively rather than rationally' (104), appealing to the all too familiar contrast between feminine intuition and masculine knowledge. Penelope cannot fully acknowledge what she intuits, because she is too afraid of being proved wrong (here, too, we may suspect that another cliché about female nature, lack of self-confidence, has been projected onto Penelope). The dream, which echoes the omens in the *Odyssey*, is Penelope's invention and a means by which she can test her intuition. But she is 'not yet ready emotionally to accept Odysseus' return' (106). Athena's intervention in Book 20 is thus 'a kind of shorthand for a psychological process', employed at a point in the narrative where there is no space for a fuller account. At the same time, it also 'symbolizes the fact that Penelope, acting only on intuition, without a full knowledge of the situation, does just the right thing at the right time' (113). Amory explains Penelope's tears as she picks up the bow as being prompted both by the memory of Odysseus that the weapon provokes and also by the 'sheer nervous tension' she feels.[131] To sum up, Amory finds that all of Penelope's reactions are 'completely credible psychologically' (120).

Norman Austin (1975) and Joseph Russo (1982) also propose a picture of Penelope as guided by intuition. Austin (1975: 235) claims that when she decides to suggest the contest of the bow, it is because she has somehow understood a whole series of signs without fully realizing it and 'relinquishes herself over to the subconscious'. For Russo (1982: 17), Penelope's sudden decision to set up the test of the

[130] Winkler 1990: 155.

[131] Amory 1963: 114: 'She weeps in part simply because the bow reminds her of Odysseus . . . sheer nervous tension too accounts for her tears.'

bow comes as 'she is caught up in a swelling current of intuitions, intimations and half-believed hopes'.

Jack Winkler's article 'Penelope's Cunning and Homer's' (1990) represented a turning point in the interpretation of Penelope's character and that of the author. Like Amory, Austin, and Russo, he accepts that Penelope suspects Odysseus' true identity from Book 19 onwards: 'There are good reasons to think that everything she says and does in book 19 is guided by her thought that the beggar might be . . . Odysseus' (Winkler 1990: 142–3). However, Penelope is no longer a woman at the mercy of her emotions and of her subconscious, nor is she merely 'a pawn in the game of male characters and of the poet' (Winkler 1990: 142). She is the embodiment of the 'shrewd and effective activity of Greek women laboring (to be sure) under great constraints' (Winkler 1990: 143) in a Mediterranean society that places value on the deliberate use of secrets and lies. She constantly tests the man whom she suspects of being her husband while carefully avoiding giving any sign of her suspicions, a cautiousness that is more than justified by the presence of the maidservants who are in league with the suitors. She thus becomes an emblematic figure for a poetic art that privileges the duplicity and disguise of Odysseus over the heroic deeds of the warrior Achilles.[132]

The study by Marylin Katz, *Penelope's Renown*, published a year after Winkler's article, in 1991, takes a similar approach. It establishes a parallel between the 'indeterminacy of narrative direction and the representation of Penelope's character' in Books 17–21 and in Books 18 and 19 in particular (Katz 1991: 192). Katz also sees Penelope as endowed with a '*metis* that entails the appearance of yielding to the suitors' importunities while in actuality remaining faithful to Odysseus' (Katz 1991: 6) and reads the supposed inconsistencies in her character as an 'indeterminacy' that 'undermines [the] notion of a coherent, essential self' (Katz 1991: 94). She also argues for a narrative structure that is characterized up until Book 23 by ambiguity and 'indeterminacy', thus creating a thoroughly modern Penelope, and justifying the application of new methods of criticism to the Homeric text.

[132] Winkler 1990: 155–6: 'Penelope is a master-weaver, and weaving is an appropriate image for the work of the epic poet who specializes not in recitals of heroic battle but the plotting and counter-plotting of a household in conflict.'

The influence of this type of interpretation on subsequent readings of the *Odyssey* is clear from the titles of books such as Ioanna Papadopoulou-Belmehdi, *Le Chant de Pénélope: poétique du tissage féminin dans l'Odyssée*, published in 1994, and Barbara Clayton, *A Penelopean Poetics: Reweaving the Feminine in Homer's Odyssey*, published in 2003. It is also evident in the works of Marilyn Katz and Nancy Felson-Rubin, who propose, in place of the 'male centered view' of Penelope, a more feminist character. In a similar way, Helene Foley aims in her article 'Penelope as a Moral Agent' to free Penelope from the passive role in which she has long been cast by showing that she takes a 'socially responsible decision' when she decides, contrary to her own feelings, to remarry and to sacrifice her own desires in order to fulfil the needs of her son (by saving his house from destruction) and to obey the instructions given by Odysseus on his departure. Penelope emerges as a tragic heroine: 'Penelope's choice is less dubious and irrational than tragic.'[133]

These interpretations, however, all rely on what is not said, attributing intuitions or intentions to Penelope that are not explicitly mentioned in the text. For this reason, I prefer a reading like that of Sheila Murnaghan which takes into account only what is said in the text of *Odyssey* 17–23.[134] I would therefore suggest, along with most critics since Antiquity, that the decision to instigate the contest of the bow and the developments that lead up to it are indeed ambivalent and opaque and that this is not just a misleading appearance that needs to be dispelled.[135] Let us, then, return to the text and to the analysis of the passages in question.

In Book 17, we see Penelope leave her room to welcome her son home and ask him 'tearfully' (ὀλοφυρομένη, 17.40) to 'tell in full what [he] saw' (ἀλλ' ἄγε μοι κατάλεξον, ὅπως ἤντησας ὀπωπῆς, 17.44). Despite her use of the imperative here, she receives no reply, as Telemachus simply gives her an order similar to the one given to her by Eurycleia in Book 4. He urges her to wash her face, put on clean clothes, go up to her room, and pray, promising unblemished

[133] Foley 1995: 101 and 103.

[134] Murnaghan 1986, 1987, 1994, and 1995.

[135] Contra Foley 1995: 97: 'as the recent and formidable studies of Murnaghan, Winkler, Felson-Rubin and Katz among others have argued, the narrative context in which Penelope acts has made both her decision to establish the contest for her hand and her behavior leading up to that decision *appear* ambivalent, opaque and/or contradictory to critics from antiquity on.'

hecatombs to the gods if Zeus brings about his revenge (17.48–51). Penelope obeys, without saying a word, as we see from lines 57–60: 'Thus he spoke and she obeyed his order without a word (ὣς ἄρ' ἐφώνησεν, τῇ δ' ἄπτερος[136] ἔπλετο μῦθος): She bathed her face and put on fresh garments; she prayed, and promised to all the gods the sacrifice of unblemished hecatombs, in hope that then Zeus would bring about requital.'

The narrative then follows Telemachus to the assembly-place and back to the palace, where another feast is under way, before returning to Penelope, sitting opposite her son, spinning wool (17.96–7). She is about to return to her room to cry once more, since Telemachus has not taken advantage of the suitors' absence to tell her what he learned about Odysseus' return (17.101–6). It is only then that he replies to her question—a gap similar to that between Odysseus' request for protection and Arete's reply in Book 7—and gives his account of his journey in lines 108–49. Penelope's reaction is then described in a single line: 'Thus he spoke and the queen's heart was moved within her' (17.150). The seer Theoclymenus then speaks, telling her of the favourable omen described in Book 15.525–8 and predicting, with a solemn oath, Odysseus' return and revenge. Penelope's reply is an exact repetition of that of Telemachus in Book 15: 'Ah, my guest, if only your words might be fulfilled! Then you would learn soon enough what friendship and multiplied gifts from me were worth; anyone then who came your way would call you a happy man' (17.163–5 = 15.536–8). What is more, she will repeat the same words a second time to the beggar in Book 19 when he announces Odysseus' imminent return (19.309–11), a repetition that seems to suggest, I would argue, the pre-eminence of Telemachus, who is the first to promise generous rewards to the bringer of good news.

We do not see Penelope again until line 492 when she learns that Antinous has struck the beggar in the great hall and expresses her indignation in lines 499–504. It is only then that she truly takes the

[136] The meaning of this expression, which recurs at 19.29, 21.386, and 22.98, is disputed and the scholia give different interpretations. I would prefer, like Chantraine *DE* 2009, s.v. πτερόν, to accept the suggestion of Latacz 1968 that the α is privative and therefore to understand that the *muthos* in question is that of Penelope and that it is 'without wings', meaning that she does not pronounce a single word. But the general meaning remains the same if we apply these words to Telemachus and understand ἄπτερος to mean 'impetuous' as do the scholiasts to line 57 who explain it as ταχὺς πρὸς τὸ πεισθῆναι καὶ ἰσόπτερος.

initiative and gives Eumaeus the order to 'command' (ἄνωχθι) the beggar to come to her so that she can ask about Odysseus (17.508–11). Her order, however, is not obeyed immediately as Eumaeus begins to praise the beggar, forcing her to repeat it in line 529: 'Go and call him here and let him speak to me face to face.' But before Eumaeus can carry out her order he is interrupted by another favourable omen, Telemachus' sneeze, and Penelope has to give it a third time in line 544: 'Go now, and ask that stranger to speak to me face to face.' Eumaeus finally obeys in line 551: 'Thus she spoke, hearing her order (*muthos*), the swineherd went' (ὣς φάτο, βῆ δὲ συφορβός, ἐπεὶ τὸν μῦθον ἄκουσε). Penelope therefore has to speak three times before her words gain the authority of a *muthos* and Eumaeus conveys it to Odysseus: 'Aged friend, you are summoned now by Telemachus' mother, wise Penelope; her spirit bids her to question you on her husband' (17.553–5). Odysseus' reply introduces a new delay. Although he says that he is willing to tell her everything 'straight away' (αἶψά 17.561), he asks Eumaeus to 'tell her to wait (ἄνωχθι μεῖναι) in the hall until after sunset' (17.569–70) and this order, which carries weight, is carried out immediately, as we see from line 574 which repeats line 551: 'Thus he spoke, hearing his order the swineherd went' (ὣς φάτο, βῆ δὲ συφορβός, ἐπεὶ τὸν μῦθον ἄκουσε). Penelope's surprise at seeing Eumaeus returning alone ('Have you not brought the beggar then?', 17.576) reveals the full incongruity of this fresh delay. Eumaeus, in fact, justifies it when he emphasizes the good sense of Odysseus' words in line 580 (μυθεῖται κατὰ μοῖραν) and Penelope says as much too in line 586: 'The stranger has his wits about him.' This whole scene seems to me to serve entirely to reveal the true meaning of the ὁμοφροσύνη between husband and wife, which inevitably involves 'the internalisation by the wife of the values of the husband' and thus underlines Penelope's subordinate role.[137] As Nancy Felson-Rubin (1994: 53) has pointed out, the meeting will only take place according to the conditions set down by the true master of the house, Odysseus.

In Book 18, after the victory of Odysseus, the false beggar, over the real beggar, Irus, and the warning that Odysseus gives, in vain, to the 'good' suitor, Amphinomus, the narrative leaves the great hall to return to Penelope: 'But now the goddess of gleaming eyes put it into the queen's mind (τῇ δ' ἄρ' ἐπὶ φρεσὶ θῆκε) to show herself before

[137] Thalmann 1998: 235.

the suitors, to open their hearts more widely (ὅπως πετάσειε[138] μάλιστα θυμὸν μνηστήρων) and win more esteem from son and husband' (18.158–62). These lines introduce one of the most controversial scenes in the whole of the *Odyssey*.[139] First of all we see Penelope manipulated from the outside by a deity who seems to make her act against her natural inclination, which is highly unusual in Homer.[140] We can of course discuss the exact meaning of the purpose clause introduced by ὅπως ('(in order) to'). It may be used here to express the intention or simply to state the result of Penelope's action, as Russo suggests.[141] If it is the former, should we see these lines as expressing the combined intentions of the divine and the human agents, interpret them as a typical example of the dual causality that is characteristic of the Homeric poems, and agree with John Finley that 'the goddess is working in her—which is not to say that she herself is not acting'?[142] Or should we, as I think preferable, attribute this intention to Athena alone, as has often been suggested.[143]

This account is followed, in line 163, by Penelope's 'laugh' (ἐγέλασσεν) described as ἀχρεῖον, which only complicates matters further since the sense of this adjective was already debated in Antiquity.[144] Russo, following the scholia, understands inappropriate.[145]

[138] The text is uncertain: some manuscripts read θέλξειε. If we keep πετάσειε as most editors do, we should probably understand 'to lift' or 'lighten' as do Hesychius who glosses it as κουφίσειε, and Russo 1985: 204 ad loc.

[139] See, for example, Hölscher 1996: 134: 'one of the most puzzling and controversial scenes in the entire *Odyssey*'; and Emlyn-Jones 1984: 10: 'one of the hardest to interpret in the whole poem.'

[140] Murnaghan 1995: 71.

[141] Russo 1985 ad 18: 160–2.

[142] Finley 1978: 9, see also Allione 1963: 76. On dual causality in the Homeric poems see Lesky 2001.

[143] See Büchner 1940: 43, Katz 1991: 81–3, and Felson-Rubin 1994: 28. Emlyn-Jones 1984: 10: 'So it seems likely that both reasons given in 160–162 are those of Athena.' Contra Winkler 1990: 146: 'Penelope descends the stairs . . . intending to soften up the suitors, to enhance her own domestic honor as wife and mother.'

[144] As Büchner 1940: 141–3 notes, ἀχρεῖον is only found elsewhere at *Iliad*, 2.269 where it applies to Thersites (ἀλγήσας δ' ἀχρεῖον ἰδὼν ἀπομόρξατο δάκρυ), and the meaning of the word in these two passages was a subject of debate in Antiquity. It has even been suggested that the meaning might be different in each case. Chantraine 2009, s.v. χρή understands 'in vain' at *Iliad*, 2.269 and 'pretending to laugh' at *Odyssey*, 18.163.

[145] Russo 1985 on 18.163 follows the scholia that gloss ἀχρεῖον with ἄκαιρον μηδενὸς προκειμένου, οὐ χρειῶδες, οὐδὲ πρὸς χρείαν ἁρμοζόμενον. Cf. Emlyn-Jones 1984: 10: 'she does not really know what she is doing'; and Wohl 1993: 40: 'it clearly must mean something like "idly" or "without reason".'

But Büchner and Levine both compare Penelope's laugh with the laugh that, in the *Odyssey*, precedes an act of deception or expresses the character's admiration for an effective trick played on another character and suggest that ἀχρεῖον should be translated as 'sardonically', while Nancy Felson-Rubin sees this involuntary laugh, whose meaning Penelope herself does not understand, as a sign of awakening desire ('her forced and aimless laugh may also indicate a new susceptibility to eros, perhaps in response to the charming stranger').[146]

To complicate the reader's task still further, Penelope immediately goes on to give a completely different explanation to Eurynome in lines 164–8:

Eurynome, my heart is eager now, though it never was before, to show myself before the suitors whom I detest (θυμός μοι ἐέλδεται, οὔ τι πάρος γε, μνηστήρεσσι φανῆναι, ἀπεχθομένοισί περ ἔμπης); moreover I wish to give Telemachus a warning that may be of service to him, not to mix so much with these overwheening men; they speak kindly to him, but are plotting to harm him.

This explanation completely contradicts the narration it follows because it ascribes the decision to Penelope's *thumos* alone. Moreover, its logic is hard to follow, to say the least: it is difficult to see why Penelope would need to show herself *to the suitors* in order to give a warning *to her son*. It is not surprising, therefore, that critics are divided over its interpretation.[147] Some solve the problem by avoiding it: Penelope's decision to show herself to the suitors has been read as a means of extracting presents from them, which at best implies that she is secretly attracted to the suitors or at worst that she is behaving here like a prostitute (*regina prope ad meretricias artes descendit*), an 'often cited judgement of scholarship'.[148] For Analysts like Merkelbach (19.1: 13) the solution is simple. The passage results from the juxtaposition of two different versions: one, by poet A, presents Penelope as an autonomous agent, the other, by poet B, makes her the instrument of Athena's will. It is also possible to put it down to an oversight on the part of the poet: *aliquando bonus dormitat Homerus* ('sometimes even the great Homer nods', *Ars Poetica*, 359); or a trace of the folktale and a remainder of the cunning Penelope, who is otherwise absent

[146] Felson-Rubin 1994: 29.

[147] See the lengthy discussion in Katz 1991: 81–8.

[148] This judgement by Kayser is cited by Hölscher (1996: 135) among others.

from the epic.[149] Others, like Hölscher (1996: 137), are prepared to be more generous to Homer and explain the discrepancy between the objective purpose of the scene that coincides with the intentions of the goddess and its subjective one as a way of distancing 'the sensible and mourning Penelope of the epic' from 'the cunning Penelope of the folktale'. Others, such as Murnaghan, Katz, and Wohl, claim that Homer's text is irredeemably ambiguous and that it would be futile to try to clarify the question of motivation when it has been left deliberately unclear.[150] I find this last approach preferable, for what seems to emerge from all the discussions is the mystery surrounding Penelope's motivation even for herself, since she is unaware of Athena's influence.[151] At the very moment when she presents her decision as emanating from herself alone she emphasizes its strangeness. She hates the suitors' company and has done everything she could in the past to avoid them. We should also note her uncertainty. She seems to need Eurynome's approval, which is given straightaway in lines 170–1: 'My child, all that you say is well said (*ναὶ δὴ ταῦτά γε πάντα, τέκος, κατὰ μοῖραν ἔειπες*). Go then and give your son the message without concealment.'

Penelope nevertheless rejects Eurynome's advice in lines 172–4 to improve her appearance by bathing her body and anointing her cheeks, saying, in lines 178–9, 'Eurynome, do not in your affection try to coax me to wash myself and anoint myself with unguents.' Athena will have to take care of Penelope's looks, as she did for Odysseus in Books 6, 8, and 23 and as she will do for Laertes in Book 24. She begins, as she does several times in the *Odyssey*,[152] by pouring sweet sleep upon her: 'Penelope lay back on the couch she was resting on and all her limbs were relaxed in slumber (*λύθεν δέ οἱ ἅψεα πάντα*)', 189–90.[153] Then Athena cleanses her face with

[149] As summarized by Hölscher 1996: 135.

[150] See Murnaghan 1987: 130: 'The text makes her state of mind hard to assess'; Katz 1991: 88: 'The text suspends judgment'; Wohl 1993: 40 speaks of 'confusion about her motives'.

[151] See Emlyn-Jones 1984: 10, Pedrick 1994: 102–3, Holmberg 1995: 115.

[152] *Odyssey*, 18.187–8. See also 1.363–4, 16.450–1, 19.603–4, 21.357–8.

[153] I do not think that we can interpret this detail in terms of sexuality and see in it a sign of Penelope's awakening sensuality, as suggested by Wohl 1993: 40. The Greek phrase *λύθεν δέ οἱ ἅψεα πάντα* has nothing to do with *τῶν δ' αὐτοῦ λύτο γούνατ'* used to describe the effects of desire on the suitors in line 212. The same expression recurs at 4.794 where it expresses the relaxation brought to Penelope by sleep which is elsewhere described as *λυσιμελής* ('limb loosening') (*Odyssey*, 20.57, 23.343).

ambrosia, makes her appear taller and fuller than she is, and makes her face whiter than ivory (18.190–6). This scene has been rightly compared with the *Dios apaté* (the deception of Zeus) of *Iliad* 14.[154] But I do not think that we should see this episode as a prelude to a deliberate act of deception, as is clearly the case with Hera. Instead, it is important to emphasize all that distinguishes Hera's manoeuvres from the involuntary seduction exercised by a woman who never ceases to declare her fidelity to her absent husband and is beautified against her will. As Ingrid Holmberg points out: 'Despite the fact that Penelope seduces the suitors, the text is very careful to distance Penelope from a conscious and active role in their seduction.'[155]

When Penelope appears before the suitors, she has an irresistible effect on them through her appearance alone: 'their knees weakened (*τῶν δ' αὐτοῦ λύτο γούνατ'*), their hearts were transported with desire (*ἔρῳ δ' ἄρα θυμὸν ἔθελχθεν*) and they voiced a prayer, every one of them, to share her bed and lie beside her' (18.212–13). As she had announced, Penelope then speaks to Telemachus, but her words are entirely different from what she claimed she was going to say. The reproaches she addresses to him serve in fact to emphasize her qualities as a hostess as she criticizes him for having allowed a guest to be mistreated (18.215–25). Telemachus accepts her criticism but informs her that the beggar came out best from his fight with Irus and ends by expressing his desire to see the suitors suffer the same treatment as Irus one day. The image of 'limbs weakening' recurs in Telemachus' speech where it takes on an entirely new meaning. It no longer serves to convey the impact of desire, as in line 212, but rather the suitors' powerlessness in the face of their impending deaths or the impossibility of return for Irus.[156]

The speech by Eurymachus that follows is a twofold homage to Penelope's beauty and wisdom which, ironically, echoes Arete's praise of Odysseus in Book 11.[157] The queen's reply, which begins with a

[154] See Levine 1983: 174–5 and Wohl 1993: 40.

[155] Holmberg 1995: 116. See also Winkler 1990: 146–7: 'Penelope is thus protected from any imputation of wanting to appear desirable in the eyes of strange men. Homer arranges both that she seduces and that she not be blamable for any seduction.'

[156] *Odyssey*, 18.238 and 242. Felson 1994: 62–3 sees the ambiguity of this expression that can describe the effects of desire (cf. 23.205–6) but can also be used of the vanquished warrior (18.235–42).

[157] *Odyssey*, 18.248–9. Line 249 (*εἶδός τε μέγεθός τε ἰδὲ φρένας ἔνδον ἐΐσας*) is applied to Odysseus at 11.337.

denial of her beauty (18.251–53) and repeats the theme of her response to Eurynome in 18.180–1, serves first and foremost to reassure the reader (and Odysseus) of her fidelity by showing that she has precisely followed his orders, which she quotes in lines 267–70: '"Keep in mind my father and mother in this place no less than you do now, or keep them in mind more perhaps when I am far from home. But when you see this son of ours grown to bearded manhood, then leave your own palace and marry whom you will".' She goes on to emphasize her reluctance to contract a 'hated marriage' in line 272.

As this is the only reference to the order given by Odysseus to his wife as he left for the war it has sometimes been suggested that it is Penelope's own invention, which would then explain why Odysseus, who knows the truth, is able to guess Penelope's real objective in talking of marriage to one of the suitors.[158] But there is no conclusive evidence to support this interpretation. The end of Penelope's speech, with its indirect invitation to the suitors to give her presents, also raises problems. Should we interpret it as proof of her duplicity, as Odysseus does and as do critics like Büchner, Allione, Levine, and Russo?[159] For Odysseus' wife, according to her husband's interpretation, is not content simply to charm the suitors with her beautiful appearance, she also charms their hearts with her gentle words (θέλγε δὲ θυμὸν μειλιχίοισ' ἐπέεσσι) though she has something else in mind (νόος δέ οἱ ἄλλα μενοίνα, 18.282–3). This would be a precise parallel to her previous action when she encouraged the suitors to hope for marriage when she had finished weaving the shroud that she, in reality, never intended to finish 'since she had something else in mind', as both Antinous and Athena say, using the same words.[160] I would suggest instead that we should see these words, which have no logical relationship with what precedes them, as a further result of

[158] See for example Winkler 1990: 147: 'We might well suppose that Penelope's account of Odysseus' parting words about Telemakhos' beard is her own invention, on the spur of the moment, and that this is an added reason why Odysseus is perfectly sure of her fidelity even as she acts out the opposite'. See also De Jong 1994: 41 and 2001: 467.

[159] Büchner 1940: 139–40, Allione 1963: 71–4, Levine 1983, Russo 1985 on 18.283.

[160] *Odyssey*, 2.92 (Antinous) and 13.381 (Athena). As De Jong 1994: 41 notes, the context is different: 'the implication of νόος δέ οἱ ἄλλα μενοίνα in *Odyssey*, 2.91–2 and 13.380–1 is clearly that Penelope is promising to remarry, but does in fact have other plans, i.e. is not considering remarriage. There, however, the νόος δέ clause contrasts with a promise of marriage μέν clause, but in [this] passage it contrasts with an "eliciting gifts and charming through sweet words" μέν clause.'

Athena's intervention aimed at 'making her win more esteem from husband and son' (*ὅπως . . . τιμήεσσα γένοιτο μᾶλλον πρὸς πόσιός τε καὶ υἱέος ἢ πάρος ἦεν*, 18.160–2) thanks to the gifts she will manage to extract from the suitors. To achieve this end, the goddess not only transforms Penelope's appearance to make her more attractive, she also manipulates her words, just as she worked earlier, unbeknownst to Penelope, on her *thumos*. In this case, Odysseus would be projecting his own *mētis* onto his wife on the basis of her past actions.[161] There is nothing to indicate that he is correct in this. We may even compare this passage with Book 24.167–9 where Amphinomus claims, erroneously, that Penelope was working with Odysseus who 'told (*ἄνωγε*) her to set out before us suitors his own bow and the axes of grey iron' and wrongly attributes an active role to her in the massacre of the suitors.

We may also choose, as does Hölscher (1996: 135–7), to interpret the phrase *νόος δέ οἱ ἄλλα μενοίνα* as meaning 'she desired something entirely different', that is, Odysseus' return. Odysseus' joy would therefore be a response to the way in which Penelope expresses her hostility to the idea of a new marriage and unintentionally proves her fidelity, as well as reflecting his certain knowledge that this new marriage will not take place, since he has returned (De Jong 1994: 41). What seems certain to me is that a reading like that of Wohl (2003: 41), who sees Penelope as making use of her sexuality here in order to exert her power in the only way possible for women, is not in accordance with the text, which is more interested in the impact of the queen's appearance than in the precise nature of her intentions. The scene ends, moreover, with Antinous' speech at 285–9, inviting Penelope to accept the presents that the suitors are about to give her, and with a list of these presents, while Penelope returns to her room 'with her waiting-women carrying the gorgeous gifts' in lines 302–3.

The beginning of Book 19 is framed by two lines, 2 and 52, describing Odysseus in the great hall 'pondering how with Athena's aid he should slay the suitors' (*μνηστήρεσσι φόνον σὺν Ἀθήνῃ μερμηρίζων*). The rest of the book is entirely devoted to the meeting between him and Penelope. This meeting opens with lines 53–4: 'Now Penelope began to descend from her room, looking like Artemis or

[161] Katz 1991: 89: Odysseus here is constructing Penelope's intentions in accordance with the overall narrative action and is reading the incident against the paradigm articulated by Athena in 13.381 (cf. 2.92).

like golden Aphrodite.' These lines are an exact repetition of 17.36–7, immediately preceding the reunion of Penelope and Telemachus, and thus seem to be a prelude to a recognition scene.[162] This is certainly how the lines are interpreted by those critics who see the meeting in Book 19 as the moment when Penelope 'intuitively' or 'unconsciously' recognizes Odysseus (see pp. 287–8 above).

The dialogue between Penelope and Odysseus which we have been expecting since Book 17 is delayed at first by Melantho's fresh insults to Odysseus in lines 65–9.[163] He responds with threats that are reiterated by Penelope.[164] A further delay is introduced in lines 96–102 by the order given to Eurynome to bring a chair and by the account of its execution. It is only then that Penelope is able to enquire about Odysseus' identity in terms that are paralleled in the meeting between Odysseus and Arete and nowhere else.[165] And, like Arete in Book 7, she does not receive a reply to her question. Instead, Odysseus skilfully precedes his refusal with a compliment, the famous comparison of Penelope, whose 'fame (*κλέος*) goes up to wide heaven', to a good king.[166]

Penelope then tells of her current plight and her suffering.[167] The story she tells of the stratagem that allowed her to keep the suitors at a distance for three years only serves to show that she is now in an impossible situation (19.157–61): she cannot avoid remarriage because she cannot invent another trick and she is under pressure both from her family, who are urging her to marry,[168] and from her son, who is suffering as a result of the suitors' devouring of his resources (159) but refuses to send his mother back to her father Icarius or to expel her from his house 'against her will' (*ἀέκουσαν*) by a 'compelling order' (*μύθῳ ἀναγκαίῳ*), as he will say later on (20.343–4). It is only after this long parenthesis that she repeats her question: 'But, however that may be, tell me what race you come from and what place' (19.162).

[162] Everywhere else (*Odyssey*, 1.332, 16.413, 18.207, 21.66) Penelope enters with two handmaidens.

[163] Melantho had already insulted Odysseus at 18.326–36.

[164] *Odyssey*, 19.87–8, Odysseus: *τὸν* [Telemachus] *δ' οὔ τις ἐνὶ μεγάροισι γυναικῶν λήθει ἀτασθάλλουσ'* and 91–2 Penelope: *οὔ τί με λήθεις | ἕρδουσα μέγα ἔργον*. See Rutherford 1992 on 19.91.

[165] *Odyssey*, 19.104–5a = 7.237–8a. On the connection between these two scenes see De Jong 2001: 459.

[166] *Odyssey*, 19.108–14. See Segal 1996: 206–8.

[167] *Odyssey*, 19.129: *νῦν δ' ἄχομαι.*

[168] See *Odyssey*, 15.16–18.

Odysseus replies with another 'Cretan' tale in lines 165–202, claiming to have suffered at least as much as Penelope, and mentioning his meeting with Odysseus, which makes Penelope cry again, emphasizing by contrast Odysseus' ability to control himself and disguise his feelings (19.210–12). But, from line 215 onwards, Penelope proves herself to be a spouse worthy of Odysseus by her caution as well as her hospitality. She puts the beggar to the test by asking him questions which will enable her to be sure that he has really met Odysseus (19.215–19). As Chris Emlyn-Jones (1984: 8) has remarked, Homer makes use here of elements which normally occur in the recognition type-scene but he alters their meaning since, rather than leading to a true recognition, they simply serve to establish the beggar's veracity. Odysseus naturally emerges triumphant from this test (19.220–48). He then tries to comfort his wife by announcing Odysseus' imminent return (19.262–307) though she is not convinced (19.312–16). As has been noted, Penelope's scepticism is revealed by her use, when talking of Odysseus, of the formula εἴ ποτ' ἔην γε (315) 'if it was ever really so' which, in both the *Iliad* and the *Odyssey*, is spoken by characters who have suffered, or think they have suffered, an irremediable loss.

The reminder of the qualities of Odysseus, who was unequalled for his generosity in welcoming guests and ensuring their safe return home, leads into a scene of hospitality. Like the other female characters in the *Odyssey*, Penelope knows how to ensure that her guest is well looked after. In lines 317–18 she orders her maidservants to wash his feet and prepare a bed for him. She also orders them to prepare a bath for him on the next day and anoint him with oil so that he can be dressed appropriately for the feast to be held the next evening (19.319–28). Here again, it is important to note that, as in Book 17, these orders are only carried out once they have been modified and endorsed by Odysseus. He refuses the bed and only accepts the foot bath on condition that it is given by a devoted old serving woman (19.336–48). Here again, as in Book 18, Penelope accepts the 'sensible' advice of the beggar[169] and orders Eurycleia to wash his feet (19.357–60).

Penelope now disappears from the narrative during the recognition scene that is played out between Eurycleia and Odysseus. She is only mentioned once, in lines 476–9, when Eurycleia looks at her to tell her

[169] *Odyssey*, 19.350–2: "ξεῖνε φίλ'· οὐ γάρ πώ τις ἀνὴρ <u>πεπνυμένος</u> ὧδε | ξείνων τηλεδαπῶν φιλίων ἐμὸν ἵκετο δῶμα, | ὡς σὺ <u>μάλ' εὐφραδέως πεπνυμένα πάντ'</u> ἀγορεύεις.

that her husband has returned. But here again Athena makes a decisive intervention, acting on Penelope's *noos* ('mind', 'thoughts') which she turns elsewhere (*τῇ γὰρ Ἀθηναίη νόον ἔτραπεν*) in line 479. The conversation between the beggar and Penelope does not resume until line 508, where she mentions a last small question she wants to ask him (*ξεῖνε, τὸ μέν σ' ἔτι τυτθὸν ἐγὼν εἰρήσομαι αὐτή*). But before asking it she speaks once again of the sorrow and mourning that fill her days and nights (19.512, 516–17), emphasizing her suffering by comparing it with the nightingale's lament for her son (19.518–23). Then, she starts by setting out the dilemma which faces her in terms that are very close to the description given by Telemachus at 16.73–7: 'my mind shifts hither and thither (*ὣς καὶ ἐμοὶ δίχα θυμὸς ὀρώρεται ἔνθα καὶ ἔνθα*), wondering if I should stay with my son and keep everything unchanged—my estate, my waiting-women, my lofty-roofed house itself—respecting my husband's bed and the people's voice; or if I should now go with (*ἦ ἤδη ἅμ' ἕπωμαι*) whatever Achaean lord seems noblest as he woos me here and offers my kinsmen countless gifts' (19.524–9).

In contrast to Book 4, this is a real case of deliberation involving a choice between two alternatives that are both equally possible, which was not the case before since, as Penelope herself remarks at 19.530–1, 'my son, when he was a child and unreflecting, would say that I must not marry and leave my husband's house'. Now, however, Telemachus no longer opposes his mother's remarriage and is even keen for her to leave: 'he prays heaven that I may depart, because he frets at the suitors' wasting of his possessions' (19.533–4).[170] But here again, the deliberation fails to lead to a decision. Penelope changes the subject and asks the beggar to interpret a dream she has had. This dream has several unusual features:[171] it is the only Homeric dream that takes the form of a symbolic image. It is also the only one (apart from the ones briefly mentioned by Odysseus, posing as a Cretan, in Book 14 or by Penelope in Book 20) to be known only through the words of the dreamer, which explains why it has been interpreted as an invention, like that of Cretan Odysseus.[172] It is also not hard to see why modern readers have been tempted by psychoanalytical interpretations and have seen it as an expression of the pleasure

[170] See also 20.341–2.

[171] On dreams in the *Odyssey*, see below Chapter 10, pp. 336–41.

[172] See, for example, Büchner 1940: 149 n. 1, Harsh 1950: 16, Winkler 1990: 153–4.

Penelope feels subconsciously at being wooed by the suitors[173] or, alternatively, of her intense desire to see her husband again.[174] But this dream seems to fulfil a more immediately practical function and to belong to the series of signs and prophecies that point to Odysseus' imminent return from Book 15 onwards. It even contains its own interpretation in the form of the speech by the eagle Odysseus in lines 544–50. Penelope's request may therefore seem surprising, as Winkler (1990: 153) has remarked. The beggar can only confirm the eagle's words: 'It is not possible to interpret your dream (*ὑποκρίνασθαι ὄνειρον* in any other way,) since Odysseus himself has revealed to you how he will fulfil it' (19.555–7). It is strange, to say the least, that the same woman who asked the beggar to interpret her dream in line 535 (*ἀλλ' ἄγε μοι τὸν ὄνειρον ὑπόκριναι*) states categorically a few lines later at 19.560 that dreams are 'beyond interpretation' (*ἦ τοι μὲν ὄνειροι ἀμήχανοι ἀκριτόμυθοι*).

There is, moreover, no clear link between this passage and what follows, that is Penelope's declaration (19.570–81) that she will leave Odysseus' house the next day and her decision to propose the trial of the bow to the suitors as a means of deciding who will win her hand, while all the time claiming that the dawn of this day is 'loathsome' to her and that she will continue to remember 'even in her dreams' the house she is about to leave. There is nothing in the text to suggest that she has any other purpose in mind here than the one she mentions: to decide on her future husband. We can therefore concur with the observation of Ingrid Holmberg (1995: 117) that, at this point in the plot 'when Penelope finally does settle upon a course of action, the contest of the bow, we know that her stated plans are in direct contradiction to the plot of the *Odyssey* and Odysseus' "plans"'. This is preferable to reading her proposal as designed to allow the beggar to dissuade her, if he is not Odysseus (Amory 1963: 106) or as a machiavellian strategy: 'She *knows*, when she proposes the contest, that she is choosing a move that will fit into more than one strategy' (Felson-Rubin 1994: 33). It is as if Penelope, before actually proposing the contest to the suitors, needed Odysseus' approval in the eyes of the author. And approve he does, urging her with the use of the imperative not to put off the trial (*μηκέτι νῦν ἀνάβαλλε δόμοισ' ἔνι*

[173] Devereux 1957, Rankin 1962, Russo 1982: 9, Felson 1994: 32, Clayton 2003: 45. See the comments of Katz 1991: 147.

[174] Emlyn-Jones 1984: 4.

τοῦτον ἄεθλον, 19.584), since Odysseus will return before the suitors have managed to accomplish the task. The book ends with Odysseus remaining in the great hall where he will sleep on the ground and Penelope going back up to her room where, once again, 'she weeps for Odysseus her dear husband till Athena of the gleaming eyes sends welcome slumber upon her eyelids' (19. 603–4).

We next see Penelope when she wakes at line 57 of Book 20 and begins weeping again, showing the continuity between the end of Book 19 'then she wept for Odysseus her dear husband' (κλαῖεν ἔπειτ' Ὀδυσῆα φίλον πόσιν, 19.603) and the beginning of Book 20 where her tears (κλαῖεν δ', 20.58) lead into expressions of despair. She longs for death in an episode that was prefigured by her reaction at 18.201–5 just before she appeared in front of the suitors, resplendent in her beauty. Both of these scenes serve to establish her fidelity beyond any doubt by showing her desire to see Odysseus again, even if it is in the Underworld, and the disgust she feels at the idea of taking another husband who will be inferior to Odysseus (20.82), before two scenes that could call this fidelity into question. At the same time, the contrast between husband and wife created at the beginning of the book (one is sleeping, the other is not) is a way of indirectly emphasizing their shared preoccupations, since each one is thinking of the other, while also contrasting them. Penelope sees her husband in what she describes as 'an evil dream sent by some god' (20.87) because the presence by her side of a man resembling Odysseus as he was when he set out for Troy (20.88–9) is only an illusion and not a vision of reality, as she at first thought (ἐπεὶ οὐκ ἐφάμην ὄναρ ἔμμεναι, ἀλλ' ὕπαρ ἤδη, 20.90). When, by contrast, Odysseus seems to see Penelope standing by his head, as is characteristic of dreams in Homer, it is not a dream but the effect of the imagination of a man who is awake: 'In his fancy it seemed to him that even now she stood at his bedside and knew him for who he was' (δόκησε δέ οἱ κατὰ θυμὸν ἤδη γινώσκουσα παρεστάμεναι κεφαλῆφι, 20.93–4); even though it is introduced by what will become, in later literature, the standard formula for introducing dreams.

The brief dialogue between Telemachus and Eurycleia that follows (20.128–43) is also focused on Penelope. It serves to show, once again, her qualities as a hostess as the doubts expressed by Telemachus about the quality of the welcome that his mother has extended to the beggar are immediately dispelled by Eurycleia. But during the ensuing feast Penelope is simply a mute presence, mentioned by the suitor Agelaus when he invites Telemachus to take a seat next to his mother and tell her to marry the best man among the suitors, the one who gives the most generous gifts (20.334–5), then by Telemachus himself when he refuses, out of respect (αἰδέομαι), to force his mother to leave the palace against her will (ἀέκουσαν) (20.343), and then in the narrative which tells how she listens to the men's *muthos* in lines 387–9.

Book 21, by contrast, is dominated by Penelope and her decision to propose the trial of the bow to the suitors. But here too, while the decision itself is clear, its origin is left opaque by the author. We have seen how, in Book 18, Penelope's decision to appear before the suitors is explained in different ways in the space of a few lines, first as a result of Athena's intervention in line 158 and then, by Penelope herself, as coming from her *thumos.* We find the same contrast between the explanation given in Book 19, where the decision to propose the trial of the bow is attributed to the speaker herself, designated as 'I', in lines 572, 'now I shall propose a contest' (νῦν γὰρ καταθήσω ἄεθλον), and 576, 'now I shall send this contest upon the suitors' (νῦν δὲ μνηστήρεσσιν ἄεθλον τοῦτον ἐφήσω), and that of Book 21, where it is attributed to Athena, 'the goddess of the gleaming eyes put it into the queen's mind' (τῇ δ' ἄρ' ἐπὶ φρεσὶ θῆκε θεὰ γλαυκῶπις Ἀθήνη, 21.1). The description of Penelope's action not only places emphasis on the queen's energy when she takes the key 'with a sturdy hand'[175] but also, as in Book 18, accentuates Penelope's fidelity: she weeps loudly when she picks up her husband's bow (21.56–7).

Her entrance into the great hall is described using the same lines as in Books 1, 16, and 18.[176] But her words are introduced for the first time by the formula φάτο μῦθον in line 67, which is used of speech that carries a certain authority.[177] Here, she presents Odysseus' bow to the suitors, promising to marry the victor, while still declaring her fidelity to her first husband, just as she did when she first revealed her plan to Odysseus in Book 19: she will, she claims, remember the

[175] On the implications of the formula χειρὶ παχείῃ see Chapter 2 above (p. 53).

[176] *Odyssey*, 21.64–6 = 1.333–5 and 18.209–11; 21.64–5 = 16.415–16.

[177] This formula, which occurs six times in the *Odyssey*, serves to introduce the speech of a male character on four occasions (Odysseus: 6.148, 13.37; Athena disguised as Telemachus: 2.384; Alcinous' herald: 8.10) and is only once used to introduce the speech of another female character, Helen, when in 15.171 she acts as a seer and predicts Odysseus' return and revenge.

house she came to as a bride even in her dreams.[178] She also asserts her authority when she orders (*ἀνώγει*, 21.80) Eumaeus to hand the bow and the axes to the suitors. But once again the meaning of her decision is altered by Telemachus' intervention. By participating in the contest himself, he introduces the possibility of a different outcome: if he is the victor, his mother will not have to leave the palace (21.102–17). During the preparations for the contest (21.118–23) and the attempts to string the bow made by Telemachus and the suitors, with the exception of their two leaders (124–87) there is no mention of Penelope. From lines 188 to 241 the narrative recounts the actions of Odysseus who leaves the hall to reveal his identity to his two loyal servants, give them instructions, and tell Eumaeus in particular to be sure to give him the bow, even if the suitors object (21.232–5).

Penelope is just as absent from the second phase of the contest: Odysseus' return to the great hall, Eurymachus' failure, and Antinous' decision to put off the rest of the trial until the next day (21.242–73). She does not re-enter the narrative until Odysseus has asked to attempt the task and has been, as he predicted, vehemently rebuffed by the suitors and their leader Antinous (20.285–310). It is then that Penelope intervenes to criticize Antinous' behaviour as a breach of the laws of hospitality, telling him that 'it is neither honourable nor just to deny his due to any guest of Telemachus' (21.312–13), and to reassure him at the same time. No one, least of all the beggar himself, expects Penelope to marry him even if he does succeed at the test. The conversation that follows between Penelope and Eurymachus, who now takes Antinous' place as the leader of the suitors, serves to point out Odysseus' superiority over those who seek his wife's hand in marriage, a superiority that is not only demonstrated in the narrative, but also acknowledged by Eurymachus, the last to attempt the challenge.[179] Eurymachus also contrasts the shame that will be attached to their names in the future if they fail to bend Odysseus' bow with the glory that their failure will bring to Odysseus.[180]

In her reply (21.331–3), Penelope contrasts this glory, won through victory in a contest, with the 'good reputation' granted by the people

[178] *Odyssey*, 21.77–9 = 19.579–81.

[179] *Odyssey*, 21.185: *πολλὸν δὲ βίης ἐπιδευέες ἦσαν*, 253–4: *εἰ δὴ τοσσόνδε βίης ἐπιδευέες εἰμὲν ἀντιθέου Ὀδυσῆος*.

[180] *Odyssey*, 21.255: *ἐλεγχείη δὲ καὶ ἐσσομένοισι πυθέσθαι* and 329: *ὣς ἐρέουσ᾽, ἡμῖν δ᾽ ἂν ἐλέγχεα ταῦτα γένοιτο*.

to those who pay due respect to a hero and his house. This is the reason why the suitors need not fear dishonour, since they have already been shamed by the outrages they have committed against Odysseus' house. Penelope then tries to take control of the contest which she has instigated and to be more than just its prize: in line 336 she orders the bow to be given to the beggar, using the imperative δότε.[181] She then utters a formula that elsewhere, in both the *Iliad* (on four occasions) and the *Odyssey* (two occasions), is always a sign that the character is asserting his authority: 'I will tell you this and it will certainly be done' (ὧδε γὰρ ἐξερέω, τὸ δὲ καὶ τετελεσμένον ἔσται, 21.337), when she states the prize that the beggar will win if he succeeds: 'I will clothe him in a fine cloak and tunic (ἕσσω μιν χλαῖνάν τε χιτῶνά τε, εἵματα καλά); I will give him a cutting javelin to protect him against dogs and men, and a two edged sword, and sandals for his feet; and I will find him passage to wherever he may choose to go' (21.339–42). With the exception of just one line, this passage repeats Telemachus' promise to the beggar when he meets him in Eumaeus' hut, and thus on his own estate (16.79–81). It is surprising to find it attributed to Penelope here. It is true that she remains firmly within her own sphere when she promises him clothing. But she steps outside it when she adds the javelin and the sword. These are weapons and, normally, swords only feature among the gifts exchanged between men (like the sword given to Odysseus by the Phaeacian Euryalus, or the one which Odysseus once gave to Eurytus in exchange for his bow (8.406 and 21.34). Finally, her promise to convey the beggar wherever he wants to go contrasts with the words of Alcinous who states in Book 11 that 'to send him home shall be the concern of men and in the first place of myself, since mine is the supremacy in the land' (11.352–3). But, as in Book 1, Penelope's assertion of her authority[182] meets opposition from Telemachus who puts his mother in her place: 'No one among all the Achaeans has a better title than myself to give the bow or to deny it to whomsoever I may decide . . . Go up to your room again and look to your own province, distaff and loom, and tell your women to ply their task. The bow shall be the concern of men, and my concern most of all. Authority in this house is mine' (21.344–53). The reuse of the

[181] As Thalmann 1998: 234 remarks: 'Initiator as well as prize of the contest, [Penelope] plays an unusually active part.'

[182] See Katz 1991: 151.

same formulae as were used in Book 1 to express Penelope's subordinate position, and the poet's approval of Telemachus' good sense shown in the words, 'at this she withdrew to her room in wonder, laying to heart her son's wise words (*μῦθον πεπνυμένον*)' (21.354–5) make perfectly clear the limits imposed on women's actions.

Penelope is completely absent from the end of Book 21 and from the whole of Book 22, given Odysseus' refusal to allow Eurycleia to go upstairs to speak to Penelope when she asks permission to do so (22.428–31). It is only at the beginning of Book 23 that Eurycleia finally goes up to tell her mistress that her husband is present. But her arrival is described using the formula 'she stood above her head' (*στῆ δ' ἄρ' ὑπὲρ κεφαλῆς*) which elsewhere always serves to introduce a dream[183] or a supernatural apparition that is very close to a dream as it occurs during the night.[184] Could this be a subtle way of preparing the reader for Penelope's incredulous response as she calls Eurycleia a fool and accuses her of mocking her? Even when she does accept that the suitors are dead, because Eurycleia has seen their bodies, she prefers to attribute this to the action of a deity. Her scepticism is not even shaken by the 'clear sign' (*σῆμα ἀριφραδὲς*, 23.73) of the scar that convinced Eurycleia, Eumaeus, and Philoetius. She does however agree to go down to the hall, even though she is unsure how to behave. This is one of the rare moments when the text describes her thoughts unfolding and shows her truly weighing the alternatives: 'She was wondering (*πολλὰ δέ οἱ κῆρ ὥρμαιν*') whether to stand apart and question her husband thus or whether to go up close to him and to clasp and kiss his head and hands' (23.85–7).

As we saw above (Chapter 2, pp. 63–4), these deliberation scenes usually end with a decision, introduced by 'this seemed in his heart to be the best plan' or with a divine intervention. But here the decision remains implicit. It is evident only in the description of Penelope seated by the wall opposite Odysseus and racked once again by doubt: 'she thought him at one moment like Odysseus and then again could not see him so because of his miserable rags' (23.94–5). Her mistrust prompts Telemachus to reproach her in lines 100–3: 'No other wife would be heartless enough (*τετληότι θυμῷ*) to keep aloof from her

[183] *Iliad*, 2.20, 59 (Agamemnon's dream), *Odyssey*, 4.803 (Penelope's dream) and 6.21 (Nausicaa's dream).

[184] *Iliad*, 23.68: the appearance of Patroclus' ghost to Achilles, 24.682: the appearance of Hermes to Priam; *Odyssey*, 20.32: Athena's appearance to Odysseus.

husband so, when after much trial and tribulation she had him again, in the twentieth year, in his own country. But you have always been stony-hearted.' The same mistrust, however, earned Odysseus the compliments of Athena at 13.333–6.[185] We can also compare Penelope's 'stony heart' with the appreciative description of Odysseus' reaction to Penelope's tears in Book 19.211–212: 'beneath his eyelids his eyes kept as firm as horn or iron; he still dissembled and showed no tears'.

The recognition itself is further delayed by a parenthesis (23.117–52) describing the stratagem invented by Odysseus to hide the massacre of the suitors from the people of Ithaca by pretending to celebrate a wedding. We might expect the recognition to take place once Odysseus has taken a bath and has regained his handsome appearance, since Penelope's hesitation in line 95 was explained by his rags. But this is not the case. Odysseus responds by echoing his son's reproaches, concluding, in line 172, 'she has a heart of iron'. Penelope then puts her husband to the test, showing that she equals her husband in cautiousness. It is the marital bed, built by Odysseus from an olive tree and placed in the centre of the house, that will bring about the reunion of husband and wife. These clear signs (σήματ' ἀριφραδέα, line 225), known only to the couple, combine nature and culture (the bed is both a tree and a product of human skill) and its stability (it is ἔμπεδόν, 23.203) symbolizes the essence of marriage.[186] This and this alone overcomes Penelope's resistance and persuades her heart, despite its hardness. Her emotion reveals itself physically, as does that of old Laertes in Book 24, by her failing knees and her melting heart.[187] At this point she tries to excuse her incredulity by attributing it to her fear of being deceived. In this context, her allusion to the story of Helen, which the ancient commentators, as well as many modern scholars as we have seen above,[188] wanted to remove, is problematic. The excuses made by a faithful wife for the behaviour of an adulteress have been seen as proof of 'Penelope's independence of judgment',[189] or alternatively as an expression of her subconscious

[185] See Katz 1991: 163.

[186] As the scholia to 23.188 say: ἀκίνητον δὲ λέγων εἶναι τὸ λέχος, ἔοικεν αἰνίττεσθαι ὅτι τὴν γαμικὴν κοίτην ἀδιάλυτον εἶναι δεῖ.

[187] *Odyssey*, 23.205 and 24.345 ὣς φάτο, τῆς (τοῦ) δ' αὐτοῦ λύτο γούνατα καὶ φίλον ἦτορ.

[188] See n. 55 above.

[189] Schein 1995: 25: 'Penelope refuses to join in the otherwise universal condemnation of her [Helen].'

and an implicit admission of the desire she felt for the suitors,[190] or of her 'awareness of herself as the subject (as well as object) of desire and her ensuing fear and guilt',[191] or as a way of 'tacitly aknowledg[ing] to her husband how close she came to adultery . . . and seek[ing] to exonerate herself from blame'.[192] But this defence of Helen, which echoes that of Helen herself in Book 4, can only, in this context, be interpreted as an a fortiori argument as Marilyn Katz has noted:[193] if Helen, who was guilty of committing adultery, can be excused, then I can certainly be excused given that I am only guilty of a delay in recognizing my husband. Odysseus' emotion at this point is manifested only in his tears while that of Penelope is portrayed in a simile comparing her 'joy'[194] with that of a shipwrecked man who arrives on dry land and alludes not only to the description of Odysseus' shipwreck before he lands on Phaeacia but also to line 13 of the prologue to the poem which associates homecoming and the wife.

Book 23 continues with an exchange of stories in which each spouse recounts his or her many trials. But Penelope's trials are summarized in just four lines (23.302–5) while those of Odysseus are told at length (23.306–41). It concludes with two orders given by Odysseus to his wife.[195] The first defines the respective spheres of activity of the two sexes, with the man waging war outside the house in order to amass wealth and the woman staying inside to take care of it: 'You must keep watch in the house itself over all the possessions left to me. As for the flocks the proud suitors ravaged, much of the loss I mean myself to retrieve by pillage, and the rest our Ithacans shall make good till they have filled all my folds again' (23.355–8). The second command sends Penelope back to her room and

[190] See Devereux 1957: 384, Marquart 1985: 44–5, Felson 1994: 39–40. This type of interpretation is rightly criticized by Katz 1991: 184–6.

[191] Wohl 1993: 43.

[192] Felson-Rubin 1987: 66–7 and 1996: 170–1 followed by Foley 1995: 103: 'It is certainly possible to interpret this exemplum as a recognition by Penelope that she inadvertently flirted with adultery.' Zeitlin 1996: 49–50: 'at worst . . . it might sound like an unconscious vindication of what we do not know (will never know) with regard to Penelope herself.'

[193] Katz 1991: 182–6.

[194] *Odyssey*, 23.233: ἀσπάσιος γῆ, 238: ἀσπάσιοι, 239: ὣς ἄρα τῇ ἀσπαστὸς ἔην πόσις εἰσοροώσῃ.

[195] *Odyssey*, 23.349: ἀλόχῳ δ' ἐπὶ μῦθον ἔτελλεν; and 361: σοὶ δέ, γύναι, τόδ' ἐπιστέλλω.

condemns her to silence: 'Go to the upper-room with your waiting-women. Sit there, look at no one and question no one' (23.364–5).

After this, Penelope disappears from the story. She is only mentioned on two occasions. First of all, in the second *nekuia* in Book 24 in the speeches of the suitor Amphimedon and Agamemnon who give two contrasting pictures of her. According to Amphimedon, she planned the suitors' deaths along with Odysseus and her decision to instigate the trial of the bow was just another 'trick', like the shroud for Laertes (24.128): she was simply obeying Odysseus' orders and helped him prepare the final massacre.[196] But Agamemnon portrays her as a model of good sense (ἀγαθαὶ φρένες, 24.194, ἐχέφρονι Πηνελοπείῃ, 24.198) and conjugal fidelity (ὡς εὖ μέμνητ' Ὀδυσῆος ἀνδρὸς κουριδίου, 24.195–6) who has won, thanks to her excellent qualities (*aretē*), a glory that will never perish (τῷ οἱ κλέος οὔ ποτ' ὀλεῖται ἧς ἀρετῆς, 24.196–7). Then, in lines 404–7, she is mentioned in the brief dialogue between Dolius, who asks whether Penelope should be informed of what has happened, and Odysseus, who says no: 'Old friend, she knows already; trouble yourself no further.'

What, then, are we to make of Penelope? And how can we explain the sudden, apparently unmotivated, decisions attributed to her from Book 18 onwards? Rather than trying to find the motives that are never explained in the poem, we should accept, as Thalmann, for example, does, that this silence is intentional and try to understand why it is that the text is only interested in the effects that these decisions will have upon the action.[197] This indifference to Penelope's motivation is entirely attributable, I suggest, to the paradoxical place she occupies within the plan that Athena and Odysseus worked out together in Book 13. While Telemachus, Eurycleia, Eumaeus, and Philoetius are involved in the plan and play an active role in it from the moment at which each recognizes Odysseus, she remains in ignorance of it until the end, with the result that her actions, as when she shows herself to the suitors or instigates the contest for

[196] *Odyssey*, 24.153: ἡμῖν φραζομένη θάνατον καὶ κῆρα μέλαιναν, and 167–9: τὼ δὲ μνηστῆρσιν θάνατον κακὸν ἀρτύναντε.

[197] Thalmann 1998: 233: 'although it may be reductive to read Penelope's motives and evaluate her actions only from the vantage point of the ending . . . there is a sense in which the poem does ask us to read the story's final significance in just that way . . . Thus the question of Penelope's motives or more broadly her subjectivity is not significant to the narrative, even though it may matter greatly to us as modern readers.'

her own hand in marriage, are utilized by Odysseus and given a significance that she had not foreseen.[198] This also explains why her actions, despite becoming more and more important from Book 16 onwards (16.409–33, 17.36–44, 18.157–302, 19.53–9 to 19.603–4, 21.4 to 344–58), are cut short every time and why she is always, in the end, kept out of the action and sent back to her quarters, as Rutherford has remarked.[199]

The way in which Penelope becomes the instrument of the goddess comes out most clearly if we compare Athena's cooperation with Odysseus with her behaviour towards his wife. The goddess does not just help Odysseus indirectly on many occasions. She also appears to him in person in Book 13, to 'weave a plan together with [him]' (*ἵνα τοι σὺν μῆτιν ὑφήνω*, 13.303), the two of them place (*θείομεν*, 13.364) his treasures in the Cave of the Nymphs and 'plan how things may be ordered best' (*αὐτοὶ δὲ φραζώμεθ', ὅπως ὄχ' ἄριστα γένηται*, 13.365). She also speaks with him in Book 20 to reassure him that she will protect him in the trials to come and to speak openly to him (*διαμπερὲς ἤ σε φυλάσσω ἐν πάντεσσι πόνοισ'. ἐρέω δέ τοι ἐξαναφανδόν*, 20.47–8). And during the massacre of the suitors in Book 22 as well as the final battle of Book 24 she intervenes directly. Penelope, by contrast, is constantly manipulated by the goddess. Athena sends her to sleep several times[200] and sends her a reassuring dream at 4.795–839. She 'puts into her mind' (*Τῇ δ' ἄρ' ἐπὶ φρεσὶ θῆκε*) the idea of showing herself to the suitors in at 18.158 (and enhances her beauty while she is asleep at 18.187–97) and the idea of the trial of the bow at 21.1.

It is true, however, that the conclusion of the *Odyssey*, according to Agamemnon, demonstrates the *aretē* and the *kleos* of Penelope: 'Happy son of Laertes, resourceful Odysseus, you have indeed won a wife with great virtue! How single-hearted was your incomparable Penelope, how faithfully did she keep remembrance of the husband she had wedded! And therefore the fame of her virtue will never die' (24.192–8).

[198] Murnaghan 1986: 109: 'Like her appearance before the suitors in book 18, Penelope's setting of the contest of the bow involves a dichotomy between the meaning her action has for her as she takes it . . . and the meaning it acquires through its actual consequences.'

[199] Rutherford 1985: 137: 'in short she plays a progressively greater and more effective role, but is always cut short, dismissed or baffled.'

[200] *Odyssey*, 1.363–4, 16.450–1, 18.188, 19.603–4, 21.357, 22.429.

> *ὄλβιε Λαέρταο πάϊ, πολυμήχαν' Ὀδυσσεῦ,*
> *ἦ ἄρα σὺν μεγάλῃ ἀρετῇ ἐκτήσω ἄκοιτιν·*
> *ὡς ἀγαθαὶ φρένες ἦσαν ἀμύμονι Πηνελοπείῃ,*
> *κούρῃ Ἰκαρίου, ὡς εὖ μέμνητ' Ὀδυσῆος,*
> *ἀνδρὸς κουριδίου. τῶ οἱ κλέος οὔ ποτ' ὀλεῖται*
> *ἧς ἀρετῆς . . .*

This passage is itself more ambiguous than it at first appears. For it is unclear whether we should understand *σὺν μεγάλῃ ἀρετῇ*, 'with great virtue', as qualifying *ἐκτήσω* 'you won'[201] (in which case Agamemnon is praising Odysseus' virtue) or with *ἄκοιτιν*, 'wife', (in which case the virtue is Penelope's). Most critics, however, are in agreement that the *kleos* of the *aretē* in lines 196–7 is that of Penelope.[202]

This raises the further question of how we should understand 'valour' (*aretē*) and 'glory' (*kleos*) in the *Odyssey* when they are applied to female characters. A rapid survey of the uses of *aretē* (which occurs twenty-one times) and *kleos* (which occurs sixty-one times, not including the two references to *eukleia*) confirms that they are very rarely attributed to women (four and five times respectively). This can be explained by the definition of excellence and glory, which are applied above all to the valour of the warrior, the athlete, or the avenger, like Odysseus, or the man who completes a successful journey, like Telemachus, even if there are some examples of both terms being used with moral connotations. At 14.402–4, for example, Eumaeus links good reputation and excellence (*ἐϋκλείη τ' ἀρετή τε*) closely to respect for the laws of hospitality. Similarly, the glory of the good king to whom Penelope is compared at 19.108–15 does not derive solely from the number and wealth of his subjects but also from his respect for the gods (*θεουδής*), his wise judgements (*εὐδικίας*), and his good governance (*ἐξ εὐηγεσίης*). Penelope herself contrasts the glory that derives from goodness (*ὃς δ' ἂν ἀμύμων αὐτὸς ἔῃ καὶ ἀμύμονα εἰδῇ*) with the curses hurled against those who are harsh (*ὃς μὲν ἀπηνὴς αὐτὸς ἔῃ καὶ ἀπηνέα εἰδῇ*, 19.329–34).

[201] In support of this interpretation we could cite the lines in which Cretan Odysseus boasts of having married into a wealthy family thanks to his valour: *ἠγαγόμην δὲ γυναῖκα πολυκλήρων ἀνθρώπων | εἵνεκ' ἐμῆς ἀρετῆς* (*Odyssey*, 14.211–12).

[202] See for example Heubeck 1986 on 24.183, Segal 1996: 208, Katz 1991: 21. But Nagy 1979: 37–9 understands the reference to be to the *aretē* and *kleos* of Odysseus.

The *aretē* of Penelope, who is the prize for which the suitors compete (2.205–6), is not easy to define. Twice it is associated with her beauty and stature (*ἐμὴν ἀρετὴν εἶδός τε δέμας τε*, 18.251 = 19.124). Here there are two possible interpretations: according to one, her excellence is identified with her stature and beauty, according to the other her moral or intellectual qualities complement her beautiful appearance.[203] In both these passages Penelope presents her glory as dependent on her husband, declaring to Eurymachus in Book 18, and then to the beggar in Book 19: 'The Deathless Ones took away my form and presence and everything that was worth praise in me, when the Argives went up to Ilium and Odysseus my husband went with them. If he came back to have the care of this life of mine, then indeed my repute would be nobler and more widely spread' (*μεῖζόν κε κλέος εἴη ἐμὸν καὶ κάλλιον οὕτω*, 19.124–9 = 18.251–6). The extent of a woman's *kleos* is thus linked to the presence by her side of a husband who 'takes care of her life (*bios*)' in the most concrete sense of the term, that is, of the wealth which is at the root of the prosperity and the reputation of a house. Feminine *kleos* is thus comparable to the *aretē* of a slave: the former grows with the presence of a husband while the latter is reduced by half with slavery and the existence of a master.[204] We may also see these lines as a much delayed reply to the words of Antinous in Book 2, who dissociated the two, making the ruin of Telemachus' wealth—and thus of the house of Odysseus—the flipside of the 'glory' (*kleos*) that Penelope wins by refusing to take another husband,[205] since the suitors refuse to leave the palace and to stop eating up Odysseus' possessions until Penelope decides to marry one of them.

But Penelope's glory or her good reputation, to put it in less grandiose terms, depends in the end on her fidelity to her husband. This is what Antinous' words show as does Agamemnon's praise, cited above. This is also shown indirectly in two passages, one spoken by Telemachus at 16.73–7 and the other by his mother at 19.524–9. Both describe in almost identical terms the dilemma facing Odysseus'

[203] In support of this interpretation we could cite the lines where Odysseus contrasts the apparent beauty of words to their true value (*Odyssey*, 8.167–75).

[204] *Odyssey*, 17.322–3. Foley (1995: 96) makes the comparison but draws no conclusions from it.

[205] *Odyssey*, 2.125–6: *μέγα μὲν κλέος αὐτῇ | ποιεῖτ', αὐτὰρ σοί γε ποθὴν πολέος βιότοιο.*

wife and treat respect for the marital bed as inseparable from fear of public opinion (*εὐνήν τ' αἰδομένη πόσιος δήμοιό τε φῆμιν*, 17.75 = 19. 527). Similarly, in Book 23 the people condemn what they take to be Penelope's remarriage: hearing the noise of celebrations coming from the palace and assuming wrongly that the queen has decided to marry one of the suitors they say, 'Doubtless one of her many suitors has married the queen at least. Heartless woman! She had not the courage (*οὐδ' ἔτλη*) to keep to the house of her true husband until he came' (23.149–51).

It is clear, then, that Penelope's excellence consists in having stayed in the palace with her son to keep everything safe. This is the reassuring image of her that is given, in identical terms, by Anticleia in Book 11 and Eumaeus in Book 16 in response to the questions of Odysseus and Telemachus: 'Indeed she remains in your halls most patiently (*τετληότι θυμῷ*); each night, each day wears to its ending for her amid her grief and tears' (11.181–3 = 16.37–9). Athena gives a similar picture when she describes to Odysseus in Book 13 a wife 'seated there in the hall as ever, each night, each day wears to its ending for her amid grief and tears' (13.336–8). Finally, it is what the narrative from Book 1 to Book 23 never ceases to emphasize.

If we accept this definition of Penelope's excellence and glory we may wish to go further and to contrast this one-dimensional female *aretē*, totally identified with fidelity founded on endurance as well as on caution (as when she refuses to recognize Odysseus in Book 23 until she has put him to the test), and a masculine *aretē* which can manifest itself in many different ways: on three occasions the *Odyssey* in fact underlines the multiple nature of Odysseus' excellence (*παντοίη ἀρετή*).[206] As we saw above, Odysseus' excellence involves the ability to come through trials and to endure, but it has many other aspects. We should also contrast the passive, feminine heroism with its masculine counterpart. Nothing brings this out more clearly than the contrast between the stories told by Penelope and Odysseus of their trials. Those of Penelope illustrate a passive capacity to endure the spectacle of the suitors' depredations and are entirely set within the confines of the palace (*ὅσ' ἐν μεγάροισιν ἀνέσχετο δῖα γυναικῶν*

[206] *Odyssey*, 4.725 = 815, 18.205.

ἀνδρῶν μνηστήρων ἐσορῶσ', 23.302–3) while those of Odysseus are both active and passive in nature, involving all the suffering he inflicted on others (*ὅσα κήδε' ἔθηκεν ἀνθρώποισ'*, 23.306–7) as well as all the suffering he underwent himself (*ὅσα τ' αὐτὸς ὀϊζύσας ἐμόγησε*, 23.307).

10

The World of the Gods

The *Odyssey* is not only concerned with the human world but, like the *Iliad*, it devotes a great deal of space to the gods.[1] However, the Pantheon of the *Odyssey* is smaller.[2] Only Zeus, Athena, Poseidon, Hermes, and Calypso play an active role in the main story, Odysseus' homeward journey from Ogygia. But, if we take into consideration the whole of the adventures recounted by Odysseus in Books 9 to 12, as well as the secondary stories of the Achaeans' return journeys told by Nestor and Menelaus and the songs of the bards, Phemius and Demodocus, the narrative is enriched by a whole series of minor deities like Proteus and his daughter Eidothea, Circe, Ino Leucothea, Charybdis, Scylla, and the Sirens, not to mention Helios, Ares, Aphrodite, Hephaestus, and all the gods who are present to see them being punished.

Homer represents these gods in stories, recounts their words, and reports what men say about them. This means that these representations belong to very different levels of discourse and we need to draw careful distinctions between what the gods say and what is said about them, between the poet who, thanks to Muse, is omniscient and his heroes who are not necessarily able to identify divine interventions.[3] In this chapter I will begin by presenting the way in which the gods are shown interacting among themselves, before going on to look at their role in the action and their relationships with humans.

[1] See Chantraine 195, Severyns 1966, Lloyd-Jones 1971: 1–32, Fenik 1974: 208–30, Griffin 1980a: 144–78, Strauss Clay 1997: 133–85, Kullmann 1985, Segal 1992a, Olson 1995: 205–23, Kearns 2004, Graziosi and Haubold 2005: 65–75, 80–94, Allan 2006: 15–27.

[2] Kearns 2004: 67.

[3] This is emphasized by Rutherford 1986: 153 n. 43 and Winterbottom 1989: 33.

1. THE GODS AMONG THEMSELVES

In both the *Iliad* and the *Odyssey* we occasionally see the gods in their own domain: Olympus. Book 1 and Book 5 of the *Odyssey* both begin with assemblies of the gods who prompt Telemachus to act and set in motion Odysseus' return. In addition, there is at Book 8.266–366 the 'beautiful song about the loves of Ares and Aphrodite of the lovely crown' (8.266–7), the dialogue between Zeus and Poseidon in Book 13.125–64 that seals the Phaeacians' fate, and, in Book 24.472–87, the conversation between Athena and Zeus who decide to re-establish peace on Ithaca. It is striking that there is also a scene set on Olympus in Book 12.374–88, that is, within the story told by Odysseus, who has no direct access to the world of the gods given that he is neither a poet nor a seer. This anomaly is only possible because Odysseus has divine sources, whom he cites: 'All this I heard from Calypso of the lovely hair, who herself had heard it, so she told me, from Hermes, messenger of the gods' (12.389–90). We also get brief glimpses of the gods among themselves, with the conversation between Hermes and Calypso, which is followed by a meal in Book 5.75–147. Mostly, however, the gods appear on earth in various disguises or, more rarely, in their own form, unless they choose to reveal themselves through signs.

The gods, as they are portrayed in the Homeric poems, are immune from old age and death (they are ἀθάνατοι (eighty-seven occurrences) and ἀγήραοι (three occurrences)), they are superior beings: larger, more beautiful, and stronger than men, and their possessions are not subject to the decay that affects those of men (4.78–9). In their supreme power we can see an inverted image of human weakness.[4] The encounter between Apollo and Diomedes on the battlefield in *Iliad* 5 is emblematic of this disparity. Three times Diomedes rushes at Apollo and three times Apollo pushes him back, the fourth time 'Apollo called to him with a fearful shout: "Think, son of Tydeus, and shrink back! Never think yourself gods' equal—since there can be no likeness ever between the make of immortal gods and of men who walk on the ground"'. (*Iliad*, 5.440–2).

[4] Griffin 1980a; 167–8, Strauss Clay 1997: 139–43.

In the *Odyssey*, the gods' superiority emerges most clearly in the massacre of the suitors. They are over a hundred in number while Odysseus is supported by Athena alone. Indeed, in Book 13.390–1, he says he is ready to fight as many as 300 men, if the goddess is by his side. In Book 16 he calms Telemachus' concerns about the unequal strength of the two sides by saying, 'Ask yourself this—will Athena and father Zeus together be helpers enough for us two, or must I call to mind some other' (16.260–1). And Telemachus replies, 'True; those you speak of are both good helpers, though they sit aloft among the clouds; they have sway over mortal men and over immortal gods as well' (16.263–5).

In Book 20, Athena reassures Odysseus, who is afraid of the consequences of his murder of the suitors and of their families' vengeance, by reminding him once again of the superiority of the gods:

> Unbelieving one, most men are ready to trust a comrade, a mortal man without my strength and without my cunning; yet I am a goddess, one who through all your trials has guarded you continually. I will speak plainly. If fifty squadrons of mortal men were to close on the two for us, all of them eager to slaughter us in battle, even then you would carry off the plunder of the herds and fat flocks that once were theirs. (20.45–51)

As well as being all powerful, the gods are blessed (μάκαρες)[5] and their happiness only serves to emphasize the misery of human lives. This contrast is expressed most clearly by Achilles in Book 24 of the *Iliad*: 'This is the fate the gods have spun for poor mortal men, that we should live in misery, but they themselves have no sorrows' (lines 525–6).

Their home is depicted as the antithesis of the human world with its upheavals and its storms, as we see in the following description with its series of negations:[6] Olympus is 'unrocked by tempest, undrenched with rain, unassailed by snow; a cloudless sky stretches out above and a white radiance is everywhere. It is in this place that the blessed gods take their pleasure through all their days' (6.43–6).

It is this opposition that underlies Demodocus' song of the loves of Ares and Aphrodite and gives it its meaning.[7] At first sight, this is simply a burlesque episode of everyday life on Olympus which would not be out of place in an operetta by Offenbach, as the following

[5] This epithet occurs twenty-four times.

[6] Griffin 1980a: 168.

[7] See Burkert 1997.

summary suggests: two lovers are making love in the husband's house, a third party tells the husband. He lays a trap for the lovers, manages to catch them *in flagrante*, invites all the gods on Olympus to come see the spectacle, and only frees the couple after he has been promised a monetary compensation. This story has often been dismissed as a Phaeacian story (as in Athenaeus for example),[8] fitting for a people who spent their time in the pursuit of pleasure and who conceived of the gods in their own image. But this is to overlook the fact that there are parallels to this story in the *Iliad*. First of all, there is the assembly of the gods at the end of *Iliad* 1 in which Hephaestus provokes 'uncontrollable laughter' (*Iliad*, 1.599) among the gods by his story of his misadventures and by the way he bustles around the tables. Then there is the 'seduction of Zeus' in Book 14 (or, to give it its Greek title, the 'deception of Zeus') where Zeus gives way to Hera and makes exactly the same suggestion to her as Ares does to Aphrodite: 'Come, let us go to bed now and enjoy our lovemaking.'[9] All of these scenes show 'the sublime unseriousness' of the Olympians.[10]

More importantly, this episode has numerous echoes in the *Odyssey*. Aphrodite is the embodiment of infidelity in opposition to the ever-faithful Penelope. But she also contrasts with the figure of Clytemnestra whose adultery makes her the accomplice of Aegisthus and leads to Agamemnon's death for, among the gods, adultery has no consequences: everything ends amid laughter as the guilty couple slip away:

> Unshackled thus, the lovers were up and off at once; Ares went on his way to Thrace, and Aphrodite the laughter-lover to Paphos in Cyprus, where she has her precinct and fragrant altar. In this home of hers the Graces washed her, anointed her with the celestial oil that gleams on the limbs of the immortals, and clad her in lovely garments that ravished the gazing eye. (8.360–6)

It is nothing more than a minor incident that can be washed away with a bath. It seems that among the gods, who have no fear of death, nothing is truly serious, neither moral failings nor physical injuries. We can draw a further parallel with Book 5 of the *Iliad* in which Aphrodite, again, is wounded by Diomedes. Here, her mother, Dione, simply has to place her hand on her daughter's arm for 'the hand [to be] healed, and the heavy pains soothed away' (*Iliad*, 5.417).

[8] Athenaeus, *Deipnosophistae*, 12.511b–c.

[9] *Iliad*, 14.314 and *Odyssey*, 8.292.

[10] Reinhardt 1997b: 180.

2. GODS AND MEN

(a) Varieties of divine intervention

1. Epiphanies, transformations, and miracles

In both the *Odyssey* and the *Iliad*, the gods can appear to men or make themselves invisible as and when they wish. Often, when they are visible to men, we are not told what form they take. Thus, in Book 15 nothing is said about the appearance of Athena 'when she stands close' (ἀγχοῦ δ' ἱσταμένη) to Telemachus and urges him to return home (15.9).

They can reveal themselves as gods, and do so regularly among certain specially honoured peoples. They appear in clearly visible form (αἰεὶ γὰρ τὸ πάρος γε θεοὶ φαίνονται ἐναργεῖς ἡμῖν, 7. 201–2) and 'without concealment' (οὔ τι κατακρύπτουσιν, 7.205) to the Phaeacians, who are 'close to the gods',[11] and frequently visit the Ethiopians.[12] They also reveal themselves to certain privileged individuals. This is the case in Odysseus' story to the Phaeacians, in Book 10, when he tells of his encounter with Hermes as he was going to Circe's palace to find out about his companions' fate: 'I was met by golden-wanded Hermes; he seemed a youth (νεηνίῃ ἀνδρὶ ἐοικώς) in the lovely spring of life with the first down upon his lip' (10.277–9). Here, the comparison to the young man is simply a way of suggesting, by analogy, the physical appearance of the god. In the same way, when Athena abandons her disguise to reveal herself to Odysseus in Book 13, or when she appears to him in Book 16, the description takes the form of a comparison to a 'woman, tall and lovely, with skill to make works of beauty' (δέμας δ' ἤϊκτο γυναικὶ καλῇ τε μεγάλῃ τε καὶ ἀγλαὰ ἔργα ἰδυίῃ, 13.288–9 = 16.157–8). The same applies in Book 20 where she is simply compared to a woman (δέμας δ' ἤϊκτο γυναικί, 20.31).

Conversely, the gods can also make themselves invisible, as in Book 10: 'Circe had already passed before us and tethered a ram and black ewe beside the vessel. She had slipped past us unperceived with ease (ῥεῖα παρεξελθοῦσα); what eyes could discern a god in his comings and his goings if the god himself should wish it otherwise?'

[11] *Odyssey*, 5.35, 7.205, 19.279. [12] *Odyssey*, 1.22, 5.287.

(10.571–4). And in Book 3.435–6, Athena is present at Nestor's sacrifice without being noticed by anyone. It is certainly the case that when she appears to Odysseus in Book 16 she is invisible to Telemachus: 'She stood outside the cottage gateway, making herself visible to Odysseus. Telemachus did not see her before him or sense her coming, because it is not to every man that divinities make themselves manifest' (16.159–61).

They can also take on all sorts of different appearances,[13] as Odysseus says to Athena: 'For a mortal who meets you, goddess—be the man never so wise—it is hard to know you as yourself; there is no semblance you may not take' (σὲ γὰρ αὐτὴν παντὶ ἐΐσκεις, literally 'you can make yourself look like anything') (13.312–3). Any human being may therefore be a god in disguise. Nothing shows this better than the reaction of the suitors when Antinous strikes Odysseus the beggar: 'Antinous, it was an ugly thing to assault this unhappy beggar so; you will rue it if this proves to be some god from heaven. Gods often take upon themselves the likeness of strangers from far countries (ξείνοισιν ἐοικότες ἀλλοδαποῖσι); they assume this shape and that (παντοῖοι τελέθοντες) and wander about our towns, watching to see which men keep the laws, and which are violent' (17.483–7). This explains why, when characters see an exceptionally beautiful young woman, like Nausicaa, or a tall and handsome stranger, like Odysseus, or hear someone singing a beautiful song, like Circe, they wonder if they might not in fact be in the presence of a god.[14]

The best example of a divine metamorphosis in the *Odyssey* is no doubt that of Athena. First of all, in Book 1, she is described in her true form as she prepares to set out for Odysseus' palace: 'She fastened sandals beneath her feet, the immortal sandals of lovely gold . . . she took the great spear, tall, strong, heavy and brazen-tipped, with which she, the child of a mighty father, strikes down the ranks of warriors who have aroused her wrath' (1.96–101). She appears to Telemachus first of all in the shape of a foreigner, Mentes, the leader of the Taphians (εἰδομένη ξείνῳ, Ταφίων ἡγήτορι, Μέντῃ, 1.105). But in this initial disguise she retains a trace of her true form since 'Mentes', like Athena, carries a spear in his hand (παλάμῃ δ' ἔχε χάλκεον ἔγχος, 1.104) In reply to his prayer in Book 2 she appears to him in the form of

[13] See Strauss Clay 1974.

[14] *Odyssey*, 6.149–50, 276 (Nausicaa), 280–1 (Odysseus), 10. 228, 255 (Circe).

Mentor, whom she now resembles in stature and in voice (*σχεδόθεν δέ οἱ ἦλθεν Ἀθήνη, Μέντορι εἰδομένη ἠμὲν δέμας ἠδὲ καὶ αὐδήν*, 2.267–8). Then she makes herself like Telemachus himself (*Τηλεμάχῳ εἰκυῖα*, 2.3) in order to gather a crew and to borrow a ship from Noemon in lines 383–7, before assuming the appearance of Mentor once again (2.401 = 2.268) to escort him out of the palace and board the ship with him to sail to Pylos. Later on, however, Noemon, who saw Mentor embark with Telemachus only to see him shortly afterwards on Ithaca, is puzzled and suspects that he may have seen 'some god who at all points resembled Mentor' (*ἠὲ θεόν, τῷ δ' αὐτῷ πάντα ἐῴκει*, 4.653–4).

In Book 3.371–2 she takes the form of a bird of prey (perhaps a sea-eagle) to leave Pylos: *ὣς ἄρα φωνήσασ' ἀπέβη γλαυκῶπις Ἀθήνη φήνῃ εἰδομένη· θάμβος δ' ἕλε πάντας Ἀχαιούς*. And the astonished reaction of the Achaeans shows that this is not simply a simile but an account of a real metamorphosis. In Book 6, when she appears to the sleeping Nausicaa, she 'takes the form of the daughter of Dymas, famed for his prowess at sea' (*εἰδομένη κούρῃ ναυσικλειτοῖο Δύμαντος*, 6.22). When Odysseus is about to enter the city in Book 7 she goes before him 'in the form of a young girl carrying a pitcher' (*παρθενικῇ εἰκυῖα νεήνιδι κάλπιν ἐχούσῃ*, 7.20). In Book 8 she goes through the town in the shape of one of wise Alcinous' heralds (*εἰδομένη κήρυκι δαΐφρονος Ἀλκινόοιο*, 8.8). Then, at the games, she measures the distances in the discus competition disguised as a man (*ἔθηκε δὲ τέρματ' Ἀθήνη ἀνδρὶ δέμας εἰκυῖα*, 8.193–4).

When Odysseus arrives on Ithaca, in Book 13, she chooses first to appear to him 'wearing the guise of a young shepherd, with the gentle air of a king's son; a lovely mantle fell in two folds around her shoulders; there were sandals on her glistening feet, and she held a javelin in her hand' (13.222–5). In Book 22.205–7 she appears to Odysseus and his followers in the shape of Mentor. But Odysseus recognizes her, as we see from the use of the feminine pronoun in line 207 (*τὴν δ' 'Οδυσεὺς γήθησεν ἰδών*) and in line 210 'So he spoke, not doubting in truth that this was Athena the gatherer of armies' (*ὣς φάτ', ὀϊόμενος λαοσσόον ἔμμεν' Ἀθήνην*), even though he addresses her as 'Mentor' in line 208. In lines 239–40 she goes and perches on the smoke-blackened rafters 'looking like a swallow' (*χελιδόνι εἰκέλη*), just as, in Nestor's palace, she arrived in the form of Mentor and left in the form of a bird of prey (although there is no mention here in Book 22 of the spectators' amazement, which may suggest that we are dealing with a simile comparing her to a swallow rather than a true metamorphosis into a swallow). Finally, at 24.502–3 she arrives disguised as Mentor, yet again, as Odysseus and his supporters leave the house, here too the use of the feminine pronoun suggests that Odysseus, who rejoices on seeing her (τὴν μὲν ἰδὼν γήθησε, 504), recognizes her.

In the *Odyssey* only Proteus, whom Menelaus encountered on his travels, surpasses Athena in the number and variety of transformations he undergoes. As Eidothea announces to Menelaus: 'He will seek to foil you by taking the shape of every creature that moves on earth, and of water and of portentous fire' (4.417–18). When they encounter Proteus, Menelaus and his companions rush at him and try to seize him, 'but the ancient god had not forgotten his craft and cunning. He became (γένετ') in turn a bearded lion, a snake, a panther, a monstrous boar; then running water, then a towering and leafy tree' (4.455–8).

The gods are not only capable of making themselves invisible and transforming themselves. They can act in the same way on the human world, rendering invisible or transforming any object or being, as they wish.[15] They can change the appearance of landscapes, for example. In Book 13 Odysseus does not recognize Ithaca through the mist that Athena has spread over it (13.189–96). They are also able to make individuals, or even a group, invisible to others. In Book 7, Odysseus walks through the Phaeacian city and enters Alcinous' palace without anyone noticing, thanks to the mist that Athena has created around him.[16] They can make night fall in the middle of the day. In Book 23, as dawn breaks over the earth, 'Athena cloaked the four [Odysseus and his companions] in the darkness of night (νυκτὶ κατακρύψασα) and swiftly led them out of the town' (23.371–2).

They can also completely transform the appearance of human beings, for better or for worse (or even prevent them from being transformed through the use of magic plants like the famous *moly* that allows Odysseus to escape from Circe's spell).[17] In Book 10, Circe transforms Odysseus' companions into pigs: 'The men had the form of swine—the snout and grunt and bristles' (10.239–40). But when she returns them to human form she can also make them 'younger

[15] Severyns 1966: 56, Strauss Clay 1997: 161–7.
[16] *Odyssey*, 7.14–17, 39–42, 139–40.
[17] *Odyssey*, 10.286–92.

than they had been before, and taller and handsomer' (10.395–6). The same applies to Odysseus himself. Athena is able to transform him into a beggar in Book 13 but can also turn him back into his former self in Book 16.[18] On several occasions she also enhances his beauty with a divine grace. Thus, in Book 6, when Odysseus puts on the clothes he has been given by Nausicaa after his bath,

> Athena the child of Zeus gave him ampler stature and ampler presence (*θῆκεν, Διὸς ἐκγεγαυῖα, μείζονά τ' εἰσιδέειν καὶ πάσσονα*), and over his head she made the hair curl and cluster like hyacinth. It was as when a man adds (*περιχεύεται*) gold to a silver vessel, a craftsman taught by Hephaestus and Athena to master his art through all its range, so that everything that he makes is beautiful; just so the goddess poured beauty (*κατέχευε χάριν*) over the head and shoulders of Odysseus. (6.229–35)

She works the same effect on his son when she enhances his looks with godlike beauty in Book 2 and does the same for Penelope in Book 18 where the poet describes Athena's intervention in detail after sending Penelope to sleep.[19] However, the precise vocabulary used (the verb *χεύειν* 'to pour') as well as the similes (the application of gold to silver) reveal the limits of these divine transformations. They are merely a question of surface appearance; even once they have been transformed into swine, Odysseus' companions have the same mental capacities as before: 'their minds remained unchanged' (*αὐτὰρ νοῦς ἦν ἔμπεδος ὡς τὸ πάρος περ*, 10.240).

We must also be careful not to exaggerate the role of the marvellous in the *Odyssey*.[20] With the exception of these changes in appearances, miraculous events are few and far between. Some are extremely prosaic. In Book 4, when Menelaus and his companions are suffocating under the stinking sealskins they are using as a disguise, Eidothea saves them with a 'good remedy' (*μέγ' ὄνειαρ*, 4.444): 'She brought every one of us ambrosia and put it underneath his nostrils; it smelt delectably; and so she countered the bestial stench' (4.445–6). And in Book 19, when Odysseus and Telemachus are removing the weapons from the hall, Athena lights their path quite literally: 'Pallas Athena walked before them carrying a lamp of gold and shedding a most lovely light. Telemachus instantly exclaimed: "Father, I see before me now a thing that is

[18] *Odyssey*, 13.429–38 and 16.172–6.

[19] *Odyssey*, 2.12: *θεσπεσίην δ' ἄρα τῷ γε χάριν κατέχευεν Ἀθήνη*, and 18.190–6.

[20] See Griffin 1980a: 165–7.

marvelous indeed (μέγα θαῦμα). The walls of the hall... seem to my eyes to be lit as it were from a flaming fire. Surely some god must be present here (ἦ μάλα τις θεὸς ἔνδον)"' (19.33–40).

In the *Odyssey*, Athena is also able to prolong the duration of the night for Odysseus and Penelope, just as Hera was able, in the *Iliad*, to shorten the day.[21] Poseidon can also turn the Phaeacians' ship to stone (13.159–64). But, as has been pointed out, disruptions of the natural order, like the sun leaving the earth to shine on the inhabitants of the Underworld (12.382–3), are only threats that are never realized, due to the intervention of Zeus.[22]

In fact any unforeseen event can appear to be miraculous and cause characters to suspect the intervention of some deity. Odysseus claims that it was 'the Nymphs' who 'started some hillside goats to give a meal to my companions' (9.154–5) and that a stag that crosses their path at another moment only does so because 'some divinity pitied [him]' (10.157).

2. *The gods and the natural world*

Usually, the gods in the *Odyssey* affect nature without altering its normal functioning. They grant sleep to men, either to allow them to rest (as happens on eleven occasions) and to release them from their cares or, on the contrary, to prevent them from keeping watch (as when Odysseus' companions open the bag of the winds or sacrifice the cattle of the Sun while he sleeps).[23] Above all, they control navigation, just as they can control the outcome of battles.

(a) The gods and navigation

The storms that occur with great frequency in the Odyssey are stirred up by Zeus[24] and by Poseidon.[25] Aeolus, too, is able to make the winds 'rise or fall at his own pleasure', 'because Zeus had made him warden of all the winds' (10.21–2). Athena is also able to calm the

[21] *Odyssey*, 23.241–6 and *Iliad*, 18.239–41.

[22] Strauss Clay 1997: 159 commenting on *Odyssey*, 12.377–83.

[23] *Odyssey*, 10.31–33 and 12.338 and 372.

[24] *Odyssey*, 3. 288–90 (Nestor's story) and 9. 67 (Odysseus' story).

[25] *Odyssey*, 5.282–381, 7.270–4, 11.399–400.

winds (5.382–4) or to make a favourable wind blow.[26] Secondary deities, like Circe and Calypso, also have this power.[27]

This is why Nestor and Menelaus attribute their uneventful journeys to the favour of the gods who 'smoothed the sea with its underworld of waters' and gave them a following wind.[28] Odysseus explains his arrival in a safe harbour in a similar manner, as a sign that some god was leading him.[29] Conversely, storms are understood to be caused by Poseidon's anger, as we see from the identical questions that Odysseus asks Agamemnon in Book 11 and Agamemnon in turn asks Amphimedon in Book 24: 'Did Poseidon rouse some hideous blast of contrary winds and destroy you among the ships that went down with you?' (11.399–400 = 24.109–10). When telling his adventures to Alcinous, Athena, or Eumaeus, Odysseus, like Nestor, explains the storms that scattered the Achaeans as the result of the action of some god,[30] and attributes the loss of his companions to the intervention of a divinity who deprived them of their return.[31] Menelaus and Odysseus both suspect that a god is responsible when the winds stop blowing.[32]

(b) The gods and war

In the Homeric poems, the gods also intervene in battle. The *Iliad* contains many examples of the gods intervening physically on the battlefield.[33] They strike warriors, guide their arrows to their marks, and help their spears to pierce their enemies' skin or, conversely, transport their favourites out of the battle zone, deflect their opponents' arrows, or stop a spear from wounding them too deeply. The gods also intervene indirectly by giving men the 'energy' (*menos*) or the courage (*alkē*) to stay and fight or to attack or, on the contrary, by stirring up panic.[34] Such interventions are naturally less common in the *Odyssey*, given the subject matter of the poem. But the account of

26 *Odyssey*, 2.420–1.
27 *Odyssey*, 11.7–8, 12.149–50 (Circe), 5.268 (Calypso).
28 *Odyssey*, 3.158, 182–3 (Nestor), 4.585–6 (Menelaus).
29 *Odyssey*, 10.141: καί τις θεὸς ἡγεμόνευεν.
30 *Odyssey*, 3.131 (Nestor) =13.317 and 14.232 (the Cretan Odysseus).
31 *Odyssey*, 12.419 (to Alcinous) and 14.309 (to Eumaeus).
32 *Odyssey*, 4.351–3: Menelaus, 12.168–9: Odysseus.
33 Kearns 2004: 65.
34 Lesky 2001: 170.

the massacre of the suitors in Book 22 and the description of the battle between the families of the suitors and Odysseus in Book 24 both have many points in common with the Iliadic *aristeiai*. It is interesting to note that the role of divine intervention is most obvious in the narrative of the herald Medon: 'I myself saw a deathless god standing by Odysseus in Mentor's likeness. This same immortal showed himself now in front of Odysseus, urging him on, and now again rushing down the hall and driving the suitors wild with fear till they fell down one upon another' (24.445–9). This can be explained by the fact that his speech is aimed at demonstrating to the people of Ithaca that 'it was not without the gods' consent that Odysseus planned and did these things' (24.443–4).

In the principal narrator's account in Book 22, by contrast, Athena does not intervene as soon as we might expect her to. Odysseus—and the reader—expect the gods to intervene almost immediately, as we see from his words to Telemachus in Book 16: 'Those two [Athena and Zeus] will not hold aloof for long from the din and stress of the battle when the martial mettle of both the suitors and ourselves is put to the proof in my own hall' (16.267–9). The conclusion of Athena's speech to Odysseus, when she is disguised as Mentor, creates the same expectation: 'Come, dear friend, stand by me and mark my actions, see how well Mentor son of Alcimus will repay your service among these warriors who are your foes' (22.233–5). But, in the place of the Iliadic formula telling how Zeus 'was turning the battle to victory for the Trojans' (*Ζεύς, ὅτε δὴ Τρώεσσι δίδου ἑτεραλκέα νίκην*, *Iliad*, 17.627), here we find, on the contrary, 'but she did not yet fully turn the battle to his favour' (*καὶ οὔ πω πάγχυ δίδου ἑτεραλκέα νίκην*, 22.236). It is only after she has 'made trial of the strength and courage (*σθένεός τε καὶ ἀλκῆς πειρήτιζεν*) of Odysseus and his son' (22.237–8) that the goddess acts, first by sending all the suitors' weapons astray (22.256), or most of them (22.273), then by brandishing her 'man-destroying aegis', which 'panics the suitors' wits' (*τῶν δὲ φρένες ἐπτοίηθεν*, 22.297–8). This contrast is extremely revealing: it sums up all that separates the tragic vision of the *Iliad* from the world of the *Odyssey*, where the emphasis is on human responsibility.

Athena is far more present, by contrast, in Book 24. Like the gods of the *Iliad*,[35] she 'breathes energy' (*ἔμπνευσε μένος*, 24.520) into the

[35] The expression *ἔμπνευσε μένος* is also found at *Iliad*, 10.482 with reference to Athena, and at 15.262 and 20.110 with reference to Apollo.

aged Laertes. Then her voice inspires panic in the people of Ithaca: 'So spoke Athena, and ashy terror seized on them all; in their dismay the weapons flew from their hands and dropped on the ground as the goddess sent forth her voice. They began to turn back towards the city, eager to save their lives' (24.533–6). But this panic, which has parallels in the *Iliad*,[36] does not lead to a massacre. Instead, it follows an invitation to lay down arms and cease hostilities.

(c) The gods and the human soul

It is not just in battle that the gods influence the minds or emotions of humans. There are many other occasions on which the narrative shows the gods working an effect on the φρένες, νόος, θυμός, and κραδίη of men.[37] It is difficult to make clear distinctions between these different terms which often seem to be interchangeable (even if translators tend to translate the first two as 'mind' and the second two as 'heart' it would be inappropriate to look for a Platonic dualism and a distinction between a rational and an irrational part of the soul in Homer).[38]

As Albin Lesky (2001) showed, the omniscient narrator sometimes gives two different causes for the same phenomenon, one human and one divine. The generosity of the Phaeacians towards Odysseus is said to be due to their innate nobility, but also to Athena's intervention (13.120–1); the massacre of the suitors is planned by Odysseus and Athena together (19.1–2, 51–2), and the death of Amphinomus is the result of the joint action of Athena and Telemachus (18.155–6). Odysseus and Penelope are able to explain the reaction of their interlocutors both as the result of a human thought process and as a divine intervention affecting their *thumos*.[39]

In certain cases, mortals' changes of heart are simply the indirect consequence of changes in their situation that have been brought

[36] See, for example, *Iliad*, 8.75–7.

[37] Chantraine 1954: 48.

[38] See the critiques of the theories of Dodds 1951 and Snell 1953 in Russo and Simon 1968 and Austin 1975: 81–129, Jahn 1987, and Williams 1993: 33–69, chapter 2, 'Centres of agency'. As Jahn 1987 *passim* has shown most of the formulae in which these words occur are equivalent in meaning and the choice of one over another is motivated purely by metrical concerns.

[39] *Odyssey*, 19.485 (Odysseus) and 23.260 (Penelope): ἀλλ᾽ ἐπεὶ ἐφράσθης καί τοι θεὸς ἔμβαλε θυμῷ.

about by Zeus. As Odysseus tells the 'good' suitor Amphinomus: 'The father of gods and men makes one day unlike another day, and mortals change their thoughts on life in accordance with this' (*τοῖος γὰρ νόος ἐστὶν ἐπιχθονίων ἀνθρώπων, οἷον ἐπ' ἦμαρ ἄγησι πατὴρ ἀνδρῶν τε θεῶν τε*, 18.136–7).

In the *Odyssey*, it is Athena who intervenes most frequently to inspire thoughts in men that enable them to escape from difficulties. Sometimes her intervention 'is described merely in terms of having affected the agent's mind . . . without our being told exactly how it was affected' (Williams 1993: 29–30). Thus, in Book 3, Athena gives Telemachus the 'courage' (*θάρσος*) to question Nestor (3.75–7). She also gives Nausicaa the steadfastness she needs to stop her running away when she sees the shipwrecked Odysseus emerge from the bushes, in contrast to her companions who run away across the beach: 'The princess alone kept where she was, for Athena put courage in her heart and took away the trembling from her limbs' (*οἴη δ' Ἀλκινόου θυγάτηρ μένε· τῇ γὰρ Ἀθήνη θάρσος ἐνὶ φρεσὶ θῆκε καὶ ἐκ δέος εἵλετο γυίων*, 6.139–40).

On several occasions she puts a good idea into Odysseus' mind. In Book 5, he would have drowned 'if the bright-eyed goddess Athena had not put it into his mind' (*εἰ μὴ ἐπὶ φρεσὶ θῆκε θεὰ γλαυκῶπις Ἀθήνη*,) to cling onto a rock with both hands (5.427–8) and if she 'had not given him the idea' (*εἰ μὴ ἐπιφροσύνην δῶκε γλαυκῶπις Ἀθήνη*, 5.437) of swimming parallel to the shore. It is Athena again who prompts him to beg from the suitors in Book 17 so that he can find out which of them are just and which are unjust (17.360–3). Similarly, in Book 18 Athena gives Penelope the idea (*τῇ δ' ἄρ' ἐπὶ φρεσὶ θῆκε θεὰ γλαυκῶπις Ἀθήνη*, 18.158) of showing herself to the suitors, without the queen realizing, as we see from her words to Eurynome at 18.164–5, when she explains her decision by referring to her *thumos*. The same applies to the trial of the bow. At the very beginning of Book 21 we are told that Athena 'puts in the queen's mind' (using the same formula as in Book 18). It is clear, however, that the queen knows nothing of this divine influence since she does not mention it when, in Book 19.572, she tells Odysseus that she is going to propose this contest to the suitors. In Book 19 Athena intervenes once more to distract Penelope's attention and prevent her from seeing the signal that Eurycleia makes to her when she recognizes Odysseus (19.479).

Deities can also influence humans through the words they speak to them while they are in disguise. In order to 'rouse' (ἐποτρύνω) Telemachus and 'put fresh eagerness in his heart' (οἱ μένος ἐν φρεσὶ θείω, 1.88–9), she speaks to him disguised as Mentes. By the time she leaves him in the middle of Book 1, she has 'put in his heart strength and courage, and more than ever she brought his father before his mind' (τῷ δ' ἐνὶ θυμῷ θῆκε μένος καὶ θάρσος, ὑπέμνησέν τέ ἑ πατρὸς μᾶλλον ἔτ' ἢ τὸ πάροιθεν, 1.320–2).[40] This divine intervention is not only noticed by the narrator and the audience but later becomes evident to the recipient too: 'He had felt what she did and was astonished; it came to him that this was a god' (1.322–3). It is for this reason that he is able to reassure Eurycleia in Book 2 when she is worried about him leaving on his travels, saying, 'Take heart, dear nurse; this purpose of mine came from a god' (ἐπεὶ οὔ τοι ἄνευ θεοῦ ἥδε γε βουλή, 2.372). And through the words she utters while in the shape of one of Alcinous' heralds, she works on the *menos* and *thumos* of the Phaeacians, making them go to the assembly to see Odysseus (8.7–15). In Book 24 it is Athena, yet again, who stands near to Laertes, speaks to him, advises him to pray to the goddess, and breathes *menos* into him (καί ῥ' ἔμπνευσε μένος μέγα Παλλὰς Ἀθήνη, 24.520).

But the gods do not confine themselves to implanting good ideas in humans. They can also lead them to their destruction by robbing them of their wits or by inspiring disastrous ideas in them, as we see in the story of the seer Melampus in Book 15. While he was a prisoner in Phylacus' palace, Neleus plundered his possessions because he had dared to attempt to capture Neleus' flocks in order to win his daughter's hand in marriage, a decision that turned out to be 'a lamentable folly which the grim Erinys had laid upon his mind' (εἵνεκα Νηλῆος κούρης ἄτης τε βαρείης, τήν οἱ ἐπὶ φρεσὶ θῆκε θεὰ δασπλῆτις Ἐρινύς, 15.233–4). In the same way, Athena regularly inspires the suitors to commit acts that only seal their fate. In Books 18 and 20, she 'would not let the suitors refrain from new and biting insult; she meant indignation to sink more deeply still into the heart of Laertes' son' (18.346–8 = 20.284–6) and in Book 20 she provokes 'uncontrollable laughter' in them and 'drives their wits astray' (ἄσβεστον γέλω ὦρσε, παρέπλαγξεν δὲ νόημα, 20.346).

[40] As Lesky (2001: 183) remarks: 'Here then it is not [only] a new impulse that originates with the deity, but something already present is increased by divine intervention.'

In this context, it is not hard to understand why men frequently identify the gods (usually in the vaguest of terms) as at the origin of a decision, or of their good or bad behaviour. Thus Nestor explains the quarrel that broke out between the two sons of Atreus as resulting from Athena's intervention (3.135–6). In Book 4, Helen attributes her own decision to abandon her homeland, her daughter, and her husband to *atē*, sent by Aphrodite (*ἄτην . . . ἣν ᾿Αφροδίτη δῶχ'*, 4.261–2), and Penelope echoes this at 23.222–4. In Book 4, when Menelaus recounts Helen's stratagem of imitating the voices of the Achaeans' wives to make them leave their hiding places in the wooden horse, he explains it as the result of the action of some god: 'You approached the spot, doubtless at the prompting of some divinity who wished to give glory to the Trojans' (4.274–5). He also attributes her decision to go away from the horse to Athena's intervention (4.289). In Book 9, Odysseus attributes to a divinity (*daimon*) the courage displayed by his companions when they help him to blind the Cyclops (9.381). In his false tale in Book 14, the Cretan Odysseus evokes divine interventions on several occasions: Ares and Athena are responsible for his *tharsos* and his bravery, Zeus made his companions panic but also gave him the good idea of presenting himself as the suppliant of the Egyptian king who spared him, finally, during the Trojan War, a divinity (*daimon*) misled him by giving him the bad idea of keeping watch without a cloak.[41] Penelope, in Book 23, can only explain Eurycleia's words, which seem senseless to her, as the result of an intervention by the gods who 'have power to make a wise man foolish or set a weak-witted one on the path to wisdom' (23.11–13).

On occasion, a character who cannot understand why he or she acts as she does explains it as the result of divine intervention. One example is Telemachus in Book 21. When Penelope proposes the trial of the bow to the suitors and announces that she will marry the winner, her son bursts out laughing and exclaims: 'Surely the son of Cronos has taken my wits away (*ἦ μάλα με Ζεὺς ἄφρονα θῆκε Κρονίων*). My own dear mother, for all her wisdom, is saying now she will leave this house in another's company, yet here am I, thoughtlessly (*ἄφρονι θυμῷ*) laughing and making merry' (21.102–5).

[41] *Odyssey*, 14.216–17, 268–9, 273–4, 488–9.

This type of explanation is so expected that it is possible for characters to use it in a false speech, as Odysseus suggests to Telemachus in Book 19, to justify to the suitors the disappearance of the weapons from the hall:

> You must lead the suitors astray with a gentle answer (*αὐτὰρ μνηστῆρας μαλακοῖσ᾽ ἐπέεσσι παρφάσθαι*): 'I put them away out of the smoke, because they had lost the look they had when Odysseus went to Troy and left them.... There is this too, a graver matter—some god has brought it before my mind (*πρὸς δ᾽ ἔτι καὶ τόδε μεῖζον ἐνὶ φρεσὶν ἔμβαλε δαίμων*): I fear that when you are in your cups and have started some quarrel among yourselves, you may wound one another and bring disgrace on your banqueting'. (19.5–13)

When characters do not know what lies behind another's actions, they can explain them as the result of divine intervention, or hesitate between a human and divine cause. This is the response of Nestor to Telemachus' account of the suitors' excesses in Book 3, a response that is repeated word for word by Odysseus the beggar in Book 16: 'Tell me then—do you consent to be thus humbled, or have the people throughout your land conceived detestation for you, moved by some divine message (*ἐπισπόμενοι θεοῦ ὀμφῇ*)' (3.214–15 = 16.95-6). Similarly, when Penelope questions the herald Medon about the causes of Telemachus' departure, he hesitates: 'I cannot say if some god impelled him or if his own heart felt the prompting to go to Pylos (*οὐκ οἶδ᾽, ἤ τίς μιν θεὸς ὤρορεν, ἦε καὶ αὐτοῦ θυμὸς ἐφωρμήθη ἴμεν ἐς Πύλον*) to gather news of his father's homecoming or of his fate' (4.712–14). Even though Calypso says nothing about Hermes' visit and claims that she is letting him go of her own free will (5.161), Odysseus is unsure about her motivation when he tells his story to Alcinous: she did it 'perhaps because Zeus had sent her warning, perhaps because her own mind had changed' (*Ζηνὸς ὑπ᾽ ἀγγελίης, ἢ καὶ νόος ἐτράπετ᾽ αὐτῆς*, 7.263). In Book 9, he is similarly unsure of the reasons why the Cyclops chose to bring the whole of his flock inside the cave: 'had he some foreboding, or was it a god who directed him?' (*ἤ τι ὀϊσάμενος, ἢ καὶ θεὸς ὣς ἐκέλευσεν*, 9.339). And in Book 14, Eumaeus also gives two possible reasons why Telemachus left to find out about his father: 'the rightmindednesss that he had has been somehow warped, whether by a god or by a man' (*τὸν δέ τις ἀθανάτων βλάψε φρένας ἔνδον ἐΐσας ἠέ τις ἀνθρώπων*) (14.178–9).

3. Divine commands and signs

(a) Divine commands

The gods can also influence men by explaining why they should act in a particular way. Thus, in Book 15 when Athena goes to Sparta 'to rouse remembrance in [Telemachus] and urge him to hasten home again' (*νόστου ὑπομνήσουσα καὶ ὀτρυνέουσα νέεσθαι*, 15.3), she pronounces a lengthy speech (15.10–42) in which she lists all the reasons why he should not stay for too long in Menelaus' palace. The Homeric poems also depict gods who appear in their own form to give an order to a mortal. In Book 24 of the *Odyssey*, when Odysseus and his followers are about to massacre the suitors' relatives, Athena, in the form of Mentor, speaks to the people of Ithaca, ordering them to 'cease from the toil of warfare' (*ἴσχεσθε πτολέμου, Ἰθακήσιοι, ἀργαλέοιο*, 24.531) and then addresses Odysseus, telling him in turn to 'restrain' himself (*σὺ δ' ἴσχεο*, 24.543) and make an end of the battle. Readers of the *Iliad* will immediately think of the famous scene in Book 1 in which the same goddess stops Achilles, who is drawing his sword to kill Agamemnon, using the same formula 'restrain yourself' (*σὺ δ' ἴσχεο*, *Iliad*, 1.214) and giving him, as she does with Odysseus, a good reason to obey by, first of all, revealing to him that she was sent by none other than Hera: 'The white-armed goddess Hera sent me, as she loves both of you alike in her heart and cares for you equally' (*Iliad*, 1.207–8) and then by holding out the hope of future gain (212–14). After this, Achilles obeys willingly. Odysseus does likewise. In these two cases, the divine intervention is therefore anything but mechanical. As Bernard Williams notes (1993: 30), 'The goddess has done more than help him to see that one course of action is better than the other in terms he was already considering; in this case, she has given him an extra and decisive reason, which he did not have before, for thinking that it is better.' We can also note that the distance between god and mortal has increased: the goddess does not appear in person in the *Odyssey* but 'had the form and the voice of Mentor' (*Μέντορι εἰδομένη ἠμὲν δέμας ἠδὲ καὶ αὐδήν*, 24.547) and is simply the messenger of Zeus who threatens Odysseus with his anger.

(b) Signs, omens, and dreams

In both the *Odyssey* and the *Iliad*, the gods also reveal their will indirectly through signs, omens,[42] and dreams. Sometimes, the reader is not told of the nature of the sign but only its meaning. In Book 3, for example, Nestor tells how, on his return journey, he and his companions asked the god to send them a sign (*teras*, 3.173), which he does, telling them to sail in mid ocean towards Euboea to escape disaster (3.173–5). But mostly, the text is much more explicit. The gods can send terrifying portents (τέραα, 12.394), like those that occur on the island of the Sun in Book 12 after Odysseus' men have sacrificed the cattle of the Sun: 'The beasts' hides began to move; the flesh on the spits, raw or roasted, began to bellow, and there was a noise like the sound of cattle, (12.395–6). Thunderclaps are a sign that can be favourable.[43] At the moment when Odysseus draws his bow: 'Zeus gave a sign (σήματα φαίνων) and thundered loud, and much-enduring Odysseus was filled with joy that the son of Cronos had sent him such an omen (τέρας)' (21.413–15).But the thunder that occurs at 24.539–44, like the thunderbolt that lands in front of Diomedes' chariot in the *Iliad*,[44] is a sign of the wrath of Zeus.

Words overheard by chance can also be interpreted as a sign sent by a deity and constitute what Homer calls a κλεηδών, which makes the hearer glad. Thus, when Telemachus, in Book 2.33–5, and his father in Book 18.112–17, hear someone expressing the hope that their wishes will come true, they rejoice, just as Odysseus does again in Book 20, when he hears one of the serving women express her wish that the meal she is preparing will be the suitors' last (20.112–20).[45] A simple sneeze, that occurs at the same moment as a wish, is also a favourable omen,[46] as we see from Penelope's reaction when she 'laughs' on hearing Telemachus sneeze loudly (20.540–1) just as she says 'If Odysseus returned to his own country, he with his son would soon requite the outrages of these men' (17.539–40).

The signs *par excellence* are those provided by birds[47] (the Greek term for 'bird', οἰωνός, can have the general meaning 'omen'). Thus

[42] See Stockinger 1959: 51–85 and Podlecki 1967.
[43] Podlecki 1967: 16–17.
[44] See, for example, *Iliad*, 8.133–4, 139–44.
[45] Podlecki 1967: 15–16.
[46] Podlecki 1967: 17.
[47] Podlecki 1967: 12–14.

Odysseus, in the false tale he tells to Laertes in Book 24, is careful to include a mention of the 'favourable birds' (ἦ τέ οἱ ἐσθλοὶ ἔσαν ὄρνιθες ἰόντι, 24.311) which accompanied Odysseus when he left his house. In the main narrative of the *Odyssey* this role is always fulfilled by birds of prey who appear alone, like the eagles in Book 2.146–55, or with their prey, like the eagle in Book 15 who carries off a goose in its talons (160–2) or the hawk tearing a dove to pieces (525–8), or the eagle in Book 20 that grips a timid dove (242–3). Their meaning is always clear.

In Book 2, the meaning is evident above all from the context: the eagles which fly down from the top of the mountain (ἐκ κορυφῆς ὄρεος, 2.147) and are harbingers of death (ὄσσοντο δ' ὄλεθρον, 2.152) who tear at each other's neck and head (δρυψαμένω δ' ὀνύχεσσι παρειὰς ἀμφί τε δειράς, 2.153) as they pass over the assembly before flying off to the right (δεξιὼ ἤϊξαν, 2.154) (a favourable sign) are sent by Zeus in response to Telemachus' appeal for help. Their significance is further suggested by the reaction of the spectators who are amazed when they see the birds (θάμβησαν δ' ὄρνιθας, ἐπεὶ ἴδον ὀφθαλμοῖσιν, 2.155). Finally, their meaning is made explicit by the interpretation given by Halitherses who is 'versed in the lore of birds and wise in expounding it' (2.158–9) and announces that a great disaster is about to overwhelm the suitors, as Odysseus is not far away and is preparing their deaths (2.163–7).

In Book 15, the eagle that appears as Telemachus leaves Sparta also flies 'to his right' (15.160) and flies off in the same direction (15.164). Again, the omen is interpreted, this time by Helen who says that she is inspired by the gods:

> Listen while I expound this thing as the Deathless Ones put it in my heart and as I am sure will come to pass. Just as yonder eagle left that mountain that holds his eyrie and his brood, just as he snatched the goose that was fattening in this house, so, after all his trials and travels, Odysseus will come back home and will be avenged; or it may be he is home already, sowing for all the suitors the seeds of doom. (15.172–8)

The importance of this sign is further underlined by the echoes which refer back to the omen of Book 2: in both cases, the predators come from the mountains and the fate that is in store for the suitors is expressed in identical terms.

This first omen is echoed in the same book by a second that appears just as Telemachus arrives back in Ithaca: 'As he ceased speaking, a bird flew up to the right of him (δεξιὸς ὄρνις), a hawk, the swift messenger of Apollo; in its talons it held a dove plucking out its feathers and strewing them on the ground between Telemachus and the ship' (15.525–8). Here too the omen is favourable since the bird flies to the right and its meaning is interpreted by an expert: Theoclymenus, a descendant of the famous seer Melampus (15.225):

> Telemachus, it is not without some god's intention that this bird flew up to the right of you (οὔ τοι ἄνευ θεοῦ ἤλυθε δεξιὸς ὄρνις); when I saw it before me, I knew it for a bird of omen (ἔγνων γάρ μιν ἐσάντα ἰδὼν οἰωνὸν ἐόντα). No family in the land of Ithaca is to be kinglier than your own; the supremacy is with you for ever. (15.531–4)

Moreover, this first interpretation is supplemented in Book 17 by Theoclymenus' announcement of Odysseus' imminent return and revenge to Penelope in lines that almost repeat those in Book 2 and at the beginning of Book 15: '[I tell you] in solemn truth, Odysseus is in his own land already sitting or walking as it may be, acquainting himself with these deeds of iniquity and sowing the seeds of evil for all the suitors' (ἀτὰρ μνηστῆρσι κακὸν πάντεσσι φυτεύει)' (17.157–9).

By contrast, the last omen which appears to the suitors as they plot to kill Telemachus in Book 20 echoes the first omen of Book 2: 'Suddenly on their left there appeared a bird of omen (ἀριστερὸς . . . ὄρνις), an eagle of lofty fight, with a cowering dove in its talons' (20.242–3). It is a bad omen indeed for the suitors coming as it does from their left. And its meaning, which is interpreted by the 'good' suitor Amphinomus at 20.245–6, makes them abandon their plans.

This subtle interplay of echoes is intensified, as has been pointed out, by a whole series of correspondences with the contents of dreams, with similes, or with divine epiphanies.[48] First of all, there is a marked similarity with the famous dream described by Penelope to Odysseus in Book 19.535–53, in which an eagle flies down from the mountains and kills all the geese in the palace. There is a further correspondence with the similes comparing Odysseus and his son to birds of prey in Book 16, 'sea-eagles or vultures' (φῆναι ἢ αἰγυπιοὶ, 16.217), and, in Book 22, during the massacre of the suitors, comparing them to 'vultures with crooked claws and with hooked beak' (22.302) which swoop down from the mountains to catch other

[48] Podlecki 1967: 14–15.

birds (ἐξ ὀρέων ἐλθόντες ἐπ' ὀρνίθεσσι θόρωσι, 22.303) and comparing their victims to doves (22.468). Finally there is the similarity to the appearance of Athena at Pylos, who disappears in the form of a 'sea-eagle', to the amazement of the assembled Achaeans (ἀπέβη γλαυκῶπις Ἀθήνη φήνῃ εἰδομένῃ· θάμβος δ' ἕλε πάντας Ἀχαιούς, 3.371–2).

With the exception of the portents on the island of the Sun, which are recounted by Odysseus and foretell the death of his companions, these omens are all closely linked to the main action of the poem (Odysseus' return and his revenge) and serve first and foremost to foreshadow these events. Within the first part of the *Odyssey*, they are concentrated in Book 2. But they become more frequent from Book 15 onwards, after Odysseus' arrival on Ithaca. But, yet apart from the birds whose appearance prompts the suitors to abandon their plans in Book 20 and the thunderbolt that lands at Athena's feet in Book 24 and puts an end to the threat of civil war, these signs and portents have no influence on the development of the action. They serve mainly to keep alive hopes of a happy ending for Odysseus and his family. They are also, in Book 2, a means of drawing attention to the blind folly and the impiety of the suitors: instead of listening to Halitherses' warning, they reply, through Eurymachus: 'Enough of this now, old prophesier; go home and interpret omens there; save your own children from threats of doom. This morning's omens I claim to interpret better than you. There are many birds that cross the sunlight, and not all of them have fateful meaning' (2.177–82).

Dreams are more complex.[49] Unlike divine epiphanies or omens they do not only serve to signify the will of the gods or to announce the future. They also have a psychological dimension, which modern readers of Freud have no doubt overemphasized, but which is certainly present nonetheless. The most famous dream in the *Odyssey*, that told by Penelope to Odysseus the beggar in Book 19 so that he can interpret it,[50] is a symbolic dream which has no parallel in the *Iliad* but which is closely related to the omens of Book 15:

I have twenty geese belonging here, and I love to watch them leaving their pond and eating their wheat; but a great eagle with crooked beak swooped down from the mountain-side and broke all their necks and killed them. So

[49] On dreams in Homer see Hundt 1935, Rankin 1962, Kessels 1978: 25–174, Levy 1982, Morris 1983, Brillante 1990. This section owes a great deal to an unpublished work by Danièle Auger.

[50] See Latacz 1994.

there they lay heaped up inside the house (οἱ δ' ἐκέχυντο ἀθρόοι ἐν μεγάροισ') while the eagle soared skywards. Still in my dream I wept and moaned, and Achaean ladies with lovely tresses came and stood round me as I lamented this eagle's slaughtering of my geese. (19.536–43)

As with the omens, its meaning is unambiguous as it contains its own interpretation:

The eagle returned; he perched upon a projecting roof-beam, he spoke with a human voice to check my grief: 'Take heart again, daughter of great Icarius. This was no dream but a waking vision, a happy one, destined to be fulfilled for you (οὐκ ὄναρ, ἀλλ' ὕπαρ ἐσθλόν, ὅ τοι τετελεσμένον ἔσται). The geese were the suitors, and I who was the eagle am now your own husband, at home again and about to bring a hideous death upon all the suitors (ἀεικέα πότμον ἐφήσω)'. (19.544–50)

This interpretation is immediately confirmed by Odysseus himself in lines 555–8 as well as by the similarities between this passage, the allusions to the terrible fate that Odysseus will bring about for the suitors,[51] and the description in Book 22 of the suitors' bodies 'lying in heaps' (ὣς τότ' ἄρα μνηστῆρες ἐπ' ἀλλήλοισι κέχυντο, 22.389).

But in contrast to the omens, which are always recounted by the principal narrator, this dream is only known through the dreamer's own account, which explains why its reality has been questioned (see Chapter 9 above, p. 300). It is also remarkable for the psychological responses that it portrays in Penelope, which have been the subject of much discussion. How are we to interpret the 'feeling of warmth' (which is the precise meaning of the verb ἰαίνομαι) which the sight of the geese (who represent the suitors) inspires in Penelope and her tears and lamentations at their death (while in the main narrative, it is the disloyal maidservants who, when they are about to be killed for having slept with the suitors, 'lament terribly' and 'shed tears in abundance')?[52] Readers of Freud were tempted to see in these details the expression of a repressed desire,[53] for why should a mature woman like Penelope not feel some pleasure at being so ardently courted by the young suitors? But it is probably simpler—and preferable—to explain this in a more prosaic manner: it is normal for a

[51] *Odyssey*, 19.550: ὃς πᾶσι μνηστῆρσιν ἀεικέα πότμον ἐφήσω; 4.340 and 17.131: ὣς Ὀδυσεὺς κείνοισιν ἀεικέα πότμον ἐφήσει.

[52] *Odyssey*, 22.447: αἴν' ὀλοφυρόμεναι, θαλερὸν κατὰ δάκρυ χέουσαι.

[53] See, for example, Rankin 1962: 621–2.

farmer's wife to rejoice when she sees her geese growing fat and to lament their destruction.

Like the *Iliad*, with Agamemnon's famous dream at the beginning of Book 2, the *Odyssey* also contains 'messenger-dreams'. These have much in common with divine epiphanies. In both cases, the deities can reveal themselves in their true form.[54] They can also appear to men in a disguise which is carefully chosen to win their trust and thus lend more weight to the message. But these epiphanies occur during the day, to a recipient who is awake, while dreams occur at night while the recipient is asleep. Thus, Athena takes on the form of Mentes and Mentor to appear to Telemachus and to win his trust (because both of these men were friends of Odysseus), but when she appears to Nausicaa in a dream she does so 'taking the form of Dymas' daughter . . . who was of Nausicaa's age and a special favourite with her' (6.22–3). Similarly, in Book 4 she sends a semblance of Penelope's sister to her in a dream: 'She fashioned a wraith in the likeness of a woman (εἴδωλον ποίησε, δέμας δ' ἤϊκτο γυναικί), Iphthime, daughter of bold Icarius and wife of Eumelus who lived in Pherae and sent this wraith to the house of Odysseus' (4.796–8). We find a similar phenomenon in the *Iliad* where the dream took on the appearance of Nestor, the wise counsellor in whom Agamemnon had the most confidence, to convince him to launch an assault upon Troy (2.20–1).

The line separating such dreams from divine epiphanies is a very fine one,[55] particularly when the deity appears during the night to a mortal who is not sleeping, as happens to Telemachus in Book 15 and to Odysseus in Book 20. In Book 15 the only difference is in the introduction, which makes clear that Telemachus is not asleep: '[Athena] found Telemachus and Peisistratus in the vestibule of Menelaus' palace; they were both in bed, but while Peisistratus slumbered peacefully, Telemachus was held back from sleep by troubled night-thoughts about his father (μελεδήματα πατρὸς ἔγειρεν)' (15.4–8), and the use of formula 'standing near him' which is never used to describe a dream.[56] In Book 20, the difference is even more subtle: Athena who addresses Odysseus 'in the shape of a woman' (δέμας δ' ἤϊκτο γυναικί, 20.31) stands, as is

[54] *Iliad*, 24.679–88 (Hermes appears to Priam in his sleep) and *Odyssey*, 10. 277–9 (epiphany of Hermes to Odysseus).

[55] See Brillante 1990.

[56] This formula, ἀγχοῦ δ' ἱσταμένη | ἱστάμενος, occurs eighteen times in the *Iliad* and six times in the *Odyssey*.

usually the case with dreams, 'above his head' (στῆ δ' ἄρ' ὑπὲρ κεφαλῆς, 20.32).[57] The only indication that this is not a dream is to be found in the first words of her message. Instead of beginning by saying 'you are sleeping' (εὕδεις), as do the dreams of Agamemnon, Achilles, and Priam in the *Iliad*, or the dream of Penelope in the *Odyssey*,[58] she asks Odysseus, 'Why are you awake, most wretched of men' (20.33).

In contrast to the *Iliad*, in which dreams are objective realities (they are always described first of all by the main narrator, who is usually the only source),[59] several dreams in the *Odyssey*, like the dreams of Penelope in Books 19 and 20, are only known to the reader through the account of the dreamer him- or herself. This also applies to the dream recounted in Odysseus' false tale in Book 14, which he claims was invented by Odysseus in order to procure a cloak for the Cretan. The story of this dream is told to Eumaeus in order to inspire him to act in a similar fashion. Like all good lies, it is entirely true to life, that is to say, it conforms entirely to the conventions of the dream type-scene in the *Iliad*. It is introduced by the same formula that is used by Agamemnon when he recounts his dream to the Achaean leaders: 'Listen friends. A divine dream came to me' (κλῦτε, φίλοι· θεῖός μοι ἐνύπνιον ἦλθεν ὄνειρος, *Odyssey*, 14.495 = *Iliad*, 2.56). Like Agamemnon's dream, that of Odysseus is a deceptive dream whose significance lies entirely in the message it brings and the events that will be set in motion by this message. Just as in the *Iliad*, the dream has the desired effect: first in the secondary narrative, 'In response to this, the son of Andraemon, Thoas, leapt up at once, threw aside his scarlet cloak and ran off to the ships, while I could wrap myself blissfully in the garment he left behind' (14.499–502). And then, in the main narrative, Eumaeus responds: 'Old guest, this tale you have told is excellent; not a word of it was misjudged or went to waste, so you shall not go short either for covering' (14.508–10).

It should also be noted that this invented dream is the only one that prompts, in an almost mechanical fashion, a human to act. Even Nausicaa's dream, which also moves the action forward and constitutes a means for Athena, who is 'planning return for bold

[57] *Iliad*, 2.20, 59, 23. 68, 24.682; *Odyssey*, 4.803, 6.21.

[58] *Iliad*, 2.23, 60, 23.69, 24.683; *Odyssey*, 4.804.

[59] The only exception is Agamemnon's dream which is told twice, first by the main narrator (*Iliad*, 2.23–34) then by Agamemnon himself (2.60–70). But this second version reproduces the first almost exactly, except for a single line.

Odysseus' (6.14), to achieve her end, is more subtle in its effects. By suggesting to the young girl, in the voice of one of her friends, that she go and wash clothes near to where Odysseus fell asleep after the shipwreck, the goddess prepares the ground for their meeting. But she does so indirectly, speaking only of the good reputation she will earn as a future bride. Moreover, when Nausicaa goes to her father to ask his permission to borrow the chariot and the mules so that she can go to the washing place, she makes no mention of the dream, even though lines 49–51, 'She remembered her dream with wonder and went her way through the palace halls to tell her tale to her dear parents, her father and her mother', clearly lead the reader to expect an account of the dream itself. What is more, she gives him a reason which did not feature in Athena's speech: 'She was too shy in the presence of her father to speak of her own happy bridal day' (*αἴδετο γὰρ θαλερὸν γάμον ἐξονομῆναι | πατρὶ φίλῳ*, 6.66–7) but explains her desire to wash the clothes by the need for her father and her brothers to have freshly laundered garments when they preside over the council or take part in choruses (6.60–5). The way in which the dream is told thus contributes to the depiction of the young girl's character.

In contrast to Nausicaa's dream, Penelope's two messenger-dreams, in Book 4 and in Book 20, do not affect the action in any way and have a purely psychological significance. Her dream in Book 4, which is part of the reality of the poem (it is described by the principal narrator), is simply a way for Athena to 'rescue stricken sobbing Penelope from tears and mourning and lamentation' (*εἷος Πηνελόπειαν ὀδυρομένην γοόωσαν παύσειε κλαυθμοῖο γόοιό τε δακρυόεντος*, 4.800–1) by reassuring her that Telemachus will return safely. But, in contrast to the *Iliad*, the scene does not end when the *eidolon* has finished delivering its message but continues with a dialogue in which Penelope attempts to find out about the fate of her husband, attempts that are met with refusal. The dream nevertheless fulfils its function. When Penelope wakes up at 4.839–1 she is comforted (*φίλον δέ οἱ ἦτορ ἰάνθη*) 'so vivid had been this apparition that winged its way to her through the gloom' (*ὥς οἱ ἐναργὲς ὄνειρον ἐπέσσυτο νυκτὸς ἀμολγῷ*).

We only hear of the 'bad dreams' in Book 20, 'sent by some god for [Penelope's] distress' (*αὐτὰρ ἐμοὶ καὶ ὀνείρατ' ἐπέσσευεν κακὰ δαίμων*, 20.87), through the queen's prayer to Artemis: 'This very night someone lay beside me in the likeness of Odysseus himself when he went from here with the other warriors; and my heart was glad, because I thought that this was no dream, but waking truth (ἐπεὶ οὐκ ἐφάμην ὄναρ ἔμμεναι, ἀλλ' ὕπαρ ἤδη)' (20.88–90). But these dreams, which are soon to become reality, are neither 'bad' nor deceptive, as Penelope believes. It is Penelope who is mistaken about their interpretation.

In fact, when we look more closely, it is clear that there are in fact no deceptive dreams in the *Odyssey*, with the exception of the dream invented by the Cretan Odysseus which is clearly presented as false. This is in accordance with the strong emphasis on divine justice that is discernible throughout the poem. It is, however, in the *Odyssey* that we find a general theory of dreams which underlines the difficulties involved in their interpretation, even if this theory is presented indirectly, through the character of Penelope who, as we have seen, is capable of misunderstanding the significance of her own dreams:

> Dreams are beyond our unravelling—who can be sure what tale they tell? Not all that men look for comes to pass. Two gates there are that give passage to fleeting dreams; one is made of horn, the other of ivory. The dreams that pass through sawn ivory are deceitful, bearing a message that will not be fulfilled; those that come out through polished horn have truth behind them, to be accomplished for men who see them. (19.560–7)

> ἦ τοι μὲν ὄνειροι ἀμήχανοι ἀκριτόμυθοι
> γίνοντ', οὐδέ τι πάντα τελείεται ἀνθρώποισι.
> δοιαὶ γάρ τε πύλαι ἀμενηνῶν εἰσὶν ὀνείρων·
> αἱ μὲν γὰρ κεράεσσι τετεύχαται, αἱ δ' ἐλέφαντι.
> τῶν οἳ μέν κ' ἔλθωσι διὰ πριστοῦ ἐλέφαντος,
> οἵ ῥ' ἐλεφαίρονται, ἔπε' ἀκράαντα φέροντες·
> οἳ δὲ διὰ ξεστῶν κεράων ἔλθωσι θύραζε,
> οἵ ῥ' ἔτυμα κραίνουσι, βροτῶν ὅτε κέν τις ἴδηται.

The distinction between the two gates of dreams, one of horn for dreams that will come true and one of ivory for dreams that will not come true, can probably be explained as Eustathius suggested,[60] by a double pun on the word for ivory (*elephas*) which is close to *elephairo* ('to deceive') and the word for horn (*keras*) which is close to *krainein* ('to accomplish').

[60] Eustathius, *Ad Odysseum*: 218, 30–7.

(c) Prophets and seers

This survey of the means used by the gods to communicate with men would be incomplete without mention of the prophets and seers who announce the future to men and forewarn them of the choices they will have to make. These figures have a relatively prominent role in the *Odyssey*. It is important, in analysing them, to distinguish between the 'mythical' seers encountered by Menelaus and Odysseus on their travels and the 'real' seers on Ithaca.

Both Proteus and Tiresias are to tell Menelaus and Odysseus 'the path before [them] and how [they are] to return home over the teeming sea' *ὅς κέν τοι εἴπῃσιν ὁδὸν καὶ μέτρα κελεύθου νόστον θ', ὡς ἐπὶ πόντον ἐλεύσεαι ἰχθυόεντα*, 4.389–90 = 10.539–40). Menelaus, who suspects that he may have committed some offence, asks both Eidothea and her father Proteus: 'Which of the deathless ones is it who has thwarted me in my journeying and how am I to return home over the teeming sea?' (4.380–1 = 469–70),

> *ὅς τίς μ' ἀθανάτων πεδάᾳ καὶ ἔδησε κελεύθου,*
> *νόστον θ', ὡς ἐπὶ πόντον ἐλεύσομαι ἰχθυόεντα*

The seer tells him the precise nature of his offence: 'You should have made choice offerings to Zeus and the other gods' (4.472–3). He also tells him how to atone for it: he must return to Egypt to make sacrifices to the gods and put an end to their anger by this means (4.475–85). Tiresias similarly reveals to Odysseus that he is being held up because of the wrath of Poseidon, who is angry because he blinded his son (11.101–2). Knowledge of the future is thus intimately linked to knowledge of the past.

In Book 4, the knowledge of Proteus, like that of Calchas in the *Iliad* (1.70), encompasses both time and space. He can tell of the fates of Ajax son of Oileus and of Agamemnon (4.499–537) and describe how he saw (*ἴδον*, 4.556) Odysseus weeping on Calypso's remote island and predict that Menelaus will go to the Elysian Fields after his death. But his predictions leave certain details open, as we see at 4.544–7: 'Endeavour as soon as may be to return to your land again. Perhaps you will find the murderer living (*ἢ γάρ μιν ζωόν γε κιχήσεαι*); perhaps Orestes already will have slain him (*ἤ κεν Ὀρέστης κτεῖνεν ὑποφθάμενος*), and you may join in the funeral feast.' And the same is true of Tiresias' predictions in Book 11. Twice he leaves open alternative endings, first with regard to Odysseus' return, which will depend on whether he and his companions leave the cattle of the Sun untouched (11.105–15), then concerning his revenge which will either be accomplished 'by guile' or 'openly with the keen bronze' (ἠὲ δόλῳ ἢ ἀμφαδὸν ὀξέϊ χαλκῷ, 11.120).

Circe's predictions in Book 12 are equally indeterminate as she leaves Odysseus to decide between Scylla and Charybdis, after he has passed by the Sirens: 'When your crew have rowed past the Sirens, I will not expressly say to you which of two ways you ought to take (ἔνθα τοι οὐκέτ' ἔπειτα διηνεκέως ἀγορεύσω, ὁπποτέρη δή τοι ὁδὸς ἔσσεται); you must follow your own counsel there (ἀλλὰ καὶ αὐτὸς θυμῷ βουλεύειν); I will only give you knowledge of both' (12.55–8). Like Tiresias, she leaves open the outcome of their stay on the island of the Sun (12.137–41 = 11.110–15). We should also add the predictions revealed at the moment of their fulfilment by the Cyclops, Circe, or Alcinous.[61]

Human seers are very different. It is important to distinguish the 'specialists' δημιοεργοί,[62] who can tell which birds are bearers of omens (because they do not all do so)[63] like Halitherses, who 'was versed in the lore of birds beyond the rest of his generation and wise in expounding it' (ὁ γὰρ οἶος ὁμηλικίην ἐκέκαστο ὄρνιθας γνῶναι καὶ ἐναίσιμα μυθήσασθαι, 2.159) or Theoclymenus, the descendant of Melampus, whose father was Polypheides 'the best of all seers' (15.252–3), and occasional seers who can make prophecies when 'the gods inspire them'[64] like Athena/Mentes who is 'not a prophet, and [has] no certainty with omens' in Book 1,[65] or Helen in Book 15. All their prophecies concern Odysseus' return and revenge. All these prophecies echo each other[66] and are arranged in a chiasmus: Halitherses' prophecies to the people of Ithaca in Book 2.157–76 and their reminder in Book 24.451–62 frame those of Theoclymenus to

[61] *Odyssey*, 9.507–12 (the prediction of the seer Telemus to the Cyclops); 10.330–2 (Hermes' prediction to Circe); 13.172–8 (the old predictions made to the father of Alcinous).

[62] *Odyssey*, 17.383–4.

[63] *Odyssey*, 2.181–2, 15.531–2.

[64] *Odyssey*, 1.200–1(Athena/Mentes) = 15.172–3 (Helen): αὐτὰρ ἐγὼ μαντεύσομαι, ὡς ἐνὶ θυμῷ ἀθάνατοι βάλλουσι καὶ ὡς τελέεσθαι ὀΐω.

[65] *Odyssey*, 1.202: οὔτε τι μάντις ἐὼν οὔτ' οἰωνῶν σάφα εἰδώς.

[66] *Odyssey*, 2.163–7 Halitherses, 15.176–8 Helen, and 17.157–9 Theoclymenus. In these three passages the verb φυτεύει occurs with an object like φόνον (2.165) or κακὸν (15.177, 17.159) and alludes to the killing of the suitors.

Telemachus in Book 15.529–34—complemented by that given to Penelope in Book 17.151–61—and to the suitors in Book 20.351–7. They are all based on the interpretation of birds with the exception of Theoclymenus' last prophecy which leaves no room for doubt:

> Unhappy men, what is this thing that has come upon you? Your heads and your faces and your knees are wrapped in darkness; the air is alive with lamentation (οἰμωγὴ δὲ δέδηε); your cheeks are streaming with tears; the walls and the fashioned tie-beams are dank with blood (αἵματι δ' ἐρράδαται τοῖχοι καλαί τε μεσόδμαι); the entrance and court beyond are thronged with ghosts speeding down to the murk of Erebus; the sun has been blotted out from heaven, and a ghastly mist (ἀχλύς) hovers over all.

This hallucinatory vision, which is unparalleled in the Homeric poems,[67] prefigures precisely the massacre in Book 22, in which 'darkness' (ἀχλύς) spreads over the eyes of the dying Eurymachus (22.88), the terrible moaning that rises up (τῶν δὲ στόνος ὤρνυτ' ἀεικής, 22. 308), the ground steaming with blood (δάπεδον δ' ἅπαν αἵματι θῦεν, 22.309),[68] and the 'ghosts' that Hermes leads to the Underworld.[69]

(b) The motivations for divine intervention

When they intervene in the human world, the gods of the *Odyssey*, like those in the *Iliad* and like the heroes, are above all moved by their concern to protect their honour and to punish those who have offended them.[70] When Poseidon visits his wrath upon the Phaeacians, it is because they have slighted him by conveying Odysseus back to his homeland against his will (13.128–38). It is also possible that the fact that they 'take home all manner of men'[71] provoked the god's anger as it placed limits on his power. Whatever the case, Poseidon has no problem in obtaining the agreement of Zeus (13.140–5) who safeguards the stability of the cosmos and each god's sphere of influence in which he or she is all-powerful.[72]

67 See Stanford 1964–5 on *Odyssey*, 20.351.

68 Podlecki 1967: 19.

69 On the equivalence between ψυχή and εἴδωλον, see *Odyssey*, 24.14: ψυχαί, εἴδωλα καμόντων.

70 Allan 2006: 17.

71 *Odyssey*, 8.566 = 13.174. See Winterbottom 1989: 35.

72 See Allan 2006: 19.

The gods also destroy those who dare to challenge them and to question their power: in the *Odyssey* (8.226–9), Apollo killed Eurytus when he challenged him to a contest in archery, just as, in the *Iliad*, 2.594–600, the Muses blinded Thamyris and deprived him of the power of song when he boasted that he would beat them in a contest. They also pursue those who attack their associates or their possessions. Just as, in the *Iliad*, 1.93–100, Apollo visits his wrath upon Agamemnon for having failed to show respect to his priest, Poseidon hates Odysseus for having blinded one of his sons (11.101–3) and fulfils the Cyclops' prayer to the letter.[73] Similarly, Helios destroys the men who dared to consume his cattle with the support of Zeus, who strikes their boat with his thunderbolt (12.374–419). They also punish those who, like Menelaus, neglect to offer sacrifices to them before embarking on a journey, 'for the gods want us always to remember their commandments' (4.353).

As in the *Iliad*, too, the gods punish the group for the crimes committed by one of its members and pay no heed to attenuating circumstances, nor do they feel pity. On their return from Troy, all the Achaeans are punished by Zeus 'because they were not all wise or righteous' (3.133–4) just as all the Trojans paid the price for Paris's crime. The same applies to the suitors since Amphinomus and Leiodes are not spared:[74] Athena ensures that Amphinomus dies by Telemachus' spear,[75] and Odysseus rejects Leiodes' prayers.[76] It is equally vain to attempt to appease the wrath of the gods by sacrifices and offerings once the offence has been committed, as we see from the examples of Agamemnon and Odysseus' companions,[77] and, in all probability, the Phaeacians, even if the story leaves them at 13.187, in the middle of their prayers and sacrifices to Poseidon, and does not show their punishment.

As well as having enemies, the gods have protégés whom they help. The special relationship between Odysseus and Athena existed in the *Iliad*;[78] in the *Odyssey* it is explained by the similarities between a hero and a goddess who both excel in cunning and intelligence, as Athena herself states: 'Both of us are subtle—you excel all mankind in

[73] *Odyssey*, 9.528–42. See Winterbottom 1989: 34.
[74] See Silk 2004: 37.
[75] *Odyssey*, 18.155–6.
[76] *Odyssey*, 22.310–29.
[77] *Odyssey*, 3.143–7, 159–61; 12.345–7.
[78] *Iliad*, 10.245, 23.782–3. See Kearns 2004: 67.

stratagem and well-chosen words, I am renowned among all the gods for wiles and wisdom' (13.296–9). The gods also favour those who are related to them: Menelaus will be transported to the Elysian Fields after his death because his 'wife is Helen and her father is Zeus himself' (4.569). Nor do they forgot those who, like Odysseus, have been particularly assiduous in offering sacrifices (1.65–7). All these reactions are paralleled by the gods of the *Iliad*.[79] As in the *Iliad*, too, the gods observe an aristocratic code of behaviour and are careful not to encroach on others' domains. At the end of Book 6 of the *Odyssey*, Athena hears Odysseus' prayer but does not appear to him since she 'shrank from offending (*αἴδετο*) her father's brother, who kept unquenched his anger against godlike Odysseus, until his arrival in his own country' (6.329–31).

There are, however, a number of differences between the gods of the *Iliad* and those of the *Odyssey*. These differences may sometimes be exaggerated by critics, but they are real, nevertheless.[80] The cast of divine characters in the *Odyssey* is less rich. A goddess like Hera, who plays an important role in the *Iliad*, only intervenes in the pre-history of the *Odyssey* to save Agamemnon and Jason and to grant beauty and intelligence to the daughters of Pandarus.[81] There is also less conflict between the gods. The two divine assemblies that decide on Odysseus' return both take place in the absence of his principal enemy, Poseidon, and Athena's twofold plan meets no opposition. Even when there are direct conflicts of interest, the gods of the *Odyssey* respect the rules that ensure the smooth functioning of an aristocratic society and never question the division of powers. It is noticeable that there is no conflict, in the *Odyssey*, between the respective interventions of Poseidon and Athena, as we can see from the construction of Book 5 in particular. Athena does not intervene during the storm sent by Poseidon (5.282–381). But from line 382 onwards she mobilizes her energies: first of all she bars the paths of all the winds except for the North Wind, to allow Odysseus to land in Phaeacia (382–7), then she gives him the idea of clinging on

[79] On two occasions in the *Iliad*, Zeus mentions the size of the sacrifices made by the Trojans (4.44–9) and by Hector (24.66–70) as justification of his support for them.

[80] See in particular Allan 2006 who mounts a vigorous critique of the tendency to contrast the theology of the *Iliad* to that of the *Odyssey* in such works as Lloyd-Jones 1971: 28, Griffin 1980b: 51–2, 1987: 77–8, Kullmann 1985: 5–12, and more recently, Kearns 2004: 67–9, Graziosi and Haubold 2005: 80–1.

[81] *Odyssey*, 4.513; 12.72; 20.70–1.

to the rocks (5.428) and swimming parallel to the coast (5.437), and finally sends him to sleep to put an end to his exhaustion as quickly as possible (5.491–3). In Book 6, she continues to help him indirectly by sending the dream to Nausicaa and, at the beginning of Book 7, she guides him in the form of a young child, while making him invisible to the Phaeacians. But, as Odysseus reminds her in Book 13, during the whole journey that took him from Troy to the coast of Phaeacia, she did not intervene:

> Once we had sacked Priam's tall city, when we had embarked and the god had scattered us far and wide, from then onwards, daughter of Zeus, I never saw you. I caught no glimpse of you boarding my ship to keep off trouble from me there. No, I wandered on all the time with my heart and mind in despair, until the gods released me from hardship. Only when I had reached the rich land of the Phaeacians did you comfort me with your words and guide me into the town yourself. (13.316–23)

Athena accepts this but justifies her inaction in lines 339–43 by her conviction that he would eventually return home and by her respect for her father's brother. Conversely, Poseidon knows full well that once Odysseus has landed in Phaeacia, where 'he is destined to be delivered from the sorrow that has been his' (5.288–9), he can do nothing more to harm him.

In the *Odyssey*, the king of the gods seems to have no difficulty ensuring that the other gods obey him. In the *Iliad* (8.399–408) he has to threaten to smash Hera and Athena's chariot to stop them coming to the Achaeans' aid and sees his plans thwarted, temporarily at least, by Hera and Poseidon. But in the *Odyssey*, both Hermes and Calypso obey his orders without question in Book 5, one by going to the ends of the earth and the other by letting Odysseus go because they know that 'once the master of the aegis has fixed his own purpose, no other god can cross or thwart it' (5.103–4 = 137–8). In Book 13, likewise, Poseidon admits that he could not prevent the return that Zeus had solemnly promised to Odysseus (13.131–3) and must ask the king of the gods for his permission to punish the Phaeacians, because he 'fears and shuns [his] anger' (ἀλλὰ σὸν αἰεὶ θυμὸν ὀπίζομαι ἠδ' ἀλεείνω, 13.148). We may contrast this with the *Iliad* in which the same god did not hesitate to disobey Zeus in Book 14, in order to help the Greeks, and only obeyed with great reluctance in Book 15.[82]

[82] *Iliad*, 14.361–78 and 15.173–219.

But even if we agree with William Allan (2006: 2) that there is no fundamental divergence between the gods of the *Iliad* and those of the *Odyssey*, it is undeniable that there is a difference in the way men talk about them. Characters in the *Odyssey* do sometimes speak about the gods in ways that can be directly paralleled in the *Iliad*. Both Helen and Eumaeus recognize the overwhelming power of the god who 'gives good and evil' (4.237) and 'gives one thing and withholds another . . . all things are within his reach, (14.444–5). Nestor encourages Telemachus to recognize mortals' dependence when he reminds him that 'all men stand in need of the gods' (3.48). A god can 'easily (ῥεῖα) save a man, if he so chooses, no matter from how far away' (3.231) as Athena states (in the form of Mentor). And Odysseus is the first to admit that things that are impossible for men are made possible if a god comes to their aid (23.184–6).

The gods are also responsible for mortals' qualities as well as for their faults. For example, it is they who gave to Penelope and to the women of Phaeacia the gift of weaving fine cloth, they gave the gift of deceit to Autolycus, and the gift of song to Demodocus and Phemius.[83] But this distribution of gifts is not entirely a matter of chance: the gods tend to keep a degree of balance. The story of the jars in *Iliad*, 24.527–33 made this clear: when Zeus gives gifts to a man he never takes them only from the jar of blessings. At best he mixes good and ill fortune; at worst, he only gives from the jar of evils. In just the same way, Odysseus claims that

> the gods do not give their favours all together, form, and wisdom and eloquence. A man may seem in outward aspect unworthy of much regard, yet heaven hangs beauty about his words, and those who hear him gaze at him in delight while he speaks unfalteringly and with winning modesty; he stands out among those assembled there, and as he goes his way through the city, men look at him as if at a god. Another man is in aspect like the Deathless Ones, but then no grace attends on his words at all. (8.167–75)

In both the *Odyssey* and the *Iliad* there is however a limit to the gods' power. Zeus may 'know all things perfectly, what is fated and what not fated for mortal men' (ὁ γάρ τ' ἐῢ οἶδεν ἅπαντα, μοῖράν τ' ἀμμορίην τε καταθνητῶν ἀνθρώπων, 20.75–6) but he cannot alter

[83] *Odyssey*, 2.116–17 (Penelope), 7.110–11 (Phaeacian women), 19.396 (Autolycus), 8.44–5 (Demodocus), and 22.347–8 (Phemius). Lesky 2001: 185 shows that the same is true of the *Iliad* (5.51–2: Scamandrius; 15. 411–12: the carpenter; 23.306–8: Antilochus).

the outcome, as Athena/Mentor reminds Telemachus: 'Death comes to all, and the gods themselves cannot ward it off, even from one they love, on the day when he is overtaken by the grim doom of death' (3.236–8). But in contrast to the *Iliad*, the *Odyssey* reserves a privileged destiny for certain mortals: Menelaus will be sent to the Elysian Fields where he will live a life of ease, very similar to that of the gods, for all eternity: 'There men live unlaborious days. Snow and tempest and thunderstorms never enter there, but for men's refreshment Ocean sends out continually the high-singing breezes of the west' (4.565–8). And Heracles only leaves his 'phantom' in the Underworld while 'he himself feasts with the immortal gods and has Hebe of the lovely ankles as his wife' (11.601–3).[84]

The characters of the *Odyssey*, including Telemachus, sometimes still hold Zeus responsible (αἴτιος) for what happens to mortals, Zeus who 'allots to bread-eating men whatever he chooses' (ὅς τε δίδωσιν ἀνδράσιν ἀλφηστῇσιν ὅπως ἐθέλῃσιν ἑκάστῳ, 1.348–9). According to Nausicaa, 'Zeus gives prosperity to men, to the good or the bad, as he pleases' (ὅπως ἐθέλῃσιν) (6.188–9). Thus, as Menelaus remarks, Zeus granted Nestor an old age lived in prosperity surrounded by sons who are both wise and brave (4.209–11).

More frequently, the heroes of the *Odyssey*, like those of the *Iliad*, accuse the gods of being the cause of their suffering. Telemachus reproaches the gods for 'plotting evil' (κακὰ μητιόωντες, 1. 234) and keeping his father in obscurity; he also holds them responsible for his troubles and for the suitors' excesses (1.244). Menelaus echoes this when he regrets the fact that Odysseus was unable to come and live in Argos with him, as he wanted him to do: 'But that was begrudged (ἀγάσσασθαι) us by the god himself, who robbed that unhappy man of the hope of homecoming (ὅς κεῖνον δύστηνον ἀνόστιμον οἷον ἔθηκεν)' (4.181–2). Penelope also considers the gods to be the cause of all the troubles that overwhelm her. When she hears that Telemachus has left Ithaca she cries out: 'To me, above all other women born and bred in my generation, Olympian Zeus has allotted sorrow (ἄλγε' ἔδωκεν)' (4.722–3). Nestor draws the same lesson from the story of Clytemnestra (or of Agamemnon's bard): 'it was the gods' purpose (μοῖρα θεῶν) that ordained that she [or 'he'] should yield' ἀλλ' ὅτε δή μιν μοῖρα θεῶν ἐπέδησε δαμῆναι, 3.269). In Book 18,

[84] These lines are omitted by some editors and by Shewring's translation.

Odysseus claims that 'when the Blessed Ones send a man sorrow' (ὅτε δὴ καὶ λυγρὰ θεοὶ μάκαρες τελέωσι, 18.134) he must bear it with endurance. And when, in Book 19.75–80, he speaks of his past prosperity to Melantho he identifies the will of Zeus as the cause of his downfall. Similarly, when Philoetius sees Odysseus the beggar, 'a poor man who looks like a lord', he draws the conclusion that 'when the gods weave sorrow into men's lot (ἐπικλώσωνται ὀϊζύν)—even into the lot of kings—they send them wandering and plunge them into misery' (20.195–6) and exclaims, using a line pronounced by Menelaus in the *Iliad*: 'O father Zeus, no god is ruthless (ὀλοώτερος) as you are ruthless. You bring men into the world yourself, yet you have no more compassion for them than to plunge them into suffering and bitter tribulation' (μισγέμεναι κακότητι καὶ ἄλγεσι λευγαλέοισιν). (20.201–3).[85] But this discourse on the gods is no longer central, as was the case in the *Iliad*. It is put into perspective first of all by the prologue, but also by significant changes of emphasis and by a series of statements that reveal a belief in divine justice. Above all, the narrative shows divine justice at work in the events related.

Since Werner Jaeger,[86] critics have emphasized the importance of the speech in Book 1 in which Zeus defends himself against the criticisms of mortals and refuses to accept responsibility for *all* human suffering: 'O the waywardness of these mortals! They accuse the gods, they say that their troubles come from us, and yet by their own presumptuousness[87] they draw down sorrow upon themselves that outruns their allotted portion' (1.32–4).

> ὢ πόποι, οἷον δή νυ θεοὺς βροτοὶ αἰτιόωνται.
> ἐξ ἡμέων γάρ φασι κάκ' ἔμμεναι· οἱ δὲ καὶ αὐτοὶ
> σφῇσιν ἀτασθαλίῃσιν ὑπὲρ μόρον ἄλγε' ἔχουσιν.

He thus seems to respond to Agamemnon who, in the *Iliad*, placed the entire responsibility for his disastrous decision onto the gods:[88]

[85] *Odyssey*, 20.201 = *Iliad*, 3.365.

[86] Jaeger 1960 (1st pub 1921).

[87] Allan 2006: 16 n.73 rightly points out the importance of the καί in line 33 and translates 'and yet they too themselves through their own reckless acts have sorrows beyond their destined share'.

[88] Silk 2004: 32; 'It is as if Zeus has been brooding on Agamemnon's apology in the *Iliad*.'

I am not to blame, but rather Zeus and Fate and Erinys that walks in darkness: they put a cruel blindness in my mind at the assembly on that day when by my own act I took away his prize from Achilles. But what could I do? It is god who brings all things to their end. (*Iliad*, 19.86–90)

> . . . ἐγὼ δ' οὐκ αἴτιός εἰμι
> ἀλλὰ Ζεὺς καὶ Μοῖρα καὶ ἠεροφοῖτις Ἐρινύς,
> οἵ τέ μοι εἰν ἀγορῇ φρεσὶν ἔμβαλον ἄγριον ἄτην,
> ἤματι τῷ ὅτ' Ἀχιλλῆος γέρας αὐτὸς ἀπηύρων.
> ἀλλὰ τί κεν ῥέξαιμι; θεὸς διὰ πάντα τελευτᾷ.

There are also significant shifts in emphasis between the *Iliad* and the *Odyssey* that become clear when one pays more attention than has been done in the past to the context, which tends to question the accusations made by mortals against the gods. The fulfilment of the will of Zeus does not guide the action of the poem as it did in the *Iliad*, where it features in the prologue (Διὸς δ' ἐτελείετο βουλή, *Iliad*, 1.5 = *Odyssey*, 11.297).[89] In the Odyssey, the will of Zeus only serves to explain the story of the seer Melampus, 'entangled by a god's hard sentence' when he was 'caught by herdsmen and galled with chains' (11.292–3). When Odysseus, echoing Agamemnon in *Iliad* 19, claims that the gods were responsible for the judgement of the arms of Achilles: 'No other was the cause of all this but Zeus; he it was who bore hate unbounded against the host of Achaean spearsmen' (11.558–60).

> οὐδέ τις ἄλλος
> αἴτιος, ἀλλὰ Ζεὺς Δαναῶν στρατὸν αἰχμητάων
> ἐκπάγλως ἤχθηρε, τεῒν δ' ἐπὶ μοῖραν ἔθηκεν.

It is difficult to see this as anything other than an excuse that allows him to avoid admitting his responsibility. His son accuses a god of presenting him with a man who looks like his father in order to deceive him in Book 16.194–5 but admits later that he was wrong. Similarly, when Philoetius in Book 20 echoes Menelaus' words in Book 3 of the *Iliad*, accusing Zeus of being a 'ruthless' god, he is only partially correct since Odysseus the beggar is about to regain his royal status.

Finally, it is important to acknowledge the importance of the belief in divine justice in the *Odyssey*,[90] and the fact that the narrative

[89] These are the only two occurrences of this expression in Homer. See Lesky 2001: 174.

[90] Kearns 2004: 68. On this theme in the *Iliad* see Winterbottom 1989: 33, Allan 2006: 3 who cite *Iliad*, 3.351–4, 4.157–69, and 13.620–7.

depicts this justice in action on several occasions. Telemachus, for example, believes that the gods are angered by transgressions and visit their wrath (*mēnis*) upon those who fail to act when they witness crimes (2.66–7). This is why he begs them on two occasions to take appropriate revenge.[91] Odysseus, for his part, reminds the Cyclops that Zeus avenges suppliants and guests, that he protects them and ensures that they will be respected (9.270–1). When he suspects that Phaeacians have tricked him he calls upon Zeus to punish them for not fulfilling their duty to their guest (13.213–14). Eumaeus also claims that 'the blessed gods are no friends of wickedness; they honour justice and righteous action' (14.83–4) and Philoetius also acknowledges that the gods watch over justice and punish the guilty (20.215). Even the suitors, speaking in chorus, admit that the gods 'observe both outrage and righteous dealing among mankind' (17.487). We should also not forget Penelope's prayers to Athena and to Zeus, which are essentially appeals for divine vengeance.[92]

Conversely, mortals justify at least some suffering as brought about by a crime. If Zeus gave the Achaeans a disastrous return from Troy it is because 'not all of them were wise or righteous' (3.132–4), as Nestor acknowledges. Proteus explains to Menelaus that Ajax son of Oileus was destroyed as a result of his arrogance and folly: he was saved by Poseidon but 'said that he had escaped from the sea despite the gods' (4.504). Odysseus claims that Zeus and the other gods punished the Cyclops for his failure to respect strangers and for having dared to commit the supreme impiety and devour his guests instead of offering them a feast, as tradition demanded (9.475–9). When, disguised as a beggar, he presents his life as an example to the 'good' suitor Amphinomus, he explains his present misery as the result of his past crimes: 'I did many reckless deeds to sate my desire for power and mastery, putting great faith in my father and my brother. And so I would have no man be lawless, rather let each man accept unquestioningly whatever gifts the gods may grant him' (18.139–42). Menelaus also suspects that he has committed some offence that has provoked the wrath of the gods when his ship is becalmed (4.377–8).

The opposite also applies: the righteous do not suffer. It is for this reason that Penelope's sister is able to reassure her, about Telemachus' fate, telling her 'your son is to come home again; in no way has he

[91] *Odyssey*, 1.378–9 = 2.143–4.

[92] *Odyssey*, 4.762–6, 17.59–60.

offended the gods' (οὐ μὲν γάρ τι θεοῖσ' ἀλιτήμενός ἐστι) (4. 806–7). The prologue shows that these ideas are shared by the narrator of the *Odyssey*. From the outset the poet, who has often been accused of partiality towards his hero (according to Eustathius he is φιλοδυσσεύς, 'pro-Odysseus'),[93] holds Odysseus' companions alone responsible for their suffering because of their own wild recklessness (αὐτῶν γὰρ σφετέρῃσιν ἀτασθαλίῃσιν ὄλοντο, 1.7) as the story of Book 12 shows clearly. The companions were warned, not once but twice. First, Odysseus tried to dissuade them from stopping on the island of the Sun: 'listen to what I say, sad though your plight is; I must tell you of the prophetic words of Theban Tiresias and of Circe. They urged me solemnly, both of them, to shun this island of the all-gladdening sun-god, because there, they said, the direst of perils awaited us' (12.271–5). Then, once they have landed, he attempts to avert the sacrilege by making them swear an oath: 'swear a solemn oath, all of you, that if we come on a herd of cows or a great flock of sheep, not one among you in fatal folly will slay either cow or sheep. No, take your ease and eat the food that immortal Circe gave us' (12.298–302). But his efforts are vain and the companions will pay for their crime with their lives.

Zeus himself cites the example of Aegisthus (1.35–43). He was warned by Hermes of what would happen to him if he seduced Agamemnon's wife and killed the king on his return. But he ignored the warning and brought disaster upon himself, which was not originally part of his lot. The suitors, who attack Odysseus and his house by courting his wife, eating up his wealth, and plotting to kill his son, are also given several warnings. In Book 2, the seer Halitherses urges them to 'check themselves—they will gain most by doing so now' (168–9). In Book 20 another seer, Theoclymenus, announces that he can see a night of death descending upon them (351–7). But they ignore these warnings and finally succumb to Odysseus who draws a clear moral from the story: 'These men have perished because the gods willed it so and because their own deeds were evil. They had no regard for any man, good or bad, who might come their way; and so by their own presumptuous follies they brought on themselves this hideous end' (22.413–16).

τούσδε δὲ μοῖρ' ἐδάμασσε θεῶν καὶ σχέτλια ἔργα·
οὔ τινα γὰρ τίεσκον ἐπιχθονίων ἀνθρώπων,

[93] *Ad Odysseam*, 2.220.30.

> *οὐ κακὸν οὐδὲ μὲν ἐσθλόν, ὅτίς σφεας εἰσαφίκοιτο·*
> *τῶ καὶ ἀτασθαλίῃσιν ἀεικέα πότμον ἐπέσπον.*

The massacre of the suitors is also interpreted by Penelope and Laertes as a manifestation of the wrath of the gods.[94]

We should not, however, exaggerate the contrast between the theology of the *Odyssey* and that of the *Iliad*, or attempt to see in the author of the *Odyssey* a philosopher who holds, like Plato in the *Republic* (379c), that the god is the sole cause of good and that we must 'look for some factors other than good as cause of the evil'.[95]

In the *Odyssey*, where the distinction between human and divine spheres is more clear cut,[96] there seems to be a clearer distinction than in the *Iliad* between two sorts of ills: those that mortals bring upon themselves by their crimes,[97] and those that they were always destined to suffer and which they have done nothing to deserve. This explains why the Phaeacians are destined to be destroyed in a manner that appears unjust (they are punished for fulfilling their role as hosts too well) and why Odysseus undergoes trials that are not justified by any crime. We can also note that in the *Odyssey* the only event that occurs *ὑπὲρ μόρον* is a crime while, in the *Iliad*, it is always events that would occur before their time, like the return of the Achaeans in Book 2.155–6, the killing of Sarpedon by Odysseus in Book 5.674–5, the capture of Troy by Patroclus in Book 16. 698–701 or Achilles in Book 21.544–6, or the death of Aeneas in Book 20.290–1, but which are stopped by a god. We can therefore, to a certain extent, continue to speak of a moralized presentation of the gods in the *Odyssey*.

[94] *Odyssey*, 23.63–7: Penelope, 24.351–2: Laertes.

[95] Translation by D. Lee (London, 2007).

[96] Lesky 2001: 189.

[97] In the Homeric poems, the story of Aegisthus (*Odyssey*, 1.34, 35) is the only example of an event that occurs *ὑπὲρ μόρον* or *ὑπὲρ μοῖραν*. In every other case (*Iliad*, 20.336; 21.517: *Odyssey*, 5.436) a god (Poseidon, Apollo, or Athena) intervenes in time to prevent it.

11

The Ideology of the *Odyssey*

1. THE HOUSE

The *Odyssey* is not just the story of a man promised in the prologue, it is also the story of the house that plays a central role in the poem.[1] The house is the end point towards which Odysseus is constantly striving and returning, for him, means not only being reunited with his wife and living once again in his own land, it is also a 'homecoming',[2] seeing once more his 'possessions, [his] own servants and the tall roof of [his] own great house' (7.225).

This house has a physical existence, as we see it through Odysseus' eyes in Book 17: 'Eumaeus, this house is surely Odysseus' own; one could tell it at once among a hundred. Each part of it opens out from another, the courtyard has been made complete with a corniced wall, and there are double doors for protection; no man alive could hope to storm it' (17.264–8). The house also has a 'wide vaulted' storeroom whose interior is described on two occasions, when Telemachus enters to get provisions (2.337–45) and then when Penelope goes in to fetch Odysseus' bow (21.8–12). We hear of Odysseus' 'treasures, bronze, gold and wrought iron' as well as 'his pliant bow with its ample quiver' (21.9–11); it also contains 'gold and bronze piled up, clothing in chests and an abundance of fragrant oil with big jars of old sweet wine' (2.338–41).

The house is also the centre of an estate with land, sometimes situated far away, and many herds of animals, as Eumaeus proudly tells the beggar:

[1] Halverson 1992: 177 and Thalmann 1998: 124–33.

[2] See, for example, *Odyssey*, 1.17–18: *οἶκόνδε νέεσθαι*; 5.220: *οἴκαδέ τ' ἐλθέμεναι καὶ νόστιμον ἦμαρ ἰδέσθαι.*

'My master's wealth was huge; no other lord had as much as he, either on the dark mainland or here in Ithaca; not twenty together could equal such abundance. I will reckon it up for you. On the mainland twelve herds of cattle and as many of swine, twelve flocks of sheep and as many of wide-ranging goats, tended by either his own herdsmen or others from outside his household.' (14.96–102)

The house and all its lands and contents should, in normal circumstances, be passed on intact, or even enriched, to his rightful heirs. Odysseus himself prays that Arete and her guests will 'bequeath their children the wealth that they have in their own halls' (7.149–50). The situation on Ithaca, where the house is gradually being pillaged by outsiders who 'can scarcely wait to parcel out the possessions of the long-absent king' (20.215–16), is therefore a scandalous outrage.

The house is also, and above all, the people who live in it: the wife and son, as well as the servants. Their loyalty and fidelity are essential to the survival of the whole. The image presented by the *Odyssey* is entirely shaped by a patriarchal ideal, certain aspects of which could be compared to the worlds portrayed in *Uncle Tom's Cabin* or *Gone with the Wind*.

(a) Masters and servants

Good servants, like Eumaeus, are 'loyal and love Telemachus and Penelope' (13.405–6).[3] The expressions of goodwill and affection by Eumaeus and Philoetius in Book 21.222–7, the maidservants in 22.497–501, and Dolion and his six sons in Book 24.391–411 make this abundantly clear. The good servants are reliable allies who carry out orders to the letter, something that is easy to show in a formulaic style which uses exactly the same words to describe an order being carried out as are used in the order itself, as we can see if we compare Telemachus' order to Eurycleia (2.373–6) and its implementation (4.746–9) to give just one example. There is a distinction between male and female servants: the good male servant makes efforts to increase his master's wealth, as Eumaeus does when, during Odysseus' absence, he 'himself, unhelped by his mistress or old Laertes, had walled in the yard to enclose the swine while his master was away' (14.7–10). The female servants, like Eurycleia, see it as their duty to

[3] *Odyssey*, 13.405–6: ἤπια οἶδε | παῖδά τε σὸν φιλέει καὶ ἐχέφρονα Πηνελόπειαν.

protect the goods accumulated in the house by guarding the door of the storeroom day and night and keeping watch over everything (2.345–7).

These good servants have an equally good master, that is, a master who knows how to recognize the work that has been done on his behalf. As Eumaeus says, if Odysseus was there, 'he would have shown [him] generous favour and given [him] possessions for [his] own—a farm, a farmhouse, a wife any man would be glad to wed—such gifts as a kindly master does give a servant who has worked for him hard and has had his work prospered by heaven' (14.62–6). And this is exactly what does happen when Odysseus returns, as we see from the promises he makes to his two loyal servants: 'If the god delivers the suitors into my hands, I will find wives for you both and give you possessions and well-built houses near my own; and from henceforward in my eyes you two shall be comrades and brothers (ἑτάρω τε κασιγνήτω τε) of Telemachus' (21.213–16).[4]

It is an idyllic tableau. And the reward is even greater than Eumaeus expects: he will not only have a house, it will be 'a well-built house' close to that of Odysseus and he will become, metaphorically at least, a member of the family,[5] like Eurycleia, whom Laertes regarded as highly as he did his own wife (1.432).

The *Odyssey* also depicts a very close and informal relationship between the servants and the mistress of the house: they speak frankly to her, ask questions, and receive gifts which they take back to the countryside, which 'comfort a servant's heart' (15.368–70). We could be (despite the divide of several centuries between the two works) in Xenophon's *Oeconomicus*, with Penelope prefiguring the ideal wife of the Athenian gentleman farmer, Ischomachus. But, if we look more closely, the *Odyssey* contains a certain number of details that suggest a less rosy picture. The rewards are not simply given for effort, to the servant who has 'laboured' for the master, but for results (the gods must ensure that the work bears fruit, and the field must bear a good crop). The master is free to have sexual relations as he pleases with any of his female servants and the care taken by the poet to point out that Laertes did not sleep with Eurycleia suggests that such restraint was exceptional. The lying speech that Athena addresses to Telemachus in Book 15, when she urges him to return home, confirms this

[4] On the idea of the companion (ἑταῖρος) see Spahn 2006: 175–83.

[5] Thalmann 1998: 86–7.

impression, as she advises him to 'entrust this or that prized possession to whichever maidservant seems to you the trustiest, until the gods grant you a noble bride' (15.24–6); that is, to take a concubine. (Even if this speech is deceptive, any lie has to be plausible to its addressee, so that such a speech might say more about real social relations than an 'objective' description of reality.) Similarly, Eumaeus' words in Book 17 suggest that fear is as important as respect in master–servant relationships and that harsh rebukes are a common phenomenon in the world of the *Odyssey*: 'I reverence [my master] and have fears of being upbraided later—a master's rebukes are hard to bear' 17.188–9). This point of view is shared by the master: Odysseus does not separate respect from fear when dealing with his servants.[6]

(b) The family

The house is also the household, the family members whose solidarity must be perfect. In Book 6, Odysseus praises the 'harmony between husband and wife (*ὁμοφρονέοντε νοήμασιν*), a thing which brings much distress to the people who hate them and pleasure to the well-wishers, and for them the best reputation' (6.183–5), since it constitutes the most solid foundation for the prosperity of the household. But, as we saw in Chapter 9 (p. 291), this harmony, despite claims to the contrary,[7] does not imply the elimination of 'gender hierarchy and reverse domination and subordination' as it invariably involves the acceptance by the wife of the husband's ideas. This is illustrated in the *Odyssey* by two contrasting examples: one positive, Odysseus' house, saved by Penelope's fidelity, and one negative, Agamemnon's house, destroyed by Clytemnestra's infidelity.

As well as demonstrating the importance of agreement between husband and wife, the *Odyssey* also emphasizes the bonds between fathers and sons. In the Underworld, once Odysseus has discovered the causes of his mother's death, his first question to her is about his father and his son: 'Tell me of my father and of the son I left behind' (11.174). Agamemnon too is only concerned about his own son

[6] *Odyssey*, 6.306: *ἠμὲν ὅπου τις [δμώων ἀνδρῶν] νῶι τίει καὶ δείδιε θυμῷ.*
[7] Felson-Rubin 1994: 64.

(11.457–60) and, a little later on, Achilles also asks Odysseus about his son and then about his father (11.492–7).

The similes reinforce this impression. The joy of a shipwrecked man who finally sees land is compared to that felt by a son on learning that his father has recovered from an illness (5.394–9). Conversely, Eumaeus' joy at Telemachus' safe return is conveyed through the image of a father welcoming home his only son who has returned from abroad after a ten-year absence (16.17–21).

We should also mention the happiness of Nestor who is blessed with 'an old age of comfort in his own palace and sons who are wise and who are excellent warriors' (4.210–11) or Laertes who, at the end of Book 24, sees his son and grandson 'vying for the prize of valour' (24.515), thus demonstrating that they are worthy members of a family renowned throughout the world for its courage and strength. In the aristocratic world of the *Odyssey*, valour and wisdom are both hereditary, as Menelaus emphasizes after listening to the words of the son of the wise Nestor: 'Friend, those were wise words and an older man could speak and act no better. You are your father's son; your wisdom in speech comes from him. There is no mistaking the child of a man whom the son of Cronos marked out for happiness both at birth and at his wedding' (4.204–8) As we saw above (Chapter 9, pp. 243–4), the portrait of Telemachus, also reveals a son who shows himself to be the image of his father in intelligence, self-control, and, finally, in Books 22 and 24, courage in battle, thus proving that he is really Odysseus' son and his worthy successor.

The example of Telemachus also seems to show that, although the son remains under the authority of his father, he has authority over his mother from the moment when he attains adulthood. I will not reopen here the vexed question of Penelope's *kurios* or ask who really has the power to give her hand in marriage (the various contradictory indications in the text can be perfectly well explained by the fact that this question is always going to remain purely theoretical, given that Odysseus is alive and Penelope will not remarry).[8] Twice, however, the son is able to send his mother back to her quarters[9] and, although

[8] At *Odyssey*, 2.113–14, for example, Antinous cites Telemachus' order to his mother, the authority of Penelope's father, and the queen's own choice as possible reasons for her remarriage.

[9] *Odyssey*, 1.356–9, 21. 350–53.

he refuses to send her away against her will,[10] there is nothing in the text to indicate that he could not do so if he wished. For, during Odysseus' absence, Telemachus is the true master of the house, as he declares on several occasions.[11] This is only to be expected in a work which states that, despite women's responsibility to look after the household, they only do this under their husbands' authority.[12]

(c) The honour of the house

All the various elements of the house combine to form a single entity. The house has its own collective honour which is indistinguishable from that of its master. Dishonouring Odysseus' house is the same thing as dishonouring Odysseus himself.[13] And any act of aggression towards any of the members of the household is an attack on the master's honour which he must avenge. The clearest illustration of this principle is of course the story of Odysseus who 'will be revenged on whoever affronts his wife and his noble son' (14.163–4). The Greek, *καὶ τείσεται ὅς τις ἐκείνου ἐνθάδ' ἀτιμάζει ἄλοχον καὶ φαίδιμον υἱόν* (literally 'whoever dishonours his wife and son'), emphasizes the fact that Odysseus' wife and child are, in a way, merely extensions of him and that any dishonour inflicted upon them dishonours him above all. This also explains the change of persons and the easy slippage from 'we' (or more precisely, 'the two of us', since it is a dual) to 'you' (singular) when Odysseus is speaking to his son after the recognition scene in Book 16: 'we should do well to test the menservants too—where among them are those who still have regard and heartfelt reverence for you and me (*νῶι τίει καὶ δείδιε*), and who are those who care nothing for us and disesteem you (*σὲ δ' ἀτιμᾷ*) as you now are' (16.305–7). The misdeeds of the maidservants who sleep with the suitors are also described, using the same half line (*αἵ τέ σ' ἀτιμάζουσι* '[the women] who are disloyal to you'), as outrages committed against Telemachus,[14] at one moment, and against

[10] *Odyssey*, 2.130–1, 20.343–4.
[11] *Odyssey*, 1.251, 397–8, 2.64, 16.128, 20.264–5.
[12] *Odyssey*, 7.68: *ὅσσαι νῦν γε γυναῖκες ὑπ' ἀνδράσιν οἶκον ἔχουσιν*.
[13] *Odyssey*, 16.431: *τοῦ νῦν οἶκον ἄτιμον ἔδεις*; 21.332–3: *οἶκον ἀτιμάζοντες ἔδουσιν | ἀνδρὸς ἀριστῆος*.
[14] *Odyssey*, 16.317 (Odysseus speaking to Telemachus).

Odysseus himself at another.[15] Similarly, when the consumption of the house's wealth and the insults suffered by Penelope are mentioned they are always explicitly defined as the wealth and the wife of Odysseus, showing that it is his honour that is at stake.[16] Even insults to Eurycleia, to whom Odysseus has given a certain degree of authority, are considered by Odysseus to be insults directed against him (22.417–25).

From the moment when the guest is first invited inside the house he is under the protection of its master and thus has the right to be well treated and respected by everyone in it. The insults and blows that he receives therefore represent attacks on the honour of the head of the household who is obliged to intervene. This is why, at 18.215–25, Penelope reproaches Telemachus for having allowed the beggar to be insulted in his palace and condemns his inaction which is a source of dishonour for him because he has been insulted through his guest. Telemachus accepts this interpretation when he expresses his indignation after Ctesippus mistreats Odysseus, saying: 'It would be far better for me to perish than to watch such monstrous things continually—guests maltreated and maidservants dragged in shame down the noble hall' (20.316–19). It makes no difference that the same maidservants are willing accomplices, as we see at the beginning of Book 20. What counts is the will of the master of the house. Any man who sleeps with his serving maids without his consent is guilty of rape and of insulting his honour.

If the integrity of the house is the central theme of the *Odyssey* it is because the house is always presented as an extension of its master. But it would also be possible to reverse the situation and to say that the master is only ever the embodiment of his house, so inextricably linked are they. As John Halverson has rightly pointed out,[17] even for Penelope, attachment to the house and attachment to her husband are indissolubly linked, as we see from the lines in which Penelope explains her dilemma to the beggar: 'My mind shifts hither and thither, wondering if I should stay with my son and keep everything unchanged—my estate, my waiting-women, my lofty-roomed house

[15] *Odyssey*, 19.498: *αἵ τέ σ᾽ἀτιμάζουσιν* (Eurycleia speaking to Odysseus). See also 22.418 (Odysseus speaking), *αἵ τέ μ᾽ ἀτιμάζουσι.*

[16] *Odyssey*, 18.144–5: *κτήματα κείροντας καὶ ἀτιμάζοντας ἄκοιτιν | ἀνδρός*: 24.459–460: *κτήματα κείροντες καὶ ἀτιμάζοντες ἄκοιτιν | ἀνδρὸς ἀριστῆος.*

[17] Halverson 1992: 186–7.

itself—respecting my husband's bed and the people's voice; or if I should now go with whatever Achaean lord seems noblest as he woos me and offers my kinsmen countless gifts' (19.524–9). We may also quote the lines in which she laments the fact that she will one day have to leave a house (δῶμα) that she calls κουρίδιον ('of her marriage').[18] This is not a purely romantic attachment to the past since she goes on to describe the house as 'beautiful and full of treasures'. What she refuses to leave here is her 'marital home' to which she is married at least as much as she is married to Odysseus seeing that, in both the *Iliad* and the *Odyssey*, the adjective κουρίδιος (usually translated 'wedded') is used of the 'husband' (πόσις or ἀνήρ) or the wife (ἄλοχος or γύνη) with the exception of these two passages, where it is used of the house, and at *Iliad* 15.40 where it is used of the bed. In the *Odyssey* the marital bed symbolizes the permanence of the couple and of the house that belongs, first and foremost, to Odysseus. The ferocity with which he carries out his vengeance shows exactly how much value Homeric men attach to the integrity of their house.

2. THE CITY

Unlike the world of the Cyclopes, Odysseus' world is not one where the household can exist in isolation, cut off from other households. They are an integral part of a political sphere and are linked by ties of collaboration and competition. This is not the place to join in the historians' debates about the extent to which Ithaca can be defined as a city-state (*polis*), as the answer will always depend on the exact definition of the *polis* we choose to use. My purpose here is simply to sketch a picture of the social strata in the *Odyssey* and to ask about the complex relationships that link the members of the elite to each other and about the role played—or not played—by the common people in a work that adopts the point of view of the elite[19] and presents an idealized image of a patriarchal monarchy.[20]

[18] *Odyssey*, 19.579–80 = 21.77–8.

[19] See Strasburger 1997: 55, Morris 1986: 120–7, Raaflaub 1991: 248–50, van Wees 1992: 153–7, Thalmann 1998, 285.

[20] Rose 2009: 310.

(a) The elite and the people

Like the *Iliad*, the *Odyssey* depicts a society that is clearly divided in two, as was noted by Hermann Strasburger (1997: 49) and Moses Finley (1978: 63), with, on the one hand, an upper class composed of noble families (that is to say, landowners) and, on the other, the people. The gulf between the two groups is immense. It is even expressed in physical terms: in Odysseus' world, the members of the elite recognize one another at first glance, as we see from the words of Menelaus when he first sets eyes on Telemachus and the son of Nestor: 'You belong to the race of heaven-protected and sceptred kings; no lesser parents could have such sons' (4.63–4).

This difference in nature is, of course, reflected in the different treatment accorded to the two groups. I will illustrate this with one example that, although indirect, is highly revealing. It needs, however, to be read in the light of an episode from the *Iliad* which I will deal with first. This is the moment in *Iliad* 2 when Agamemnon's attempt to test the morale of his troops nearly goes disastrously wrong. He had hoped that his suggestion that they give up the expedition and return home (2.139–41) would be violently rejected by his soldiers. But the exact opposite happens. Agamemnon has hardly finished speaking when the Achaeans start to run 'cheering to the ships' (2.142–54). At Hera's request, Athena urges Odysseus to intervene, telling him to 'use gentle words to turn the men back one by one' and not to 'let them haul their balanced ships down to the water' (2.180–1). But Odysseus' actions are rather different, and it is this difference that is of interest to us here. In fact, it is only 'kings and men of importance' (ὅν τινα μὲν βασιλῆα καὶ ἔξοχον ἄνδρα κιχείη, 2.188) whom he turns back 'with gentle words' (2.189). By contrast, 'whenever he sees a commoner and finds him shouting' (ὃν δ' αὖ δήμου τ' ἄνδρα ἴδοι βοόωντά τ' ἐφεύροι, 2.198) he: 'strikes him with the sceptre and berates him, saying: "Friend, sit quiet and listen to what others tell you, your superiors (καὶ ἄλλων μῦθον ἄκουε οἳ σέο φέρτεροί εἰσι)—you are a coward and a weakling, of no account either in war or in counsel"' (2.199–202). Neither the words nor the actions here could be described as gentle and this episode points to the treatment Odysseus will mete out to Thersites, with the same sceptre, a little later in Book 2.244–66. This common man will also be beaten for his speech, which in parts repeats word for word the insults thrown at Agamemnon by Achilles in

Book 1. There could hardly be a clearer illustration of the difference in treatment received by nobles and common men, between an Achilles and a Thersites, in the Homeric world.

Book 24 of the *Odyssey* contains a similar scene. Athena, wishing to put an end to the civil war that is in danger of breaking out, gives orders to the people of Ithaca and to Odysseus in turn. When speaking to the people, she simply gives commands and does not justify her orders: 'Men of Ithaca, cease from the toil of warfare; separate at once, and shun bloodshed' (24.531–2). The resulting panic causes them to turn on their heels at once (24.533–6). When speaking to Odysseus, however, she addresses him using a full range of honorific titles and takes the trouble to argue her case: 'Son of Laertes and seed of Zeus, Odysseus of many subtleties, now control yourself, make an end of the strife of inexorable war, lest Zeus the Thunderer should be angry with you' (24.542–4).

The massacre of the suitors had already shown, in its way, that the nobility and commoners are not equal in death. All the suitors, who are 'elite young men' (*κοῦροι κεκριμένοι*, 16.248) and 'all noble' (*πάντες ἄριστοι*, 16.251), are killed honourably in combat by Odysseus and his supporters. But, as we have seen, the goatherd Melanthius suffers a horrible and shameful fate: his body is mutilated and his sexual organs thrown to the dogs (22.475–7).

(b) The ideal *polis*

The ideal *polis* should overcome this divide. When this occurs 'the whole people is in festivity' (9.6), as among the Phaeacians.[21] This implies, as we saw in Chapter 6 above (p. 182), perfect harmony between the members of the ruling class, that is, the twelve 'kings' whom Homer usually calls 'leaders and lords of the Phaeacians' (*Φαιήκων ἡγήτορες ἠδὲ μέδοντες*, eight occurrences). These are distinguished by the honours paid to them by the people—and good order requires that this be always vested in the same families[22]—and by their regular participation in the banquets given by the king. For Phaeacia is a hereditary monarchy: Alcinous, after his father Nausithous and his brother Rexenor, 'has the supremacy in the land' (11.353) and 'the people listened to him as to a god' (7.11). And even

[21] See Olson 1995: 184–9.

[22] *Odyssey*, 7.148–50.

if Odysseus describes himself as the 'suppliant of the king and all the people' (8.157), the decision to transport him home is made by Alcinous alone who also decides on the presents he should be given.

The Ithaca of former times, in the days of Odysseus' reign, is also an image of order in a patriarchal monarchy whose structure is closely modelled on that of the family, as Moses Finley remarked long ago.[23] Odysseus ruled Ithaca 'like a good father' as the *Odyssey* states on two occasions,[24] and dispensed justice in a manner that is described above all in negative terms by the absence of exactions and of favouritism (4.687–93). He thus embodied the ideal of the good king as depicted in the famous simile in Book 19 evoking

> a virtuous king who fears the gods and who rules a strong well-peopled kingdom. He upholds justice, and under him the dark soil yields wheat and barley; trees are weighed down with fruit, sheep never fail to bear young and the sea abounds in fish—all this because of his righteous rule, so that thanks to him his people prosper (19.109–14)

The same ideal is also to be found in Hesiod's *Works and Days*, 225–37.

A reign such as this should be followed by an uneventful succession, as in the scenario described to Odysseus by his mother at 11.184–6, with Telemachus, inheriting the kingdom, ruling his inheritance 'in peace and tranquillity' (ἕκηλος) and organizing banquets as a king should. This is, in fact, what will happen after the end of the *Odyssey*, when Odysseus regains power, as Tiresias promises him that he will die amid general prosperity,[25] and an omen interpreted by Theoclymenus in Book 15 predicts that power will remain with the house of Odysseus since 'no family in the land of Ithaca is more kingly than your own' (15.533–4).

(c) The threat of civil war

In the city of Argos the *Odyssey* also contains an image of total disorder, where the murder of the king forces the people to submit to the usurper Aegisthus (even if this is only a temporary state which ends when the legitimate heir, Orestes, regains power (3.304–5)).

[23] M. Finley 1978: 79 (see also 83).

[24] *Odyssey*, 2.234 = 5.12: πατὴρ δ' ὣς ἤπιος ἦεν.

[25] *Odyssey*, 11.136–7: ἀμφὶ δὲ λαοὶ | ὄλβιοι ἔσσονται.

Throughout the poem we also see vivid illustrations of the crisis which threatens to overthrow the royal family on Ithaca and could have done so elsewhere, in every place in which a king went off to war leaving an aged father and son who was too young to rule, as we see from the fears voiced by Achilles in Book 11. He asks whether his father is still honoured as before or whether people have taken advantage of his age to dishonour him (11.494–7).

It is, therefore, possible to claim that the *Odyssey* gives us the first analysis of a phenomenon that will haunt classical Greece: civil war (*stasis*). Long before Thucydides, Homer analyses the possible causes in the dialogue between Odysseus and Telemachus in Book 16. In lines 95–8 Odysseus suggests two causes: opposition between the royal family and the 'people' (*λαοί*) who have taken against them because of 'some oracle from a god' or, alternatively, conflict within the ruling family itself, struggles which pit brother and against brother (one thinks immediately of the classic example of the rivalry between the two sons of Oedipus, Eteocles and Polynices). But Telemachus, in his reply to Odysseus, proposes a third, which is the right one: the appearance of divisions within the elite with, on one side, Telemachus, and on the other 'the great island chieftains in Dulichium, in Same, in forested Zacynthus, and those who are princes in craggy Ithaca' (16.122–4).

But it is above all the consequences of such divisions that are emphasized in the *Odyssey*. First of all there is the attempt to assassinate Telemachus, which the *Odyssey*, being steadfast in its support of the right of succession, condemns through the words of Amphinomus. In Book 16.400–5, he reminds the suitors that it is a 'serious matter (*δεινόν*) to kill a prince of the blood' and insists that they first consult the gods, who in fact show themselves to be entirely opposed by sending the omen at 20.241–3. There are also the threats uttered by suitors at 22.213–23 against anyone, like Mentor, who supports Telemachus: death and the confiscation of his possessions (including those abroad) as well as exile for all the members of his family.

It is in this context that the people may intervene. When Telemachus calls the assembly in Book 2 it is in order to try to provoke the indignation of the people at the suitors' plundering of his house, to ask them to put an end to the disorderly behaviour that is causing them to lose the respect of their neighbours, and to threaten them with the wrath of the gods (2.64–7). Mentor's speech, in which he reproaches the people for their failure to act and to restrain the suitors by reprimands even though they have the advantage of numbers, says much the same (2.229–41). Penelope, in Book 4, also thinks that Laertes may be able to go to the people and provoke them to act (4.735–41). And in Book 16.374–82, the suitors express their concern that a skilful speech by Telemachus might prompt the people to take action, and that the assembly might formally condemn their crimes and force them to leave the country. Such an intervention by the people would not be without precedent, as the poem makes clear through Penelope's reproaches to Antinous:

> Do you not know that your own father fled here for refuge in terror of the people? They were raging violently against him because he had joined the Taphian pirates to harass the Thesprotians, though these were close friends of ours. The people were set on killing him, making an end of him, devouring his patrimony themselves—it was rich and tempting. Yet Odysseus checked their passion and held them back. (16.424–30)

A popular uprising is thus a possibility and represents a permanent threat to the members of the elite.

During internal struggles between members of the elite (and here we find yet another feature of what will later be the classic definition of *stasis*) it is perfectly possible for one party to appeal for help to allies from abroad in order to vanquish its opponents. In Book 2, what the suitors fear, and what explains their desire to stop Telemachus leaving, is that he might 'bring back men to fight for him, from sandy Pylos or else from Sparta' (*ἤ τινας ἐκ Πύλου ἄξει ἀμύντορας ἠμαθόεντος ἢ ὅ γε καὶ Σπάρτηθεν*, 2.326–7). Conversely, Laertes expresses the fear in Book 24.353–5 that the suitors' kinsmen might send messengers throughout Cephallenia. But Zeus finally decides to intervene to put an end to the civil war and to impose, through Athena, a reconciliation backed up by oaths. In so doing, he founds the Ithacan dynasty anew, requiring the deaths of brothers and sons to be forgotten, and re-establishes concord, prosperity, and peace on Ithaca (24.482–6).

3. THE STRANGER

The *Odyssey* is also a traveller's tale. It tells of Odysseus' travels in Books 5 to 13, but also Telemachus' travels in Books 1 to 4, and we can even include under this heading Odysseus' travels to and on Ithaca in Books 13 to 22, seeing that he disguises himself as a foreigner. The question of hospitality therefore lies right at the heart of the poem.[26] In the Homeric world, giving hospitality is a religious duty because 'Zeus is patron of every stranger and every beggar, and to such as these, even a humble gift means much' (6.207–8). He is the 'protector of guests' (*ξεῖνιος*, 14.284) and of suppliants (*ἱκετήσιος*, 13.213). He 'accompanies' them (*ὀπηδεῖ*),[27] feels a righteous anger (*νεμεσσᾶται*, 14.284) against anyone who mistreats them, watches out for transgressions of the laws of hospitality and 'avenges' them (*ἐφορᾷ καὶ τίνυται ὅς τις ἁμάρτῃ*, 13.214). For this reason, suppliants and guests deserve respect[28] and must be treated as 'brothers' (8.546), that is, as equals.

Hospitality is regulated by very precise rules: the stranger must be offered a bath and clean clothes. He must be invited to join his hosts at the table, which is the best way of demonstrating his temporary integration into the community, and must take part in the feast where he is honoured by being given the best place and a choice piece of meat. Finally he must be given a gift (*ξείνιον*), which may take the form of the meal itself,[29] and be given, if necessary, the means to return home.

Hospitality also implies reciprocity. As Moses Finley and, more recently, Evelyne Scheid-Tissinier and Walter Donlan have shown, the Homeric world relies for its smooth functioning on a system of gifts and counter-gifts.[30] As in many traditional societies, the gift marks the beginning of a process of exchange and places the recipient under an obligation. This is shown most clearly in the dialogue between Odysseus and Laertes in Book 24. Odysseus, who has introduced himself as former host of Odysseus, begins by enumerating with great satisfaction the gifts he gave him: 'I offered him at his departure the presents that such a guest deserved. I gave him seven talents of worked gold, a mixing bowl, all of silver and patterned with flowers, twelve single cloaks and as many rugs and fine robes and

[26] See Scheid-Tissinier 1994: 115–76 and Spahn 2006: 201–8.

[27] *Odyssey*, 7.165 and 181, 9.271.

[28] They are *αἰδοῖοι*: *Odyssey*, 7.165 and 181 and 9.271.

[29] *Odyssey*, 5.91–2, Calypso's welcome to Hermes, *ἀλλ' ἕπεο προτέρω, ἵνα τοι πὰρ ξείνια θείω*, is immediately followed by her setting a table: *ὣς ἄρα φωνήσασα θεὰ παρέθηκε τράπεζαν*.

[30] Finley 1978, Scheid-Tissinier 1994, and Donlan 1997.

tunics, and besides all this, four women of his own choice, handsome and skilled in all proper tasks' (24.273–9). But Laertes replies, in tears, that he has given all this for nothing:

As for all the gifts you bestowed so lavishly on your guest, they were given in vain (*δῶρα δ' ἐτώσια ταῦτα χαρίζεο*), though had you found him alive in Ithaca he would have responded with equal gifts and warm hospitality before he let you depart (*τῷ κέν σ' εὖ δώροισιν ἀμειψάμενος ἀπέπεμψε καὶ ξενίῃ ἀγαθῇ*); such return of hospitality is just and right (*ἣ γὰρ θέμις*). (24.283–6)

Travel can also be a means of testing the morality of the various peoples encountered along the way. This means that recounting a journey does not just involve identifying the peoples but also saying whether they are just or unjust, as we see from Alcinous' question to Odysseus: 'But come now, tell me fully and faithfully: what lands have you wandered through, what countries of men have you visited? What of the men themselves, what of their pleasant-sited cities? Who among them were harsh and lawless and barbarous (*ὅσοι χαλεποί τε καὶ ἄγριοι οὐδὲ δίκαιοι*)? Who were hospitable and god-fearing (*οἵ τε φιλόξεινοι, καί σφιν νόος ἐστὶ θεουδής*)?' (8.573–6). The welcome extended to Odysseus and his companions is one way of distinguishing the just, that is the good hosts, from the impious who show no respect for strangers or suppliants.

The Cyclopes, who have no fear of or respect for the gods (9.275–6) belong to the second category and are the very embodiment of injustice (9.106, 215). Instead of giving his guests food to eat, Polyphemus 'feels no shame to devour [his] guests in [his] own home' (9.478–9). He also mocks the practice of giving presents 'as custom expects from host to guest' (*ξεινήιον ... δωτίνην ἥ τε ξείνων θέμις ἐστίν*, 9.267–8). The first gift (*ξεινήιον*, 9.370) he gives Odysseus is the promise to eat him last of all, the second gift (*ξείνια*, 9.517) is more ironic still: he asks Poseidon to 'grant him his homecoming' (9.518) but it is to be in the worst possible circumstances: 'If he is fated to see his kith and kin and to reach his high-roofed house and his own country, let him come late and come in misery, after the loss of all his comrades, and carried upon an alien ship; and in his own house let him find mischief' (9.532–5).

The injustice of the Laestrygonians is also expressed through their inversion of the rites of hospitality: instead of welcoming the strangers with a feast, Antiphates 'clutched one of [Odysseus'] men at once and made a meal of him' (10.116) and his subjects, after crushing

Odysseus' fleet with rocks, go fishing for the crew, 'spearing men like fish and carrying home their monstrous meal' (10.123–4). The monster Scylla, who is also compared to a fisherman, also devours Odysseus' companions in a similar manner (12.251–7).

Good hosts, by contrast, respect the rules of hospitality scrupulously. The first example, Aeolus, 'treated [Odysseus] as a guest-friend (φίλει) for a whole month' (10.14) He invites him to his banquets and 'speeds his return' (10.18) by giving him the 'gift' of the bag of winds. Once Odysseus' identity has been revealed, Circe also acts as the perfect hostess. She gives baths, clothes, and banquet first to Odysseus and then to his companions (10.348–73, 449–52). She promises to 'give [him] passage home' (10.483–4) and keeps her promise: through two sets of prophecies she sets out the path that Odysseus must follow to the Underworld and then to the island of the Sun, passing by Scylla and Charybdis (10.488–540, 12.37–110). She also gives him what he needs to make the proper sacrifices to the gods of the Underworld (10.571–2). The last people encountered by Odysseus on his travels are also the most hospitable. The Phaeacians are not content to perform the rites on one occasion only but repeat them several times. We have already seen this in the case of the gifts (see Chapter 6, p. 183). But it applies just as much to the rest. First of all Nausicaa offers him a bath, clothing, and food (6.209–16, 246–8). Once he arrives at Alcinous' palace, Odysseus is given another meal followed by the promise of a fresh banquet and passage home to his country (7.162–76, 190–6). In Book 8, Odysseus is given another bath and another feast, before being conveyed home in Book 13.

In comparison to these perfect hosts, Calypso is a rather more ambiguous figure. At the beginning, she acts according to the rules: 'she welcomes him and tends him'[31] and even offers to make him immune to old age and death. After learning of Zeus' decision from Hermes she gives him advice 'without concealment' (5.143), promises to give him provisions and clothing for the journey and to make a favourable wind blow (5.165–8). She gives him a meal, gives him the equipment he needs to construct his raft, and keeps all her promises faithfully, after bathing him and giving him fragrant clothes. But in contrast to Circe and the Phaeacians who refuse to keep Odysseus any

[31] *Odyssey*, 5.135, 7.255–6, 12.450.

longer than he wishes (10.489, 7.315), she 'forces' him to stay on her island for seven years (5.14–15, 154).

When we go from the mythical universe of Odysseus' travels to the infinitely more real world in which his son's travels take place, we find a society in which hospitality is the rule. As we saw above (Chapter 5, pp. 141 and 144), Nestor in Pylos and Menelaus in Sparta act as perfect hosts towards Telemachus. At the beginning of Book 15, Menelaus even offers to accompany Telemachus on a journey around Greece that would allow him to collect even more guest-presents: 'If you wish to visit more of Hellas and of Argos and have me with you, then I will harness the horses and guide you to the cities of men; no one will send us on empty-handed; each will give us something at least, a fine bronze tripod or a cauldron, a pair of mules or a golden goblet' (15.80–5).

We can also add the stories of Cretan Odysseus who often mentions the generous hospitality that he either gave or received in the past, which is an indirect, but very effective, way of ensuring that he is well treated by his hosts. He also tells Eumaeus how, in Egypt, he was protected from the anger of the people by the king: 'The king kept them away from me, fearing the wrath of Zeus who protects strangers and who more than all other gods shows his displeasure at deeds of wickedness. In that place I stayed for seven years, and I gathered much wealth among the men of Egypt, because they all made me gifts' (14.283–6). In conversation with Penelope, he gives a detailed account of how he once received Odysseus: 'I myself brought him into the house and gave him all hospitality, entertaining him unstintingly from the wealth of things the palace offered; and besides this, I drew on the public store to give the comrades sailing with him supplies of barley and glowing wine and cattle for slaughter enough for their desire' (19.194–8).

We saw above (Chapter 7, pp. 191, 197–201) how his time on Ithaca, from the moment when he arrives at Eumaeus' home up to the moment when he reveals his identity to the suitors and begins the massacre, provides Odysseus with the opportunity to tell the 'good', characterized by their respect for the rules of hospitality, and the 'bad' who constantly break them. In the first group are Eumaeus, who knows that it is 'a monstrous thing (οὔ μοι θέμις ἔστ') not to honour any guest who comes to me, even one more miserable than you' (14.56–7), Telemachus, who refuses to drive away by force (μύθῳ ἀναγκαίῳ, literally 'with an order that constrains', 17.399) a guest from his house, and Penelope, who tells her serving women to prepare a bath for Odysseus before taking him to the feast and seating him near her son (19.317–22). In the second are the suitors who interrupt the system of exchanges of which the feast should normally be part and fail to invite others in return, preferring to waste the resources of Odysseus' house without making any return (1.376–7) and greet the stranger with blows and insults.

The *Odyssey* can thus be read, if not as a guide to proper behaviour, at least as a collection of examples illustrating how to act and how not to act in relation to others.

Conclusion: The *Odyssey*: An Epilogue to the *Iliad*?

According to the author of the treatise *On the Sublime*, the *Odyssey* is nothing other than an 'epilogue to the *Iliad*' (9.12). It is certainly true that it features the same characters, depicted in very similar ways. In particular, there is a definite continuity between the hero of the *Odyssey* and the Odysseus of the *Iliad* who was characterized by his courage in war, his cunning intelligence, and his powers of endurance,[1] to the extent that he was said to be able to 'go through blazing fire and come back safe [as] the skill of his mind is without equal' (*Iliad*, 10.246–7). Twenty years later, the Nestor encountered by Telemachus on his travels, ruling peacefully over Pylos surrounded by his sons and respected by the people, is the same pious and prudent old man that we see in the *Iliad*.

But other characters have changed. Helen is no longer the unfaithful wife for whose sake the Trojans and Achaeans suffered so much. She now plays the role of the model wife alongside Menelaus, who lives in luxury surrounded by the treasures he has brought back from his wanderings in faraway lands, and invites a crowd of relatives to a banquet to celebrate the marriages of his two children.

The two *nekuiai* of Book 11 and Book 24 also show the heroes transformed in death: Agamemnon is now just the victim of Clytemnestra and Aegisthus, Achilles would prefer to lead the miserable life of a serf rather than reign, as he does, in the Underworld, and Ajax

[1] We can see this from the epithets *πτολίπορθος* (two occurrences), *πολύμητις* (eighteen occurrences), *ποικιλομητής* (one occurrence), *πολμήχανος* (seven occurrences), *πολύτλας* (five occurrences), and *ταλασίφρων* (one occurrence) used to qualify him in the *Iliad*.

retains his incurable resentment against Odysseus, because of his failure to win the arms of Achilles. But the *Odyssey* does more than simply show the heroes of the *Iliad*, it is haunted by the war at Troy 'where the Greeks endured sufferings' (3.100) both 'roving for plunder over the misty sea, wherever Achilles led the way' and 'fighting round the great city of King Priam' (3.104–5). Through the stories told by various characters and the songs of the bards, Phemius and Demodocus, it even continues the story and fills in the gaps in the *Iliad*, by relating the events that occurred between the funeral of Hector, at the end of the *Iliad*, and the fall of Troy. The *Odyssey* scrupulously avoids repeating the subject matter of the *Iliad*:[2] when Demodocus sings of the 'quarrel' (νεῖκος) of Achilles it is not the quarrel with Agamemnon with which the *Iliad* opens and which marks the beginning of the Achaeans' misfortunes, but a quarrel between Achilles and Odysseus that pleased Agamemnon because it was a sign that victory for the Greeks was near (8.75–82). It also continues the story of the war by telling the tales of the returns of the various Greek leaders and providing a detailed account of the last and longest of these homecomings, that of Odysseus who is still kept back by Calypso when 'all those others who had escaped the pit of destruction were safe in their own lands' (1.11–12).

The *Odyssey* also represents the continuation of the *Iliad* in its structure as well as its content. Just as the *Iliad* avoids treating the whole of the Trojan War, only covering a short period of time, the *Odyssey* does not recount the whole of Odysseus' adventures following the fall of Troy. It only tells of the end. The organization of the narrative also has much in common with that of the *Iliad*. In both poems the gods hold a discussion in Book 1, there is an assembly of the people in Book 2, the violence reaches a peak in Book 22 with the death of Hector in the *Iliad* and the massacre of the suitors in the *Odyssey*, and, finally, Book 24 brings peace and reconciliation.

It is also possible to detect, as has been done in several places in this book, a series of echoes and variations which are too precise to be explained by the fact that both works derive from the same oral tradition and draw on the same stock of formulaic poetry. This occurs at the level of individual words, as we saw in the case of the three variants on the famous formula used by Hector as he sends

[2] See Rutherford 2001: 120–1 on the various reasons that have been put forward to explain this silence.

Andromache back to the female domain: 'war will be the men's concern.' But it also occurs at the level of gesture: Achilles and Telemachus are the only heroes who throw their sceptres to the ground after speaking at the assembly. But this gesture has a very different significance in each case. In this sense, the *Odyssey* could be called the first palimpsest text in Western literature, justifying an intertextual reading of the type undertaken by Alfred Heubeck in his study of 'The *Odyssey*-Poet and the *Iliad*' (*Der Odyssee-Dichter und die Ilias*) and, more recently, by D. N. Maronitis, 'Hidden References to the *Iliad* in the *Odyssey*', Pietro Pucci in a book entitled *Odysseus Polutropos: Intertextual Readings in the Odyssey and the Iliad*, and R. B. Rutherford in his article 'From the *Iliad* to the *Odyssey*'. But this type of reading does not, in my opinion at least, imply any presuppositions about the written nature of these two texts. Nor am I sure that it is necessary to identify the approach of the critic, whose judgements are always the result of comparisons, with that of the author (if, indeed, there ever was a 'Homer'!).

It is also true that the two poems display at least as many differences as they do similarities,[3] in the personality of their heroes, their tone, and the worlds they portray. Although both celebrate 'great suffering' the relationships established between this suffering and their respective heroes are diametrically opposed. In the *Iliad*, this suffering is first of all brought by the hero upon his companions: the prologue contains an implicit criticism of the 'accursed wrath of Achilles, son of Peleus' which 'brought countless sufferings to the Achaeans and hurled down to Hades many mighty souls of heroes' (1.2–4). In the *Odyssey*, by contrast, the suffering is endured by the hero in order to save his companions: the prologue celebrates the man who 'suffered many troubles in his heart, labouring to save himself and to bring his comrades home' (1.4–5).

Achilles is a solitary hero. It is true that, like his father Peleus, he is one of the descendants of Aeacus. On several occasions he is defined as 'the son of Peleus' (fifty-two occurrences) and is once called the father of Neoptolemus (*Iliad*, 19.326–7). But the special bond between him and Patroclus is stronger than these blood ties, as is clear from his lament at the death of Patroclus: 'There could be no worse suffering for me, not even if I heard of the death of my

[3] See Rutherford 2001: 135–45.

father . . . or the death of my dear son, godlike Neoptolemus, who is being brought up in Scyros, if indeed he still lives', *Iliad*, 19.321–7). He may be the leader of the Myrmidons, but no one would think of defining him as 'the man from Phthia'.

Odysseus, by contrast, introduces himself to Alcinous as the man who 'lives in far-seen Ithaca', 9.21. He places himself within a network of family relationships as the 'son of Laertes' (thirty occurrences), whose own son is Telemachus (referred to twenty-one times as 'son of Odysseus') and whose wife is Penelope (referred to as the 'wife of Odysseus' on eight occasions). This wanderer is the most rooted of men, which is what enables him to travel for so long without losing sight of his ultimate destination. Despite Calypso who 'seeks continually with her soft and coaxing words to beguile him into forgetting Ithaca' (1.56–7) and urges him to stay with her by announcing the troubles that await him on his voyage home and when he arrives (5.206–7), he dreams only of his homecoming, of seeing the smoke rise from his native land once again, of being reunited with his family and seeing his wife again.[4]

These two heroes also differ in the choices they make. As was revealed to him by his mother Thetis, Achilles was able to choose between two fates, staying in Troy and dying there in battle and acquiring 'glory that will never die' or returning home to live a long life, but without glory (*Iliad*, 9.410–16). In Book 18 he seals his fate when he decides to fight Hector and gives up any hope of return, as the text emphasizes on several occasions. Odysseus, however, owes his glory to his 'perilous journey home' (*Odyssey*, 9.37, 23.351). He is the man who chooses life and embodies 'the heroic refusal of immortality' (Vernant 1996: 188) despite the fact that he could have stayed with Calypso who promised to spare him the trials of old age and death. It took the arrival of the 'decadent' Imperial period and the irony of Lucian to make Odysseus express his regrets at this choice in a letter that he passes secretly to the Nymph.[5]

In Antiquity, the sophist Hippias contrasted Achilles, the embodiment of simplicity and truth, to Odysseus, who represented duplicity and lies.[6] Jean Starobinski has developed this contrast and provided a superb analysis of everything that distinguishes the two heroes: Achilles, who 'hates like the gates of Hades the man who hides one

[4] *Odyssey*, 1.58–9, 5.114, 11.161–2.
[5] Lucian, *True Histories*, 2.35.
[6] Plato, *Hippias Minor*, 364e–365c.

thing in his mind and speaks another' (*Iliad*, 9.312–13), and the 'man of many turns' who owes his glorious reputation to his stratagems and even echoes Achilles' words ironically at *Odyssey*, 14.156–7, at the very moment when he is skilfully mixing truth (the news that Odysseus is about to return) and falsehood (a life story that is a pure tissue of lies). The hero who undergoes a noble death and is willing to risk everything in the moment is able to indulge in the luxury of not dissembling. He would, moreover, be incapable of dissimulation because doing so would mean that he was able to follow his father's advice to 'hold down [his] heart's high passion in [his] breast' (*Iliad*, 9.255–6). For Achilles to be able to master his passions requires nothing less than the intervention of Athena who tells him to 'stop [his] fury', to put an end to the quarrel, and to 'restrain [him]self'.[7] Much-enduring Odysseus, by contrast, who chooses to confront the difficulties of life and to exist in the long term, is the very embodiment of self-control: he knows how to 'defer the moment of action',[8] how to command his soul to endure, how to restrain himself, and he also sometimes—though not always—manages to restrain the impulses of others. This is what allows him to hide behind 'temporary fictions' which are ways of 'safeguarding a permanent project'[9] and to achieve a goal that remains unchanging.

Achilles was a hero who cared nothing for the necessities of life, refusing to eat or drink until Patroclus' death was avenged. It was Athena who protected him from hunger by instilling nectar and ambrosia, the nourishment of the gods, in his breast. He was even willing to order the Achaeans to fight immediately, 'hungry and unfed' (*Iliad*, 19.207), until Odysseus wisely reminded him that it was essential for the troops to eat and drink if they were to fight courageously (*Iliad*, 19.160–70). The Odysseus of the *Odyssey*, although he curses his stomach on several occasions,[10] knows that its demands must be satisfied and that the body has needs that cannot be ignored.

This realism and this ability to adapt to circumstances enable Odysseus to survive in a world that is in constant flux. The hero is well aware that the world is, in the words of Montaigne, a 'perpetual see-saw' ('une branloire perenne'), that the human condition, in

[7] *Iliad*, 1.207, 210, 215. [8] Starobinski 1989: 279.
[9] Starobinski 1989: 281.
[10] *Odyssey*, 7.216–22, 17.286–9, 473–7, 18.53–4.

contrast to that of the gods, is unstable, and that the human must adapt to circumstances:

Earth mothers nothing more frail than man. As long as the gods grant him prosperity, as long as his limbs are lithe, he thinks he will suffer no misfortune in times to come; but when instead the Blessed Ones send him sorrow, he bears these also with endurance, because he must. The father of gods and men makes one day unlike another day, and earthlings change their thoughts on life in accord with this. (*Odyssey*, 18.130–7)

The world of the *Iliad* was characterized by its stability and by the correspondence between appearance and reality: Achilles, 'the best of the Achaeans', was also, along with Nireus, 'the most handsome' (*Iliad*, 2.673–4) while Thersites, the anti-hero who inspired disgust in both Achilles and Odysseus, was 'the ugliest man that went to Troy' (*Iliad*, 2.216). The world of the *Odyssey* is, by contrast, a world of constant change where appearances are often deceptive. The sons of kings can become slaves or beggars, as in the story of Eumaeus and in the life stories of Cretan Odysseus. A king can take on the appearance of a beggar. Thanks to Athena's magic, Odysseus is transformed into an aged, bald beggar with wrinkled skin and dull eyes. His father, Laertes, is an unkempt and badly dressed old man who lives in the countryside like the most humble peasant. Conversely, Antinous seems to be 'the best of the Achaeans'—he is a 'kinglike man' (*Odyssey*, 17.415–16)—but behaves like the worst of villains.

It is certainly the case that the *Odyssey* concludes with the re-establishment of order: Odysseus regains his power both in his palace and in his city, confident that in Telemachus he has a son who resembles his father and a worthy successor; thanks to Athena, his father regains his looks and his stature; harmony reigns on Ithaca, bringing with it peace and prosperity. But the threats he faced, as well as the awareness of his own fragility and of the instability of human affairs, no doubt explain why the world of Odysseus, unlike that of the *Iliad*, is not confined to the elite and encompasses bards, beggars, and servants like swineherd Eumaeus or Eurycleia the nurse. It was for very similar reasons that Herodotus in his *History* mentions small cities alongside large ones, because he is well aware that 'those which were great once are small today' and that 'human prosperity never abides long in the same place' (1.5).[11]

[11] Translation by A. de Sélincourt (Harmondsworth, 1954).

While the *Iliad* presented a homogeneous world in which Achaeans and Trojans shared the same values (not until the Persian Wars do the Trojans become 'barbarians'), the *Odyssey* represents 'the savage' in contrast to the civilized world which is defined by agricultural labour, the practice of sacrifice and of cooking.[12] It thus offered the Greeks for the first time a mirror-like image of the Other in which they would never cease to contemplate themselves and, before even Herodotus, lays the foundations of an enquiry (*ἱστορίη*, 'history') of which modern ethnography is just another manifestation.

How can we explain these differences? By the advancing age of the author, as ancient authors like Pseudo-Longinus thought?[13] By positing two different authors, as most modern critics believed? Or two different dates? There is no simple solution. But even if the causes remain unclear, the consequences are not: alongside the archaic monumentality of the *Iliad*, the *Odyssey* seems astonishingly modern thanks to the personality of its hero who, from Greek tragedy to James Joyce and Kazantzakis, has undergone the most numerous and diverse reincarnations, thanks also (or perhaps above all) to its complex organization and its ironic presentation which have never ceased to fascinate modern readers of narrative literature.

[12] Vidal-Naquet 1996.
[13] Pseudo-Longinus, *On the Sublime*, 9.13–15.

Bibliography

Allan, W. 2006. 'Divine Justice and Cosmic Order in Early Greek Epic', *JHS* 126: 1–35.

Allen, T. W. 1912. *Homeri opera*, V. Oxford.

Allione, L. 1963. *Telemaco e Penelope nell'Odissea*, Turin.

Amory, A. 1963. 'The Reunion of Odysseus and Penelope', in C. H. Taylor (ed.), *Essays on the Odyssey*, Bloomington, Ind.: 100–21.

Amory-Parry, A. 1971. 'Homer as an Artist', *CQ* 65: 1–15.

Andersen, Ø. 1973. 'Der Untergang der Gefährten in der *Odyssee*', *SO* 49: 7–27.

—— 1977. 'Odysseus and the Wooden Horse', *SO* 52: 5–18.

Antonaccio, C. 1995. *An Archeology of Ancestors: Tomb-Cult and Hero-Cult in Early Greece*, Lanham, Md.

Arend, W. 1933. *Die typische Szenen bei Homer*, Berlin.

Armstrong, J. L. 1958. 'The Arming Motif in the Iliad', *AJP* 79: 337–54.

Auerbach, E. 1968. *Mimesis: The Representation of Reality in Western Literature*, trans. W. R. Trask, Princeton.

Austin, N. J. E. 1969. 'Telemachos Polymechanos', *California Studies in Classical Antiquity*, 2: 45–63.

—— 1972. 'Name Magic in the Odyssey', *California Studies Classical Antiquity*, 5: 1–20.

—— 1975. *Archery at the Dark of the Moon*, Berkeley.

—— 1983. 'Odysseus and the Cyclops: Who is Who?', in Rubino and Shelmerdine 1983: 3–37.

Bader, F. 1976. 'L'Art de la fugue dans l'Odyssée', *REG* 89: 18–39.

Bakker, E. 2002. 'Polyphemos', *Colby Quarterly*, 38: 135–50.

—— and Fabricotti, F. 1991. 'Peripheral and Nuclear Semantics in Homeric Diction: The Case of Dative Expressions for Spear', *Mnemosyne*, 44: 63–84.

Beck, G. 1965. 'Beobachtungen zur Kirke-Episode in der *Odyssee*', *Philologus*, 109: 1–24.

Bennet, J. 1997. 'Homer and the Bronze Age', in Morris and Powell 1997: 511–33.

Bergk, T. B. 1872. *Griechische Literaturgeschichte*, vol. i, Berlin.

Bergren, A. 1981. 'Helen's Good Drug: *Odyssey* IV 1–305', in S. Kresic (ed.), *Contemporary Literary Hermeneutics and Interpretation of Classical Texts*, Ottawa: 201–14.

Beye, C. R. 1974. 'Male and Female in the Homeric Poems', *Ramus*, 3: 87–101.

Bittlestone, R., Diggle, J., and Underhill, J. 2005. *Odysseus Unbound: The Search for Homer's Ithaca*, Cambridge.

Blok, J., and Mason, P. (eds.). 1987. *Sexual Asymmetry: Studies in Ancient Society*, Amsterdam.

Blümlein, G. 1971. *Die Trugreden des Odusseus*, diss. Frankfurt.

Bollack, J. 1997. 'Ulysse chez les philologues', repr. in *La Grèce de personne*, Paris: 29–59 (1st pub. 1975).

Bremer, J. M. 1975. 'Het elfde boek van de Odyssee', *Lampas*, 8: 115–43.

—— De Jong, I. J. F., and Kalff, J. 1987. *Homer: Beyond Oral Poetry. Recent Trends in Homeric Interpretation*, Amsterdam.

Brillante, C. 1990. 'Scene oniriche nei poemi omerici', *Materiali e discussioni*, 24: 95–111.

Büchner, W. 1937. 'Probleme der homerischen Nekya', *Hermes*, 72: 104–22.

—— 1940, 'Die Penelopeszenen in der Odyssee', *Hermes*, 75/2: 129–67.

Burkert, W. 1987. 'The Making of Homer in the Sixth Century BC: Rhapsodes versus Stesichorus', in D. von Bothmer (ed.), *Papers on the Amasis Painter and his World*, Malibu, 1987: 43–62; repr. in C. Riedweg (ed.), *Kleine Schriften I. Homerica*, Göttingen, 2001.

—— 1997. 'The Song of Ares and Aphrodite', in G. M. Wright and P. V. Jones (eds.), *Homer: German Scholarship*, Oxford: 249–62 (1st pub. 1960).

Butler, S. 1897. *The Authoress of the Odyssey: Where and When She Wrote, Who She Was, the Use She Made of the Iliad, and How the Poem grew under her Hands*, London (repr. 1922).

Buxton, R. 2004. 'Similes and Other Likenesses', in Fowler 2004a: 139–55.

Cairns, D. (ed.). 2001. *Oxford Readings in Homer's Iliad*, Oxford.

Calame, C. 1977. 'Le Mythe des Cyclopes dans l'Odyssée', in B. Gentili and G. Paioni (eds.), *Il mito greco: Atti del Convegno Internazionale Urbino 1973*, Rome: 369–91.

Carpenter, R. 1946. *Folklore, Fiction and Saga in Homeric Epic*, Berkeley.

Cartledge, P. 1996. 'La nascita degli opliti e l'organizzazione militare', in S. Settis (ed.), *I Greci: Storia, cultura, arte, societa*, i: *Noi e i Grece*, Turin: 681–714.

Chantraine, P. 1954. 'Le Divin et les dieux chez Homère', in *Entretiens Hardt 1*, Geneva: 47–94.

—— 1965–73. *Grammaire Homérique*, 2 vols., Paris.

—— 2009. *Dictionnaire étymologique de la langue grecque: Histoire des mots*, 2nd edn., Paris.

Charles, M. 1995. *Introduction à l'étude des textes*, Paris.

Clausing, A. 1913. *Kritik und Exegese der homerischen Gleichnisse im Altertum*, diss. Freiburg.

Clayton, B. 2003. *A Penelopean Poetics: Reweaving the Feminine in Homer's Odyssey*, Lanham, Md.

Coffey, M. 1957. 'The Function of the Homeric Simile', *AJP* 78: 113–32.

Cohen, B. (ed.). 1995. *The Distaff Side: Representing the Female in Homer's Odyssey*, Oxford.

Coldstream, N. J. 1976. 'Hero-Cults in the Age of Homer', *JHS* 96: 8–17.
—— 1977. *Geometric Greece*, London.
Collombier, A.-M. 2002. 'Le Destin d'Eumée (*Odyssée* xv, 400–484): Trafics d'esclaves dans les poèmes homériques', in M. Garrido-Hory (ed.), *Routes et marchés d'esclaves*, 26e colloque du GIREA, Besançon: 7–19.
Combellack, F. 1959. 'Milman Parry and Homeric Artistry', *Comparative Literature*, 11: 193–208.
Cook, E. 1995. *The* Odyssey *in Athens: Myths of Cultural Origins*, Ithaca, NY.
—— 1999–2000. 'Active and Passive Heroics in the Odyssey', *CW* 93/2: 149–67.
—— 2004. 'Near Eastern Sources for the Palace of Alcinoos', *AJA* 108/1: 43–77.
Cook, J. M. 1992. 'The Topography of the Plain of Troy', repr. in Emlyn-Jones, Hardwick, and Purkis 1992: 167–74 (1st pub. 1984).
Crane, G. 1988. *Calypso: Background and Conventions of the Odyssey*, Athenäum Monografien 191, Frankfurt am Main.
Creuzer, G. F. 1845. *Die Historische Kunst der Griechen in ihre Entstehung und Fortbildung*, Leipzig.
Crielaard, J. P. (ed.). 1995a. *Homeric Questions: Essays in Philology, Ancient History and Archaeology*, Amsterdam.
—— 1995b. 'Homer, History and Archaeology: Some Remarks on the Date of the Homeric World', in Crielaard 1995a: 201–88.
Danek, G. 1998. *Epos und Zitat: Studien zu den Quellen der Odyssee*, Wiener Studien Beiheft 22, Vienna.
—— 2002. 'Odysseus between Scylla and Charybdis', in Hurst and Letoublon 2002: 15–25.
Davies, J. K. 1992. 'The Reliability of the Oral Tradition', repr. in Emlyn-Jones, Hardwick, and Purkis 1992: 211–25 (1st pub. 1984).
De Jong, I. J. F. 1987. *Narrators and Focalizers: The Presentation of the Story in the Iliad*, Amsterdam.
—— 1992. 'The Subjective Style in Odysseus' Wanderings', *CQ* 42: 1–11.
—— 1993. 'Studies in Homeric Denomination', *Mnemosyne*, 46: 289–306.
—— 1994. 'Between Words and Deeds: Hidden Thoughts in the Odyssey', in I. J. F De Jong and J. P. Sullivan (eds.), *Modern Critical Theory & the Classics*, Leiden: 27–50.
—— 1997. 'Homer and Narratology', in Morris and Powell 1997: 305–25.
—— 2001. *A Narratological Commentary on the* Odyssey, Cambridge.
Delebecque, E. 1958. *Télémaque et la structure de l'Odyssée*, Aix en Provence.
Detienne, M. 1996. *Masters of Truth in Archaic Greece*, New York.
—— and Vernant, J. P. 1974. *Les Ruses de l'intelligence: La Mètis des Grecs*, Paris.
Devereux, G. 1957. 'Penelope's Character', *Psycho-analytic Quarterly*, 26: 378–86.
Di Benedetto, V. 1994. *Nel laboratorio di Omero*, Turin.

—— 1998. 'Letteratura del secondo grado: L'Odissea tra riusi e ideologia del potere', *Rivista di cultura classica e medioevale*, 40/1–2 (repr. in V. Di Benedetto, *Il richiamo del testo: Contributi di filologia e letteratura*, Pisa, 2007: ii. 705–39).

—— 2003. 'Ulisse: conoscere o regnare?', in S. Nicosia (ed.), *Ulisse nel tempo: La metafora infinita*, Venice: 79–105 (repr. in V. Di Benedetto, *Il richiamo del testo: Contributi di filologia e letteratura*, Pisa, 2007: ii. 741–67).

Dimock, G. E. 1963. 'The Name of Odysseus', repr. in C. H. Taylor Jr. (ed.), *Essays on the Odyssey*, Bloomington, Ind.: 54–72 (1st pub. 1956).

Dirlmeier, F. 1971. *Das serbokroatische Heldenlied und Homer*, Heidelberg.

Dodds, E. R. 1951. *The Greeks and the Irrational*, Sather Classical Lectures 25, Berkeley.

Doherty, L. E. 1995a. 'Sirens, Muses and Female Narrators in the Odyssey', in Cohen 1995: 81–92.

—— 1995b. *Siren Songs: Gender, Audience and Narrators in the Odyssey*, Ann Arbor.

—— 2009. *Oxford Readings in Classical Studies: Homer's Odyssey*, Oxford.

Donlan, W. 1997. 'The Homeric Economy', in Morris and Powell 1997: 649–67.

Dougherty, C. 2001. *The Raft of Odysseus: The Ethnographic Imagination of Homer's 'Odyssey'*, Oxford.

Dubel, S., and Rabau, S. (eds.). 2001. *Fiction d'auteur: Le Discours biographique sur l'auteur de l'Antiquité à nos jours*, Paris.

Duckworth, G. E. 1966. *Foreshadowing and Suspense in the Epics of Homer, Apollonios and Vergil*, New York (1st pub. 1933).

Dueck, D. 2000. *Strabo of Amasia: A Greek Man of Letters in Augustan Rome*, London.

Dupont-Roc, R., and Le Boulluec, A. 1976. 'Le Charme du récit (Odyssée IV. 219–289)', in *Écriture et théorie poétique: Lectures d'Homère, Eschyle, Platon, Aristote*, Paris: 30–9.

Durante, M. 1957. 'Il nome di Omero', *Rendiconti morali dell'Accademia dei Lincei*, ser. 8, 12/1–2: 94–111.

Eaton, D. E. 1984. 'Hittite History and the Trojan War', in Foxhall and Davies 1984: 23–35.

Edwards, M. 1966. 'Some Features of Homeric Craftsmanship', *TAPhA* 97: 115–79.

—— 1970. 'Homeric Speech Introductions', *HSCP* 74: 1–36.

—— 1975. 'Type-Scenes and Homeric Hospitality', *TAPhA* 105: 51–72.

—— 1986. 'The Conventions of Homeric Funerals', in J. H. Betts, T. T. Hooker, and J. R. Green (eds.), *Studies in Honour of T. B. L. Webster*, Bristol: 84–92.

—— 1987. 'Topos and Transformation in Homer', in Bremer, De Jong, and Kalff 1987: 47–60.

—— 1989. 'On Some Answering Expressions in Homer', *CP* 64: 82–7.

Edwards, M. 1991. *The Iliad: A Commentary. Books 17–20*, Cambridge.
—— 1992. 'Homer and the Oral Tradition: The Type-Scene', *Oral Tradition*, 7: 284–330.
—— 1997. 'Homeric Style and "Oral Poetics" ', in Morris and Powell 1997: 261–83.
Eide, T. 1980. 'A Note on the Homeric *χείρ παχείη*' *SO* 55: 23–6.
—— 1986. 'Poetical and Metrical Value of Homeric Epithets: A Study of the Epithets Applied to *χείρ*', *SO* 61: 5–17.
Emlyn-Jones, C. 1984. 'The Reunion of Penelope and Odysseus', *G&R* 31: 1–10.
—— 1986. 'True and Lying Tales in the Odyssey', *G&R* 33: 1–10.
—— 1992. 'The Homeric Gods: Poetry, Belief, and Authority', in Emlyn-Jones, Hardwick, and Purkis 1992: 91–103.
—— Hardwick, L., and Purkis, J. (eds.). 1992. *Homer: Readings and Images*, London.
Erbse, H. 1972. *Beiträge zum Verständnis der Odyssee*, Untersuchungen zur antiken Literatur und Geschichte 13, Berlin.
Eustathius. *Ad Iliadem*: Eustathius, *Commentariii ad Homeri Iliadem pertinentes ad fidem codicis Laurentiani*, ed. M. van der Valk, Leiden, 1971–87.
—— *Ad Odysseam*: Eustathius, *Commentarii ad Homeri Odysseam. Ad fidem exempli romai*, ed. G. Stallbaum, Leipzig, 1825–6.
Feeney, D. C. 1991. *The Gods in Epics: Poets and Critics of the Classical Tradition*, Oxford.
Felson-Rubin, N. 1987. 'Penelope's Perspective: Character from Plot', in Bremer, De Jong, and Kalff 1987: 61–83.
—— 1994. *Regarding Penelope: From Character to Poetics*, Princeton.
—— 1996. 'Penelope's Perspective: Character from Plot', in Schein 1996: 163–83.
—— and Slatkin, L. 2004. 'Gender and Homeric Epic', in Fowler 2004a: 91–114.
Fenik, B. 1968. *Typical Battle Scenes in the Iliad*, Wiesbaden.
—— 1974. *Studies in the Odyssey*, Hermes Einzelschriften 30, Wiesbaden.
—— (ed.). 1978. *Homer: Tradition and Invention*, Leiden.
Finkelberg, M. 1986. 'Is kl°ow êfyiton a Homeric Formula?', *CQ* 36: 1–5.
—— 1989. 'Formulaic and Nonformulaic Elements in Homer', *CP* 84: 179–87.
—— 1990. 'A Creative Oral Poet and the Muse', *AJP* 111: 293–303.
Finley, J. H. 1978. *Homer's Odyssey*, Cambridge, Mass.
Finley, M. 1964. 'The Trojan War', *JHS* 84: 1–10.
—— 1977a. *The World of Odysseus*, 2nd edn. London.
—— 1977b. 'Lost the Trojan War', repr. in *Aspects of Antiquity*, 2nd edn. London (1st pub. 1967).
—— 1978. *The World of Odysseus*, New York (1st pub. 1954).
Focke, F. 1943. *Die Odyssee*, Stuttgart.

Foley, H. P. 1978. 'Reverse Similes and Sex Roles in the Odyssey', *Arethusa*, 11: 7–26.

—— 1995. 'Penelope as Moral Agent', in Cohen 1995: 93–115.

—— 2001. *Female Acts in Greek Tragedy*, Princeton.

Foley, J. F. 1990. *Traditional Oral Epic: The Odyssey, Beowulf and the Serbo-Croatian Return Songs*, Berkeley.

—— 1991. *Immanent Art: From Structure to Meaning in Traditional Oral Epic*, Bloomington, Ind.

—— 1997. 'Oral Tradition and its Implications', in Morris and Powell 1997: 146–73.

Ford, A. 1992. *Homer: The Poetry of the Past*, Ithaca, NY.

Fornara, C. 1983. *The Nature of History in Ancient Greece and Rome*, Berkeley.

Fowler, R. 2004a. *The Cambridge Companion to Homer*, Cambridge.

—— 2004b. 'The Homeric Question', in Fowler 2004a: 220–32.

Foxhall, L., and Davies, J. K. (eds.). 1984. *The Trojan War: Its Historicity and Context*, Bristol.

Fränkel, H. 1921. *Die homerischen Gleichnisse*, Göttingen, 1921: 98–104 (trans. as 'Essence and Nature of the Homeric Similes', in G. M. Wright and P. V. Jones (eds.), *Homer: German Scholarship in Translation*, Oxford, 1997: 103–23).

Friedrich, R. 1975. *Stilwandel im homerischen Epos: Studien zur Poetik und Theorie der epischen Gattung*, Heidelberg.

—— 1987a. 'Thrinakria and Zeus' Ways to Men in the *Odyssey*', *GRBS* 28: 375–400.

—— 1987b. 'Heroic Man and Polymetis Odysseus in the Cyclopeia', *GRBS* 28: 121–33.

Garvie, A. F. 1994. *Odyssey Books VI–VIII*, Cambridge.

Germain, G. 1954. *Genèse de l'Odyssée*, Paris.

Goldhill, S. 1988. 'Reading Differences: Juxtaposition and the Odyssey', *Ramus*, 17: 1–31.

—— 1991. *The Poet's Voice: Essays on Poetics and Greek Literature*, Cambridge.

Gomme, A. W. 1954. *Greek Attitude to Poetry and History*, Berkeley.

Goody, J., and Gandah, W. K. 1972. *The Myth of the Bagre*, Oxford.

Grafton, A. 1991. *Defenders of the Text: The Tradition of Scholarship in an Age of Science, 1450–1800*, Cambridge, Mass.

Grandolini, S. 1998. *Canti e aedi nei poemi omerici*, Pisa.

Gray, D. 1947. 'Homeric Epithets for Things', *CQ* 61: 109–21.

Graziosi, B. 2002. *Inventing Homer: The Early Reception of Epic*, Cambridge.

—— and Haubold, J. 2005. *Homer: The Resonance of Epic*, London.

Greene, E. S. 1995. 'The Critical Element in the Embarkation Scenes of the Odyssey', *GRBS* 36: 217–30.

Griffin, J. 1977. 'The Epic Style and the Uniqueness of Homer', *JHS* 97: 39–53.

Griffin, J. 1980a. *Homer on Life and Death*, Oxford.
—— 1980b. *Homer*, Oxford.
—— 1986. 'Homeric Words and Speakers', *JHS* 106: 36–57.
—— 1987. *Homer: The Odyssey*, Cambridge (repr. 2003).
—— 2003. *Homer: The Odyssey*, 2nd edn., Cambridge.
Griffith, M. 1983. 'Personality in Hesiod', *CA* 2: 37–65.
Grossardt, P. 1998. *Die Trugreden in der Odyssee und ihre Rezepzion in der antiken Literatur*, Sapheneia 2, Bern.
Groten, F. J., Jr. 1968. 'Homer's Helen', *G&R* 15/1: 33–9.
Güterbock, H. G. 1986. 'Troy in Hittite Texts? *Wilusa, Ahhkiyawa* and Hittite History', in Mellink 1986: 33–44.
Hainsworth, J. B. 1966. 'Joining Battle in Homer', *G&R* 13: 158–66.
—— 1970. 'Criticism of an Oral Homer', *JHS* 90: 90–8.
—— 1984. 'The Fallibility of an Oral Heroic Tradition', in Foxhall and Davies 1984: 111–35.
—— 1993. 'Formulas', in *The Iliad. A Commentary*, iii: *Books 9–12*, Cambridge: 1–31.
Halverson, J. 1992. 'Social Order in the *Odyssey*', repr. in Emlyn-Jones, Hardwick, and Purkis 1992: 177–90 (1st pub. 1985).
—— 1986. 'The Succession Issue in the Odyssey', *G&R* 33: 119–28.
Hampl, F. 1961. 'Die Ilias ist kein Geschichtsbuch', *Serta Philologica Aenipontana*, 1: 37–63.
Hansen, W. 1997. 'Homer and the Folktale', in Morris and Powell 1997: 442–62.
Harder, R. 1960. 'Odysseus und Kalypso', in *Kleine Schriften* (Munich): 148–63.
Harsh, P. W. 1950. 'Penelope and Odysseus in *Odyssey* XIX', *AJPh* 71: 1–21.
Haslam, M. 1997. 'Homeric Papyri and Transmission of the Text', in Morris and Powell 1997: 55–100.
Heath, J. 2001. 'Telemachus PEPNUMENOS: Growing into an Epithet', *Mnemosyne*, 54: 129–57.
Heath, M. 1998. 'Was Homer a Roman?', *Papers of the Leeds International Latin Seminar*, 10: 23–56.
Helleman, W. E. 1995. 'Homer's Penelope', *EMC* 39: 227–50.
Hellwig, B. 1964. *Raum und Zeit im homerischen Epos*, Spudasmata 2, Hildesheim.
Hermann, G. 1832. *De interpolationibus Homeri*, Lipsiae.
Heubeck, A. 1974. *Die homerische Frage*, Darmstadt.
—— 1978. 'Homeric Studies Today', in Fenik 1978: 1–17.
—— 1979. 'Geschichte bei Homer', *Studi Micenei ed egeo-anatolici*, 20: 227–50.
—— 1983. *Odissea vol. III (Libri IX–XII)*, ed. A. Heubeck, Fondazione Lorenzo Valla.
—— 1984. 'Homer und Mykene', *Gymnasium*, 91: 1–14.
—— 1986. *Odissea vol. VI (libri XXI–XXIV)*, ed. M. F. Galiano and A. Heubeck, Fondazione Lorenzo Valla.

—— 1991. 'Studien zur Struktur der Ilias', repr. in J. Latacz, *Homer: Die Dichtung und ihre Deutung*, Wege der Forschung 634, Darmstadt: 450–74 (1st pub. 1950).

—— and Hoekstra, A. 1989. *A Commentary on Homer's Odyssey*, ii: *Books IX–XVI*, Oxford.

—— and West, S. 1981. *Odissea vol I (libri I–IV)*, ed. A. Heubeck and S. West, Fondazione L. Valla.

—— —— and Hainsworth, J. B. 1988. *A Commentary on Homer's Odyssey I: Introduction and Books I–VIII*, Oxford.

Hillgruber, M. 1994–9. *Die pseudoplutarchische Schrift De Homero*, Beiträge zur Altertumskunde 57–8, Stuttgart.

Hoekstra, A. 1965. *Homeric Modifications of Formulaic Prototypes*, Amsterdam.

—— and Privitera, G. A. 1984. *Odissea vol. IV (Libri XIII–XVI)*, ed. A. Hoekstra, trans. G. A. Privitera, Fondazione Lorenzo Valla.

Holmberg, I. E. 1995. 'The Odyssey and Female Subjectivity', *Helios*, 22: 103–22.

Hölscher, U. 1960. 'Das Schweigen der Arete', *Hermes*, 88: 257–65.

—— 1988. *Die Odyssee: Epos zwischen Märchen und Roman*, Munich.

—— 1996. 'Penelope and the Suitors', Eng. trans. in Schein 1996: 133–40 (1st pub. 1967).

Hommel, H. 1976. 'Aigisthos und die Freier', repr. in *Symbola: Kleine Schriften zur Literatur und Kulturgeschichte der Griechen*, Hildesheim: 1–17 (1st pub. 1955).

Horrocks, G. 1997. 'Homer's Dialect', in Morris and Powell 1997: 193–217.

Hundt, J. 1935. *Das Traumglaube bei Homer*, Greifswald.

Hunzinger, C. 1997. 'Comment décider qu'un passage est interpolé? Les Interprétations des *Amours d'Arès et d'Aphrodite*: bilan bibliographique', *Lalies*, 17: 125–38.

Hurst, A., and Letoublon, F. (eds.). 2002. *La Mythologie et l'Odyssée: Hommage à Gabriel Germain*, Geneva.

In Iliadem: *Scholia Graec in Homeri Iliadem (scholia vetera)*, recensuit Hartmut Erbse, Berlin, 1969–88.

In Odysseam: *Scholia Graeca in Homeri Odysseam*, ed. G. Dindorf, Oxford, 1855.

Jacoby, F. 1933. 'Homerisches I: Der Bios und die Person', *Hermes*, 68: 1–50 (repr. in F. Jacoby, *Kleine Philologische Schriften*, ed. H. J. Mette, vol. i, Berlin, 1961).

Jaccottet, P. 1982. *Homère: L'Odyssée*, trans. and notes by P. Jaccottet. Paris.

Jaeger, W. 1960. 'Solons Eunomie'; repr. in *Scripta Minora* (Rome): i. 315–37 (1st pub. 1921).

Jahn, T. 1987. *Zum Wortfeld Seele-Geist in der Sprache Homers*, Zetemata 83, Munich.

Janko, R. 1981. 'Equivalent Formulas in the Greek Epos', *Mnemosyne*, 34: 251–64.

—— 1982. *Homer, Hesiod and the Hymns: Diachronic Development in Epic Diction*, Cambridge.

—— 1990. 'The *Iliad* and its Editors: Dictation and Redaction', *CA* 9: 326–34.

Jones, P. V. 1988. 'The Kleos of Telemachus: Od.1.95', *AJPh* 109: 495–506.

Jörgensen, O. 1904. 'Das Auftreten der Götter in den Büchern *i-k* der *Odyssee*', *Hermes*, 39: 357–82.

Kahane, A. 1992. 'The First Word of the Odyssey', *TAPhA* 122: 115–31.

—— 1994. *The Interpretation of Order: A Study in the Poetics of Homeric Repetition*, Oxford.

—— 1997. 'Quantifying Epic', in Morris and Powell 1997: 326–42.

Kakridis, J. T. 1949. *Homeric Researches*, Lund.

—— 1962. 'Helena and Odysseus', in R. Muth (ed.), *Serta Philologica Aenipontana*, Innsbruck: 27–36 (repr. in Kakridis 1971: 40 ff.).

—— 1971. *Homer Revisited*, Lund.

Katz, M. A. 1991. *Penelope's Renown: Meaning and Indeterminacy in the Odyssey*, Princeton.

Keaney, J. J., and Lamberton, R. 1996. [Plutarch,] *Essay on the Life and Poetry of Homer*, Atlanta.

Kearns, E. 2004. 'The Gods in the Homeric Epics', in Fowler 2004a: 59–73.

Kessels, A. H. M. 1978. *Studies on Dreams in Greek Literature*, Utrecht.

Kindstrand, J. F. 1990. [Plutarchus,] *De Homero*, Leipzig.

Kirchhoff, A. 1879. *Die homerische Odyssee*, Berlin (1st pub. 1859).

Kirk, G. S. 1962. *The Songs of Homer*, Cambridge.

—— 1976. *Homer and the Oral Tradition*, Cambridge.

Klingner, F. 1997. 'The Fight for Justice and the Departure of Telemachus', in Wright and Jones 1997: 192–216 (1st pub. 1944).

Korfmann, M. 1986a. 'Troy: Topography and Navigation', in Mellink 1986: 1–16.

—— 1986b. 'Besik Tepe: New Evidence for the Period of the Trojan Sixth and Seventh Settlements', in Mellink 1986: 17–28.

Kreuzer, F. 1845. *Die historische Kunst der Griechen in ihrer Entstehung und Fortbildung*, Leipzig (1st pub. 1803).

Krischer, T. 1971. *Formale Konventionen der homerischen Epik*, Zetemata 56, Munich.

—— 1985. 'Phäaken und Odysee', *Hermes*, 113: 9–21.

Kuhn, A. 1859. *Herabkunft des Feuers und des Göttertranks: Ein Beitrag zur vergleichenden Mythologie der Indogermanen*, Berlin.

Kullmann, W. 1960. *Die Quellen der Ilias*, Hermes Einzelschriften 14, Wiesbaden.

—— 1984. 'Oral Poetry and Neo-Analysis in Homeric Research', *GRBS* 25: 307–23.

—— 1985. 'Gods and Men in the *Iliad* and the *Odyssey*', *HSCPh* 89: 1–23.

—— 1992. 'Ergebnisse der motivgeschichtlichen Forschung zu Homer (Neoanalyse)'; repr. in *Homerische Motive*, Stuttgart: 100–34 (1st pub. 1991).

Lachmann, K. 1847. *Betrachtungen über Homers Iliad*, Berlin.

Lamberton, R. 1986. *Homer the Theologian: Neoplatonist Allegorical Reading and the Growth of Epic Tradition*, Berkeley.

—— and Keaney, J. J. 1992. *Homer's Ancient Readers*, Princeton.

Lambin, G. 1995. *Homère le compagnon*, Paris.

Latacz, J. 1968. 'APTEROS MUYOS, APTEROS FATIS, ungeflügelte Worte?', *Glotta* 46: 27–47.

—— 1977. *Kampfparänese, Kampfdarstellung und Kampfwirklichkeit in der Ilias, bei Kallinos und Tyrtaeus*, Zetemata 66, Munich.

—— (ed.). 1978. *Homer: Tradition und Neuerung*, Darmstadt.

—— (ed.). 1991a. *Zweihundert Jahre Homer-Forschung: Rückblick und Ausblick*, Colloquium Rauricum 2, Stuttgart.

—— (ed.). 1991b. *Homer: Die Dichtung und ihre Deutung*, Wege der Forschung 634, Darmstadt.

—— 1994. 'Lesersteuerung durch Träume: Der Traum Penelopes im 19. Gesang der Odyssee', in *Erschliessung der Antike: Kleine Schriften zur Literatur der Griechen und Romer*, Stuttgart: 205–24.

—— 1996. *Homer: His Art and his World*, trans. J. P. Holoka, Ann Arbor.

Lefkowitz, M. L. 1981. *The Lives of the Greek Poets*, London.

Lesky, A. 2001. *Göttliche und menschliche Motivation im homerischen Epos*, Heidelberg; Eng. trans. in Cairns 2001: 170–202 (1st pub. 1961).

Levine, D. B. 1983. 'Penelope's Laugh', *AJPh* 104/2: 172–8.

Levy, E. 1982. 'Le Rêve homérique', *Ktema*, 7: 23–41.

Lloyd-Jones, H. 1971. *The Justice of Zeus*, Sather Classical Lectures 41, Berkeley.

Lohmann, D. 1970. *Die Komposition der Reden in der Ilias*, Berlin.

Long, A. A. 1970. 'Morals and Values in Homer', *JHS* 90: 121–39.

Lonsdale, S. 1990. *Creatures of Speech: Lion, Herding and Hunting Similes in the Iliad*, Beiträge zur Altertumskunde 5, Stuttgart.

Lord, A. 1953. 'Homer's Originality: Oral Dictated Texts', *TAPhA* 84: 124–34.

—— 1960. *The Singer of Tales*, Cambridge, Mass.

—— 1971. 'Homer, Parry, and Huso', repr. in Parry 1971: 465–78 (1st pub. 1948).

Lorimer, H. L. 1950. *Homer and the Monuments*, London.

Luther, A. (ed.). 2006a. *Geschichte und Fiktion in der homerischen Odyssee*, Zetemata 25, Munich.

—— 2006b. 'Die Phaiaken der Odyssee und die Insel Euboia', in Luther 2006a: 77–92.

McDonald, W. E. 1997. 'On Hearing the Silent Voices: Penelope and the Daughters of Pandareus', *Helios*, 24: 3–22.

MacLeod, C. 1983. 'Homer on Poetry and the Poetry of Homer', in his *Collected Essays*, ed. O. Taplin, Oxford: 1–15.

Mactoux, M.-M. 1975. *Pénélope: Légende et mythe*, Besançon.

Maehler, H. 1963. *Die Auffassung des Dichtersberuf im frühen Griechentum bis zur Zeit Pindars*, Hypomnemata 5, Göttingen.

Marg, W. 1956. 'Der erste Lied des Demodokos', in *Navicula Chilonensis: Studia Philologica für F. Jacoby*, Leiden: 16–29.

—— 1971. *Homer über die Dichtung: Der Shield des Achilleus*, Münster.

Maronitis, D. N. 1981. 'Die erste Trugrede des Odysseus in der Odyssee: Vorbild und Variationen', in G. Kurz, D. Müller, and W. Nicolai (eds.), *Gnomosyne, Menschliche Denken und Handeln in der frühgriechischen Literatur: Festschrift W. Marg*, Munich: 117–34.

—— 1983. 'Références latentes de l'Odyssée à l'Iliade', in *Mélanges Édouard Delebecque*, Aix en Provence: 277–91.

Marquart, P. 1985. 'Penelope *Polutropos*', *AJPh* 106: 32–48.

Martin, R. P. 1989. *The Language of Heroes: Speech and Performance in the Iliad*, Ithaca, NY.

—— 1993. 'Telemachus and the Last Hero Song', *Colby Quarterly*, 29: 222–40.

Mattes, W. 1958. *Odysseus bei den Phäaken. Kritisches zur Homeranalyse.* Diss. Frankfurt Würzburg.

Matthiessen, K. 1988. 'Probleme der Unterweltsfhart des Odysseus', *GB* 15: 15–45.

Mehmel, F. 1955. 'Homer und die Griechen', *A&A* 4: 16–41.

Mellink, M. J. (ed.). 1986. *Troy and the Trojan War: A Symposium Held at Bryn Mawr College October 1984*, Bryn Mawr.

Merkelbach, R. 1951. *Untersuchungen zur Odyssee*, Munich (2nd edn. 1969).

Millar, C. M. H., and Carmichael, J. W. S. 1954. 'The Growth of Telemachus', *G&R* 1: 58–64.

Montanari, F. (ed.). 2002. *Omero tremila anni dopo*, Rome.

Morris, I. 1986. 'The Use and Abuse of Homer', *CA* 5: 81–138.

—— 1997. 'Homer and the Iron Age', in Morris and Powell 1997: 535–59 (revised in Cairns 2001: 57–91).

—— and Powell, B. (eds.). 1997. *A New Companion to Homer*, Leiden.

Morris, J. F. 1983. 'Dream Scenes in Homer: A Study in Variation', *TAPhA* 113: 39–54.

Most, G. 1989. 'The Structure and Function of Odysseus' Apologoi', *TAPhA* 119: 15–30.

Moulton, C. 1977. *Similes in the Homeric Poems*, Göttingen.

Mueller, M. 2007. 'Penelope and the Poetics of Remembering', *Arethusa*, 40: 337–62.

Murdock, G. P. 1981. *Atlas of World Cultures*, Pittsburgh.

Murnaghan, S. 1986. 'Penelope's *Agnoia*: Knowledge, Power and Gender in the Odyssey', *Helios*, 13/2: 103–15.

—— 1987. *Disguise and Recognition in the Odyssey*, Princeton.

—— 1994. 'Reading Penelope', in Oberhelman, Kelly, and Goslan 1994: 76–96.

—— 1995. 'The Plan of Athena', in Cohen 1995: 61–80.

Murray, O. 1980. *Early Greece*, London.

Myres, J. L. 1958. *Homer and his Critics*, ed. D. Gray, London.

Naerebout, F. G. 1987. 'Male–Female Relationships in the Homeric Epics', in Blok and Mason 1987: 109–27.

Nagler, M. N. 1967. 'Towards a Generative View of the Oral Formula', *TAPhA* 98: 269–311.

—— 1974. *Spontaneity and Tradition: A Study in the Oral Art of Homer*, Berkeley.

—— 1996. 'Dread Goddess Revisited', in Schein 1996: 140–61.

Nagy, G. 1979. *The Best of the Achaeans: Concepts of the Hero in Heroic Greece*, Baltimore.

—— 1990. *Pindar's Homer: The Lyric Possession of an Epic Past*, Baltimore.

—— 1996. *Homeric Questions*, Austin, Tex.

Notopoulos, J. A. 1964. 'Studies in Early Greek Oral Poetry', *HSCP* 63: 1–77.

Oberhelman, S. M., Kelly, V., and Goslan, R. J. (eds.). 1994. *Epic and Epoch: Essays on the Interpretation and History of a Genre*, Lubbock, Tex.

Olson, D. S. 1989a. '*Odyssey* 8: Guile, Force and the Subversive Poetics of Desire', *Arethusa*, 22: 135–45.

—— 1989b. 'The Stories of Helen and Menelaus (*Odyssey* 4.240–289) and the Return of Odysseus', *AJPh* 110/3: 387–94.

—— 1990. 'The Stories of Agamemnon in Homer's *Odyssey*', *TAPhA* 120: 57–71.

—— 1995. *Blood and Iron: Stories and Storytelling in Homer's Odyssey*, Mnemosyne Suppl. 148, Leiden.

Ong, W. J. 1982. *Orality and Literacy: The Technologizing of the Word*, London.

Osborne, R. 2004. 'Homer's Society', in Fowler 2004a: 206–19.

O'Sullivan, J. N. 1987. 'Observations on the Kyklopeia', *SO* 62: 5–24.

Page, D. 1955. *The Homeric Odyssey*, Oxford.

—— 1973. *Folktales in Homer's Odyssey*, Cambridge, Mass.

Palmer, P. L. 1962. 'The Language of Homer', in Wace and Stubbings 1962: 75–178.

Papadopoulou-Belmehdi, I. 1994. *Le Chant de Pénélope*, Paris.

Parry, A. M. 1989a. 'The Language of Achilles', repr. in Parry 1989d: 1–7 (1st pub. 1956).

Parry, A. M. 1989b. 'Have we Homer's *Iliad?*', repr. in Parry 1989d: 104–40 (1st pub. 1966).
—— 1989c. 'Language and Characterization in Homer', repr in Parry 1989d: 301–26 (1st pub. 1972).
—— 1989d. *The Language of Achilles and Other Papers*, Oxford.
Parry, H. 1994. 'The Apologos of Odysseus: Lies, All Lies', *Phoenix*, 48: 1–20.
Parry, M. 1971. *The Making of Homeric Verse: The Collected Papers of Milman Parry*, ed. A. M. Parry, Oxford.
Patzer, H. 1971. *Dichterische Kunst und poetische Handwerk im homerischen Epos*, Frankfurt.
Pedrick, V. 1988. 'The Hospitality of Noble Women in the Odyssey', *Helios*, 15: 85–103.
—— 1994. 'Eurycleia and Eurynomé as Penelope's Confidantes', in Oberhelman, Kelly, and Goslan 1994: 97–116.
Peradotto, J. 1990. *Man in the Middle Voice: Name and Narration in the Odyssey*, Princeton.
—— 1993. 'The Social Control of Sexuality: Odyssean Dialogics', *Arethusa*, 26: 173–82.
Pestalozzi, H. 1945. *Die Achilleis als Quelle der Ilias*, Zurich.
Pfeiffer, R. 1968. *History of Classical Scholarship*, Oxford.
Podlecki, A. J. 1967. 'Omens in the *Odyssey*', *G&R* 14: 12–23.
Porter, D. H. 1972–3. 'Violent Juxtaposition in the Similes of the Iliad', *CJ* 68: 11–21.
Powell, B. 1991. *Homer and the Origin of Greek Alphabet*, Cambridge.
—— 1997. 'Homer and Writing', in Morris and Powell 1997: 3–32.
Pralon, D. 1998. 'Homère et la poésie orale. 3', *Connaissance Hellénique*, 75: 11–21.
Privitera, G. A. 1993. 'L'*aristia* di Odisseo nella terra dei Ciclopi', in *Tradizione e innovazione nella cultura greca da Omero all'età ellenistica: Scritti in onore di B. Gentili*, Rome, i. 19–43.
Pucci, P. 1987. *Odysseus Polutropos: Intertextual Readings in the Odyssey and the Iliad*, Ithaca, NY.
—— 1998. *The Song of the Sirens: Essays on Homer*, Lanham, Md.
Raaflaub, K. 1991. 'Homer und die Geschichte des 8 Jahrhunderts v. Chr.', in Latacz 1991a: 205–56.
—— 1997. 'Homeric Society', in Morris and Powell 1997: 624–48.
Rabau, S. 1995. 'Une rivalité narrative: Hélène et Ménélas au chant IV de L'Odyssée 219–284', *Ktema*, 20: 273–85.
—— 1997a. 'Interpolation et lacune: Introduction', *Lalies*, 17: 103–12.
—— 1997b. 'Les Phéaciens sont des passeurs d'hommes', *Uranie*, 7: 91–114.
—— 2000. *Fictions de présence: La Narration orale dans le texte romanesque du roman antique au XXe siècle*, Paris.

—— 2001. 'Inventer l'auteur, copier l'œuvre: Des *Vies d'Homère* au *Pétrone romancier* de Marcel Schwob', in Dubel and Rabau 2001: 97–115.

Raddatz, G. 1913. 'Homeros', *RE* 8: 2188–213.

Rankin, A. V. 1962. 'Penelope's Dreams in Books XIX and XX of the Odyssey', *Helikon*, 2: 617–24.

Redfield, J. M. 1983. 'The Economic Man', in Rubino and Shelmerdine 1983: 218–47.

Reece, S. 1993. *The Stranger's Welcome: Oral Theory and the Aesthetics of the Homeric Hospitality Scene*, Ann Arbor.

—— 1994. 'The Cretan Odyssey: A Lie Truer than Truth', *AJPh* 115: 157–73.

Reinhardt, K. 1996. 'Die Abenteuer der Odyssee', Eng. trans. in Schein 1996: 63–132 (1st pub. 1948).

—— 1997a. 'Homer and the Telemachy, Circe, Calypso, the Phaeacians', Eng. trans. in Wright and Jones 1997: 217–48 (1st pub. 1948).

—— 1997b. 'The Judgement of Paris', Eng. trans. in Wright and Jones 1997: 170–91 (1st pub. 1960).

Rengakos, A. 1995. 'Zeit und Gleichzeitigkeit in den homerischen *Epen*', *A&A* 41: 1–33.

—— 1998. 'Zur Zeitstruktur der Odyssee', *WS* 111: 45–66.

—— 2002. 'Narrativität, Intertextualität, Selbstreferentialität', in M. Reichel and A. Rengakos (eds.), *Epea Pteroenta: Beiträge zur Homerforschung: Festschrift für W. Kullmann*, Stuttgart: 173–91.

Richardson, N. J. 1980. 'Literary Criticism in the Exegetical Scholia to the Iliad: A Sketch', *CQ* 30: 265–87.

—— 1981. 'The Contest of Homer and Hesiod and Alcidamas', *CQ* 31: 1–10.

—— 1984. 'Recognition Scenes in the Odyssey and Ancient Literary Criticism', *Liverpool Latin Seminar*, 4: 219–35.

—— 1987. 'The Individuality of Homer's Language', in Bremer, De Jong, and Kalff 1987: 165–84.

Richardson, S. 1990. *The Homeric Narrator*, Nashville.

Roisman, H. M. 1987. 'Penelope's Indignation', *TAPhA* 117: 59–68.

—— and Ahl, F. 1996. *The Odyssey Re-formed*, Ithaca, NY.

Romilly, J. de. 1985. *Homère*, Paris.

Rose, G. P. 1969. 'The Unfriendly Phaeacians', *TAPhA* 100: 387–406.

Rose, P. W. 2009. 'Class Ambivalence in the *Odyssey*', in Doherty 2009: 288–313 (1st pub. 1975).

Rubens, B., and Taplin, O. 1989. *An Odyssey round Odysseus*, London.

Rubino, C. A., and Shelmerdine, C. W. (eds.). 1983. *Approaches to Homer*, Austin, Tex.

Ruijgh, C. J. 1995. 'D'Homère aux origines proto-mycéniennes de la tradition épique: Analyse dialectologique du langage homérique, avec un excursus sur la création de l'alphabet grec', in Crielaard 1995a: 1–96.

—— 2000. 'La Genèse du dialecte homérique', *ZAnt* 50/1–2: 213–29.

Russo, J. 1966. 'The Structural Formula in Homeric Verse', *YCS* 20: 219–40.
—— 1968. 'Homer against his Tradition', *Arion*, 7: 275–95.
—— 1982. 'Interview and Aftermath: Dream, Fantasy and Intuition in Odyssey 19 and 20', *AJPh* 103: 4–18.
—— 1994. 'Homer's Style: Non Formulaic Features of an Oral Aesthetics', *Oral Tradition*, 9: 371–89.
—— 1997. 'The Formula', in Morris and Powell 1997: 238–60.
—— Galiano, M. F., and Heubeck, A. 1992. *A Commentary on Homer's Odyssey, III: XVII–XXIV*, Oxford.
—— and Privitera, G. A. 1985. *Omero, Odissea vol. V (libri XVII–XX)*, Fondazione Lorenzo Valla.
—— and Simon, B. 1968. 'Homeric Psychology and the Oral Epic Tradition', *Journal of History of Ideas*, 29: 483–98.
Rutherford, R. B. 1985. 'At Home and Abroad: Aspects of the Structure of the Odyssey', *PCPS* 31: 133–50.
—— 1986. 'The Philosophy of the Odyssey', *JHS* 106: 145–62.
—— 1992. *Homer Odyssey: Books XIX and XX*, Cambridge.
—— 2001. 'From the *Iliad* to the *Odyssey*', repr. in Cairns 2001: 117–46; 1st pub. 1991–3.
Ruyer, R. 1977. *Homère au féminin*, Paris.
Saïd, S. 1978. *La Faute tragique*, Paris.
—— 1979. 'Les Crimes des prétendants, la maison d'Ulysse et les festins de l'Odyssée', *Études de littérature ancienne*, Paris: 9–49.
Sale, W. 1989. 'The Trojans, Statistics and Milman Parry', *GRBS* 30: 341–410.
Schadewaldt, W. 1938. *Iliasstudien*, Darmstadt (repr. 1966).
—— 1952. *Von Homers Welt und Werk: Aufsätze und Auslegungen zur homerischen Frage*, Stuttgart (repr. 1965).
—— 1959. 'Kleiderdinge', *Hermes*, 87: 13–26.
—— 1960. 'Der Helios-Zorn in der *Odyssee*', in *Studi in onore di L. Castiglione*, Florence: 861–76.
—— 1970. 'Neue Kriterien zur Odyssee-Analyse: Die Wiedererkennnung des Odysseus und Penelope', in *Hellas und Hesperien: Gesammelte Schriften zur Antike und zur neueren Literatur in zwei Bänden*, 2nd edn., Zurich: i. 58–77.
—— 1991. 'Neue Kriterien zur Odyssee-Analyse. Die Wiedererkennung des Odysseus und der Penelope', repr. in Latacz 1991b: 340–65 (1st pub. 1959).
Scheid-Tissinier, E. 1994. *Les Usages du don chez Homère: Vocabulaire et pratiques*, Nancy.
Schein, S. L. 1970. 'Odysseus and Polyphemus in the *Odyssey*', *GRBS* 11: 74–83.
—— 1995. 'Female Representations and Interpreting the Odyssey', in Cohen 1995: 17–27.
—— (ed.). 1996. *Reading the Odyssey*, Princeton.

—— 2002. 'Mythological Allusion in the Odyssey', in Montanari 2002: 85–101.

Schenkeveld, D. M. 1976. 'Strabo on Homer', *Mnemosyne*, 29: 52–64.

Schmidt, J.-U. 2002. *Die Lügenerzahlungen des Odysseus als Spiegel eines neuen Weltbildes*, Hamburg.

Schmidt, M. 2006. 'Der Welt des Eumaios', in Luther 2006a: 117–38.

Scholia Graeca in Homeri Odysseam, ed. W. Dindorf, Oxford, 1855.

Schwartz, E. 1924. *Die Odyssee*, Munich.

Schwinge, E. R. 1991. 'Homerische Epen und Erzählforschung', in Latacz 1991b: 482–512.

Scott, J. A. 1918. 'Eurynome and Eurycleia in the *Odyssey*', *CQ* 12: 75–9.

Segal, C. P. 1962. 'The Phaeacians and the Symbolism of Odysseus' Return', *Arion*, 1: 17–64.

—— 1968. 'Circean Temptations: Homer, Vergil, Ovid', *TAPhA* 99: 419–42.

—— 1971. *The Theme of the Mutilation of the Corpse in the Iliad*, Leiden.

—— 1992a. 'Divine Justice in the *Odyssey*: Poseidon, Cyclops, and Helios', *AJPh* 113: 489–518.

—— 1992b. 'Bard and Audience in Homer', in Lamberton and Keaney 1992: 3–29.

—— 1994. *Singers, Heroes and Gods in the Odyssey*, Ithaca, NY.

—— 1996. '*Kleos* and its Ironies in the *Odyssey*', in Schein 1996: 201–21 (1st pub. 1983).

Severyns, A. 1963. *Recherches sur la chrestomathie de Proclos IV: Vita Homeri et les sommaires du Cycle*, Paris.

—— 1966. *Les Dieux d'Homère*, Paris.

Sherratt, E. S. 1995. 'Reading the Texts: Archaeology and the Homeric Question', repr. in Emlyn-Jones, Hardwick, and Purkis 1995: 145–65 (1st pub. 1990).

Silk, M. 2004. 'The *Odyssey* and its Explorations', in Fowler 2004: 31–44.

Singor, H. 1995. '*Eni prôtoisimachesthai*': Some Remarks on the Iliadic Image of the Battlefield', in Crielaard 1995a\: 183–200.

Skiadas, A. D. 1965. *Homer im griechischen Epigramm*, Athens.

Skinner, M. (ed.). 1986. *Rescuing Creusa*, *Helios*, 13/2.

Slatkin, L. 1986. 'Genre and Generation in the Odyssey', *Metis*, 1: 259–68.

Snell, B. 1953. *The Discovery of the Mind: The Greek Origins of European Thought*, New York; Eng. trans. by T. G. Rosenmeyer of *Die Entedeckung des Geistes* (1948).

Snipes, K. 1988. 'Literary Interpretation in the Homeric Scholia: The Similes of the *Iliad*', *AJP* 109: 196–222.

Snodgrass, A. M. 1974. 'An Historical Homeric Society?', *JHS* 94: 114–25.

—— 1980. *Archaic Greece: The Age of Experiment*, London.

—— 1997. 'Homer and Greek Art', in Morris and Powell 1997: 560–97.

Spahn, P. 2006. 'Freundschaft und Gesellschaft bei Homer', in Luther 2006a: 163–216.

Stanford, W. B. 1950. 'Homer's Use of *Polu* Compounds', *Classical Philology*, 45: 108–10.
—— 1954. *The Ulysses Theme: A Study in Adaptability of a Traditional Hero*, Oxford.
—— 1964–5. *The Odyssey of Homer*, 2 vols., 2nd edn., London.
Starobinski, J. 1989. 'Je hais comme les portes de l'Hadès', repr. in *Le Remède dans le mal: Critique et légitimation de l'artifice à l'âge des lumières*, Paris: 263–86 (1st pub. 1974).
Stein, E. 1990. 'Probleme der Entwicklung vom Sänger zum Autor', in W. Kullmann and M. Reischel (eds.), *Der Übergang von der Mündlichkeit zur Literatur bei den Griechen*, Tübingen: 265–70.
Stockinger, H. 1959. *Die Vorzeichen im homerischen Epos: Ihre Typik und ihre Bedeutung*, diss. Munich.
Strasburger, G. 1952. *Die kleine Kämpfer der* Ilias, diss. Frankfurt.
Strasburger, H. 1982. 'Homer und die Gescheitsschreibung', repr. in *Studien zur alten Geschichte*, 2: 1057–97 (1st pub. 1972).
—— 1997. 'The Sociology of the Homeric Epics', Eng. trans. in Wright and Jones 1997: 47–70 (1st pub. 1953).
Strauss Clay, J. 1974. 'Demas and Aude: The Nature of Divine Transformation in Homer', *Hermes*, 102: 129–36.
—— 1997. *The Wrath of Athena: Gods and Men in the Odyssey*, Lanham, Md. (1st pub. 1983).
—— 2002. 'Odyssean Animadversiones', in Montanari 2002: 73–83.
Suerbaum, W. 1968. 'Die Ich-Erzählungen des Odysseus: Überlegungen zur epischen Technik der Odyssee', *Poetica*, 2: 150–77.
Tarrant, R. J. 1987. 'Towards a Typology of Interpolations in Latin Poetry', *TAPhA* 117: 281–98.
—— 1989. 'The Reader as Author: Collaborative Interpolation in Latin Poetry', in J. Grant (ed.), *Editing Greek and Latin Texts*, New York: 121–62.
Thalmann, W. G. 1984. *Conventions of Form and Thought in Early Greek Epic Poetry*, Baltimore.
—— 1998. *The Swineherd and the Bow: Representation of Class in the Odyssey*, Ithaca, NY.
Thapar, R. 1989. 'Epic and History: Tradition, Dissent and Politics in India', *Past and Present*, 125: 3–26.
Theiler, W. 1950. 'Vermutungen zur Odyssee', *MH* 7: 102–22.
Thomas, C. G. 1988. 'Penelope's Worth: Looming Large in Early Greece', *Hermes*, 116: 257–64.
Thornton, A. 1970. *People and Themes in the* Odyssey, London.
Todorov, T. 1977. 'Primitive Narrative', in *Poetics of Prose*, trans. R. Howard, Ithaca, NY: 53–65.
Trahman, C. R. 1952. 'Odysseus' Lies (Odyssey. Books 13–19)', *Phoenix*, 6: 31–43.

Turner, F. M. 1997. 'The Homeric Question', in Morris and Powell 1997: 123–45.

Van Nortwick, T. 1979. 'Penelope and Nausicaa', *TAPhA* 109: 269–76.

Vansina, J. 1965. *Oral Tradition: A Study in Historical Methodology*, Chicago.

—— 1985. *Oral Tradition and History*, Madison.

Van Wees, H. 1992. *Status Warriors: War, Violence and Society in Homer and History*, Amsterdam.

—— 1994. 'The Homeric Way of War: The Iliad and the Hoplite Phalanx (I and II)', *G&R* 41: 1–18, 131–55.

—— 1997. 'Homeric Warfare', in Morris and Powell 1997: 668–93.

Vernant, J. P. 1996. 'The Refusal of Odysseus', in Schein 1996: 185–9.

Vidal-Naquet, P. 1996. 'Land and Sacrifice in the Odyssey', Eng. trans. in Schein 1996: 33–53 (1st pub. 1970).

Visser, E. 1988. 'Formulae or Single Words? Towards a New Theory on Homeric Verse-Making', *Würzburger Jahrbuch für Altertumswissenschaft*, 14: 21–37.

Vivante, P. 1982. *The Epithets in Homer: A Study in Poetic Values*, New Haven.

Voigt, C. 1933. *Üeberlegung und Entscheidung*, Berlin.

Von der Mühll, P. 1940. 'Odyssee', in *RE* Suppl. 7: 696–768.

Wace, A. J. B., and Stubbings, F. H. (eds.). 1962. *A Companion to Homer*, London.

Wade-Gery, H. T. 1952. *The Poet of the Iliad*, Cambridge.

Walcot, P. 1977. 'Odysseus and the Art of Lying', *Ancient Society*, 8: 1–19.

Watkins, C. 1982. 'Aspects of Indo-European Poetics', in *The Indo-Europeans in the Fourth and Third Millenium*, ed. E. C. Polome, Ann Arbor: 104–20.

—— 1986. 'Aspects of Indo-European Poetics', in E. C. Polomé (ed.), *The Indo-Europeans in the Fourth and Third Millennium*, Ann Arbor: 104–20.

Webster, T. B. L. 1963. Review of G. S. Kirk, *The Songs of Homer*, *JHS* 83: 157–8.

Wehrli, F. 1959. 'Penelope und Telemachus', *Museum Helveticum*, 16: 228–37.

Welcker, F. G. 1865–82. *Der epische Cyclus oder die homerischen Dichter*, 2 vols., 2nd edn. Bonn.

Wender, D. 1978. *The Last Scenes of the Odyssey*, Mnemosyne Suppl. 52, Leiden.

West, M. L. 1967. 'The Contest of Homer and Hesiod', *CQ* 17: 433–50.

—— 1988. 'The Rise of the Greek Epic', *JHS* 108: 151–72.

—— 1999. 'The Invention of Homer', *CQ* 49: 364–82.

—— (ed.). 2003. *Homeric Hymns, Homeric Apocrypha, Lives of Homer*, Cambridge, Mass.

Whallon, W. 1969. *Formula, Character and Context*, Washington.

Whitley, J. 1991. 'Social Diversity in the Dark Age of Greece', *Annual of the British School of Athens*, 86: 341–65.

Whitman, C. 1958. *Homer and the Heroic Tradition*, Cambridge, Mass.

Whittaker, H. 1999. 'The Status of Arete in the Phaeacian Episode of the Odyssey', *SO* 74: 140–50.

Wilamowitz-Moellendorf, U. von. 1884. *Homerische Untersuchungen*, Berlin.

—— 1916. *Die Ilias und Homer*, Berlin.

—— 1927. *Die Heimkehr des Odysseus*, Berlin.

Willcock, M. 1997. 'Neoanalysis', in Morris and Powell 1997: 174–89.

Williams, B. 1993. *Shame and Necessity*, Sather Classical Lectures 57, Berkeley.

Winkler, J. 1990. 'Penelope's Cunning and Homer's', in *The Constraints of Desire: Anthropology of Sex and Gender in Ancient Greece*, Princeton: 129–61.

Winterbottom, M. 1989. 'Speaking of the Gods', *G&R* 36: 33–41.

Wohl, V. 1993. 'Standing by the Stathmos: The Creation of Sexual Ideology in the *Odyssey*', *Arethusa*, 26: 19–50.

Wolf, F. A. 1985. *Prolegomena to Homer* (1795), trans. and ed. A. Grafton, G. W. Most, and J. Zetzel, Princeton.

Wood, R. 1976. *An Essay on the Original Genius of Homer* (1775), ed. E. Fabian, New York.

Woodhouse, W. J. 1969. *The Composition of Homer's Odyssey*, Oxford (1st pub. 1930).

Wright, G. M., and Jones, P. V. 1997. *Homer: German Scholarship in Translation*, Oxford.

Wyatt, W. F. 1978. 'Penelope's Fat Hand', *CPh* 36: 343–4.

Zeitlin, F. 1996. 'Figuring Fidelity in Homer's *Odyssey*', in *Playing the Other: Gender and Society in Classical Greek Literature*, Chicago: 19–52.

Index